Transitional Justice

Volume III
Laws, Rulings, and Reports

Transitional Justice includes:

Volume I: General Considerations
Volume II: Country Studies
Volume III: Laws, Rulings, and Reports

Transitional Justice

HOW EMERGING DEMOCRACIES RECKON WITH FORMER REGIMES

Volume III
Laws, Rulings, and Reports

NEIL J. KRITZ
EDITOR

Foreword by
Nelson Mandela

UNITED STATES INSTITUTE OF PEACE PRESS
Washington, D.C.

United States Institute of Peace
1550 M Street NW, Suite 700
Washington, DC 20005-1708

First published 1995

Printed in the United States of America

The paper used in this publication meets the minimum requirements of American National Standard for Information Sciences—Permanence of Paper for Printed Library Materials, ANSI Z39.48-1984.

Library of Congress Cataloging-in-Publications Data
Transitional justice : how emerging democracies reckon with former
 regimes / Neil J. Kritz, editor.
     p.   cm.
     Includes bibliographical references and indexes.
       Contents: v. 1. General considerations — v. 2. Country studies —
 v. 3. Laws, rulings, and reports.
       ISBN 1-878379-47-X. — ISBN 1-878379-43-7 (pbk.)
       1. Political crimes and offenses.   2. Crimes against humanity.
 3. Political persecution.   4. Criminal justice, Administration of.
 I. Kritz, Neil J., 1959– .
 K5250.T73   1995
 345'.0231—dc20
 [342.5231]   95-24363
                                                           CIP

Volume III: LAWS, RULINGS, AND REPORTS

Summary of Contents

Volume III: LAWS, RULINGS, AND REPORTS

Contents

FOREWORD

This important publication on transitional justice comes at a time when the world is grappling with the problems of governance, legitimacy, democracy, and human rights. In recent years, particularly during the past decade, there has been a remarkable movement in various regions of the world away from undemocratic and repressive rule towards the establishment of constitutional democracies.

In nearly all instances, the displaced regimes were characterized by massive violations of human rights and undemocratic systems of governance. In their attempt to combat real or perceived opposition, they exercised authority with very little regard to accountability.

Transition in these societies has therefore been accompanied by enormous challenges. While it has signified new hopes and aspirations, it has at the same time brought into sharp focus the difficult choices that these countries would have to make on their road to democracy and economic progress.

Ironically, the advent of democracy has also put the welcome endeavors for national consensus to a test. In South Africa, for instance, it has highlighted the deep divisions that have existed within society.

As all these countries recover from the trauma and wounds of the past, they have had to devise mechanisms not only for handling past human rights violations, but also to ensure that the dignity of victims, survivors, and relatives is restored. In the context of this relentless search for appropriate equilibria, profound issues of policy and law have emerged. They have arisen out of the question of how a country in transition should respond to allegations of gross human rights violations by individuals of either the predecessor or extant authority. The issue that has concerned the international community is the problem created by the incompatibility of such amnesties with a state's international obligations.

In so far as these volumes on *Transitional Justice* bring together under one roof the diverse experiences of transitional societies, they provide an impetus for the creation of an international community predicated on human dignity and justice. The variety as well as the richness of experiences contained in this publication will certainly be a useful guide not only to students and researchers in retrospective justice, but also in the popular endeavors to reorganize civil society.

My heartfelt congratulations to the United States Institute of Peace for this timely and well-organized publication.

Nelson Mandela
President of the Republic of South Africa

PREFACE

The movement from repressive regimes to democratic societies has become a worldwide phenomenon as humanity approaches the twenty-first century. The transitions in South Africa, Central and Eastern Europe, and large parts of Latin America provide inspiring recent examples of this trend. The legacy of past political repression, however, can be an emotional and practical burden, affecting the stability of many a transition. How can a new society peacefully integrate those former officials who were associated with a past of repression as well as those who were its victims? How can an emerging democracy respond to public demands for redress of the legitimate grievances of some without creating new injustices for others? From 1989 to 1992, I observed the practical import of these complex questions while negotiating the United Nations Peace Agreement for Cambodia. The ultimate success of Cambodia's effort to build a participatory political order will be at least partly determined by the way the country handles its own recent past of genocidal violence and revolutionary repression.

The national culture, the history of the former regime, and the political realities of the transition process all influence the approach adopted by any society emerging from a period of repression. A constant in each case, however, is the search for a political process that will achieve justice as well as social stability and reconciliation. The history of the last fifty years provides a wealth of positive examples of the transition process as well as some notable missteps and failures.

The United States Institute of Peace is exploring these challenging questions through an ongoing project entitled "Transitional Justice," under the direction of our Rule of Law Initiative. The present three-volume collection, *Transitional Justice: How Emerging Democracies Reckon with Former Regimes*, is a major outcome of that project. *Volume I: General Considerations* addresses legal, political, and philosophical perspectives. *Volume II: Country Studies* examines more than twenty transitions in the period from World War II to the present. *Volume III: Law, Rulings, and Reports* includes over 100 samples of legislation, constitutional provisions, judicial decisions, and reports of official commissions of inquiry, as well as relevant treaty excerpts.

This collection should become a standard reference for governments, private organizations, scholars, and other individuals dealing with these difficult issues. Some of the models of a transition process documented here may suggest approaches that would facilitate a just and peaceful transition; others might best be consigned to the history books. The United States Institute of Peace does not endorse any one approach, but offers these volumes in the belief that a comparative review can provide insights and examples for leaders in emerging democracies as they confront the challenges of transitional justice.

Richard H. Solomon
President
United States Institute of Peace

INTRODUCTION

When the communist world began its collapse in the late 1980s and the post–Cold War period opened, newly democratic nations, some with vibrant histories of democracy, others ruled only by tyrants, and a few enjoying the promise of new nationhood, looked to the democracies, especially the United States, for help in creating democratic institutions and the complex foundation of a citizenry of democrats so necessary to traverse the inevitable rough waters ahead. How, they asked, might we best inspire our people with the habits of democracy and establish legal institutions to propel and protect our new freedoms?

Without question, the new historical era offers the most exciting opportunity for durable peace since the end of the First World War. With that prospect in mind, the United States Institute of Peace responded in a variety of ways, among them by establishing a Rule of Law Initiative and directing all programs—grants, fellowships, in-house projects, education and training, and library and communications—to pay special attention to the integral relationship between the rule of law and international peace with justice and freedom. By creating the initiative, the Institute underscored law as a crucial component of both scholarship and practice in peacemaking and peacebuilding, based upon the following propositions:

- Although in practice imperfect, democracy is by nature peaceful: on the international plane, democracies generally do not wage war against each other.
- Democratic structures require governance under the rule of law, which includes separate and independent lawmaking and judicial branches of government and incorporates basic norms of human rights and civil rights.
- The rule *of* law—not simply rule *by* law—ensures a system governed by openness, security, and accountability such that citizens may enjoy trust in their institutions and among each other.

In designing the initiative, we were intrigued by the immediate problem of how new leaderships in former totalitarian countries would treat previous governments. People had been ruled on a daily basis by violence, terror, and division, whether for decades or a few years. Civil trust had been impossible, economic opportunity crushed, and congenial social relations hard. With democracy now in the air, there were penetrating cries for retaliation against old rulers and for revelations about the past. Amnesties were discussed as were prosecutions. Decisions about the personnel and activities of the earlier governments came to mark a critical phase of this era of democratization. The Western world watched, commented, in some instances sent experts to advise. If judgments lacked fairness and if truth was subverted by bias and propaganda, the democratic foundation would be built on sand. If prosecutions (or decisions not to prosecute) complied with due process standards and if reports protected individual rights, then the symbols, structures, and operations of the new state would be built upon justice and the start would be strong. In short, democracy would not be safe over time without a thorough and careful application of normative rules to ensure that justice was achieved upon a foundation of the rule of law.

We believed that, while each country's experience was not only dramatic but unique, their problems were not unique, in particular with respect to the treatment of former officials. We were confident that similar issues were being struggled with across the world and that studies from the recent past would hold lessons for today. We determined to create a set of first-rate readings on basic questions of "transitional justice," demonstrating that, despite the uniqueness of each society and its historical and political context, there are unifying themes common to nations moving from despotism to democracy and lessons that each nation might bring to others.

These volumes are a major compilation of carefully selected excerpts from studies as well as primary documents on transitional justice, a subject that is itself a defining theme of the second half of the twentieth century and is likely to endure well into the new millennium as suppressed ethnic, religious, and political disputes continue to be unleashed and the struggle for democracy continues. The readings show continuity of issues across continents and time, while demonstrating remarkable complexity: readers will find passages rich in legal, moral, political, and social content and, perhaps most tellingly, deep historical context.

This project proceeded from the belief that the collection, editing, and organization of the best existing material would be an important contribution to the field, facilitating comparative analysis of issues that many countries have previously viewed as unique to their own experience. The project began with a review of over 17,000 books and articles of possible relevance to the project. With the exception of Volume III, the search was mostly limited to English-language materials. We also consulted extensively with political scientists, historians, legal experts, psychologists, theologians, human rights activists, philosophers, and specialists on various countries for ideas and references in the literature. And above all, we read, edited, and structured the volumes as our findings developed.

These volumes are limited, as the subtitle indicates, to the way that emerging *democratic* societies address the legacy of their repression of their own people. This approach has excluded consideration of non-democratic successor states (for example, the transition from the Pahlavi to Khomeini regimes in Iran, or from Somoza to the Sandinistas in Nicaragua). It has also excluded most material on the transition policies of occupation authorities (such as post–World War II Japan). Lastly, although proper handling of the transitional justice issue is integral to the process of democratization, these two issues are conceptually distinct; the present study therefore does not examine democratization per se.

Each volume stands on its own, and each reinforces the others. *Volume I: General Considerations* provides a range of views on the broad issues entailed in transitional justice. Political, historical, legal, psychological, and moral perspectives are all included.

Volume II: Country Studies examines the handling of these nettlesome issues in twenty-one countries during the last fifty years. These case studies are arranged in chronological order: five countries that dealt with the issues of transitional justice in an immediate post–World War II context (Germany, France, Denmark, Belgium, and Italy); South Korea's democratic interlude in the 1960s (with a brief discussion of that country's subsequent return to these issues nearly three decades later); transitional justice in Southern Europe in the 1970s (Greece, Portugal, and Spain); emergence from dictatorships in the 1980s in Latin America (Argentina, Uruguay, Brazil, and Chile) and in Uganda; and, finally, selected post-communist transitions in the former Soviet bloc (Czechoslovakia, Germany, Hungary, Bulgaria, Albania, Russia, and Lithuania). Because few authors have examined the full range of transitional justice issues in any one country, most of these chapters weave together material from several sources. Often, various excerpts from the same source are interspersed throughout a country study to permit thematic organization of the material.

Volume III: Laws, Rulings, and Reports contains samples of primary documents from the transitions in twenty-eight countries. Among the more than one hundred documents included are legislative charters for "truth commissions" along with lengthy excerpts from their resulting reports, amnesty and purge laws and their evaluation by the judiciary, and detailed provisions for the rehabilitation of victims of the former regime. While some of these are official translations, most are unofficial translations that we commissioned or obtained from a variety of sources.

Except as indicated, the articles and documents reprint the original text. With each of the 224 individual selections included, we have generally adhered to the style, format, and footnote numbering of the original material. As a consequence, the style may vary from selection to selection.

Finally, it is important to point to a fact that too often is left unsaid: readers should know that while they are using these books, people in many other countries are studying them too. We hope these volumes raise the profile of scholarship on transitional justice; it is extraordinarily important for the success of democracy and a world with greater freedom.

Charles Duryea Smith
Former General Counsel and Director
Rule of Law Initiative
United States Institute of Peace

ACKNOWLEDGMENTS

The compilation and editing of these volumes—involving tracking down thousands of books, documents, and articles, extensive consultations and research, conceptualization of the major issues as well as historical analysis—would not have been possible without the assistance of a great many people. Space does not permit the recognition of everyone who gave of their time and knowledge, but I would like to express my heartfelt appreciation to the following individuals: John Herz, Guillermo O'Donnell, Herman Schwartz, and Ruti Teitel, who reviewed a draft of the volumes and provided valuable advice and perspective; Tim Phillips and Eric Nonacs of the Project on Justice in Times of Transition; Dwight Semler at the Center for the Study of Constitutionalism in Eastern Europe; Susan Scharf, Jocelyn Nieva, and especially Donald Gressett, who, serving in succession on the staff of the Institute's Rule of Law Initiative, each ably managed myriad tasks to keep this project on course; the Institute's capable Publications staff; Bob Schmitt, the Institute's computer guru, who solved numerous technical problems; and last but far from least, my wife Francesca, for her patience and support.

THE DILEMMAS OF TRANSITIONAL JUSTICE

In March 1992, some fifty participants from twenty-one countries gathered in Salzburg, Austria for a two-day conference organized by the New York-based Charter Seventy-Seven Foundation. The group included a Czech journalist, members of the Lithuanian and Uruguayan parliaments, a former president of Argentina, a Hungarian philosopher, a professor of history from Madrid, and a member of the Bulgarian Constitutional Court. The subject of the meeting was the one thing this diverse collection of individuals had in common: each came from a country which had suffered through a brutal and repressive regime, been liberated, and was obliged to cope with the legacy of that ousted system.

One major theme of the conference (and of the effort to compile the present three-volume collection, which had begun in 1991) was the extent to which the Central and Eastern Europeans and former Soviets who were just emerging from communist rule could learn any useful lessons from the Latin American transitions of the previous decade.

A fascinating undertone seemed to dominate the first day of the conference, as the assembled began to describe the experience of their respective nations. In words spoken and unspoken, in skeptical glances and general body language, the Latin Americans and Europeans seemed to be expressing the same thing to one another: the suffering of our people during the old regime and the difficulties resulting from our legacy is far worse than any hardship you endured. Ours is the greater pain; there is little we can learn from your experience.

There is, of course, some legitimacy to each point of view. On the one hand, communism was entrenched for forty-five years in East Germany, seventy years in Russia—so long that whole generations of the citizenry knew no other way of life. Though the most horrific and large-scale abuses of the Stalinist period had yielded to milder forms of repression in later years, the entire culture and fabric of their societies had been decimated during those decades; in dealing with the legacy of the old system, those in the former Soviet bloc had to reconstruct both government and the private sector virtually from scratch. On the other hand, though the military dictatorships which seized power in Argentina, Uruguay, Chile, and elsewhere in that region ruled for much shorter periods of time, the brutality with which they systematically tortured, killed, and caused large numbers of their citizens to "disappear" numbs in its detail. Numerous other contrasts exist between the legacy problems of Latin America and of post-communist Europe.

And yet. By day two of the proceedings, there was a gradual but palpable recognition that many of the details and dilemmas were not so different. How best, for example, to highlight the division between old and new government, so as to instill public confidence in the latter? This was a key issue for the participants from both regions. How should they handle those perceived as having served the old regime—as senior officials and architects of the system, as bureaucrats who implemented the old policies and may continue to be obstacles to reform, as members of the military or secret police, or as paid or volunteer collaborators with the secret police? In some countries of the former Warsaw Pact, more than half the population was potentially implicated in one of these categories. The challenge, as one participant put it, was to strike the proper balance between a whitewash on the one hand and a witch-hunt on the other. Could victims of the old regime be fairly compensated? For that matter, was it possible to achieve consensus as to *who* were the victims of a system that, by its design, affected everyone in society? Above all, how to achieve authentic reconciliation and prevent the future recurrence of abuses of the sort inflicted by the old regime?

Over lunch one day at that meeting, I described to Raul Alfonsín, the courageous former president of Argentina who returned his country from military junta to civilian democracy, the "transitional justice" project underway at the United States Institute of Peace and some of the questions emerging from our examination of transitions from repressive regimes to democracy from the Second World War to the present. I pointed out that there were intriguing parallels between the cases of Argentina and Greece. (1) In both cases, a military junta ruled the country for a period of seven years. The relatively short duration is relevant in determining whether there are people who have "clean hands" and who can bring pre-regime experience and training to the job in replacing those affiliated with the ousted regime—or whether, as in Russia, nearly every qualified person was a part of the system in which they grew up. (2) In both Greece and Argentina, the regime was driven by a virulent, right-wing, anti-communist ideology. (3) Both were characterized by human rights abuses on a massive scale, including extensive use of torture, which prompted gradually increasing international condemnation and ostracism of the country. (4) In both cases, the junta had promised economic improvement, but was faced with a faltering economy by the end of the seven-year rule. (5) Both regimes were finally forced to relinquish power immediately following a failed military venture (in Cyprus and the Falklands respectively).

In Greece, President Karamanlis assumed power from the junta and dealt with the issues of "transitional justice"—including prosecution of ousted officials, purging from governmental and quasi-governmental agencies those affiliated with the former regime, access to and use of the surveillance and interrogation records of the military police, and compensation and rehabilitation of victims—in an unusually firm and swift manner in 1974-75. Certainly there were important differences between the Greek and Argentine cases. Given the striking continuities, however, I asked President Alfonsín whether he had had any information on Greece and the Karamanlis program when formulating his own government's approach to these same issues nine years later. Alfonsín was intrigued by the parallels between the two cases, but confirmed that, as he and his advisors grappled with these difficult questions in the transition from repressive rule, they had no such information to draw upon; they "invented" their approach from nothing. They would probably not have followed the identical course as Greece, he assured me, but having material regarding the Greek experience on the table would have been extremely valuable in helping them to frame the issues and the options. President Alfonsín urged that we at the United States Institute of Peace pursue the present project so as to ease the transition process in future cases.

In countries undergoing the radical shift from repression to democracy, this question of transitional justice presents, in a very conspicuous manner, the first test for the establishment of real democracy and the rule of law—the very principles which will hopefully distinguish the new regime from the old. Strong political pressure for victor's justice in dealing with those who served the repressive regime, and the need to demonstrate a separation between the old and the new governments, may call for immediate and harsh retribution against a large number of individuals. New terms are created for the country or region in question—*denazification* in Germany after Hitler, *defascistization* in Italy, *dejuntafication*, *decommunization*—but they all express the same attempt of a liberated society to purge the remnants of its vilified recent past. If handled incorrectly, however, such action may deepen rather than heal the divisions within the nation. The temptation exists to compartmentalize, by viewing the need to "clean up old business" as unrelated to the democratization process. A vivid demonstration to the contrary, however, is the kangaroo trial and execution of former dictator Nicolae Ceausescu immediately following the fall of his government in Romania: with that one act seen on television around the world, the new government damaged its ability to move forward and the credibility of its interest in democracy and the rule of law—in the eyes of both other nations and its own citizens. Dealing firmly and aggressively with those who participated in, or benefitted from, the repression of the past is one way to demonstrate a clear break between the old regime and the new order. Adhering to the new government's pronounced commitments to principles of democracy and the rule of law, particularly in the tough cases, is another. The tension between the two is a theme which runs through each of the basic components of "transitional justice."

Criminal Sanctions

A basic question confronting all transitional governments, of course, is whether to undertake the prosecution of the leaders of the ousted regime or their henchmen for the abuses they inflicted upon the nation. Some will argue that trial and punishment of these people is not only essential to achieve some degree of justice, but that a public airing and condemnation of their crimes is the best way to draw a line between the old and new governments, lest the public perceives the new authorities as simply more of the same. Others will claim that these are simply show trials unbefitting a democracy, that they are manifestations of victor's justice, that the best way to rebuild and reconcile the nation is to leave the past behind by means of a blanket amnesty. In some cases, abuses have been committed both by the former government and by its opponents, and it can be argued that the best approach is to forgive the sins of both sides.

The debate recurs time and again. Following the death of Franco, the relatively peaceful Spanish transition was marked by such a mutual amnesty. In Greece, nearly twenty years after the conviction of junta leaders who had overseen the torture of hundreds, plans to release them from prison still prompted huge protests. In newly democratic Argentina and Chile, the prospect of trials for the gross violations of human rights that had occurred under the old regime provoked bald threats of military intervention and a return to the terror of the past. In post-apartheid South Africa, disagreements at the end of 1994 regarding amnesty were reported to threaten the stability of the new coalition government. International standards are evolving which help deal with this question; there is a growing consensus that, at least for the most heinous violations of human rights and international humanitarian law, a sweeping amnesty is impermissible.

When a decision is made to prosecute, the desire to use criminal sanctions against those who served the old regime may run directly counter to the development of a democratic legal order. The principles of *ex post facto* and *nulla poena sine lege*, for example, form one of the basic concepts of that legal order, barring the prosecution of anyone for an act which was not criminal at the time it was committed. At the very time that countries emerging from repressive regimes are committing themselves to these basic principles, the reality is that many of the acts that they desire to punish today were not crimes when they were committed under the former regime; they were often laudable and encouraged under the old system. In post-war France, for example, this issue was fiercely debated. Ultimately, thousands of people were prosecuted under a 1944 law establishing the new offense of "national indignity" for acts they had committed prior to the law's adoption. In the immediate post-communist period, largely owing to this same *ex post facto* dilemma, German officials initiated proceedings against Erich Mielke, the former head of East Germany's Stasi secret police, not for any abuses of the hated Stasi, but for a murder he had allegedly committed half a century earlier—based on evidence extracted by Nazi police. Although some sort of justice might have been served by this trial, the Mielke prosecution could not provide for East Germans the kind of catharsis that would be achieved through a public airing and trial of secret police wrongdoing.

Some of the worst abuses inflicted by former regimes *were* crimes under the old system, but they obviously were not prosecuted. If the statute of limitations for these crimes has already elapsed by the time of the transition, can the new authorities still hold the perpetrators accountable for their deeds? In both Hungary and the Czech Republic, post-communist legislators argued that since these crimes (particularly those committed to suppress dissent in 1956 and 1968 respectively) had not been prosecuted for wholly political reasons, it was legitimate to hold that the statute of limitations had not been in effect during the earlier period. Now, freed of political obstacles to justice, the statutory period for these crimes could begin anew, enabling the new authorities to prosecute these decades-old crimes. Legislation was adopted accordingly. In both countries, the matter was put to the newly created constitutional court for review. In a fascinating pair of rulings, each court handed down a decision which eloquently addressed the need to view this question of legacy and accountability in the context of the new democracy's commitment to the rule of law. On this basis—with plainly similar fact patterns—the Czech constitutional court upheld the re-running of the statute of limitations for the crimes of the old regime as a requirement of justice; the Hungarian court struck down the measure for violating the principle of the rule of law.

How widely should the net be cast in imposing sanctions on those who served the former regime? How high up the chain of command should superiors be responsible for abuses inflicted by their underlings? What standard of evidence is required to demonstrate that, rather than random events, these acts of persecution, corruption, and violence were designed, or at least condoned, by those at the top? Conversely, how far down the chain should soldiers or bureaucrats be held liable for following the orders of their superiors in facilitating these abuses? In dealing with the legacy of the former East Germany, several young border guards were prosecuted in 1991 for implementing shoot-to-kill orders that produced nearly 600 deaths of East Germans attempting to escape across the border. Many criticized the first of these trials for punishing the "small fry" at the end of the chain of responsibility who actually pulled the trigger, while leaving untouched the party leaders who had designed the repugnant system and given the orders. (In January 1995, seven former senior East German officials *were* eventually charged, in a 1,600-page indictment, with manslaughter and attempted manslaughter for their roles in developing and overseeing the system.) In Rwanda, after ousting a regime that organized genocidal killings of at least half a million people, if the new government were to undertake prosecution of every person who participated in this heinous butchery, some 30,000-100,000 Rwandan citizens could be placed in the dock—a situation that would be wholly unmanageable and extremely destabilizing to the transition. Moving the nation forward toward both justice and reconciliation plainly precludes an absolutist approach to the chain of responsibility.

In bringing those who served the former regime to account for their actions, what kind of deeds should be scrutinized? Should prosecution be limited to egregious violations of human rights? Should they be extended to charges of corruption and economic mismanagement? In Bulgaria, for instance, several former officials were convicted because of their role in specific foreign aid decisions that contributed to the country's economic ruin.

Should there be limits on the penalties imposed in these criminal cases? Some will argue that, even in those countries in which capital punishment is used, it should not be available in transitional purge trials. Given the high emotion and political pressures inherent in these trials, they suggest that use of the death penalty will further aggravate tensions within the society.

The temptation of victims of ghastly human rights violations under the old regime to make short shrift of the criminal procedural rights of those put in the dock for the crimes of that regime—to pay them back for the abuses they inflicted—is certainly understandable. Providing yesterday's dictators and torturers with the judicial guarantees and procedural protections that they never afforded their victims may be a source of short-term frustration during the transition, prompting cynicism of the sort expressed by an East German activist: "what we wanted was justice; what we got was the rule of law." Nonetheless, if these defendants are not afforded all the same rights granted to common defendants in a democratic order, the rule of law does not exist and the democratic foundation of the new system is arguably weakened.

Non-Criminal Sanctions

At least as great a challenge to the installation of democracy and the rule of law comes in the context of administrative penalties. Most frequently, the issue is that of purging from the public sector those who served the repressive regime. In post-war France, the process was called *epuration*; in the Czech and Slovak Federal Republic, *lustration*. A variety of effective arguments are made in favor of this process. The new democratic authorities must find ways to restore public confidence in the institutions of government. The public may reasonably be skeptical when told they will now be treated differently, if these institutions simply retain all their existing personnel. These, after all, are the same people who kept the engine of the repressive state operating; it is unlikely that many of them have undergone a sudden epiphany that has turned them into committed democrats. Even if they do not actively attempt to sabotage the changes undertaken by the new authorities, these people are set in the old ways and will serve as obstacles to the process of democratic reform. Finally, jobs in public service, whether as senior ministers or as clerks, should be granted first and foremost to those who have demonstrated loyalty to the democratic ideals of the new order.

Depending on the country, those perceived as having supported the old regime might include senior officials and architects of the system, bureaucrats who implemented the old policies and may continue to be obstacles to reform, members of the military or police, paid or volunteer collaborators with the secret police, or even simply party members. Perhaps the most difficult of these categories in one country after another is the vague description of "collaborators." In some emerging democracies, those who fit into one of these categories potentially comprise more than half the population.

On the other hand, particularly in those countries where the ousted regime was in power for many years, these people may be the only ones with the knowledge and experience to staff the ministries and the banks and the other institutions without which the national infrastructure would surely collapse. Practical considerations may make them indispensable.

How to undertake such a purge while rebuilding on the basis of democratic principles? These programs of administrative sanctions do not, as a rule, provide individuals with the same level of due process protections from which they would benefit in a criminal proceeding. Driven by the fact that they involve a large number of people, purges tend to be conducted in summary fashion. Beyond procedural considerations, the rule of law rejects collective punishment and discrimination on the basis of political opinion or affiliation. In establishing accountability, even in a non-criminal proceeding, the burden of proof should be on the authorities making the accusation, not on the accused to prove his or her innocence. When large numbers of people are removed from their places of employment purely because they had worked there under the old system or because of their membership in a political party, without any demonstration of individual wrongdoing, they may legitimately cry foul and question the democratic underpinnings of the new government. Rather than contributing to reconciliation and rebuilding, the result may be the creation of a substantial ostracized opposition that threatens the stability of the new system.

In much of the former communist bloc, the issue of lustration was a source of great controversy during the first years after the revolutions of 1989. In Poland, for example, only 38 percent of those polled in late 1991 supported creation of a system for disqualification of former communists, officials, and collaborators from public offices; a March 1992 poll showed an increase to 64 percent in favor of disqualification. Some observers suggested that the trend was related to the complex questions of privatization and redistribution of wealth: necessary austerity programs and wrenching efforts to overhaul the entire economic system result in many people becoming more impoverished, and the desire consequently grows to assign blame for society's ills. In addition, a perception exists that many former communist officials gave themselves "golden parachutes" as they exited their government posts, in the form of embezzled funds and property or controlling interests in the newly privatized companies; rather than being punished, in other words, the old guard had won once again.

The courts reflect an interesting problem relative to the purge process. On the one hand, the rule of law requires an independent judiciary insulated from political pressures. This generally means that judges are not easily removable from their posts. Even if judges were easily purged, it might take years to train a qualified class of new lawyers and judges to replace them on the bench. On the other hand, in most cases of transition from totalitarian or authoritarian regimes, the judiciary was severely compromised and was very much a part of the old system, implementing the repressive policies and wrapping them in the mantle of law. In post-war Germany, when victims of Nazi persecution were authorized to file claims for damages, some of them were stunned to find their claims assigned to the very same judge who had sentenced the claimants or their relatives in the first place. In order to enhance the power and independence of the judiciary as part of the democratization process in post-communist Poland, a law was enacted establishing the irremovability of judges. One consequence, subsequently recognized, was that many tainted communist judges thereby became entrenched in the "new" court system. An effort followed to create a system for the verification of judges based on their past activity and affiliation, and apply that system to both prospective new judges and those already in office.

In Ethiopia, it was proposed that all members of the former ruling party be denied the right to vote in elections. Such denial of suffrage based on previous party affiliation has occurred in other places, such as Norway after World War II. Other countries may attempt to ban the former ruling party and its successor parties. In Russia, President Boris Yeltsin's decree banning the Communist Party and seizing its assets was hotly debated and resulted in a closely watched case before the country's new constitutional court, which ultimately struck down half of the ban while leaving significant elements of it intact.

Once again, these efforts can rub against the intention to create a new, freer society wholly unlike the old regime. Administrative purge programs can easily be abused for purely political motives. In many cases, the old regime actually used the same methods, banning political parties, denying people a say in choosing their government. Citizens' rights to vote, to run for office, or to exercise their freedom of association are fundamental elements of a democracy. The balancing act for countries feeling their way through transitional justice is not an easy one.

Acknowledging the Past

In all cases of transition from a repressive regime, history has been controversial. Even after its ouster, the old guard will still have its defenders, who will deny that the evil acts of which it is accused ever took place, or will claim that they were actually perpetrated by others, or will suggest that they were justified by exigent circumstances. If left uncontested, these claims may undermine the new government and strengthen the hand of those determined to return the former regime to power. They will also add insult to the injury already inflicted on the victims.

Establishing a full, official accounting of the past is increasingly seen as an important element to a successful democratic transition. Criminal trials are one way in which the facts and figures of past abuses may be established. The establishment of a "truth commission," several variations of which are covered at length in each of the three volumes, is another. Following the initial phase of transition, this history may be reaffirmed in the long-term through national days of remembrance, the construction of museums and commemorative monuments, and the incorporation of this recent history into the curriculum of the nation's schools.

Compensation, Restitution, and Rehabilitation

In Russia, during the early stages of the transition from communist rule, there was no program to provide restitution of property or material compensation to victims. There was also initially no attempt to deal with recent abuses. Instead, efforts focused on restoring to victims of Stalinism their good names. On a case-by-case basis, hundreds of these victims were granted posthumous rehabilitation. While acknowledging the wrongs inflicted decades earlier, such an approach is, of course, far less costly to the new government—in both material and political terms—than compensation of recent victims.

In Chile, where the terms of the transition proscribed the criminal prosecution of former officials—and the sense of justice and catharsis which might be achieved thereby—the new democracy undertook instead one of the most comprehensive programs of compensation and rehabilitation of those described herein, encompassing life-long pensions for the survivors of those who died in General Pinochet's prisons, compensation for prison time and for lost income, educational benefits, a national network of medical and psychological services for victims and their families, and exemptions from military service.

More often than not, the legacy left by departing totalitarian or authoritarian regimes includes a weak economy and empty government coffers, depleted through corruption or mismanagement. The nascent democratic government must use its limited resources to turn the economy around, restructure the bureaucracy to restore public trust in government and better fulfill its basic functions, and invest in new present- and future-oriented programs (such as overhaul of the educational system where it was previously infused with the ideology of the old regime) to ensure the security of democracy. In this circumstance, many will ask, how much of its limited funds should the new democracy be obliged to allocate for victims' compensation, paying for the sins of the old guard? In addition, some will argue, since it is impossible to adequately compensate all victims for their loss, perhaps it is unjust to divert precious resources when the only result is to make some more whole than others.

To be sure, the parents whose daughter was tortured to death by the former regime, which then disposed of her body without a trace, or the man who spent a dozen years in prison for his political beliefs when he should have been completing his professional training, building his career, and watching his toddlers become young adults cannot be made whole for their loss. Nevertheless, compensation serves at least three functions in the process of national reconciliation. First, it aids the victims to manage the material aspect of their loss. Second, it constitutes an official acknowledgment of their pain by the nation. Both of these facilitate the societal reintegration of people who have long been made to suffer in silence. Third, it may deter the state from future abuses, by imposing a financial cost to such misdeeds. There is a growing consensus in international law that (a) the state is obligated to provide compensation to victims of egregious human rights abuses perpetrated by the government, and (b) if the regime which committed the acts in question does not provide compensation, the obligation carries over to the successor government.

Internationalization of the Issues

In our ever-smaller world, the handling of transitional justice has increasingly become a source of interplay between new successor governments and those outside the country. When the Czech and Slovak Federal Republic adopted its "lustration" law to screen and purge a range of former communist officials and collaborators, it became a major focus of international attention. The Council of Europe and the International Labor Organization each analyzed it, as did numerous foreign non-governmental organizations. Foreign attention is often welcome. The report of the Chadian "Commission of Inquiry into the Crimes and Misappropriations Committed by Ex-President Habré, his Accomplices and/or Accessories" begins with a map and profile of the country—obviously meant mostly for foreign consumption.

Foreign governments are forced to play a role in either providing refuge to those from the former regime or facilitating their exclusion or extradition for trial. Assisting in the tracing and return of assets which have been moved out of the country by the former leaders and their cohorts may also be appropriate. Some functions may be performed by wholly international bodies, such as the truth commission for El Salvador or the UN war crimes tribunal for Rwanda. Alternatively, foreign governments may play a part in advising, critiquing, or participating in the new leaders' plans with respect to such issues as amnesty, purging, and retraining for government personnel; the United States has arguably played such a role in Haiti.

These issues of transitional justice are highly charged flashpoints in many countries emerging from repression, with societal wounds still open and in need of treatment. Having recognized that the way in which these dilemmas are handled can directly affect the short- and long-term stability of the transition in many countries, foreign policy makers would be well-advised to keep this lens in focus as they monitor, anticipate, and respond to such transitions around the world.

Financing Transitional Justice

In theory, all victims of past repression are entitled to maximum compensation from a new government emerging from years of repression, but who is going to pay for it? High profile trials of former officials, particularly when they are looking farther back in time, can be expensive propositions, but justice done on the cheap is inadequate. Truth commissions, if they are to credibly research and create an unimpeachable historical record, need human, financial, and technical resources. Each of the aspects of transitional justice discussed above has a price tag attached—a serious problem for most emerging democracies struggling to rebuild their society anew. Most observers will agree, of course, that the long-term price of not dealing with these issues is greater still.

A recent Polish example drives home the point. A victim of human rights abuses under the old regime filed a successful lawsuit for damages from the government, resulting in an order to pay a huge sum to the plaintiff. Following a public outcry over holding the new, financially strapped government accountable for the sins of its communist predecessor, all the money was donated to charity.

If the transitional government cannot afford to pay for these efforts, foreign governmental or private funding is obviously an option. The truth commission for El Salvador received $1 million, some forty percent of its total budget, from the United States government. The commission in Uganda has received major infusions of funding from the Ford Foundation in the U.S. and Danita in Denmark. The Rwandan court system will hopefully receive foreign funding for the genocide trials it will undertake. In a lengthy bulletin produced "for NGOs and the media," the Special Prosecutor's Office created to investigate and prosecute crimes of the Mengistu regime in Ethiopia includes a section on "foreign support" which lists the contributions of six countries to the effort, ranging from a Canadian donation of $40,000 to $403,000 from Sweden. A recently established United Nations Voluntary Fund for Victims of Torture may also be of assistance in certain cases.

Some observers are wary of moving to foreign funding too quickly, particularly for victim compensation programs. If the national government is freed to allocate its resources and fiscal priorities without factoring in this issue, if it does not reach into its own coffers to acknowledge the victims of repression in a material sense, then the new regime may less effectively integrate the lessons of the past, and the sense that the state is paying its respect to the victims and restoring to them their dignity may be lessened—weakening both long-term democratization and rehabilitation.

The national resources so often embezzled by the leadership of totalitarian and authoritarian regimes—yet another issue facing emerging democracies—offers an interesting source of financing. Whether this entails efforts like that undertaken by the Philippine government to lay legal claim to millions of dollars worth of foreign assets and accounts controlled by Ferdinand and Imelda Marcos, or the efforts in Bulgaria and Albania to seize properties amassed by the former ruling clique and order them to reimburse the state millions of dollars, there is a certain sense of justice and balance to recapturing these ill-gotten gains and applying them directly to pay for other aspects of transitional justice. A curious variation on this was a legislative proposal in Poland to impose a special tax on communists, with a sliding scale based on one's position within the Communist Party hierarchy.

Particularly in countries emerging from communism or other centrally controlled economies, property restitution is not only a form of justice for victims, it is also a highly complex issue of economic conversion and privatization with obvious consequences for clarity of ownership and for business and investment opportunities in the emerging democracy. This may provide an additional incentive for foreign governments or businesses to help the restitution process along, including through subsidization.

As a rule, these are not problems that disappear quickly or easily. A half-century after the Second World War, the scars of Nazism are still felt in Germany. After the fall of the Berlin Wall and reunification, many acknowledged that the debate over decommunization was in many ways a shadow debate among East and West Germans over the success of denazification and was significantly colored by a desire to "do it better this time." The trials of Klaus Barbie and Paul Touvier for their crimes as part of the Vichy regime exposed still-raw nerves and soul-searching in France some fifty years after the facts in question. In Namibia, several years after the transition, officials claim that it is still too soon for an investigation and accounting of those who disappeared on both sides of the conflict, that such an effort would threaten Namibian stability; others argue that this past will haunt the country until it is dealt with. And in Cambodia, talk of bringing charges against leaders of the Khmer Rouge for the genocide they inflicted on their country twenty years ago will continue to affect the reconstruction process.

This is, of course, an ongoing process. A full accounting is yet to be written of transitional justice in countries such as South Africa, El Salvador, or Ethiopia. The current global trend from totalitarian and authoritarian systems to democratic ones will hopefully continue, producing new cases of transitional justice in the years to come. Through the publication of these volumes and the ongoing work of the United States Institute of Peace and others on this subject, one can hope that positive lessons will be derived from past experience, that future transitions will bolster their own stability by achieving justice and reconciliation through the rule of law.

Neil J. Kritz, Editor

1

COMMISSIONS OF INQUIRY

ARGENTINA: *NUNCA MÁS*—REPORT OF THE ARGENTINE COMMISSION ON THE DISAPPEARED*

(September 1984)

Prologue

During the 1970s, Argentina was torn by terror from both the extreme right and the far left. This phenomenon was not unique to our country. Italy, for example, has suffered for many years from the heartless attacks of Fascist groups, the Red Brigades, and other similar organizations. Never at any time, however, did that country abandon the principles of law in its fight against these terrorists, and it managed to resolve the problem through the normal courts of law, guaranteeing the accused all their rights of a fair hearing. When Aldo Moro was kidnapped, a member of the security forces suggested to General Della Chiesa that a suspect who apparently knew a lot be tortured. The general replied with the memorable words: "Italy can survive the loss of Aldo Moro. It would not survive the introduction of torture."

The same cannot be said of our country. The armed forces responded to the terrorists' crimes with a terrorism far worse than the one they were combating, and after 24 March 1976 they could count on the power and impunity of an absolute state, which they misused to abduct, torture and kill thousands of human beings.

Our Commission was set up not to sit in judgment, because that is the task of the constitutionally appointed judges, but to investigate the fate of the people who disappeared during those ill-omened years of our nation's life. However, after collecting several thousand statements and testimonies, verifying or establishing the existence of hundreds of secret detention centres, and compiling over 50,000 pages of documentation, we are convinced that the recent military dictatorship brought about the greatest and most savage tragedy in the history of Argentina. Although it must be justice which has the final word, we cannot remain silent in the face of all that we have heard, read and recorded. This went far beyond what might be considered criminal offenses, and takes us into the shadowy realm of crimes against humanity. Through the technique of disappearance and its consequences, all the ethical principles which the great religions and the noblest philosophies have evolved through centuries of suffering and calamity have been trampled underfoot barbarously ignored.

---

* Excerpts from NUNCA MAS: THE REPORT OF THE ARGENTINE NATIONAL COMMISSION ON THE DISAPPEARED, pp. 1-7, 9-10, 20, 51-53, 63-64, 209-210, 233-236, 241-242, 248, 252-255, 263-265, 270-272, 284-286, 305, 312, 321-322, 325, 328, 332, 337-338, 355-356, 362-364, 386-387, 395-400, 412-413, 428-441, 446-449, Translation copyright © 1986 by Writers and Scholars International Ltd. Reprinted by permission of Farrar, Straus & Giroux, Inc. Reprinted in Great Britain by permission of Faber and Faber Ltd.

Throughout the ages there have been many pronouncements on the sanctity of individual rights. In modern times, these have ranged from the rights enshrined in the French Revolution to those expressed in the universal declarations of human rights and the great encyclicals of this century. Every civilized nation, including our own, has laid down in its constitution guarantees which can never be suspended, even in the most catastrophic state of emergency: the right of life; the right to security of person; the right to a trial; the right not to suffer either inhuman conditions of detention, denial of justice or summary execution.

From the huge amount of documentation we have gathered, it can be seen that these human rights were violated at all levels by the Argentine state during the repression carried out by its armed forces. Nor were they violated in a haphazard fashion, but systematically, according to a similar pattern, with identical kidnappings and tortures taking place throughout the country. How can this be viewed as anything but a planned campaign of terror conceived by the military high command? How could all this have been committed by a few depraved individuals acting on their own initiative, when there was an authoritarian military regime, with all the powers and control of information that this implies? How can one speak of *individual excesses?* The information we collected confirms that this diabolical technology was employed by people who may well have been sadists, but who were carrying out orders. If our own conclusions seem insufficient in this respect, further proof is furnished by the farewell speech given to the Inter-American Defence junta on 24 January 1980 by General Santiago Omar Riveros, head of the Argentine delegation: "We waged this war with our doctrine in our hands, with the written orders of each high command." Those members of the Argentine military juntas who replied to the universal outcry at the horror by deploring "excesses in the repression which are inevitable in a dirty war", were hypocritically trying to shift the blame for this calculated terror on to the individual actions of less senior officers.

The abductions were precisely organized operations, sometimes occurring at the victim's place of work, sometimes in the street in broad daylight. They involved the open deployment of military personnel, who were given a free hand by the local police stations. When a victim was sought out in his or her home at night, armed units would surround the block and force their way in, terrorizing parents and children, who were often gagged and forced to watch. They would seize the persons they had come for, beat them mercilessly, hood them, then drag them off to their cars or trucks, while the rest of the unit almost invariably ransacked the house or looted everything that could be carried. The victims were then taken to a chamber over whose doorway might well have been inscribed the words Dante read on the gates of Hell: "Abandon hope, all ye who enter here."

Thus, in the name of national security, thousands upon thousands of human beings, usually young adults or even adolescents, fell into the sinister, ghostly category of the *desaparecidos*, a word (sad privilege for Argentina) frequently left in Spanish by the world's press.

Seized by force against their will, the victims no longer existed as citizens. Who exactly was responsible for their abduction? Why had they been abducted? Where were they? There were no precise answers to these questions: the authorities had no record of them; they were not being held in jail; justice was unaware of their existence. Silence was the only reply to all the habeas corpus writs, an ominous silence that engulfed them. No kidnapper was ever arrested, not a single detention centre was ever located, there was never news of those responsible being punished for any of the crimes. Days, weeks, months, years went by, full of uncertainty and anguish for fathers, mothers and children, all of them at the mercy of rumours and desperate hopes. They spent their time in countless attempts at wringing information from those in authority: whether officers in the armed forces who were recommended to them, bishops, military chaplains or police inspectors. They received no help.

A feeling of complete vulnerability spread throughout Argentine society, coupled with the fear that anyone, however innocent, might become a victim of the never-ending witch-hunt. Some people reacted with alarm. Others tended, consciously or unconsciously, to justify the horror. "There must be some reason for it," they would whisper, as though trying to propitiate awesome and inscrutable gods, regarding the children or parents of the disappeared as plague-bearers. Yet such feelings could never be wholehearted, as so many cases were known of people who had been sucked into that bottomless pit who were obviously not guilty of anything. It was simply that the "anti-subversive" struggle, like all hunts against witches or those possessed, had become a demented generalized repression, and the word "subversive" itself came to be used with a vast and vague range of meaning. In the semantic delirium where labels such as: *Marxist-Leninist, traitors to the fatherland, materialists and atheists, enemies of Western, Christian values,* abounded, anyone was at risk—from those who were proposing a social revolution, to aware adolescents who merely went out to the shanty towns to help the people living there.

All sectors fell into the net: trade union leaders fighting for better wages; youngsters in student unions; journalists who did not support the regime; psychologists and sociologists simply for belonging to suspicious professions; young pacifists, nuns and priests who had taken the teachings of Christ to shanty areas; the friends of these people, too, and the friends of friends, plus others whose names were given out of motives of personal vengeance, or by the kidnapped under torture. The vast majority of them were innocent not only of any acts of terrorism, but even of belonging to the fighting units of the guerrilla organizations: these latter chose to fight it out, and either died in shootouts or committed suicide before they could be captured. Few of them were alive by the time they were in the hands of the repressive forces.

From the moment of their abduction, the victims lost all rights. Deprived of all communication with the outside world, held in unknown places, subjected to barbaric tortures, kept ignorant of their immediate or ultimate fate, they risked being either thrown into a river or the sea, weighed down with blocks of cement, or burned to ashes. They were not mere objects, however, and still possessed all the human attributes: they could feel pain, could remember a mother, child or spouse, could feel infinite shame at being raped in public. They were people not only possessed of this sense of boundless anguish and fear, but also, and perhaps indeed because of feelings such as these, they were people who, in some corner of their soul, clung to an absurd notion of hope.

We have discovered close to 9000 of these unfortunate people who were abandoned by the world. We have reason to believe that the true figure is much higher. Many families were reluctant to report a disappearance for fear of reprisals. Some still hesitate, fearing a resurgence of these evil forces.

It is with sadness and sorrow that we have carried out the mission entrusted to us by the constitutional President of the Republic. It has been an extremely arduous task, for we had to piece together a shadowy jigsaw, years after the events had taken place, when all the clues had been deliberately destroyed, all documentary evidence burned, and buildings demolished. The basis for our work has therefore been the statements made by relatives or by those who managed to escape from this hell, or even the testimonies of people who were involved in the repression but who, for whatever obscure motives, approached us to tell us what they knew.

In the course of our investigations we have been insulted and threatened by the very people who committed these crimes. Far from expressing any repentance, they continue to repeat the old excuses that they were engaged in a *dirty war*, or that they were saving the country and its Western, Christian values, when in reality they were responsible for dragging these values inside the bloody walls of the dungeons of repression. They accuse us of hindering national reconciliation, of stirring up hatred and resentment, of not allowing the past to be forgotten. This is not the case. We have not acted out of any feeling of vindictiveness or vengeance. All we are asking for is truth and justice, in the same way that the churches of different denominations have done, in the understanding that there can be no true reconciliation until the guilty repent and we have justice based on truth. If this does not happen, then the transcendent mission which the judicial power fulfills in all civilized communities will prove completely valueless. Truth and justice, it should be remembered, will allow the innocent members of the armed forces to live with honour; otherwise they risk being besmirched by an unjust, all-embracing condemnation. Truth and justice will permit the armed forces as a whole to see themselves once more as the true descendants of those armies which fought so heroically despite their lack of means to bring freedom to half a continent.

We have been accused, finally, of partiality in denouncing only one side of the bloody events which have shaken our nation in recent years, and of remaining silent about the terrorism which occurred prior to March 1976, or even, in a tortuous way, of presenting an apology for it. On the contrary, our Commission has always repudiated that terror, and we are glad to take this opportunity to do so again here. It was not our task to look into the crimes committed by those terrorists, but simply to investigate the fate of the disappeared, whoever they were, and from whichever side of the violence they came. None of the relatives of the victims of that earlier terror approached us, because those people were killed rather than "disappeared". Also, Argentinians have had the opportunity of seeing an abundance of television programmes, of reading countless newspaper and magazine articles, as well as a full-length book published by the military government, in which those acts of terrorism were listed, described, and condemned, in minute detail.

Great catastrophes are always instructive. The tragedy which began with the military dictatorship in March 1976, the most terrible our nation has ever suffered, will undoubtedly serve to help us understand that it is only democracy which can save a people from horror on this scale, only democracy which can keep and safeguard the sacred, essential rights of man. Only with democracy will we be certain that NEVER AGAIN will events such as these, which have made Argentina so sadly infamous throughout the world, be repeated in our nation.

Ernesto Sabato

Authors' Note

The cases outlined in this report are drawn from the documents and evidence we received. They have been selected solely in order to substantiate and illustrate our main arguments. These in turn were formed on the basis of all the material in our possession—the evidence given by first-hand witnesses of the events described. We can discount neither the possibility of occasional errors, nor the existence of many other cases which might have illustrated our points more adequately.

As regards any persons named here according to the function they were carrying out, or who are included in the transcription of statements which implicate them in events that may have legal consequences, the National Commission in no way seeks to imply their responsibility for any of the cases mentioned. The Commission has no competence in this respect, since authority for this belongs to the judicial power, in accordance with the statutes of the constitution of Argentina.

Part One
The Repression

General Introduction

Many of the events described in this report will be hard to believe. This is because the men and women of our nation have only heard of such horror in reports from distant places. The enormity of what took place in Argentina, involving the transgression of the most fundamental human rights, is sure, still, to produce that disbelief which some used at the time to defend themselves from pain and horror. In so doing, they also avoided the responsibility born of knowledge and awareness, because the question necessarily follows: how can we prevent it happening again? And the frightening realization that both the victims and their tormenters were our contemporaries, that the tragedy took place on our soil, and that those who insulted the history of our country in this way have yet to show by word or deed that they feel any remorse for what they have done.

With this first stage of investigations complete, the Commission on Disappeared People takes the weighty but necessary responsibility for affirming that everything set out in this report did indeed happen, even if some of the details of individual cases may be open to question. These questions can only be resolved conclusively by the testimony of those who took part in the events.

Month after month of listening to accusations, testimonies and confessions, of examining documents, inspecting places, and doing all in our power to throw light on these terrifying occurrences, has given us the right to assert that a system of repression was deliberately planned to produce the events and situations which are detailed in this report. The typical sequence was: *abduction—disappearance—torture*. Each of the testimonies included in this report is representative of the thousands of cases which tell a similar story. Our selection represents only a tiny fraction of the material collected. A single one of these testimonies would in itself be enough to permit the moral condemnation which the Commission has expressed; but it is the sheer number of similar and inter-related cases which makes us absolutely convinced that a concerted plan of repression existed and was carried out.

The cases highlighted in the report were not due to any "excesses", because no such thing existed, if by "excess" we mean isolated incidents which transgress a norm. The system of repression itself, and its planning and execution, was the greatest "excess"—transgression was common and widespread. The dreadful "excesses" themselves were the norm.

It has repeatedly been claimed that those members of the security forces who committed any kind of "excess" during the anti-subversive campaign were properly brought to justice on the initiative of their commanders. This Commission wishes to deny strongly any such assertion. From the information we have collected, there is not a single instance of any member of the security forces being charged with involvement either in the forced abduction of a person, with the use of torture, or with causing the death of anyone held in the secret detention centres. The military commanders of the Process of National Reorganization reserved the term "excess" for any offence committed by military or police personnel for their own ends, without the authority of their superiors. It was not related to the repression itself.

As the report shows, murder, rape, torture, extortion, looting and other serious crimes went unpunished, as long as they were carried out within the framework of the political and ideological persecution unleashed during the years 1976 to 1982.

Abduction

There are some 600 instances of abductions recorded in the Commission's files which are said to have taken place prior to the 24 March 1976 coup. After that date the number of people who were illegally deprived of their liberty throughout Argentina rises to the tens of thousands. Eight thousand, nine hundred and sixty of them have not reappeared to this day....

When the victims entered the secret detention centres, the decisive stage of their disappearance was reached.

Torture

...In nearly all the cases brought to the attention of the Commission, the victims speak of acts of torture. Torture was an important element in the methodology of repression. Secret torture centres were set up, among other reasons, to enable the carrying out of torture to be carried out undisturbed.

The existence and widespread use of different forms of torture is particularly frightening because of the perverse imagination demonstrated, and the character of the people who carried it out, as well as of those who supported its use and employed it as a means to an end. In drawing up this report, we wondered about the best way to deal with the theme so that this chapter did not turn into merely an encyclopedia of horror. We could find no way to avoid this. After all, what else were these tortures but an immense display of the most degrading and indescribable acts of degradation, which the military governments, lacking all legitimacy in power, used to secure power over a whole nation?

We have included the full version of the first of these cases, since it is typical of all of them. From it we can understand both the physical and mental suffering inflicted on the victims. We are quoting it in full to show the extent to which it affected the personality of the person whom the torturers were trying to destroy. In the other cases we mention, we have kept only those parts describing the methods of torture used.

Lastly, we are well aware of, and share, the feeling of dismay which the bald narration we set down here will arouse in torture victims and their families, who were made to suffer so much. We know only too well the anguish that a detailed knowledge of this barbarity causes....

Secret Detention Centres (SDCs)

General Considerations

The policy of the disappearance of persons could not have been carried out without the detention centres. There were about 340 of them throughout the country. Thousands of men and women illegally deprived of their freedom passed through them, often being kept in detention for years, sometimes never returning. This was where they lived through their "disappearance"; this was where they were when the authorities would reply in the negative to requests for information in the habeas corpus appeals. There they spent their days at the mercy of others, with minds twisted by the practice of torture and extermination, while the military authorities (who frequently visited these centres) would respond to national and international public opinion by asserting that the disappeared were abroad, or that they had been victims of feuding amongst themselves. (Statements of this nature are included in the answers given by the *de facto* government to the Inter-American Commission on Human Rights of the OAS—see "Report on the Situation of Human Rights in Argentina", 1980.)

The characteristics of these centres, and the daily life led there, reveal that they had been specifically conceived for the subjection of victims to a meticulous and deliberate stripping of all human attributes, rather than for their simple physical elimination.

To be admitted to one of these centres meant to cease to exist. In order to achieve this end, attempts were made to break down the captives' identity: their spatio-temporal points of reference were disrupted, and their minds and bodies tortured beyond imagination.

These centres were only secret as far as the public and the relatives and people close to the victims were concerned, inasmuch as the authorities systematically refused to give any information on the fate of the abducted persons to judicial appeals and national and international human rights organizations. It goes without saying that their existence and operation were only possible with the use of the State's financial and human resources, and that, from the highest military authorities down to each and every member of the Security Forces who formed part of this repressive structure, these centres were their fundamental basis of operation.

The reality was continually denied, the military government also making use of the total control it exercised over the media, to confuse and misinform the public. It would subsequently be seen during the hostilities of the war in the South Atlantic, to what extent covering up the truth and misinformation were essential to the most important acts of the military governments between 1976 and 1983.

> I categorically deny that there exist in Argentina any concentration camps or prisoners being held in military establishments beyond the time absolutely necessary for the investigation of a person captured in an operation before they are transferred to a penal establishment. (Jorge Rafael Videla, 22 December 1977, *Gente* magazine.)

> There are no political prisoners in Argentina, except for a few persons who may have been detained under government emergency legislation and who are really being detained because of their political activity. There are no prisoners being held merely for being political, or because they do not share the ideas held by the Government. (Roberto Viola, 7 September 1978.)

From the highest levels of the military government they attempted to present to the world a situation of maximum legality. Disregarding all limits—even the exceptional *de facto* legislation—the dictatorship kept up a secret, parallel structure. At first categorically denied, later—faced with a mass of evidence resulting from accusations made by relatives and the testimonies of prisoners who were released—they had to admit the existence of this structure, though with false explanations....

A substantial number of reports and testimonies received by this Commission corroborate the presence of high-ranking military officials in the detention centres....

Personnel

Conscripts were for the most part kept on the fringes of SDC activity. The centres at Formosa and El Palomar Air Base were exceptions, since some of them were made to participate in the camp's operation. Nor did the whole of the military or security personnel take part. The order was to keep the SDCs isolated, as a secret structure. Personnel assigned to guard such centres comprised members of the *Gendarmería*, of the Federal Penitentiary system, or of the police, always under the command of armed forces officers. This guard personnel was not generally the same as those who tortured in the systematic interrogation sessions designed to obtain information. Testimonies have been gathered from which it is clear that some of the soldiers assigned to guarding the camps demonstrated signs of humanity, showing concern for the appalling condition of the prisoners:

> I was abducted and held in the Pozo de Quilmes from 12 November 1977. On one occasion, when they couldn't bring our daily rations as usual from a nearby army unit, the corporal on guard, nicknamed "Chupete", bought food with his own money and cooked it for us himself. In addition, the corporal on duty, Juan Carlos, who seemed to belong to the Army, would give us cigarettes when conditions of imprisonment improved....
>
> (Fernando Schell, file No. 2825.)

However, this is not the case with the majority of personnel attached to the SDCs, who generally contributed to the physical and mental breakdown of the prisoners, punishing them unnecessarily and capriciously justifying it.

Food

The infrequency and inferiority of meals constituted another form of torment. Prisoners were fed—depending on the centre—once or twice a day, but on many occasions several days went by when they were given no food at all. At other times they were given water with flour or raw offal. In general, rations were barely enough, and anybody who tried to give some to another person in a worse state than themselves was severely punished. Solidarity was forbidden.

In spite of all this, mealtimes were eagerly awaited since it meant not only eating but also the chance to lift one's hood and possibly to establish contact with another person, although conversation between prisoners was brutally punished....

All those released coincide in mentioning the appalling food, which, it should be borne in mind, remained unchanged throughout their confinement, causing the physical deterioration of the prisoners....

Death as a Political Weapon: Extermination

In the course of our work we have frequently had to confront the subject of death: death as a result of torture, electric shock, submersion in water, suffocation; death *en masse*, collective or individual, premeditated, by drowning at sea or firing squad.

It is a subject which by its very nature deeply disturbs our consciences, not just because of the huge numbers involved, but because of the circumstances surrounding these deaths, which affect the ethical and legal foundations of our civilized society.

The death penalty has traditionally been systematically banned from the legal system in this country. Under the military government this policy was abandoned and it was incorporated into penal legislation. It was argued that it was necessary to prevent the worst subversive crimes.

Even so, there was still an instinctive reluctance to apply the death penalty. It was believed its introduction would discourage anti-social elements from committing the more serious crimes, or that preliminary trials by military courts would reserve its application for exceptional cases. No council of war formally tried anyone who deserved such a terrible punishment.

But the reality was different. There were thousands of deaths. None of these came about through an ordinary or military trial, none was the result of a sentence. Technically speaking, they were murders, murders into which no proper investigation was ever carried out and for which those responsible were never, as far as we know, punished in any way.

To conclude, the regime which considered it necessary to change our legal tradition by introducing capital punishment, never used it as such. Instead, it organized a collective crime, a veritable mass extermination, on which the evidence is now coming to light in the morbid form of hundreds of nameless corpses and the testimony of the survivors, telling of those who died in agony.

It was not an excess of repressive activity, it was not a mistake. It was the implementation of a cold-blooded decision. There are so many examples and proofs that there can be no doubt about this conclusion.

Mass Executions by Firing Squad: The "Pit" on the Loma del Torito

Soon after the work of the Commission began, we started receiving a large number of depositions about the "disappearances" of people in Córdoba. Their stories all converged on the La Perla secret detention centre. The most horrific violations of human rights were committed here. Mass executions were also carried out.

In their testimony the survivors speak of their fear of "transfers", carried out regularly in a sinister Mercedes-Benz lorry which would return after a brief interval without its human cargo. They associated transfers with the repeated threats by their gaolers that they would be taken "to the pit".

This awful reference was to the execution of many prisoners by firing squad on the edge of a pit, dug in advance to bury their bodies. The place was in the area known as the Loma del Torito, inside the La Perla camp, under the military jurisdiction of the base of the 4th Airborne Cavalry Reconnaissance Squadron in Córdoba.

This Commission obtained legal authorization to excavate the land, and did so on 22 March 1984, without any positive result. Nevertheless, confirmation by a witness, who had farmed in the area for many years, that the earth had been disturbed, backed up by other testimony and accounts of the exhumation of human remains there, tends to indicate that the prisoners' fear for their lives was well-founded. Let us look at some of the statements....

Why did the Bodies Disappear?

It is hard for us, after our difficult and complex search for living disappeared prisoners, to accept that many of them are dead and that their bodies have been scattered or destroyed as part of a planned policy of making them disappear.

This evidence necessarily leads us to ask, why such an evil policy? Why should the bodies be destroyed? Was it on the same basis as an individual criminal trying to wipe out all traces of his act? We do not think this sufficient explanation.

There was something more, which had to do with the methodology of disappearance. First it was the people, their absence giving hope to the relatives that the kidnap victim would be freed and return; then the concealment and destruction of documentation, which undoubtedly existed in every case, prolonging the uncertainty about what had happened; and finally, the nameless bodies, without identity, driving people distraught at the impossibility of knowing the specific fate of their loved one. It was a bottomless pit of horror.

This is why we think that the nameless bodies fit into the same way of thinking that took the initial decision to make people disappear: wiping out the identity of the corpses magnified the shadow hanging over the thousands of disappeared of whom all trace was lost after their arrest or kidnapping.

It was another way of paralysing public protest, of ensuring the silence of the relatives. By giving them hope that their loved ones might be alive, in the nebulous category of missing persons, an ambiguity was created which forced the relatives into isolation, frightened to do anything which might annoy the government. They were terrified by the mere idea that their own actions might decide whether their son, daughter, father or brother joined the lists of the dead.

It was also a way of trying to stall investigation into the facts. By the covering-up process, the apportioning of individual responsibility was blurred. The shadow of suspicion was cast over a great many military officers—unless they could prove otherwise, which was almost impossible—as to their personal role in the direction or execution of these crimes.

Lastly, at the heart of this policy of total disappearance lay the prevention by every possible means of solidarity being shown by the population in general, with all the protests and demands this would lead to within the country, and the knowledge abroad that behind the facade of a fight against a terrorist minority lurked genocide.

The Implications of "Impunity"

Every society without exception has always been concerned with the possibility that some crimes go unpunished. Concern turns into alarm when impunity becomes a planned component in the execution of the crime, incorporated like an armour plate around events, and part of the *modus operandi* of systematic criminal behaviour. Then this is a case of state terrorism. Hobbes in *Leviathan* argued that there is no greater crime than that perpetrated in the knowledge of its impunity. The institutional subversion inherent in such a situation seriously undermines the ethical basis intrinsic to government acts, and for a period which is difficult to measure. Such is the case with the government of the so-called "Process of National Reorganization".

The fact that they take advantage of the victim's state of defencelessness says everything about the nature of the oppressors. This phenomenon takes on additional dimensions when those in power from the very beginning of their administration award themselves special authority to plan a complete system of illicit acts. The views of the constitutional President of Argentina are clear in this regard, in his justification of Decree 158/83 for the prosecution of those responsible for ordering and executing illicit acts: "The Military Junta which usurped power conceived and instrumentalized a plan of operations ... based on manifestly illegal methods."

If we take note of this presidential statement, the criminal events which took place cannot be considered "excesses" or chance occurrences, undesired by their authors. On the contrary, in line with the above definition, they were from the beginning created as part of a network of crime with no historical precedent; this network was based on the assumption that the responsibility for planning and performing these illegal acts lay with the consciences of those who carried them out, and whose actions were checked by no judicial or legal constraint or consideration.

Tragically, this presidential statement was fully corroborated in the investigation carried out by this Commission. The context of impunity within which those responsible acted reveals itself more clearly in the case of arbitrary detainment, disappearance and/or murder of individual Argentinians who were well known both nationally and internationally. We are referring to men and women who held distinguished positions in public life, were known for the importance of their roles in scientific, diplomatic, religious, political, business, trade union and literary circles; their fate symbolized the conviction of those responsible for State terrorism that they would never be called to account for their acts.

Representatives of this particular group in society have always had access to sources of power and decision, to which they once again appealed, but in this case found no remedy for the clandestine kidnapping and ungrounded accusations of which they were victims. Their relatives immediately resorted to any sources of power—particularly within the Armed Forces—to which they had access. In spite of this, they were unable to reverse injustices which at times turned into tragedies. In addition to those who were special cases because of their outstanding position in the community, there were others who, although not members of these groups, became well known to the public. The traumatic experiences which they suffered were extensively publicized since eminent individuals or institutions—diplomatic, political, etc.—became actively concerned for their protection, and attempted to save them from uncertainty, darkness and horror. They too failed.

The aim was to seek to instill in the population as a whole a sense of utter defencelessness in the face of a multi-faceted power, through carrying out selective attacks which went unpunished and were impossible to redress, and through demonstrating that traditional methods of personal protection, whether social or legal, were entirely inefficacious. A general conviction that nothing can change the course of events can be a great advantage in the execution of a terrorist, repressive, policy.

We shall make a brief reference to cases of disappearance, torture and death of people whose detention, for very different reasons, mobilized the intervention of highly respected institutions, which were in fact unable to modify the absolute impunity within which illegal repression operated. Without doubt, however, the greatest evidence for this impunity is the thousands of ordinary human beings who disappeared and whose cases have not been clarified....

Agents and Structures of Repression

The National Commission on Disappeared People has been presented with a number of depositions and testimonies from people who acknowledged their involvement in task forces and other forms of operation of the repressive apparatus. These depositions were linked to the knowledge they had of the methods used for repressive purposes, as well as containing accounts of kidnapping, torture and physical elimination.

In several instances this spontaneous collaboration came from repressive agents who had themselves been punished before 10 December 1983 by the Armed Forces and Security Forces for illicit action which was marginal to the anti-subversive struggle and motivated by individual interests. These same crimes went unpunished when they were part of a planned operation by the whole repressive apparatus.

In these cases, giving testimony was motivated not so much by the search for moral support, repentance, moral sanction or military honour, as by the conviction that they had been "abandoned by their own superiors", after having

> contributed to the anti-subversive war, in some cases losing their career, in others risking their own lives, while they observed their superiors becoming wealthier, the generalized corruption of those of their own rank, and the loss of the aims which had originally been given as motivation for the struggle. (Testimonies Nos. 683, 1901 and 3675.)

Some of those who gave testimony were influenced by the knowledge of the physical elimination of several brothers-in-arms "because they were no longer of any use to their superiors or because they knew too much" (testimony No. 683). Only exceptionally did any of them show signs of repentance or moral responsibility for their experiences.

In some cases (testimonies Nos. 3157 and 3675), those giving testimony were resentful towards their superiors "for having used us", involving them in a political and economic project which finally betrayed the "nationalist ideals" for which they had joined the Army, the Police or paramilitary groups in the first place.

Feelings of guilt were expressed in perhaps two or three cases; others were sickened by the "madness of it all"; others expressed a desire to denounce the atrocities they had witnessed or been responsible for, "to prevent them from happening again" or to prevent "my children from having to live through anything like it" (testimony No. 3675).

Any sign of disagreement within the Armed Forces and the Security Forces about the methods used for detention or elimination was brutally punished. To provide any information to the relatives about the arrested-disappeared, concerning their whereabouts, physical condition or destination, was tantamount to signing their own death warrant. They were forbidden even among members of their own ranks to comment about the operations carried out; they were punished with maximum severity if any sign of humanity were shown towards any prisoner:

> My husband was a Federal Police Inspector in the Department of Political Affairs at Federal Security. He was an idealist within the Police; he was against torture and anything that could be considered cheating or corruption. His service record was impeccable and at twenty-five years old he was already an Inspector. His only mistake was to have provided information to relatives on the disappearance of detainees. Only two days after the disappearance of my husband, Carlos María,... the wife of a second lieutenant ... let me know that I should "no longer search for him because they have already killed him". (Mónica De Napoli de Aristegui, file No. 2448.)

Any attempt to escape from the repressive structure, which members called the "blood pact," could mean their persecution and even elimination....

The Attitudes of Some Members of the Church

The bishops of the Argentinian Church repeatedly condemned the repression which this Commission investigated. Scarcely two months had passed since the coup on 24 March 1976 when the Episcopal Conference in a General Assembly described the methods used as "sinful". In May 1977, after making representations to members of the Military Junta, it published a strongly worded document on similar lines.

Regrettably, some individual members of the clergy by their presence, their silence or even by direct involvement supported the very actions that had been condemned by the Church as a whole.

The following testimonies made reference to members of the clergy:...

Questionnaires Sent to Former Officials of the De Facto Government

Once the work of this Commission was well advanced it was decided to send out lengthy questionnaires to those former State officials who, because of the positions they held in the command of the Armed Forces or Security Forces of the *de facto* government, or in the carrying out of operations, could be expected to have the information necessary to answer such questions.

The decision to send out the questionnaires was prompted by the clear knowledge of the members of the Commission of the difficulties involved in locating the whereabouts of the disappeared persons and by their requiring information regarding:

- The criteria used by the Joint Forces in interpreting and implementing the instruction to "neutralize and/or annihilate the action of subversive elements" contained in Decrees No. 261/76 and 2772/75, and also the principles which served to legitimize the methods used in the so-called anti-subversive struggle.
- The objective criteria used to decide who should be arrested.
- The list of places where these were held and the authorities responsible for their administration and custody.
- The special arrangements made for the disposal of the remains of those who died and the identification of the judicial authority acting in each case.
- The decisions regarding the form of the documentation relating to the orders, execution and outcome of operations and the uses to which it was put, and regarding the computing centre which processed this information.

In addition to the other measures taken by the Commission to investigate thousands of depositions on the disappearance of people, the questionnaire was used to obtain any further information which could help in the task assigned to us.

Replies to the questionnaires were requested through the Ministry of Defence and the Ministry of the Interior by Decrees No. 2107/84 from the following members of the Military Junta and Presidency; Ministers of the Interior and Chiefs of Staff of the three branches of the Armed Forces; Commanders of the Army; Chiefs of the Intelligence Services; Chiefs of the Argentine Federal Police; of the *Gendarmería*, of the Argentine Naval Prefecture and others: [The report then lists the names of 44 military officers who received these questionnaires.]...

There were a few cases in which no answer was forthcoming, and none of the replies received by this Commission have been of use in clarifying the circumstances surrounding the disappearance of people or in helping to trace them.

The Coordination of Repression in Latin America

The illegal repressive operations undertaken by the government and the activities of persecution linked to them were not confined by geographical boundaries. The security organizations of neighbouring states collaborated with these activities in reciprocal arrangements whereby people were arrested with no regard for legality, in blatant violation of the international treaties and conventions on political asylum and refuge to which our country subscribes. The agents of foreign repressive regimes operated in our country and arrested Uruguayans, Paraguayans, Bolivians and other nationals.

Foreigners were clandestinely abducted with impunity and handed over to the authorities of their respective countries. Some of these people were refugees, some were legal residents and others were under the protection of the High Commission of the United Nations. The violation of their status as refugees represented clear breaches of internationally recognized conventions and constituted a blatant contempt for long-established precedents relating to political asylum.

The method used consisted basically of a linking-up of illegal, repressive groups, which acted together as a single force. This operation, because of its clandestine nature, constituted a clear violation of national sovereignty.

The events which occurred demonstrated the existence of a typically "multi-national" repressive apparatus. Under its protection the foreign forces of repression were integrated into the task groups and became involved in kidnapping, interrogation under torture, assassination or the transfer of their nationals to secret detention centres in their own countries.

Although the largest number of foreigners involved were Uruguayans, there were significant numbers of Paraguayan, Bolivian and even Chilean citizens who had been given asylum. They all suffered the consequences of the close association between authoritarian political models imposed on this part of South America....

The Argentinian constitutional authorities should examine this evidence with the utmost care to guarantee the exercise of the nation's full sovereignty through complete control over potential unlawful links between officials of our country and others.

Documentation

Decree No. 187/83 which created the Commission on Disappeared People directs in article 2, paragraph d, that the organization should "Denounce any attempt to conceal or withhold evidence relating to matters being investigated". The work undertaken since the Commission came into operation has established the existence of a considerable amount of documentation which has been destroyed or is being concealed by the perpetrators of repressive action.

The immense and complex machinery built up to carry out clandestine repressive activity required a gigantic infrastructure which was based on orders, directions and communications which inevitably were recorded in writing. Considerable resources were made available, staff allocated and entire buildings constructed or rehabilitated as secret detention centres. Such an enterprise presupposes the existence of essential recorded information. All the people kidnapped were identified and complete dossiers were made out for each of them, with copies distributed to each different security and intelligence organization.

Where is that vast quantity of written material which must have been in the hands of those who made such a huge and sinister machine work? Intensive investigation has been able to identify only a minimal amount of it. This does, however, form the basis for the reconstruction of part of the jigsaw puzzle of the terror which reigned over the country.

Recently, journalistic sources revealed information from the Ministry of the Interior which indicated that orders had been issued by authorities in the military government to destroy the entire secret documentation relating to repressive activities.

The former *de facto* President General Reynaldo Benito Bignone himself gave orders, in a confidential Decree No. 2726/83, to destroy documentation relating to those detained at the disposition of the National Executive under the state of siege. The difficulties encountered by the Commission in their task of investigation were put to the President of the Nation, Dr Raúl Alfonsín, in a letter of 3 May 1984 which stated:

> There is no doubt that the Governments of the former military Juntas, by establishing absolute control in order to guarantee state monopoly in the exercise of force, received, recorded and filed relevant detailed information. Furthermore, if, as was maintained by the ex-Commanders and high-ranking officers involved, the methods and procedures used in the so-called anti-subversive struggle were based on a formal legal structure, then the existence of a minimum of documentation following from this institutional character of the repression was unavoidable. At the very least, this should include the instructions which preceded decisions of guilt or innocence, the registration of names of detainees or of the dead, and the places of imprisonment or burial.
>
> However, we have so far been able to obtain little of this information. Those who know they are responsible remain silent, and hiding behind the anonymity provided by military secrecy, avoid or delay responding fully to our inquiries, or do not respond at all.
>
> The first task assigned to this Commission—to determine the whereabouts of the disappeared persons—is therefore hindered by an essential lack of documentary information regarding the specific operational orders of the repression, the identification of those arrested, prosecuted, sentenced, freed or killed, and the places where they were held or should have been given a decent burial.
>
> As you will no doubt observe, Mr President, in order to make clear the limits of our accountability to public opinion, the report with which our task concludes should make explicit the sources of information upon which it is based as well as the channels which were closed to us.

The destruction and concealment of the documentation concerning the grave crimes committed by the *de facto* government placed on the Commission, the judicial powers and the population, the extremely difficult task of reconstructing what occurred using the scanty documentation available. Nevertheless, on the basis of testimonies from those freed, from the relatives of disappeared prisoners, from members of the security forces and the few documents found, we have been able to discover the fundamental information about the illegal action of the repression.

Registration of those Arrested-Disappeared

Those who were arrested and transferred to the secret detention centres were interrogated, mostly by use of unlawful methods, to discover their political, trade union or student activities and affiliations.

In each case a card was made out assigning a number to each detainee, which was then used to identify them during their captivity. In many detention centres prisoners were photographed and the declarations obtained from them were tape-recorded. Testimonies made by those freed from various centres throughout the country concur on this particular aspect of procedure.

Carlos Muñoz (file No. 704) relates what occurred at the Navy Mechanics School:

> ...in January they took the sixty (referring to the number of detainees held) down into the basement and a photograph was taken of each one. In February I was given a job in photography as that was work I knew how to do, and I was transferred to the laboratory.
> All the cases were filed on microfilm containing descriptions of procedures used, past record and sentence....

Falsification of Documents

According to testimonies, the terrorist apparatus had an administrative structure which falsified documents for use in carrying out new unlawful activities. Evidence of this is shown in the operation of the detention centre established at the Navy Mechanics School.

The testimonies of Miriam Lewin de García (file No. 2365), Lázaro Jaime Gladstein (file No. 4912) and Víctor Melchor Basterra (file No. 5011) indicate that as "arrested-disappeared" they had to work in the basement of the officers' mess at the Navy Mechanics School, where a printing press used for the production of false documentation operated, producing "passports, identity cards, property deeds, driving licences, credentials for the Federal Police, university degrees, etc."

This unlawful behaviour was important in facilitating the carrying out of other crimes detailed in this report: the sale of properties, use of stolen vehicles, use of houses belonging to the disappeared, entry and exit from the country of task force members and their infiltration into different sectors and activities of society....

Alteration of Documents

Cases of the alteration or concealment of existing documentation to obliterate traces of criminal action have been brought to light by our investigation.

The case of Silvia Isabella Valenzi (file No. 3741) is an example of this. She was kidnapped and held in Pozo de Quilmes and was taken to the Quilmes Hospital to have her baby. Both her admission and the birth of her daughter, Rosa Isabella Valenzi, were recorded in the register of births. The Commission obtained a copy of the register of births and found page 156 crudely altered. "Identity unknown" had replaced the patient's name: Silvia Isabella, and by the number 82019 which recorded the birth of Rosa Isabella Valenzi had been added the word "deceased". The nurse and midwife at the hospital were kidnapped for the "crime" of letting Silvia Isabella Valenzi's family know what was going on....

The Profits of Repression

It is worth repeating that the violations committed by those responsible for repression involved not only attacks against the freedom and security of individuals, but also the systematic and simultaneous transgression of other legal rights, such as property and public documents to facilitate the transfer of goods or to set up non-existent transactions. False deeds, false documents, false car registrations and certificates of ownership were made out to expedite looting and theft. We are referring here to crimes committed in the course of carrying out the official policy of making people "disappear", leaving aside the limitless number of economic crimes which were committed by the *de facto* authorities during their administration, as those go beyond the aims of the present investigation.

The mentors of the so-called Process of National Reorganization often used the term "illicit", perhaps in order to refer to the lucrative aspects of the "excesses" they themselves acknowledged having committed during the anti-subversive struggle....

Part Two
The Victims

Introductory Note

The Commission on Disappeared People has compiled two lists of victims of the repression. The first of these is of those persons who disappeared; the second, of those who although they are still missing, have been seen in secret detention centres.

In the first category there are 8,960 people, but clearly the list is not exhaustive. It was compiled on the basis of depositions received by this Commission (the number for each respective file is also given alongside the name) and compared with other lists drawn up by other national and international organizations.

Up until the last minute the list was being cross-referenced by computer. However, there may still be mistakes, for instance, in an individual case—though not in a series of cases—as someone may have failed to inform the relevant organizations that they are no longer missing.

We also know that in many cases depositions were not filed at all, either because the victims had no relatives or because the relatives were frightened or lived a long distance from the centre of town. This was confirmed by the Commission when we went to the interior of the country. Relatives of people who had disappeared said that in the past few years they had not known where to go for help.

The list of people seen in secret detention centres is also a partial one: we could find the complete names and surnames of only 1,300 people.

However, we know that thousands of people passed through these camps, who were only known by their nicknames to prisoners who were freed; or by a superficial physical description; or by their province of origin; profession, political affiliation or some other isolated characteristic. There are 800 cases of this type. Nonetheless, by continuing to work patiently—and with adequate technical support—it will be possible to increase this provisional list. Finally, it has to be said that a complete list of people who disappeared and an account of what happened to them may only be provided by those who were responsible for causing the disappearances, so long as a record of their deeds was kept intact and not tampered with or destroyed, which constitutes a crime under the Penal Code and which has been formally denounced when necessary by the Commission.

The Disappeared by Age Group

Age	%		Age	%
0-5	0.82		41-45	3.40
6-10	0.25		46-50	2.41
11-15	0.58		51-55	1.84
16-20	10.61		56-60	1.17
21-25	32.62		61-65	0.75
26-30	25.90		66-70	0.41
31-35	12.26		70+	0.25
36-40	6.73			

The Disappeared According to Sex

If one analyses these figures, it is clear that women suffered from the repression on a large scale. It is striking that 10 per cent of the women who disappeared (3 per cent of all the disappeared people) were pregnant women.

Women who disappeared	:	30%
(Pregnant women	:	3% of total)
Men who disappeared	:	70%

Children and Pregnant Women Who Disappeared

"Woe to those who abuse a child," say the Scriptures. Never, perhaps, has this maxim become such a horrific reality as in the cases related in this chapter.

When a child is forcibly removed from its legitimate family to be put in another, according to some ideological precept of what's "best for the child's welfare", then this constitutes a perfidious usurpation of duty. The repressors who took the disappeared children from their homes, or who seized mothers on the point of giving birth, were making decisions about people's lives in the same cold-blooded way that booty is distributed in war. Deprived of their identity and taken away from their parents, the disappeared children constitute, and will continue to constitute, a deep blemish on our society. In their case, the blows were aimed at the defenceless, the vulnerable and the innocent, and a new type of torment was conceived.

This most painful situation was rapidly challenged by the extraordinarily indefatigable and discreet work begun by the Grandmothers of the Plaza de Mayo, which has so far resulted in the registration of 172 cases of children who disappeared, most of whom were seized at the time of their mother's detention, or who were born in prison. Of these, twenty-five have been traced, but the remaining 147 have not, even though there are many leads, and investigations are under way which suggest that they may be found in the future....

The Effects on Children

Many pregnant women were kidnapped, and in captivity they endured all kinds of suffering. Some were released and managed to have their babies either at home or in hospitals. However, both the mothers and their children suffered the sequels of their descent into hell. These after-effects were difficult to overcome even with clinical and psychological treatment, and enormous efforts had to be made by the mother and child for them to adjust back to family and social life....

Adolescents

...Almost 250 boys and girls aged between thirteen and eighteen years disappeared, kidnapped in their homes, in the street, or on leaving school. It is enough to look at the mural that the Commission prepared with the photographs of adolescents who had disappeared for the television programme *Nunca Más*, for the question "Why?" to remain unanswerable.

Many adolescents also disappeared as a consequence of the repression against their parents....

A Father's Memory

Enrique Fernández Meijide remembers the disappearance of his son Pablo (file No. 4807) in this way:

They took away my son who, at the age of seventeen, was at the end of his adolescence. As well as feeling the loss of someone I loved, anger at the possibility of his being maltreated, physically and mentally, and fear about his future, there was the frustration of knowing that his education was not completed. I was (I felt) responsible because he still did not have autonomy. Everyone knows that to be able to move about freely in this country, an adolescent needs written authorization from his father, and that without a father's authorization going abroad is unthinkable. His brothers were stunned. They could not understand why I was so powerless and incapable of preserving the family unit. This forced me to face up to a feeling of emptiness, to my own misery. Isn't it a nightmare? Every day I have to come to terms with the fact that I am still living....

The Family as Victim

It is a feature of the disappearance syndrome that the stability and structure of the family of the person who disappears is profoundly affected. The arrest (generally carried out in the presence of the family or of people connected to the family); the anxious search for news at public offices, law courts, police stations and military garrisons; the hope that some information will arrive; the fantasy of a bereavement that is never confirmed; these are factors that destabilize a family group just as much as the individual members. Behind each disappearance, there is often a family that is destroyed or dismembered, and always a family that is assaulted in what is most intimate: its right to privacy, to the security of its members, and to respect for the profoundly affectionate relations that are the reason for its existence.

This attack on the family has extreme consequences. However, that is only part of the problem. In causing people to disappear, the attack on the family went much further and took on the cruellest, most merciless of forms. There is evidence that on several occasions members of the family were used as hostages for people who were being sought; or that sometimes the presumed responsibility of the person who the police were after rebounded with full force on that person's family, in the form of robbery, physical violence and even disappearances, while at other times the torture was shared or witnessed by members of a suspect's family. To have a person suspected of subversion in the family was more than sufficient reason for punishing the family as a group or individually. To show any solidarity, however minimal, was reason enough for torture, suffering and even disappearance.

The Family as Hostage

It was common practice during the repression to seize one or more members of the family of the person sought, to obtain information on their whereabouts by threats and violence, or with the aim of provoking him/her to come forward and surrender. Thus siblings, mothers, fathers and even grandparents were illegally arrested, violently treated, and at times made to disappear in the search for one member of the family who was under suspicion....

Families Who Disappeared

Such was the impetus of the repression that it exceeded even the use of relatives as hostages and the total lack of respect for family values. This Commission has depositions which are proof of the disappearance of entire families, without the existence of any reasons, however distorted, that may have influenced such an action. We think it important to mention three such cases:...

People Over Fifty-Five Still Among the Disappeared

Thousands of young people, hundreds of babies, children and adolescents disappeared. But the "pensioners" were not spared repression and torture either. Our file shows 150 people aged fifty-five or more, who disappeared after March 1976. Generally they were taken from their homes, where often they were acting as grandparents. Neither the advanced age, nor, in many cases, the precarious state of health of the victims were respected....

It is very difficult in the context of a struggle against subversion to find a valid reason for imprisoning and torturing people of the age we have referred to. The majority were taken as hostages. The real search was for their children and they could be the most direct way of finding them. They were captured, robbed, tortured, and made to disappear, in many cases with the intention of forcing them to betray their children. On other occasions they were kidnapped because they refused to be intimidated by the reign of terror imposed by a military dictatorship and went on struggling to find their children alive....

Members of the Clergy and Religious Orders

It does not seem redundant to repeat once more that the drama of the illegal repression in Argentina was that each and every sector of society suffered. The clergy and lay members of the Catholic Church and other churches were affected.

Members of the Church who were committed to helping the least fortunate, or who denounced the systematic violation of human rights, were persecuted by state terrorism in a way that was particularly cruel. Thus, Catholic priests and nuns, seminarists and catechists, and members of other faiths were kidnapped, beaten, tortured and, in many cases, killed.

The Christian faith of the Armed Forces contrasted with the un-Christian nature of the repression. The contradictions in those who were responsible for the repression know no limits: while advocating a Western, Christian style of life the lack of respect shown towards human beings was constant. In April 1976 the then Colonel Juan Bautista Sasiaiñ, who later became Head of the Federal Police, declared that "The Army values a human being as such because the Army is Christian" (*La Nación*, 10 April 1976)....

It is also worth remembering how, more recently, General Jorge Rafael Videla referred to the "Final Report on the Disappeared," which was published by the Military Junta (April, 1983), as "an act of love".

Let us see how this love for one's neighbour was interpreted, through a few witnesses' accounts:

> For Christmas 1977 the internal security measures were reinforced and something extraordinary happened. About fifteen of us prisoners were taken to attend a Mass in the officers' mess of the Navy Mechanics School. In the hall of the dormitories a simple altar had been erected and benches had been laid out. We were all in chains, with our hands tied behind our backs and our heads covered with hoods. They removed our hoods and Captain Acosta said that to celebrate the feast of Christmas in a Christian manner he had decided that those of us who were believers should be allowed to hear Mass, go to confession and receive communion, and that those of us who were not believers could attend, to benefit from spiritual peace; and that all of us should think that life and peace were possible and that everything was possible in the Navy Mechanics School. Meanwhile we could hear the shrieks of people....

Conscripts

The depositions presented to this Commission referring to soldiers and conscripts who disappeared were of special significance, both because of the large number of depositions and their characteristics. It is necessary to analyse the situation of these young conscripts, most of whom were not more than eighteen years old.

1. In the first place they had been entrusted by their parents to the most senior commanders in the military service where they were enrolled.

2. At the same time, at the moment of embarking on military service, an administrative relationship was formally established between the young soldiers and the State that implied rights and duties that had to be fulfilled by both parties: by the soldier and by each branch of the Armed Services and their respective commanders-in-chief. It was a fundamental duty of the latter that they could never be ignorant or uninformed about what was happening to soldiers under their command.

3. Furthermore, all the activities of conscripts take place under, and are in the total and permanent control of, their superiors. Thus, in considering them to be involved in actions outside the law, the Armed Forces had all the legal means at their disposal to sanction the presumed lawbreaker legally.

Methods of Imprisonment

Away from their families, where the young men had enjoyed the protection of their parents, and from the moment when the leadership of the Armed Forces took charge of them, two developments occurred which are repeated in more than 135 cases of disappearances among citizens doing their military service. Because of the young men's lack of defence, their captors could take advantage of all the facilities that the situation offered them. On the other hand, those who were in command did not take responsibility, or share the responsibility, for their omissions, or for the alleged orders that they may have given to facilitate the illegal detentions. These detentions were carried out in the same place that the soldiers were stationed in 35 per cent of the cases, in the soldiers' sleeping quarters in 18 per cent of the cases, in 29 per cent of the cases when the soldier was on "leave" or "on a mission"; in 7 per cent of the cases in the streets by people dressed in civilian clothes; in 4 per cent of the cases immediately after being discharged from active service; and in 5 per cent of the cases in other circumstances....

In all the cases the reports given to the judiciary by the authorities contacted simply stated that the victim in question was not detained on the orders of the National Executive or on anyone's authority, with the result that the writs of habeas corpus were refused....

Journalists

If one is to point to a sector of Argentine society that was singled out to be closely watched by the whole repressive and persecutory apparatus of the military government, then, inevitably, one must mention journalists. There was nothing casual or mistaken about the fact that the number of victims in proportion to the number of professionals working in this field was extremely high. Besides being directed against culture in a general sense, which is always treated with suspicion by dictatorships, it is clear that this attack on journalists was an attempt to silence a very important group in society, in order to prevent all public debate. Naturally, journalism attracts a very wide range of intellectuals, artists and literary personalities as well as people with a high level of concern for politics and sociology. Furthermore, journalists' trade unions are renowned for strongly defending their members. Because of this they stand out among those struggling for the freedom of thought. On 24 March 1976, the Junta of the Commanders-in-Chief let it be known in their communiqué No. 19 that "anyone who by any means emits, spreads or propagates news, communiqués or images with a view to upsetting, prejudicing or demeaning the activity of the Armed, Security, or Police Forces, will be liable to a punishment of up to ten years in prison." In time the meaning and scope of this warning became evident. The military took over the Argentine Journalists Federation (Federación Argentina de Trabajadores de Prensa). Foreign news agency correspondents were expelled from the country, and numerous books in private and public libraries were seized and burnt.

It was reported in *La Razón* on 29 April 1976 that Lieutenant Colonel Jorge Eduardo Gorleri, head of the 14th Regiment of the Airborne Infantry, which is under the command of the 3rd Army Corps, based in Córdoba, had invited journalists to witness a public burning of books by Marxist authors, or those with a similar philosophy, that had been confiscated from different bookshops in the city. On this occasion Lieutenant-Colonel Gorleri declared they were going to burn "pernicious literature which affects our intellect and our Christian way of being ... and ultimately our most traditional spiritual ideals, encapsulated in the words God, Country and Home".

Many journalists were imprisoned, or disappeared, or were killed. Those responsible for the repression saw journalists as a threat to the consensus that was meant to exist for the government's highly controversial and compromising actions. Journalists were also seen as a threat to the secrecy that was meant to surround the illegal, repressive system of disappearances, which was aimed at paralysing the nation with fear. The mere possibility of some testimonies eventually being published, or of someone being given information on what was going on, was considered by the regime a major threat to its policies. Something had to be done that would be more than the application of measures of control against those voices that were critical, or simply trying to report the situation objectively. Those who were engaged in journalism had to feel the full weight of the repression, to discourage the slightest criticism of the government right from the start, and so avoid any public confirmation of the ghastly fate of thousands of citizens who had been kidnapped.

Although this was one of the most serious problems in the country, or, perhaps because of this, public opinion was kept misinformed about what was going on. In these circumstances the media generally refrained from giving information about those who were arrested and were considered subversives by the authorities. Everyone knew that people were being seized, but they were prevented from knowing how many, who they were, and where they were taken. In the first few years the big-circulation newspapers even thought it prudent to refrain from publishing classified advertisements with the names of people being sought by relatives.

Characteristic of this atmosphere was Internal Memorandum No. 44 in *La Voz del Interior*, a Córdoba newspaper, dated 22 April 1976. It was addressed to the Editorial Department and stated: "Córdoba 22.4.1976. By a decision of the Management, and in accordance with the instructions of the 3rd Army Corps Command, no information can be published on requests by relatives for information on the whereabouts of people who are presumed detained." The result was that large sections of the population ingenuously believed that the kidnappings were not going on, or, when they heard of a specific case, they were incredulous or considered it of little importance. It was also during the first few months of government, when the groundwork was being laid by the government for achieving its objectives, that most journalists were kidnapped. In the course of 1976 at least forty-five journalists were detained in an illegal fashion, and to this day nothing more has been heard of them. In the first eight months of 1977, a further thirty journalists disappeared; and it is estimated that the total number of journalists who suffered the same fate was about 100.

To give a complete picture of the situation it must be noted that a further 100 journalists were actually imprisoned without ever being brought to trial after 24 March 1976. In addition, a number of journalists fled the country when faced with the danger of a threat to their lives. The Commission drew up its information with a wealth of evidence on what had become all too frequent an occurrence: the participation of State forces in kidnappings and the destruction, ransacking and extortion of money from the relatives of victims....

Part Three
The Judiciary during the Repression

Once it has been clearly demonstrated that an enormous number of people disappeared and thousands of abductions were carried out involving the deployment of a great many vehicles and men, that big, well-organized detention and torture centres situated in densely populated areas housed hundreds of rapidly changing prisoners, and that the families of the disappeared exhausted practically all the available legal procedures, the following questions have to be asked: "How could so many crimes with the same *modus operandi* and often with numerous witnesses be carried out with such impunity? How was it that judges failed to locate a single kidnap victim, even after the experiences of those fortunate enough to have been released had been public knowledge for several years? What prevented them from investigating a single one of those detention centres?" These are painful questions, but they must be clarified.

After the Armed Forces took power on 24 March 1976, Argentine institutions were drastically subverted. A kind of "executive-legislative-constituent power" was created. It assumed extraordinary governmental powers and supreme public authority.

The composition of the highest levels of the judiciary, that is, the Supreme Court, the Attorney-General, the Provincial High Courts, changed on the first day of the coup. At the same time all other members of the judiciary were suspended from duty. All judges, whether newly appointed or confirmed in their posts, had to swear to uphold the Articles and objectives of the "Process" instigated by the Military Junta.

From then on, the activities of the judiciary assumed very distinctive features. Although intended by the Supreme Law of the Nation to protect citizens from excesses of authority, it now condoned the usurpation of power and allowed a host of judicial aberrations to take on the appearance of legality. With a few exceptions, it recognized the discretionary application of the powers of arrest under the state of siege, and accepted the validity of secret reports from the security services as justification for the detention of citizens for an indefinite period. At the same time, it turned the writ of habeas corpus into a mere formality, rendering it totally inefficient as a means of combating the policy of forcible abduction.

Instead of acting as a brake on the prevailing absolutism as it should have done, the judiciary became a sham jurisdictional structure, a cover to protect its image. Free expression of ideas in the press was denied through control of the mass media and through self-censorship practiced as a result of the state terrorism unleashed on dissident journalists. Legal representation in court was seriously affected by the imprisonment, exile or death of defence lawyers. The reluctance and even complacency with regard to human rights shown by many judges complete the picture of a total absence of protection for Argentine citizens.

Nevertheless, there were judges who, in the face of tremendous pressure, carried out their duties with the dignity and decency expected of them. It is also true, however, that although it is a judge's duty to protect individuals and their property, many did not do so. Many who could have limited the abuses of arbitrary detention endorsed the imposition of sentences without trial. And many showed complicity with the abductions and disappearances by their indifference. People came to feel that it was useless to appeal to the judiciary for protection of their basic rights. This situation became so notorious internationally that a Swiss court once refused to extradite five Argentines even though all the requirements of the relative treaty had been met, on the grounds that the lives of the criminals, once extradited, could not be guaranteed.

Our conclusion is that during the period in which large numbers of people disappeared, the judicial process became almost inoperative as a means of appeal. Furthermore, it could almost be said that under the military regime, the right to life, security of person and individual liberty had little to do with the decisions of the judges; the sole arbiters of these decisions were the members of the State's repressive apparatus.

The following cases are eloquent proof of this:...

As we have said, none of these deaths—all the results of violent acts—produced any investigation on the part of the judicial authorities, despite the condition of the bodies and their irregular delivery by soldiers.

The deposition presented by lawyers in Buenos Aires calling for an administrative investigation, caused the Supreme Court of justice to open dossier No. 1306/82; however, the proceedings were halted by a resolution of 7 June 1983 on the grounds that the investigation "does not reveal irregularities which merit disciplinary action by the Court".

The magistrates who acceded to the Court with the advent of the Constitutional Government did not agree. Their resolution No. 908/84 has just ordered reopening the case since the arguments on which suspension of the investigation was based "do not comply with the law; neither is there sufficient basis in the evidence of the proceedings undertaken".

The reasoning of the newly constituted High Court forms a solid base of argument for the juridical support due to this decision; and, at the same time, it reveals an unmistakable desire to make judicial action reinforce and exhaust any investigations which throw light on the tragic problem of the disappeared.

Habeas Corpus

No official or extra-official procedure was left unexplored by the families of the disappeared. They appealed to the country's rulers and the most influential people in society, they went through all the administrative channels laid down by the Ministry of the Interior, they begged the various Churches to intervene, and reported their terrible experiences to national and international human rights organizations. Only on very few occasions did these measures bring any positive result.

The families also appealed to the law. They covered the whole range of possibilities offered by the legal process. In an overwhelming majority of cases, they took the most obvious step: they repeatedly filed writs of habeas corpus to establish where their loved ones had been taken and who was detaining them.

Habeas corpus is the fruit of a long and often difficult historical evolution. It has become the fundamental guarantee of freedom of movement and is, with good reason, the legal mechanism despotism hates most. A free and just society is almost unimaginable without it.

In our country, it has always been thought of as one of the implicit guarantees in our Constitution. It is the basic right to ask a judge to order, through a rapid, summary, procedure, the cessation of any action by an official which restricts the right of personal freedom. The magistrate must be informed if the beneficiary of habeas corpus is being detained, which official is holding him, the legitimacy of the detention, and also whether there is reasonable cause for arrest when it is ordered by the National Executive under a state of siege.

The statistics of the Federal Criminal Court are very eloquent in this respect. Not counting renewed applications, the number of writs presented in the period 1976/9 in Buenos Aires city alone reached 5,487 against 1,089 for the period 1973/5 and 2,848 for the period 1980/3. The same proportions, but with lower figures, apply in the main provincial cities.

It must be said, however, that not a single case of habeas corpus fulfilled the hopes put in it. A substantial modification, decreed in February 1976, already affected the summary and rapid nature of recourse to habeas corpus; this was ratified on 18 May by Law 21,312 which greatly altered Article 639 of the Penal Code. This Article previously prescribed that, if the court decision secured the freedom of the protected person, he would without exception be released while an appeal was dealt with by a higher court. The revised wording stipulated in practice that if the beneficiary of the writ was arrested at the disposition of the National Executive, a decision in his favour to release him would not take immediate effect if the public prosecutor appealed against it. Since this was invariably the case, the protected person remained in custody while the appeal was dealt with. Through a succession of appeals the case went up to the Supreme Court and several years could pass, with the gravest consequences for the person urgently in need of protection.... Similarly, when a case reached the Supreme Court, the decision almost invariably went against release.... In this way, all the verdicts from the lower courts in favour of release—either total or conditional—could not be put into effect until a final decision had been made in the Supreme Court.* It is not surprising, therefore, that from 1973

---

*On 9 February 1984 Congress passed Law No. 23.050, which revoked the modification to the original text of Article 639 of the Penal Code, recognizing that appeal against a favourable decision by a habeas corpus judge should not postpone the execution of the release.

on, judges did not manage to locate or rescue a single one of the many disappeared.

We can find only one reason for such a dramatic fact. The blueprint for the techniques employed in forcible and systematic abduction included eliminating recourse to habeas corpus from the constitutional guarantees in our country. This criterion for the government's position was set out in a statement attributed to General Tomás Sánchez de Bustamante by the Rosario newspaper *La Capital*, on 14 June 1980:

> There are judicial norms and standards which do not apply in this instance: the right of habeas corpus, for example. In this type of struggle, the secrecy with which our special operations must be conducted means that we cannot divulge whom we have captured and whom we want to capture; everything has to be enveloped in a cloud of silence.

Such clear, explicit statements explain why in the majority of cases when a magistrate made official inquiries to the police, military or prison authorities as to the beneficiary of the habeas corpus writ, he accepted the standard reply which informed him that the person was not being detained. The authority against which the writ was issued was the very one whose negative response determined that the investigation be closed.

This deliberate withholding of information was, however, met by growing evidence brought by the families of the victims. The situation became more and more dramatic. Although government policy did not change in the slightest in this respect, the dubious verdicts of the Courts became more widely known.... The direction events were now taking prompted the government to adopt even more stringent norms for restricting the sacred guarantees for the protection of the individual more efficiently. We refer to the modification of Article 618 of the Penal Code, the original wording of which was altered by Law 22, 383 of 28 March, 1981.

As from that date, the Federal Criminal Court was designated the only body authorized to deal with writs of habeas corpus. It was impossible therefore to appeal to ordinary magistrates, at the very time when "detention-disappearance" and arrests without trial were becoming more frequent. It was prohibited, then, to appeal to judges in the provinces, and this damaged the Constitution with respect to the federal organization of the country. This legal position remains unchanged, and represents an obstacle to the historically recognized right to file a writ of habeas corpus with a judge of one's own choosing....

While we recognize that the main responsibility for what occurred lay with the bodies which exercised a monopoly of state power, we feel it is only fair to point out that the judiciary did not urge firmly enough the exceptional measures needed in the circumstances to compensate for the loss of authority they faced. Not once did a judge go to any of the places controlled by the bodies issuing the false reports. If they had, they would have seen the grossly untrue version of events which had become public knowledge. They used no special methods of investigation, despite the fact that there was a general awareness of the extraordinary magnitude of the cases involved.

And except for the timid steps taken by some of them in the final moments of the tragedy, they did not bring to trial a single person who due to his position in the repressive apparatus must have been directly involved in the disappearances under investigation.

It is inadmissible—and in this the judges should have concurred—for so many families to have been subjected to such an overwhelming feeling of impotence. On top of their fear, pain and grief, they had to endure the frustration of having no adequate legal channel to protect their rights. Recourse to habeas corpus, this simple but vital procedure which was considered the "cornerstone of liberties", was totally ineffective in preventing abductions by force. As we have said, thousands of writs proved to be nothing but useless formalities, offering no possibility of locating or releasing the individual illegally deprived of his freedom. In fact, habeas corpus totally failed to achieve what it was intended to do, since the formal way in which it was implemented operated in practice like the "other face" of disappearance.

In no way can it be inferred from what we have said, however, that the failure lay in habeas corpus itself as a guarantee of liberty. It was made deliberately ineffective through the perverse exercise of power by a government which instructed officials to ignore the norms governing its application. The majority of cases mentioned in this report are examples of this....

The detention of persons for an indefinite period, without precise charges, without trial, without defence counsel or any effective defence measures, constitutes without doubt a violation of human rights and the due process of law. This is much more serious if we remember that prisoners were judged and absolved by civil or military courts, but still remained at the disposition of the National Executive. When the period of detention is longer than the time required to collect enough evidence to bring the prisoner to trial, then its *raison d'etre* is only maintained by the crudest and most willful repression. From what we have seen this was commonplace during the government of the Military Junta.

Disappearance of Lawyers

A fundamental pillar of the constitutional system of individual rights and guarantees is undoubtedly the inviolable "right to the defence in court of a person and his rights" (Article 18 of the Constitution). This applies to all citizens. The most perfect array of freedoms and the most exhaustive catalogue of rights are meaningless if they do not have the guarantee of an efficient defence when under attack.

The defence lawyer plays a central role in these guarantees. He is the "trusted lawyer" of traditional jurisprudence and his importance in the administering of justice was recognized in Argentine law when it placed him on a par with the judges in terms of the respect and consideration due to him. Without his backing, his representation and his professional skills, any victim of the abuse of power is seriously hindered in his attempt to obtain judicial protection.

This is in fact what happened in Argentina. As just one more technique in the machinery of state terrorism, the harshest reprisals fell on the lawyers who defended the victims of the state. Arbitrary detention, assault, ill-treatment by the security organizations, disappearance and death of defence lawyers were everyday events in the early years of the military regime.

The Military began by identifying defence lawyers with their defendants. Anyone who supported or merely inquired about an assumed subversive was suspected of connivance with subversion, and anyone actually defending "terrorists" was considered a member of the same illicit organization until he could prove the contrary. In most cases he was not given the time to do this.

Such an aberrant criterion is absurd since it would actually mean that any lawyer defending someone accused of murder would himself have homicidal tendencies. Taken further still, this view would leave a valuable professional skill in the hands of the depraved and unscrupulous and, consequently, condemn the accused to a position of total defencelessness.

The facts indicate that the concept of the independence of a lawyer exercising his profession changed substantially during the military dictatorship. With predictable consequences, they associated the political idea and motivations of the defendant with the defence counsel, and turned him into an accomplice of or accessory to serious crimes.

In other cases, absolute and arbitrary power in the hands of the forces of repression was used to persecute worthy professionals who steadfastly defended their clients' interests, and also to punish by means of false accusations lawyers who were simply defending labour rights.

The results are evident. Lawyers' associations estimate that twenty-three of their colleagues were assassinated for political motives after 1975. Over and above this traumatic situation, 109 lawyers were kidnapped and their fate is still unknown. Ninety per cent of these "disappearances" took place between March and December of 1976. More than 100 lawyers were imprisoned—the majority without trial—and a much larger number retained their freedom, and perhaps saved their own lives by going into exile abroad. The exact number is difficult to ascertain.

The following cases illustrate, albeit partially, our case:…

Part Four

Creation and Organization of the
National Commission on the Disappeared

One of the most important tasks facing resurgent democracy in Argentina was tackling the problem of the disappeared and determining the fate of the victims. The first indispensable reparation demanded by society after fundamental institutions had been restored was to ascertain the truth of what had happened, to "face up" to the immediate past and let the country judge.

The National Executive recognized this when it stated that "the question of human rights transcends governments, it is the concern of civil society and the international community". This was the first clause of Decree No. 187 of 15 December 1983 which set up the National Commission on Disappeared People. Its aim was to clarify events relating to the disappearance of persons in Argentina and investigate their fate or whereabouts. The Commission was to receive depositions and evidence concerning these events, and pass the information on to the courts where crimes had been committed. Its brief would not extend, however, to determining responsibility. It would be the task of the courts receiving the material emanating from the Commission's investigations to determine responsibility and try the guilty parties.

In order to guarantee objectivity, the National Executive resolved that the Commission be comprised of individuals who enjoyed national and international prestige, chosen for their consistent stance in defence of human rights and their representation of different walks of life. The President of the Republic called upon the following people to carry out their function independently and *ad honorem*: Ricardo Colombres, René Favaloro, Hilario Fernández Long, Carlos T. Gattinoni, Gregorio Klimovsky, Marshall T. Meyer, Jaime F. de Nevares, Eduardo Rabossi, Magdalena Ruiz Guiñazú and Ernesto Sabato.

By the same decree, the government invited both Chambers in Congress to send three representatives to join the Commission. Only the Chamber of Deputies complied, and on 6 March 1984 elected the members Santiago Marcelino López, Hugo Diógenes Piucill and Horacio Hugo Huarte, all three from the Radical Party.

Prior to this, on 29 December 1983, Ernesto Sabato was unanimously elected President of the Commission. Five departments were created to deal with the different aspects of the Commission's work:

a) Depositions Department under Sra Graciela Fernández Meijide.
b) Documentation and Data Processing Department under Dr Daniel Salvador.
c) Procedures Department under Dr Raúl Aragón.
d) Legal Affairs Department under Dr Alberto Mansur.
e) Administrative Department under Dr Leopoldo Silgueira.

Embarking on something completely new to Argentina, the Commission started work in a climate charged with tension not only due to the nature of the task in hand but also because of incredulity shown in some quarters, disagreement in others and criticism in many more.

We must also remember that the setting up of the Commission caused resentment among those who favoured other channels of investigation (e.g. parliamentary), or who saw the Commission as an attempt to circumvent any more profound clarification of the matter.

Nevertheless, the Commission's first steps, within the framework of the precise powers laid down for it by the Decree, stimulated immediate public response in an incredible process of reconstructing collective memory. A kind of popular wave of support for the Commission was evident from the start, and this no doubt provided the enthusiasm, the courage and the large dose of imagination which we needed to respond to the magnitude of the task in hand and the desire for the truth emanating from all sectors of society.

We must emphasize here the invaluable assistance the Commission received from human rights organizations. They provided manpower, technical resources and all the experience acquired under the very difficult conditions in which they worked during the *de facto* government. The Commission was also helped by the work done by the UN, the OAS and other international organizations on the disappeared in Argentina. They compiled and processed an enormous amount of data which investigated important aspects and disseminated conclusions on a phenomenon which moved world opinion. This international solidarity was what the military authorities insultingly called the "international campaign to discredit Argentina" when it clumsily attempted to minimize the clear demonstration of universal fraternity which, without a doubt, helped bring the hitherto uncontrolled actions of state terrorism to an end.

The contribution made by the staff was fundamental. Most of them regarded their task as a civic duty rather than a job. They could not otherwise have worked all the extra hours at weekends and holidays which the task demanded. It should be remembered that at the outset we had only two offices staffed by employees on temporary loan from the Civil Service, who had no experience at all in these matters, and who found it difficult to cope with the frightful tales which emerged with every testimony. These were lengthy, exhausting, horrendous depositions in which a father, a mother, a wife recounted their pilgrimages through the courts, ministries, police stations and army barracks, searching in vain for information about the fate of their loved ones. Or, worse still, descriptions, interspersed with sobs, of the ways in which their children were tortured in their presence.

These early collaborators were unable to stand the strain and left, their shocked reaction in itself a testimony to just how little they had known of what was going on. The ones who stayed, those who occupied the vacant jobs and those who gradually joined the team as secretaries or lawyers came face to face—perhaps for the first time—with the horrifying vision of what had happened in Argentina. Each and every one of them increasingly felt a need to provide answers for our society as a whole and especially for the relatives of the disappeared, who came in their thousands hoping to discover something more about them. There was certainly no room for bureaucracy. Every person who received a deposition, and every lawyer who processed it to facilitate its passage through the courts, acted with a dedication born of a real awareness of what was at stake. It was that dedication which enabled us to receive so many depositions and testimonies, and study and process so many dossiers for the courts in so short a time.

No sooner had the Commission started work than it became obvious from the flood of depositions and testimonies that we had to take on more people and obtain more space in the San Martín cultural complex. Its director, Javier Torre, resolved the problem immediately and even surpassed our own expectations. The whole of the second floor, fully furnished and equipped, was put at the Commission's disposal. This gave the public better access and the staff more comfortable working conditions. The Commission was, therefore, able to act with greater speed and efficiency as the workload increased through massive popular response, and the deadline laid down by the Decree came nearer every day.

The creation of the different departments was aimed at carrying out the tasks according to the following work schedule. The Depositions Department, which had more staff than the others, saw as many people as it could from 9.30 a.m. to 5.30 p.m. from Monday to Friday initially and subsequently from Monday to Thursday, leaving Fridays free to process the vast amount of material collected. Each deposition was given a number corresponding to a file containing all the information relevant to that particular disappearance (publications, letters, press cuttings, habeas corpus, etc). This was complemented by taking statements from witnesses and liaising with the appropriate government departments.

For information about events which took place in areas at some distance from the Commission's headquarters where there was no permanent delegation, representatives of the Commission travelled to fifteen of the provinces, collecting more than 1,400 depositions. In addition to the full Commission members and heads of delegations forty-seven people undertook this work. These testimonies, especially in the most isolated areas, revealed some of the cruellest methods mentioned in this report, visited on our poorest and therefore most defenceless compatriots.

Testimonies were not only collected in the provincial capitals. The Commission members often went out into the countryside.... In the town of Libertador General San Martín, Jujuy province, they verified the mass abduction of 200 people in one night, sixty of whom are still missing. We have to thank the Mothers of the Plaza de Mayo for their tireless efforts in this locality. With their cooperation, we were able to collect in one day more than seventy testimonies from simple peasant people who were obviously deeply distressed at not knowing the fate or whereabouts of close members of their family.

CONADEP's arrival in a province was generally an important event. There were press conferences, interviews, round tables for information purposes at which the media were present. The legislative bodies and human rights organizations cooperated with CONADEP in the task of receiving depositions, and on most occasions the delegations met with top officials in the provincial government who lent their support.

The visits also served to coordinate the process of verifying the existence of secret detention centres. For this we had to visit witnesses in their own homes, which were often more than 50 kilometres away. This operation proved that the scope of the tragedy extended to the furthest corners of the country. We were sure, however, that the speed with which we had to cover each area we visited prevented us from obtaining all the existing information. We would have needed to visit many more places to be able to complete the full picture of what happened.

Given the fact that a large number of Argentines (it is not yet certain exactly how many) had to leave the country, we decided to ask our diplomatic representatives abroad to receive depositions. We also decided that members of the Commission would travel to obtain new evidence and testimonies. We received the support of the Foreign Secretary, Dante Caputo, and the active collaboration of Dr Elsa Kelly of the Foreign Office, and Ambassador Dr Horacio Ravena in charge of human rights at the Foreign Office. They arranged for the staff of the Argentine missions abroad to cooperate fully with the Commission....

The depositions, testimonies, evidence, and information collected on these journeys abroad generally made a valuable contribution to the Commission's Legal Department.

One point worth noting was the enormous concern expressed for our work by the people of the countries we visited. This was reflected both in the large amount of space dedicated to the problem of the disappeared in the press at the time of our visit, and the more general support for the Commission, related to the high expectations for the outcome of judicial proceedings already under way.

In cases where some urgent supplementary action had to be taken (exhumations, obtaining documents outside the Commission's terms of reference, inspection of secret detention centres, impounding and/or proof of ownership of personal effects and documents etc.) the corresponding file was passed to the Government Procedures Department for the completion of formalities. Searching the labyrinth to pinpoint the exact moment at which traces of many thousands of people had been lost was a difficult and often painful task, since it revived bitter memories for those who had been released.

The procedure was generally as follows:

1. Identifying "*in situ*" the secret detention camps with people released from these camps.
2. Visiting the morgues to obtain information about irregular admissions.
3. Making inquiries in neighbourhoods and workplaces as to the exact location of secret detention camps or the different ways in which the disappeared had been abducted.
4. Receiving declarations in places other than the Commission's headquarters from people either in active service with the Armed Forces or Security Forces, or retired from them.
5. Checking prison registers.
6. Checking police registers.
7. Investigating crimes committed concerning the property of the disappeared.

The Commission also made investigations on the basis of information provided by people who had been told their loved ones might be in a certain place. We accompanied relatives even though the chances of success were very slight and the procedures were difficult and time-consuming. Investigating the fate or whereabouts of disappeared persons who might be detained but still alive proved fruitless. The Commission was asked by relatives to check the Río Negro Military District in Viedma, the 29th Rural Infantry Regiment in Formosa, and the National Atomic Energy Commission, all to no avail. On other occasions, relatives of the disappeared received telephone calls, usually anonymous, indicating that the victims might still be alive in various psychiatric or medical institutions.... The Commission accompanied relatives to all these institutions and thoroughly checked the lists of patients, especially those designated "NN" (identity unknown).

They then went through the wards to study the patients. In each ward they questioned the nurses, doctors and even the patients themselves, showing them photographs and describing special features to help them recognize the victims or jog some memory they might have in the back of their minds. None of these visits proved positive in terms of finding people, but perhaps they were positive inasmuch as they put an end to the terrible anguish and false expectations of families who by now no longer had the strength to bear them.

The Legal Department, which was in charge of preparing the presentations made to the courts, scrutinized each file in great detail and processed it like a proper legal indictment. With the primary objective of determining the fate and ultimate whereabouts of the disappeared always in mind, it organized, selected and linked the large number of depositions and evidence received, paying special attention to any relevant details which would point the investigation in a fruitful direction.

As the efforts to locate the disappeared proved more and more hopeless, however, the presentation of depositions to the courts increased. Both the material received testifying to events which had occurred and the results of the statements, the information solicited and the inspections carried out, led to a wide range of crimes being identified.

The Department began from the moment the victim was kidnapped and followed the itinerary of the abduction to the detention centres where most of the crimes were committed. As we said before, this was a totally new situation; investigating clandestine activity by the State which, by acting quite outside licit norms and procedures, itself became a criminal organization. Some of the serious obstacles the Department came up against in their work were: clues and documents had been destroyed; the perpetrators of the crimes were masked, used false names or nicknames and had forged credentials; buildings which had served as operational bases were altered; land used for secret cemeteries had been dug over; and in many cases it was impossible for the victims to recognize their captors since they were blindfolded or hooded from the outset.

One prime consideration in the work was that when coming to a conclusion the Department should not be influenced by anything that was not reliably checked. The findings to emerge from the investigations, however, more than confirmed the veracity of the accounts contained in the depositions. When an investigation was considered to be sufficiently far advanced, the file was presented to the courts. When it was felt, on the other hand, that no further progress could be made for the time being, it was filed away until such time as it was reactivated by fresh evidence.

Working methods improved as we went along, especially when we realized that if the files were grouped together according to detention centre or "camp" where a disappeared person had been seen alive, or where a released prisoner had been held, there was a greater chance of testimonies coinciding, and this made the proof more conclusive. From this emerged the so-called "packages", or combined depositions, testimonies and evidence, containing several files with a common link such as reference to a certain camp. In some cases a "package" of depositions or evidence was put together according to the common circumstances of the victim—for example, the 100-odd conscripts who disappeared while doing their military service.

The part played in all this by released prisoners was decisive. While in no way detracting from the mentions they are given in other chapters, we would like to stress their courage and solidarity here. They came forward from the very start, despite having themselves suffered terrible deprivation and torture. Civic values and unquenchable ethical considerations overcame the fear they still felt. It was they who provided concrete information about other disappeared persons, gave details of the camps and agreed to identify the places used for imprisonment and torture, that is, "their" places of imprisonment and torture. The fact that this Commission is able to present concrete, irrefutable evidence to the courts—as we are sure we can—is certainly due to the testimonies of these released detainees. What we have achieved in the course of these investigations would not have been possible without their collaboration.

We must point out, however, that our work was hindered by the destruction and/or removal of a vast amount of documentation containing detailed information on the disappeared. We appealed to various institutes and organizations of the military and security forces for instructions, organizational diagrams, orders and the names of certain of their members who, because of the central role they played in the repression, could have supplied us with vital evidence.

Approximately 1,300 requests for information were made, broken down as follows:

Ministry of Defence	280
Foreign Ministry	30
Ministry of the Interior	60
Federal Police	100
Provincial Police	100
Federal Prison Service	70
Government of Buenos Aires Province	10
National and Provincial Courts	290
National Register of Persons, Property and Automobiles	80
Various bodies (official and private)	280
	1,300

For bureaucratic reasons, and for others unknown to us, many of our questions remained unanswered, since the organizations connected to the

Armed Forces did not reply satisfactorily to the Commission's requests for information. A similar lack of cooperation was shown by some judges, both in Buenos Aires and in the provinces, who returned our letters and refused us the benefit of their status and experience. We even had to ask the President to order certain administrative and security bodies to comply with our requests and to annul the provision which allowed members of the Armed Forces to refuse to answer our questions on the pretext of "military secrets" (Decree No. 2107/84).

Although the work of this Commission will undoubtedly not satisfy some quarters, we believe that it carried out its brief to get to the root of these events which had few—if any—precedents in other parts of the world. In a few short months, the staff of CONADEP processed an amount of data and files which would have taken years had it not been for the spirit which fired them. A look at the list of cases sent to the courts is proof enough of this.

Other Aspects of the Work Undertaken by the National Commission on the Disappeared

1. From the outset the National Commission held weekly plenary sessions which began around 10 a.m. and went on without interruption until late in the afternoon or until the agenda had been dealt with. The Executive Committee met almost every day.

The Commission made continual statements to the press and received numerous individuals and delegations from both Argentina and abroad. Most significant among these were: Edmundo Vargas Carreño, Executive Secretary of the OAS Human Rights Commission; Juan E. Méndez, Director of Americas Watch based in Washington; Martin Pérez from the Pro-Human Rights Association in Spain; Rafael de Campagnola, Counsellor in the Italian Embassy; European and Israeli parliamentarians, Jorge Santistevan, Director of the UN High Commission on Refugees, and Dr José Figueres, ex-President of Costa Rica.

The National Commission also met with [several ambassadors, members of parliament, representatives of various organizations,] and innumerable other representatives of national and international public opinion. All these people offered their support for the work of the Commission.

2. The Commission also invited to Argentina members of the Committee for Scientific Freedom and Responsibility, of the American Association for the Advancement of Science. Their contribution in terms of research into matters of interest to human rights organizations, and particularly to this Commission, was invaluable. The members of the Commission were: Dr Lowell Levine, Dr Lesli Lukash, Dr Marie-Claire King, Dr Clyde Snow and Dr Luke Tedeschi, who were accompanied by Dr Cristian Orrego and Mr Eric Stover.

They took part in a symposium during which they explained the latest advances in genetic analysis to help determine biological links. This could help identify the children of disappeared parents. They also advised our authorities on the scientific possibilities of determining the cause of death from examining a person's remains. They offered their assistance to the Grandmothers and Mothers of the Plaza de Mayo. In addition, they accompanied the Commission's delegations to Córdoba, Mar del Plata and La Plata on specific missions.

3. The Commission asked the National Executive to make Argentine Embassies and Consulates abroad available for exiles to present their depositions and evidence. This they did. We would like to mention here one particular gesture by the President. We made the request to the National Executive on 10 January 1984. Late in the afternoon that very same day we received a personal note from the President with a copy of his instructions to all Argentine missions abroad.

4. The Commission sent a representative to the session of the UN Working Group on the Enforced or Involuntary Disappearance of Persons held in June 1984 in New York, and to the International Committee on Human Rights in Geneva. On both occasions the delegate was Rabbi Marshall Meyer.

5. In January 1984, without intending to prejudge the conduct of any one individual, the Commission decided to request that the appropriate State authorities adopt precautionary measures to ensure that certain individuals, whose testimonies would aid the investigations of either the Commission or the courts, remain in the country in case they be called on to testify.

6. The Commission created branches in Bahía Blanca, Mar del Plata, Córdoba, Rosario and Santa Fe, and another small office in Resistencia, Chaco province.

7. It arranged for members of the Commission to visit the interior of the country to organize centres for receiving depositions and evidence. For this, four work zones were created: The Coast, the Centre, the North and the South.

8. It agreed on a data processing method with CUPED (Centre for Electronic Data Processing) and installed the appropriate terminals, provided free of charge by IBM.

9. It decided to photocopy or microfilm all the documents gathered to date and keep them in safes in official banks.

10. It worked in conjunction with organizations such as the International Red Cross, the Parliamentary Committee for Human Rights for the Province of Buenos Aires, the Vicariate of Solidarity in Chile, etc., and contacted organizations like the United Nations, UNESCO, Amnesty International, CLAMOR, the International Commission of Jurists, the International Association of Democratic Jurists, and other no less important bodies.

11. It set out its own internal rules and designated a four-person Executive Committee to deal with everyday matters.

12. It arranged for Committee members, parliamentarians Piucill and Huarte, and Heads of Departments Meijide and Mansur to travel to various countries in America and Europe to collect valuable evidence the Commission did not yet have. These delegations were entirely successful.

13. As spokesman for the Commission, its President Ernesto Sabato gave over 100 press, radio and television interviews, both in Argentina and abroad.

14. More than thirty press conferences were held on both specific and general questions, many with the participation of witnesses and released prisoners.

15. It produced the television documentary "Never Again".

16. Sixty press communiqués were issued on the state of the different investigations. The Commission members on special missions gave press conferences in the places they visited to organize branches in the interior.

Work Carried out by the Computer Department

The Commission was faced with the task of listing all the names and particulars of the victims of repression—the disappeared, those who had disappeared and were later freed, and those killed. Since the list contained many thousands of names, it was decided to set up a computerized data bank.

To this end help was sought from CUPED (which deals with pensions, the national lottery, etc). This organization lent staff and equipment to the Commission free of charge in accordance with the Decree setting up the Commission and subsequent additional legislation.

CUPED prepared programs and set up a data bank drawing on the lists prepared by the Permanent Assembly on Human Rights, CLAMOR, OAS, United Nations and so on. The programs contained information with names, surnames, age, identity documents, date of the event, place of disappearance and the profession of the victims. As new lists were incorporated, their information was checked against that already existing in the data bank, to avoid repetition.

Two terminals were installed in the Commission's offices, enabling staff to enter information directly and to see it on a screen. The lists could then be complemented by further information provided from other sources, such as the testimonies given directly to the Commission. Everything was given a file number, to facilitate the checking and cross-checking of information. The terminals were used to carry out an exhaustive check of the data bank information. As some of the names contained were not supported by any documentary evidence, it was impossible to tell from the computer program whether two names such as Pérez Susana and Perel Susana were in fact the same person. The checking of facts like this had to be done manually, by going through all the available data on the screen and eliminating those which belonged to the same person.

To help speed up the flow of data, another two terminals were installed in June 1984. Since by then other members of the Commission were using the terminals to discover information, a printer was installed so that this information could be obtained speedily without immobilizing either of the terminals.

CUPED's central computer was used to print out lists of the victims in alphabetical order, by document number, by age, by date of disappearance, and so on.

Finally, two other important tasks were carried out:

1. The work of checking and double-checking continued, in order to separate in as many cases as possible the disappeared from those who were freed, those who have been accounted for as dead, so that a final list and statistics could be prepared.

2. Work to include the places and dates the disappeared were seen in detention centres....

Part Six

Recommendations

The facts presented to this Commission in the depositions and testimonies speak for themselves. They lead us to recommend to the various State authorities certain measures which will help to ensure that this curtailment of human rights is never repeated in Argentina. The aim of these recommendations is also to press for a judicial investigation into the facts denounced to us. We therefore recommend:

a) That the body which replaces this Commission speeds up the procedures involved in bringing before the courts the documents collected during our investigation.

b) That the courts process with the utmost urgency the investigation and verification of the depositions received by this Commission.

c) That the appropriate laws be passed to provide the children and/or relatives of the disappeared with economic assistance, study grants, social security and employment and, at the same time, to authorize measures considered necessary to alleviate the many and varied family and social problems caused by the disappearances.

d) That laws be passed which:

1. Declare forced abduction a crime against humanity.
2. Support the recognition of and adhesion to national and international human rights organizations.
3. Make the teaching of the defence and diffusion of human rights obligatory in state educational establishments, whether they be civilian, military or police.
4. Strengthen and provide ample support for the measures which the courts need to investigate human rights violations.
5. Repeal any repressive legislation still in force.

Conclusions

Up to the time of the presentation of this report, CONADEP estimates that 8,960 people are still missing. It bases this estimate on the information it received and comparisons made with figures given by national and international human rights organizations.

This is not a final figure, since CONADEP realizes that many cases of kidnapping have not been reported. The figure may also include people who did not communicate their release to the appropriate organization in time.

• Abduction was also used as a method of repression prior to the military coup of 24 March 1976. It was, however, from the date on which the forces usurping power took absolute control of the resources of the state, that the method became widespread.

The kidnappings were carried out by members of the Security Forces who concealed their identity. The victim was then taken to one of the approximately 340 secret detention centres in existence. In the course of its investigations, CONADEP inspected a large number of these establishments used by the *de facto* government. They were under the command of high-ranking officers in the military and security services. The prisoners were kept in inhuman conditions and subjected to all kinds of torture and humiliation. Our investigations to date show that a provisional figure of 1,300 persons were seen in these secret centres prior to their ultimate disappearance.

• Seeing proof of the extent of the use of torture in these centres, and the sadism with which it was carried out, is horrendous. Some of the methods used have no precedent elsewhere in the world. Some depositions referred to the torture of children and old people in front of their families to obtain information.

• CONADEP has shown that as a result of these methods, prisoners were murdered, their identities concealed, and in many cases their bodies destroyed, to prevent subsequent identification. We also established that people alleged by the forces of repression to have been killed in combat were in fact taken alive from a secret detention centre and killed in simulated military confrontations or in fake attempts to escape.

• Among the victims still missing and those who were subsequently released from secret detention centres are people from all walks of life:

Blue-collar workers	30.2
Students	21.0
White-collar workers	17.9
Professionals	10.7
Teachers	5.7
Self-employed and others	5.0
Housewives	3.8

Military conscripts and members of the security forces	2.5
Journalists	1.6
Actors, performers, etc.	1.3
Nuns, priests, etc.	0.3
	100.0

• We can state categorically—contrary to what the executors of this sinister plan maintain—that they did not pursue only the members of political organizations who carried out acts of terrorism. Among the victims are thousands who never had any links with such activity but were nevertheless subjected to horrific torture because they opposed the military dictatorship, took part in union or student activities, were well-known intellectuals who questioned state terrorism, or simply because they were relatives, friends, or names included in the address book of someone considered subversive.

• This Commission maintains that it was not just a question of some "excesses", if that means aberrant acts, being committed. These atrocities were common practice; the normal methods used daily during the repression.

• Despite their claim in the "Final Document of the Military Junta on the War Against Subversion and Terrorism" that the forces of subversion had 25,000 recruits of whom 15,000 were "technically able and ideologically trained to kill," the Military Courts set up to judge these crimes sentenced only approximately 356 individuals. This demonstrates clearly that other measures were used to annihilate thousands of people who opposed them, terrorists or not.

• Hence the claim that subversion and terrorism were in effect defeated is invalid: certain terrorist organizations were wiped out, but in their stead a system of institutionalized terror was implemented which undermined the most basic human, ethical and moral principles and was backed by a doctrine which was also foreign to our national identity.

• CONADEP prepared 7,380 files, comprising depositions from relatives of the disappeared, testimonies of people released from secret detention centres, and statements by members of the security forces who had taken part in the acts of repression described above. It carried out numerous investigations in different parts of the country and collected information from the Armed Forces, the Security Forces and other private and public organizations.

• As a result of its investigations, CONADEP was able to present evidence before the courts, comprising 1,086 dossiers proving the existence of the main secret detention centres, giving a partial list of the disappeared seen alive in these centres, and a list of members of the Armed Forces and

Security Forces mentioned by victims as responsible for the serious crimes they denounced.

• The destruction or removal of documentation providing details of the fate of the disappeared before government was handed over to the constitutional authorities hindered the investigation with which this Commission was entrusted by decree.

Nevertheless, there is enough evidence to allow us to confirm that people who are still missing passed through the secret detention centres and that the truth as to their subsequent whereabouts will come out as progress is made in determining which individuals are responsible for the acts of repression committed.

National Commission on the Disappeared (CONADEP)
Buenos Aires, September 1984.

CHAD: DECREE CREATING THE COMMISSION OF INQUIRY INTO THE CRIMES AND MISAPPROPRIATIONS COMMITTED BY EX-PRESIDENT HABRÉ, HIS ACCOMPLICES AND/OR ACCESSORIES

Decree No. 014 /P.CE/CJ/90 (December 29, 1990)

THE PRESIDENT OF THE COUNCIL OF STATE,
CHIEF OF STATE.

Pursuant to:

- the program of the Constituent Congress of the Patriotic Movement of Salvation, held 8-11 March 1990;
- the Charter of the Patriotic Movement of Salvation;
- Decision No. 002/P.CE/MB/90 of 4 December 1990 relative to the creation of the Council of State;
- Decree No. 001/P.CE/90 of 4 December 1990 relative to nomination of members of the Council of State.

THE COUNCIL OF STATE at its meeting of 19 December 1990, acting ON THE PROPOSAL of the Commissioner of Justice,

DECREES:

Article 1

There is hereby created a Commission called the "Commission of Inquiry into the crimes and misappropriations committed by the ex-president, his accomplices and/or accessories."

Article 2

The mission of the Commission is:

- to investigate the illegal imprisonments, detentions, assassinations, disappearances, tortures and practices of acts of barbarity, the mistreatment, the other attacks on the physical or mental integrity of persons, and all violations of human rights and illicit trafficking in narcotics;

- to collect documentation, archives and exploit them;

- to confiscate and secure under seal all objects and premises required for elucidating the truth;

- to preserve in their present condition the torture chambers and the equipment utilized;

- to hear testimony from all victims and invite them to produce documentation attesting to their physical and mental condition following their detention;

- to take the testimony of interested parties and invite them to furnish any relevant or necessary documents;

- to hear testimony from any person whose deposition may be useful to elucidation of the truth;

- to determine the total cost of the war effort and how the money was spent beginning in 1986;

- to audit the financial operations and bank accounts of the ex-president, his accomplices and/or accessories;

- to take inventory of all the goods and properties, both in country and abroad, belonging to or having belonged to the ex-president, his accomplices and/or accessories.

Article 3

The Commission is composed of:

President:	Mahamat Hassane Abakar, first deputy prosecutor
1st Vice President:	Ali Abdoulaye, director of Police Security Branch
2d Vice President:	Isseine Djibrine, principal police superintendent
Members:	Beassoum Ben N'Gassoro, magistrate
	Dimanche Beramgoto, director of research in the Commissariat of the Interior and Security
	Bemba Jonas, police officer
	Wadar Moudalbaye, administrative officer in the sub-directorate of external finance
	Sam Manang, military police warrant officer
	Ousmane Mahamat, records clerk
	Naindo Dalroh, records clerk
Secretaries:	Madjitoloum Ngardedji, police secretary
	Koh Djabou, magistrate's clerk

Article 4

The Commission may summon any natural or legal person in a position to assist it in the investigation.

Article 5

If the investigation so requires, members of the Commission may travel both within and outside the country.

Article 6

To this end, the material resources necessary will be put at the disposal of the Commission to enable it to carry out its mission.

Article 7

The Commission shall submit its report within 6 months, however this period may be extended if necessary at the request of the President of the Commission.

Article 8

When the work is concluded, a decree of the President of the Council of State will terminate the mandate of the Commission.

Article 9

The Commissioner of Justice, Keeper of the Seal, is directed to implement the present Decree, which takes effect from the date of signature, and will be recorded and published in the official journal of the Republic.

CHAD: REPORT OF THE COMMISSION OF INQUIRY INTO THE CRIMES AND MISAPPROPRIATIONS COMMITTED BY EX-PRESIDENT HABRÉ, HIS ACCOMPLICES AND/OR ACCESSORIES

Investigation of Crimes Against the Physical and Mental Integrity of Persons and their Possessions

(May 7, 1992)

Introduction

Before entering into the main subject of the report, it would be useful to give the reader of this document and annexes a brief overview of modern-day Chad.

Brief Overview of Chad

Area:	11,284,000 km^2
Population:	about 6 million
Religions:	Islam, Christianity, animism
Capital:	Ndjamena
Principal towns:	Sarh, Moundou, Abéché
Official languages:	French and Arabic. But several other unwritten languages are spoken in Chad.
Political parties:	Chad is governed currently by the Patriotic Movement of Salvation (MPS); several political parties were established and legalized in late 1991. These are: - Rally for Democracy and Progress (RDP) headed by Lol Mahamat Choua; - Union for Democracy of the Chadian People (UDPT) headed by Elie Romba; - National Rally for Democracy and Progress (RNDP) headed by Nouradine Kassiré Delwa Coumakoye; - Union for Democracy and Rally (UDR) headed by Jean Bawoyeu Alingué; Others have been formed and are awaiting legalization.
Head of State:	Idriss Déby

Succinct Chronology of Successive Political Regimes

Chad is an African country which faced problems of every kind in the first years of independence: guerrilla movements, civil wars, and fratricidal, murderous and interminable struggles for control of the central government. In addition, there has been an almost steady stream of natural calamities such as drought and famine.

All these misfortunes have wounded, weakened, and retarded it politically, economically, and socially for entire decades. Until quite recently, Chad has suffered 26 years of instability and insecurity. Few countries have known such a wretched fate.

These painful events, which have left such deep scars on Chad, may be summarized briefly as follows:

11 August 1960: Chad is proclaimed independent. Mr. François Tombalbaye becomes first president of the republic. He is a native of southern Chad.

Late October 1965: Exasperated by excessive assessments of civic taxes (head taxes), the peasants of Mangalmé (a locality in central Chad) rise up against the local administrative authorities, massacring several of them.

22 June 1966: creation at Nyala (Sudan) of the Chadian National Liberation Front ("FROLINAT"). Initially, this front includes natives of the central, east-central and northern parts of the country, which feel marginalized and oppressed by those in power, their fellow citizens from the south.

This is the beginning of a long, very long period of political instability.

1 September 1969: Colonel Qadhdhafi seizes power in Libya and topples King Idriss from his throne. Qadhdhafi's coming to power would have incalculable repercussions on Chad's political future. Qadhdhafi would continually support armed movements that wanted to take power.

13 April 1975: The military take power and kill Tombalbaye. General Malloum is named president of the republic and president of the Higher Military Council (CSM).

28 August 1978: Hissein Habré, rebel leader of an armed dissident faction, joins forces with the government. He is named prime minister.

12 February 1979: Beginning of the armed conflict between supporters of President Malloum and partisans of Prime Minister Hissein Habré. This conflict would allow FROLINAT to enter Ndjamena without a fight and lead to the removal of the military from the government.

10 November 1979: A Transitional National Union Government (GUNT) is created. The president is Goukouni Oueddeï, ex-rebel leader; Colonel Kamougué is vice president; Hissein Habré, minister of State for defense; Mahabat Abba, minister of State for interior; Acyl Ahmat, minister of foreign affairs. This new government confirms the victory of FROLINAT, as all key positions are taken by leaders of this armed movement.

21 March 1980: War breaks out in Ndjamena, the capital, between the Northern Armed Forces (FAN) of Hissein Habré and the People's Armed Forces (FAP) of Goukouni Oueddeï, who was president of the country. This civil war is extremely murderous. It leaves thousands dead and wounded

and drives hundreds of thousands to seek refuge in neighboring countries. Ndjamena, the capital city, is destroyed.

14 December 1980: Hissein Habré, beaten by GUNT's forces, retreats to eastern Chad, to the Sudan border. Outraged Ndjamena residents discover a large burial ground on the banks of the river, not far from Habré's residence in the Sabangali quarter. This is the work of Hissein Habré.

7 June 1982: Hissein Habré seizes power in Ndjamena as Goukouni Oueddeï flees to Cameroon.

1 December 1990: Eight years later, the all-powerful Habré flees Ndjamena and takes refuge in Cameroon; taking with him the entire treasury of the Chadian State and killing in cold blood all the political prisoners detained at the presidency. His former commander in chief of the Chadian National Armed Forces, Colonel Idriss Déby, who launched his rebellion on 1 April 1989, takes power.

The Commission of Inquiry

After Hissein Habré took flight, the new government headed by Colonel Idriss Déby created, in Decree No. 014/P.CE/CJ/90 of 29 December 1990, a Commission called "Commission of Inquiry into the Crimes and Misappropriations Committed by Ex-President Habré, his Accomplices and/or Accessories."

The mandate of the Commission is:
- to investigate the illegal imprisonments, detentions, assassinations, disappearances, tortures and practices of acts of barbarity, the mistreatment, other attacks on the physical or mental integrity of persons, and all violations of human rights and illicit trafficking in narcotics;
- to collect documentation, archives and exploit them;
- to confiscate and secure under seal all objects and premises required for elucidating the truth;
- to preserve in their present condition the torture chambers and equipment utilized;
- to hear testimony from all victims and invite them to produce documentation attesting to their physical and mental condition following their detention;
- to take the testimony of interested parties and invite them to furnish any relevant or necessary documents;
- to hear testimony from any person whose deposition may be useful to elucidation of the truth;
- to determine the total cost of the war effort and how the money was spent beginning in 1986;
- to audit the financial operations and bank accounts of the ex-president, his accomplices and/or accessories;
- to take inventory of all the goods and properties, both in country and abroad, belonging to or having belonged to the ex-president, his accomplices and/or accessories.

The Commission was composed initially of 12 members, including two magistrates, four officers of the judicial police, two civil administrative officers, two records clerks, and two secretaries.

It was given 6 months to submit its report. Due to lack of resources and office space, it was unable to begin its work until 1 March 1991, 2 months late. Unable to find anything better, it was obliged to set up its offices, after some hasty reconstruction work, in the former offices of the loathsome Directorate of Documentation and Security (DDS), the political police of the Habré regime.

After many démarches to the authorities concerned, the Commission was allocated operating funds totaling 4.8 million francs, to be disbursed in three installments.

With the financial problem partly resolved, it was the lack of transport that paralyzed the Commission for a considerable time. At the start, the Commission was furnished two small urban automobiles, a 504 and a small Suzuki, whereas all-terrain vehicles were actually required for travel to the provinces and the outskirts of Ndjamena.

On 25 August 1991 a Toyota all-terrain vehicle was put at the disposal of the Commission. But during the events of 13 October 1991, unfortunately, the Toyota and the little Suzuki were taken off by combatants. A month later the Toyota was recovered, but the Suzuki was not found until 3 January 1992. This act of brigandage, which deprived the Commission of its means of transportation, paralyzed it for several more months. This is why the Commission was unable to send investigators to the interior of the country during the entire initial period.

In the course of its investigations, the Commission ran into many obstacles, both material and psychological. The victims of Habré's repression were afraid to give testimony because they had doubts about the Commission's precise mission. They feared it might be a trap designed to identify them and persecute them afterward. They also feared Habré would come back for the "nth" time and their lives would be forfeit. Others, however, did not want to talk about these painful sufferings because they were loath to revive the trauma and violent shocks they endured.

It must also be conceded that the location of the Commission headquarters itself was not such as to encourage victims to come forward with depositions. As mentioned above, due to the shortage of available sites, the Commission set up its offices in the former building of the sinister DDS. And it took a great deal of tactful persuasion to reassure and allay the anxieties of hesitant, frightened people.

Obtaining testimony from former DDS agents rehired in the new, rehabilitated intelligence service, called the General Directorate of the Center for Investigation and Intelligence Coordination, was a grueling ordeal for the Commission. These unscrupulous criminals believed—with good reason, moreover—that being "rehabilitated" they did not have to account to anyone for their actions. Some even tried to intimidate witnesses who had come to testify to the Commission. It was with great difficulty that we succeeded in interviewing the majority of them.

On several occasions, but without success, the Commission has drawn the attention of the competent authorities to the real danger involved in rehiring these agents, who in the recent past participated in acts of genocide against the Chadian people. The sad truth is that these agents were trained by Habré to kill, pillage and terrorize. Thus there are no grounds for hoping they will make a positive contribution.

Likewise, interviewing high-ranking former Habré officials who were hastily given responsible positions by the new government has not been easy.

Within the Commission, some members judged the task too hazardous and disappeared altogether. Others reappeared only at the end of the month to pick up their pay and vanished again.

This is why, when its 6-month mandate expired, the Commission through its president, requested the replacement of certain members and the enlargement of the Commission. This request was granted by the competent authorities, as a result of which the second decree, No. 382/PR/MJ/91 of 29 July 1991, was promulgated. This decree extended by 4 months the deadline for submission of the report. Three-fourths of the Commission members were replaced by new appointees, and their number was increased from 12 to 16.

The new composition of the Commission is as follows:...

The Commission's mission is essentially twofold:

The first mission relates to crimes against the physical and mental integrity of persons, such as arbitrary detentions, tortures, assassinations, disappearances, etc.

The second concerns misappropriations of public resources.

To meet this heavy responsibility, the members of the Commission divided into two sections, criminal and financial.

The methods followed in these investigations are those utilized in judicial proceedings, notably criminal proceedings. To wit, the taking of testimony from parties concerned, such as former political detainees, close relatives of people who died or were executed, former DDS agents, former high-ranking security officials, and even several ministers. In a word, the Commission listens to anyone able to throw light on the matter. It also collects written and material evidence such as lists of persons who were executed or died in prison, photographs of torture, burial ground premises, etc.

Generally, each investigator takes individual depositions from the attestant. But when the attestant conceals important information, a team of investigators, often headed by the president in person, conducts the cross-examination. This was done in the case of former directors and high officials of the DDS, several ministers, and survivors of mass executions.

After several months of intense investigation, and in order to further accelerate the work, the Commission drew up a series of questionnaires:
- for former political detainees;
- for close relatives of victims who died in detention or were executed;
- for prisoners of war;

- for former DDS agents.

With the help of these pre-established questionnaires the daily output of the Commission more than quintupled.

But the work of the Commission would be incomplete if it did not include the provinces in its program of investigation. That is why a team of investigators composed of two magistrates and an officer of the judicial police was dispatched to the southern part of the country on 19 November 1991. It stayed there more than a month to scour the prefectures and subprefectures. It produced an impressively large volume of work. More than 700 persons were heard, and four prefectures and 10 subprefectures were visited, namely:

- Prefecture of Moyen-Chari: Sarh, Kyabé, Maro, Koumra, Moîssala
- Prefecture of Logone Occidental: Moundou, Beinamar, Bénoyé,
- Prefecture of Logone Oriental: Doba, Bébidja, Goré, Mbaibokoum
- Prefecture of Tandjilé: Laï, Kélo

As in the rest of the country, the repression in the south was both brutal and disastrous. Entire villages were burned with their inhabitants, worshippers praying in churches or temples were locked inside and burned alive. (The reader will find ample details in the chapter reserved for the provinces.) It should also be noted that the investigators did not have time to visit Mayo-Kebbi, although it did not escape the murderous madness of Habréist agents, particularly the administrative station at Gagal;

Another team composed of a judicial police officer and two gendarmes was dispatched on 24 December 1991 to the central, east-central and extreme northeast parts of the country. It was on the road for 21 days, during which it combed the following localities: Abéché, Biltine, Tiné, Arada, Oum-Hadjer, Ati, Djaddaâ.

For reasons of security, investigators did not visit the Guerra region. That zone was the victim of an odious genocide that lasted several years. The Commission however was able to gather a great deal of testimony from natives of Guerra living in Ndjamena. This will to some extent make up for this large gap. But the enthusiasm of the young investigators sent to the central part of the country was crushed by the numerous obstacles they encountered on their journey. The first difficulty: Arriving at Tiné (a locality situated in the extreme northeast of the country near the Sudanese border), their driver suddenly died on 29 December 1991 after a short illness. The second major obstacle: the armed attacks unleashed at Lake Chad by partisans of Hissein Habré in late 1991. This attempt to return Habré to Ndjamena created anxiety and made many victims of the Habré regime understandably unwilling to talk for fear of reprisal. Bichara Djibrine Ahmat, a survivor of a mass murder, felt too threatened even in Ndjamena to make a deposition before the Commission.

For all these reasons, the results of this trip were very meager, though nevertheless instructive. In all, 143 people were interviewed, including 120 relatives of victims, 21 former political detainees, and two former prisoners of war. The investigators located two mass graves, a pit excavated to provide a place for burning regime opponents alive. They took the names of 420 persons who died in detention or were executed.

In bringing its investigation to a close, the Commission summarizes its hearings as follows:
- 662 former political detainees or prisoners of conscience;
- 786 close relatives of victims who died in prison or were executed;
- 236 former prisoners of war;
- 30 former DDS agents;
- 12 former holders of high political position under Habré.

Altogether, the testimony of 1,726 attestants was recorded by the Commission. The Commission located several charnel-houses in the vicinity of the capital city, Ndjamena, and open-air execution sites where remains of victims trail off into the bush.

Also noteworthy were the corpses floating on the Chari river near Milézi after summary executions, a daily sight for inhabitants living on the banks.

On the outskirts of Ndjamena alone, the Commission counted five large charnel-houses and four open-air execution sites (the executioners did not even condescend to bury them).

At the Commission's behest, three exhumations were performed just outside Ndjamena. The first, performed on 15 July 1991 at the Hamral-Goz cemetery about ten kilometers northwest of Ndjamena, uncovered the corpses of political detainees buried in large plastic bags. On 16 January 1992 a second exhumation was performed, again at Hamral-Goz, where 30 bodies were counted in two adjacent mass graves. On 6 February 1992, a final exhumation took place 25 km northwest of Ndjamena and one kilometer from the village of Ambing, where 150 people were executed summarily by the DDS in 1983.

The Commission at first believed it was dealing with a major massacre. But the further the investigation proceeded, the clearer it became that it was a veritable genocide carried out against the Chadian people. It is only honest to point out to the reader that this investigation actually covers only an infinitesimal part of the actions committed by the dictator Habré. Neither the time given to the Commission nor the means at its disposal nor its access to victims was sufficient to carry out such an exhaustive labor.

This work covers only 10 percent of the crimes of the tyrant Habré.

The current government should be given credit for having taken this initiative to enlighten the Chadian public concerning the disastrous reign of the tyrant Habré.

It would also be appropriate to ensure very wide distribution of this report so that the public—in Chad, first of all, but internationally as well—will know what the Chadian people as a whole endured during these interminable eight years of despotism.

Readers should also be advised that this first part of the report deals only with crimes against the physical and mental integrity of persons, and their property; the second part will be devoted to misappropriation of public funds.

Chapter One: The Hissein Habré Regime

When Hissein Habré seized power on 7 June 1982, many Chadians foresaw the tragedy that would engulf Chad under his rule, for he is a man without scruples. In working to achieve his ends, neither law nor religion could restrain his impulsiveness. Thus he would join with the armed rebellion one moment and with the government the next. To win over public sympathy, he portrayed himself by turns as a convinced Maoist and a fervent Muslim.

His long and tumultuous path to power is filled with conspiracies, intrigues, perfidies, and the physical elimination of his adversaries. It was he in 1976 who slipped out on his fellow rebel, Goukouni Oueddeï, to join the central government headed by General Félix Malloum. Named prime minister under the provisions of the 1978 Khartoum (Sudan) accords, Hissein took advantage of his entry into Ndjamena to declare war on Gen. Malloum, who had extended the open hand of friendship. Realizing the inadequacy of his forces, owing to attrition in the ranks of his soldiers, Hissein turned the battle into a civil war between Muslims and Christians (Hissein is a Muslim from the north, President Malloum a Christian from the south). He fanned and in a remarkably machiavellian way exploited ethnic, religious, and regional cleavages, setting Chadians against each other. Unfortunately, Muslim Chadians naively followed him, and there was a rupture between north and south.

Following these events, the government of Gen. Malloum was pushed aside, allowing all the armed factions that had been vegetating in the central, east-central and northern part of the country to enter Ndjamena. Now it was necessary to redistribute the political prizes and ensure that each faction had a position in the new government. Thus a new government was born on 10 November 1979: the "Government of National Union and Transition," or GUNT, headed by former rebel leader Goukouni Oueddeï. Hissein occupied the position of minister of State for defense in that government.

Goukouni and Habré came from the same prefecture, they spoke the same language, and they practiced the same religion, Islam. But none of these similarities and affinities stopped Habré from declaring war against him in March 1980, only 5 months after having engineered the sudden fall of Gen. Malloum. The most murderous war in the country's history was fought between its president (Goukouni) and its defense minister (Habré). The great majority of casualties in this massacre were northerners.

Chadians have not forgotten, nor will they ever forget, that it was Habré who in December 1980, beaten by the GUNT coalition forces, left behind him a horrible charnel-house near his residence in the Sabangali quarter of Ndjamena. It was he, in the same period, who physically liquidated a number of high-level officials, northerners and southerners, and decimated an entire family, the Djallals.

It is obvious that Habré's penchant for crime is not the result of special circumstances or blind chance, but rather an innate predisposition.

Taking over as head of State after sweeping out the heterogeneous GUNT coalition, which proved unable to govern the country, Habré quickly focused on consolidating his own personal and absolute power. The enthusiasm of the allies whom he brought to power—mainly from the Hadjaraï and Zaghawa—yielded very soon to disappointment and bitterness. They discovered early on that Habré trusted only his own ethnic group—the Goranes, especially the Anakaza—while for the others he had only distrust and contempt.

The reader should note that Habré is not illiterate; in fact, he is a cultivated intellectual, educated at distinguished French universities. In daily life, however, his comportment and thinking are not much different from those of a camel thief.

After just a few months under his rule, Chad became, to the great surprise of its citizens, an exclusively Gorane state. To ensure control and keep his grip on the whole country, Habré installed his brethren in all strategic governmental positions: in the security services, the army, and finance. He planned and maneuvered in such a way that no act or decision, however pedestrian, that affected their interests could be taken without their knowledge.

For example, the directorate of customs, the primary organ of government revenue collection, was never entrusted to anyone outside their family in all his years in power. But the worst part is that these officials, chosen because of their tribal connections, were often illiterate, with a resulting paralysis of institutions. The purpose of these appointments was to enable members of his own clan to enrich themselves by diverting revenue for their personal benefit.

Within the Chadian National Army, Habré created his personal army, the Presidential Security (SP), composed mainly of members of his tribe and those that had been won over to his cause. Elements of the SP not only enjoyed special rights and privileges but were allowed to engage in extortion, at a time when the rest of the army was reduced to beggary and abandoned to its own devices, without salary or other compensation. The principle of military hierarchy was turned upside down: high-ranking officers walking around in patched trousers while simple enlisted with no rank or training had vehicles and housing and issued orders to those who normally would be their superiors.

The whole country was painstakingly divided into security zones, and the populace was terrorized by those bloody agents of the political police, the DDS. This sinister institution watched everything people said and did. A single word deemed "out of place," the smallest gesture perceived as suspect, and its author's life would be forfeit.

The more he consolidated his power in blood and terror, the more Habré believed himself endowed with supernatural qualities comparable to those of God. He believed he was all-knowing and all-powerful. And at all his public appearances, the militants of his single party, the National Union for Independence and Revolution (UNIR), hailed him with slogans like "Hissein Habré the savior, Hissein Habré the liberator, Hissein Habré the messenger of peace," and even "With Hissein Habré can you have any doubts?" to which the public would chorus back in response "No! No!" But Habré's delusions of grandeur extended even further, as shown by this slogan so dear to his heart: "Hissein Habré here, Hissein Habré there, Hissein Habré everywhere, Hissein Habré for always... for always," intoxicated by absolute and limitless power, Hissein Habré shamelessly and unabashedly usurped the attributes of God. He felt himself so strong, so durable, that he identified with Him.

But it was in daily life that the despotism of Hissein and his brethren was most revolting. There were in fact two distinct classes in Chadian society. The first was that of the rulers, the masters of the country. The second was that of the governed, the slaves. The slave class was subjected day after day to persecutions, humiliations, and arbitrary actions. To illustrate this depraved state of affairs, it suffices to cite a few examples selected at random:

- On 25 October 1989 an Issa KoKi of the Gorane ethnic group forced his victim, livestock specialist Dayangar Moudjinia, to kneel before his work colleagues, then murdered him in cold blood with a fire-arm. The motive for the public punishment of the victim was his refusal to tend the poultry of the Gorane master. The perpetrator has never been touched. He has been neither arrested nor tried. A master is not accountable for the murder of his subject.

- Law enforcement agencies, such as the judicial police and the gendarmerie, were in the hands of the same tribe. That is why they never intervened to arrest a Gorane, despite the urgent injunctions of magistrates. But if one of their own were in a tight spot, they would help him escape.

- Abdelkader Mahamat, a young man of about 30 from Abéché, was fatally stabbed in 1989 following a minor dispute with a Gorane soldier. The arrested offender was released a few days later by his brethren in the gendarmerie. He was never found again.

- On 23 January 1987, Jeremy Djere, a volunteer militiaman, was on duty with one of his colleagues in the second municipal arrondissement. They were asked to stop a brawl between some Goranes and private citizens at the "Domino Bar". Unfortunately, the brawl ended with a death on the Gorane side. The people panicked and everyone cleared out. The only thing the two militiamen did was report the facts. When the family of the victim learned the news, it reacted by abducting Jeremy and his companion. The latter was executed and thrown into the Chari river. As for Jeremy, he was brutally tortured before being assassinated. To hide their crime, the killers filled a large sack with pebbles and pieces of heavy iron, then tied the sack to the corpse's back before throwing him into the backwater next to the Diguel community building.

- The guilty parties were a group of Goranes headed by a close friend of Habré named Hissein Hamita. The criminals would go unpunished, to the great indignation of all Chadians.

People who did not live through the Habré regime cannot believe or even imagine what took place.

To the great stupefaction of magistrates, Gorane customs took precedence over the laws of the republic. They were enforceable by Kalachnikovs. Goranes did not recognize that a traffic accident might be solely the fault of the victim, nor did they accept self-defense, much less the statute of limitations.

If you had the misfortune to run over a Gorane, even if it was entirely his own fault, you had to come up straightway with 4 million francs in damages if you valued your life. This sum represents the value of 100 camels, according to their local customs. And so much the worse for you if the court declared you not guilty—the order would remain a dead letter.

Dizzy with power and arrogant with the impunity afforded them by the regime, the Goranes regarded their fellow citizens with disdain and treated them as slaves.

Section 1: Organs of Repression of the Habré Regime

The pillars of the dictatorship on which Habré built his regime were the Directorate of Documentation and Security (DDS) or political police, the Presidential Investigation Service (SIP), the security branch (RG) of the police force, and the State party, the National Union for Independence and Revolution (UNIR).

All these organs had the mission of controlling the people, keeping them under surveillance, watching their actions and attitudes even in the smallest matters, in order to flush out so-called enemies of the nation and neutralize them permanently.

I. DDS: The Principal Organ of Repression and Terror

Among all the oppressive institutions of the Habré regime, the DDS distinguished itself by its cruelty and its contempt for human life. It fully carried out its mission, which was to terrorize the population to make them better slaves.

Habré laid all the foundations for his future political police in the first days after he seized power. Initially it existed in embryonic form as the "Documentation and Intelligence Service" headed by Mahamat Fadil and Saleh Batraki. The said service was attached at the time to the Directorate of National Security. The DDS as it is known today was created by Decree No. 005/PR of 26 January 1983.

A. Functions and Structures of the DDS...

At the National Level

No sector public or private, not one scrap near or far, escaped the eye of the DDS. Agents were everywhere in the country, beginning with the prefectures, the subprefectures, the cantons and even the villages. It had a branch in every electoral borough. To oversee its territory, it recruited local agents as spies and informers. Each branch was composed of a chief and a deputy. In addition to the salaries of its staff, the branch each month received operating funds totaling between 50,000 and 100,000 CFA francs, depending on the size of the urban area, to be used for paying snitches.

In terms of nationwide surveillance, Saleh Younouss, ex-director of the DDS, says "we placed agents in every sector: administration, neighborhood, shopping center, etc. At the start, it was we who placed them, but later on people came forward on their own to offer their services. Some earned promotions with the information they furnished."

Finally, a powerful transceiver installed at DDS headquarters collected the daily reports from the provincial branches....

DDS Attached Directly to the Office of the President

Article 1 of the decree creating the DDS provided that it was responsible to the Office of the Presidency because of the confidential nature of its activities. There were no intermediaries between the DDS and Hissein Habré; communication between them was direct. He transmitted all his orders and directives to it; in turn, the DDS sent memoranda to him every day reporting back all their activities in fullest detail. The DDS was his personal affair; nobody else was involved in managing it. The all-powerful Djimé Togou, ex-minister of interior and ex-commissioner for orientation and mass organizations in UNIR, confirmed this, telling the Commission of Inquiry: "Everything having to do with the DDS was reserved for the president, and no one at the time, regardless of rank or function, was allowed to meddle in the affairs of that directorate."

The Structures of the DDS

...At the time of its creation in 1983, the DDS had only three services and four secretariats.... Six years later, this oppressive apparatus had grown astonishingly. The number of services had increased from 3 to 23. The authorities had created an average of three new services per year....

A constant atmosphere of distrust and suspicion reigned at the DDS; each agent had to be on his guard. To avoid indiscretions and intelligence leaks, services were rigidly compartmentalized, and there were no horizontal communications between them. Each service was responsible only to the directorate.

From its creation to the end of the Habré regime, DDS had four directors, successively:
- Saleh Younouss
- Guihini Koreï
- Ahmat Allatchi
- Toke Dadi.

All these directors came from Habré's ethnic group, a fact that says a great deal about the latter's distrust of Chadians from different groups.

The Personnel of DDS

The Commission of Inquiry enumerated 1,076 permanent civilian agents, and 584 soldiers belonging to the redoubtable BSIR, the armed branch of the DDS.

Naturally, one finds in this organization Chadians from all over the country, but the majority of agents were recruited in Gorane areas and

Kanembou. Their educational level is generally very low, and it is rare to find any with more than a secondary education.

The director of DDS had a great deal of latitude in recruitment. There were no objective criteria for hiring; the factors determining the decision were personal connections or friendship, tribal connections, and militancy in the UNIR....

Except for a few policemen and gendarmes seconded to DDS, most personnel had absolutely no understanding of the delicate mission that was to be entrusted to them. There was nothing in their recent path to predispose them to such activities. Their erstwhile trades say a lot about them: peddlers, stock growers, peasants, students who failed to complete primary school, simple soldiers, and the jobless.

No plans for training, not even short courses, were envisaged at the time of their recruitment. It was only several years later that officials decided to train a few hand-picked elements. The personnel were relatively young, often immature, and without any experience in life. The average age varied between about 25 and 35.

Professional Training

Professional training was not a priority in this directorate. It was doled out sparingly and only to a select few. The hierarchy preferred to have blind robots always ready to carry out whatever dirty work needed doing rather than deal with educated, principled and responsible men. Moreover, many of these agents were not intelligent enough to be trained....

Oath Taking

Beginning in early 1990, all DDS agents were required to take an oath. Agents swore on the Bible, Koran, or "Diro" depending on whether they were Christian, Muslim or animist. This oath was taken before a three-member commission consisting of Adoum Galmaye, the controller; Warou Fodou Ali, head of the investigations service; and Mbang Ilanan, head of the training and recruitment service.

The language of the oath was as follows:

"On my honor I swear loyalty and devotion to the president and the institutions of the Third Republic. I solemnly pledge to uphold and never betray the confidentiality of all DDS activities, whatever the circumstances, regardless of the consequences."

The DDS director or his proxy accepts the oath by pronouncing the following words: "in the name of the president, I acknowledge your oath."

The purpose behind the administration of this oath was apparently to put an end to leaks of information about the atrocities for which the organization was responsible.

Habré, irritated by the constant flood of correspondence addressed to him by active members of Amnesty International calling on him to end summary executions and other violations of human rights, believed these indiscretions came from DDS employees, hence the resort to an oath.

B. DDS Budget for 1988

The DDS had a substantial budget consisting of operations and personnel funds. The funds came from multiple sources: the general treasury, the presidency, money confiscated from persons arrested, and so-called friendly countries like the United States and Iraq....

Money Confiscated from Arrested Persons

Arrestees were systematically stripped of their possessions, especially money. The director of DDS put it into a strong-box and prepared a memo to Habré, who controlled its utilization. Often this money was enough to offset the directorate's entire budget allocation. The Commission estimates the value of funds arbitrarily confiscated at more than 1 billion CFA francs per year....

In short, the total budget for DDS for 1988 (operating funds plus personnel expenses) was close to 688,100,000 CFA francs.

Aid from Foreign Countries to DDS

The United States of America heads the list of countries that actively provided DDS with financial, material, and technical support.

America took the DDS under its wing in the very first months of its existence. It trained it, supported it, and contributed effectively to its growth, up to the time of the dictator's fall. As was mentioned earlier in the paragraph on "DDS Budget," the world's greatest power did not scrimp on resources for its protégé. It provided 5 million CFA francs per month. According to some sources, this sum was raised to 10 million in 1989. Add to that vehicles, arms, clothing, and other sophisticated observation and communication devices too numerous to mention....

America also provided training for many intelligence agents.

In addition, France, Egypt, Iraq, and Zaire all contributed (depending on their means and experience) financing, training, and equipment, or shared information.

Security cooperation between the intelligence services of the above-mentioned states and the DDS was intense and continued right up to the departure of the ex-tyrant....

C. Deviation of the DDS from Its Initial Mission to Become an Instrument of Terror and Oppression

The powers of the DDS as envisioned by the Decree of 26 January 1983 scarcely differ from those of similar services in countries where democracy and respect for human rights are venerated. A vigilant observer who looks through the list of this intelligence service's original competencies will find nothing disquieting or mysterious. No hint of what it would become.

However, it would be a serious mistake to rely only on this eloquently and brilliantly drafted decree, to fail to recognize the congenital duplicity of Habré, who has always been two-faced. He projects a legalist and conformist image for public consumption, but hidden behind it is his true face, the incarnation of evil.

The espionage and counter-espionage directorate, whose mission was to thwart the destabilizing activities of Libya, was transformed within just a few months of its creation into an instrument of terror and oppression.

Among the critical factors which led DDS to veer off from its initial functions and become an oppressive monster were the tyrannical and perverse character of Habré on the one hand, and the frustration and greed of DDS agents on the other.

Hissein Habré cultivated a unique philosophy about his real and imagined political enemies, which consisted of physically eliminating them. This philosophy may be summed up as follows:

> Hissein is a man determined to exterminate all who do not share his opinions; according to Habré, those who don't think like him are against him, and those who are against him don't deserve to live.

During his 8 years in power, Hissein Habré did not change by one iota his macabre attitudes, which led him to subject the 6 million people of Chad to total enslavement by establishing terror and insecurity throughout the country.

By way of example, on 10 August 1983, 150 Chadian prisoners of war, who had been captured in the northern part of the country and represented many different ethnic groups, were taken out one afternoon from the jail in Ndjamena to be executed 25 km northeast of the capital near Ambing village. Their corpses were abandoned in the open air for nearly 2 years. No one could approach them to bury them, no one dared say a word.

It was these kinds of actions that Hissein Habré liked to carry out to deter his potential adversaries. Thus DDS became a privileged instrument of terror, by which Habré meant to govern the country.

DDS agents, coming from the most disadvantaged social classes, had always been on the margins of Chadian society. When suddenly they were propelled, with no preparation, to the forefront of the national scene and given absolute, unlimited power, they believed that Chad was their personal property. And that they could do whatever they wanted with people and their possessions. Such power, such nectar of the gods, could not fail to pervert the humblest of citizens. Inflated by all that, and disposing of a weapon as terrifying as the DDS, these latter could neither contain nor master their impulse to take vengeance on those who not too long ago had considered them trash.

Very soon they began arresting people all over the place, day and night, usually without cause or for trivial reasons that had nothing to do with the security of the state. Once the unfortunate was arrested, the possessions for which he had worked long, hard years were pillaged; but that was not all: "Roomers" at DDS had no chance of getting out alive.

The objective pursued by DDS was quickly attained. The people were terrorized; every citizen was apprehensive and knew not what tomorrow might bring. With every passing day their anxiety increased.

This life of deliberately maintained terror and oppression was summed up by former DDS director Saleh Younouss, who says: "It must be admitted that the original mission assigned to the DDS was gradually modified by the president (Hissein Habré) himself. At first, the directorate was supposed to concern itself with the country's internal and external security, and in particular to thwart any operation by Libyans against Chad. But little by little the president himself gave a new orientation to the directorate and made it into an instrument of terror."

II. Auxiliary Organs of the DDS

In its daily activities, the DDS was often back-stopped or reinforced by other parallel security organs. These auxiliary organs were the Police Security Branch (RG), the Presidential Investigation Service (SIP), and the National Union for Independence and Revolution (UNIR).

Habré is a paranoid who could not be satisfied with just one intelligence service, hence the proliferation of these organs....

B. Presidential Investigation Service (SIP)

This is a parallel intelligence service whose powers are somewhat unclear; this service, which had its finger in everything, was attached directly to the Office of the President.

SIP was also an organ of terror; its mandate in matters of oppression knew no limits.

The other services, such as DDS and RG, though they committed their share of atrocities, constantly complained to Habré about SIP interference in their own special domains. SIP, as noted above, was interested in everything: politics, contraband, diversion of public funds, social problems. In short, it did whatever it wanted.

Mr. Abdel-Aziz Ahmat, a young economist arbitrarily arrested by the SIP, summarizes for us the service's activities during the course of one night: "The first person I encountered in the cell was arrested for public drunkenness. She came in 2 days ahead of me, and when I was freed 48 hours later, she was still there. I have the impression she had been forgotten. As for the two other people arrested at the same time as me, the first was accused of falsifying his motor-bike registration and the second, a mere driver, of having removed the effects of the late Ibrahim Mahamat Itno, a former minister of interior and territorial administration whom Habré assassinated during the events of April 1989.

"The same night, SIP agents brought in a group of people who were arguing about a 'DIA' affair (damages awarded to relatives of the person killed). These people were beaten all night long, they shouted, howled, and cried.

"Finally, they arrested two young people suspected of using drugs. They too were tortured all night. By morning their faces were swollen, and they had wounds all over their bodies."

Arrestees were transferred to the president's detention center after interrogation and torture.

It should also be noted that SIP does not occupy an official building: Its headquarters are situated on private property belonging to a certain Doudji, a Treasury employee; this property is located in a slum neighborhood called "Moursal." The personnel in this service all belonged to Habré's praetorian guard, the Presidential Security (SP). It is headed by Captain Hissein Ramadan, Mahamat Hassaballah Oudi, and a certain "Allatchi" of the Tubu ethnic group.

C. National Union For Independence and Revolution (UNIR)

The National Union for Independence and Revolution (UNIR) is a State party created on 22 June 1984 in Ndjamena, after the dissolution of the political-military movement called "Northern Armed Forces" [FAN] which carried Hissein Habré to power.

When this State party was created, all Chadians were obliged to join; those who refused or dragged their feet were watched and considered enemies of the regime. All Chadians knew what happens to unfortunates tagged with that label. To avoid problems with the DDS and be left in peace, the majority of Chadians took out UNIR membership cards whether they wanted to or not.

The most important mission for UNIR militants was to keep watch on the people, to unmask enemies of the party, i.e. opponents of the Habré regime. Thus all so-called "earnest" militants were eyes and ears of the despot. They constituted the main reservoir of informants for the intelligence services.

Interrogated on this subject, Saleh Younouss, ex-director of the DDS, says: "Our informers were mostly UNIR militants. They received bonuses from the Directorate, the amount depending on the importance of the information furnished."

Section 2: The Directorate of Documentation and Security in Action

I. Arrests and Interrogations

A. Arrests

In Chad, legal and procedural provisions for arrest are specified in the Code of Criminal Procedures. All persons arrested are theoretically subject to these provisions. But in practice, this procedure was never applied to political prisoners or prisoners of conscience....

Every DDS Agent had Power of Arrest

Arrests could be ordered by the president, who often gave out instructions over the telephone.

In that connection, Abbass Abougrène, ex-DDS agent, says: "On 1 April 1989 at 0600 hours, Guihini Koreï, ex-director of the DDS, summoned all the service chiefs and told them to arrest all Zaghawa nationals without exception. He told them these were the instructions of the president."

The director had unlimited powers of arrest. Finally, the service chiefs and even simple agents could make an arrest, so long as they could answer for it to the director. Once the individual was arrested, no one, whatever his political or social standing, dared inquire as to the place of detention or reason behind the arrest: He might incur the same fate....

A commission was created in 1987 to take charge of arresting members of the Hadjaraï ethnic group. It was composed of Al Hadj Djada (president), Mahamat Wakaï, Mahamat Djibrine, Absakine Abdoulaye, Warrant Officer Sabre Ribe, and Lieutenant Ketté Moïse.

In 1989, an analogous commission was created to deal with the Zaghawa problem. This commission was composed of Mahamat Djibrine, Ndojigoto Haunan, Mahamat Sakher, Issa Arawaï, Warou Fodou, Doudet Yalade, Abdelaziz Philippe, Mbang Elina Jéremie, Ndjinan Jérôme, and Saleh Nambe.

Grounds for Arrest

Grounds for arrest were generally trivial, even laughable. Arrests were often motivated by desire for self-enrichment or simply score-settling....

Some examples:

Ngaressoum Ngarkol: Government employee working in Mao, was arrested by the DDS branch in the said locality on 30 September 1987. He was accused of having said in a tavern that Hissein Habré's father was a southerner. Transferred to Ndjamena and held at DDS headquarters, he died on 11 August 1988.

Dilnodji Belaloum: arrested on 5 September 1987 in Ndjamena for having stolen kerosene, died on 13 January 1988....

Guideo Pierre: was arrested on 27 February 1986 at Pala. He was accused of having listened to Radio Bardaï....

Brahim Bourma: who tried to travel to the CAR from Maro without a pass, was arrested on 18 January 1988. Transferred to Ndjamena and held at DDS headquarters, he succumbed on 12 July 1988.

Moussa Ahmat: was arrested by the DDS in Dourbali on 21 May 1988 for having expressed his joy at [news of] the death of Hissein Habré's father. He succumbed on 20 August 1988....

As we have noted, none of the above-mentioned charges has the least connection with the security of the state, the ostensible reason people were arrested at all hours of the day and night. Thus they were arbitrary arrests, motivated solely by the whim of those who felt themselves invested with the power of life and death over their fellow citizens.

B. The Interrogators

Everyone arrested had to be interrogated. Interrogations were instituted by DDS to force detainees to admit the allegations made against them, to denounce their accomplices, and to sign confessions. In the view of DDS, anyone suspected or accused was presumed guilty....

Generally, detainees were interrogated late at night. Under exceptional circumstances, for example during political crises, interrogations were held during the day.

It was during interrogation that the torturers practiced their arts....

Interrogations were conducted in such a way that it was impossible for detainees to deny the allegations made against them. Victims were usually forced, by means of torture and abuse, to admit the facts and allegations, none of which were true, simply to end their agony.

The Commission noted, in reading numerous investigative reports prepared by DDS, that the following accusations reappear time and again:
- Performing magical rites to aid the enemy
- Transmitting information to the enemy
- Agent in the pay of the enemy
- Crossing the border without documents
- Sheltering suspects
- Fraudulent importation of merchandise
- Comments maligning the Goranes, the president, or his regime
- Recruitment of elements for the Islamic Legion
- Listening to enemy radio stations....

Interrogation reports were generally sent to the director of DDS, who decided what was to be done. When the case was of great importance, or when the detainee was arrested on orders from Habré, the director of documentation and security forwarded the reports to him. Once the report on a detainee was sent to Hissein Habré, his fate was in the president's hands.

Questioned on this subject, Saleh Younouss, ex-director of the DDS, said: "I could not release a detainee unless the offense was minor, and only before a report went to the president, because after that, he alone could decide the detainee's fate."

II. Torture and Arbitrary Detention

Torture was an institutional practice in the DDS. Arrestees were systematically tortured, then kept in tiny cells under terrible and inhumane conditions.

A. Torture

This was the procedure of choice used by DDS to obtain confessions, or quite simply to inflict suffering.

Most DDS detainees, the great majority of whom were arrested arbitrarily, had no knowledge of the deeds they were alleged to have committed—if indeed they were even accused of a specific misdeed. A great number of people were arrested without being accused of any criminal act, simply because of their ethnic background or wealth.

Those accused of an offense were tortured so they would admit their guilt, regardless of the consequences, and sign confessions, in many cases despite their obvious innocence; after all, their innocence was irrelevant: What mattered was getting the confession. Often, even after a spontaneous confession, detainees were tortured atrociously.

Those arrested because of their ethnic affiliation or wealth were tortured as a reprisal or with a view to intimidation: In other words, the DDS elevated torture virtually to the status of a standard procedure, and almost all detainees were subjected to it one way or another, regardless of sex or age.

1. Who Ordered People Tortured?

Actually, within the DDS, torture was a natural concomitant of the very mission of the interrogators. In fact, DDS had a permanent commission responsible for interrogation of detainees.

Its role being to make detainees "confess," it resorted systematically to torture during its interrogations. The commission had no need to order detainees tortured, since the practice was routine. However, the president and the director often gave specific instructions to torture a particular individual, group of individuals, or ethnic group.

In the provinces, apart from instructions received from the director, the heads of DDS branches also arrested and tortured people on their own initiative.

2. Agents Responsible for Torture

Within the DDS, interrogations and torture were primarily the responsibility of the above-mentioned commission. Members of this commission included Abakar Torbo, Mahamat Sakher ("Bidon"), Mahamat Djibrine ("El Djonto"), Issa Arawaï, and Adoum Galmaye.

Apart from this commission, special interrogation and torture missions were often entrusted to specific service chiefs trusted by the president or the director. People like Issa Arawaï.

One particular form of torture, the "black diet," was also practiced by the penitentiary service under Abakar Torbo, its chief.

3. Torture of Arrestees was Systematic

Everyone arrested by the DDS, in Ndjamena or in the provinces, was systematically subjected to at least one interrogation session, following which an interrogation report was prepared. Torture being the tool of choice during interrogation, DDS agents resorted to it systematically.

A number of former DDS detainees told the Commission of Inquiry about the torture and abuse to which they were subjected during their detention. Scars from these tortures and medical examinations have corroborated their testimony....

5. Diverse Forms of Torture

To extract confessions during interrogation, DDS agents used an infinite variety of tortures. Sometimes they resorted to these atrocities out of pure sadism, simply to make their prisoners suffer.

Here are some of the methods of torture practiced.

a) The "Arbatachar" Binding

This is a form of torture that consists in tying the two arms to the back, pulling the cord until the two elbows are almost touching behind the prisoner and his chest is thrust out as far as it can go. A variant of the "arbatachar" involves tying the arms to a piece of wood set crosswise behind the back.

Several persons subjected to this torture for long enough periods of time completely lost the use of their arms; others remained deformed, their chests permanently stuck out.

b) Forced Swallowing of Water

After being tightly bound, the detainee is laid down on his back with his mouth held wide open and his torturers make him swallow an incredible amount of water, often until he faints. Sometimes, a torturer would get on top of his distended stomach, ultimately smothering him.

c) Spraying of Gas

Some detainees, after being tightly bound, had gas sprayed in their eyes, nose, ears and mouth. Many died, and almost all of those few that survived lost their eyesight.

d) Exhaust Pipe

This form of torture consists in forcing the mouth of the tied-up detainee around the end of the exhaust pipe of a car whose engine is running. A little pressure on the accelerator is enough to make the wretched victim lose consciousness and inevitably burns his mouth.

e) Burns with Incandescent Objects

Burning match sticks and lit cigarettes were frequently used to torture DDS prisoners. These burns were inflicted on the most sensitive parts of the body.

f) Cohabitation with Corpses

This is an especially odious form of mental torture which consists in not removing bodies from the cells of prisoners for several days, while the corpse reaches an advanced stage of decomposition.

g) The Chopsticks Torture

This form of torture consists in placing a piece of wood over each temple and attaching the ends to ropes. As the ropes are pulled tighter, the victim begins to feel as if his head is going to explode.

Other tortures included the black diet, which consists of allowing the victim to die of hunger and thirst, roughing-up, flagellation, deprivation of oxygen, electric shocks, and as many other forms of torment as the sadistic imaginations of the torturers could devise.

6. The Most Feared Torturers

By their cruelty, sadism and inhumanity, certain DDS agents have acquired a sad notoriety among former political detainees, who speak of them constantly. To these pitiless tormentors, the life of a prisoner means very little. The list includes:
- Guihini Koreï (former DDS director)
- Mahamat Sakher alias "Bidon" (deputy commander of BSIR)
- Mahamat Djibrine alias "El-Djonto" (coordinator)
- Issa Arawaï (chief of documentation service)
- Abakar Torbo (head of penitentiary service)
- Abba Moussa (penitentiary service agent)
- Adoum Galmaye (controller)
- Warou Fodou (head of investigations service)
- Yaldé Samuel (head of training and recruitment)
- Doudé Yaladé (deputy chief of internal security service)
- Bandjim Bandoum (chief of exploitation service)
- Mahamat Fadil (ex-director of National Security)
- Nodjigoto Haunan (ex-director of National Security)
- Bichara Chaïbo (ex-deputy director of DDS)

B. Detention Centers and Living Conditions

One of the characteristics of the Habré dictatorship was the proliferation of detention centers throughout the country. In Ndjamena alone there are seven detention centers, not to mention additional incarceration facilities such as the interrogation cells of the judicial police and the prisons.

Once arrests were made, detainees were sent to different detention centers and divided up according to the threat they posed to the regime.

Once the prisoner, alone or with others, was assigned to a cell, he was not allowed to leave it.

1. Detention Centers

...*Underground Prison or "Swimming Pool."* This is located on the DDS premises across from USAID. It is an old swimming pool from the colonial era that was turned into an underground detention facility in 1987 and covered with a reinforced concrete slab. The building measures 21.47 meters in length and 9.62 m in width. It has 10 cells with tiny barred windows. The dimensions of the cells vary between 2.98 and 3.13 m in length, and between 2.97 and 3.2 m in width. The windows in the cells measure 75 cm in length and 34 cm in width. A double door 1.38 m wide and 1.96 m high gives access to the cells.

These cells, which theoretically should not hold more than 15 people, were often crammed with 90 or more. When the weather was hot, especially in March, April and May, the cells were veritable furnaces, the atmosphere was stifling and quickly became fatal for human beings. Barring a miracle, the prisoners died one by one of asphyxiation.

The blind repression did not spare the weaker sex or children. Thus women were held in the same prisons as the men. Some of them even gave birth to a child in this macabre setting.

Such an event serves to remind us all of the sacred value of human life, because while babies were being born in complete innocence, men were being sent to their death by their fellows to satisfy their base ends.

To lighten their suffering, detainees sometimes resorted to pathetic ploys. Thus, doubtless in hope of currying favor with her jailer, when detainee Billah Hamit gave birth to a child, she named the newborn after the head of the penal system, Abakar Torbo, a dreaded torturer. In the absence of testimony, it is impossible to say whether this gesture succeeded in bringing out the man's more humane sentiments, because by their very nature all DDS agents are perverted beings, insensitive to the suffering of others....

2. Living Conditions in the Detention Centers

When someone was interned in the DDS jails, he had little prospect of ever returning to the world of the living. If he withstood the tortures, the heat, the suffocation, and disease, he died of starvation....

b) Clothing

Before being locked into the cells, any valuable personal possessions were taken from the prisoners, except for their clothing. After that, they never got another change of clothes. However long they were in detention, they continued to wear that one outfit. As prisoners never washed, their clothes became filthy and veritable breeding grounds for lice, which caused skin maladies. Eventually, prisoners were reduced to wearing rags.

Thus some prisoners, when they were released on 1 December 1990, were in tatters and others almost naked, which made them unrecognizable and quite pathetic....

k) Released Prisoners had to take Oath

To avoid any leakage of information concerning the dark activities of the DDS, the latter imposed a black-out on everything happening within its precincts. To enforce this, it forced the few prisoners it released to take oaths. The Commission brought to light the case of 12 prisoners from the first army who were ordered released on 20 November 1989. Their names were Moussa Youssouf Adoum, Souleymane Issa Moussa, Alio Taltal Ali, Mahamat Abdoulaye Djibrine, Annour Gaday Rado, Adef Abdelkerim Doudoum, Alhabo Sanda Alkidjer, Moussa Ali Acyl, Khalil Adoum Ibrahim, Wal Ibedou Diare, Ahmat Hassan Moussa, and Abdoulaye Idriss.

These prisoners were administered the following oath, which was termed a "Solemn pledge":

> By these presents I, the undersigned Souleymane Issa Moussa, born in 1962 at Karal (Chari-Baguirmi), solemnly swear, on being released this day, 20 November 1989, from the custody of the Directorate of Documentation and Security, that I have seen and heard nothing, and will say nothing whatsoever about the facilities or the detainees remaining in prison.
> I swear by God never to say anything about what happens there.
> By my signature I acknowledge my responsibility before God, and subject myself moreover to prosecution under the law as provided in your statutes, in the event I should reveal any of these secrets.
>
> Done on 19 November 1989
>
> Subject   Chief of DDS Penitentiary Service

After which, prisoners affixed their signature or thumbprint on the document. Thus prisoners, after their release, were always followed by the DDS. If they violated their oath, culprits were subject to capital punishment. This is why some agents and prisoners, having witnessed the death of their relatives, have chosen to keep quiet, in order to save their own lives and those of their families.

3. Physical and Emotional Consequences of Torture and Detention

Detention under abominable conditions, torture, and ill treatment have in the case of many prisoners left profound physical and psychological after-effects from which they will continue to suffer for the rest of their lives, unless appropriate medical assistance could alleviate their suffering.

In that connection, the president of the Commission, at the recommendation of Amnesty International, appealed on 10 June 1991 to "AVRE," a French humanitarian organization dedicated to providing care for victims of political repression, to come to Chad to treat the many victims of the Habré regime. The request was favorably received, and the response was immediate. Thus Dr. Hélène Jaffé, accompanied by her assistant, Sibel Agrali, came to our country in July 1991 to evaluate the situation and make contact with Chadian authorities.

At the conclusion of this visit, it was agreed the practitioner and her team would spend 2 weeks in Ndjamena every 2 months.

By the end of January 1992, 242 patients had been examined and received free medical care and medicines. Thanks to the solicitude of Dr. Jaffé and her team, patients were given new hope, comforted, and reassured of gradual improvement in their condition.

We must also mention the case of our two seriously ill countrymen, whose condition requires treatment at a specialized hospital complex, for which AVRE obtained financial assistance from the French Government, which will allow them to be evacuated very soon to France....

III. Deliberate Determination to Exterminate So-Called Opponents of the Regime

During his 8-year reign, Hissein Habré created a regime where adherence to any political opinions contrary to his own could mean physical liquidation. Thus, from the time he came to power in June 1982 through November 1990 when he fled, a large number of Chadians were persecuted for their efforts to modify his autocratic policies. That is why entire families were arrested and imprisoned with no trial of any kind, or simply hunted down and wiped out. This policy, based mainly on tribalism and regionalism, forced other Chadians, some of them his former comrades in arms, to flee into exile.

Individuals arrested by DDS had very little chance of coming out alive. This sad reality was known to all Chadians. Detainees died in one of two ways: either slowly, following days or months of imprisonment, or quickly, in the first few days after arrest, at the hands of Hissein Habré's executioners.

Death by Physical Exhaustion, Asphyxiation or as a Result of Torture

Testimony from former political prisoners has provided ample evidence about the ways their comrades died in prison. Some died of physical exhaustion due to inhuman prison conditions, inadequate and poor-quality food, or the total lack of hygiene and medical attention. The body, weakened and with all its defenses run down, was assailed by a host of maladies that lead inexorably to death. Others died from asphyxiation. Packed into minuscule cells with no ventilation for 2 or 3 days in intense heat approaching 45° in the shade, deprived moreover of water and nourishment, prisoners died one after another.

Lacking gas chambers like those of Hitler, Hissein Habré—an equally demonic man—simply substituted airless cells....

Prisoners Died Every Day

...DDS regulations did not permit the body of a prisoner to be turned over to his relatives, or relatives even to be informed of his death. Thus families of detainees continued to hope for their return and were often cheated and swindled by DDS agents.

Poisoning of Prisoners

Habré and his torturers stopped at nothing that could help them exterminate their adversaries. They even resorted to poisoning.

Godi Bani, arrested in 1987 and held at Bitkine (Guéra subprefecture), recounts: "I miraculously escaped poisoning, since one day our jailers served us poisoned millet; 93 of our comrades who ate that ration died. We spent 3 days among the corpses.

"At the end of the fourth day, our guards came to select several prisoners to bury the decomposed bodies. After the burials, our executioners told us: 'Let this be a lesson to anyone who dares to revolt against the government of Hissein Habré.'"

In corroboration of this testimony, the Commission of Inquiry has found, in the notebook of DDS controller Adoum Galmaye, the names of poisoned prisoners....

The Cemetery of Hamral-Goz

The bodies of prisoners who died in DDS prisons were generally taken away 24-48 hours later, in a state of advanced decomposition, by Moussa Adoum Seïd, alias "Abba Moussa," with the help of a few prisoners who were still healthy. After bundling them up in two large empty plastic bags, the bodies would be loaded into the sinister 404 covered pick-up with license plates RT 1247 AP to be thrown into a common grave, usually on the northwest outskirts of Ndjamena, more specifically at Hamral-Goz. Traditional funeral rites were never allowed; the pits were shallow, and the bodies were thrown one over another in all positions. No prayers were said over the victims, whether Muslim or Christian.

The Commission of Inquiry during its investigations discovered several grave sites, the largest of which was the ... one at Hamrol-Goz, located about 5 km west of the French military base, in a civilian cemetery.

The huge charnel house—140 meters long and 41 meters wide—is marked out with pits where four, five, 10 or even more people were buried. Thanks to information furnished by former detainees who provided the manpower for DDS to inter its victims, the Commission of Inquiry conducted two exhumations in this cemetery. The first took place on 15 July 1991, when the Commission found several bodies wrapped in plastic bags. The second exhumation, carried out on 16 January 1992, uncovered human skeletons, including 30 skulls, in two adjacent pits....

The Executioners

These were confidential agents of Habré, recruited if possible from Goranes in the BSIR or Presidential Security. At various times they worked under the direction of Guihini Koreï, Issa Arawaï, or Mahamat Saker. But other agents often took their place, such as Mahamat Djibrine alias "El-Djonto," Adoum Galmaye, Warou Ali Fodou, Lieutenant Ketté Ndoji, and personally directed the slaughter....

Another investigation undertaken [by the Commission of Inquiry] at villages along a 20-km stretch of the Chari river west of "Ndjamena Abba Djellou" village confirmed the executions carried out in these localities. People living near the river unanimously report that "human corpses, decomposing, floating on the river, carried by the current toward Lake Chad," were an almost-daily spectacle during the 8 years of Habré's reign. They also say that some corpses, during times when the water level was low, "ran aground on the sand banks and were devoured by birds." The powerless and terrorized river-dwellers could not approach the corpses for fear of meeting the same fate.

The Discovery of Written Documents about the Executions and the Destruction of Villages

As a result of investigations of the archives of the ex-DDS, the Commission of Inquiry discovered documents concerning the executions and the destruction of villages. One hand-written three-page document, undated, which we reproduce here in its entirety, discusses the number of persons arrested or killed as well as villages destroyed or abandoned....

Another important document was discovered in the DDS archives, in which the informant provides details to his superiors on the massacre that took place at Koumra (Moyen-Chari subprefecture).

Reproduced below is the full text of the said document:...

All the executions, the physical eliminations, and the poisonings were ordered directly by Hissein Habré. In that connection, the former director of DDS, Saleh Younouss, a trusted confidential agent of Habré, told the Commission of Inquiry: "It is true that many prisoners died of exhaustion or maladies in DDS jails. But others were removed at night from the jails or directly from their homes and disappeared. These operations, or more precisely these executions, were always ordered by President Hissein Habré and frequently carried out by Issa Arawaï."

Mahamat Djibrine, alias "El-Djonto," the redoubtable coordinator of the DDS, greatly feared by the political detainees, confirmed the revelations made by his director: "It is the head of State who personally gave the order for liquidations," he asserts.

IV. Physical Elimination of Opponents

Opponents of Habré were hunted down wherever they might be; in Chad or outside the country. Public awareness campaigns were often undertaken to persuade people who had fled into exile abroad to return to the fold. It was part of the famous national reconciliation policy that was a constant theme in the speeches of Habré and his supporters, but once former opponents returned to Ndjamena, their actions and words were systematically monitored and they were arrested at the least provocation. As for those who never allowed themselves to be taken in by these idle promises and soothing words, they were abducted and transferred to Ndjamena or killed wherever they were found. Thus the "headhunters" in the "Terrorist Mission" service were sent to different countries to track down dissidents. The victims include members of the opposition, their relatives and friends, and simple traders suspected of having sheltered opponents.

The political and administrative authorities of the countries concerned, deluded by Habré's deceitful rhetoric, closed their eyes to the tragedy overtaking Chadians within their borders.

To carry out abductions and assassinations abroad more effectively, DDS created a special service, Terrorist Mission, known by the acronym "MT."... MT was responsible for a number of abductions and executions committed abroad. The majority were abducted or killed while residing in countries that share borders with Chad. Dissident refugees in Togo, Benin, and even Saudi Arabia were victims of DDS revenge....

Arabic instructor Mahamat Issa, a native of Ouaddaï, paid with his life for his opposition to the Habré regime. He was killed at Fotokol, Cameroon, in 1987, while he and several other persons were worshipping in a mosque....

Survivors of Executions Testify

In the course of its investigations, the Commission of Inquiry encountered several former prisoners of conscience and political detainees who miraculously escaped the massacres organized by the DDS. All these miraculously saved persons will carry on their bodies for the rest of their lives the indelible scars of the executioners' bullets. Four survivors presented their testimony; their gripping accounts are incredible but true.

By reason of the importance of these affidavits, the Commission deemed it indispensable to reproduce them in their entirety....

Neldi Wa Moramngar: another survivor of a mass execution in the subprefecture of Moïssala in Moyen-Chari, recounts:

> On 27 July 1985, while I was on vacation in the village of Ngalo, 52 km from Moïssala, about twenty soldiers in two vehicles swarmed into the village and rounded up the entire population. Next they pulled aside the women and some children. That done, the soldiers stripped us of all the belongings we had on our persons, that is watches, glasses, and shoes. All the houses were also pillaged; then, after about 1-1/2 hours, that is close to 1600 hours, and after first being tied up hands behind our backs, we were taken to a clearing about 300 meters west of the village. After packing us close together in the clearing, the soldiers began executing us in groups of five. The first group of five was shot, then a second, and when the soldiers ran into a little resistance with the third group, they decided to open fire on all of us huddled together. An AA52 (1952

automatic weapon) was pulled into firing position, and several people were riddled with bullets, then those who were not hit by the AA52 were shot at almost point-blank range by two rows of soldiers. Then we were sprayed with an insecticide, ULV, and they set fire to us.

For my part, I was only wounded on the right buttock, because when the fusillade was fired I was under my big brother, who was killed by a bullet in the throat, and whose blood completely covered me.

When the fire was ignited, the hair on my left side caught fire but I quickly turned over on that side and extinguished the flame.

Noticing that I was not dead, the soldiers began firing on me, but I was only hit in the buttock, as I said earlier.

Their despicable work finished, the soldiers retired. Several minutes after they left, the survivors, including me, picked ourselves up. We were eight men and a child.

The same night, about midnight, after burying our dead relatives, I left the village on foot and went to Bédaya, an administrative post about 25 km away. Next I went to Sarh, where I stayed for a month before returning to the village.

Such was the sad reality, such was the curse, that laid low a submissive population shattered and terrorized by a tyranny without precedent in the history of our country.

Chapter Two: Extent of the Calamity of the Habré Regime

The Hissein Habré regime was a veritable hecatomb for the Chadian people; thousands of people died, thousands of others suffered in mind and body and continue to suffer.

Throughout this dark reign, in Ndjamena and everywhere else in the country, systematic repression was the rule for all opponents or suspected opponents of the regime.

The possessions of persons arrested or hunted were pillaged and their relatives persecuted. Entire families were decimated.

In the interior, villages were completely burned down and their populations massacred. Nothing was immune to this murderous madness, and the entire country was in a state of terror.

Section 1: More than a Massacre, Habré
Committed Genocide against the Chadian People

During his eight years of bloody dictatorship, Hissein Habré committed a veritable genocide against the Chadian people. Never in the history of Chad have there been so many deaths, never have there been so many innocent victims. When the Commission of Inquiry began its work, it believed that at worst it would be dealing with massacres, but the further it proceeded in its investigations, the larger loomed the dimensions of the disaster, until finally it was a question of extermination. No ethnic group, no tribe, no family was spared, except the Goranes and their allies. The killing machine made no distinction between men, women, and children. The mildest protest was equated with revolt and triggered horrible reprisals. The silenced and submissive population watched powerless its own gradual asphyxiation. Starting in 1982, political prisons sprang up all over Chad, and they were not emptied until the fall of the regime in 1990. In Ndjamena as well as the provinces, arrests were made at a frenetic pace. People were arrested on any pretext, even without any pretext. A slip of the tongue, an old grudge never forgiven by a Gorane or DDS agent, even an incident fabricated of whole cloth was enough for one to find himself in the grim dungeons of the DDS.

In these dungeons, a very large number of people died. The number of political prisoners counted by the Commission of Inquiry for the period 1982-1990 and the number who died during the same period boggle the imagination.

I. The Statistics Speak for Themselves

During the whole time the Commission of Inquiry was given to carry out its mission, it worked tirelessly, first in Ndjamena and later in the provinces, to get as many names as possible of people killed by the Hissein Habré regime, as well as those arbitrarily detained.

A. The Number of Deaths Recorded by the Commission for the Period 1982 to 1990

It should be kept in mind that these figures do not include opponents who died fighting, to whose memory the nation remains profoundly grateful.

These are only innocent victims of the regime, persons who died in prison or were killed for their beliefs, and prisoners of war assassinated in cold blood after their capture.

1. Nationals

The Commission of Inquiry counted no less than 3,780 dead.

2. Foreigners

The Commission also counted 26 foreigners who died in DDS prisons or were executed, including 6 Cameroonians, 5 Libyans, 4 Central Africans, 2 Senegalese, 2 Nigerians, 1 Malian, 1 Nigerian, 1 Zairian, 1 Ethiopian, 1 Syrian, 1 Yemeni, and 1 Frenchman.

3. Estimated Number

Far from being an exhaustive enumeration of the atrocities committed by the Habré regime, the figures published by the Commission of Inquiry constitute only an indicator giving some idea of the scope of the calamity.

The Commission estimates in fact that the work it has done covers no more than 10 percent of everything that happened, because many people for diverse reasons did not come forward to testify before the Commission. Some people saw no need to give such testimony; others did not want to revive evil memories; most numerous, finally, are those whose abstention is motivated by fear or distrust. In the view of the latter, the work of the Commission might serve only to identify all the malcontents of the old regime with a view to possible future repression. Some of them went so far as to call the Commission merely a new version of the DDS.

Thus, by the reckoning of the Commission, the number of persons who died in prison or were executed by the Habré regime is estimated at more than 40,000 nationwide.

B. The Number of Political Prisoners Counted by the Commission for the Period 1982-1990

The number of detainees (living or dead) counted under the Habré regime is more than 54,000.

II. Suspected Individuals Despoiled of Their Possessions

During the Habré era, mere suspicion was sufficient to bring on arrest. An arrested person had no rights. He therefore lost ownership of all his possessions: Looting, theft of belongings, and arbitrary occupation of others' houses became commonplace.

A. Houses of Arrested Persons Systematically Sacked

When someone was arrested, DDS agents and elements of Presidential Security (SP) quickly descended on his house and stripped it of all effects so rapidly that one is often led to wonder what was the real reason for the arrest.

1. Orders to Plunder came from Higher Up

The looting and theft of the possessions of arrestees was not carried out solely at the initiative of the agents who perpetrated it; they received orders for the arrest of high officials and important businessmen from their service chiefs or from the DDS director himself, who in turn received them from the head of state.

2. Beneficiaries of the Plundering

The plundering was carried out both by DDS agents and by elements of the Presidential Investigation Service (SIP) or Presidential Security (SP).

When the plundering was done by the SIP or SP, the objects collected were taken directly to the office of the president. When the DDS went to work, the pillaged goods were first of all taken to the DDS then put in a storehouse used for this purpose. Then the booty was evaluated and divided up into what strictly speaking were shares.

Goods of great value (deluxe carpets, vehicles, gold jewelry, etc.) went to the presidency, the rest being divided between the director and his close associates. From time to time the agents too received a portion of these goods, but they first had to submit a written request to the director, who decided whether it was appropriate....

Several relatives of victims and a few survivors of the DDS jails brought the Commission of Inquiry testimony regarding the pillaging, including the following examples:...

In addition to this testimony amassed by the Commission of Inquiry, several documents relative to the plundering have been discovered in the archives of DDS, among them an inventory report dated 22 April 1989, from which we reproduce several extracts:...

Documents itemizing the contents of DDS storehouses were also found. In reality, the DDS had three storehouses for storing confiscated goods: one at the DDS, another at BSIR, and a third at the National Police College.

An accounting prepared by the DDS controller's office itemizes the contents of these storehouses as of 4 August 1990. The following inventory of the National Police College is reproduced as an example....

B. Families of Arrestees Evicted from Their Own Homes

When someone was arrested, his family was evicted from the house. No distinction was made between a person's own house and the house of a relative with whom the family was living. So women and children were thrown homeless into the street and exposed to inclement weather, disease, and poverty.

1. The Habré Dictatorship did not Stop with Punishing the Suspect Alone

As soon as an individual was sought or arrested, whether for good cause or no, all the members of his family were punished with him. In fact, making the whole family suffer was a typical example of Habré's sadism and cynicism. It was a sort of collective punishment: Everyone had to pay. This sanction, which frequently entailed pillaging the family's possessions and expelling it from the house, was inflicted with the intention of making sure the arrestee was not the only one to suffer.

2. Arbitrary Occupations of Detainees' Houses

As soon as the wretched family was expelled from its abode, it was quickly occupied.

The new occupants were generally members of the president's ethnic group. These takeovers were not as anarchic as they might seem. Records discovered by the Commission of Inquiry in DDS archives indicate these houses were assigned to a variety of petitioners. The DDS director chose recipients carefully. In fact, several requests sent to him asking for assignment to these houses were also discovered. For example, on 10 July 1983, one Abakar Tchotoya, who was already unlawfully occupying someone else's house, wrote to the director, first to inform him that the house he occupied had just fallen to pieces, and second to ask him for "one of the houses that has just been inventoried."

Some of these houses were rented to individuals by UNIR, which collected the rent each month. Others were rented by close associates of the president.

Found in DDS archives was a report dated 25 February 1985 and signed by Police Chief Tamia Animba, head of the commission assigned to inventory properties of opponents seized in Ndjamena, which mentions 436 properties already recorded. The report was summarized in a detailed chart giving for each property the first and last name and nationality of the dissident, location of the property (quarter, arrondissement, block, property number), first and last name and profession of the new occupant, and "remarks."

Under this last category one can read "gratis" or "so many francs per month to UNIR" depending on whether the house was provided free of charge or in consideration of rent paid to UNIR....

The practice of arbitrary occupation of houses enabled Hissein Habré to provide cost-free lodgings to newly arrived members of his ethnic group, who generally had nowhere to stay....

III. Repression in the Provinces

Outside the capital, the provinces did not escape the heavy hand of the DDS. Repression there was equally if not more barbarous.

A. DDS Branches Established Throughout the Country

DDS was a monstrous and tentacular organization that covered the length and breadth of the country. Its branches were installed in every city and all the big market towns of the country. Local agents were recruited in almost every remote village and reported regularly on everything the people said and did.

B. Repression in Central and East-Central Chad

In 1987, several military and political officials from Guéra, harassed by the government, entered into rebellion against the regime.

The origin of this discontent goes back some years, to 1984 and the sudden disappearance of Idriss Miskine, one of Hissein Habré's comrades in arms, the circumstances of his death remaining a mystery to this day. Some accused ex-president Hissein Habré himself of being responsible for his death. Members of the Hadjaraï community maintain that on 7 January 1984, Idriss Miskine was poisoned with cyanide, though the allegation was never formally proven. Nevertheless, this incident, along with all the daily extortion and injustice, led to a revolt among the Hadjaraï in 1987. This revolt precipitated a brutal and overwhelming reaction on the part of the regime. A veritable manhunt was organized. At first, only members of the intellectual elite and the bourgeoisie were affected, but the pogrom was rapidly extended until it became blind repression against all the Hadjaraï. All Hadjaraï were considered to be enemies of the regime. These so-called enemies, the majority of whom had no idea what was happening, were first hunted down in Ndjamena, and later throughout the country, particularly in Guéra, where several dozen villages were destroyed and their populations massacred;...

C. Repression in the Extreme Northeast

There were also arrests, arbitrary detentions, and summary executions in the extreme northeast part of the country.

In 1989 occurred an event that would trigger an outburst of violence in the region. On 1 April 1989, driven to desperation by the regime, a number of Zaghawa civilian and military officials, among them Hassan Djamous, Idriss Déby and Ibrahim Mahamat Itno, decided to launch a guerrilla campaign; it was the only course open. Hissein Habré quickly branded it treason—he who had deliberately pushed them to that point. The same day, at 0600 hours, according to the testimony of former DDS agents (including Abbas Abougrène, chief of the waterway security service), Guihini Koreï, former DDS director, convoked all the service chiefs and told them to arrest all Zaghawa indiscriminately. He then told them that these were the instructions of the president himself. The Zaghawa were hunted down all over the country. There were mass arrests, they were tortured and executed, or at best kept in prison under deplorable conditions.

In the prefecture of Biltine, where hundreds of Zaghawa died, the repression was particularly horrible. Innocent victims for the most part, these people were in many cases summarily executed and sometimes burned alive. In fact, about 300 meters from Tiné, on a hill between the transit camp and the squadron, a hole was carved out of the rocks and turned into a crematory oven. The individuals were tightly bound, doused with kerosene or gasoline, and pushed into the pit. Then a lit match stick was tossed into the hole and the victims were burned to death.

Three members of the Commission of Inquiry traveled to this macabre site and verified the truth of the testimony. This was during an investigatory mission that took place between 24 December 1991 and 14 January 1992 in the prefectures of Batha, Biltine, and Ouaddaï.

D. Repression in the South

A mission similar to the one sent to the northeast visited southern Chad from 19 November to 22 December and combed the prefectures of Moyen-Chari, Logone Occidental and Oriental, and Tandjilé. The testimony of several hundred witnesses was taken, and facts were physically verified.

In the south, repression began in 1982, when Habré came to power, and started to intensify in 1984. Throughout almost the entire south, arrests, executions, and exactions were carried out with such fury, such murderous madness, during the month of September 1984 that it was called "Black September."

In Moyen-Chari, the repression was especially inhuman: Dozens of villages were burned and their inhabitants massacred. This was the case for several villages in the subprefectures of Maro and Moïssala, where after having executed the villagers at point-blank range, soldiers carried off objects of value and then set fire to the livestock and provisions.

In the canton of Bédjo in Maro subprefecture, the entire population was rounded up and gunned down. Only one person survived this massacre.

In Ngalo village in Moïssala subprefecture, on 27 July 1985, after rounding up all the inhabitants of the village on the pretext of communicating instructions from the government, FAN combatants held them at gunpoint while tying them up in groups of three to five people, before mowing them down with their AA52s (1952 automatic weapons). Several victims were then burned while writhing in their death throes. Despite the ruthless actions of the soldiers, a few people miraculously survived the barbarism....

Finally, at Kélo, worshippers performing religious observances were locked inside their church and burned alive.

To justify this series of massacres, the government of the day accused the natives of this zone of being in collusion with the armed opposition groups known as "codos." These reprisals had a twofold objective: first to subjugate these populations, which had always challenged Hissein Habré's authority, and second to further isolate the codos, the better to hunt them down.

IV. Social Consequences of the Repression of the Habré Regime

Naturally, the regime of a man as bloodthirsty as Hissein Habré left many victims in its wake. Virtually no family in Chad was spared, and throughout these 8 long years of absolute dictatorship, the people mourned an ever growing number of their sons and daughters. This reign engendered the largest number of orphans, widows and destitutes in the country's history.

A. Orphans

The Commission of Inquiry recorded 3,519 orphans who lost father or mother in DDS cells, or in some unknown place or clearing in the bush converted to an execution site. However, that is only a small part of it. The Commission estimates there are more than 80,000 orphans.

B. Widows

The Habré dictatorship made widows of hundreds of women. The Commission has recorded 807 widows, but this is nowhere near the real figure, which is estimated at more than 30,000. These poor women generally had no idea why their mates died. Some never knew where their spouses were imprisoned, others were cheated ruthlessly for years by DDS agents who brought them false news about their husbands, some of whom were long dead. Many others continued to nourish hope of seeing them again one day, but their hopes evaporated with the fall of the Habré regime.

C. Dependents Deprived of All Support

The genocide perpetrated by Hissein Habré on the Chadian people deprived a great number of persons of their moral and material support. Chadian families, like families everywhere in Africa, are typically large. The paterfamilias not only supports his children and wives, but provides for the whole extended family: father and mother, uncles and aunts, cousins, nephews and nieces. The approximate number of individuals deprived of support is on the order of 200,000.

Thus the Hissein Habré regime precipitated a real social calamity. Many of these unfortunates have become homeless and destitute. There are orphans living in the streets who survive only by begging. Some have become drug users, others have turned to prostitution.

Section 2: National and International Reaction

Undeniably, the great political changes that have taken place in East Europe and especially in Africa could not have occurred without popular pressure—or without pressure from the international community. It took nationwide clamor and persistence to force authoritarian regimes to step aside.

International opinion has been an equally indispensable support in facilitating a democratic transition....

A. Reaction of Domestic Opinion

The Habré regime nurtured an ignoble culture of denunciation and mutual suspicion between all strata of society, to the point that everyone was afraid of everyone else, even of his own shadow. Everyone withdrew into himself, and no one dared mention the tyranny reigning in the country for fear of reprisals.

Reaction of the Average Citizen

The average citizen soon felt himself under suspicion and became suspicious of everyone else. There seemed no hope for a rapid change of regime, so his attitude became one of powerlessness, indifference, and resignation.

Despite the climate of terror that reigned, some Chadians—both individuals and groups—conquered their fears. They opted for peaceful struggle, resorting to tracts, open letters, and consciousness-raising journals published by opposition groups in exile in France, Belgium, Libya, Nigeria, Benin, Burkina Faso, and Congo (Brazzaville).

We will give a few examples....

Some citizens who had enough of the dictatorship and its police methods distributed tracts denouncing the totalitarian regime of Hissein Habré and his regime's flagrant and repeated violations of human rights. As a result of their courageous stand, the authors were arrested on 16 August 1990.

They survived only because the Patriotic Movement of Salvation (MPS) headed by Colonel Idriss Déby came to power.

Others went into armed rebellion against the regime....

Hissein Habré ran an implacable dictatorship, surrounding himself with men of the Gorane ethnic group. Other groups were subjected to savage repression to secure their total submission to the regime. Habré did not even shrink from physical elimination of his old comrades in arms, once they became an annoyance. Repression was visited on the Hadjaraï in 1987 and the Zaghawa in 1989. These massacres led his former companions to denounce the autocratic regime and its police-state methods. They entered into open rebellion against him....

Culpable Passivity of High Officials

Human history teaches us that the advance of national liberation movements has helped bring about the advent of liberal and democratic societies.

In the face of the tyranny and oppression of the Habré regime, the Chadian people reacted in some instances with violence, in others by waging a political struggle based on nonviolence to obtain a peaceful change of institutions.

Except for a very timid reaction from the average citizen—very quickly nipped in the bud—high officials kept quiet while everything was destroyed before their eyes.

By their culpable passivity, the country's administrative, political, and military leaders abetted and contributed to the survival of one of the bloodiest dictatorships on the African continent. They maintained a conspiratorial silence in the selfish hope of continuing to enjoy the privileges accorded by the regime, to the detriment of the suffering majority.

To hang onto their positions in government or the bureaucracy, or even to obtain favors and boons from the regime, some officials went so far as to issue scathing denials of reports concerning the human rights violations and atrocities committed by Hissein Habré and exposed by the mass media and international humanitarian organizations.

In that regard, one of Chad's most prominent diplomats in Europe, while denying prisoners were subjected to torture and extrajudicial execution, admitted in August 1989 that there were what he called "exceptional detentions" of government opponents. He gave people to understand that these cases did not fall under the ordinary criminal code and that the participation of these individuals in the armed opposition justified the "exceptional" treatment they received; others practiced an ostrich policy, closing their eyes and ears to atrocities, despite the urgent letters of Amnesty International. As examples, here are summaries of five letters sent by members of Amnesty International to Djime Togou, Nouradine Kassire Coumakoye, Gouara Lassou, Ahmed Korom, and Youssouf Sidi Gougoumi—respectively the former minister of interior and territorial administration, the minister of justice and keeper of the seals, the minister of foreign affairs and cooperation, special presidential delegate to the Inspectorate General and Government Auditing Office, and the secretary general of the Ministry of Government....

B. Reaction of International Opinion

Two contradictory attitudes are observed in this domain, one positive and the other negative.

The people of the Western countries deeply feel for the suffering endured by the Chadians. Without exception, their reaction to the violations of human rights perpetrated by Hissein Habré has been magnificent and fortifying. By contrast, their governments nevertheless continued to support this pariah regime, even though their vital interests were not threatened.

Attitude of the Western Powers

It is unthinkable that the great Western powers represented by their chancelleries in our country can have failed to realize what was happening in Chad. Were they deluded by Hissein Habré into letting him do whatever he wanted, or did they willingly close their eyes to what was transpiring, because their own interests were not threatened and the massacre of innocent victims was not a compelling enough argument to move them?

The answer probably lies in the machiavellianism of Hissein Habré, who deceived everyone. In fact, to stay in power, Hissein Habré was continually brandishing in the face of the Western countries and the Americans the specter of international terrorism and the threat of Qadhdhafi's Islamic Legion. He presented himself as the only bulwark against the Libyan invader.

Their guard lowered, Western countries and the United States thought they had found in him a solid ally. So they closed their eyes to the horrible crimes he was committing, thus allowing a despotic and bloodthirsty regime to continue.

Reaction of International Humanitarian Organizations, Notably Amnesty International

Although the Western and American governments failed to react at all, international humanitarian organizations made many energetic démarches. Among the international humanitarian organizations, Amnesty International was probably first to understand what was happening in the jails of Hissein Habré, and it tried in vain to get the Western countries and the United States to turn their attention to the genocide already under way in Chad. Amnesty

International's energy and commitment to humanitarian solidarity gave new hope to thousands of detainees and their families.

The Commission has enumerated 50,092 pieces of correspondence addressed to Hissein Habré, including 32,915 cards and 17,177 letters divided as shown in the table on the following page:

Summary Table of Cards and Letters Sent to Ex-President Hissein Habré and His Close Collaborators by Members of Amnesty International Demanding the Release of Prisoners of Conscience, Speedy and Fair Trials of Political Detainees, and an End to Torture and Summary Executions

Rank Order	Country	Cards	Letters	Total
01	Sweden	6,864	917	7,781
02	Germany	4,024	3,439	7,463
03	Netherlands	6,604	723	7,327
04	England	3,450	1,481	4,931
05	Australia	4,200	586	4,786
06	Canada	2,196	1,940	4,136
07	France	1,185	2,740	3,925
08	United States	170	3,391	3,561
09	Belgium	1,678	554	2,232
10	Finland	1,111	109	1,220
11	Norway	606	195	801
12	Israel	510		510
13	Italy	200	194	394
14	Denmark	32	331	363
15	Switzerland	24	233	257
16	Portugal		180	180
17	New Zealand	3	58	61
18	Greece		44	44
19	Japan	12	29	41
20	Luxembourg	3	27	30
21	Ivory Coast	20		20
22	Egypt	17		17
23	Brazil	4	6	10
24	Mauritius	2		2
TOTALS		32,915	17,177	50,092

However, this figure is not exhaustive, because a large number of cards and letters sent to the authorities were never answered and were destroyed by the latter.

With its back to the wall, the regime continued to run from the pressures of international organizations.

It is fitting at this point to pay glowing tribute to Amnesty International and exhort it to persevere in the struggle for the defense of human rights with the same determination and dedication. The Commission of Inquiry expresses its thanks to these men and women residing in countries as diverse as they are distant who sympathized with the misfortunes of the Chadians and mobilized on their own initiative to send tens of thousands of letters and postcards to Hissein Habré and the authorities to demand the release of prisoners of conscience, an end to the torture and summary executions, speedy and fair trials for political detainees, and respect for defendants' rights. Likewise, we cannot omit mention of the humanitarian operations mounted on behalf of prisoners of war by the International Committee for the Red Cross (ICRC) in Geneva and its representatives in our country, which made it possible to renew contacts and correspondence between detainees and their families, and also increased pressure for their eventual release. Thanks to its unselfish efforts beginning in March 1984, the International Red Cross saved the lives of thousands of prisoners. There could be no better place to pay homage to the ICRC for its humanitarian action and its humanism.

Chadians Must Do Everything Possible to Prevent the Rise of Another Dictatorship

The reign of terror and despotism that came to an end on 1 December 1990 was knowingly maintained and encouraged by small, corrupt cliques that were more concerned about protecting their privileges than with the survival of the nation. Motivated too, we should add, by indifference, contempt for others, and fear, all of which helped perpetuate a despotic regime reviled by all. This deplorable fact causes us to wonder about the future of our country. The time has come for everyone to leave his egoism behind and give priority to the general interest, while at the same time cultivating national solidarity. Chadians must feel themselves to be parts of a greater whole, concerned by the sufferings and misfortunes of their fellow citizens.

In the jails of DDS, no distinction was made between Christians and Muslims. All were subject to the same treatment and bound for the same tragic end.

In the face of adversity and death, a spirit of brotherhood and active solidarity arose to bind them to each other. We will never know how many Muslims breathed their last breath in the arms of Christian brothers, and vice versa, with no regard for ethnic or religious affiliation. Such behavior should excite the admiration of all and encourage us to continue on the same path.

Already, the feeling of belonging to a nationwide community and faith in a common destiny urges every citizen to struggle against culpable indifference and to banish forever the "every man for himself" ethic. In a world increasingly ruled by the law of the jungle, nothing comes without effort and struggle. Freedom is not given: It must be grasped, sometimes at the cost of one's life. So every Chadian should be willing to make minimal sacrifices to prevent the resurgence of dictatorship.

However, it must be acknowledged that dictatorship has a thick skin and must be extirpated at its deepest roots. The Habré system was supported by a special service responsible for internal and external security. The DDS quickly became the regime's political police. The authorities' retention of the old DDS structures and personnel in the new special service may pose a mortal danger to nascent democracy.

DDS Structures and Personnel
Should Step Aside for New Men

Intended originally to be a counter-espionage service whose mission would be to thwart subversive intrigues and Libyan expansionism, DDS metamorphosed into a formidable political police dedicated solely to the service of one man: Hissein Habré. It is composed of a bunch of unscrupulous men with no training. Such agents know only how to kill and pillage. Many of them blithely continue to this day to enjoy with impunity the goods they amassed on all sides. Some have returned to their former functions in the army, the gendarmerie and the police; others have been rehabilitated by the new government, which has recruited them into its own intelligence services. They continue to exhibit the same contempt and arrogance as in the past for the relatives of victims and for the public....

[T]he collective memory cannot forget the crimes and atrocities committed. DDS agents were thieves, torturers, and executioners, and as such, they should be excluded from the new special service.

Certainly, a country like ours cannot do without a modern and effective intelligence service staffed by competent personnel. To ensure that it does its job properly, however, the structures, the methods, and the personnel should be changed. To avoid repeating the errors of the past, the General Directorate of the Center for Investigation and Intelligence Coordination (DGCRCR) should do away entirely with the old DDS structures and methods, especially its reliance on illiterate, untrained men with no professional scruples and no consideration or respect for the individual or human life. Such men, even if they have close ties to the regime, should be discarded to make room for educated, intellectually mature and morally irreproachable men.

Therefore, the CRCR should establish new structures and operate with transparent methods and new men thoroughly trained in their mission.

Conclusion

The record of Habré's 8-year reign is terrifying. The Commission still wonders how a citizen, a child of the country, could have committed so much evil, so much cruelty, against his own people. The stereotype of the hard-core revolutionary idealist quickly gave way to that of a shabby and sanguinary tyrant.

Recapitulating the evils he has wrought on his fellow citizens, the toll is heavy and the record grim:
- more than 40,000 victims
- more than 80,000 orphans

- more than 30,000 widows
- more than 200,000 people left with no moral or material support as a result of this repression.

Add to that the movable and immovable goods plundered and confiscated from peaceful citizens—an amount estimated at ONE BILLION CFA FRANCS each year.

Eight years of rule, 8 years of tyranny, genocide, terror and plunder on all sides. Why so much evil, so much hatred of his own people? Was it worth the pain of struggling for a whole decade to win power, just to do that? For what ideal and to what end was Habré fighting?

In seeking power and taking it, Habré was satisfying a personal and selfish ambition. Today, after his fall, only his tribe, which he elevated above all others, misses him. And a handful of cynical profiteers who encouraged and applauded him while he shed the blood of innocents for no reason.

Yesterday Habré and his tribe acted like conquerors; they trampled on their compatriots and allowed themselves to take whatever they wanted, because they naively thought they would stay in power forever. They had no regard or consideration for other Chadians, whom they treated as second-class citizens. What have they reaped, now that the regime has fallen, but hatred—yes, the hatred of all other Chadian communities without exception? Today the Goranes walk with heads down, hugging the walls. They are ashamed, they are afraid, and they even avoid the main roads.

The Habré regime and what became of it should serve as a lesson to all Chadians, and in particular to the country's rulers. A wise man once said: "Power is like a shadow, and shadows are never eternal."

Recommendations

To prevent Chad from falling again into the horrors and injustice of the past;

To guarantee present and future generations that their basic rights and dignity will be respected;

To enable Chad and Chadians to return to peace, stability, and national concord;

And finally to bar the road to any sanguinary and despotic regime in the future, the Commission of Inquiry recommends:

1) the establishment of a real democracy and an independent and sovereign judiciary, which are essential if Chadians are to be guaranteed a stable and happy life; to do so, it exhorts the current authorities to accelerate and strengthen the democratic process now under way so that the country may rapidly reach the haven of peace and stability;

2) creation now of a National Human Rights Commission, whose mission will be:

- to investigate violations of human rights;
- to protect and promote human rights at the national level;
- to issue advisories and make proposals in the domain of human rights, to bring suits in court for violations of said rights;

3) an end to illegal occupation of houses and confiscation of others' possessions;

4) speedy establishment of a Commission whose task will be to restore to the rightful owners those movable and immovable goods illegally confiscated or plundered under both the old and the current regime;

5) sequestration, after full inventory has been taken, of the movable and immovable goods belonging to former DDS agents implicated in crimes and looting, which possessions will be held in trust by the Ministry of Justice pending the outcome of legal proceedings;

6) prosecution without delay of the authors of this horrible genocide, who are guilty of crimes against humanity;

7) erection of a monument to the memory of the victims of the Habré repression, and the promulgation of a decree making the second Sunday of December a day of prayer and remembrance for the said victims;

8) conversion of the old DDS headquarters and subterranean prison into a museum to remind people of Habré's dark reign;

9) re-examination of the powers and structures of the new special service, the General Directorate of the Center for Investigation and Intelligence Coordination (DGCRCR), so that this institution may become an instrument in the service of the people and their well-being, not a machine of oppression and torture;

10) removal from their positions, once the present report is published, of all former DDS agents who have been rehabilitated and employed by the DGCRCR;

11) respect for and enforcement of the laws in force (Criminal Code, Code of Criminal Procedures), with regard to offenses against the internal or external security of the state;

12) elimination of detention centers under the control of the DGCRCR and the Police Security Branch (RG), maintaining only those provided for in the Code of Criminal Procedures;

13) initiation and promotion of the teaching of human rights in the schools, universities, police academies, and gendarmerie, as well as in the army;

14) Finally, we recommend that His Excellency, the Head of State, guarantor of the institutions of the republic and the security of all Chadians, take all necessary steps to punish impartially anyone guilty of human rights violations, especially assassinations, abductions, sequestrations, and torture.

DONE IN NDJAMENA, 7 May 1992

CHAD: QUESTIONNAIRES DEVELOPED BY THE COMMISSION OF INQUIRY

Questionnaire for the Taking of Testimony from a Former Political Detainee

REPUBLIC OF CHAD   UNITY - WORK - PROGRESS
MINISTRY OF JUSTICE
COMMISSION OF INQUIRY

No._____/PVCE/91

OFFICIAL REPORT OF INVESTIGATION

The Year Nineteen Hundred Ninety-One and the

WE   MAHAMAT HASSAN ABAKAR   (President)

    _____   (Member)

of the Commission of Inquiry into the crimes and misappropriations committed by ex-President Habré, his accomplices and/or accessories; pursuant to Decrees No. 014/PCE/CJ/90 of 29 December 1990 and No. 382/PR/MJ/91 of 29 July 1991;

EXAMINATION OF WITNESS

"We shall now take testimony from: _____"

LAST NAME, FIRST NAME:
Alias:
Date and Place of Birth:
Child of:
        And of:
Nationality:
        Ethnic Identification:
Profession:
Marital Status:
Military Status:
Court Record:
Complete Address:
Documents Produced:

Who submits to us the following deposition:

When were you arrested?

With whom?
Where?
In the daytime or at night?
Who arrested you?
Was he alone or in a group?
Do you know the reason for your arrest?
Where were you taken after your arrest?
Were you interrogated?
By whom?
What questions were you asked?
Were you the object of extortion?
By whom?
Were you tortured?
By whom?
How?
Do you still bear the marks of torture?
On what parts of your body?
Who gives the orders for torture?
Where were you held in detention?
For what length of time?
Were you alone or with others in your cell?
What are the dimensions of your cell?
Did you relieve yourselves in the cell or elsewhere?
Were you transferred to other prisons?
How were you fed?
What kind of food were you given?
Did you fall ill while in detention?
When you were ill, were you given medical care?
From what ailment did you suffer in prison?
Did anyone die in prison while you were in detention?
How many?
Do you know them and can you give us their names?
Were there executions?
When and how were the persons to be executed selected?
Can you give us the names of those executed?
Who ordered the executions?
Were your possessions taken when you were brought to the DDS?
What was taken?
Was your domicile plundered after your arrest?
By whom?
What was taken?
Was your family evicted from your house?
Who took over your house?
Do you have a bank account?
Did the DDS take the money out?
Were your relatives blackmailed by DDS agents?
How?
Can you give us the names of the crooks?

What would you estimate is the value of the material losses you sustained?
Do you recall the names of anyone who worked for DDS? Who?
Did the ex-president visit the DDS prisons?
Did he watch people being tortured?
Are there any mass graves?
Do you know where they are located?
In your opinion, which agents or torturers are most feared?
Which of the agents you encountered are most amiable?
Are you seeking damages?

Having nothing further to depose, deposition having been read to and translated for deponent, deponent attests to accuracy of same and affixes his signature with ours to this Report of Investigation.

The President of the Commission: MAHAMAT HASSAN ABAKAR
The Investigator:
The Deponent:

➤—— ⊨◆⊒ ——◄

Questionnaire for the Taking of
Testimony from the Relative of a Victim

REPUBLIC OF CHAD   UNITY - WORK - PROGRESS
MINISTRY OF JUSTICE
COMMISSION OF INQUIRY

No._____/PVCE/91

OFFICIAL REPORT OF INVESTIGATION

The Year Nineteen Hundred Ninety-One and the

WE   MAHAMAT HASSAN ABAKAR   (President)

      _____   (Member)

of the Commission of Inquiry into the crimes and misappropriations committed by ex-President Habré, his accomplices and/or accessories; pursuant to Decrees No. 014/PCE/CJ/90 and No. 382/PR/MJ/91 of 29 December 1990 and 29 July 1991;

EXAMINATION OF WITNESS

"We shall now take testimony from: _____"
LAST NAME, FIRST NAME:
Alias:
Date and Place of Birth:
Child of:
       And of:
Nationality:
       Ethnic Identification:
Marital Status:
Profession:
Court Record:
Complete Address:
Documents Produced:

IDENTITY OF VICTIM(S)

FIRST VICTIM

LAST NAME:
       First Name:
Alias:
Date and place of birth:
Nationality:
       Ethnic identification:
Profession:
Marital Status:
Profession:
Complete Address Prior to his/her Arrest:

SECOND VICTIM…

THIRD VICTIM…

How are you related to the victim?
When was he/she arrested?   Where?
During the day or at night?
With whom?
Who arrested the victim?
Was the victim alone or with others?
Do you know the reason for the arrest of your relative?
Where was your relative taken after being arrested?
Where was your relative kept in detention?
For what period of time?
Did you regularly get news about your relative?
How?
Were you the object of threats or extortion?

Were you expelled from your house?
By whom?
Who took it over?
Were your possessions plundered?
By whom?
Were you blackmailed by DDS [Directorate of Documentation and Security] agents?
Do you know their names?
What would you estimate is the value of the material losses you sustained?
When and how did you learn of the disappearance of your relative?
Did your relative die in prison or was he executed?
How many children did the victim leave behind?
How many widows?
How many dependents?
Did you recover your property and some of your valuables?
Are you seeking damages?

Having nothing further to depose, deposition having been read to and translated for deponent, deponent attests to accuracy of same and affixes his signature with ours to this Report of Investigation.

The President of the Commission: MAHAMAT HASSAN ABAKAR
The Investigator:
The Deponent:

⋯ ⧏◆⧐ ⋯

Questionnaire for the Taking of
Testimony from an Ex-DDS Agent

REPUBLIC OF CHAD   UNITY - WORK - PROGRESS
MINISTRY OF JUSTICE
COMMISSION OF INQUIRY

No._____/PVCE/91

OFFICIAL REPORT OF INVESTIGATION

The Year Nineteen Hundred Ninety-One and the

WE   MAHAMAT HASSAN ABAKAR   (President)

        _____   (Member)

of the Commission of Inquiry into the crimes and misappropriations committed by ex-President Habré, his accomplices and/or accessories; pursuant to Decrees No. 014/PCE/CJ/90 and No. 382/PR/MJ/91 of 29 December 1990 and 29 July 1991;

EXAMINATION OF WITNESS

"We shall now take testimony from: _____"

LAST NAME, FIRST NAME:
     Alias:
Date and Place of Birth:
Child of:
     And of:
Nationality:
     Ethnic Identification:
Profession:
Marital Status:
Court Record:
Complete Address:

Who submits to us the following deposition:_____

How were you recruited into the DDS?
When?   Where?
By whom?
What positions have you filled?
What were your duties in these various positions?
What is your total salary?
Do you receive bonuses in addition to your salary?
What orders did you receive once you became a DDS agent?
Did you take an oath?   When?
How are your services organized?
How many personnel?
How do they operate?
Are there any foreigners in your ranks?
What are their nationalities?
Their names?
From whom do you receive your orders?
Directly or through an intermediary?
Who gives orders for arrests?
Which service attends to arrests?
Besides the DDS, are there other agencies involved with arrests?
Are the individuals to be arrested identified by name or left to your own judgment?
Did you take part in the mass arrests of the Hadjaraye and the Zaghawa?
How do you explain these arrests?
When and how were these arrests made?
Who ordered the plundering of goods and occupations of houses?

What do you do with the plundered goods?
Who are the people responsible for interrogations?
What methods have you used to obtain confessions?
Have you resorted to torture?
What kinds of torture have you carried out?
Who are the people responsible for torturing people?
Who are the people in charge of the penitentiary service?
Can you give us the names of your closest associates?
How are your agents and informers recruited?
How are they paid?
Who has the authority to recruit?
How long on average are prisoners detained?
Who gives orders for detainees to be released?
How are detainees fed?
How many rations do they get each day?
How big are the rations?
What are they composed of?
Do ill detainees get medical care?
Do you allow your detainees to perform their religious observances?
In case of death, do you properly wash and bury the corpse and offer a prayer for the deceased?
Do you inter the bodies naked or in funereal shrouding?
Are there any mass graves?
Do you know where they are located?
Do you have anything to add?

Having nothing further to depose, deposition having been read to and translated for deponent, deponent attests to accuracy of same and affixes his signature with ours to this Report of Investigation.

The President of the Commission: MAHAMAT HASSAN ABAKAR
The Investigator:
The Deponent:

CHILE: DECREE ESTABLISHING THE NATIONAL COMMISSION ON TRUTH AND RECONCILIATION[*]

Supreme Decree No. 355 (April 25, 1990) Executive Branch, Ministry of Justice Undersecretary of the Interior

Considering:

1. That the moral conscience of the nation demands that the truth about the grave violations of human rights committed in our country between September 11, 1973 and March 11, 1990 be brought to light;

2. That only upon a foundation of truth will it be possible to meet the basic demands of justice and create the necessary conditions for achieving true national reconciliation;

3. That only the knowledge of the truth will restore the dignity of the victims in the public mind, allow their relatives and mourners to honor them fittingly, and in some measure make it possible to make amends for the damage done;

4. That the judiciary has the exclusive responsibility, in each particular case, to establish what crimes may have been committed, to identify those persons guilty and to apply the proper sanctions;

5. That the nature of such legal procedures makes it unlikely that the judiciary will quickly provide the country with an overall sense of what has happened;

6. That delaying the formation of a serious common awareness in this regard may potentially disrupt our life as a national community and militates against the yearning among Chileans to draw closer together in peace;

7. That without in any way affecting the responsibilities of the judiciary, it is the duty of the president as the person charged with governing and administering the state and the person responsible for promoting the common good of society to do all within his power to help bring this truth to light as quickly and effectively as possible;

8. That a conscientious report by highly respected people with moral authority in our country, who are to receive, gather, and analyze all the evidence given to them or that they can obtain on the most serious cases of human rights violations, will make it possible for national public opinion to come to a rational and well-grounded idea of what has happened and will offer the various branches of government information that will make it possible or easier to take the measures appropriate to each one;

9. That in order to meet their objective these people must carry out their task in a relatively brief period, and hence the investigation must be limited

---

[*] Reprinted from a complete English translation of the report, *Report of the Chilean National Commission on Truth and Reconciliation,* translated by Phillip E. Berryman (University of Notre Dame Press, 1993), pp. 5-9.

to instances of disappearance after arrest, executions, and torture leading to death committed by government agents or people in their service, as well as kidnappings and attempts on the life of persons carried out by private citizens for political reasons, so as to provide the country with an overall picture of the events that have most seriously affected our common life together as a nation;

And exercising the faculties conferred on me by Article 24 and Article 32, No. 8, of the Constitution, and in accordance with Article 1, paragraphs 4 and 5, and Article 5, paragraph 2, as well,

I decree

Article One:

Let there be created a National Truth and Reconciliation Commission for the purpose of helping to clarify in a comprehensive manner the truth about the most serious human rights violations committed in recent years in our country (and elsewhere if they were related to the Chilean government or to national political life), in order to help bring about the reconciliation of all Chileans, without, however, affecting any legal proceedings to which those events might give rise.

Serious violations are here to be understood as situations of those persons who disappeared after arrest, who were executed, or who were tortured to death, in which the moral responsibility of the state is compromised as a result of actions by its agents or persons in its service, as well as kidnappings and attempts on the life of persons committed by private citizens for political purposes.

In order to carry out its assigned task, the Commission will seek:

a)   To establish as complete a picture as possible of those grave events, as well as their antecedents and circumstances;
b)   To gather evidence that may make it possible to identify the victims by name and determine their fate or whereabouts;
c)   To recommend such measures of reparation and reinstatement as it regards as just; and
d)   To recommend the legal and administrative measures which in its judgment should be adopted in order to prevent actions such as those mentioned in this article from being committed.

Article Two:

In no case is the Commission to assume jurisdictional functions proper to the courts nor to interfere in cases already before the courts. Hence it will not have the power to take a position on whether particular individuals are legally responsible for the events that it is considering.

If while it is carrying out its functions the Commission receives evidence about actions that appear to be criminal, it will immediately submit it to the appropriate court.

Article Three:

The Commission is to be made up of the following persons:

> Raúl Rettig Guissen, who will serve as president
> Jaime Castillo Velasco
> José Luis Cea Egaña
> Mónica Jiménez de La Jara
> Ricardo Martin Díaz
> Laura Novoa Vásquez
> Gonzalo Vial Correa
> José Zalaquett Daher.

Article Four:

In order to carry out its assigned task the Commission is to:

a) Receive the evidence provided by alleged victims, their representatives, successors, or relatives within the time period and in the manner that the Commission itself will determine;
b) Gather and weigh the information that human rights organizations, Chilean and international, intergovernmental and non-governmental, may provide on their own initiative or upon request about matters within their competence;
c) Carry out as much investigation as it may determine suitable for accomplishing its task, including requesting reports, documents, or evidence from government authorities and agencies; and
d) Prepare a report on the basis of the evidence it has gathered in which it is to express the conclusions of the Commission with regard to the matters mentioned in Article One in accord with the honest judgment and conscience of its members.

The report is to be presented to the president, who will then release it to the public, and will adopt the decisions or initiatives that he regards as appropriate. With the submission of its report the Commission will conclude its work and will automatically be dissolved.

Article Five:

The Commission will have six months to carry out its work. If it cannot do so in that period it may obtain an extension for no more than three months, by passing a resolution to that effect along with providing a justification for so doing.

Article Six:

Jorge Correa Sutil will serve as Commission secretary. The secretary's functions will be to organize and manage the office with sufficient staff to carry out its task, as well as to perform other functions the Commission may entrust to him.

Article Seven:

The Commission will prepare its own by-laws to guide its operation. The Commission's activities will be confidential.

The by-laws will determine which activities the Commission can delegate to one or more of its members or to the secretary.

Article Eight:

Either on its own initiative or upon request, the Commission may take measures to protect the identity of those who provide information or assist it in its tasks.

Within the scope of their competency, government authorities and agencies are to offer the Commission all the collaboration it may request, furnish the documents it may need, and provide access to such places as it may determine necessary to visit.

Article Nine:

The members of the Commission will carry out their tasks without pay. The secretary and the secretariat staff will be paid as contract employees. The Ministry of Justice will provide whatever technical and administrative support may be necessary.

CHILE: REPORT OF THE NATIONAL COMMISSION ON TRUTH AND RECONCILIATION

(February 9, 1991)

[Editor's note: The narrative portion of the report of the National Commission on Truth and Reconciliation comprises approximately 900 pages in two volumes. The excerpts which follow are reprinted from a complete English translation of the report, *Report of the Chilean National Commission on Truth and Reconciliation*, translated by Phillip E. Berryman (University of Notre Dame Press, 1993), pp. 13-24, 33-35, 39-44, 453.]

Methodology and Work of the National Commission on Truth and Reconciliation in Preparing This Report

Objectives of the Commission

On May 9, 1990, by publishing Supreme Decree No. 355 of the Ministry of the Interior in the *Diario Oficial*,[a] His Excellency, the President of the Republic, created this National Commission on Truth and Reconciliation. Its purpose has been to help the nation come to a clear overall understanding of the most serious human rights violations committed in recent years in order to aid in the reconciliation of all Chileans.

At that time the president believed that for the sake of the nation's moral conscience the truth had to be brought to light, for only on such a foundation, he said, would it be possible to satisfy the most basic requirements of justice and create the necessary conditions for achieving true national reconciliation.

This Commission was charged with four tasks:

- To establish as complete a picture as possible of those grave events, as well as their antecedents and circumstances;
- To gather evidence that might make it possible to identify the victims by name and determine their fate or whereabouts;
- To recommend such measures of reparation and the restoration of people's good name as it regarded as just; and
- To recommend the legal and administrative measures which in its judgment should be adopted in order to prevent further grave human rights violations from being committed.

---

[a] *Diario Oficial:* Chile's journal in which all presidential decrees and laws must be published, and therefore made public, within five working days following processing. It is published daily.

As it began to operate, the Commission believed that its primary duty was to determine what really had happened in every case in which human rights had been seriously violated. Only by clearly determining what had happened in each individual instance would the Commission be able to draw up as complete a picture as possible of the overall phenomenon of the violations of these basic rights. Knowing this individual truth was also the indispensable basis for measures to repair, insofar as possible, the harm done to families, to identify the victims, and to recommend measures that might be taken to prevent such actions from recurring....

The decree ... made quite clear the differences between this Commission and the courts. In accordance with a solid and well-established principle in the area of human rights, it was determined that in no case was the Commission to take on legal functions proper to the courts nor to interfere in cases already pending. In order to make the matter even more explicit, the Commission was expressly prohibited from making pronouncements on whether and to what extent particular persons might be responsible for the events it investigated....

Thus the task was understood as being moral in character: to examine as much evidence as possible about the most serious human rights violations of this period and report its findings based on its honest and considered judgment. The aim was to enlighten the country and its government officials, so that knowing this truth might help them to make the decisions they determined most apt for bringing about national reconciliation.

Knowledge of the Truth

Deciding Which Cases the Commission Should Consider

After approving an overall work plan and by-laws, and hiring the first staff members, the Commission sought to invite all the relatives of the victims of these events to register their cases, and to make an appointment to meet with the commission. They could register in the Commission's offices in Santiago, in regional offices of the national government, and in many of the provincial governorships, which provided space for this purpose. Outside the country they could go to Chilean embassies and consulates. Notices were published several times in different publications. Cases were registered during June 1990.

Meanwhile, as the Commission was planning its work in greater detail and approving procedures for the work of its staff, lists of those who had died as a result of human rights violations were sought and received from the various branches of the armed forces and from the police as well as from other organized groups, such as business, labor, and professional organizations, which had gathered evidence of such violations. Thus seven professional associations, the army, the navy, the air force, the police, the investigative police, the Socialist party, the Communist party, the MIR (Revolutionary Left Movement), the Vicariate of Solidarity, the Chilean Human Rights Commission, FASIC (Christian Churches Foundation for Social Welfare), CODEPU (Commission for the Rights of the People), the

Pastoral Office for Human Rights of the Eighth Region, the Sebastián Acevedo Movement Against Torture, CORPAZ (the National Corporation to Defend Peace), FRENAO (National Front of Independent Organizations), the Group of Relatives of those Arrested and Disappeared, the Group of Family Members of those Executed for Political Reasons, the CUT (Unified Labor Federation), and the National Commission of the Organization of Democratic Neighbors all brought their lists of victims to the Commission.

Through registration by family members and information presented by these agencies, the Commission was able to decide on the overall body of cases it should examine. After duplications and errors had been eliminated, a little more than 3,400 cases remained.

When the family members registered their cases with the Commission, in addition to the basic information about what had happened, they were asked to mention which agencies, groups, or organizations had already made some inquiry concerning the case. These agencies were then asked to provide the evidence they had been able to gather. Copies of initial court records were requested. Thus began the effort of consulting the archives of human rights organizations, particularly that of the Vicariate of Solidarity. The Commission could thus draw on a great deal of information already gathered about these matters.

Staff Organization

Determining the overall body of cases that the Commission should investigate made it possible to organize the staff more specifically. Certified lawyers and law school graduates were hired. Each lawyer, working with a law school graduate, began to study approximately two hundred cases.

The Commission also hired a group of social workers in order to come to a proper understanding of the effects of these events on the victims' families, to reflect this truth in its report, and to lay the groundwork for its recommendations for reparation. The staff was aided by a computer team which was responsible for properly storing and retrieving all the information the Commission gathered, and a files and documentation unit, which was responsible for filing all documents received. Together with secretaries, technicians, and their assistants, the staff consisted of more than sixty people.[1] All the professional people were chosen by the Commission, while support staff was proposed by the secretary and appointed by the president of the Commission. No more than ten percent of these people had prior experience with human rights organizations. The Commission's intention was that its staff take a fresh look at the cases it was to examine and report upon.

In accordance with the terms of the decree, Commission members were not paid for their work, while the staff was hired to work by contract. All Commission expenses were paid with government funds provided by the Ministry of Justice, which offered continual support and assistance.

---

[1] [omitted]

Testimony from Family Members

By the end of June, the Commission had a file on each case received, including the registration form and the request for an interview, along with all the relevant evidence previously gathered. The family members in the Metropolitan Region [Santiago and environs][2] who had requested an interview session were assigned a particular date and time.

The lawyer, the social worker, and the law school graduate were present at these sessions; however, during the busiest periods only two of them might be present and in a very few exceptional cases only one of these people was able to be present. There was always one Commission member present in the office, taking part in the sessions and helping resolve any emergency problems that might present themselves.

Each session lasted from forty-five minutes to an hour, although some lasted much longer. The Commission sought to obtain from relatives any information they could supply about the events. It particularly wanted any evidence that might serve to advance the investigation, such as the names of witnesses, and any information concerning proceedings initiated in the courts, human rights organizations, and other agencies. Relatives were also asked to explain the impact of these events on the family so that this aspect of the truth could be made known. This information was also intended to help provide the basis for devising policies for making reparation....

When the Commission had determined how many sessions had been requested through the regional and provincial government offices throughout the country,[3] it organized a schedule of visits to all these places and set dates for giving testimony. From July to September two members of the Commission, one or two social workers, and a varying number of lawyers and law school graduates visited each regional capital and practically all provincial capitals. Families were gathered in small groups so that they could express what they had suffered as a result of the grave human rights violations. This method proved very valuable, since it enabled many of them to share their experience and support one another. After these joint meetings, each family group met with a law school graduate and a lawyer, who after becoming familiar with the cases and gathering evidence where possible, recorded their accounts and testimony. Commission members organized their time so as to be present during as many interviews as possible.

Subsequent Investigations

Once the interviews had taken place and the materials had been obtained from human rights organizations and the families themselves, further steps were taken to obtain new evidence and corroborate the accounts already received. The Commission approved a general plan for that purpose. Article 4c of Supreme Decree No. 355 authorized the Commission to carry out all the investigation it deemed useful in order to accomplish its

---

[2] There were 1,845 such requests in the Metropolitan Region.

[3] The number of interviews requested in other regions of the country was 1,688.

task, including requesting reports, documents or evidence from government officials and agencies. In addition, Article 8, paragraph 2, of that decree declared that these officials and agencies were obliged to "offer the Commission all the collaboration it may request, furnish the documents it may need, and provide access to such places as it may determine necessary to visit."

Many of the procedures ordered were of a general nature. Thus the Civil Registrar's Office was asked to supply the birth certificates for all those presented as victims, so as to assure from the beginning that their existence was legally recognized. Death certificates and autopsy reports were requested for those reported as having been killed, so as to provide information on the date and cause of their death and relevant evidence. In the case of those presented as disappeared after arrest, death certificates were always requested along with birth certificates, in view of the possibility that a death might have been registered unbeknownst to the family. In addition, the international police [whose task is to monitor entrance into, and departure from, the country] was asked if the victims might have left the country. Inquiries were also made with the Civil Registrar and the Electoral Registrar to see whether they might have registered in some fashion during the period in which they were presented as disappeared....

Whenever there had been a judicial investigation, the Commission sought to obtain copies. In the metropolitan area law students were especially contracted for this purpose; elsewhere regional officials of the Ministry of Justice or of the bar association or other persons often provided help. Many official requests were sent to hospitals in order to provide documentation for the medical treatment mentioned in the evidence that had been gathered. The National Archives, the General Comptroller's Office,[b] and the Chilean Police were also frequently consulted. The Commission sent out more than two thousand formal requests and received a response in approximately eighty percent of the cases.

In practically all cases in which the evidence gathered indicated that agencies of the armed forces or police might have been involved, the head of the respective branch was consulted as well as the chief of staff when appropriate, and they were asked for any evidence their institution might have on those events. The Chilean Army replied to more than two-thirds of these requests. In most of its replies it pointed out that in keeping with the legislation in force and its own by-laws, the evidence on such events that might have existed had been burned or destroyed when the legal period for doing so had passed. In other cases the response was that the institution did not have any evidence or could not respond unless the Commission provided further information. In those cases in which the army turned over the requested information, it proved valuable for determining what had happened.

The Chilean Police almost always responded to such requests by indicating that the documents from that period had been legally burned. In most cases they indicated that they had made some investigation to find the

---

[b] [omitted]

requested information, but these efforts proved fruitless except in a small number of cases. On other occasions, the police answered that the evidence was part of a judicial investigation, and they invoked legal provisions currently in force to justify not sending it. The Chilean Air Force sometimes provided the evidence requested; in other cases, however, it said that it did not have records of the events or that they had been legally burned. The Chilean Navy replied to all the Commission's requests and sent material that proved very useful for the investigations. In some cases, it replied that it did not have evidence on the situations about which inquiries were being made....

When information on the involvement of their security agencies was requested, the army, the navy, and the air force pointed out that they were legally prohibited from providing information having to do with intelligence activities....

When the evidence gathered indicated the involvement of uniformed personnel not identified by name but by rank, by their unit, or by the functions they were carrying out at a particular moment, official inquiries were sent to their institutions requesting their names or the names of all those who were serving on a particular squad or unit....

In almost every case in which the evidence gathered made it possible to pick out a particular person, the Commission asked that person to give testimony in order to learn his or her version of the events and to take it into account in discerning what had happened. If the person was still on active duty, the Commission made such a request through the commander-in-chief of each branch and through the chief of staff where appropriate. After explaining that the individual member had been mentioned in a document the Commission had received, noting that such testimony was voluntary and could be made confidentially, and that it was not the Commission's role to determine whether individuals were guilty of crimes, these officers were asked to inform the individual members how important their testimony was considered to be. The Commission requested the testimony of one hundred and sixty members of the armed forces and the police. The commanders-in-chief answered that the names of some of these people were not listed as belonging to their institution or were now retired. Even in these cases, the police attempted to locate these people and inform them of the Commission's interest. In other cases, the heads of these branches did inform those cited that the Commission wanted to receive their testimony. With the exception of a few cases, which will be noted below, those who were on active duty refused to offer testimony to this Commission. They offered a number of reasons for doing so: they generally indicated that they had no knowledge of the events for which they had been summoned; that they had already stated all they knew in court proceedings; or that, since compliance was voluntary, they chose not to appear. One member of the police who was on active duty and one in the air force indicated their willingness to offer testimony. A considerable number of policemen and one air force officer agreed to answer questions in writing. When such persons did not belong to the armed forces or were now retired, these requests were delivered directly to them. In these cases a larger number came forward to testify.

The investigative police passed on all the Commission's requests except those in which it was noted that there were no records in its files. Its members were often willing to provide testimony to the Commission.

Because of the limited amount of time, it was impossible to take testimony from all persons who were mentioned as witnesses of the events under investigation. Hence the Commission chose those it regarded as more relevant and whose testimony was not to be found in other reliable documents. The lawyers and law school graduates visited almost all regions of the country a second time in order to record the testimony of the most important witnesses.

Individual Decision on Each Case

By the beginning of October, the Commission had established a schedule and laid down a procedure whereby each of the lawyers could prepare information on the cases he or she had been assigned to investigate under the supervision of the Commission members. At this point the lawyers focused on drawing up a written report in accordance with Commission guidelines in order to give an account of all the evidence they had gathered in each case and to suggest that the Commission adopt a particular conclusion....

The first cases were presented to the Commission at the end of October 1990. In sessions lasting until mid-January 1991, the Commission individually examined about 3,400 cases, until it had reached agreement over how it was going to present each case in which human rights had been gravely violated or in which people had been killed as a result of political violence. In other cases it concluded that it had not been able to come to such a determination or that the case was beyond its competence. In only a small number of instances did it reach agreement by a simple majority, and in none of these cases were the differences over matters of principle. Hence the Commission agreed to leave dissenting opinions only in its minutes and to omit them in this report.

As a result of the time available to the Commission for completing its tasks some of its official inquiries remained unanswered and consequently a number of cases were left unresolved. Hence in this report the Commission recommends that the government continue to investigate these situations to determine whether they also constituted grave human rights violations.

An Account of the Truth about Individuals and the Country as a Whole

As it was weighing information, the Commission was also deciding the structure and characteristics of the present report. In order to provide an account of the episodes in which the Commission concluded that grave violations of human rights had taken place, the staff first had to provide concise accounts of these cases and present them in draft form to the Commission. Given the nature of this report, information on many circumstances connected to the most serious violations, such as prior surveillance or pursuit, treatment in prison, and arrest procedures had to be omitted, except where they were necessary for the Commission's decision. Hence what is written in the accounts are basically those elements that directly or indirectly led the Commission to conclude that a grave human rights violation had taken place. This procedure has enabled the Commission to identify every single victim of grave human rights violations, as well as the people who were killed as a result of political violence, and to indicate its conclusion and reasoning in each case....

The Commission was also charged with providing evidence that might make it possible to determine the fate of the victims and their whereabouts. From the beginning efforts were focused on this vital task. Whether it could be accomplished was basically dependent on whether people who could offer evidence were willing to appear voluntarily before the Commission. The information thus gathered can be found in this report as well as in what was presented to the courts, since whenever evidence concerning the whereabouts of the remains of someone who had disappeared after arrest was obtained, it was immediately submitted to the courts....

The final volume [not included in the English translation] of this report is simply auxiliary in nature. It provides an alphabetical list of all [2,279] of those persons whom this Commission has regarded as having suffered grave human rights violations or political violence. It seeks to indicate who these persons were and is limited to a brief mention of the events that led to their death or disappearance, in accordance with the Commission's conclusion, as presented in the body of this report.

Sending Evidence to the Courts

The second paragraph of Article 2 of the Commission's founding decree states that if "while it is carrying out its functions," the Commission "receives evidence about actions that appear to be criminal, it will immediately submit it to the appropriate court."

In compliance with this obligation, the Commission sent to the courts all the evidence it gathered of whatever seemed to be an illegal burial in order to help determine the fate or whereabouts of those who disappeared after arrest. In other cases, the Commission decided to send the courts whatever evidence it gathered that seemed new, useful, or relevant for judicial investigations....

In no case did the Commission refrain from sending evidence because a criminal action might be ruled out, or because the amnesty law might go into effect. The Commission determined that such decisions were to be made by the courts, and hence it should not decide such circumstances on its own.

In sending evidence to the courts, the Commission was careful to observe the norms laid down in its founding presidential decree, namely that the identity of those who wanted to testify confidentially should be protected. In no case has this concern hindered the Commission from sending to the courts all available evidence about sites where the remains of someone who disappeared after arrest might be found.

Acknowledgement of Harm Inflicted
and Proposals for Reparation and Prevention

...In addition to examining what the relatives of the victims of grave human rights violations had suffered, the Commission consulted with relevant experts and persons who could offer guidance on proposals for reparation and prevention such as the decree had urged it to prepare. The Commission consulted with a large number of national and international organizations by asking them what they believed would be the most fitting measures of reparation and prevention. Naturally, the Commission was quite aware that complete reparation for the damage done was impossible, and that any proposal for reparation should be made with complete respect for the dignity of the people involved. Moreover, the Commission had to bear in mind that its primary duty was to clarify the truth, which in itself had undeniable effects in terms of reparation and prevention. Starting with these premises, the Commission consulted each one of these organizations and institutions and inquired which measures of symbolic or cultural reparation, whether legal or administrative, or in the form of services or aid, they regarded as most fitting for repairing, insofar as possible, the harm that has been done. Likewise they were asked about measures that might strengthen the legal order and institutional framework, or promote a culture more respectful of human rights in order to assure that such events never again take place in our country. One hundred and nine organizations were consulted in this fashion, including those of the victims' family members, human rights agencies, the main universities and centers of learning, the political parties, the churches, and other moral authorities. Internationally, the request was sent primarily to those intergovernmental and private bodies with the greatest experience in protecting and promoting human rights. The Commission received more than seventy extensive and well-documented presentations, which it then studied and carefully processed, until it finally came to the proposals and recommendations included in this report.

Chapters Dealing with Relevant Prior Circumstances

[B]efore beginning its accounts of the events themselves, this report notes some of the legal, political, and social features of the period that are more directly related to human rights violations. While fully aware that nothing can excuse or justify these violations, the Commission has sought to take into account some characteristics of the climate in Chile before and after September 11, 1973 that may have contributed to such violations. The Commission believes it is thereby carrying out a duty imposed by the decree that it should set forth the antecedents and circumstances of these violations, while also helping recall the climate that enabled such violations to take root. The purpose of these observations is to help prevent them from ever occurring again.

We have also considered the main legal institutions which made such violations possible, as well as those legal mechanisms that proved most effective for countering them. The Commission believes that acknowledging such antecedents will always be useful for enabling us to examine our cultural and legal institutions and as a basis for determining the changes required in order to prevent such events from recurring....

A Truth for Reconciliation

The tasks assigned to the Commission were clearly and precisely described in its founding supreme decree, as were its duties and powers. In carrying out these tasks, the Commission worked with complete and utter independence. The administration that had created the Commission did not seek to influence its decisions in any way nor did any other branch or agency in the government do so. The Commission's decisions were always made in accordance with the members' conscience.

Nevertheless, from the beginning the Commission understood that the truth it was to establish had a clear and specific purpose: to work toward the reconciliation of all Chileans. In view of the magnitude of such a task, the Commission sought the opinion of the main actors in our national life and especially those most concerned with this undertaking, in order to draw upon their ideas about the work that was to be done. Thus from the time it began its work until it moved into the stage of analyzing cases, the Commission met with all of the groups of victims' relatives, human rights agencies, those professional associations that sought meetings, and all the political parties. Discussions with groups of relatives and human rights organizations dealt primarily with the objectives and methods the Commission was to use to gather the evidence they had in their possession and to seek the truth both in individual cases and as a whole. The Commission also sought to keep in mind the expectations of the organizations of family members about its work, and it often sought the opinion of those who brought individual cases before it. In the case of the churches, the moral authorities in the country, and the political parties, the Commission sought to become familiar with, and analyze, their perspectives about how the Commission, within its limitations, could best reach the truth and truly aid national reconciliation.

Thus after a hundred working sessions, this Commission has come to the end of its task and presents to His Excellency, the President of the Republic, this report on its work....

The State's "Moral Responsibility"

The decree creating the Commission mentions "acts in which the moral responsibility of the state is seen to be compromised as a result of actions by its agents or by persons in their service." As far as the Commission has been able to determine, this concept of the "moral responsibility of the state" does not have a precise legal or technical meaning.

The Commission has understood that phrase to mean the kind of responsibility which may rightly be attributable to the state due to acts committed by its agents (or by persons serving them) in compliance with policies or orders from state agencies, or due to actions carried out by such persons without specific policies or orders, provided that their actions were subsequently approved by state agencies or that the protection of, or inaction by, state agents allowed their behavior to go unpunished....

Other Kinds of Responsibility: Those which Fall on Individuals and those which Fall on the Institutions to which They Belong

...The Commission believes that it must state clearly its opinion on the individual and institutional responsibility that may stem from the human rights violations it has had to examine. More explicitly it must state what responsibility—if any—should fall on the armed forces and security forces for human rights violations committed by individuals on active duty in their respective institutions.

One opinion repeatedly expressed by representatives of a wide range of political parties as well as by other voices which help shape public opinion in our country, holds that the responsibility for such actions is always that of individuals and in no way affects the institutions they serve....

Indeed it is correct to say that the responsibilities of a criminal character and other legal responsibilities that may derive from human rights violations are personal in nature and do not affect the institution to which the perpetrator belongs. It is also true that the fundamental role played by the armed forces and security forces in the history of the country should be fully appreciated, as should be their character as permanent and essential national institutions. Finally, it is praiseworthy to strive to avoid any use of the issue of human rights to attempt to sully these institutions, or to detract from their contribution to the country and the role they are called to play in the future.

Nevertheless, these points cannot be invoked to deny the historic or moral responsibility that may befall one institution or another as a result of the practices it ordered, or to which it consented, or with regard to which it failed to do all that was required to impede or prevent their recurrence. Just as we have spoken of the moral responsibility of the state, which would be inconceivable if the actions of its officials could never affect it, we can also speak properly of the moral or historical responsibility of political parties, of other institutions or sectors of national life, and of society as a whole. The armed forces and the security forces are no exception. It is human beings who forge and make institutions great, and it is also human beings who can affect them negatively.

It is not a purely conceptual concern, however important it might be, that prompts this Commission to make these distinctions. This Commission believes that if matters came to the point that an institution would always be immune from any harm or loss of respect no matter what the behavior of its individual members might be, there would be a danger of falling into an attitude of complacency, the result of which could be serious damage to the institutional integrity and prestige that everyone rightly seeks to preserve.

When the nation's institutions acknowledge their historic and moral failures—and few if any are completely free of such failures—they are in fact ennobled, made better, and enabled to serve more fully the high purposes for which they were created....

The Victims

Victims of Human Rights Violations

Based on these formulations, the Commission has defined as victims of human rights violations those who were subjected to:

- forced disappearance, that is, those who disappeared after being arrested;
- execution, in any of its forms;
- use of undue force leading to death;
- abuse of power resulting in death, if the government has condoned the action or permitted it to go unpunished;
- torture resulting in death;
- murder attempts leading to death, committed by private citizens, including acts of terrorism, whether indiscriminate or selective, as well as other kinds of attacks on life.

The Commission has also regarded as victims of human rights violations those who have taken their own life, if the circumstances make it possible to come to a reasonable and honest judgment that the person committing suicide was led to despair or impelled to make such a decision due to physical or psychological torture, or to the conditions of imprisonment or some other situation for which the government was responsible, and which itself violated human rights....

Persons who were Killed in Armed Clashes or who were, in a General Sense, Victims of the Situation of Political Confrontation

We refer here to people who strictly speaking cannot be regarded as victims of human rights violations. Their death is nonetheless directly connected to the political conflict in our country or to its effects. The Commission has also declared them victims (although clearly distinguishing them from the victims of human rights violations). The decree creating the Commission does not formally consider these situations. Nevertheless, given the complexity of the cases it examined, the Commission judged that it was its moral duty to consider each case of those who perished in this manner....

Criteria

Honest Decision on the Basis of the Information Gathered

...The Commission reached a reasonable and honest conviction about each case based on the testimony of the victims' relatives, of eyewitnesses to relevant events, of current and former government agents, uniformed and civilian, including statements by now-retired high and mid-level ranking officers of the armed forces and police and by former agents of state security; press reports; expert testimony and opinion; some visits to the places where events took place; documentation from human rights Organizations; official documents and certificates such as birth certificates, death certificates, autopsy reports, voter registration rolls, criminal records, immigration service records about entry into and departure from the country and many other official documents; copies of court records and responses to official requests that the Commission sent to institutions under the authority of the executive branch, including the armed forces and security forces.

The utilization of all these items as the basis for examining thousands of cases made it possible to achieve a thorough vision of the context of the events under study throughout the country and in each region or location during various periods. It also made it possible to understand the working methods of particular government bodies as well as those of the various political opposition groups as they evolved over time.

Thus it was possible to evaluate the veracity of testimony and documents not only directly but by comparing them with information already established concerning the same events or related events....

The Commission has examined these cases very rigorously, especially when the remains of the victim have not been found. However, it cannot entirely rule out the possibility that in one or other isolated case it may have made the mistake of qualifying a person as "disappeared" and presuming him or her to be dead. Nevertheless, the Commission fears that even more numerous will be the cases of genuine victims about which, given its own rigorous standards and the fact that the investigation could not be pursued further, it has been forced to state that it could not reach a conviction about whether the person's human rights were violated or not. The Commission hopes that in the future it will be possible to determine the truth about what has happened in such cases.

The Perpetrators and Their Motivations

The Decision not to Assign Blame to Particular Individuals

In carrying out its investigations, the Commission received information about the identity of government agents, both uniformed and civilian, and about people in their service, as well as about members of political parties or armed groups opposed to the military government, all of whom were said to have been involved in one or more of the events it was examining.

The Commission has not included those names in this report. Its founding decree forbade it to take a stand on the potential responsibility of individual persons in these events in accordance with existing legislation. The reasons for that prohibition are both clear and compelling: only the courts of justice can determine the responsibility of particular persons for crimes committed. If this report had included the names of those presumed responsible, whether of government agents or private citizens, the practical result would be that a commission appointed by the executive branch would be publicly accusing of committing crimes people who had not been able to defend themselves. Indeed, they had no such obligation to defend themselves since the Commission did not have any judicial authority, nor indeed did it prosecute any case. Such a procedure would have been an obvious violation of the principles of the rule of law and of the separation of the powers of government, as well as of the basic norms of respect for human rights.

Those considerations notwithstanding, in all relevant cases the Commission has sent the respective items of evidence to the courts.

Determining the Institution or Group

In this report the Commission is offering as much information as it could obtain about actions committed by government agents except for the names of the individuals alleged to have participated. Thus when such information is available the report names the branch or branches of the armed forces or police forces or the security or intelligence agencies said to have participated, and specifically the regiment, base, police precinct, garrison, or group from which the official forces came. When the Commission was unable to obtain such information but did come to the conviction that the person was killed by, or disappeared in the hands of, government agents, it has stated so.

When available, the Commission has also provided information on the political affiliation of private citizens who committed terrorist acts or other kinds of politically motivated attacks....

Determination of Causal Connections and the Fate of the Victims

Connection Between Torture and Death

As has already been noted, the Commission judged that it was obligated to come to a reasonable and honest judgment on whether the torture a person had undergone either caused, led to, or contributed to his or her death. Making such a determination is especially difficult when a relatively long time has elapsed between the treatment suffered and subsequent death. The medical specialists whose opinion the Commission sought whenever there was doubt, always pointed out that in most cases medical science can only provide estimates of probability. Nevertheless, their expert opinions proved extremely valuable for establishing the parameters within which the Commission made its decision in conscience.

The Fate of the Disappeared

After examining all the available evidence about individual cases and the relevant context, this Commission concluded that it was morally obliged to declare its conviction that in all the cases which it has accepted as disappearances, the victims are dead; that they died at the hands of government agents, or persons in their service; and that these or other agents disposed of the victims' mortal remains by throwing them into a river or the sea, by covertly burying them, or by disposing of them in some other secret fashion....

Human Rights Violations Committed by Private Citizens for Political Reasons

Overview

In this section the Commission will deal with human rights violations committed by private citizens for political reasons, as well as deaths occurring as a result of political violence. Those killed were primarily government forces. These deaths were the result of armed clashes which occurred during the first few days after the military intervention and also of attacks perpetrated in that context of violence....

According to information gathered by the Commission, the armed forces and security forces faced no organized rebel troops. Nevertheless, as has been mentioned, there was some armed resistance from groups who supported the previous government.... None of this resistance lasted very long.

This climate of violent confrontation should be understood in light of the legitimacy that each side was claiming as its own. Without taking a stand on this matter, this report views each side's defenders from that standpoint from which each believed it was operating: obeying either the established government or what had been the established government within the previous legal framework. Hence, whatever their position in the struggle, the report regards them as having been killed in armed clashes or as victims of the situation of political violence.

Thirty members of the armed forces and security forces were killed during the period in question. Fifteen belonged to the armed forces, fourteen to the police, and one to the investigative police. Most of the victims were killed on September 11 and immediately thereafter. Twenty-four were killed in the Metropolitan Region, three in Tarapacá, one in Maule, one in Bío, and one in Los Lagos. We should note that most of these victims were young; their average age was only 26.... The institutions in which these men served honor their memory. We hope that our whole society will remember them among the victims of a painful situation that we must not repeat.

[Editor's note: The excerpts which follow are reprinted from *Summary of the Truth and Reconciliation Commission Report* (Chilean Human Rights Commission and Centro IDEAS, 1991), pp. 21-94.]

Political Context

The condition of the country at that time, which must be described as an acute crisis in the nation's life, represents the destruction and deterioration of a large part of the consensus among Chileans with regard to institutions, traditions and assumptions on social and political coexistence.

It is essential to comprehend the 1973 crisis in order to understand the genesis of subsequent human rights violations and to avoid their repetition.... This must not be understood to mean that the crisis in 1973 justifies or excuses said violations....

The Chilean Situation until September 11, 1973

The crisis of 1973 can be described, in general, as an acute polarization of the political positions of civilians into two camps—governmental and opposition.... Among the most important factors of the polarization and crisis was the so-called "Cold War," which began in the early 50's, and which, given its opposing interests and ideologies at the global level, in itself implied a polarization.

The second was the ideologization of movements and political parties, through which were favored complete models of society in which there could be no compromise....

In certain political groups, of both the "left" and the "right," the idea took hold that force was a priority, and the only way, to impose the favored change or preservation of a model of society....

Final Phase of the Polarization of the Crisis

After 1970, the year in which the [leftist] Popular Unity assumed power, the aforementioned phenomena became more acute.

Within the framework of the Cold War, the victory of the Popular Unity was seen as a triumph for the Soviet Union and a defeat for the United States. This explains the interventionist policy of this latter country in the internal affairs of Chile, which, after having failed to block the assumption of power of Salvador Allende, promoted the economic destabilization of the new government.

Related to this last point, an acute economic crisis unfolded in 1972, characterized by inflation, the break-down of production and a progressive paralysis of economic activity....

Among the circumstances that can explain the position of extreme rebelliousness held by professional and trade associations, and by the leadership of opposition parties, are the numerous violations to the right to property in the form of "takeovers" which occurred after 1970. [T]hose who were victimized by the existing disorder and lawlessness ... thought that the only alternative was self-defense, and promoted the idea of irregular pressure on the government and of armed groups to defend property and personal security.

This led, at the same time, to the formation of pro-government paramilitary groups.

By 1973, Chile was objectively experiencing a climate favorable to civil war.

The Role of the Armed Forces and Police

Until September 1973, the Armed Forces and Police remained outside the crisis, in a professional role, of obedience to civilian authorities and the neutrality assigned them by the Constitution. The unfolding of the crisis began to distance them from their role.

The reasons that led the Armed Forces to assume power were:...

- The magnitude of the crisis—or the possibility of a civil war—whetted foreign appetites and implied, therefore, a threat against external security, which is the specific mission of the Armed Forces and Police.
- "Armed struggle" and "ungovernability" implied, as was demonstrated daily, a permanent and ever-increasing disturbance in public order, internal security and the functioning of the economy in its most essential aspects, which the Armed Forces understood as their responsibility.

It is very probable that besides theses causes, the Armed Forces and Police were also impelled to assume power because of an ideological current that existed within them. It suited this ideological current and its distorted concepts of counter insurgency and national security to have an authoritarian regime. And the circumstances of the crisis favored soldiers that supported that doctrine, while not favoring the probably majoritarian sector which would have preferred to continue in the traditional constitutional role, as advocated in the military institutes.... Finally, as the crisis accelerated, the clamor of many civilians that the Armed Forces and Police intervene became more and more insistent....

The Political Context 1973-1990 and Human Rights

The Armed Forces and Police as Collective Actors in Politics

The Armed Forces and Police, through the Government Junta, assumed first the Executive Power and then the Constituent and the Legislative.

The Judicial Power kept only the legal appearance of its power and autonomy, since the majority of the members of the Supreme Court sympathized with the new regime.... The National Congress was dissolved, and communications media which were not closed were subject to censorship.

When the time came to build a "political regime" the Armed Forces and Police faced serious internal contradictions: they did not have a clear program for their course of action of the duration of the military regime.... And there were many political differences among the officers.

In the confusing ideological picture which existed among officers there was, nevertheless, a group of officers, essentially from the army, who acted in secret; a group that had a remarkable ideological coherence and initiative and that had a decisive impact on the problem of human rights.

This ... so called DINA group was one composed of Army majors and colonels that began to act in the Military School from September 11, 1973, and which later became the "DINA Commission" and then DINA itself.

This group showed great audacity and cohesion and the capacity to take extreme actions, assigning itself as its essential task the liquidation of those considered to be extreme left, especially MIR. Among the possible explanations for the prevalence of this group is the fact that they were experts in secrecy, compartmentalization and disinformation, along with the self-justification that the Armed Forces and Police were at war, and the fear that challenging the group and its growing violations of human rights would mean an institutional loss of prestige and would damage "Chile's image."

Finally, another fear that played a role in the consolidation and impunity of the group was its efficiency in maneuvering within the Armed Forces, and specifically, within the Army.

The Chain of Political Command

...Presiding over the Government Junta was the Commander in Chief of the Army, who was given the title of Supreme Commander of the Nation and, later, President of the Republic.

Thus was born a new institution, the Presidency of the Republic-Commander in Chief, with the powers unprecedented in Chile. Its head not only governed and administered the country, but was also a member of and presided over the Government Junta—such that it was not possible to legislate or to amend the Constitution without him—as well as commanding the Army.

In this way, the regime of the Armed Forces and Police stopped being directed by the collective leadership or even the top commanders, and was centralized and unified in the President of the Republic-Commander in Chief of the Army....

Civilians as Political Actors of the Military Regime

The military action in 1973 was carried out without civilian collaboration.... [T]hose civilian groups which became political actors in the regime, although some of them knew about the problem or harmfulness of the DINA group, lacked the necessary instruments to face the situation or believed that human rights violations had ceased. Others asserted that their jobs were technical and not political....

The Constitutional Context

The Months After September 11, 1973...

The Functioning of Political Power

The new legislation expressed a range of values and political principles which were profoundly different from the ones contained in the preceding legal system. The democratic orientation of that system was replaced by one of strengthening the coercive apparatus of the State and authoritarianism as a model of government. Widespread powers were concentrated in the authoritarian regime that began in Chile on September 11, 1973.

Among the events that made this concentration evident is the dissolution of the National Congress and the Constitutional Tribunal.

With the destitution of the President and the dissolution of the Congress, the essential political institutions of Chilean democracy were dismantled. The effect of the Junta's decisions was extended to the associations that had made the functioning of said institutions possible: the political parties. Those parties, entities, groups of movements which believed in Marxism were declared dissolved and considered illegal organizations. Their legal status was canceled and their property was transferred to the State.

All of the political parties, entities, factions, or movements of a political nature, not involved with the first group were declared in recess.

Finally, the Electoral Rolls were incinerated and activities of Mayors and Aldermen were made to cease. The Junta thereafter appointed all mayors, who thus owed it their alliance.

Effects on Constitutional Guarantees

On September 11 a State of Siege was declared throughout the country, and a State of Emergency in some provinces and departments. Chile remained subject to a regime of exception of State of Siege, which was renewed every six months for years to follow....

The practical result of those precepts was to remove from the regular courts all cases for violations of the rules of the State of Siege and shift them to military jurisdiction.

During the State of Siege the government was also empowered to expel from the country, through decree, Chileans and foreigners "when required by the higher interests of the State."

Control of labor activities and intervention of universities were also among the effects on constitutional guarantees provoked by the actions of the Junta....

The Years 1978 to 1990

General Amnesty

In 1978, the Government Junta decreed an amnesty for the perpetrators, accomplices and accessories after the fact of criminal acts occurring during the State of Siege between September 11, 1973 and March 10, 1978, insofar as these were not being tried or sentenced at the time the decree entered into force. Also amnestied were those persons sentenced by military courts after September 11, 1973. Excluded from the amnesty were those persons who would appear responsible as perpetrators, accomplices or accessories after the fact in the murders of Orlando Letelier and Ronni Moffitt in Washington, D.C....

The Constitution of 1980

[T]he Government Junta, exercising its constituent power, approved the text of the Constitution presently in effect, and then called a plebiscite to ratify it.

That plebiscite, carried out on September 11, 1980, under a State of Siege and Emergency, ratified said text. On March 11 of the following year it entered permanently into effect, with the exception of the 29 transitory articles, the majority of which were in force until March 11, 1990.

States of Constitutional Exception

...For the Government Junta, the State of Siege decreed due to internal commotion as of September 11, 1973 was understood as a "state or time of war" insofar as this affected the application of penalties established by the Code of Military Justice.

The decree laws that declared the country under state of siege, or a "state or time of war," although taking into account the country's situation of internal commotion, dispensed with the legal requirement that there be "organized rebel forces" or "any kind of rebel or seditious forces organized militarily."...

The Courts

General Behavior of the Judiciary

During the period that concerns us, the Judiciary did not react with sufficient energy with regard to violations of human rights....

The Judiciary was the only one of the three powers that continued to function without intervention or dissolution by the authorities that assumed control on September 11.

The new authorities were especially careful with the judges, declaring on September 11, that the Junta would guarantee the full effectiveness of the power of the Judiciary.... This ... could have permitted the Judiciary to assume a more resolute attitude in the defense of human rights. Nevertheless, jurisdictional authority in the field of human rights was conspicuously deficient.

Such an attitude was unexpected in a country accustomed to see in the Judiciary a tenacious defender of the rule of law.

The attitude adopted by the Judiciary during the military regime produced, in important measure, an intensification in the process of systematic violation of human rights, both in the short term, since the persons detained were not protected, and also by affording those involved in repression a growing certainty of impunity for their criminal actions.

Behavior of the Judiciary from the Point of View of the Application of the Most Relevant Procedural Institutions Related to the Obligation to Defend Human Rights

...The courts had broad discretion in order to protect the affected parties. This latitude, nevertheless, was generally used. Moreover, on numerous occasions persons were left unprotected without any legal justification.

Among the violations of legal norms, it is sufficient to point out:

- The principle of "immediacy" was not applied. This principle sets a period of 24 hours for a decision on habeas corpus.
- The courts also did not accept habeas corpus for arrests ordered by DINA and later by CNI.
- The courts did not oversee compliance with the restrictions regarding places of detention. The courts did not require the application of the constitutional precept according to which no one my be arrested, subjected to preventive detention or jailed except in his home or in public places designated for that purpose. In fact, for many years there were detention centers to which judicial personnel did not have access.
- The courts did not monitor the complete observance of the norms relating to incommunicado detention.

During the years to which this report refers, administrative incommunicado detention was extensively applied as punishment. During the period 1973-1980 there were cases of persons held incommunicado for 109, 300 and even 330 days.

During the period in which the 1980 Constitution was in effect, administrative incommunicado detention of up to 20 days was common.

The Commission believes that if the courts had respected the constitutional mandate to act immediately; or observed the mandate to decide on habeas corpus within 24 hours, or exercised the legal power which is the essence of the remedy, which consists of physically seeing the detainee; or had they observed the norm which requires passing of judgment before the harm resulting from unjust imprisonment becomes grave, then death, disappearance and torture could have been prevented in many cases and, moreover, the perpetrators would have been notified that their actions were rejected by at least one of the powers of the State, which could eventually punish them.

Other Factors

Impunity for the Violators

This Commission concluded, after rigorous analysis, that the number of fatal victims of violations of human rights attributable to government agents is more than 2,000, the majority of these being victims of political repression. Except in very exceptional cases, violations were not investigated by the courts, nor their authors legally punished.

In trying to systematize the extent to which judicial conduct contributed to impunity, the following situations can be mentioned.

   a. In the matter of prosecuting crimes committed by government agents, the excessive rigor and legal formalism with which the courts weighed the prosecution's proof against the perpetrators, in many cases hindered the application of the corresponding punishment. Had this not been the case, these persons could have been sentenced in accordance with the reality of the events proven.
   b. The courts' acceptance of the version of events given by the authorities contributed to preventing the punishment of those responsible.
   c. Application of the Amnesty Law was such that it prevented the investigation of events. The courts ruled dismissal of cases based on the amnesty of April 1978, whenever the Armed Forces and Police were implicated in a case covered by the law. This thesis overrides the argument emanating from Article 413 of the Code of Criminal Procedure, which requires that "definitive dismissal may not be decreed except after an investigation in which all efforts to uncover evidence of the crime and to determine the identity of the criminal have been exhausted."
   d. Non-exercise on the part of the Supreme Court of its power to oversee the military courts in times of war. The non-exercise of this power over said courts hindered the Supreme Court from demanding that the actions of the war-time courts martial be carried out according to the rule of law.

Other Actions of the Courts

Several other questionable actions of the courts could be analyzed, especially those of the Supreme Court, which facilitated the violations of human rights, such as the recognition of secret laws never challenged by the courts; the approval of abusive searches in marginal neighborhoods, which in 1986 alone totaled 688; its rulings and protection remedies resulting from the aforementioned; its exaggerated formalism in the interpretation of the law; its acceptance of confessions obtained under torture as proof, and the application of sanctions and poor annual qualifications to judges who adopted a courageous attitude in the investigation of human rights violations.

A more detailed analysis of this and other situations is beyond the scope of this Commission....

September - December 1973

This period, defined as the consolidation of the military regime, includes the period from September 11, 1973 to December 31, 1973.

Violations of Human Rights Perpetrated by the Government or Persons at its Service

After September 11, 1973, the Armed Forces and Police achieved their most immediate objective, the effective control of the country, in a few days, without encountering any significant armed resistance on the part of supporters of the deposed regime....

It must also be noted that, in the country as a whole, the general rule was that the deposed authorities voluntarily turned over their positions to the new authorities, without any difficulties and even in a formal fashion and that those people required in officials edicts to turn themselves in for detention did so voluntarily in large numbers....

Detention and Imprisonment

Detention Methods

- Edicts requiring named persons to present themselves before military authorities. After doing so, they were arrested.
- Specific search for a person in his house, place of work, or the street.
- "Roundups" in rural areas and searches in large cities.

The detentions were carried out by patrols of uniformed Police (Carabineros), sometimes assisted by plainclothes Investigations Police (Investigaciones) and civilians. When large-scale, the detentions were carried out by other branches of the Armed Forces and Police. In these searches or selective detentions there was no resistance.

Places of Detention

Regiments, police stations, Investigations Police, barracks, and other places were used as prison camps (Pisagua, Tejas Verdes, Quiriquina Island, Dawson Island and others), and ships and sports stadiums (Estadio Nacional, Estadio Chile, among others), as were educational establishments of the Armed Forces and Police.

With the exception of police stations and one of the prison camps, these places were not authorized to receive prisoners.

Ill-Treatment and Torture

Ill-treatment and torture, in different degrees and forms, was routinely used on prisoners, both in vehicles for transference, in the police stations and when they arrived at their definitive place of imprisonment.

Torture

The torture methods were extremely varied. Violent blows were used almost universally. Also widespread was the increase in severity of imprisonment until it became torture. For example, prisoners were kept face down on the ground or on their feet for many hours without moving, kept naked for hours or days; subjected to constant light or rendered sightless by blindfolds or hoods, or tied up, forced to sleep in cubicles so narrow that it was impossible to move; held incommunicado under one of these conditions; denied food and water or warm clothing or sanitary facilities. It was also common to hang prisoners by their arms, without their feet touching the floor, for prolonged periods. Different forms of semi-asphyxia were used, in water, in foul-smelling substances and in excrement. Sexual abuse and rape were frequently denounced, as were the applications of electricity or burns. Simulated executions were also widely used. In some centers sophisticated tortures were used, such as the *"paudearará"* [*"Parrot's perch:" a forced position in which the detainee is hung by wrists and ankles which are tied behind his back. Ed. Note]*, attack by dogs, and abuse of the prisoner in the presence of their relatives and vice versa....

The Commission, in conscience, concludes that the accusations which are the source of the aforementioned descriptions have not been devalued or mitigated by any of those—from the other side—who should also know the same facts. The aggregate of facts gathered, due to their huge number and virtual uniformity, seems to compose an undeniable reality of torture which, as atonement and example, cannot remain secret or forgotten.

Deaths and Disappearances

The Victims

The majority of deaths and detentions followed by disappearances were the result of actions undertaken against prominent officials of the deposed regime, against its highest authorities and mid-level officials.

In the selection of those to be arrested, some role was played by civilians, especially farm owners, merchants, truckers, etc., and a small number of them supplied the means for detention—vehicles, rooms for interrogation—or participated in the executions.

Motivation of Government Agents to Cause Death and Disappearance

    a. Selective executions of a political nature: these especially affected the national and local authorities of the deposed regime and the leaders and most active militants of the parties that supported it.

    b   Executions of persons sympathizing with the deposed government, often those without any party membership and generally from low-income sectors....

    c. Selective executions of alleged criminals.

    d. Deaths perpetrated by government agents, using unnecessary or excessive force.

    e. Selective executions for personal vengeance.

The Procedures Employed

Courts Martial

In some of the deaths it was announced that the action was a result of a court martial. The Commission has concluded that this, presumably, never took place and was only a way of explaining an illegal execution.

In others, the courts martial were carried out.... The Commission has decided that the deaths resulting from courts martial violated the human rights of the victims, due to their substantive and formal irregularities. In all of the courts martial in 1973, the accused and sentenced did not enjoy the right to due process.

Executions Outside any Law

...The Commission was forced to point out that death was preceded by torture and cruelty whose only aim was to increase the suffering of the victims. There were cases in which victims were mutilated prior to death and their bodies maimed afterwards.

These executions were explained by the authorities as "shot while trying to escape" or confrontations....

Disappearance of the Corpses

During this period the denial or concealment of those executed or detained-disappeared was an irrational, anarchic procedure. There was a practice of not handing over the bodies, concealing them in different ways, in clandestine graves or mine shafts, throwing them into rivers or the sea, and dynamiting them.

Treatment of Families

The disposal of the bodies is the first demonstration of the ill-treatment of the families of the detainees. The following practices repeat themselves monotonously.

For example:

- Denying to the family that the person was detained.
- Concealing the death of the prisoner.
- Destruction or theft of objects and furniture during house searches.
- Extortion of relatives under false promises of freeing the prisoner.
- Handing over the remains in a sealed casket.
- Direct order to leave the city or town....

Violations of Human Rights by Region

[Editor's note: This section—comprising 300 pages of the Commission's report—outlines the particular circumstances in each of thirteen regions of Chile. Within each region, in chronological order, the Commission reviews the case of each individual victim and its conclusion regarding their fate. The section is omitted for reasons of space.]

Reactions of Various Sectors of Society with Regard to the Violations of Human Rights in the Months Immediately After September 11, 1973.

Attitude of Chilean Society

The military intervention of September 11, 1973 meant, immediately and throughout the period, a permanent violation of basic human rights (principally the rights to personal liberty, to a fair trial, to physical integrity and to life) of many persons who—supposedly or actually—had belonged to or sympathized with the deposed regime. This situation did not produce in Chile, during that initial period, practically any public critical reaction, except on the part of churches, especially the Catholic Church.

The absence of reaction from the society can be attributed to fear, surprise, ignorance of what was happening and the deficiencies of our national culture with regard to the subject of human rights.

As the facts began to become known, vast sectors of public opinion permitted, tolerated and even supported the violations of the rights of persons accused of belonging to or sympathizing with the Popular Unity, justifying this attitude by reference to acts allegedly committed or about to be committed by said persons.

There did not exist in our country the profound conviction that the human rights of all persons must be respected, especially the most basic rights, no matter what charge is imputed to those persons or what harm they allegedly have caused.

It is not our role to determine the moral responsibility which society as a whole might have as a consequence of its lack of a timely and strong reaction to what was taking place. We believe, nevertheless, that what occurred must make every Chilean reflect on the serious omission which incurred....

The Reaction of the Churches

The only really significant reaction with the regard to violations of human rights came from the churches.

The Catholic Church expressed itself on two fronts: educationally through the different statements of the Permanent Episcopal Committee, and concretely in the action of helping and protecting victims. With this aim it became a part of the Committee of Cooperation for Peace in Chile, jointly with the Lutheran Evangelical Church, Evangelical Methodist, Orthodox, Pentecostal and Hebrew Community of Chile; and the National Refugee Commission, also of an ecumenical nature.

Attitude of the Communications Media

One of the first measures adopted by the new government was to establish control of the communications media, closing them or subjecting them to a strict prior censorship.

In general, the few communications media which survived supported the new government. Therefore, especially in the beginning, they published or disseminated the information requested by the new government without verifying the truth of said information, which, in many cases, as was later demonstrated, did not correspond to reality, and which affected the good name and dignity of many persons.

Disinformation in these matters certainly contributed to the perpetuation of human rights violations in the country....

The Attitude of Professionals and their Organizations

In the matter of human rights many professionals did not behave in accordance with the ethics demanded by their respective professions. Such was the case of physicians who participated in torture sessions; and of lawyers who participated as prosecutors in courts martial that did not respect the norms of due process.

Professional associations, as such, did not exercise their normal faculties of supervising the ethical behavior of their members. On the other hand, it must be pointed out that various professionals began to react as individuals, adopting a clear position of defense of human rights....

The Attitude of Intermediate Organizations

Intermediate organizations [*unions, students federations, community organizations. Ed. Note.*] were not permitted any type of reaction to military measures.

The Reaction of the International Community

The military intervention that deposed the regime of President Allende, interrupting existing institutionality, was harshly received by various countries of the international community, which perceived that a democratic and constitutional President had been deposed.

Many countries participated in the expatriation of persons who had sought asylum in different embassies accredited in our country. [M]any of them broke diplomatic relations with Chile.

With regard to international organizations concerned with the protection of human rights, the most important during this period were the Inter-American Commission on Human Rights of the Organization of American States (OAS), whose Executive Secretary visited Chile in October 1973; the United Nations High Commissioner for Refugees and the International Red Cross, in attention to political prisoners.

Also during this period persons from Amnesty International and from the International Commission of Jurists visited Chile. The two institutions requested United Nations intervention on September 15, 1973, in view of threats to life in Chile....

1974 - August 1977

...It is important to underscore that during this period, the disappearance of persons responded to a pattern of prior planning and central coordination that reveals a resolve to exterminate certain categories of persons: those considered highly dangerous politically.

Violations of Human Rights by Agents of the Government or Persons at its Service

The principal intelligence service in charge of political repression during the 1974-1977 period was DINA. It was born of the Government Junta's need to create a government intelligence organization to fight the political forces which, though defeated, nevertheless had the potential to reorganize underground and outside the country.... In addition to its intelligence function, DINA was engaged in repressing those persons it perceived at political enemies....

In 1976, at the initiative of DINA and apparently coordinated by that organization, a collaboration began among the intelligence services of the Southern Cone (Chile, Argentina, Uruguay and Paraguay) which permitted the implementation of joint activities through an operational plan called "Condor" which included the elimination of political opponents....

The intelligence services of the different branches of the Armed Forces and Police were also active in this period....

Intelligence Organizations that Carried out Political Repression in the Period 1974 - August 1977

DINA

DINA was formally created in June 1974 (December Law No. 521). Nevertheless, the origins of this organization go back to November 1973 or even earlier. DINA was dissolved in August 1977 and was replaced by the National Information Center (CNI). DINA must be characterized as an organization with virtually all-embracing power, which permitted it to affect the basic rights of persons and even use its power to conceal its activities and ensure its impunity.

Specific characteristics which permitted its actions:

- It was a government intelligence organization and, therefore, had centralized capacity for action and government resources and means.
- It was an organization which, in practice, was secret and above the law. Its internal organization, composition and activities were not only unknown by the public but also outside the effective control of the law.
- Although formally controlled by the Government Junta, in practice the DINA answered only to the Presidency of the Government Junta, and later the Presidency of the Republic.
- It had the broad mission of gathering and evaluating information which would later be employed to adopt important governmental decisions. DINA extended its mission to encompass the investigation of government officials and members of the Armed Forces....

Operational and Command Structure of DINA

[T]he leadership and the personnel and operational teams came from the Armed Forces and Police. The highest positions were in the hands of Army personnel, with the participation of an occasional Navy and Air Force officer. The operational leadership comprised essentially Army and Police Officers.

On the other hand, DINA also had collaborators that worked in government offices and companies, both in Chile and abroad. It also enjoyed the collaboration of professionals, such as physicians, both for the care of its personnel and for supervising torture sessions to determine the capacity of prisoners to withstand torment....

The Joint Command

The so-called Joint Command was an intelligence group that operated approximately between the end of 1975 to the end of 1976, whose central objective was repression of the Communist Party. It was composed principally of agents from the Intelligence Directorate of the Air Force

(DIFA), the Intelligence Directorate of Carabineros (DICAR), or the Naval Intelligence Service (SIN), and to a lesser degree agents from the Intelligence Directorate of the Army (DINE). Also participating in the Joint Command were members of the Investigations Police and civilians from nationalist and extreme right groups.

The birth of the Joint Command can be explained in the context of Armed Forces resistance to the unchecked operations of DINA. This jealousy was expressed with greatest clarity in the Air Force, which in fact created the group.

The group nevertheless undertook joint operations with DINA....

Intelligence Organizations of the Air Force

During 1974, the repressive actions of the Intelligence Service of the Air Force (SIFA), which later became the Intelligence Directorate of the Air Force (DIFA), were notorious....

There was also another organization of a different nature, called the Intelligence Community. Its aim was to centralize administrative aspects of intelligence work, exchange relevant information and train personnel.... The directors of the respective intelligence services gathered in weekly meetings also attended by the director of DINA.

Each directorate or intelligence service continued to work independently in operational repressive tasks until the end of August 1975.

Places of Detention and Torture and Other Facilities used by Political Repression Organizations in the 1974 - 1977 Period

...In this category there were secret detention and torture facilities; places of detention where there was no torture; detention camps where people were held under the orders of the Executive Power; jails and penitentiaries where people awaiting or sentencing were held....

Villa Grimaldi

This was DINA's most important detention and torture facility.... It was located in Santiago, in José Arrieta Avenue in the borough of La Reina.

The operations teams had their headquarters in Villa Grimaldi. There, prisoners were taken for their first interrogations after detention and places and objects specially designed for different forms of torture were kept there.

Villa Grimaldi had practically uninterrupted activity. The operations teams went in and out 24 hours a day, and prisoners were brought in at any moment and tortured at any time.

Inside Villa Grimaldi was an atmosphere of generalized degradation. In addition to torture during interrogations, the officers as well as other operations personnel and some guards permanently beat and abused prisoners.

The Discotheque or Venda Sexy

The "Discotheque" was one of the places where, during the period that concerns us, many of the DINA prisoners who would later become the detained-disappeared were held. The "Venda Sexy" or "Discotheque" was a house located in Santiago, in the Quilín sector, at N° 3037 Irán Street. The installation had permanent music, which was the reason why it was called the "Discotheque."

Here torture methods were different from other torture centers, because sexual abuses were emphasized. Frequently, episodes of torture alternated with periods of relaxation and even kindness on the part of agents as a way of obtaining the required information....

Cerrillos hangar

In April 1975, this facility began to be used as a secret detention and torture center. DINA agents and civilians from nationalist or extreme rightist groups acted there.

Torture was practiced throughout the day....

Nido 18

Located at N° 9053 Pení Street, borough of La Florida, in Santiago, operated by members of DIFA, DICAR and civilians, it was used exclusively as a secret installation for torture.

Anti-Aircraft Artillery Regiment in Colina (Remo Cero)

In 1974 SIFA used the existing holding cells of this base as a detention facility. Later, further construction was carried out for use by the Joint Command.

From this place several prisoners were taken in helicopters to be thrown into the sea. In this facility some detainees died as a consequence of torture....

Why Forced Disappearances?

It is very difficult to attribute motives, and more so if we are dealing with acts such as the planning, ordering and execution of a policy of forced disappearances. This presupposes not only being subjective, but also trying to discern rationality in acts which are repugnant to conscience.

From the study of all the cases of detained-disappeared, it is evident that this practice had a double objective: to kill and to conceal, in order to destroy an enemy who must be exterminated.

This motivation or priority, with a strong ideological connotation, is intrinsically contrary to the rule of law which inspires the norms of human rights.

Moreover, the method of disappearance fulfilled other objectives such as permitting the government and the security forces to evade responsibility for their actions....

Repressive Methods: Detention, Torture and Cover-up

The apprehension or detention of persons by security forces evolved in such a way that it facilitated the concealment of facts, that is, avoided the presence of eyewitnesses. In the beginning, DINA detained victims in their homes, but then there evolved an apparent working method prior to the detention of the victim: study of his habits and a thorough selection of the method, place and hour in which he was to be detained. Sophisticated methods were used for the interception of private communications.

The Joint Command did not exercise the same care, which permitted knowledge not only of the facts of an arrest but also the identity of agents responsible.

Detainees were taken to secret DINA installations (or those of other services) where they were systematically tortured. The principal objective of torture was to obtain information from the victim. A second objective was to break down detainees' resistance or their physical and moral courage, as well as to frighten others who witnessed or heard the torture and to intimidate third parties who would eventually hear about it.

There was also treatment considered cruel, inhuman and degrading. This had as an objective, not the pursuit of information as such, but rather to punish and intimidate the prisoner; for this reason it was the expression of the cruelty and amorality of an agent or guard.

The routine methods of torture applied to practically every prisoner in the secret installations were: the grill [*electric shock applied while prisoner was tied to a metal frame, often a bedframe. Ed. Note*], hanging by the extremities, immersions or "submarines," the dry submarine [*near-asphyxiation. Ed. Note*], and beatings of every type. Other frequently applied methods included psychological tortures (kidnapping and/or threat of torture of a relative in the presence of the prisoner); traumas caused by bullet or knife wounds; rapes and/or other threats of sexual abuse; burns with boiling liquids; aberrant acts with animals and the injection of drugs.

With regard to the execution of prisoners, it seems that the majority of detained-disappeared were taken from the secret centers where they were held and executed near the place where they would be buried or their bodies would be disposed of.... Other executions were carried out inside the same detention centers, in the street, shooting victims in the back, and in foreign countries with the use of bombs.

A type of execution was practiced which consisted of taking the prisoners asleep or semi-awake, under the influence of strong sedatives, in a helicopter flying over the sea and throwing them into the water, their abdomens previously cut open so that their bodies would not float.

The disposal of bodies was carried out in different ways, generally by clandestine burial or by throwing the corpse into the sea or some river. In other cases bodies were left in the street or even taken to the Legal Medical

Institute [*morgue. Ed. Note*]. There were also cases of persons who were buried in a cemetery as NN [*no name. Ed. Note*] and even in some exceptional cases, their bodies were returned to their relatives.

It is important to point out that in the majority of cases of bodies buried clandestinely by the Joint Command, the cadavers were mutilated and the faces disfigured to prevent identification.

For carrying out their crimes, the security forces needed to conceal what had happened with the victims and for this end they used several methods:

Concealment of prisoners from the family. To this end, false identities were used in the detention, and the presence of witnesses to the arrest was avoided.

After the detention, government officials systematically denied the fact to the relatives or gave them false information. No list of prisoners was kept.

Concealment from different national and international authorities. At the national level when writs of habeas corpus and other legal remedies were presented, frequently the courts went to government authorities, particularly the Ministry of the Interior, inquiring as to the whereabouts of the person in question. In the majority of cases, the detention itself was denied through responses which began to have a standard content. The tone of these responses was understood by the courts as a denial on the part of the government that the person was detained, although the text of the response did not expressly deny that he had been arrested. At the international level, the government denied the detention or gave manifestly false versions to organizations such as the United Nations or the Inter-American Commission on Human Rights.

Disinformation to the public. This is attributable to the restrictions on freedom of the press during this period, which would explain the meager public information on these events. Moreover, DINA had disinformation operations.

Final Consideration

When stating the objectives of DINA it is impossible to forget that the long pattern of violations of human rights was not the work of an abstract entity.

Said institution, or any similar one, was conceived and implemented by human beings who planned and gathered all the essential tools.

It was necessary to choose the personnel. These personnel had to have a willing mentality or one that could slowly adapt so as not to perceive the suffering of others, even when it reached an extreme degree. Having recruited or trained them for that work is also a responsibility which must be assumed....

Reactions of Relevant Sectors of Society

Attitude of Chilean Society

During this period, once the public commotion of the first period diminished, the reaction of different social sectors began to increase with regard to the defence of human rights, as cases of persons detained, tortured, executed or made to disappear began to be known.

A slow rebirth of the social habit of solidarity began, which later became a platform from which society as a whole would be able to react....

The Reaction of the Churches

As in the first period, the Catholic Church worked on two fronts: teaching and the concrete work of aid and protection.

In its ecumenical work to aid and protect victims, the Committee for Peace was one of the essential actors. When it intensified its efforts, the government detained ten of its members between September and November, and prohibited the return to the country of its chairman, the Lutheran pastor Helmut Frenz. Finally, General Pinochet asked the Cardinal Archbishop of Santiago to dissolve the Committee for Peace on December 31, 1975.

The Committee for Peace gave legal aid in a total of 6,994 cases of political persecution in the provinces, 6,411 cases of persons dismissed from their jobs for political reasons, and a total of 16,992 persons benefited from the medical assistance program.

On January 1, 1976, the Catholic Church created the Episcopal Vicariate of Solidarity, with similar objectives to those of the Committee for Peace.

On April 1, 1975, the Social Aid Foundation of Christian Churches (...FASIC) was born as an ecumenical institution, with the aim of supporting prisoners who had been sentenced. From this initial work, it extended its scope to assist political prisoners and their families....

The Attitude of the Communications Media

As a general rule, communications media during this period maintained a tolerant attitude with regard to violations of human rights and abstained from using their influence to try to prevent continued abuses....

At the end of the period, publications appeared that were critical of the military regime's policies....

With regard to radio, the authorities introduced measures that encroached on freedom of information, permanently or temporarily closing some radio stations. Television stations were in the hands of the government.

The Attitude of Political Parties

...The situation reached its critical point in 1977, at which time decree laws dissolved all undissolved parties, confiscated their goods and prohibited all partisan political activity.

The Attitude of Professionals and their Organizations

The same basic reactions as in the first period were maintained....

In the first half of 1976, during the celebration of the Sixth General Assembly of the Organization of American States (OAS) held in Chile, four prominent lawyers presented to the participating Foreign Ministers, including the one from Chile, a document denouncing the violations of human rights which were being carried out in Chile. A short time afterwards, two of them were expelled from the country.

The Reaction of Organizations of Relatives of the Victims, of Human Rights Organizations and Intermediate Institutions

Through the Committee for Peace, different groups of victims and relatives of victims were organized.

The first group to be formed was the Relatives of the Detained-Disappeared at the end of 1974....

With regard to intermediate organizations of society (labor unions, student and community organizations), they did not have an official public position with regard to human rights due largely to their disintegration.

The Reaction of the International Community

In the first years of the military regime, it is estimated that no less than 20,000 people left the country for political reasons. The majority were received as refugees by foreign governments.

Relations with numerous countries deteriorated as a consequence of the human rights problem in Chile. Relations with the United States, nevertheless, remained relatively normal, and economic aid from that country to Chile increased in the period 1974-1976.

The terrorist act that caused the deaths of Orlando Letelier and his associate in the United States, in which DINA agents were involved, produced important effects in the repressive policies of the military regime. The arrival of the Undersecretary of State for Latin American Affairs of the United States coincided with the announcement of the end of DINA in August 1977. The Organization of American States maintained its concern about the fate of victims of the regime, as can be seen by its periodic reports and visits to the country.

The United Nations, beginning in 1974, prepared special reports on the situation of human rights in Chile. There were also resolutions in the General Assembly and the Human Rights Commission and the designation of an Ad Hoc Working Group on Chile....

August 1977 - March 1990

This period extends from August 1977 to March 1990. In contrast to the previously studied periods, which have similar and relatively homogeneous characteristics, this one has different stages and exhibits great variation in the number and methods of human rights abuse resulting in death, both in the cases of those committed by government agents and those perpetrated by private citizens who acted for or under political motives.

The following stages can be pointed out as milestones during this period:

- In August 1977 the National Information Center (CNI) was created, maintaining practically the same pattern as DINA.
- Between November 1977 and mid-1980, the CNI was oriented more towards political intelligence than repression.
- Starting in 1979, and more systematically after 1980, MIR began its return operation, which involved the clandestine entry of its militants into the country to prepare themselves for armed struggle against the military government. Subsequently, the Manuel Rodríguez Patriotic Front (FPMR) and later the "Lautaro Group" were organized.
- Starting in mid-1980 and for the rest of the period, the CNI carried out much more intensive repression....

Violations of Human Rights Perpetrated by Government Agents or Persons at its Service

...The CNI

This was the principal government organization in charge of political repression and counterinsurgency during the 1977-1990 period. The CNI legally ceased to exist in February 1990.

Its definition, characteristics, functions and objectives were very similar to those of DINA. The greatest difference consisted in its coming legally under the control of the Ministry of the Interior and that it had a new generic function, which was to defend existing institutions.... With the exception of the 1978-1980 period, the CNI systematically committed illegal actions in the fulfillment of the tasks entrusted to it....

The operational function of CNI was concentrated on direct actions against leftist groups which had taken up armed struggle against the regime. In addition to the methods used by DINA, CNI is presumed to have created paramilitary organizations such as the Comando 11 de Septiembre and the ACHA to cover up its activities and those of the people who acted on its behalf.

It also had an important role in the attempt to create political and labor union organizations supportive of the government....

To undertake all these activities, the CNI had absolute certainty of impunity....

Victims of the CNI and of Other Government Repressive Groups

The fatal victims during this period were chosen much more selectively than in previous periods. The vast majority belonged to MIR, the FPMR and the Communist Party. These organizations were the most tangible enemy, according to the rationale of the CNI, since its aim was to combat armed insurgency. Within this same rationale, it can be understood that executions and other repressive methods were seen by the government as a necessary harshness in the context of an irregular war, methods also used by the adversary.

There were also persons chosen as victims to avenge a terrorist act or some other attack, which were seen as reprisals or punishment....

Methods of Repression

In comparison to the previously analyzed period (1974-1977), methods of repression change as evident in the double methodology used by the CNI. On the one hand, some arrests were recognized and the alleged perpetrators handed over to military prosecutors; on the other hand, violations of human rights were carried out which were concealed or were presented with disinformation as legitimate self-defence in confrontations....

Torture, Executions and Forced Disappearances

Torture continued to be a systematic practice during this period.... Torture methods were essentially the same as those employed in the previous period.

There was, nevertheless, a difference. Torture was more selective and not as indiscriminate as during the DINA period, when practically everyone who passed through the secret centers was tortured.

Disappearances continued to occur, although during the 1981-1989 period, carried out in such a way so that there were no witnesses.

There were three types of executions. In some cases there actually was a confrontation between security forces and those they were going to detain or kill. In several of these cases, they killed persons already captured or wounded. In other cases, an ambush was arranged to kill the person sought, and was later characterized as an armed confrontation....

Disposal of the Body and Methods of Concealment

The bodies of people killed in real or simulated confrontations were generally given to their relatives. The bodies of the executed were thrown in fields or at the side of the road. With regard to the detained-disappeared, there is no information on the whereabouts of their remains....

Violations of Human Rights Perpetrated by Private Citizens Under Political Pretext, August 1977 - March 1990

Victims

During this period there were essentially two types of victims: persons who were at the site of a terrorist attack and who were completely unrelated to the situation that affected them, and members of the Armed Forces and Police....In selecting victims, among uniformed personnel, the aim was to provoke an effect on society more than to harm an individual person, turning the individual into a mere instrument, which does not accord the appropriate value to a human life.

The Evolution of Violence

Beginning in 1980, violent acts began to occur with ever-increasing regularity; they declined in the years 1981-1982, to begin once again in 1983 and through 1989.

This is the period in which terrorist activities increase in an important manner.

The organizations that acted were essentially two, MIR and the FPMR (the latter appearing in 1983), and at the end of this period, the MAPU-Lautaro....

The Methods

- Urban guerrilla actions
- Selective killings
- Shooting of Carabineros in the back
- The use of large quantities of explosives
- Bank robberies
- Arms smuggling...

Deaths in Protests and Collective Demonstrations

Many deaths occurred in the context of political demonstrations of different types.... On May 11, 1983, the first national protest day was called by the National Confederation of Copper Workers. Between 1983 and 1985, 14 national protest days took place. There were also social mobilizations, strikes, and slowdowns which continued until the general strike on July 2 and 3, 1986....

The protests were essentially peaceful. Nevertheless, there were expressions of violence especially in shantytown settlements and during the evening and night. Political and social leaders began to be overtaken by events beginning in 1984 and, therefore, the degree of violence and disorder increased.

Government measures and police actions to prevent alteration of public order were often excessive. The climate of confrontation became exacerbated and the most unprotected social actors suffered the greatest consequences....

Reactions of the Relevant Sectors of Society Before the Violations of Human Rights Occurring Between August 1977 and March 1990

August 1977 - May 1983

The Attitude of Chilean Society

As a result of the dissolution of DINA, which marks the beginning of this period, the replacement of the State of Siege by the State of Emergency and other important facts for the issue of human rights, some spaces opened up which permitted society to begin to react in more organized and effective fashion with regard to human rights violations and the military regime.

Opposition to the regime was channeled, from the beginning to the end of this period, essentially in two different and opposing positions: the stance that adopted all forms of struggle against the military regime and the peaceful stance.... Nevertheless, in this subperiod there was no significant reaction on the part of society showing open solidarity with the victims of violations. There was more of an indifferent attitude or one of disbelief, but, nevertheless, an increasing awareness of the subject.

The Attitude of those who were Part of the Regime

Suppression of dissidence essentially consisted of the prohibition against those opposed to the regime who were abroad to enter Chile; administrative internal banishment of labor and student leaders to different parts of the country and administrative exile for political leaders, who were also insulted and abused.

On the other hand, the number of detained-disappeared and deaths decreased significantly during this period.

On April 19, 1978, the Amnesty Law was decreed, reflecting the government's intention to leave behind the stage considered as civil war and of confrontation with subversion, giving full immunity to the violations of human rights committed until that date....

The Reaction of Communications Media

The end of the State of Siege and the suppression of DINA meant the creation of growing spaces of freedom of information. Despite this, self-censorship became a habit which was difficult to overcome. During this period the magazine *Cauce* and the newspaper *Fortin Mapocho* appeared, which carried out ... denunciations of human rights violations.

The Reaction of Political Parties

Although political parties still did not have a legal existence, they were able to achieve greater organization, which permitted the public expression of their respective opinions on the subject of violation of human rights.... Rightist political parties and organizations condemned terrorist acts openly and unequivocally, and theoretically condemned human rights violations without clearly recognizing that said violations existed in Chile. Centrist political parties and organizations had a clear and unequivocal position of condemnation of human rights violations perpetrated by the authorities as well as of terrorist acts of both the left and the right. Leftist political parties, which were somewhat reorganized after the persecution they had endured, had an attitude of permanent denunciation ... of the violations of human rights and of the military regime in general. Nevertheless, they did not have an equally clear position on terrorist acts allegedly carried out by extreme leftist groups.

Reactions by Professionals and their Organizations

...On February 1, 1981, Decree Law 3621 was dictated, repealing the legal provisions that empowered professional organizations to hear and punish violations of professional ethics; it gave them the character of trade associations and canceled the requisite of affiliation to an organization to exercise the respective profession.

Reaction of Organizations of Victims and Relatives of Victims and of Human Rights Organizations

Besides the activities that the Association of Relatives of the Detained-Disappeared continued to carry out, other organizations of victims or relatives of victims were formed, among them the Association of Relatives of Persons Executed for Political Reasons, which became public in November 1978.

The principal aim of this latter organization was, and is, to bring to trial those responsible for the deaths of their relatives and in general to denounce the responsibility of the military regime with regard to those deaths. During this period, [several] new human rights organizations were born....

The Reaction of the International Community

A critical attitude persisted on the part of the international community towards the government of Chile due to the human rights situation.... The Organization of American States (OAS) during 1977 and 1980 approved resolutions stating its concern for the situation of human rights in Chile. In May 1981, the Chilean government decided to suspend relations with the Inter-American Commission on Human Rights.

The United Nations, every year between 1978 and 1982 in its General Assembly, condemned Chile for the violation of human rights. In 1979, the

General Assembly named a Special Rapporteur to investigate the evolution of human rights in Chile.

May 1983 - March 1990

The Reaction of the Opposition and Moderate Supporters.

As in the preceding phase, the two options on how to oppose the military government were maintained.

The violent option led to a number of terrorist acts.... [T]here was a counterreaction by ultra-rightist groups, which also carried out terrorist acts. The growing degree of violence that the protests acquired was due, in large part, to the provocation of these groups.

On the other hand, persons in opposition to the government who favored peaceful actions promoted the protests, and when these began to lose their peaceful character due to the actions of interested groups, the organizers began to seek other formulas for peaceful opposition. Concurrently, peaceful opposition was achieving a large degree of coherence, through the reorganization of political parties and professional organizations, the creation of multiparty organizations and the celebration of agreements which encompassed large numbers of people.

This process culminated with the triumph of the NO vote in the October 5, 1988 plebiscite; with the approval of the constitutional amendments through a plebiscite in 1989 and with the presidential election on December 14, 1989. In every one of these events the subject of human rights had paramount importance.

Moderate sectors that had supported the military regime, as they began to know the violations of human rights perpetrated earlier, developed a critical attitude to the military regime's conduct, which although it did not mean the withdrawal of support, did mean a certain distancing....

Cases Declared "Without Conviction"

These are cases that the Commission investigated but in which it did not have sufficient objective information to declare them as victims of violations of human rights. Among the reasons why it was not able to gather evidence were:

- The lack of time
- The lack of witnesses during the moment of detention
- The disappearance of bodies
- The incineration of documents
- The fear or reluctance of witnesses to give statements
- The death or disappearance of witnesses
- The lack of previous information in human rights organizations
- The dispersion of relatives of the victims in exile

The cases considered as without conviction represent the situations of 642 persons.

Summary Table of Victims, 1973-1990

Victims of violations		
of human rights abuses	2,115	
Victims of political violence	164	
Total Victims	2,279	

Cases in which the Commission		
could not reach a conviction	641	

TOTAL CASES	2,920	

Another 508 cases were presented to the Commission which were not within its mandate and 449 in which only a name was given, which was insufficient to carry out an investigation

Victims of violations of human rights

Victims of Government agents or persons at its service

A. Deaths		
In courts martial	59	2.8%
During protests	93	4.4%
Allegedly while trying		
to escape	101	4.8%
Others executions		
and deaths due to torture	815	38.5%
Total deaths	*1,058*	*50.5%*
B. Detained-disappeared	**957**	**45.2%**

Victims of private citizens acting under political pretext

Deaths	90	4.3%
Subtotal victims	2,115	100%

Victims of political violence

Fallen during 1973	87	53.0%
Fallen in protests	38	23.2%
Confrontations and others	39	23.8%
Subtotal victims	164	100%
TOTAL VICTIMS	2,279	

Victims according to marital status

Single	960	42.1%
Married	1,172	51.5%
Widowed	12	0.5%
Not specified	135	5.9%
Total	2,279	100%

Victims according to sex

Women	126	5.5%
Men	2,153	94.5%
Total	2,279	100%

Victims according to age

Less than 16	49	2.1%
Between 16 and 20	269	11.8%
Between 21 and 25	557	24.4%
Between 26 and 30	512	22.4%
Between 31 and 35	287	12.6%
Between 36 and 40	152	6.7%
Between 41 and 45	164	7.2%
Between 46 and 50	97	4.3%
Between 51 and 55	53	2.3%
Between 56 and 60	34	1.5%
Between 61 and 65	15	0.7%
Between 66 and 70	8	0.4%
Between 71 and 75	3	0.1%
Older than 75	2	0.1%
Unspecified age	77	3.4%
Total	2,279	100%

Victims according to party membership

Socialist Party	405	17.8%
M.I.R.	384	16.9%
Communist Party	353	15.5%
M.A.P.U.	24	1.0%
F.P.M.R.	9	0.8%
Radical Party	15	0.7%
Christian Democrats	7	0.3%
Christian Left	5	0.2%
National Party	4	0.2%
Other Parties	15	0.7%
Without known		
affiliation	1,048	46.0%
Total	2,279	100%

Number of Victims According to their Activities

1. Professionals	207	4. *Workers and Campesinos*		686
2. Administrators, Managers, and		Campesinos		65
High officials	45	Carpenters		14
3. Office workers	305	Domestic workers		3
4. Workers and Campesinos	686	Drivers		33
5. Self-employed	314	Workers		571
6. Students	324			
7. Armed Forces and Security		5. *Self employed*		314
Services	132	Artisans		61
8. Other	226	Artists		7
9. Unknown	40	Farmers		59
		Salesmen		102
TOTAL	2,279	Self-employed		85

		6. *Students*	324
Details of activities		Primary education	17
		Secondary education	48
1. *Professionals*	207	University	165
Architects	5	Other	94
Contractors	9		
Economists	3	7. *Armed Forces and*	
Engineers	37	*Security Services*	132
Journalists	10	Air Force	3
Lawyers	13	Army	37
Medical Doctors	24	Carabineros	69
Nurses	2	Detectives	7
Priests	3	DINA	1
Professors	20	Navy	3
Social workers	5	Unspecified	12
Sociologists	5		
Teachers	71	8. *Other Activities*	226
		Housewives	17
2. *Administrators, Managers and*		Other activities	130
High Officials	45	Retired	17
Administrators	33	Unemployed	48
Businessmen	12	Did not work	14
3. *Office workers*	305	9. *No information*	40
Secretaries	11		
Other office workers	294	Total	2,279

[Editor's note: The excerpts which follow are reprinted from *Report of the Chilean National Commission on Truth and Reconciliation*, translated by Phillip E. Berryman (University of Notre Dame Press, 1993), pp. 777-778.]

Impact of the Most Serious Human Rights Violations on Families and Social Relations

...The Commission believes the truth would remain incomplete if the relatives of these victims were not allowed to testify on what they have suffered as a result of these grave human rights violations. Throughout these years their voices and their pain have been little heard....

The Commission received this testimony in private and group sessions. The aim was to assure that people who came forward would feel welcome and that in the interview itself they would experience some acknowledgement and reparation. As a rule family members felt free to express their emotions and feelings, and they reclaimed the good name and dignity of their relatives by telling of their life and personal qualities.

The Commission honestly believes that it must allow these voices and this testimony to be heard directly. Hence this chapter is organized differently from the rest of the report. To present all these personal accounts would be impossible. We had to choose a few that could serve to present as faithfully as possible the overall message we heard in thousands of interviews....

The suffering that such grave losses and such unjust actions have caused relatives is one and the same no matter who the victims might be, and is entitled to equal respect. The fact that most of the quotes presented here are from the relatives of those who were killed by government agents rather than from those killed by private citizens acting for political reasons should not be regarded as indicating greater sensitivity to the pain of some than to that of others. The fact is that far more of the families interviewed fell into that group. However, beyond numbers—which it should be repeated, do not affect the respect each family deserves—there are certain kinds of harm such as the uncertainty caused by disappearance, or the experience of being outcast, that affected some families and not others.

[Editor's note: The excerpts which follow are reprinted from *Summary of the Truth and Reconciliation Commission Report* (Chilean Human Rights Commission and Centro IDEAS, 1991), pp. 99-103, 111-114.]

Many of the victims' relatives were denied the possibility of knowing why their loved ones had been killed, and of being able to see the bodies, bury the remains with dignity and express and share their grief.

"When we were told that he had been shot, we were forbidden to say mass and wear mourning."

"He always said that he wanted a wake with all his friends, a large funeral. It wasn't that way at all, there was no funeral, and in the cemetery we were beaten with gun butts."

Grief Without Resolution

The relatives of the detained-disappeared have been condemned to live in permanent uncertainty. It is an uncertainty which becomes chronic, and which permeates all existence.

"For years I wanted to get home urgently after work to see if he had returned."

"My mother has kept the room the way it was when they took him away. His clothes, his notebooks and his books, and in his bed an altar where she places flowers waiting for him to return."…

Torture

Many of the victims were tortured. The family knows this because they saw it in the bodies or through information from other prisoners. The way in which they died becomes a harsher nightmare than death itself.

"If they had only just killed him, it would be less hard. But since one knows that he was tortured and one doesn't really know what they did to him, imagination is more punishing than death itself."…

The Search for the Missing

All of life revolves around looking for them, nothing else is important. The search is permanent, only with time its form changes. First there was the pilgrimage through jails, detention centers, clinics, the morgue. Today it is the search for the body.

"Until recently were waiting for them alive, today we are looking for the bones."…

Damage to Personal Integrity

…Relatives bear the feeling of having been hurt in their most intimate condition as persons, affecting future plans, feelings, attitudes, identity, capacity to adapt, physical and mental well-being.…

"I got married August 8 and on October 5 I was already a widow. Why did they take away the possibility of being happy with my husband?"…

"I was 13 and they took me to the regiment to interrogate me and to make me tell them where my father was. I didn't continue to study or anything, all I wanted was to die."…

Disorders in Mental and Physical Health

Individual and social trauma has repercussions in the physical and mental health of the affected families.…

"When my brother disappeared my father was old, and he went insane. He died walking in the roads screaming his son's name."…

"I told my son to give himself up, that nothing would happen to him. I feel guilty."…

"I must get rid of this pain and also, why not say it, all of this hate I have inside; because hate is like a disease and when one hates inside one cannot live."

"I have no love for life. I am permanently afraid. I'm afraid of people."...

Damage to Family Life

"They didn't condemn only him, they condemned the whole family."

Most descriptions narrate with nostalgia and impotence the deterioration of family ties and the dispersal of family members....

Economic difficulties, exile or the need to protect the life of other members of the family meant the dispersal of the family....

"I've just met my son again.... After the death of his father, we were separated for 10 years. I was in jail and he was with my family abroad."...

"I looked for my 17-year-old son everywhere. I had to do everything on foot because I had no money for the bus. I never heard anything about him."

The Families Experience the Death as Related to a General Situation of Change

The city is no longer the same. It is difficult to discriminate between what is dangerous and what is safe. Friends can no longer get together....

"After they took him away, I spent ten days awake taking care of my two babies because I was certain they were also going to take them away from me. The greatest harm that we've endured is never feeling secure."

"If they killed the mayor and innocent peasants, how could we know who would be next?"...

"We felt like pariahs in our own country."

"It is frightening to think that one is as much a human being as they are. Where could so much evil come from?"

"I don't want them to be killed as they killed my father. But I also don't want them to be running around in the streets."

Stigma and Marginality

Death or disappearance of a member of the family is followed by a history of marginality. The families suffer discrimination in work, the children in their access to schools, universities and government institutions.... Government authorities, in their official statements, referred to the persons that were killed or disappeared as criminals, terrorists, anti-social elements dangerous to society. Society began to incorporate these ideas, stripping from the victims their character as victims....

"The papers said they were terrorists, and with that everyone justified it."

"After they shot my father, the director called me and said: you are the daughter of a criminal and therefore you cannot continue to teach in this city."

"I was left with eight minors, but they only paid me a pension for six. They told me that the eldest would not receive anything because he had the same name as his father."...

Insults and ill-treatment were added to the pain of the relatives. In the process of searching in detention centers, in the handing over of bodies and in the search for the disappeared, the families tell how they were humiliated, lied to, insulted and threatened.

"I was told that he had been freed. Now we have found him in the mass grave with his eyes blindfolded and his hands tied."

"I was told to bring lunch for my husband. I went and prepared rice with a fried egg. When I returned to the police station, he said laughing: Lady, you're crazy, there's no one detained here."...

The Positive Forces

...The persons and relatives that came to the Commission expressed that amidst the pain there was always energy, the positive force that came from different sources.

"I forced myself to draw strength despite the pain. I had the duty to show society that he wasn't a criminal, I had to clear his name."...

"I'm heartened that we are capable of recognizing that this is everyone's problem."

"For us this is a very painful but important moment. It's the first time that we can speak. We need to talk about this situation with dignity and not continue hiding."...

"I am willing to forgive but I must know whom to forgive. If only they would speak, recognize what they did, they would give us the opportunity to forgive. It would be nobler if they did this. There can only be reconciliation if there is justice."...

Prevention of Human Rights Violations

...The protection that our traditional body of laws gave human rights was weak but did exist. The destruction of democracy made us appreciate this reality in all its magnitude. These circumstances demand changes at the legislative level that permit us guaranteeing protections of human rights.

Notwithstanding the aforementioned, reforms are insufficient in themselves because the real cause of human rights violations was the lack of a national culture of respect for human rights. Therefore, the introduction of the subject of human rights and of respect for the dignity of every person into formal education, and the adoption of symbolic measures that promote these values, seem essential and unavoidable steps to reach the proposed objective.

Suggestions in the Institutional and Legal Field for the Observance of Human Rights

1. Adapting national laws to international human rights law so as to have an internal body of law truly respectful and protective of these rights.

   a. Ratifying international treaties on human rights.
   b. Perfecting national laws so as to make them compatible with international human rights law.
   c. Establishing efficient mechanisms for the defense of human rights.
   d. At the international level, the government of Chile must participate and disseminate the system for the protection and promotion of human rights.

2. Existence of a judiciary which effectively carries out its role of guaranteeing personal rights.

   a. Measures that tend to ensure the independence and impartiality of the Judicial Power, such as:

      • Incorporation of the subject of human rights into the curriculum of law students and special programs in the education of judges.
      • Perfecting the present system in the appointments and promotions in the Judicial Power in the sense of making it a truly objective system that guarantees the legal career.
      • Perfecting the qualifications of members of the Judiciary so as to ensure their objectivity.
      • Effectively incorporating the Judicial Power into the system of reciprocal control which the government must have within the rule of law....
      • Increasing the number of judges as well as justices and prosecutors in the superior courts.

b. Measures of a procedural and institutional nature aimed at obtaining from the Judicial Power a better observance of its fundamental duty of defending basic rights.

- Reforming military jurisdiction to ensure respect for the constitutional guarantee to receive trial by an independent court.
- Revising the procedural rules of the Code of Military Justice to ensure respect for the constitutional guarantee of due process.
- Ensuring compliance with the orders given by the courts.
- Perfecting habeas corpus and protection remedies to make them truly effective mechanisms for the protection of human rights.
- Reestablishing the importance of consolidating an interpretation of the law that is respectful of human rights.
- Reforming criminal procedures to ensure the constitutional guarantee of due process and the respect for human rights and the right to defense.

3. Commitment by the Armed Forces and Police to performing their functions in complete accordance with the obligation to respect human rights.

The Armed Forces and Police and Security Forces are entrusted with the monopoly of the legitimate use of force given them by the nation so as to ensure defense, the rule of law and the normal functioning of institutions. Historically they faithfully upheld these precepts which, along with their honesty and professionalism, won them the respect of the country. An example of this is that in many cases persons belonging to the deposed regime voluntarily gave themselves up, with total confidence that their basic rights would be respected.

The investigation carried out by the Commission into serious violations of human rights has led it to the conviction that there was participation of persons belonging to the Armed Forces and Police. It is fact, moreover, that in the majority of cases the corresponding responsibility has not been established by the courts or by the respective military and police institutions.

The Commission considers it indispensable to correct this situation to achieve a real national reconciliation, which is the greatest guarantee of respect for human rights. It is thus essential that any measure tending to modify, change or create proposals for reparation must have the participation of the Armed Forces and Police. Therefore, the Commission deems it imperative that these measures be the result of a broad discussion between civilians and the military.

It is suggested that this discussion be carried out in two different though complementary fields: the institutional and educational fields.

4. Creation of an institution whose function is the protection of human rights.

The Commission suggests the creation in Chile of a Defender of the People or "Ombudsman," whose specific aim is to protect persons from abuses of power, and that it becomes part of our legal system.

5. Specific modifications for better protection of human rights in constitutional and criminal procedural law.

Among others, the following are suggested:

- Ensure full respect for human rights during the act of detention and in detention facilities or jails.
- Modify the relevant juridical norms.
- Raise the penalty for the violation of the physical integrity of persons (duress).
- Punish crimes perpetrated by public officials which violate the rights guaranteed by the Constitution.
- Increase the punishment for the crime of torture.
- Update the legislation referring to the inviolability of the home or any private communication.
- Characterize the forced disappearance of persons as a specific crime.
- Establish that the statute of limitations for crimes not be applied to cases of violations of human rights, so long as situations that restrict legal actions persist.
- Promulgate laws that impede the amnesty of crimes which have not been investigated.
- Revise the basis for the decree or renovation of states of constitutional exception.
- Implement the legal mechanisms that permit the supervision of the ethical conduct of persons who exercise a profession.
- Perfect and regulate the legislation on the burial and exhumation of bodies....
- Promulgate legislation that consecrates the right of relatives to recognize and bury with dignity the bodies of their loved ones.

Suggestions Aimed at the Consolidation of a Culture Truly Respectful of Human Rights

1. Creation of an adequate cultural environment for the respect of human rights.

The effective respect for human rights can only be achieved in a society that has a culture truly inspired by the unrestricted recognition of the basic rights of human beings, that comes as a natural consequence of values inherent in daily life and that manifests itself in every sphere of national activity.

2. Conceptual suggestions as a frame of reference for the teaching of human rights.

...It is important to highlight that the teaching of human rights consists of the formation of attitudes of respect and tolerance directly related to them. In other words, it is the formulation of a coherent project of life in which human rights becomes a kind of ideal aspiration, emerging from a critical position with regard to reality, and in which contradictions are expressed in social and political contexts given to the observance of those rights.

3. Some specific suggestions with regard to human rights education

[B]oth in formal and non-formal education, the curriculum must be dealt with. With respect to this type of education and cognizant of the complexity of the subject, it is necessary to implement measures for the training of human resources, as well as the elaboration of educational and promotional materials.

4. The Need to Open Spaces for the Discussion and Adoption of Prevention Measures of a Symbolic Character

5. The need to include terrorist acts in the concept of violations of human rights

> [Editor's note: The excerpts which follow are reprinted from *Report of the Chilean National Commission on Truth and Reconciliation*, translated by Phillip E. Berryman (University of Notre Dame Press, 1993), pp. 837-850, 885-893.]

Proposals for Reparation

Introduction

...Obviously, there can be no correlation between the pain, frustration, and hopes of the victims' families and the measures to be suggested here. The disappearance or death of a loved one is an irreparable loss. Nevertheless, moral and material reparation seem to be utterly essential to the transition toward a fuller democracy. Thus we understand reparation to mean a series of actions that express acknowledgement and acceptance of the responsibility that falls to the state due to the actions and situations presented in this report. The task of reparation requires conscious and deliberate action on the part of the state.

Furthermore, the whole of Chilean society must respond to the challenge of reparation. Such a process must move toward acknowledging the truth of what has happened, restoring the moral dignity of the victims, and achieving a better quality of life for those families most directly affected.

Only in this fashion will we be able to develop a more just form of common life that will enable us to look with hope toward the future.

- Although the specific measures of reparation adopted must be designed to be effective, they will obviously be unable to accomplish anything by themselves. The great ideals—truth, justice, forgiveness, reconciliation—must come first.
- Measures of reparation must aim to bring society together and move toward creating conditions for true reconciliation; they should never cause division.
- Only within an atmosphere that encourages respect for human rights will reparation take on vital meaning and shed any accusatory trait that might reopen the wounds of the past. The reparation process means having the courage to face the truth and achieve justice: it requires the generosity to acknowledge one's faults and a forgiving spirit so that Chileans may draw together.

Recommendations for Restoring the Good Name of People and Making Symbolic Reparation

Publicly Repairing the Dignity of the Victims

For some people the very fact that this Commission was created by the president and exists may constitute an initial gesture of reparation. Out of our own experience we can attest that many of the victims' relatives who attended sessions throughout Chile saw it as such a gesture.

Moreover, there are already a number of spontaneous initiatives and gestures of reparation throughout the country. Each of them is valuable in itself for what it expresses. Such initiatives need not spring from a law. Indeed it would be beneficial if initiatives for reparation were to multiply throughout the country and in every segment of society. Our hope would be that the creativity of such gestures might add to the artistic and moral endowment of our nation. Thus some day we may have symbols of reparation that are national and others that are regional or local in nature.

However, it would seem that these things are not enough: the country needs to publicly restore the good name of those who perished and to keep alive the memory of what happened so that it may never happen again. Hence the state can take the lead in making gestures and creating symbols that can give a national impetus to the reparation process. Today more than ever our country needs gestures and symbols of reparation so as to cultivate new values that may draw us together and unveil to us common perspectives on democracy and development. If we know how to be attentive to details and observe the formalities, we will also know how to overcome the obstacles still dividing us.

It is to be hoped that as soon as it is prudently possible, the government will see fit to provide the means and resources necessary to set in motion cultural and symbolic projects aimed at reclaiming the memory of the victims both individually and collectively. Such projects would lay down new foundations for our common life and for a culture that may show more respect and care for human rights, and so provide us with the assurance that violations so threatening to life will never again be committed....

Solemnly Restoring the Good Name of the Victims

...This Commission takes the liberty of suggesting that the state—whether represented by his excellency the president of the republic, or by the Congress, or by a law—solemnly and expressly restore the good name of the victims who were accused of crimes which were never proven and who were never given the opportunity or adequate means to defend themselves....

Legal and Administrative Recommendations

Unresolved Legal Issues

...In addition to the uncertainty and anguish of this situation, family members confront a long list of problems in connection with their civil status, inheritance, ownership of the disappeared person's property, school tuition for the children, wives' legal interest in marital property, and a host of situations that harm the family estate.... [One option] is to ask that the person be declared to be presumed dead in accordance with Article 81ff. of the Civil Code. The problem with this approach has been that the family members have often preferred not to utilize this procedure because it seems to imply that they are somehow giving up their efforts to discover the truth or to find the person alive, or for some other reason. These reasons should be respected....

Special Procedure for Declaring Persons Arrested and Disappeared to be Dead

...We would recommend that the conviction of this Commission should constitute sufficient proof for such a court decision and be the only evidence required. In other words, the only proof needed would be that the person's name appear on the list of victims in this report; no other procedure would be required....

Recommendations in the Area of Social Welfare

...The aim of our recommendations in the area of social welfare is to repair the moral and material harm that the immediate relatives of the victims have suffered. Their plans and hopes have been altered radically by the violations that this Commission has examined.

We believe that by its very nature the state is obligated to undertake measures which support the efforts the affected families have made to seek a better quality of life....

- The support provided should not only help people deal with particular problems concerning their welfare; it should also encourage the participation of the relatives themselves, since it is they who can best determine which of their needs are most urgent and how they may be satisfied.

- We would also suggest that the measures finally adopted aim at providing a quick and effective solution, since these problems have been mounting up all over the years and they hinder efforts to reintegrate these families into Chilean society....

Recommendations in the Area of Pensions

...Proposal for a Single Reparation Pension

[W]e think it possible to propose a single reparation pension for the immediate relatives of the victims. The only condition is that the name of the person who is the source of the right must appear on the list in this report. That is, the relatives of those who have disappeared after arrest need not go through the procedure of having the person declared to be presumed dead....

- There is a convergence of opinion that the single pension should apply to all cases starting on a single date. That date should be at least twelve months prior to the day on which the law goes into effect, and the first payment should be accumulative. The victims' relatives would thus be able to receive a lump sum of money that could serve in part to cover the costs incurred thus far.
- In view of the documentation provided by specialized agencies and taking into account the needs of most of those affected, we suggest that the monthly sum given to each family be not lower than the average income of a family in Chile....
- Laws should be enacted to determine who the beneficiaries are to be, in what order of priority and in which proportion they are to share in any single pension like the one being proposed....
- We would also like to pass on the suggestions that we have received that this pension be for life....
- We believe that in view of the reason for the reparation it would be fitting that the pension be granted quickly, easily, and in a manner that makes it accessible to the victims' relatives....

Recommendations in the Area of Health Care

- Specialized agencies have declared that the victims and their relatives have particular problems in both physical and mental health.... The permanent stress to which these people have been subjected has made them more vulnerable. They manifest grave symptoms in the area of mental health. They have had traumatic experiences so intense and so strong that their psychic structure has not been able to process them. All their subsequent efforts at reorganizing their lives will be marked by the damage done unless they receive specialized help.

- ...Many of these persons and families are from the popular sectors and have little money or have gradually become poorer from the time they were victims of human rights violations. In some instances serious nutritional problems have been observed. We are especially concerned for senior citizens and children....

- Such disruption of health is not limited to the immediate family circle of those who were killed or who disappeared after arrest, or the survivors of serious torture or acts of violence committed for political purposes. They also affect social relations, work situations, the neighborhood, and indeed the whole community. The health of individuals, families, and society has been harmed.

- Moreover, such harm is both manifest and still latent in the population. Specialists say it will be difficult to overcome such damage in the short run, since it may extend even to the third generation....

The situation is complex because these illnesses have themselves become injustices, or may have taken the form of a mute or stigmatizing pain. Some people have experienced their health problems in the form of an obscure or confused punishment, or as a comforting explanation for why they are powerless to express their truth. Sometimes the passage of time has made certain illness chronic and renders a comprehensive solution difficult or impossible. In such cases regaining health is more complex since it also requires that the person revise what he or she expects to achieve in life....

The Commission believes that it is primarily the task of the state to respond to this situation. The Ministry of Health will be best able to develop a program or a number of programs aimed at the most directly affected population.

In accordance with our observations here and with suggestions we have received, we propose that the direct beneficiaries of such health programs be all those persons who have been subjected to extreme physical or mental trauma as the result of a grave violation of their human rights committed by government agents or by private citizens who used violence for obvious political reasons. We have in mind the immediate family members of all the persons listed in this report. We would also like to explicitly recommend that those persons who have been the victims of severe physical and mental torture also be included, along with those who have been seriously injured as a result of politically motivated terrorist actions committed by private citizens.

In the context of social reparation, we want to point to the need to serve the health needs of those persons who have been involved in practicing torture in detention sites and to those who have acknowledged their participation in actions whose grave results we have investigated, as well as to those who may require such care in the future for the same reasons. It would seem that both humanitarian and technical reasons converge to urge that this population be furnished with comprehensive health care. Starting with their recovery and physical and mental rehabilitation, such care should go on to encompass levels of prevention and positive action that may extend to broader sectors of society....

- The approach to each person seeking attention should be comprehensive (biological, psychological, and social). Hence it is desirable that the teams be interdisciplinary and be familiar with the various reasons leading them to seek care. Insofar as possible, they should be alert to the needs of the family as a whole, and kindness and understanding should be part of the treatment.
- Activities should be planned so as to involve not only persons affected by human rights violations, but groups of such people, when the representational character and experience of such groups make it appropriate.
- The projected time period for such health care activities should not be too short. However, such activities should ultimately be aimed at integrating those in most need into ordinary health programs.
- Necessary services should be provided with no regard for the ability to pay of those most directly affected by human rights violations.…

Recommendations in the Area of Education

…At first glance it might seem that the educational problems of the immediate relatives of human rights victims have to do with younger children, but that is not the case. Most of the children are adolescents or even adults whose opportunities for attending school or the university can now hardly be recovered. The events that so radically altered people's future plans usually took place years ago. The situation of people who lost their opportunity to receive an education is of special concern to us.…

Here again poverty and declining living conditions have aggravated the problem of education for many of these families. In addition such children and young people have had to bear with emotional upheaval and learning problems during their elementary and high school years.

As a result of all these factors combined it has not been easy for them to enter universities and institutes for advanced technical training. Our country needs the contribution of all its youth and particularly these young people who have been excluded from formal education by the facts and circumstances presented in the earlier chapters of this report. There is no need for a lengthy diagnosis. It is obvious that we need a vast creative and perhaps unprecedented effort in our country to find ways to make reparation in the realm of education before it is too late and the situation is irremediable.…

Measures to Take as Quickly as Possible…

- A portion of scholarships for higher education should be reserved for the children of human rights victims who are ready for such studies.
- Study should be given to the possibility of canceling debts that the children, spouses, or other immediate relatives of such victims have incurred with the state or universities, provided the proper authority approves.

- Young people and adults who did not complete their studies and do not have a trade should be regarded as having a right to enroll in certain institutes and centers for technical training.
- Similar opportunities and incentives should be provided for surviving spouses or partners, or other immediate family members, should they request it.
- ...We also urge that the government assume the costs within certain limits and time frames, once the scope of the demand has been assessed. Finally we urge that the aim must always be to reincorporate the relatives of human rights victims into society and that the stigma and risks of isolation that might derive from granting special aid be avoided....

Recommendations in the Area of Housing

...In many cases the events we have investigated have forced families to move to a different area, leaving their home and even losing it. In other instances, the family did not have a house of their own when these events occurred. Had they not taken place, however, it is quite possible that the now missing head of the house would have been able to obtain a house for his family as the fruit of his work.

This Commission has also learned of land and goods being confiscated, of houses damaged by violence, of debts owed for housing payments, of situations in which insurance policies that should have paid off the mortgage when the person was killed or disappeared did not do so, problems with deeds, and so forth....

In view of these factors, we think it would be just for the government to offer special treatment for the housing problems of the relatives of victims of the most serious human rights violations whose names are listed in this report....

Further Recommendations in the Realm of Social Welfare

Recommendations for Canceling Debts

[W]e suggest that study be given to the possibility of canceling some outstanding debts to the government owed by people who were killed or who disappeared after arrest and who are listed in this report. Such debts would include those related to social security, education, housing, taxes, or others that may still exist with government agencies because requirements were not met within prescribed time periods. The aim is to alleviate the burden that the families have had to bear....

Recommendations Concerning Obligatory Military Service

In view of the evidence the Commission has in hand, and following suggestions from eminent moral authorities, we suggest that within the climate of reparation needed if the various sectors of the nation are to come together, the competent authority should study the possibility of allowing the children of those who suffered the most serious human rights violations the option to accept or reject military service without suffering discrimination in other opportunities for study or employment. The only basis for making this recommendation is the understandable problem of sensitive feelings aroused by this matter. In no way are we motivated by any lack of esteem for military service, which deserves our wholehearted respect....

Truth, Justice and Reconciliation as Preventive Measures

A Culture that Respects Human Rights Can Only Develop in an Atmosphere of a Healthy National Common Life

We have emphasized that respect for human rights demands that a culture take its inspiration from those rights. We must nonetheless acknowledge that such a cultural atmosphere cannot be expected to flourish in a situation in which there are signs of a failure to come together, as is the case in our society.

Hence it is absolutely necessary that we overcome the level of division still present as a result of our experience in recent decades. In other words, creating the cultural climate that we are urging as a preventive measure requires a society that is reconciled. Thus we are led to insist that for the sake of such preventive measures we must attain the truth and justice that are themselves prerequisites for national reconciliation. We now make some observations on truth and justice.

Truth

Establishing the truth is clearly both a preventive measure in itself and is presupposed in any other preventive measure that may ultimately be adopted. In order to fulfill its preventive function, the truth must clearly combine certain minimum requirements. It must be impartial, complete, and objective, so that public awareness may be quite clearly convinced of what the facts are and how the honor and dignity of the victims were wronged.

In this connection we recall that the decree creating the Commission on Truth and Reconciliation indicates that its central purpose is to "clarify in a comprehensive manner the truth about the most serious human rights violations committed in recent years." In order to achieve that purpose we believed we should gather as much evidence as possible about each one of the approximately 3,500 cases on which we received complaints and that insofar as possible we should listen to the family members of each of those killed and to the witnesses that they or the organizations making the complaint brought forward. This Commission trusts that the truth that has been obtained in this fashion may in itself serve the intended purpose of prevention.

Justice

We have encountered divided opinions over what justice entails. Some argue that for the sake of both reparation and prevention it is absolutely imperative that the guilty be punished. Others, however, believe that given the amount of time that has passed and the manner in which the events took place and their context, it would not be advisable to open or reopen trial procedures, since the results could be the opposite of those sought....

From the standpoint of prevention alone, this Commission believes that for the sake of national reconciliation and preventing the recurrence of such events it is absolutely necessary that the government fully exercise its power to mete out punishment. Full protection for human rights is conceivable only within a state that is truly subject to the rule of law. The rule of law means that all citizens are subject to the law and to the courts, and hence that the sanctions contemplated in criminal law, which should be applied to all alike, should thereby be applied to those who transgress the laws safeguarding human rights. The Commission's founding decree says as much in considerations 4 and 7, which state that justice must be administered through the courts.

We make this observation fully cognizant of the whole range of practical obstacles that may hinder the full realization of such an important aim, such as the fact that many of these cases have been suspended or amnestied with either no judicial investigation or only a partial investigation; the emphatic legal position taken by the Supreme Court in its decisions in the sense of declaring that it is inadmissible to delve into the facts in those cases that have fallen under amnesty; the fact that a large portion of cases are in military courts; and other limiting conditions.

Reconciliation

Truth and justice—insofar as they can be attained through the courts—are the pillars on which a reconciled society must be built, but in themselves they are not enough. The various sectors of society affected must also be brought back together. In this regard it should be noted that this Commission has heard numerous statements from those who suffered indicating their desire that the nation be brought back together and reflecting their spirit of not seeking revenge.

Hence it is to be hoped that those who are in a position to help advance reconciliation with some gesture or specific act will do so. They could, for example, make available the information they may have on the whereabouts of those who disappeared after arrest or the location of the bodies of people who were executed or tortured to death and have not yet been found.

Only by taking such steps will we advance toward the national reconciliation that is an utter necessity and is also the primary condition for avoiding a repetition of past events.

Further Recommendations

Creation of a Public Law Foundation[i]

The Commission has also come to the conclusion that it should propose to the president the creation of an institution, which we believe should be a Public Law Foundation directly connected to the president in accordance with Law No. 18.575 (Law on the Foundations of the Administration). We suggest that the ultimate authority in the foundation be a board made up of highly respected people from diverse traditions and from across the political spectrum who hold a variety of views on our history. We further believe that this board should be motivated by a spirit that acknowledges the basic norms of democracy and of the rule of law, and that it should accept the fundamental principle that the human person is to be respected because he or she is a person and because the human person is protected by inalienable rights that must not under any circumstances be violated.

This foundation should take on the functions to be indicated here. Some of them are tasks that remain to be done as we conclude our work, while others reflect needs that may arise in the future. We believe the foundation we propose should have the following functions and purposes.

Aid in the Search for Victims

Article 1 of Supreme Decree No. 355, which created the National Commission on Truth and Reconciliation, stated that one of its purposes was to gather evidence that would make it possible to determine the fate or whereabouts of the victims, since there were so many instances of people who disappeared after arrest or whose remains have not been found even though their death has been registered. Despite the Commission's efforts, it proved impossible to achieve that objective, and the scope of the problem remains practically unchanged from what it was when the president issued the decree.

We believe the state should not give up the task of trying to determine where the victims are, or of providing aid to families who are still searching. This was one of the most basic demands we encountered, and broad segments of any population share in that yearning. It will be very difficult to come to reconciliation and a shared common life in Chile as long as this problem remains unresolved.

Hence one of the functions of the proposed foundation should be to keep searching. To that end it should be authorized to become a plaintiff in judicial investigations that may be carried out for that purpose, and it should

---

[i] Public Law Foundation: Chilean Law No. 19.123 created the National Corporation for Reparation and Reconciliation, whose mandate it is to coordinate, execute, and promote the "actions necessary for complying with the recommendations contained in the Report of the National Commission on Truth and Reconciliation." The law was passed by the National Congress and signed by President Patricio Aylwin. It went into effect with its publication in the *Diaro Oficial* on February 8, 1992.

have access to the initial summary investigation, and in general it should enjoy such faculties as may facilitate its work.

Gathering and Assessment of Evidence

Even as we finish our work we continue to receive items of evidence on human rights violations. Many of them have never been presented to the courts or to specialized agencies because the relatives live in remote parts of the country or because they have not overcome their fear. However,... in a significant number of cases the Commission could not come to a conviction on whether the person whose death or disappearance was presented to us actually suffered a human rights violation. Hence work remains to be done, and there is a need for a government agency to continue that work so as to come to an assessment on the status of these persons after the presentation of the evidence not available thus far for lack of time. When a conviction is reached on those cases presented to the Commission, the relatives could have access to such reparation measures as the president may adopt.

Centralization of the Information Gathered by the Commission

A third area is connected to the research that might be undertaken in the future by academics, university students, non-governmental organizations, Chilean and foreign scholars, or simply the general public interested in learning about or coming to a deeper understanding of matters related to human rights violations in Chile. There seems to be a need for an office to centralize the files and evidence on cases and to maintain a library devoted to this topic. People could have access to this office under conditions to be laid down by law. We believe that it would be reasonable for this task to be entrusted to such a foundation and that indeed such an office would enable the foundation to better carry out its other functions.

Assistance for Relatives

We also think it necessary that this foundation be a coordinating agency so as to make such measures of reparation as the president may adopt more efficient and prompt. Should the families so wish, it could centralize the bureaucratic procedures they might have to undertake in order to obtain those benefits. It would be preferable if the relatives of those who perished did not have to go around to numerous public offices to learn what they have to do and go through bureaucratic procedures in order to benefit from the reparation measures that might be approved. Instead they could go to a single office where they would be welcomed with dignity and respect and served efficiently.

To that end such a foundation ought to be able to provide the relatives with the legal aid and social assistance they might need. It also ought to enable them to resolve the everyday needs and concerns they will certainly face in the future as well as make certain that the benefits that may be decided upon are actually disbursed.

Elaboration of Educational Proposals

As was noted in the previous chapter,... education policies must be formulated. Information and training on human rights must be presented through formal education as well as through non-formal and informal education. Given the moral authority of its board, such a foundation would be in a good position to propose programs and assure that they were carried out in coordination with the appropriate officials.

Applying Sanctions for Concealing Information on Illegal Burials and Competence in Investigating Such Matters

As we have said, there is still no way to determine the whereabouts of almost all those who disappeared after arrest and of a large number of those who were executed and whose families did not receive their remains. Of course those involved in hiding the bodies know where they are, but our law has no provision obliging people to present such evidence to the courts.

Only for reasons of conscience have some of those who have such information made it available, thus making it possible to locate the mortal remains of the victims and then turn them over to their families to receive a decent burial.

Keeping in mind that this problem is a serious obstacle to Chilean reunification, we believe that hiding this kind of information should become criminal. It should be made a specifically defined crime so that those who do not provide it within a particular time period would be punished. In tandem with such legislation, the law should exempt from prosecution those who furnish such evidence. To provide incentives for their stepping forward, they should not be exposed to the risk of being punished.

Such matters should always be handled in ordinary courts, at least until the bodies have been completely located, identified, and turned over to their families.

Truth and Reconciliation

In Conclusion—The Need to Reflect

Our task revolved around two fundamental objectives: truth and reconciliation. As defined for us, our work was to come to a comprehensive grasp of the truth of what had happened, for it was utterly necessary to do so in order to bring about reconciliation among Chileans.

We are well aware that the task we undertook goes far beyond the thinking, the interests, and the destiny of individual persons. It is an issue facing our whole society. Each and every one of us citizens must be held accountable before ourselves and before all if we wish to encounter a solution—certainly not a final solution but at least one that is gradual and satisfactory—to the issues before us. We will have to assimilate this truth, find ways to establish the justice that any society needs, make an effort to understand where everyone stood when a human life was destroyed in a manner that overstepped all norms proper to the rule of law. We will have to search for paths to reconciliation. Otherwise, democracy—which is an essential part of our culture—will never be more than a name. For democracy means that realm in which the members of society are able to come together and settle their common problems in peace and freedom.

If this report serves such an aspiration, we can only be grateful. The events documented, evidence gathered, and convictions honestly reached will enable government authorities to adopt measures related to the triad of truth, justice, and reconciliation. Those families and social groups that have suffered in their very soul or who had ties of friendship or solidarity with the victims will now be able to exercise their rights and properly demand that those responsible be brought to account. They will also have the satisfaction that the nation as such has acknowledged and restored to its lost neighbor the full dignity proper to a human being and to a citizen. Our country should never have allowed that dignity to be lost as it did.

If all our people draw together in this fashion through the institutions of a democratic state and the rich array of social organizations, it will be easier at the proper time to take the steps that are needed in our country and that a more harmonious atmosphere may make possible.

It would be a mistake, however, to encourage simplistic illusions. We are well aware that many will find it difficult even to read this report. Clashing feelings are bound to arise. There will be problems over facts and interpretation in all honesty and fairness—and unavoidably so. This report will stand on its own.

Nevertheless we believe there is one thing that no one can deny: Chile has undergone a wrenching tragedy. The report itself says clearly and repeatedly that political situations are not on trial here. That is a matter for our country and history to decide. The report does not make distinctions between victims or perpetrators from one side or the other. It presents events whose seriousness are beyond discussion—incredible situations, sufferings borne by defenseless human creatures who were abused, tortured, destroyed or whose immediate relatives and friends underwent such treatment.

The depth of this suffering must be made known. We cannot conceal it or leave it to offhand commentary, to being dismissed, or for that matter to being exaggerated. We must collectively acknowledge that all of this happened. Only from that moment on—when each individual has plumbed what it means to suffer and to cause suffering—will some be moved to repentance and others to forgiveness....

We have witnessed and documented the tragedy. We trust that whoever reads this report will appreciate even more the expression, "Never again!" It must be never again, for we cannot return to a situation in which Chileans will again be facing the vile absurdity of resolving political problems through murder, torture, and hatred. Such a "never again" therefore also means not doing to others what has been done to oneself. Legally and politically, that is tantamount to saying that respect for the rights of every human being must come into play as the basis for our common life.

That conclusion leads us to a point that we cannot overlook in these observations. The report several times observes that the Commission believes that the human rights violations that took place during this period must not and cannot be excused or justified on the grounds of previous actions by those whose rights were violated. That is a basic proposition; it must be maintained.

When people think that the violation of fundamental rights has gone beyond the bounds of a legal or political order (or indeed simply a human order), when ordinary life in common has gone beyond the breaking point, and when matters reach the point where one portion of society believes that radical change is necessary, reactions may be very strong and a nation itself may move in a very different direction. That is a fact of political life, a reality of history on which the Commission takes no position. When matters reach this point, a society that is in crisis and faces internal or external aggression certainly has a right to defend itself.

However, as long as it intends to remain human and to respect basic values, it may never—whether for the sake of change, or self-defense, or in exercising power after a successful revolution—justify further violating human rights on the basis of the errors, excesses, or crimes that may have been committed previously.

On the contrary, we maintain that human rights fully in operation constitute the foundation of the democratic order that is now accepted by the community of nations. They are its foundation in themselves and not in terms of other objectives. That means upholding the natural dignity of the human being.

We hope that truth will serve as the basis for reconciliation. We believe we have responded to the demands of those who may have hoped either that we would show understanding for the harm that they have suffered, or be fair in judging their actions that have been branded as blameworthy. We have presented all cases, and we have taken into account all explanations. We have also fulfilled our mandate by presenting measures to prevent recurrence of human rights violations and to make reparation insofar as possible for the moral and material harm done to the victims.

Hence in concluding its labors the Commission urges all Chileans, especially those who in some manner have believed or still believe that the major problems facing Chile can be solved by inflicting violence or showing contempt for the lives of others, to turn their souls toward the choice that emerges from this long and profound tragedy. The results of what took place during this period and which to some extent remain with us, cry out in sorrow from every page of this report.

CHILE: STATEMENT BY PRESIDENT AYLWIN ON THE REPORT OF THE NATIONAL COMMISSION ON TRUTH AND RECONCILIATION*

(March 4, 1991)

Fellow countrymen, I am addressing you tonight to discuss a painful subject that still divides the Chilean people—the human rights violations of the past few years. When I assumed power, I said that this subject was an open wound in our national soul that would only be cured if we sought a reconciliation on the basis of truth and justice. With this objective, we created the National Commission of Truth and Reconciliation with individuals of renowned prestige and moral authority in Chile so that after they had received, collected, and analysed all possible records on the subject, they would issue a serious report on the most severe human rights violations committed in Chile between 11th September 1973 and 11th March 1990.

To this effect, we specified that serious human rights violations were to be understood to be cases in which individuals were missing, or had been detained, executed or tortured to death, and in which the government's moral responsibility was at stake due to actions committed by its agents or people in its service; and to be [cases in which] kidnappings and attacks against human lives had been carried out by individuals on political pretexts.

After nine months of hard work, the commission issued its report, which was agreed upon unanimously by all of its members, who publicly handed it to me on 18th February. In compliance with what I announced at that time, I am releasing it to the public today; for this reason we have given copies of the full text to the nation's foremost public, social and moral authorities, as well as to the media.

After carefully reading this report I think it is my duty to reiterate the recognition that the members of the commission and their aides deserve for the total dedication, public spirit, efficiency, responsibility, and objectivity with which they complied with their task. I think their valuable contribution deserves the gratitude of all the Chilean people.

What does the report state? [President Aylwin then provides a lengthy review of the structure and substance of the report, its findings and its recommendations.]

That is a summary of the commission's report. Let us hope everyone reads it and ponders it. I invite all of you to do so. Meditation is necessary in this instance. Allow me to share with you some thoughts that linger in my consciousness as a human being, a Chilean and President of the nation, after reading the commission's report and exchanging views with representatives of various sectors of the nation.

---

* Reprinted from *Chilean President's Address and Comments on Human Rights Violations Report*, BBC Monitoring, Summary of World Broadcasts (March 6, 1991).

First is the issue of truth. Truth lies at the foundation of coexistence. This assertion is valid for the multiple aspects of social life, from life at home to life in the world community. It is valid for family relations as well as for the family of nations, nations taken individually or as a community.

Wherever truth is not respected, confidence among people fades away, doubt sprouts, objections grow and, consequently, hatred and violence. Lies are the anteroom of violence and, therefore, are incompatible with peace.

On the issue of human rights violations in our country, the truth was hidden for a long time. While some denounced the facts, others who knew the truth denied them, and those who should have investigated them, did not. Therefore, it is understandable that many people, perhaps a majority of them, did not believe the facts that were denounced. This discrepancy became a new factor of division and hatred among Chileans.

The report that I am releasing today makes the truth clearer. This truth must be accepted by all considering the background of the report and the stature of its authors, many of whom supported and cooperated with the past regime. No one can ignore it in good faith. I am not saying it is the official truth. The state does not have the right to impose the truth, but I am convinced and I call on all my fellow countrymen to accept it and act accordingly.

Shared by all of us, however cruel and painful, this truth will remove a point of dispute and division among Chileans. Recognition of this truth is independent of the judgment each one may have made of the political events that took place in those years, or of the legitimacy of 11th September 1973. History will be the final judge. Nevertheless, no judgment on those events will do away with the fact that the human rights violations described in the commission's report were actually committed.

As the report asserts, the situation on 11th September 1973, and its consequences, represented an objective risk for human rights and made their violation possible, although unjustifiable. The existence of a state of internal war or the need to defend the homeland from terrorism cannot be invoked to deny or disregard this truth. We all know—and the report reminds us of this—that the Armed Forces and security forces very quickly took total control of the country, in a few days at the most. But war also has laws. There is no justification for torturing or executing prisoners or for making their remains disappear.

Second is the issue of pardon and reconciliation. Many fellow countrymen think that it is time to end this matter finally. Chile's wellbeing demands that we look to a future that unites us more than the past that separates us. There is much to do before we can build a truly democratic society, promote development, and reach social justice. We should not waste all our efforts digging into wounds that are irreparable. I recall what His Holiness John Paul II said when visiting us. Chile has a vocation for understanding and not for confrontation. We cannot progress by digging deeper into divisions. It is time for pardon and reconciliation.

Who could not wish this? In order to accomplish it, however, we must begin by establishing who are those who were offended and who are called upon to forgive and who are those who offended and are to be pardoned. I cannot pardon anyone in the name of others. A pardon is not imposed by decree. Pardon demands repentance from one party and generosity from the other.

Because those who caused so much suffering were state agents, because the state organs could not prevent or punish the abuses and because there was no social reaction to prevent them, the state and all society are responsible, whether by action or by omission.

It is Chilean society that owes a debt to the victims of human rights violations. This is why the suggestion in the report for moral and material compensation is shared by all sectors. This is why I dare—as President of the Republic—to assume representation of the entire nation in begging forgiveness from the victims' relatives. I also ask the Armed Forces and security forces and all who participated in the excesses to recognise the pain they have caused and to cooperate in healing the wounds.

The Chilean people have always loved and admired their armed forces and security institutions. They are identified with the homeland's glories, with the virile character of the Chileans, and with unselfish actions in everyday life or in facing serious emergencies. The yearning for reconciliation in a truly united Chile demands that we remove the obstacles that are still in the way. We should all contribute to it.

I have said on more than one occasion that my dearest wish as leader is to achieve national unity in democracy. This demands that each and every one make a great effort to put himself in the other person's place and try to understand him—with humility to recognise his own mistakes and limitations and with generosity to pardon the other person's mistakes.

On the issue of justice, justice is the greatest of all social virtues. It is the precious basis of peace. We know that given the limitations of the human condition, perfect justice is generally an unattainable good in this world, although it does not prevent us from eternally wishing for the greatest justice possible. Justice is not revenge; on the contrary, it excludes it. A crime is not punished or repaired by committing a similar crime. No one has the right to harm another individual, much less to attack someone else under the pretext of seeking justice. Whoever does this is also a human rights criminal and deserves social condemnation. To approve personal revenge is to replace law with violence and to allow the law of force to prevail over reason and justice.

On the subject of human rights violations, the clarification and acceptance of truth as it is in the report is already an important part of achieving justice for the victims. Moral vindication of the victims' dignity and the payment of reparations to their relatives, as proposed in the report, are also acts of justice. This is not enough, however, justice also demands that the fate of the missing people be revealed and that responsibilities for human rights violations be determined.

As for the bodies of missing people, the truth established by the report is not complete given that, in most of the cases in which detained and missing people were executed and their bodies not delivered to their relatives, the commission has been unable to find their bodies. As for determining responsibilities, it is a task that, in a state of law, corresponds to the courts of justice, in keeping with the legal order and its corresponding guarantees. The Commission of Truth and Reconciliation has not been able to go into this aspect because the decree that created it also denied it this faculty by virtue of clear constitutional precepts. In both cases, the commission has sent the respective records to the corresponding court. I hope that the courts will comply appropriately with their mission and carry out extensive investigations for which, I understand, the current amnesty law cannot be an obstacle.

Terrorism and Violence

The criterion I have explained must not be interpreted by anyone as a sign of tolerance or weakness in the struggle against terrorism and violence by extremist sectors. It is my government's decision to combat—with the greatest energy—terrorism and all forms of violence, whoever it comes from. The important thing is to find effective mechanisms for defeating violence and putting an end to it. The experience of other countries demonstrates that the law is more effective than simple armed confrontations. We resist accepting that, in order to combat terrorism—which is repulsive because, among other reasons, it violates human rights—it is necessary to use methods that result in similar violations because such methods are morally unacceptable and in practice, they help nourish the cycle of violence.

Decisions

Considering the report I have referred to and taking into consideration the aforementioned reflections, I think that in order to face the problems stemming from human rights violations with the greatest possible responsibility, efficiency and speed, it is necessary to adopt the following measures:

First: I fervently call on my fellow countrymen to accept the truth established in the report and to adjust their conduct to that acceptance.

Second: Taking into account the suggestions made in the report, I publicly and solemnly assert the personal dignity of the victims who were denigrated by criminal charges that were never verified and against which they never had a chance or appropriate means to defend themselves.

Third: This month the government will send Congress a draft bill formalising the report's proposals on a single reparation pension for close relatives of the victims, a special process to declare the deaths of detained missing people, other social contributions, and the creation of a public law institution that will take charge of the tasks pointed out by the report.

Fourth: Today I submitted a note and a copy of the report to the Supreme Court asking that it instruct the lower courts to speed up all pending trials involving human rights violations and to begin the new trials that may result from this report. In my opinion, the current amnesty, which this government respects, cannot be an obstacle for court-ordered investigations into responsibilities for human rights violations, particularly in cases of missing people.

Fifth: The government will ask—through the Justice Minister and in accordance with Article 26 of the Penal Proceedings Code—for the intervention of the Attorney-General's office each time it is deemed necessary.

Sixth: I will personally ask the Armed Forces commanders-in-chief and the Carabineros director for their institutions' cooperation in finding the bodies of those who were arrested and are missing and of those who were executed and whose remains have not been delivered to their families.

Seventh: The government has given special instructions to all public order and security forces for their diligent cooperation with the courts in order to help in the investigations of cases that have been mentioned.

Eighth: The government will soon send a bill to Congress, as proposed by the Chilean ombudsman, creating a people's defender to watch for human rights violations.

Ninth: The Justice Ministry will form a task force as soon as possible to prepare the necessary bills to introduce the reforms that the Commission of Truth and Reconciliation has suggested to protect human rights better.

Independent of all this, I am announcing that in keeping with some of the report's suggestions, the government has prepared bills to perfect and modernise the courts. This is an issue with a lot of support in the country and I am seeking the support needed in Congress to present the bills for discussion as soon as possible.

Concluding this speech, I beg all my countrymen to make an effort to accept this truth with integrity and responsibility. We should be able to learn from this experience so that something like this can never occur again. This is everyone's task and no one can hide from it. If the pain, the horrors, and the just indignation push us to hate and promote violence, we will be falling into the same mistake that caused the horrors. It will mean a resumption of the fight among brothers, the destruction of our new democracy, and a renunciation of the peace we all yearn for.

All Chileans can be sure that the government will fulfill its duty in accordance with the moral principles guiding it, with no other purpose than accomplishing justice, reconciliation and the homeland's wellbeing. But this is not a task for the government alone. The other state branches have to play their part. The armed institutions, the spiritual authorities, the social organisations and the national community as a whole, have to play their part. I am asking them all for their cooperation so that together—respecting and helping each other with understanding and generosity—we can do what is necessary to heal the wounds of the past and build a future with justice, progress and peace for Chile. Good night.

EL SALVADOR: MEXICO PEACE AGREEMENTS— PROVISIONS CREATING THE COMMISSION ON TRUTH

(Mexico City, April 27, 1991)[*]

...Agreement has been reached to establish a Commission on the Truth, which shall be composed of three individuals appointed by the Secretary-General of the United Nations after consultation with the Parties. The Commission shall elect its Chairman. The Commission shall be entrusted with the task of investigating serious acts of violence that have occurred since 1980 and whose impact on society urgently requires that the public should know the truth. The Commission shall take into account:

a) The exceptional importance that may be attached to the acts to be investigated, their characteristics and impact, and the social unrest to which they gave rise; and
b) The need to create confidence in the positive changes which the peace process is promoting and to assist the transition to national reconciliation.

The characteristics, functions, and powers of the Commission on the Truth and other related matters are set forth in the corresponding annex.

Annex

Commission on the Truth

The Government of El Salvador and the Frente Farabundo Marti para la Liberación Nacional (hereinafter referred to as "the Parties"),

Reaffirming their intention to contribute to the reconciliation of Salvadorian society;

Recognizing the need to clear up without delay those exceptionally important acts of violence whose characteristics and impact, and the social unrest to which they gave rise, urgently require that the complete truth be made known and that the resolve and means to establish the truth be strengthened;

Considering that, although the need to put an end to impunity was raised in the discussion on the item on the armed forces of the Agenda for the negotiations adopted at Caracas on 21 May 1990, the means of investigation which the Parties themselves have been prepared to set up are addressing situations whose complexity warrants independent treatment;

Agreeing on the advisability of fulfilling that task through a procedure which is both reliable and expeditious and may yield results in the short-term, without prejudice to the obligations incumbent on the Salvadorian

---

[*] UN Doc. S/25500 (April 1, 1993).

courts to solve such cases and impose the appropriate penalties on the culprits;

Have arrived at the following political agreement:

1. There is hereby established a Commission on the Truth (hereinafter referred to as "the Commission"). The Commission shall be composed of three individuals appointed by the Secretary-General of the United Nations after consultation with the Parties. The Commission shall elect its Chairman.

Functions

2. The Commission shall have the task of investigating serious acts of violence that have occurred since 1980 and whose impact on society urgently demands that the public should know the truth. The Commission shall take into account:

(a) The exceptional importance that may be attached to the acts to be investigated, their characteristics and impact, and the social unrest to which they gave rise; and

(b) The need to create confidence in the positive changes which the peace process is promoting and to assist the transition to national reconciliation.

3. The mandate of the Commission shall include recommending the legal, political or administrative measures which can be inferred from the results of the investigation. Such recommendations may include measures to prevent the repetition of such acts, and initiatives to promote national reconciliation.

4. The Commission shall endeavour to adopt its decisions unanimously. However, if this is not possible, a vote by the majority of its members shall suffice.

5. The Commission shall not function in the manner of a judicial body.

6. If the Commission believes that any case brought to its attention does not meet the criteria set forth in paragraph 2 of this agreement, it may refer the case to the Attorney-General of the Republic, should it deem appropriate, for handling through the judicial channel.

Powers

7. The Commission shall have broad powers to organize its work and its functioning. Its activities shall be conducted on a confidential basis.

8. For the purposes of the investigation, the Commission shall have the power to:

(a) Gather, by the means it deems appropriate, any information it considers relevant. The Commission shall be completely free to use whatever sources of information it deems useful and reliable. It shall receive such information within the period of time and in the manner which it determines.

(b) Interview, freely and in private, any individuals, groups or members of organizations or institutions.

(c) Visit any establishment or place freely without giving prior notice.

(d) Carry out any other measures or inquiries which it considers useful to the performance of its mandate, including requesting reports, records, documents from the Parties or any other information from State authorities and departments.

Obligation of the Parties

9. The Parties undertake to extend to the Commission whatever cooperation it requests of them in order to gain access to sources of information available to them.

10. The Parties undertake to carry out the Commission's recommendations.

Report

11. The Commission shall submit a final report, with its conclusions and recommendations, within a period of six months after its establishment.

12. The Commission shall transmit its report to the Parties and to the Secretary-General of the United Nations, who shall make it public and shall take the decisions or initiatives that he deems appropriate.

13. Once the report has been handed over, the Commission's mandate shall be considered terminated and the Commission shall be dissolved.

14. The provisions of this agreement shall not prevent the normal investigation of any situation or case, whether or not the Commission has investigated it, nor the application of the relevant legal provisions to any act that is contrary to law.

EL SALVADOR: REPORT OF THE COMMISSION ON TRUTH

From Madness To Hope
The 12-Year War in El Salvador[*]

I. Introduction

Between 1980 and 1991, the Republic of El Salvador in Central America was engulfed in a war which plunged Salvadorian society into violence, left it with thousands and thousands of people dead and exposed it to appalling crimes, until the day—16 January 1992—when the parties, reconciled, signed the Peace Agreement in the Castle of Chapultepec, Mexico, and brought back the light and the chance to re-emerge from madness to hope.

Violence was a fire which swept over the fields of El Salvador; it burst into villages, cut off roads and destroyed highways and bridges, energy sources and transmission lines; it reached the cities and entered families, sacred areas and educational centres; it struck at justice and filled the public administration with victims; and it singled out as an enemy anyone who was not on the list of friends. Violence turned everything to death and destruction, for such is the senselessness of that breach of the calm plenitude which accompanies the rule of law, the essential nature of violence being suddenly or gradually to alter the certainty which the law nurtures in human beings when this change does not take place through the normal mechanisms of the rule of law. The victims were Salvadorians and foreigners of all backgrounds and all social and economic classes, for in its blind cruelty violence leaves everyone defenceless....

On the long road of the peace negotiations, the need to reach agreement on a Commission on the Truth arose from the Parties' recognition that the communism which had encouraged one side had collapsed, and perhaps also from the disillusionment of the Power which had encouraged the other. It emerged as a link in the chain of reflection and agreement and was motivated, ultimately, by the impact of events on Salvadorian society, which now faced the urgent task of confronting the issue of the widespread, institutionalized impunity which had struck at its very heart: under the protection of State bodies but outside the law, repeated human rights violations had been committed by members of the armed forces; these same rights had also been violated by members of the guerrilla forces....

The Commission on the Truth was so named because its very purpose and function were to seek, find and publicize the truth about the acts of violence committed by both sides during the war.

The truth, the whole truth and nothing but the truth, as the oath goes. The overall truth and the specific truth, the radiant but quiet truth. The

---

[*] Excerpted from *From Madness to Hope: The 12-Year War in El Salvador*, Report of the Commission on the Truth for El Salvador (United Nations Publication, S/25500, 1993).

whole and its parts, in other words, the bright light shone onto a surface to illuminate it and the parts of this same surface lit up case by case, regardless of the identity of the perpetrators, always in the search for lessons that would contribute to reconciliation and to abolishing such patterns of behaviour in the new society.

Learning the truth and strengthening and tempering the determination to find it out; putting an end to impunity and cover-up; settling political and social differences by means of agreement instead of violent action: these are the creative consequences of an analytical search for the truth.

C. The Mandate

Furthermore, by virtue of the scope which the negotiators gave to the agreements, it was understood that the Commission on the Truth would have to examine systematic atrocities both individually and collectively, since the flagrant human rights violations which had shocked Salvadorian society and the international community had been carried out not only by members of the armed forces but also by members of the insurgent forces.

The peace agreements were unambiguous when, in article 2, they defined the mandate and scope of the Commission as follows: "The Commission shall have the task of investigating serious acts of violence that have occurred since 1980 and whose impact on society urgently demands that the public should know the truth". Article 5 of the Chapultepec Peace Agreement gives the Commission the task of clarifying and putting an end to any indication of impunity on the part of officers of the armed forces and gives this explanation: "acts of this nature, regardless of the sector to which their perpetrators belong, must be the object of exemplary action by the law courts so that the punishment prescribed by law is meted out to those found responsible".

It is clear that the peace negotiators wanted this new peace to be founded, raised and built on the transparency of a knowledge which speaks its name. It is also clear that this truth must be made public as a matter of urgency if it is to be not the servant of impunity but an instrument of the justice that is essential for the synchronized implementation of the agreements which the Commission is meant to facilitate.

D. "Open-Door" Policy

From the outset of their work, which began on 13 July 1992 when they were entrusted with their task by the Secretary-General of the United Nations, the Commissioners could perceive the skill of those who had negotiated the agreements in the breadth of the mandate and authority given to the Commission. They realized that the Secretary-General, upon learning from competent Salvadorian judges of the numerous acts of violence and atrocities of 12 years of war, had not been wrong in seeking to preserve the Commission's credibility by looking beyond considerations of sovereignty and entrusting this task to three scholars from other countries, in contrast to what had been done in Argentina and Chile after the military dictatorships there had ended. The commissioners also saw a glimmer of hope dawn in the hearts of the Salvadorian people when it became clear that the truth would soon be revealed, not through bias or pressure but in its entirety and with complete impartiality, a fact which helped to restore the faith of people at all levels that justice would be effective and fitting. Accordingly, in their first meeting with the media upon arriving in El Salvador, the Commissioners stated that they would not let themselves be pressured or impressed: they were after the objective truth and the hard facts.

The Commissioners and the group of professionals who collaborated with them in the investigations succeeded in overcoming obstacles and limitations that made it difficult to establish what had really happened, starting with the brief period of time—six months—afforded them under the Chapultepec Agreement. Given the magnitude of their task, this time-frame, which seemed to stretch into Kafkaesque infinity when they embarked upon their task, ultimately seemed meagre and barely sufficient to allow them to complete their work satisfactorily.

Throughout its mandate and while drafting its report, the commission consistently sought to distance itself from events that had not been verified before it reached any conclusions. The whole of Salvadorian society, institutions and individuals familiar with acts of violence were invited to make them known to the Commission, under the guarantee of confidentiality and discretion provided for in the agreements. Paid announcements were placed in the press and on the radio and television to this end, and written and oral invitations were extended to the Parties to testify without restriction. Offices of the Commission were opened in various departmental capitals, including Chalatenango, Santa Ana and San Miguel. Written statements were taken, witnesses were heard, information from the sites of various incidents (e.g. El Calabozo, El Mozote, Sumpul river and Guancorita) was obtained. The Commission itself went to various departments with members of the professional team, occasionally travelling overland but more often in helicopters provided promptly and efficiently by ONUSAL. As the investigation moved forward, it continued to yield new pieces of evidence: anyone who might have been involved was summonsed to testify without restriction as to time or place, usually in the Commission's offices or in secret locations, often outside El Salvador in order to afford witnesses greater protection.

The Commission maintained an "open-door" policy for hearing testimony and a "closed-door" policy for preserving confidentiality. Its findings illustrate the horrors of a war in which madness prevailed, and confirm beyond the shadow of a doubt that the incidents denounced, recorded and substantiated in this report actually took place. Whenever the Commission decided that its investigation of a specific case had yielded sufficient evidence, the matter was recorded in detail, with mention of the guilty parties. When it was determined that no further progress could be made for the time being, the corresponding documentation that was not subject to secrecy was delivered to the courts or else kept confidential until new information enabled it to be reactivated.

One fact must be squarely denounced: owing to the destruction or concealment of documents, or the failure to divulge the locations where numerous persons were imprisoned or bodies were buried, the burden of proof occasionally reverted to the Commission, the judiciary and citizens, who found themselves forced to reconstruct events. It will be up to those who administer the new system of justice to pursue these investigations and take whatever final decisions they consider appropriate at this moment in history.

Inevitably, the list of victims is incomplete: it was compiled on the basis of the complaints and testimony received and confirmed by the Commission....

F. Phenomenology of Violence

It is a universally accepted premise that the individual is the subject of any criminal situation, since humans alone possess will and can therefore take decisions based on will: it is individuals that commit crimes, not the institutions they have created. As a result, it is to individuals and not their institutions that the corresponding penalties established by law must be applied.

However, there could be some situations in which the repetition of acts in time and space would seem to contradict the above premise. A situation of repeated criminal acts may arise in which different individuals act within the same institution in unmistakably similar ways, independently of the political ideology of Governments and decision makers. This gives reason to believe that institutions may indeed commit crimes, if the same behaviour becomes a constant of the institution and, especially, if clear-cut accusations are met with a cover-up by the institution to which the accused belong and the institution is slow to act when investigations reveal who is responsible. In such circumstances, it is easy to succumb to the argument that repeated crimes mean that the institution is to blame.

The Commission on the Truth did not fall into that temptation: at the beginning of its mandate, it received hints from the highest level to the effect that institutions do not commit crimes and therefore that responsibilities must be established by naming names. At the end of its mandate, it again received hints from the highest level, this time to the opposite effect, namely, that it should not name names, perhaps in order to protect certain individuals in recognition of their genuine and commendable eagerness to help create situations which facilitated the peace agreements and national reconciliation.

However, the Commission believes that responsibility for anything that happened during the period of the conflict could not and should not be laid at the door of the institution, but rather of those who ordered the procedures for operating in the way that members of the institution did and also of those who, having been in a position to prevent such procedures, were compromised by the degree of tolerance and permissiveness with which they acted from their positions of authority or leadership or by the fact that they covered up incidents which came to their knowledge or themselves gave the order which led to the action in question. This approach protects institutions and punishes criminals.

G. *The Recovery of Faith*

...One fundamental element of the agreements, and one which is critical for El Salvador's democratic future, is the unreserved, unconditional subordination of the military authorities to civilian authority, not only on paper but in reality: in a democratic system based on respect for the constitutional order and governed by the rule of law, there is room neither for conditions, personal compromises or the possibility of subverting order for personal reasons, nor for acts of intimidation against the President of the Republic who, by virtue of his office, is the Commander-in-Chief of the armed forces.

H. *The Risk of Delays*

The purification which is to follow the reports of the Ad Hoc Commission and the Commission on the Truth may seem inadvisable in cases where a person guilty of a serious crime in the past rectified his behaviour and contributed to the negotiated peace. This, however, is the small price that those who engage in punishable acts must pay, regardless of their position: they must accept it for the good of the country and the democratic future of the new Salvadorian society. Moreover, it is not up to the Commission to act on complaints, requests for pardon or pleas of attenuating circumstances from persons dismissed from the armed forces, because it has no binding judicial powers. It is not by resignation but by its creative attitude towards its new commitments and the new order of democratic coexistence that Salvadorian society as a whole will ultimately strike a balance in dealing with those who must take the blame for what they did during the conflict but deserve praise for what they did in the peace process....

What is more, it would tarnish the image of the armed forces if they were to retain sufficient power to block the process of purification or impose conditions on it: if the guilty were not singled out and punished, the institution itself would be incriminated; no other interpretation is possible. Those who would have the armed forces choose this course must weigh the price of such an attitude in the eyes of history.

I. *Foundation for the Truth*

The mass of reports, testimony, newspaper and magazine articles and books published in Spanish and other languages that was accumulated prompted the establishment within the Commission on the Truth itself of a centre for documentation on the different forms of violence in El Salvador. The public information relating to the war (books, pamphlets, research carried out by Salvadorian and international bodies); testimony from 2,000 primary sources referring to more than 7,000 victims; information from secondary sources relating to more than 20,000 victims; information from official bodies in the United States and other countries; information provided by government bodies and FMLN; an abundant photographic and videotape record of the conflict and even of the Commission's own activities; all of this material constitutes an invaluable resource—a part of El Salvador's heritage because (despite the painful reality it records) a part of the country's contemporary history—for historians and analysts of this most distressing period and for those who wish to study this painful reality in order to reinforce the effort to spread the message "never again".

What is to be done with this wealth of material in order to make it available to those around the world who are seeking peace, to bring these personal experiences to the attention of those who defend human rights? What is to be done when one is bound by the requirement of confidentiality for documents and testimony? What use is to be made of this example of the creativity of the United Nations at a time in contemporary history which is fraught with conflict and turmoil and for which the parallels and the answers found in the Salvadorian conflict may be of some relevance?

To guarantee the confidentiality of testimony and of the many documents supplied by institutions and even by Governments and, at the same time, to provide for the possibility of consultation by academic researchers while preserving such confidentiality, the Commission obtained the agreement of the Parties and the consent and support of the International Rule of Law Center of George Washington University in Washington, D.C., which, since 1992, has been administering and maintaining the collection of documents relating to the transition to peace in countries under the rule of oppression and countries emerging from armed conflicts. In addition, the Commission has already sought the cooperation of Governments, academic institutions and international foundations, always on the clear understanding that it holds itself personally responsible for guaranteeing confidentiality before finally handing the archives over to their lawful owners.

The Foundation for the Truth would be a not-for-profit academic body governed by statutes conforming to United States law. It would be managed by an international Board of Directors, with Salvadorian participation; a representative of the Secretary-General of the United Nations and the members of the Commission would also be members of the Board. The Foundation would be operated under the direction of Professor Thomas Buergenthal and would maintain close contacts with leaders and researchers in El Salvador, with the group of European, United States and Latin American professionals who worked with the Commission, and with scientists from around the world. For those documents which were not subject to secrecy, duplicate copies and computer terminals for accessing the collection would be available in Salvadorian institutions requesting them.

The Foundation would be inaugurated in June 1993, in Washington, with a multidisciplinary encounter to discuss the report of the Commission on the Truth....

II. The Mandate

A. *The Mandate*

The Commission on the Truth owes its existence and authority to the El Salvador peace agreements, a set of agreements negotiated over a period of more than three years (1989-1992) between the Government of El Salvador and FMLN. The negotiating process, which took place under United Nations auspices with the special cooperation of Colombia, Mexico, Spain and Venezuela..., culminated in the Peace Agreement signed at Chapultepec, Mexico, on 16 January 1992.[1]

The decision to set up the Commission on the Truth was taken by the Parties in the Mexico Agreements, signed at Mexico City on 27 April 1991.[2] These Agreements define the functions and powers of the Commission, while its authority is expanded by article 5 of the Chapultepec Peace Agreement, entitled "End to Impunity".[3] Together, these provisions constitute the Commission's "mandate".

The mandate defines the Commission's functions as follows:

"The Commission shall have the task of investigating serious acts of violence that have occurred since 1980 and whose impact on society urgently demands that the public should know the truth."

It then states that the Commission shall take the following into account:

"(a) The exceptional importance that may be attached to the acts to be investigated, their characteristics and impact, and the social unrest to which they gave rise; and

(b) The need to create confidence in the positive changes which the peace process is promoting and to assist the transition to national reconciliation."

The specific functions assigned to the Commission as regards impunity are defined, in part, in the Chapultepec Agreement, which provides as follows:

"The Parties recognize the need to clarify and put an end to any indication of impunity on the part of officers of the armed forces, particularly in cases where respect for human rights is jeopardized. To that end, the Parties refer this issue to the Commission on the Truth for consideration and resolution."

In addition to granting the Commission powers with respect to impunity and the investigation of serious acts of violence, the peace agreements entrust the Commission with making "legal, political or administrative" recommendations. Such recommendations may relate to specific cases or may be more general. In the latter case, they "may include measures to prevent the repetition of such acts, and initiatives to promote national reconciliation".

The Commission was thus given two specific powers: the power to make investigations and the power to make recommendations. The latter power is particularly important since, under the mandate, "the Parties undertake to carry out the Commission's recommendations". The Parties thus agree to be bound by the Commission's recommendations.

---

[1] Published by the United Nations under the title *El Salvador Agreements: The Path to Peace* (DPI/1208, May 1992).

[2] *El Salvador Agreements, supra,* p. 30.

[3] El Salvador Peace Agreement (signed at Chapultepec), *supra,* p. 55.

As regards the Commission's other task, the mandate entrusted it with investigating "serious acts of violence ... whose impact on society urgently demands that the public should know the truth". In other words, in deciding which acts to focus on, the Commission would have to take into account the particular importance of each act, its repercussions and the social unrest to which it gave rise. However, the mandate did not list or identify any specific cases for investigation; nor did it distinguish between large-scale acts of violence and acts involving only a handful of people. Instead, the mandate emphasized *serious acts of violence* and their impact or repercussions. On the basis of these criteria, the Commission investigated two types of cases:

(a) individual cases or acts which, by their nature, outraged Salvadorian society and/or international opinion;

(b) A series of individual cases with similar characteristics revealing a systematic pattern of violence or ill-treatment which, taken together, equally outraged Salvadorian society, especially since their aim was to intimidate certain sectors of that society.

The Commission attaches equal importance to uncovering the truth in both kinds of cases. Moreover, these two types of cases are not mutually exclusive. Many of the so-called individual acts of violence which had the greatest impact on public opinion also had characteristics revealing systematic patterns of violence.

In investigating these acts, the Commission took into account three additional factors which have a bearing on the fulfilment of its mandate. The first was that it must investigate serious or flagrant acts committed by both sides in the Salvadorian conflict and not just by one of the Parties. Secondly, in referring the issue of the impunity "of officers of the armed forces, particularly in cases where respect for human rights is jeopardized" to the Commission, the Chapultepec Agreement urged the Commission to pay particular attention to this area and to acts of violence committed by officers of the armed forces which were never investigated or punished. Thirdly, the Commission was given six months in which to perform its task.

If we consider that the Salvadorian conflict lasted 12 years and resulted in a huge number of deaths and other serious acts of violence, it was clearly impossible for the Commission to deal with every act that could have been included within its sphere of competence. In deciding to investigate one case rather than another, it had to weigh such considerations as the representative nature of the case, the availability of sufficient evidence, the investigatory resources available to the Commission, the time needed to conduct an exhaustive investigation and the issue of impunity as defined in the mandate.

B. Applicable Law

The Commission's mandate entrusts it with investigating *serious acts of violence*, but does not specify the principles of law that must be applied in order to define such acts and to determine responsibility for them. Nevertheless, the concept of serious acts of violence used in the peace agreements obviously does not exist in a normative vacuum and must therefore be analysed on the basis of certain relevant principles of law.

In defining the legal norms applicable to this task, it should be pointed out that, during the Salvadorian conflict, both Parties were under an obligation to observe a number of rules of international law, including those stipulated in international human rights law or in international humanitarian law, or in both. Furthermore, throughout the period in question, the State of El Salvador was under an obligation to adjust its domestic law to its obligations under international law.

These rules of international law must be considered as providing the basis for the criteria applicable to the functions which the peace agreements entrust to the Commission.[4] Throughout the Salvadorian conflict, these two sets of rules were only rarely mutually exclusive.

It is true that, in theory, international human rights law is applicable only to Governments, while in some armed conflicts international humanitarian law is binding on both sides: in other words, binding on both insurgents and Government forces. However, it must be recognized that when insurgents assume government powers in territories under their control, they too can be required to observe certain human rights obligations that are binding on the State under international law. This would make them responsible for breaches of those obligations.

The official position of FMLN was that certain parts of the national territory were under its control, and it did in fact exercise that control....

With few exceptions, serious acts of violence prohibited by the rules of humanitarian law applicable to the Salvadorian conflict are also violations of the non-repealable provisions of the International Covenant on Civil and Political Rights and the American Convention on Human Rights, the two human rights treaties ratified by the State of El Salvador. The two instruments also prohibit derogation from any rights guaranteed in any humanitarian law treaty to which the State is a party.

As a result, neither the Salvadorian State nor persons acting on its behalf or in its place can claim that the existence of an armed conflict justified the commission of serious acts of violence in contravention of one or other of the human rights treaties mentioned above or of the applicable instruments of humanitarian law binding on the State.

C. Methodology

In determining the methodology that would govern the conduct of the investigations essential to the preparation of this report, the Commission took a number of factors into account....

The preamble to the mandate indicates that the Commission was established because the Parties recognized "the need to clear up without

---

[4] It is important to mention that, in the San José Agreement on Human Rights, it was the understanding of the Parties to the peace agreements that "human rights" shall mean "those rights recognized by the Salvadorian legal system, including treaties to which El Salvador is a party, and by the declarations and principles on human rights and humanitarian law adopted by the United Nations and the Organization of American States".

delay those exceptionally important acts of violence whose characteristics and impact … urgently require that the complete truth be made known…".

In establishing the procedure that the Commission was to follow in performing its functions, paragraph 7 of the mandate provided that the Commission would conduct its activities "on a confidential basis". Paragraph 5 established that "The Commission shall not function in the manner of a judicial body". Paragraph 8 (a) stipulated that "The Commission shall be completely free to use whatever sources of information it deems useful and reliable", while paragraph 8 (b) gave the Commission the power to "Interview, freely and in private, any individuals, groups or members of organizations or institutions". Lastly, in the fourth preambular paragraph of the mandate, the Parties agreed that the task entrusted to the Commission should be fulfilled "through a procedure which is both reliable and expeditious and may yield results in the short term, without prejudice to the obligations incumbent on the Salvadorian courts to solve such cases and impose the appropriate penalties on the culprits".

In analysing these provisions of the mandate, the Commission thought it important that the Parties had emphasized that "the Commission shall not function in the manner of a judicial body". In other words, not only did the Parties not establish a court or tribunal, but they made it very clear that the Commission should not function as if it were a judicial body. They wanted to make sure that the Commission was able to act on a confidential basis and receive information from any sources, public or private, that it deemed useful and reliable. It was given these powers so that it could conduct an investigation procedure that was both expeditious and, in its view, reliable in order to "clear up without delay those exceptionally important acts of violence whose characteristics and impact … urgently require that the complete truth be made known…".

So it is clear that the Parties opted for an investigation procedure that, within the short period of time allotted, would be best fitted to establishing the truth about acts of violence falling within the Commission's sphere of competence, without requiring the Commission to observe the procedures and rules that normally govern the activities of any judicial or quasi-judicial body. Any judicial function that had to be performed would be reserved expressly for the courts of El Salvador. For the Parties, the paramount concern was to find out the truth without delay.

Another important overall consideration which influenced the Commission's methodology was the reality of the situation in El Salvador today[, which] had a profound impact on the Commission's investigation process and *modus operandi*. It forced the commission to gather its most valuable information in exchange for assurances of confidentiality.

It was not just that the Parties authorized the commission, in the peace agreements, to act on a confidential basis and to receive information in private; the reality of the situation in El Salvador forced it to do so for two reasons: first, to protect the lives of witnesses and, secondly, to obtain information from witnesses who, because of the climate of terror in which they continue to live, would not have provided such information if the Commission had not guaranteed them absolute confidentiality.

The situation in El Salvador is such that the population at large continues to believe that many military and police officers in active service or in retirement, Government officials, judges, members of FMLN and people who at one time or another were connected with the death squads are in a position to cause serious physical and material injury to any person or institution that shows a readiness to testify about acts of violence committed between 1980 and 1991. The Commission believes that this suspicion is not unreasonable, given El Salvador's recent history and the power still wielded or, in many cases, wielded until recently by people whose direct involvement in serious acts of violence or in covering up such acts is well known but who have not been required to account for their actions or omissions.

Even though the fears expressed by some potential witnesses may have been exaggerated, the fact is that in their minds the danger is real. As a result, they were not prepared to testify unless they were guaranteed absolute secrecy. It should be pointed out that many witnesses refused to give information to other investigatory bodies in the past precisely because they were afraid that their identity would be divulged.

The Commission can itself testify to the extreme fear of reprisals frequently expressed, both verbally and through their behaviour, by many of the witnesses it interviewed. It is also important to emphasize that the Commission was not in a position to offer any significant protection to witnesses apart from this guarantee of confidentiality. Unlike the national courts, for instance, the Commission did not have the authority to order precautionary measures; neither, of course, did it have police powers. Besides, it is the perception of the public at large that the Salvadorian judicial system is unable to offer the necessary guarantees.

The Commission also received reports from some Governments and international bodies, on condition that the source was not revealed. This information was subjected to the same test of reliability as the other information received and was used principally to confirm or verify personal testimony and to guide the Commission in its search for other areas of investigation.

From the outset the Commission was aware that accusations made and evidence received in secret run a far greater risk of being considered less trustworthy than those which are subjected to the normal judicial tests for determining the truth and to other related requirements of due process of law, including the right of the accused to confront and examine witnesses brought against him. Accordingly, the Commission felt that it had a special obligation to take all possible steps to ensure the reliability of the evidence used to arrive at a finding. In cases where it had to identify specific individuals as having committed, ordered or tolerated specific acts of violence, it applied a stricter test of reliability.

The Commission decided that, in each of the cases described in this report, it would specify the degree of certainty on which its ultimate finding was based. The different degrees of certainty were as follows:

1. Overwhelming evidence—conclusive or highly convincing evidence to support the Commission's finding;

2. Substantial evidence—very solid evidence to support the Commission's finding;

3. Sufficient evidence—more evidence to support the Commission's finding than to contradict it.

The Commission decided not to arrive at any specific finding on cases or situations, or any aspect thereof, in which there was less than "sufficient" evidence to support such a finding.

In order to guarantee the reliability of the evidence it gathered, the Commission insisted on verifying, substantiating and reviewing all statements as to facts, checking them against a large number of sources whose veracity had already been established. It was decided that no single source or witness would be considered sufficiently reliable to establish the truth on any issue of fact needed for the Commission to arrive at a finding. It was also decided that secondary sources, for instance, reports from national or international governmental or private bodies and assertions by people without first-hand knowledge of the facts they reported, did not on their own constitute a sufficient basis for arriving at findings. However, these secondary sources were used, along with circumstantial evidence, to verify findings based on primary sources.

It could be argued that, since the Commission's investigation methodology does not meet the normal requirements of due process, the report should not name the people whom the Commission considers to be implicated in specific acts of violence. The Commission believes that it had no alternative but to do so.

In the peace agreements, the Parties made it quite clear that it was necessary that the "complete truth be made known", and that was why the commission was established. After all, the Commission was not asked to write an academic report on El Salvador, it was asked to investigate and describe exceptionally important acts of violence and to recommend measures to prevent the repetition of such acts. This task, cannot be performed in the abstract, suppressing information (for instance, the names of persons responsible for such acts) where there is reliable testimony available, especially when the persons identified occupy senior positions and perform official functions directly related to violations or the cover-up of violations. Not to name names would be to reinforce the very impunity to which the Parties instructed the Commission put an end.

In weighing aspects related to the need to protect the lives of witnesses against the interests of people who might be adversely affected in some way by the publication of their names in the report, the Commission also took into consideration the fact that the report is not a judicial or quasijudicial determination as to the rights or obligations of certain individuals under the law. As a result, the Commission is not, in theory, subject to the requirements of due process which normally apply, in proceedings which produce these consequences.

Furthermore, the Commission's application of strict criteria to determine the degree of reliability of the evidence in situations where people have been identified by name, and the fact that it named names only when it was absolutely convinced by the evidence, were additional factors which influenced the Commission when it came to take a decision on this analysis. As a result, the Commission is satisfied that the criteria of impartiality and reliability which it applied throughout the process were fully compatible with the functions entrusted to it and with the interests it had to balance.

The considerations which prompted the Commission to receive confidential information without revealing the source also forced it to omit references from both the body and the footnotes of the reports on individual cases, with the exception of references to certain public, official sources. As a result, reference is made to official trial proceedings and other similar sources, but not to testimony or other information gathered by the Commission. The Commission took this approach in order to reduce the likelihood that those responsible for the acts of violence described herein, or their defenders, would be able to identify the confidential sources of information used by the Commission. In some of the reports on individual cases, the commission also omitted details that might reveal the identity of certain witnesses.

III. Chronology of the Violence...

IV. Cases and Patterns of Violence[125]

A. *General Overview of Cases and Patterns of Violence*

The Commission on the Truth registered more than 22,000 complaints of serious acts of violence that occurred in El Salvador between January 1980 and July 1991.[126] Over 7,000 were received directly at the Commission's offices in various locations. The remainder were received through governmental and non-governmental institutions.[127]

---

[125] In investigating and resolving the cases referred to below, Commssion members examined documents in El Salvador and other countries; interviewed numerous participants, witnesses, victims and relatives; requested information from Government bodies; consulted court dossiers; visited places where incidents had occurred; and requested copies of instructions and orders given.

Requests for precise information on various cases were transmitted to Ministers and heads of Government departments, and to what is now the former FMLN Command.

In the case of requests for reports that were not met and that in some cases referred to events prior to 1984, the Ministry of Defense informed the Commission that "no records exist since the General Staff was completely restructured in that year" (letter No. 10692, 27 November 1992). The Armed Forces Press Committee (COPREFA) told the Commission that it did not have any information for the period from January 1980 onwards and currently had available only the archive of press releases from January 1988 onwards (letter of 29 Ocober 1992).

The replies to requests made to FMLN were also, in some cases, incomplete. The former Command attributed the inability to provide precise information to the Commission to the irregular nature of the war and the consequent lack of records.

[126] A detailed analysis of complaints and lists of victims are to be found in the annexes. More than 18,000 complaints from indirect sources were also registered, of which over 13,000 were analysed. The figures for direct and indirect sources have not been added together. It is estimated that as many as 3,000 complaints were duplicated in the two sources. In any event the commission believes that the total number of complaints registered is at least 22,000.

[127] The Commission also received thousands of other complaints from institutions which, once registered, could not be analysed either because they did not meet the corresponding minimum requirements, even though institutions had been informed of these in good time, or because the incidents reported had occurred outside the period covered by the mandate.

Over 60 percent of all complaints concerned extrajudicial executions, over 25 percent concerned enforced disappearances, and over 20 percent included complaints of torture.

Those giving testimony attributed almost 85 percent of cases to agents of the State, paramilitary groups allied to them, and the death squads.

Armed forces personnel were accused in almost 60 percent of complaints, members of the security forces in approximately 25 percent, members of military escorts and civil defence units in approximately 20 percent, and members of the death squads in more than 10 percent of cases. The complaints registered accused FMLN in approximately 5 percent of cases.

Despite their large number, these complaints do not cover every act of violence. The Commission was able to receive only a significant sample in its three mouths of gathering testimony.

This also does not mean that each act occurred as described in the testimony. The commission investigated certain specific cases in particular circumstances, as well as overall patterns of violence. Some 30 of the cases dealt with in the report are illustrative of patterns of violence, in other words, involve systematic practices attested to by thousands of complainants.

Both the specific cases and the patterns of violence show that, during the 1980s, the country experienced an unusually high level of political violence. All Salvadorians without exception, albeit to differing degrees, suffered from this violence.

The introduction to the report and the section on methodology contain an explanation of this phenomenon.

Patterns of Violence by Agents of the State and their Collaborators

All the complaints indicate that this violence originated in a political mind-set that viewed political opponents as subversives and enemies. Anyone who expressed views that differed from the Government line ran the risk of being eliminated as if they were armed enemies on the field of battle. This situation is epitomized by the extrajudicial executions, enforced disappearances and murders of political opponents described in this chapter.

Any organization in a position to promote opposing ideas that questioned official policy was automatically labelled as working for the guerrillas. To belong to such an organization meant being branded a subversive.

Counter-insurgency policy found its most extreme expression in a general practice of "cutting the guerrillas' lifeline". The inhabitants of areas where the guerrillas were active were automatically suspected of belonging to the guerrilla movement or collaborating with it and thus ran the risk of being eliminated. El Mozote is a deplorable example of this practice, which persisted for some years.

In the early years of the decade, the violence in rural areas was indiscriminate in the extreme.

Roughly 50 percent of all the complaints analysed concern incidents which took place during the first two years, 1980 and 1981; more than 20 percent took place in the following two years, 1982 and 1983. In other words, over 75 percent of the serious acts of violence reported to the Commission on the Truth took place during the first four years of the decade.

The violence was less indiscriminate in urban areas, and also in rural areas after 1983 (95 percent of complaints concerned incidents in rural areas and 5 percent concerned incidents in more urban areas).

Patterns of FMLN Violence

The Commission registered more than 800 complaints of serious acts of violence attributed to FMLN. This violence occurred mainly in conflict zones, over which FMLN at times maintained firm military control.

Nearly half the complaints against FMLN concern deaths, mostly extrajudicial executions. The rest concern enforced disappearances and forcible recruitment.

The patterns show that this violence began with the armed conflict. It was considered legitimate to physically eliminate people who were labelled military targets, traitors or *orejas* (informers), and even political opponents. The murders of mayors, right-wing intellectuals, public officials and judges are examples of this mentality.

Members of a given guerrilla organization would investigate the activities of the person who might be designated a military target, a spy or a traitor; they would then make an evaluation and take a collective decision to execute that person; special groups or commandoes would plan the action and the execution would then be carried out. After the extrajudicial execution, the corresponding organization would publicly claim responsibility for propaganda purposes. FMLN called such executions "ajusticiamientos".

These executions were carried out without due process. The case of Romero García, alias Miguel Castellanos, in 1989 is typical of extrajudicial executions ordered by FMLN because the victims were considered traitors. He was not given a trial. After a time, FMLN claimed responsibility for having ordered the killing. It never revealed which organization had carried out the execution.

The killings of mayors and the murder of United States military personnel in the Zona Rosa were carried out in response to orders or general directives issued by the FMLN Command to its organizations.

In the Zona Rosa case in 1985, the execution of Mr. Peccorini in 1989, and the execution of Mr. García Alvarado that same year, different member organizations of FMLN interpreted general policy directives restrictively and applied them sporadically, thereby triggering an upsurge in the violence.

In the case of executions of mayors, on the other hand, instructions from the FMLN General Command were interpreted broadly and applied extensively. During the period 1985-1989, the Ejército Revolucionario del Pueblo repeatedly carried out extrajudicial executions of non-combatant civilians. There is no concept under international humanitarian law whereby such people could have been considered military targets.

The Commission was not able to verify the existence of general directives from the leadership to its constituent organizations authorizing enforced disappearances. It did receive complaints of some 300 cases of disappearance, which occurred mainly in areas where FMLN exercised greater military control. It was not possible to establish the existence of any pattern from an analysis of these complaints. Nevertheless, links were observed between disappearances, forcible recruitment by FMLN and cases of extrajudicial execution by FMLN members of individuals labelled spies or traitors.

The extrajudicial execution of the United States military personnel who survived the attack on their helicopter in San Miguel in 1991 cannot be viewed as the norm. FMLN admitted that some of its members had been responsible, and stated publicly that it had been a mistake. However, there is no record that those who carried out the execution were actually punished.

Lastly, although the number of complaints of the alleged use of land-mines by guerrilla forces was small, the Commission considered accusations made by various organizations against FMLN to that effect. Members of FMLN admitted to the Commission that they had laid mines with little or no supervision, so much so that civilians and their own members who were not sufficiently familiar with the location of minefields had been affected. The Commission did not find any other evidence an this subject.

B. Violence Against Opponents by Agents of the State

1. Illustrative Case: The Murders of the Jesuit Priests...

2. Extrajudicial Executions...

(b) The Leaders of the Frente Democratico Revolucionario

Summary of the Case

On 27 November 1980, Enrique Alvarez Córdoba,[133] Juan Chacón,[134] Enrique Escobar Barrera,[135] Manuel de Jesús Franco Ramírez,[136] Humberto Mendoza[137] and Doroteo Hernández,[138] political leaders of the Frente Democrático Revolucionario (FDR),[139] representing an important sector of Salvadorian society, were abducted, tortured and, after a short period in captivity, executed in San Salvador.

[133-138] [omitted]

[139] The Frente Democrático Revolucionario (FDR) came into being on 18 April 1980 as a result of a political agreement between the Frente Democrático (FD) and the Coordinadora Revolucionaria de Masas (CRM). It was formally established on 18 April 1980 by various political, popular and mass organizations. A number of its leaders had held prominent government posts in the first Revolutionary Junta which had overthrown General Romero on 15 October 1979. At the time, the leadership of FDR consisted of the five victims, Leoncio Pichinte and Juan José Martel.

The abduction was carried out during the morning at the Colegio San José by a large number of heavily armed men....

...Findings

The Commission finds that:

1. The abduction, torture and subsequent murder of the political and trade union leaders was an act that outraged national and international public opinion and closed the door to any possibility of a negotiated solution to the political crisis at the end of 1980. It was a very serious act which warranted the most thorough investigation by the Commission on the Truth.

2. It is not possible to determine precisely which public security force carried out these criminal operations. Nevertheless, the Commission considers that there is sufficient evidence to indicate that State bodies were jointly responsible for this incident, which violated international human rights law.

3. The Commission has substantial evidence that the Treasury Police carried out the external security operation which aided and abetted those who committed the murders.

4. There has been an obvious lack of interest in ordering an exhaustive investigation by an independent State organ to clarify the facts, find out who was responsible and bring those responsible to justice.

(c) The American Churchwomen

Summary of the Case

On 2 December 1980, members of the National Guard of El Salvador arrested four churchwomen after they left the international airport. Churchwomen Ita Ford, Maura Clarke, Dorothy Kazel and Jean Donovan were taken to an isolated spot and subsequently executed by being shot at close range.

In 1984, Deputy Sergeant Luis Antonio Colindres Alemán and National Guard members Daniel Canales Ramírez, Carlos Joaquín Contreras Palacios, Francisco Orlando Contreras Recinos and José Roberto Moreno Canjura were sentenced to 30 years in prison for murder....[149]

...Findings

The Commission on the Truth finds that:

1. There is sufficient evidence that:

(a) The arrest of the churchwomen at the airport was planned prior to their arrival.

---

[149] The Commission on the Truth interviewed eyewitnesses, diplomats, senior commanders of the National Guard and the armed forces, members of the Maryknoll Order, relatives of the victims, lawyers for the defendants and the churchwomen's relatives, and a member of the court assigned to the case. In addition, the court dossier was reviewed and governmental and non-governmental reports were analysed. Colonel Zepeda Velasco was invited, unsuccessfully, to testify on several occasions.

(b) In arresting and executing the four churchwomen, Deputy Sergeant Luis Antonio Colindres Alemán was acting on orders of a superior.

2. There is substantial evidence that:

(a) Then Colonel Carlos Eugenio Vides Casanova, Director-General of the National Guard, Lieutenant Colonel Oscar Edgardo Casanova Vejar, Commander of the Zacatecoluca military detachment, Colonel Roberto Monterrosa, Major Lizandro Zepeda Velasco and Sergeant Dagoberto Martínez, among other officers, knew that members of the National Guard had committed the murders and, through their actions, facilitated the cover-up of the facts which obstructed the corresponding judicial investigation.

(b) The Minister of Defence at the time, General José Guillermo García, made no serious effort to conduct a thorough investigation of responsibility for the murders of the churchwomen.

(c) Local commissioner José Dolores Meléndez also knew of the murders and covered up for the members of the security forces who committed them.

3. The State of El Salvador failed in its obligation under international human rights law to investigate the case, to bring to trial those responsible for ordering and carrying out the executions and, lastly, to compensate the victims, relatives.

(d) El Junquillo

Summary of the Case

On 3 March 1981, a military operation took place in the north of the Department of Morazán. Units under Captain Carlos Napoleón Medina Garay arrived at El Junquillo and stayed there for 8 to 12 days. On leaving, Captain Medina Garay ordered the execution of the civilian population in El Junquillo canton.

On 12 March 1981, soldiers and members of the Cacaopera civil defence unit attacked the population, consisting solely of women, young children and old people. They killed the inhabitants and raped a number of women and little girls under the age of 12. They set fire to houses, cornfields and barns....[167]

---

[167] In view of the total absence of investigations into the El Junquillo massacre, on 28 November 1992 the Commission on the Truth asked the Minister of Defence and Public Security, General Réne Emilio Ponce, to provide the Commission with the following information: details of the military units which took part in the military operation carried out between 10 and 12 March 1981 in the cantons of Agua Blanca and El Junquillo in the district of Cacaopera, Department of Morazán; the names of those responsible for ordering the operation and the orders they gave, together with the duties assigned to each military unit; the names of officers, non-commissioned officers and soldiers and the duties assigned to them; a copy of the operations report received by the Armed Forces General Staff and/or the Ministry of Defence concerning the results of the operation, together with the information available to the Ministry of Defence on the events which occurred in El Junquillo canton and in the hamlet of Flor Muerto in Agua Blanca canton, district of Cacaopera, Department of Morazán, between 10 and 12 March 1981.

At the time of drafting of this report, no reply to this request had been received from the Minister of Defence and Public Security.

...Findings

The commission finds that:

...There is full evidence that the Government, the armed forces and the judiciary of El Salvador failed to conduct investigations into the incident. The State thus failed in its duty under international human rights law to investigate, bring to trial and punish those responsible and to compensate the victims or their families.

The Minister of Defence and Public Security, General René Emilio Ponce, is responsible for failing to provide this Commission with information on the military operation carried out in the area of El Junquillo canton, thereby failing to honour the obligation to cooperate with the Commission on the Truth entered into by the Government when it signed the peace agreements, and thus far preventing the identification of other soldiers who took part in the massacre....

3. Enforced Disappearances...

(c) Chan Chan and Massi

Summary of the Case

The Commission on the Truth received abundant complaints of disappearances and studied most of them in depth. The present case is symptomatic of the disregard shown for family values, family feelings, maternal grief and trade union solidarity, which is why the commission chose to focus on it....

C. *Massacres of Peasants by the Armed Forces*

In 1980, 1981 and 1982, several massacres of peasants were carried out by troops of the armed forces of El Salvador. An account of three of them follows.

1. Illustrative Case: El Mozote

Summary of the Case

On 10 December 1981, in the village of El Mozote in the Department of Morazán, units of the Atlacatl Battalion detained, without resistance, all the men, women and children who were in the place. The following day, 11 December, after spending the night locked in their homes, they were deliberately and systematically executed in groups. First, the men were

---

The Commission received testimony from persons who made statements concerning the events that took place in El Junquillo canton and from other persons from whom the witnesses had sought assistance. It also requested information from the Government of El Salvador and from Military Detachment No. 6 at Sonsonate, and summonsed an army officer. No reply was received to the request for information and the officer concerned failed to appear.

All the above factors were taken into consideration.

tortured and executed, then the women were executed and, lastly, the children, in the place where they had been locked up. The number of victims identified was over 200. The figure is higher if other unidentified victims are taken into account.

These events occurred in the course of an anti-guerrilla action known as "Operación Rescate" in which, in addition to the Atlacatl Battalion, units from the Third Infantry Brigade and the San Francisco Gotera Commando Training Centre took part.

In the course of "Operación Rescate", massacres of civilians also occurred in the following places: 11 December, more than 20 people in La Joya canton; 12 December, some 30 people in the village of La Ranchería; the same day, by units of the Atlacatl Battalion, the inhabitants of the village of Los Toriles; and 13 December, the inhabitants of the village of Jocote Amarillo and Cerro Pando canton. More than 500 identified victims perished at El Mozote and in the other villages. Many other victims have not been identified.

We have accounts of these massacres provided by eyewitnesses and by other witnesses who later saw the bodies, which were left unburied. In the case of El Mozote, the accounts were fully corroborated by the results of the 1992 exhumation of the remains.

Despite the public complaints of a massacre and the ease with which they could have been verified, the Salvadorian authorities did not order an investigation and consistently denied that the massacre had taken place.

The Minister of Defence and the Chief of the Armed Forces Joint Staff have denied to the Commission on the Truth that they have any information that would make it possible to identify the units and officers who participated in "Operación Rescate". They say that there are no records for the period.

The President of the Supreme Court has interfered in a biased and political way in the judicial proceedings on the massacre instituted in 1990....

2. Sumpul River

Summary of the Case

On 14 May 1990, units of Military Detachment No. 1, the National Guard and the paramilitary Organización Nacional Democrática (ORDEN) deliberately killed at least 300 non-combatants, including women and children, who were trying to flee to Honduras across the Sumpul river beside the hamlet of Las Aradas, Department of Chalatenango. The massacre was made possible by the cooperation of the Honduran armed forces, who prevented the Salvadorian villagers from landing on the other side.

The Salvadorian military operation had begun the previous day as an anti-guerrilla operation. Troops advanced from various points, gradually converging on the hamlet of Las Aradas on the banks of the Sumpul river. In the course of the operation, there had been a number of encounters with the guerrillas.

There is sufficient evidence that, as they advanced, Government forces committed acts of violence against the population, and this caused numerous people to flee, many of whom congregated in the hamlet, consisting of some dozen houses.

Troops attacked the hamlet with artillery and fire from two helicopters. The villagers and other people displaced by the operation attempted to cross the Sumpul river to take refuge in Honduras. Honduran troops deployed on the opposite bank of the river barred their way. They were then killed by Salvadorian troops who fired on them in cold blood....

Action taken by the Commission

The Commission received some 100 direct testimonies on the incident and examined an equivalent number of testimonies presented to other organizations. It examined the documentation available, including photographs, and interviewed the original complainants. A Commission official travelled to Honduras to gather direct testimony. Members of the Commission personally inspected the scene of the massacre.

The Commission repeatedly requested the cooperation of the Salvadorian military authorities in conducting the investigation, but the only reply it received was that there were no records for that period. The Commander of Military Detachment No. 1 at the time, Colonel Ricardo Augusto Peña Arbaiza, was summonsed to testify but did not appear.

Findings

...The Commission believes that the Salvadorian military authorities were guilty of a cover-up of the incident. There is sufficient evidence that colonel Ricardo Augusto Peña Arbaiza, Commander of Military Detachment No. 1 in May 1980, made no serious investigation of the incident.

The Sumpul river massacre was a serious violation of international humanitarian law and international human rights law....

4. Pattern of Conduct

In addition to the massacres described here, the Commission received direct testimony concerning numerous other mass executions that occurred during the years 1980, 1981 and 1982, in which members of the armed forces, in the course of anti-guerrilla operations, executed peasants—men, women and children who had offered no resistance—simply because they considered them to be guerrilla collaborators.

Because the number of such individual and group executions is so high and the reports are so thoroughly substantiated, the Commission rules out any possibility that these might have been isolated incidents where soldiers or their immediate superiors went to extremes.

Everything points to the fact that these deaths formed part of a pattern of conduct, a deliberate strategy of eliminating or terrifying the peasant population in areas where the guerrillas were active, the purpose being to deprive the guerrilla forces of this source of supplies and information and of the possibility of hiding or concealing themselves among that population.

It is impossible to blame this pattern of conduct on local commanders and, to claim that senior commanders did not know anything about it. As we have described, massacres of the peasant population were reported repeatedly. There is no evidence that any effort was made to investigate them. The authorities dismissed these reports as enemy propaganda. Were it not for the children's skeletons at El Mozote, some people would still be disputing that such massacres took place.

Those small skeletons are proof not only of the existence of the cold-blooded massacre at El Mozote but also of the collusion of senior commanders of the armed forces, for they show that the evidence of the unburied bodies was there for a long time for anyone who wanted to investigate the facts. In this case, we cannot accept the excuse that senior commanders knew nothing of what had happened.

No action was taken to avoid incidents such as this. On the contrary, the deliberate, systematic and indiscriminate violence against the peasant population in areas of military operations went on for years.

D. Death Squad Assassinations

1. Illustrative Case: Archbishop Romero (1980)...

2. The Death Squad Pattern

The Commission on the Truth received a great many complaints of serious acts of violence allegedly perpetrated by death squads. The direct testimony received concerns a total of 817 victims of abductions, disappearances and executions that occurred between 1980 and 1991.[415]

There is no question that what have been classified as murders committed by the death squads in rural areas account for a significant proportion of all killings in El Salvador between 1980 and 1991. The Commission on the Truth has obtained extensive information from the testimony of many witnesses, including several members of the armed forces and civilian members of the death squads, who admitted and gave details of their involvement at the highest levels in the organization, operation and financing of the death squads.

The undeniable impact of the extensive evidence received about the death squads leads us to share the fervent conviction of the Salvadorian people that it is crucial not only to comprehend the scope of this phenomenon in El Salvador but also to inform the international community about what it was that, by commission or omission, caused the death squads to insinuate themselves so perniciously into the formal State structure. Decisive action is needed to root out this infamous phenomenon that has so grievously compromised human rights.

Between 1980 and 1991, human rights violations were committed in a systematic and organized manner by groups acting as death squads. The

---

[415] Of these 817 cases, 644 (79 percent) were extrajudicial executions.

members of such groups usually wore civilian clothing, were heavily armed, operated clandestinely and hid their affiliation and identity. They abducted members of the civilian population and of rebel groups. They tortured their hostages, were responsible for their disappearance and usually executed them.[416]

The death squads, in which members of State structures were actively involved or to which they turned a blind eye, gained such control that they ceased to be an isolated or marginal phenomenon and became an instrument of terror used systematically for the physical elimination of political opponents. Many of the civilian and military authorities in power during the 1980s participated in, encouraged and tolerated the activities of these groups. Although there is no evidence of latent structures for these clandestine organizations, they could be reactivated when those in high Government circles issue warnings that might trigger the resumption of a dirty war in El Salvador. Since the death squad phenomenon was the problem *par excellence* of that dirty war which ultimately destroyed all vestiges of the rule of law during the armed conflict, the Salvadorian Government must not only be ready and willing to prevent the resurgence of this phenomenon but also seek international cooperation in eradicating it completely.[417]...

...Findings

Because of the clandestine nature of their operations, it is not easy to establish all the links existing between private businessmen and the death squads. However, the Commission on the Truth has absolutely no doubt that a close relationship existed, or that the possibility that businessmen or members of moneyed families might feel the need and might be able to act with impunity in financing murderous paramilitary groups, as they did in the past, poses a threat to the future of Salvadorian society.

At the same time, it must be pointed out that the United States Government tolerated, and apparently paid little official heed to the activities of Salvadorian exiles living in Miami, especially between 1979 and 1983. According to testimony received by the Commission, this group of exiles directly financed and indirectly helped run certain death squads. It would be useful if other investigators with more resources and more time were to shed light on this tragic story so as to ensure that persons linked to terrorist acts in other countries are never tolerated again in the United States.

1. The State of El Salvador, through the activities of members of the armed forces and/or civilian officials, is responsible for having taken part in, encouraged and tolerated the operations of the death squads which illegally attacked members of the civilian population.

2. Salvadorian institutions must make serious efforts to investigate the structural connection that has been found to exist between the death squads and State bodies. The fact that there are hundreds of former civil defence

---

[416] Left-wing actions that fell into the same category as violence perpetrated by the death squads are dealt with in the section of this report on abuses committed by the guerrillas.

[417] For details of how the death squads operated, see the account in this report of the assassinations of Monsignor Oscar Arnulfo Romero and Mario Zamora and the Sheraton case.

members in rural areas who are still armed is particular cause for concern. These people could easily mobilize to commit new acts of violence in future if they are not clearly identified and disarmed.

3. It is especially important to call attention to the repeated abuses committed by the intelligence services of the security forces and the armed forces. It is crucial for the future of El Salvador that the State pay attention to the use of intelligence services and to the exploitation of this arm of the Government to identify targets for murder or disappearance. Any investigation must result both in an institutional clean-up of the intelligence services and in the identification of those responsible for this aberrant practice.

4. The lack of effective action by the judicial system was a factor that reinforced the impunity that shielded and continues to shield members and promoters of the death squads in El Salvador.

5. The links of some private businessmen and moneyed families to the funding and use of death squads must be clarified.

6. The Government must recognize that, given their organizational structure and the fact that they possess weapons, there is a serious danger that the death squads may become involved, as has happened in some cases, in illegal activities such as drug trafficking, arms trafficking and abductions for ransom.

7. The issue of the death squads in El Salvador is so important that it requires special investigation. More resolute action by national institutions, with the cooperation and assistance of foreign authorities who have any information on the subject, is especially needed. In order to verify a number of specific violations and ascertain who was responsible, it will be necessary to investigate the serious acts of violence committed by death squads on a case-by-case basis.

E. Violence Against Opponents by the Frente Farabundo Marti Para La Liberacion Nacional

This section deals with the use of violence by FMLN against real or alleged opponents in violation of the rules of international humanitarian law and international human rights law. It covers the use of violence against non-combatants and also the execution of alleged criminals without due process.

The section begins with a representative case, the execution of mayors in conflict zones. Then, after an explanation of the pattern observed in this type of violence, an account follows of some of the cases attributed to FMLN which had a major impact on Salvadorian society. In some cases, it has not been possible to prove who planned the attacks, in others it is impossible to determine, or to determine with certainty, who carried them out....

V. Recommendations

Introduction

As part of its mandate, the Commission is called upon to make recommendations. Indeed, under the terms of its mandate,

> The mandate of the Commission shall include recommending the legal, political or administrative measures which can be inferred from the results of the investigation. Such recommendations may include measures to prevent the repetition of such acts, and initiatives to promote national reconciliation.

The Commission decided to first comment generally on the results of its investigations, the principles on which these investigations and its recommendations are based and the persons and institutions to whom they are addressed, before making specific recommendations.

1. General Conclusions

The causes and conditions which generated the large number of serious acts of violence in El Salvador derive from very complex circumstances. The country's history and its deeply rooted relations of injustice cannot be attributed simply to one sector of the population or one group of persons. This or that Government institution, certain historical traditions, even the ideological struggle between East and West which went on until only recently, and of which El Salvador was a victim and an episode, are mere components. All these factors help to explain the complex situation in El Salvador during the 12-year period which concerns us. The Commission was not called upon to deal with all these factors, nor could it do so. Instead, it focused on certain considerations which prompted it to formulate its basic recommendations in such a way that this situation might be fully understood.

The lack of human rights guarantees in El Salvador and the fact that a society has operated outside the principles of a State subject to the rule of law imposes a serious responsibility on the Salvadorian State itself, rather than on one or other of its Governments. The political, legislative and institutional mechanisms required to ensure the existence of a society subject to the rule of law existed in theory, at least in part, but the reality was not what it should have been, perhaps as a consequence of excessive pragmatism. With the passage of time, the military establishment and, more specifically, some elements within the armed forces, having embarked upon a course from which they found it difficult to extricate themselves, ended up totally controlling the civilian authorities, frequently in collusion with some influential civilians.

None of the three branches of Government—judicial, legislative or executive—was capable of restraining the military's overwhelming control of society. The judiciary was weakened as it fell victim to intimidation and the foundations were laid for its corruption; since it had never enjoyed genuine institutional independence from the legislative and executive branches, its ineffectiveness steadily increased until it became, through its inaction or its appalling submissiveness, a factor which contributed to the tragedy suffered by the country. The various, frequently opportunistic, alliances which political leaders (legislators as well as members of the executive branch) forged with the military establishment and with members of the judiciary had the effect of further weakening civilian control over the military, police and security forces, all of which formed part of the military establishment.

The wide network of illegal armed groups, known as "death squads", which operated both within and outside the institutional framework with complete impunity, spread terror throughout Salvadorian society. They originated basically as a civilian operation, designed, financed and controlled by civilians. The core of serving officers, whose role was originally limited to that of mere executants and executioners, gradually seized control of the death squads for personal gain or to promote certain ideological or political objectives. Thus, within the military establishment and in contradiction with its real purpose and mandate, impunity *vis-à-vis* the civilian authorities became the rule. The institution as a whole was a hostage to specific groups of officers, which were sometimes formed even as their members graduated from officer training school, abused their power and their relations with certain civilian circles and intimidated fellow officers who were reluctant to join in or to collaborate with their corrupt and illegal practices.

The internal armed conflict between opposing forces grew in intensity and magnitude. The inevitable outcome was acts of violence, some of which were brought before the Commission with anxiety and anticipation. The more bloody the conflict became, and the more widespread, the greater the power of the military hierarchy and of those who commanded armed insurgent groups. The outcome of that vicious circle was a situation in which certain elements of society found themselves immune from any governmental or political restraints and thus forged for themselves the most abject impunity. It was they who wielded the real power of the State, expressed in the most primitive terms, while the executive, legislative and judicial branches were unable to play any real role as branches of government. The sad fact is that they were transformed, in practice, into mere façades with marginal governmental authority.

How else can the *modus operandi* of the death squads be understood? The disappearance of large numbers of people, the assassination attempts on important Government officials, church leaders and judges, and the fact that the perpetrators of these atrocities were only rarely brought to trial. What is ironic is that the web of corruption, timidity and weakness within the judiciary and its investigative bodies greatly impeded the effective functioning of the judicial system even where crimes attributed to FMLN were involved.

In order to avoid any risk of reverting to the *status quo ante*, it is essential that El Salvador establish and strengthen the proper balance of power among the executive, legislative and judicial branches and that it institute full and indisputable civilian control over all military, paramilitary, intelligence and security forces. The recommendations which follow are intended to outline the basic prerequisites for this transition and to ensure that it leads to a democratic society in which the rule of law prevails and human rights are fully respected and guaranteed.

2. Principles

The report which the Commission is submitting is part of a process initiated, according to the Geneva Agreement of 4 April 1990, for the purpose of ending the armed conflict by political means as speedily as possible, promoting the democratization of the country, guaranteeing unrestricted respect for human rights and reunifying Salvadorian society. The first of these objectives has already been achieved. The remaining goals, however, require a continuous and, in some respects, permanent effort. These goals are complementary: democracy loses ground when human rights are not fully respected; human rights cannot be protected from arbitrariness without the rule of law which is the expression of the democratic system of government; and unless rights and freedoms are respected and guaranteed for all, it will be difficult to speak of a reunified society.

The Commission's recommendations, while they bear fully on the results of its investigations, provide the means for pursuing these objectives, which were defined in the context of the country's recent history by the Salvadorians who negotiated the peace agreements, and by the decisive majority which supported them, as the objectives which must be achieved in the society which they are now beginning to build. Accordingly, these recommendations are based on the following principles:

One: Democracy, which leaves the fundamental decisions as to the destiny of society in the hands of the people, and which gives priority to dialogue and negotiation as basic political tools.

Two: Participation, which integrates minorities with the majority and gives pride of place to democracy as a model respectful of the individual and collective dimensions of human coexistence; also, a participation which promotes solidarity and respect among individuals.

Three: The rule of law, in which the primacy of and respect for the law is the basis of a culture which guarantees equality and proscribes all arbitrariness.

Four: Respect for human rights, which are the *raison d'être* of the above principles and the basis of a society organized to serve people, all of whom are vested with equal freedom and dignity.

The consolidation of the supremacy of civilian authority in Salvadorian society and the necessary subordination of the armed forces to it stem directly from the democratic concept of the rule of law, the primordial value of the dignity of the human person and, hence, full respect for his rights.

The peace agreements envisage a new concept of national defence and public security which represents significant progress towards establishing the supremacy of civilian authority. It is essential that all, absolutely all, the agreements on these issues be complied with fully.

The Commission also underscores the special care which must be taken in implementing the provisions of the peace agreements, and the recommendations in this report, for strengthening a comprehensive system for the protection of human rights and an independent, strong and effective judiciary. The glaring deficiencies experienced by the country in this regard were a prime cause of the occurrence and systematic repetition of extremely grave human rights violations, and such violations will be deemed to have been completely eradicated only when this objective is achieved....

I. Recommendations Inferred Directly From the Results of the Investigation

...The Commission makes the following recommendations which must be carried out without delay:

A. Dismissal From the Armed Forces

The findings on the cases investigated by the Commission on the Truth and published in this report give the names of officers of the Salvadorian armed forces who are personally implicated in the perpetration or cover-up of serious acts of violence, or who did not fulfill their professional obligation to initiate or cooperate in the investigation and punishment of such acts. For those officers who are still serving in the armed forces, the Commission recommends that they be dismissed from their posts and discharged from the armed forces. For those now in retirement or discharged, the Commission recommends application of the measure described in paragraph C below.

B. Dismissal From the Civil Service

The findings on the cases investigated by the Commission on the Truth also give the names of civilian officials in the civil service and the judiciary. These officials, acting in their professional capacity, covered up serious acts of violence or failed to discharge their responsibilities in the investigation of such acts. For these persons, the Commission recommends that they be dismissed from the civil service or judicial posts they currently occupy. For those who no longer occupy such posts, the Commission recommends application of the measure described in paragraph C below.

C. Disqualification From Holding Public Office

Under no circumstances would it be advisable to allow persons who committed acts of violence such as those which the Commission has investigated to participate in the running of the State. The Commission therefore believes that the persons referred to in the preceding paragraphs, as well as any others equally implicated in the perpetration of the acts of violence described in this report, including the civilians and members of the FMLN Command named in the findings on individual cases, should be disqualified from holding any public post or office for a period of not less than 10 years, and should be disqualified permanently from any activity related to public security or national defence. While the Commission does not have the power to apply such a provision directly, it does have the power to recommend to the National Commission for the Consolidation of Peace (COPAZ) that it prepare a preliminary legislative draft on this issue, offering proper guarantees in accordance with Salvadorian law, and that it submit such draft to the Legislative Assembly for early approval. It also has the power to recommend to the bodies authorized to make appointments to public office that they refrain from appointing the persons referred to above.

D. Judicial Reform

All aspects of the agreed judicial reform must be put into practice. Even if this reform must be complemented by additional measures, some of which will be the subject of other recommendations by the Commission, the agreements reached on this issue during the peace process must be complied with immediately and in full. Two specific aspects should be noted:

(a) Reform of the Supreme Court of Justice

The constitutional reform approved as part of the peace process provided a new procedure for the election of judges to the Supreme Court of Justice, the body which heads the judicial branch. Those innovations cannot be put into effect until the current judges' terms expire, with the result that the Court continues to consist of persons elected in accordance with the rules that applied before the constitutional reform and the peace agreements. Given the tremendous responsibility which the judiciary bears for the impunity with which serious acts of violence such as those described in this report occurred, there is no justification for further postponing the appointment of a new Supreme Court of Justice, whose current members should make way for the immediate implementation of the constitutional reform by resigning from their posts.

(b) National Council of the Judiciary

The peace agreements provided for the establishment of a National Council of the Judiciary independent from the organs of State and from political parties.... However, the National Council of the Judiciary Act, adopted in December 1992 by the Legislative Assembly, contains provisions which, in practice, leave the dismissal of some members of that Council to the discretion of the Supreme Court of Justice. The Commission recommends that this system be changed and that it be possible to dismiss members of the Council only for precise legal causes, to be weighed by the Legislative Assembly which, being the body constitutionally authorized to appoint such members, should, logically, also be the one to decide on their dismissal.

E. Judges

The Career Judicial Service Act, the amendment of which, the Commission understands, is under discussion for the date on which this report will be submitted, should establish that only those judges who, according to a rigorous evaluation made by the National Council of the Judiciary, have demonstrated judicial aptitude, efficiency and concern for human rights and offer every guarantee of independence, judicial discretion, honesty and impartiality in their actions may remain in the career judicial service.

F. Penalties

One of the direct consequences of the clarification of the serious acts which the Commission has investigated should, under normal circumstances, be the punishment which those responsible for such acts deserve....

One painfully clear aspect of that situation is the glaring inability of the judicial system either to investigate crimes or to enforce the law, especially when it comes to crimes committed with the direct or indirect support of State institutions. It was because these shortcomings were so apparent that the Government and FMLN agreed to create an instrument such as the Commission on the Truth to perform tasks which should normally be undertaken by the bodies responsible for the administration of justice.... The inability of the courts to apply the law to acts of violence committed under the direct or indirect cover of the public authorities is part and parcel of the situation in which those acts took place and is inseparable from them. This is a conclusion which emerges clearly from most of the cases of this kind examined in this report.

[T]he judiciary is still run by people whose omissions were part of the situation which must now be overcome, and there is nothing to indicate that their customary practices will change in the near future.

These considerations confront the Commission with a serious dilemma. The question is not whether the guilty should be punished, but whether justice can be done. Public morality demands that those responsible for the crimes described here be punished. However, El Salvador has no system for the administration of justice which meets the minimum requirements of objectivity and impartiality so that justice can be rendered reliably. This is a part of the country's current reality and overcoming it urgently should be a primary objective for Salvadorian society.

The Commission does not believe that a reliable solution can be found to the problems it has examined by tackling them in the context which is primarily responsible for them. The situation described in this report would not have occurred if the judicial system had functioned properly. Clearly, that system has still not changed enough to foster a feeling of justice which could promote national reconciliation. On the contrary, a judicial debate in the current context, far from satisfying a legitimate desire for justice, could revive old frustrations, thereby impeding the achievement of that cardinal objective, reconciliation. That being the current situation, it is clear that, for now, the only judicial system which the Commission could trust to administer justice in a full and timely manner would be one which had been restructured in the light of the peace agreements.

II. Eradication of Structural Causes
Linked Directly to the Acts Examined

The peace process led to a set of political agreements which are clearly supported by society as a whole and which introduce major structural reforms and address many defects which contributed to the situation described in this report. As a general principle, the Commission recommends most emphatically that all the agreements be implemented in full: that was the undertaking made by those who negotiated and concluded the agreements and it is also what the Salvadorian people expects, believes in and hopes for.

Without prejudice to these general comments, the Commission wishes to make some additional recommendations:

A. Reforms in the Armed Forces

1. The transition to the new model of the armed forces outlined in the peace agreements and in the constitutional reform should be made rapidly and transparently, under the close supervision of the civilian authorities. It is recommended that a special committee of the Legislative Assembly be appointed for that purpose, comprising the various political forces represented in the Assembly. Special attention should be paid to the subordination of the military establishment to the civilian authorities, democratic control over promotions to senior ranks and positions of command, rigorous budgetary management, greater decentralization of the military structure, application of the new doctrine and new educational system of the armed forces and steady professionalization of officers.

2. The comprehensive review of the military legislation in force should be completed without delay, in order to bring it fully into line with the new Political Constitution, the new doctrine of the armed forces and the requirements of respect for human rights.

3. Among the reforms referred to in the preceding paragraph, a simple and practical mechanism must be established to resolve the situation of subordinates who receive illegal orders, so that they are protected if they refuse to obey. The provision of article 173 of army regulations which requires a subordinate to obey, at all times and irrespective of risk, the orders he receives from a superior, should be repealed, and the pledge so to obey should be eliminated from the formula used when swearing the solemn oath of allegiance to the flag as part of military ceremonial. It must be made clear, in any case, that so-called "due obedience" does not exonerate a person who carries out an order which is clearly illegal.

4. The above-mentioned reforms should also provide that all actions whereby members of the armed forces take advantage of their status to commit abuses of power or violations of human rights are to be regarded as serious offences against the military institution, and should stipulate the administrative and legal penalties to which the perpetrators are liable, including discharge, without prejudice to the imposition of the corresponding criminal penalties, where appropriate. A strict system of discharges should not allow persons who have been discharged for the type

of conduct described, or for other reasons which adversely affect the service or the institution, to be readmitted to the institution.

5. Military curricula, from the Military College to General Staff courses, should include thorough training in human rights. The assistance of a highly qualified civilian teaching staff will be required for this.

6. In selecting advanced training courses for officers of the armed forces to follow abroad, care will have to be taken to ensure that such courses are based on a doctrine of democracy and respect for human rights.

7. The armed forces Court of Honour created by the peace agreements should give priority to the eradication of any vestige of a relationship between serving and retired members of the armed forces and now-disbanded paramilitary bodies or any illegal armed group.

B. Reforms in the Area of Public Security

One of the prominent features of the peace agreements was the decision to disband the former public security forces (CUSEP), which were organically linked to the armed forces, and to entrust civilian security to the National Civil Police, a new and absolutely civilian entity. The Commission recommends most emphatically that the guidelines for the new body be scrupulously observed. The demilitarization of the police is a big step forward in El Salvador and it must be ensured that there are no links between the National Civil Police and the former security forces or any other branch of the armed forces.

C. Investigation of Illegal Groups

One of the most horrendous sources of the violence which swept the country in recent years was the activity of private armed groups which operated with complete impunity. All necessary measures must be taken to ensure that they are disbanded. Given the country's history, prevention is essential in this area. There is always a risk that such groups may become active again. The Commission recommends that a thorough investigation of this issue be undertaken immediately and that, since the newly established National Civil Police is still in its early stages, assistance be sought, through channels which the confidentiality of the issue requires, from the police of friendly countries which are in a position to offer it.

III. Institutional Reforms to Prevent the Repetition of Such Acts

This too is an issue which is intrinsically linked to the implementation of the reforms agreed to in all the peace agreements, which are designed to provide the country with a modern, democratic institutional framework adapted to the requirements of the rule of law.

The Commission believes, however, that there are some points which should be emphasized, either because of their importance or because they were not clearly resolved in the peace agreements.

A. Administration of Justice

One of the most pressing requirements if democracy in El Salvador is to be consolidated into the genuine rule of law is the transformation of its judicial system. The judicial reform programmes currently being worked out should be intensified and put into practice as soon as possible. The effort which the Ministry of Justice is making to link judicial reform to the democratization process is highly commendable and should be carried to its conclusion.

There are also some issues which are important enough to warrant a separate comment by the Commission:

1. One of the most glaring deficiencies which must be overcome in the Salvadorian judicial system is the tremendous concentration of functions in the Supreme Court of Justice, and in its President in particular, as the body which heads the judiciary. This concentration of functions seriously undermines the independence of lower court judges and lawyers, to the detriment of the system as a whole. The formal origin of this problem is constitutional, with the result that solving it requires analysing whether the relevant provisions should be amended, through the procedure provided for in the Constitution itself, so that the Court, without losing its status as the country's highest court, is not also the administrative head of the judiciary.

2. Judges should not be appointed and removed by the Supreme Court of Justice, but by an independent National Council of the Judiciary.

3. Each judge should be responsible for administering the resources of the court under his jurisdiction and should be accountable for them to the National Council of the Judiciary.

4. The functions of granting authorization to practice as a lawyer or notary and suspending or penalizing members of those professions should be attributed to a special independent body and not to the Supreme Court of Justice.

5. The budget allocation for the administration of justice provided for in the Constitution should be used to create new courts and improve judges' salaries.

6. The Commission recommends the adoption of the following measures to reinforce the application of the right to due process:

(a) Invalidate extrajudicial confessions.

(b) Ensure that accused persons, in all circumstances, exercise their right to be presumed innocent.

(c) Ensure strict compliance with the maximum time-limits for police and judicial detention, establishing immediate penalties for violators.

(d) Reinforce exercise of the right to defence starting from the very first actions in a proceeding.

7. The utmost priority should be given to the proper functioning of the Judicial Training School, conceived as a study centre not only for professional training but also to establish bonds of solidarity among judges and a coherent overall vision of the function of the judiciary in the State—to quote the peace agreements. There is also a short-term need to train new, sound human resources to staff new courts or to replace members of the

judiciary who, according to the evaluation which the Commission has recommended, should not remain in the judiciary. This is an area susceptible to constructive, tangible international cooperation. The Commission calls on those in a position to offer such assistance to do so without delay, as part of an accelerated programme of implementation, and even ventures to appeal first and foremost to the European Economic Community, because of the similarities between the Salvadorian legal system and that of several of its member countries.

B. Protection of Human Rights

Many agreements were reached on this issue during the peace negotiations, including constitutional and legal reforms and the deployment of a United Nations human rights verification mission, something unprecedented in the history of the organization. The Commission's first recommendation is that these agreements should be complied with strictly and that ONUSAL recommendations on human rights should be implemented.

In addition to all the proposals advanced in this area as part of the peace process, the Commission would like to make the following recommendations, fully realizing that some of them can be implemented only through a constitutional reform:

1. The Office of the National Counsel for the Defence of Human Rights must be strengthened:

(a) It would be desirable if the Counsel, with the support of ONUSAL and the participation of all governmental and non-governmental sectors concerned, made an assessment of the Office's current situation and its most immediate priorities and needs, in order to secure the means, including international cooperation, to achieve those objectives.

(b) The Office's presence should be extended throughout the country through offices in the various departments.

(c) The Office should make more frequent use of its powers to inspect any site or installation in the country, especially where places of detention are concerned.

2. Measures must be taken to make the remedies of *amparo* and *habeas corpus* truly effective. To that end, the Commission recommends the following:

(a) Competence to hear these remedies should be broadened in order to make them more accessible to the population. All judges of first instance should be competent, within their sphere of jurisdiction, to hear remedies of *amparo* or *habeas corpus*, and this competence could be extended to justices of the peace. The Supreme Court of Justice should only be the final instance in such proceedings.

(b) Express provision should be made that the remedies of *amparo* and *habeas corpus*, like the rules of due process, cannot be suspended under any circumstances, including during a state of emergency.

3. The constitutional force of human rights provisions should be reaffirmed, including those not set forth expressly in the Constitution but in other instruments such as human rights conventions binding on El Salvador.

4. The system of administrative detention also warrants a number of changes. This is a matter of prime importance, since violations of integrity of person and even disappearances can occur during such detention:

(a) The restrictions as to which officials can order administrative detention, which officials can carry it out and for what reasons should be spelled out.

(b) The duration of administrative detention should be kept to the absolute minimum.

(c) The administrative authorities should be stripped of their power to impose penalties involving deprivation of liberty. Such penalties should be imposed only by the law courts, in the context of due process.

5. It is recommended that the current system of information on detainees should be expanded. Through the office of the National Counsel for the Defence of Human Rights, a centralized, up-to-date list should be kept of all persons detained for any reason, indicating their location and legal status. The competent authorities must inform the office of any detention that is carried out and the personnel involved in the arrest.

6. Any future reform of criminal legislation should give due consideration to crimes committed with the direct or indirect support of the State apparatus, either by establishing new categories of crimes, modifying existing ones or introducing special aggravating circumstances.

7. Legislation should be passed granting a simple, swift and accessible remedy to anyone who has been a victim of a human rights violation enabling them to obtain material compensation for the harm suffered.

8. Certain decisions should also be taken at the international level to reinforce the country's adherence to global and regional systems for the protection of human rights. To that end, the Commission recommends that El Salvador:

(a) Ratify the following international instruments: Optional Protocol to the International Covenant on Civil and Political Rights, Optional Protocol to the American Convention on Human Rights (Protocol of San Salvador), Conventions Nos. 87 and 98 of the International Labour Organisation, Convention on the Non-Applicability of Statutory Limitations to War Crimes and Crimes against Humanity, United Nations Convention against Torture and Other Cruel, Inhuman or Degrading Treatment or Punishment and the Inter-American Convention to Prevent and Punish Torture.

(b) Recognize the compulsory jurisdiction of the Inter-American Court of Human Rights established by the American Convention on Human Rights, as all the other Central American Republics have done.

C. National Civil Police

The Commission emphasizes the importance of the establishment and functioning of the National Civil Police, in accordance with the model defined in the peace agreements, for defending the population and preventing human rights violations. In addition to making a general recommendation to this effect, it wishes to emphasize criminal investigation, an issue closely linked to the impunity which accompanied the serious acts of violence described in this report. First, it recommends that every effort be made to put into practice as soon as possible the criminal investigation mechanism decided on in the peace agreements, which entails joint action by the National Civil Police and the office of the Attorney General of the Republic. This is also an area where international technical and financial cooperation can make a substantial contribution. Second, it recommends that the Commission for the Investigation of Criminal Acts be dissolved: it was through its omissions that serious human rights violations during the period under investigation were covered up.

IV. Steps Towards National Reconciliation

...The country must move on from a situation of confrontation to one of calm assimilation of all that has happened, in order to banish such occurrences from a future characterized by a new relationship of solidarity, coexistence and tolerance. In order to achieve this, a process of collective reflection on the reality of the past few years is crucial, as is a universal determination to eradicate this experience forever.

One bitter but unavoidable step is to look at and acknowledge what happened and must never happen again. The Commission took on the difficult task of clarifying significant aspects of this reality, which it hopes it has fulfilled through this report. The truth is not enough, however, to achieve the goals of national reconciliation and the reunification of Salvadorian society. Pardon is essential: not a formal pardon which is limited to not imposing penalties, but one founded on a universal determination to rectify the mistakes of the past and on the certainty that this process will not be complete unless it emphasizes the future rather than a past which, no matter how abhorrent the acts which occurred, cannot now be altered.

However, in order to achieve the goal of a pardon, we must pause and weigh certain consequences which can be inferred from knowledge of the truth about the serious acts described in this report. One such consequence, perhaps the most difficult to address in the country's current situation, is that of fulfilling the twofold requirements of justice: punishing the guilty and adequately compensating the victims and their families.

...In this connection, the Commission would simply add that, since it is not possible to guarantee a proper trial for all those responsible for the crimes described here, it is unfair to keep some of them in prison while others who planned the crimes or also took part in them remain at liberty. It is not within the Commission's power to address this situation, which can only be resolved through a pardon after justice has been served.

However, the Commission fervently hopes that knowledge of the truth, and the immediate implementation of the above recommendations which can be inferred directly from the investigation, will be an adequate starting-point for national reconciliation and for the desired reunification of Salvadorian society.

But justice does not stop at punishment; it also demands reparation. The victims and, in most cases, their families, are entitled to moral and material compensation. FMLN must provide such compensation where it is found to have been responsible, while this obligation devolves on the State in cases where the actions or omissions of the public authorities or their agencies were among the causes of the acts of violence described, or in cases where the persons responsible enjoyed impunity. However, since the country's financial constraints and national reconstruction needs cannot be ignored complementary mechanisms along the lines recommended below should be envisaged.

A. Material Compensation

1. It is recommended that a special fund be established, as an autonomous body with the necessary legal and administrative powers, to award appropriate material compensation to the victims of violence in the shortest time possible. The fund should take into account the information on the victims reported to the Commission on the Truth contained in the annexes to this report.

2. The fund should receive an appropriate contribution from the State but, in view of prevailing economic conditions, should receive a substantial contribution from the international community. Therefore, without prejudice to the obligations of the State and of FMLN, the Commission urgently appeals to the international community, especially the wealthier countries and those that showed most interest in the conflict and its settlement, to establish a fund for that purpose. It also suggests that the United Nations Secretariat promote and coordinate this initiative. It further recommends that not less than 1 percent of all international assistance that reaches El Salvador be set aside for this purpose.

3. The fund could be managed by a board of directors consisting of three members: one appointed by the Government of El Salvador, one appointed by the Secretary-General of the United Nations and a third chosen by mutual agreement between the two appointed members.

4. The fund must be free to establish its own rules of procedure and to act in accordance with the Commission's recommendations, Salvadorian law, international law and general legal principles.

B. Moral Compensation

The Commission recommends:

1. The construction of a national monument in El Salvador bearing the names of all the victims of the conflict.

2. Recognition of the good name of the victims and of the serious crimes of which they were victims.

3. The institution of a national holiday in memory of the victims of the conflict and to serve as a symbol of national reconciliation.

C. Forum for Truth and Reconciliation

The Commission feels it would be useful if this report and its conclusions and recommendations and progress towards national reconciliation were analysed not only by the Salvadorian people as a whole but also by a special forum comprising the most representative sectors of society which, in addition to the above-mentioned objectives, should strive to monitor strict compliance with the recommendations.

It is not for the commission to indicate how such a forum should be established. However, a National commission for the Consolidation of Peace (COPAZ) was established under the peace agreements as "a mechanism for the monitoring of and the participation of civilian society in the process of change resulting from the negotiations". It therefore seems appropriate that the task referred to by the Commission should be entrusted primarily to COPAZ. However, given the scope the importance of the subject-matter dealt with in this report, the Commission would like to suggest to COPAZ that, to this end, it consider expanding its membership so that sectors of civilian society that are not directly represented in COPAZ can participate in this analysis.

Moreover, COPAZ is the body entrusted by the agreements with preparing preliminary legislative drafts related to the peace process. In this sphere, it has a crucial role to play in the implementation of the recommendations in the present report that call for legal reforms.

D. International Follow-Up

The Commission has carried out its mandate as part of an extraordinary process which is a milestone in the history of United Nations operations for the maintenance of international peace and security. The tragedy in El Salvador absorbed the attention of the international community. As a result, the current peace process continues to arouse expectations throughout the world. The United Nations is also responsible for verifying all the agreements, which includes ensuring that the recommendations of the Commission on the Truth, which the Parties undertook to carry out, are implemented.

The Commission requests the Independent Expert for El Salvador of the United Nations Commission on Human Rights, in the report he is to submit to the Commission on Human Rights pursuant to his mandate and to the extent allowed by that mandate, to make corresponding evaluation of the implementation of the recommendations of the Commission on the Truth.

VI. Epilogue: The Seekers After Peace

Yes indeed, as the Mayan poem goes, all these things happened among us. Each one of us projected his own version of the truth as the universal truth. Each group or party saw its banner as the only banner in the Manicheism that held sway. And every individual or party loyalty was held to be the only real allegiance. In those days, all Salvadorians were so unfair in one way or another to their fellow countrymen that the heroism of some became the immediate misfortune of others. Moreover, the nation was a pawn in the East-West conflict; Salvadorians were buffeted by a turbulent sea of waning ideologies and global contradictions. Although the victims hailed from many countries, they were mainly Salvadorians. One way or another, blame for this can be attributed to a complex web of events in El Salvador's history and to unique circumstances in world history, so that it would be unfair to assign it to a particular individual, organization or party.

When there came pause for thought, each Salvadorian once again responded to the only true allegiance—allegiance to the nation. The Salvadorian nation looked deep into its soul and saw, as the preamble to the Constitution says, its destiny written in the stars. Many brilliant war-time figures have also shone in peacetime: the old contradictions and intransigence contrast sharply with the current rapprochements and agreements. Former combatants of all parties have embraced one another in a sign of reconciliation. There are neither victors nor vanquished, since every one gains from the agreements. As in classical painting, the loftier sentiments that make law the agreed bulwark against unbridled freedom and mindless anarchy triumph over the pain of battle.

The report of the Commission on the Truth records the acts of violence that occurred repeatedly during the 12 years of war in order to prevent such events from ever happening again....

The collective spirit underlying the agreements also runs through this report, which is the contribution of the Commission on the Truth to restoring the institutional fabric of El Salvador. However, it is for Salvadorians themselves to take the fundamental decisions that will lead to a full-fledged peace. Salvadorian society must decide about accountability for past actions and new statutes of limitations. It has the power to grant pardons. It is also this society, steeped in the painful lessons of war, that will have to settle the dispute about new appointments to high office.

The members of the Commission on the Truth hope—as the only compensation for the pact made with their own consciences—that this report will help the seekers after peace, the protagonists of the new history of El Salvador, to find answers.

GERMANY: LAW CREATING THE COMMISSION OF INQUIRY ON "WORKING THROUGH THE HISTORY AND THE CONSEQUENCES OF THE SED DICTATORSHIP"

Act No. 12/2597 (May 14, 1992)

A

I. To work through the history and consequences of the SED [East German Communist Party, known as the "German Socialist Union Party"] dictatorship in Germany is a joint task of all Germans. It is particularly important for the purpose of truly unifying Germany.

The legacy of the SED dictatorship continues to be a burden preventing people in Germany from coming together. The experiences of injustice and persecution, humiliation and discouragement are still alive. Many people are looking for clarification, struggling for orientation in dealing with their own and others' responsibility and culpability; they are asking questions about the roots of the dictatorial system set up in the SBZ/GDR [the former German Democratic Republic]; about the political, mental, and intellectual and emotional effects of the dictatorship; about the possibilities of political and moral rehabilitation of the victims.

To work through these issues, the commission of inquiry appointed by the March 12, 1992 resolution of the *Bundestag* (Paper 12/2230 of March 11, 1992) has a specific mandate. It carries this obligation for the people of all of Germany, but above all to the Germans in the new Federal States [German "Länder"], who had been subjected to dictatorial forms of government for nearly six decades; the *Bundestag* considers it an essential concern of the Commission to offer them help in confronting the past and assessing personal responsibility.

The *Bundestag* is aware of the inherent limits of working through issues with political-constitutional (rule of law) connotations. The effort to satisfy an injured sense of justice by revealing injustice and identifying responsibilities is thus all the more important. At the same time, it is important to make a contribution to reconciliation in society.

The commission of inquiry shall not forestall or replace the necessary historical research. The goal of its work is to contribute, in dialogue with the public, to the solidification of democratic consciousness and the further development of a common political culture in Germany.

II. In this regard, the Commission has the mandate to make contributions to political-historical analysis and to political-moral assessment. This includes:

1. to analyze the structures, strategies and instruments of the SED dictatorship, in particular the issue of responsibilities for the violation of

human and civil rights and for the destruction of nature and the environment; including:

- the decision processes of the SED,
- the relation of the SED and the government apparatus, particularly the relation between the various levels of the SED and the MfS [Ministry for State Security],
- structure and mode of operation of national security, the police and the justice system,
- the role of the mass parties, mass organizations and the media,
- the militarization of the society and the role of the "armed bodies,"
- restructuring the economy and rendering it instrumental (expropriation; forced collectivization, centrally administered economy),
- careless handling of nature and the environment;

2. to illustrate and evaluate the significance of ideology, integrative factors and disciplining practices, including:

- the function and rendering instrumental of Marxism-Leninism and anti-fascism,
- importance and misuse of education, instruction, science, literature, culture, art and sport,
- dealing with the effects and the role of career offers and privileges;

3. to examine the violation of international human rights agreements and standards and the forms of appearance of oppression in various phases; to identify groups of victims and consider possibilities of material and moral restitution, including:

- political repression by criminal law, punitive justice and execution of sentences (e.g., prison conditions, mistreatment, restrictions on liberty, deportations);
- the mechanisms of political, mental and psychosocial oppression in people's everyday life and their consequences since 1945/46;

4. to work out the possibilities and forms of deviating and resistant behavior and oppositional action in the various spheres along with the factors that influenced them;

5. to illustrate the role and identity of the churches in the various phases of the SED dictatorship;

6. to judge the significance of the international framework conditions, particularly the influence of Soviet politics in the SBZ and the GDR;

7. to examine the significance of the relation between the Federal Republic of Germany and the GDR, including:

- German political goals, guiding concepts and perspectives for action in the two nations;
- domestic political, economic, social and cultural relations and their effects on the development of the GDR;
- the significance of personal connections for the sense of belonging together;
- the influence of the media of the Federal Republic of Germany in the GDR;
- the activities of the SED and the GDR in the Federal Republic of Germany and in the international sphere;

8. to include the issue of continuities and analogies of thought, behavior and structures in 20th century German history, particularly the period of the national socialist dictatorship.

III.   Coming to terms with the history of the SED dictatorship is to be illustrated using the following data and periods:

- constitution of the dictatorship and its framework conditions, 1945-1949 (e.g.: Potsdam Treaty, land reform, forced unification of SPD [German Socialist Party] and KPD [German Communist Party] into the SED, political and social elimination of opposition, among others);
- uprising of June 17, 1953;
- forced collectivization and construction of the Berlin Wall;
- entry of the Warsaw Pact troops into Czechoslovakia in 1968;
- transition from Ulbricht to Honecker 1971;
- peaceful revolution in Autumn 1989 and German reunification.

IV.   The Commission shall strive primarily to achieve the following practical results from its work:

- contributions to the political and moral rehabilitation of the victims and to redress damages related to the dictatorship;
- to show possibilities of overcoming continuing disadvantages in education and professions;
- contributions to clarifying the matter of government criminality in the GDR;
- obtaining, securing and opening the pertinent archives;
- improving the conditions for scholarly research on the SBZ/GDR past;
- recommendation for action to the *Bundestag* with respect to legislative measures and other political initiatives,
- suggestions for coming to terms with the East German past in pedagogical and psychological terms.

V. The mode of operation of the commission of inquiry shall contain the following elements, among others:

- discussions with interested parties and citizens' groups on site. Dialogue with scientists, scholars and grass-roots groups which work through GDR history;
- public hearings and forums;
- commissioning of presentation of expert assessments and scholarly studies.

B

The Commission will be named as follows:

Commission of Inquiry on "Working through the History and the Consequences of the SED Dictatorship in Germany"...

Rainer Eppelmann, Chairman   Dr. Dorothea Wilms
Markus Meckel   Dirk Hansen
Gerd Poppe   Dr. Dietmar Keller

GUATEMALA: AGREEMENT ON THE ESTABLISHMENT OF THE COMMISSION FOR THE HISTORICAL CLARIFICATION OF HUMAN RIGHTS VIOLATIONS AND INCIDENTS OF VIOLENCE THAT HAVE CAUSED SUFFERING TO THE GUATEMALAN POPULATION

(June 23, 1994)

Bearing in mind that the contemporary history of our fatherland has been marked by serious incidents of violence, non-observance of fundamental human rights, and suffering by the population that are related to the armed confrontation;

Considering the right of the people of Guatemala to know the whole truth regarding these events, which, if clarified will help to ensure that this sad and painful chapter will not be repeated and that the process of democratizing Guatemala will be strengthened;

Reaffirming their willingness to comply fully with the Comprehensive Agreement on Human Rights of March 29, 1994;

Further reaffirming their intention to start, as soon as possible, a new chapter in Guatemalan history which, as the culmination of a broad process of negotiation, will put an end to the armed confrontation and will help to lay the bases for a peaceful coexistence respectful of human rights among Guatemalans;

Bearing in mind, in this regard, the need to foster an outlook of harmony and mutual respect that will eliminate all forms of retaliation or revenge, as a prerequisite for a firm and lasting peace;

The Government of Guatemala and the Guatemalan National Revolutionary Unity (hereinafter "the Parties") agree as follows:

A commission shall be established as follows:

Purposes:

I. To clarify, with full objectiveness, equity, and impartiality, human rights violations and incidents of violence related to the armed confrontation that have caused suffering to the Guatemalan population;

II. To prepare a report that contains the findings of the investigations conducted, offers objective information about what transpired during this period, and includes all factors, both internal and external;

III. To formulate specific recommendations to encourage national harmony and peace in Guatemala. The Commission shall recommend, in particular, measures to preserve the memory of the victims, to foster an outlook of mutual respect and observance of human rights, and to strengthen the democratic process.

Period of Coverage:

The period the Commission shall investigate shall run from the onset of the armed confrontation to the signature of the Agreement for a Firm and Lasting Peace.

Operation:

I. The Commission shall receive background and information provided by individuals or institutions that consider themselves to have been affected, and by the Parties;

II. The Commission shall be responsible for fully clarifying these situations, in detail. In particular, it shall analyze with complete impartiality the factors and circumstances that had a bearing on the aforementioned incidents. The Commission shall invite all those who may have relevant information to submit their version of the incidents. Failure of the parties concerned to come forward shall not prevent the Commission from reaching a decision on the incidents;

III. The work, recommendation, and report of the Commission shall not delineate responsibilities or have judicial purposes or effects;

IV. The activities of the Commission shall be confidential in order to guarantee the secrecy of the sources and the security of the witnesses and informants;

V. Upon its formation, the Commission shall announce, by all means possible, the fact of its establishment and its headquarters and shall invite the parties concerned to submit their information and testimony.

Membership:

The Commission shall consist of three members:

I. The current Moderator of the peace negotiations, whom the United Nations Secretary General shall be requested to appoint;

II. One citizen of unimpeachable conduct, to be designated by the Moderator, by mutual agreement with the Parties;

III. One member of academia, selected by the Moderator, by mutual agreement with the Parties, from a slate of three candidates proposed by the university presidents;

The Commission shall have the duly qualified support personnel it considers necessary to carry out its duties.

Induction and Term:

The Commission shall be formed, inducted, and begin to operate on the day the Agreement for a Firm and Lasting Peace is signed. The work of the Commission shall last for a period of six months from its induction, which may be extended for six additional months, if the Commission so decides.

Report:

The Commission shall prepare a report that shall be delivered to the Parties and to the United Nations Secretary General, who shall make it public. The fact that not all cases or situations submitted to the Commission could be investigated shall not lessen the report's validity.

Commitment of the Parties:

The Parties undertake to cooperate with the Commission in all matters necessary to fulfill its mandate. They undertake, in particular, to establish, prior to the induction of the Commission and during its operation, the conditions required to ensure that said Commission embodies the characteristics set forth in this Agreement.

International Verification:

In accordance with the Framework Agreement of January 10, 1994, compliance with the Agreement is subject to international verification by the United Nations.

Measures for Immediate Implementation after Signature of this Agreement:

The Parties agree to request the Secretary General to appoint, as soon as possible, the Moderator of the negotiations to be a member of the Commission. After his appointment, he shall be empowered to take any steps necessary to prepare for the smooth operation of the Commission once it has been composed and inducted in accordance with the provision of the agreement.

INDIA: COMMISSIONS OF INQUIRY ACT

Act No. 60 (August 14, 1952)
(as amended through August 28, 1990)

An Act to provide for the appointment of
Commissions of Inquiry and for vesting such
Commissions with certain powers

Be it enacted by Parliament as follows:

1. **Short Title, Extent and Commencement:...**

2. **Definitions: In this Act, Unless the Context Otherwise Requires,—**

    (a) "appropriate Government" means—

        (i)   the Central Government, in relation to a Commission appointed by it to make an inquiry into any matter relatable to any of the entries enumerated in List I or List II or List III in the Seventh Schedule to the Constitution; and

        (ii) the State Government, in relation to a Commission appointed by it to make an inquiry into any matter relatable to any of the entries enumerated in List II or List III in the Seventh Schedule to the Constitution:...

    (b) in sub-clause (ii) thereof, for the words and figures "List II or List III in the Seventh Schedule to the Constitution", the words and figures "List III in the Seventh Schedule to the Constitution as applicable to the State of Jammu and Kashmir" shall be substituted;

    (b) "Commission" means a Commission of Inquiry appointed under section 3;

    (c) "prescribed" means prescribed by rules made under this Act....

3. **Appointment of Commission:**

    (1) The appropriate Government may, if it is of opinion that it is necessary so to do, and shall, if a resolution in this behalf is passed by the House of the People or, as the case may be, the Legislative Assembly of the State, by notification in the official Gazette, appoint a Commission of Inquiry for the purpose of making an inquiry into any definite matter of public importance and performing such functions and within such time as may be specified in the notification, and the Commission so appointed shall make the inquiry and perform the functions accordingly:

Provided that where any such Commission has been appointed to inquire into any matter—

(a) by the Central Government, no State Government shall, except with the approval of the Central Government, appoint another Commission to inquire into the same matter for so long as the Commission appointed by the Central Government is functioning;

(b) by a State Government, the Central Government shall not appoint another Commission to inquire into the same matter for so long as the Commission appointed by the State Government is functioning, unless the Central Government is of opinion that the scope of the inquiry should be extended to two or more States.

(2) The Commission may consist of one or more members appointed by the appropriate Government, and where the Commission consists of more than one member, one of them may be appointed as the Chairman thereof.

(3) The appropriate Government may, at any stage of an inquiry by the Commission fill any vacancy which may have arisen in the office of a member of the Commission (whether consisting of one or more than one member).

(4) The appropriate Government shall cause to be laid before the House of the People or, as the case may be, the Legislative Assembly of the State, the report, if any, of the Commission on the inquiry made by the Commission under sub-section (1) together with a memorandum of the action taken thereon, within a period of six months of the submission of the report by the Commission to the appropriate Government.

4. Powers of Commission:

The Commission shall have the powers of a Civil Court, while trying a suit under the Code of Civil Procedure, 1908 (5 of 1908), in respect of the following matters, namely:

(a) summoning and enforcing the attendance of any person from any part of India and examining him on oath;

(b) requiring the discovery and production of any document;

(c) receiving evidence on affidavits;

(d) requisitioning any public record or copy thereof from any court or office;

(e) issuing commissions for the examination of witnesses or documents;

(f) any other matter which may be prescribed.

5. Additional Powers of Commission:

(1) Where the appropriate Government is of opinion that, having regard to the nature of the inquiry to be made and other circumstances of the case, all or any of the provisions of sub-section (2) or sub-section (3) or sub-section

(4) or sub-section (5) should be made applicable to a Commission, the appropriate Government may, by notification in the official Gazette, direct that all or such of the said provisions as may be specified in the notification shall apply to that Commission and on the issue of such a notification, the said provisions shall apply accordingly.

(2) The Commission shall have power to require any person, subject to any privilege which may be claimed by that person under any law for the time being in force, to furnish information on such points or matters as, in the opinion of the Commission, may be useful for, or relevant to the subject-matter of inquiry and any person so required shall be deemed to be legally bound to furnish such information within the meaning of section 176 and section 177 of the Indian Penal Code (45 of 1860).

(3) The Commission or any officer, not below the rank of a gazetted officer, specially authorised in this behalf by the Commission may enter any building or place where the Commission has reason to believe that any books of account or other documents relating to the subject-matter of the inquiry may be found, and may seize any such books of account or documents or take extracts or copies therefrom, subject to the provisions of section 102 and section 103 of the Code of Criminal Procedure, 1898 (5 of 1898), in so far as they may be applicable.

(4) The Commission shall be deemed to be a Civil Court and when any offence as is described in section 175, section 178, section 179, section 180 or section 228 of the Indian Penal Code (45 of 1860), is committed in the view or presence of the Commission, the Commission may, after recording the facts constituting the offence and the statement of the accused as provided for in the Code of Criminal Procedure, 1898 (5 of 1898), forward the case to a Magistrate having jurisdiction to try the same and the Magistrate to whom any such case is forwarded shall proceed to hear the complaint against the accused as if the case had been forwarded to him under section 482 the Code to the Criminal Procedure, 1898 (5 of 1898).

(5) Any proceeding before the Commission shall be deemed to be a judicial proceeding within the meaning of sections 193 and 228 of the Indian Penal Code (45 of 1860).

INDIA: SARMA SARKAR COMMISSION OF INQUIRY

Notification

(November 7, 1977)

(1) The Government of West Bengal by Notification No. 10115-J dated the 12th August, 1977 appointed a Commission of Inquiry consisting of Shri J. Sarma Sarkar, Retired Judge of the Calcutta High Court to enquire into allegations of persistent misuse of authority of power in West Bengal during the period from the 20th March, 1970 to the 31st May, 1976 with the following terms of reference:—

(2) (a) to enquire and to find out—

   (i) what, if any, misuse of power by public servants took place during the aforesaid period whereby the democratic rights of citizens including liberty of person, freedom of speech and expression, the right to assemble peacefully, to form associations or unions, were curbed or nullified,

   (ii) to what extent, if any, such curbs of democratic rights of citizens took place with the encouragement of or was aided or abetted by any person or persons having official authority or by any other institutions or organisations,

   (iii) for what purposes and in whose interest and under whose directions, if any, such curbs of democratic fights took place,

   (b) to consider such other matters which in the opinion of the Commission of Inquiry have any relevance to the aforesaid allegations, and

   (c) to suggest steps and measures so that violation of such democratic rights cannot recur in future.

(3) The inquiry by the Commission of Inquiry shall be in regard to—

   (i) complaints or allegations aforesaid that may be made before the Commission of Inquiry by any individual or association in such form and accompanied by such affidavits as may be prescribed by the Commission of Inquiry, and

   (ii) such instances of misuse of authority of power as may be brought to its notice by the State Government for inquiry.

(4) (a) Accordingly, complaints or allegations, giving specific instances of misuse of authority of power committed, abetted or directed by public servants in connection with the matters mentioned above

which took place during the period mentioned before may be made by individual persons, or associations or organisations, with as much particulars as possible so as to reach the undersigned at the address given below within one month from the date of this Notice.

(b) If the complaint be by an association or organisation, then it may be signed by the principal officer with his seal, or by any other officer with authority to sign and present such complaint.

(c) The Statement should contain facts divided into paragraphs to be numbered consecutively—each material statement of fact being made the subject-matter of a separate paragraph. The Statement should be written up and prepared separately against each individual or body in respect of each separate instance in each district and for a particular time. In other words, material facts relating to or done by one and the same individual person or both within the jurisdiction of any one district should be dealt with separately and each single incident of abuse or misuse should be dealt with in separate paragraphs which again are to be arranged chronologically in the order the incidents took place or were committed by the said individual or body.

(d) The complaints should preferably by written in English and should be accompanied by five extra copies; and in case the complaint be written in any other language than English, then an English translation of the same should be furnished along with five extra copies.

(e) A list of documents, if any, on which the deponent proposes to rely should be furnished with the Statement along with originals or true copies of the documents. In case any document cannot be produced not being in the possession or power of the deponent, the Statement should mention the names and correct addresses of the persons from whom such documents may be obtained.

(f) If the informant be a Government official whose identity is not intended to be disclosed, particulars of the Government file from which the relevant information would be obtained should be mentioned in the Statement.

(g) A list of witnesses, if any, whom the deponent would like to be examined in support of the Statements made by the deponent should be furnished giving correct addresses of such witnesses.

(5) The Statement or allegations may include all or any of the following matters of misuse of authority of power:—

(a) the details of instances in which powers of arrest are alleged to have been used or detention orders issued for any consideration not commensurate with the purposes of the Act under which such arrest or detention was made; the name and particulars of the person so arrested and place or places where he was arrested and/or detained,

(b) the details of cases in which the freedom of speech and expression were curbed,

(c) the details of cases of misuse whereby the right to assemble peacefully was disturbed,

(d) the details or specific instances where the right to form associations were nullified or curbed,

(e) the details of cases relating to persons or organisations directly or indirectly aiding or abetting the suppression of any of the democratic rights mentioned above, and

(f) the Statement may also contain materials for what purpose and in whose interest and under whose directions such curbs of democratic rights took place.

(6) The Statement may contain suggestions for measures which, in the opinion of the deponent, would result in the prevention of the recurrence of such misuse of authority of power.

(7) There shall be a verification at the bottom of the Statement showing which of the allegations and matters are true to the deponent's knowledge and which matter are based on information (along with sources of information) together with correct name, occupation and address of the person making the Statement.

(8) The Commission will hold its first public sitting at the address given below on the 16th December, 1977 at 11-30 A.M. to consider the terms of reference, draft regulation of its procedure, and tentative programme in the presence of parties interested.

(9) The Statements or complaints regarding matters specified above should be filed within a period of one month from the date of Notice, either personally on any working day between 11 A.M. and 4 P.M. at the office of the Commission or by registered post to be addressed to "Secretary to Sarma Sarkar Commission of Inquiry, Assembly House, Council Chamber, Calcutta-700001".

Regulation of Procedure

(January 11, 1978)

A. Sitting of the Commission

To ensure speed with justice to all concerned in connection with more than 3,000 complaints filed, the following regulations are framed under section 8 of the Commission of Inquiry Act by the Commission of Inquiry constituted by the West Bengal Government notification No. 10115J, dated the 12th August 1977, to regulate its own procedure:—

(1) Unless otherwise notified, the office of the Commission will be located at Council Chamber, Assembly House, and remain open between

10-30 A.M. and 5-30 P.M. on all weekdays except that on Saturdays the office will close at 2 P.M. Usual Government holidays will be observed. Outsiders will not be allowed entry in the office. The public may, however, have access to the Section Officer or the Secretary in the office between 11 A.M. and 1 P.M. and again between 2 P.M. and 4 P.M. on weekdays and 11 A.M. and 1 P.M. on Saturdays....

(3) The Commission may, in its discretion, hold its sittings in other places according to the necessity of each case or on the application of parties or witnesses but the date, place and time of the sitting will be duly notified.

(4) The sittings of the Commission may be adjourned from time to time at the discretion of the Chairman. Timings or dates of the sittings of the Commission may be changed with due notice to the parties concerned.

(5) The proceedings will be conducted in English but arrangement will be made, as far as practicable, for translating depositions in vernacular and the parties or their lawyers may address the Commission in vernacular understood by the Commission.

(6) The sittings of the Commission will be open to the public and the Press but they will be held *in camera* at the discretion of the Commission in respect of particular persons or incidents or on the application of witnesses or parties as the case may be.

B. Examination of the Complaint

(1) The Commission will examine the complaint filed to ascertain its jurisdiction on the basis of allegations of (i) misuse of power, (ii) by a public servant, (iii) curbing a citizen's democratic rights, and (iv) of public importance within the period 20th March, 1970 and 31st May, 1975.

(2) The complaints which are outside jurisdiction or too trivial or individual in nature will be rejected and a list will be kept in the office for inspection by the complainants. The rejected complaints with documents, if any, may either be returned to the complainant, if available, or in the discretion of the Commission, be sent to the Department concerned or the Government for necessary action.

(3) If the complaints make out a *prima facie* case and there are sufficient materials produced in support, then a process may be issued to the respondent to answer the allegations and submit the list of the documents or witnesses in support of his own case and the complainant and his witnesses or the respondent and his witnesses may be directed to supply affidavit or counter affidavit evidence in support of their respective cases in the form of affidavits mentioned in Appendix "A". The case may be disposed of without recording any evidence.

C. Investigation of the Complaint

(1) Where the *prima facie* case is not clear or the materials furnished in the complaint are not complete, the Commission may utilize the services of officers or agencies of the Central or State Government or its own agency for preliminary investigation in private. The services of Central or State

Government or their officers with the concurrence of the respective Government may be utilized under the direction and control of the Commission.

(2) The guideline will be given by the Commission to such agencies or teams for collection of the names and addresses of witnesses for the complainant and also the names and addresses of persons involved together with the relevant documents or their copies and report to the Commission. Such teams or agencies must meet the complainant for necessary help and direction and get and secure affidavit evidence of the complainant with five copies thereof.

(3) The report of the investigating team should be full and complete giving the history and background of the case materials collected and the documents or extracts or copies thereof in connection with the case.

(4) The Commission reserves the right of confidential investigation by Police or non-Police teams consisting of Police and non-Police Officials.

(5) Where there is basis for allegation against approved team or agency employed by the Commission, the investigation of such cases will be entrusted to neutral bodies as far as practicable.

(6) The Commission may scrutinize the report and examine the reporting officer or agency to ascertain the correctness and adequacy of the report and if the report is incomplete, then further investigation may be ordered.

D. Public Inquiry

(1) When a *prima facie* case for public inquiry is made out either on the basis of affidavit and counter-affidavit or on the basis of investigation report, notice or summons will be issued to the respondent to appear and answer the allegations made in the complaint either *viva voce* or in writing and the respondent will also be asked to produce a list of witnesses and documents or extracts therefrom....

(2) The Commission may issue letter of request, summons or notice as the case may be on the lines of the forms prescribed in the Code of Civil Procedure with such modifications as may be found necessary to suit the convenience and purpose and nature of the enquiries made by the Commission.

(3) The Secretary and the Section Officer to the Commission have been authorised to sign letters, summons, notices, [and] processes on behalf of the Commission.

(4) The Commission will decide whether the case can be disposed of by affidavit and counter-affidavit or by interrogatories and cross-interrogatories and whether oral evidence is necessary. The Commission, in its discretion, will decide who are to be orally examined and the Commission is not bound to examine any witness named by a party.

(5) Interested or involved parties may appear personally or through their lawyer or agent duly authorised. The statement or allegation filed before the Commission when confirmed on oath, may be treated, in the discretion of the Commission, as examination-in-chief to avoid loss of public

time. If examination-in-chief is in vernacular, it will be translated into English and made part of the record.

(6) Parties interested or involved in any item of inquiry will produce their witnesses without intervention of the Commission but if a witness cannot be produced and the Commission finds his evidence necessary, then the Commission, in its discretion, may request or summon the witness either to appear personally or send statement in the form of affidavit or the witness may be examined on commission in terms of section 4(e) of the Commission of Inquiries Act or by interrogatories and cross-interrogatories.

(7) The complainant may be examined-in-chief by the lawyer of his choice and failing him by the Government Advocate.

(8) The cross-examination of each witness tendered for evidence should be brief and to the point and always subject to the control of the Commission which may intervene at any stage to shorten cross-examination and for the ends of justice.

(9) The respondent will then be examined by the lawyer or agent, if any, of his own choice and briefly cross-examined to elicit truth first by the lawyer, if any, of the complainant and then, if necessary, by the Government Advocate and Advocate, if any, of the Commission. The Commission may put question at any stage for clarity and for ends of justice.

(10) Barring clerical and typographical mistakes or errors apparent on the face of the record, the evidence recorded before the Commission will be correct evidence on oath unless mistakes are pointed out by the witness or his lawyer or agent on the same date or by next date.

(11) The Commission will then, if necessary, briefly hear the parties or their lawyers and then record its findings on facts or reserve its findings.

(12) The Commission may arrange hearing of the cases before it either individually or in groups for the convenience of the witnesses or the persons involved or for the economy of time in recording evidence or otherwise for the ends of justice.

(13) Registered documents in original or certified copies will be admitted without requiring formal proof.

(14) Public documents, official record of Government departments or of Statutory bodies, Local authorities, State undertakings, banks and cooperative societies including the office noting, orders, etc., may, subject to any valid claim of privilege, be admitted without any formal proof, unless the Commission in any particular case requires it to be proved in any of ways laid down in the Evidence Act.

(15) When it will not be possible to supply copies of documents to the interested or involved parties, they will be permitted to inspect documents of the respective parties and final investigation report.

(16) When an item is taken up for inquiry the hearing will usually continue from day to day till finished except where in the discretion of the Commission short adjournment is found necessary for the ends of justice.

(17) No prayer for adjournment for filing objection, for producing document, for examining witness, for preparing the case for hearing on any ground including the absence of lawyer will be allowed but the Commission, in its discretion, may grant time in extreme cases.

(18) The mode of service of processes including letters, summons or notices will be either by messenger or by registered post with acknowledgement due. When the process is correctly addressed and is served personally or on any member of the family or servant or agent or caretaker as per return, it will be deemed sufficient and decisive. The Commission, in its discretion, may either proceed *ex parte* or compel the attendance of parties or witness or may issue public notice.

(19) The Commission may either in its own discretion or on the application made by any person or party delete or expunge any matter from any petition, affidavit or other documents or return any document presented to the Commission which, in the opinion of the Commission, is irrelevant or needlessly offensive, scurrilous or scandalous.

(20) The technical rules of Code of Civil Procedure or of the Evidence Act will not be applicable to the procedure before the Commission but the principles of natural justice underlying the Code and the Act will be made applicable.

(21) The Commission reserves its right to alter, modify, delete or add to any of these regulations or procedure at any time during the inquiry as and when it considers it necessary after due notice to the interested or involved parties.

E. Authority of Commission

(1) To compel attendance of parties or witnesses: If a party or witness being served with summons or processes refuses to appear or depose before the Commission or produce documents, necessary steps including fine or arrest will be taken, in the discretion of the Commission, for appearance of that person or for production of the documents.

(2) To ensure production of documents: The claim of privilege in respect of documents or oath of secrecy in respect of depositions by an individual or Government will be duly considered by the Commission which will give necessary direction in each case.

(3) To exclude public or part of it: The inquiry before the Commission will be both "public," viz., within their sight and hearing and "open" without any preconceived view but [the] public or a section of it may be excluded to prevent over-crowding, disturbance or for other reasons.

(4) To exclude Press in particular cases: To prevent mistakes or distortions in reporting the proceedings before the Commission and for the convenience of interested and involved parties the Commission may supply, as far as practicable, authentic copy of the proceedings including the record of statements of witnesses to the Government Advocate and interested and involved parties or their lawyers and to the Press but in spite of this if there is deliberate distortions of the proceedings before the Commission, then the entry of the Press indulging in such distortions may be regulated.

(5) To try summarily for perjury and contempt:...[T]he Commission may try and punish summarily:

(a) for false or fabricated evidence. The Commission will indicate how and why the evidence is false and give an able opportunity to show cause against it and thereafter on the materials on record and further evidence, if any, the case will be disposed of,

(b) for contempt. If a witness refuses to take oath, swear affidavit or produce documents in the view or presence of the Commission, then the offender may be detained in custody and after stating the facts constituting the offence and after giving the offender reasonable opportunity to show cause he may be tried and punished summarily in the course of the day.

(6) Faithful reporting of the proceeding before the Commission and fair and *bona fide* comment by the Press or the public are welcome but *mala fide* or motivated criticism of the Commission, its staff or witnesses or anticipating the decisions of the Commission may be treated as interference with the work of the Commission and as contempt.

Form of Affidavit and Counter-Affidavit

An affidavit required by the Commission to be filed shall be sworn before an authority legally empowered to administer oath. Such affidavits may be sent to the Secretary of the Commission by registered post with acknowledgment due or handed over at the Office of the Commission on a receipt or to the investigating team or agency employed by the Commission over their receipt.

2. Affidavits before the Commission shall, as far as possible, be in the English language. If the affidavit be in any language other than English, it shall ordinarily be accompanied by a translation thereof in English duly authenticated by an Advocate or a Magistrate of the first class or by any of the investigating team or agency employed by the Commission.

3. The authority before whom the affidavit is sworn shall make the following endorsements thereon:

> "Sworn before me by the deponent who has been identified to my satisfaction by.......... or is personally known to me. The affidavit has been read out in full and explained to the deponent who has signed it in my presence after admitting it to be correct. This day......... 1978 at.......

Signature of authority with seal

4. Every affidavit shall be drawn up in the first person and shall be divided into paragraphs, numbered consecutively, each material statement being made by subject-matter of a separate paragraph. The affidavit shall state the description, occupation, if any, and the ordinary place of abode of the deponent.

The affidavit at the end shall be verified in the following manner:

(a) "I declare that the statements made in paragraph .... of the affidavit are true to my personal knowledge and those in paragraph's .... from information received and believed to be true by me."

(b) If the information is derived from any document or record, the deponent shall indicate the nature and particulars of such documents and the person in control and custody thereof.

(c) If any part of the affidavit is verified from information received by the deponent, he shall disclose the source of such information in the affidavit.

(d) The deponent shall file along with his affidavit a list of witnesses with full particulars and address in support of his statement in the affidavit. The deponent shall indicate briefly the fact or facts which the witness is expected to speak to if examined before the Commission.

(e) All affidavits filed before the Commission shall be accompanied by at least five spare copies thereof.

5. The counter-affidavit, if any, will be generally on the lines of the affidavit indicated above. In particular, the counter-affidavit should traverse specifically the facts mentioned in the affidavit and if not so traversed, then that will be taken as admitted.

Summons to Involved Parties under Section 8B of the Commission of Inquiry Act

To

    1. Name   :
    2. Description :
    3. Residence :

(1) Whereas allegations have been made before the Commission as per copy of the affidavit with a list or copies of documents and name of witnesses attached for inquiry in which your conduct and reputation may be involved you are hereby summoned to appear in person with or without a lawyer or agent duly authorised on .... at .... before the Commission to state your case orally or in writing and submit a list of names and addresses of witnesses and produce documents in support, failing which the Commission may proceed *ex parte* or may take steps for ensuring your attendance, if necessary.

(2) If you do not want personal cross-examination of the allegationist and his witnesses you may send interrogatories along with your affidavit.

(3) Given under my hand and the seal of the Commission this .... day .... 1979.

INDIA: SHAH COMMISSION OF INQUIRY, INTERIM REPORT I

*Appointed under Section 3 of the
Commissions of Inquiry Act, 1952
(March 11, 1978)*

Chapter 1

In exercise of the powers under Section 3 of the Commissions of Inquiry Act, 1952, the Central Government published on May 28, 1977, a notification appointing a Commission of Inquiry.

1.2 The notification reads as follows:

"Ministry of Home Affairs
Notification"

New Delhi, the 28th May, 1977

S.O. 374(E).—Whereas there is a widespread demand from different sections of the public for an inquiry into several aspects of allegations of abuse of authority, excesses and malpractices committed and action taken or purported to be taken in the wake of the Emergency proclaimed on the 25th June, 1975 under Article 352 of the Constitution;

And whereas the Central Government is of the opinion that it is necessary to appoint a Commission of Inquiry for the purpose of making inquiry into a definite matter of public importance, that is, excesses, malpractices and misdeeds during the Emergency or in the days immediately preceding the said proclamation, by the political authorities, public servants, their friends and/or relatives and in particular allegations of gross misuse of powers of arrest or detention, maltreatment of and atrocities on detenus and other prisoners arrested under DISIR, compulsion and use of force in the implementation of the family planning programme and indiscriminate and high-handed demolition of houses, huts, shops, buildings, structures and destruction of property in the name of slum clearance or enforcement of town planning or land use schemes in the cities and towns resulting, *inter alia*, in large number of people becoming homeless or having to move far away from the places of their vocation.

Now, therefore, in exercise of the powers conferred by Section 3 of the Commissions of Inquiry Act, 1952 (60 of 1952) the Central Government hereby appoints a Commission of Inquiry consisting of the following, namely,

Chairman—Shri J. C. Shah, Retired Chief Justice of the Supreme Court of India.

2. The terms of reference of the Commission shall be as follows:

(a) to inquire into the facts and circumstances relating to specific instances of—

(i)   subversion of lawful processes and well-established conventions, administrative procedures and practices, abuse of authority, misuse of powers, excesses and/or malpractices committed during the period when the Proclamation of Emergency made on 25th June, 1975 under Article 352 of the Constitution was in force or in days immediately preceding the said Proclamation,

(ii)   misuse of powers of arrests or issue of detention orders where such arrests or orders are alleged to have been made on considerations not germane to the purposes of the relevant Acts during the aforesaid period,

(iii)   specific instances of maltreatment of and/or atrocities on persons arrested under DISIR or detained and their relatives and close associates during the aforesaid period,

(iv)   specific instances of compulsion and use of force in the implementation of the family planning programme during the aforesaid period,

(v)   indiscriminate, high-handed or unauthorised demolition of houses, huts, shops, buildings, structures and destruction of property in the name of slum clearance or enforcement of Town Planning or land use schemes, during the aforesaid period,

Provided that the inquiry shall be in regard to acts of such abuse of authority, misuse of powers, excesses, malpractices, etc. alleged to have been committed by public servants, and

Provided further that the inquiry shall also cover the conduct of other individuals who may have directed, instigated or sided or abetted or otherwise associated themselves with the commission of such acts by public servants;

(b)   to consider such other matters which, in the opinion of the Commission, have any relevance to the aforesaid allegations; and

(c)   to recommend measures which may be adopted for preventing the recurrence of such abuse of authority, misuse of powers, excesses and malpractices.

3.   The inquiry by the Commission shall be in regard to—

(i)   complaints or allegations aforesaid that may be made before the Commission by any individual or association in such form and accompanied by such affidavits as may be prescribed by the Commission, and

(ii)   such instances relatable to paragraph 2(a)(i) to (v) as may be brought to its notice by the Central Government or a State Government or an Union Territory for inquiry.

4.   The Commission shall make interim reports to the Central Government on the conclusion of inquiry into any particular allegation or series of allegations and will be expected to complete its inquiry and submit its final report to the Central Government on or before 31st December, 1977....

1.3 Subsequently, the Central Government issued the following notification extending the time for the completion of the Inquiry to June 30, 1978:...

1.4 The Commission issued notices under rule 5(2)(b) of the Commissions of Inquiry Rules. Pursuant thereto, 48,500 complaints were received in the office of the Commission.

1.5 The Government of India made the services of the following officers and staff available to the Commission for investigation of the various complaints and other cases which came for scrutiny before the Commission:—...

1.6 In a number of cases the records of the Government of India were called for by the Commission and investigations were directed by the Commission in regard to the matters appearing before it within any of the five heads of the Terms of Reference.

1.7 The Commission fixed July 31, 1977, as the last date for filing complaints. The Commission did not entertain any complaints received thereafter. The complaints received by the Commission were categorized as under:

(I)   Complaints which do not fall within the purview of the terms of reference of the Commission—to be filed and complainants informed accordingly.

(II)   Complaints which do not fall within the purview of the terms of reference of the Commission but contain serious allegations—to be referred to the Central/State Governments for inquiry and appropriate action.

(III)   Complaints falling within the terms of reference of the Commission but not serious enough to warrant inquiry by the Commission itself—to be referred to the Central/State Governments with a request to have them looked into at an appropriate level and action as deemed fit taken thereon under intimation to the complainants.

(IV)   Complaints falling within the purview of the terms of reference of the Commission which are serious enough but cannot be handled by the Commission's staff itself—to be referred to the Central/State Governments for an inquiry by a committee/authority appointed under section 11 of Commissions of Inquiry Act, 1952, and the findings and recommendations of authority to be submitted to the Commission for disposal as and when completed. The State Governments have also been requested to take whatever remedial action they deem fit in the meanwhile.

(V)   Selected complaints will be dealt with by the Commission through its own investigating agency.

1.8 From September 29, 1977 the Commission commenced hearing of oral evidence of witnesses in cases falling within its terms of reference and which were regarded as of sufficient importance.

1.9 Since the terms of reference did not name any individual or body of individuals as responsible for the commission of an excess as understood in a compendious sense, and the excesses were also set out in general terms, the Commission in the first instance invited persons, who appeared from the investigations made by the officials of the Commission and from the complaints received, either to be responsible for the excesses or to be victims of the excesses, or being otherwise able to throw light upon the commission of the excesses, and examined those persons.

1.10 At that stage, the Commission requested the persons concerned to come before the Commission and to assist the Commission in regard to certain transactions. A large number of persons appeared in pursuance of the request of the Commission. Some of those requested did not choose to appear before the Commission, some appeared at certain stages and thereafter did not appear and raised objections after appearing before the Commission and declined to participate in the proceedings of the Commission.

1.11 Evidence of the persons who showed willingness to assist the Commission was heard in all but a very few cases, in open Session. In the larger public interests, *in-camera* sittings were held in a few cases for examining certain witnesses. If on a consideration of the evidence, it appeared to the Commission necessary to inquire into the conduct of any person or the Commission was of the opinion that the reputation of any persons was likely to be affected by the inquiry, the Commission issued notices to such persons giving them opportunities of being heard in the inquiry and to furnish to the Commission, statements relating to the matters specified in the notice under rule 5(2)(a) of the Commissions of Inquiry (Central) Rules, 1972. The Commission also issued summons under section 8B of the Act affording them reasonable opportunities of being heard in the inquiry and to produce evidence regarding their versions. The Commission also afforded opportunities to these persons to cross-examine witnesses other than the witnesses produced by them and to address the Commission. The Commission also afforded opportunity to all the parties to be represented by legal practitioners.

1.12 After hearing the evidence of the persons to whom notices under section 8B were issued and of the evidence of the witnesses produced in support of the versions of those parties and also considering the evidence of the witnesses, who had been examined for the commission and whose presence was requested by the parties to whom notices under section 8B had been issued, the Commission gave to the parties or their Advocates opportunity to address the Commission on the evidence....

Chapter II

2.1 A few minutes before the midnight of June 25, 1975, the President of India proclaimed Emergency under Article 352 of the Constitution. The order promulgating the Emergency was published in the Gazette of India, Extraordinary, on the June 26, 1975. It reads:

NOTIFICATION

G.S.R. 353(E). The following Proclamation of Emergency by the President of India, dated the 25th June, 1975, is published for general information:—

"PROCLAMATION OF EMERGENCY"

In exercise of the powers conferred by clause (1) of Article 352 of the Constitution I, Fakhruddin Ali Ahmed, President of India, by this proclamation declare that a grave emergency exists whereby the security of India is threatened by internal disturbances.

2.2 There was, however, already in force a Proclamation of Emergency, which was issued on December 3, 1971, by the President of India on the ground that the security of India was threatened by external aggression. Thereafter on December 4, 1971 the Defence of India Rules, 1971 were published.

2.3 By virtue of Article 358 of the Constitution freedoms guaranteed under Article 19 of the Constitution restricting the power of the State to make any law or to take any executive action which the State would but for the provisions contained in Part III be competent to make or to take, remained suspended till the withdrawal of the Emergency proclaimed on June 25, 1975.

2.4 After the declaration of Emergency, the President of India issued an order under Article 359 of the Constitution on June 27, 1975, suspending the right to move any court for the enforcement of fundamental rights conferred by Articles 14, 21 and 22 of the Constitution....

2.6 After the declaration of Emergency a number of legislative and regulatory measures were taken with view to impose censorship on the Press....

2.9 The declaration of Emergency and the consequent suspension of the fundamental rights under Article 19, resulted in the suspension of the protection of Articles 14, 21 and 22 by the issue of the Presidential order in exercise of the powers under Article 359 of the Constitution and by the amendment of Article 352 making the satisfaction of the President final and conclusive and not liable to be questioned in any court on any ground and subject to the provisions of clause (2) taking away the jurisdiction of the Supreme Court or any other court to entertain any action on any ground regarding the validity of the declaration made by the proclamation of the President to the effect mentioned in clause (1) or to the continued operation of the proclamation, and restrictions imposed upon the authority of the courts to grant protection against the infringement of basic human rights enumerated in Article 19; all protection against arbitrary action was taken away for the duration of the Emergency. The right of equality under Article 14, the right of fundamental guarantee against deprivation of life and personal liberty according to procedure established by law also stood suspended and the protection against arrest and detention could not be challenged before the courts. The right of free speech and expression, right to assemble peacefully, to form associations and unions; to move freely throughout the territory of India; to reside and settle in any part of the territory of India; to acquire, hold and dispose of property and to practice any profession, or to carry on any occupation, trade or business, which were guaranteed under clause (1) of Article 19, could not thereafter be exercised....

Chapter 3

...3.4 The proceedings of the Commission are, neither of the nature of a civil suit, where contesting parties are arrayed on opposite sides, one pleading that a civil right has been infringed and the other contesting that claim. Nor are the proceedings of the nature of a criminal proceeding, in which it is pleaded that a person or persons have committed infraction of the law and has or have on that account incurred liability for imposition of a penalty prescribed by law. In the case for trial of a suit the function of the court is to determine the civil rights and to grant appropriate relief to the person claiming to be aggrieved; if the infraction of his right is proved, the liability of the person infringing the right is established: in a criminal trial the function of the court is to determine whether the action of a person charged with the commission of an infraction of a law is established to have been committed by him and whether such an infraction is established beyond reasonable doubt. These proceedings are adversary proceedings—one party alleging existence of a certain right and the other party denying the right or the statement of the complainant alleging infraction of the law by the other party and the other party denying such infraction.

3.5 Functions of the Commission under the Act are, however, of an entirely different nature. The Commission is not concerned with the establishment of any civil rights or the infraction of those rights. The Commission is also not concerned to determine the infraction of any laws involving the imposition of any penalty upon a person charged with the commission of infraction of a law. The proceedings before the Commission are not of an adversary character. It is the duty of the Commission appointed for that purpose to make an inquiry into the subject matter of the inquiry if the subject-matter is of definite public importance. For that purpose, the Commission is invested with certain powers, set out in section 4 and 5 of the Act.

3.6 The Commission, constituted under section 3 of the Commissions of Inquiry Act, may be called upon to hold inquiries into a variety of matters of definite public importance.... In view of the variety of transactions or subject matters in respect of which the Commission may be appointed to inquire, the Legislature has not prescribed any definite form of procedure; and has left it to the Commission by section 8 to regulate its own procedure. This power is, however, not unguided and is subject to the Rules that may be made in that behalf by the Central Government.... Certain other restrictions are also imposed by sections 8B and 8C on the power of the Commission to regulate its own procedure....

3.16 It was also emphasised that the proceedings before the Commission are for determining the truth ... by the adoption of a procedure to be devised by the Commission having regard to the nature of the inquiry and which is essentially inquisitorial in character, as prescribed by the Act....

3.26 It was pointed out that the procedure has to be devised by the Commission in each case having regard to the nature of the inquiry to be made; and rarely there would be any two Commissions which would follow the same procedure. There may be a case, where no person may be involved directly or indirectly; but only certain matters are to be investigated by the Commission. There may be cases in which no person may be named as responsible for any impropriety and such persons may have to be identified and their involvement in the impropriety determined; there may be other cases in which the person alleged to be responsible for improper conduct may be named. In each such case the procedure would be different and the Commission has to devise a procedure, subject to the Rules and affording protection or safeguards provided by the statute to the persons against whom inquiry may have to be made....

Chapter 4

4.4 Out of a number of cases which came to its notice by virtue of the complaints made to it or on the basis of the information developed by the Commission, the Commission took up for open hearing only those cases in which it appeared that there had been a blatant abuse of authority or misuse of powers relating to instances falling under one of the five heads of the terms of reference. In this regard one general principle which has been kept in mind is that the excess complained of must be a nature which would be capable of creating a crisis of confidence or which is one of national importance.

Chapter 5

In the Elections held to the Lok Sabha in 1971 from the Rai Bareily Constituency Smt. Indira Gandhi was declared elected, defeating Shri Raj Narain and others who had contested the election. Shri Raj Narain then filed a petition in the High Court of Allahabad challenging the election of Smt. Indira Nehru Gandhi on a number of grounds, *inter alia*, alleging misconduct against her. The High Court of Allahabad pronounced its judgment on June 12, 1975. Shri J. M. L. Sinha of Allahabad High Court ordered:

> In view of my findings … this petition is allowed and the election of Smt. Indira Nehru Gandhi respondent No. 1 to the Lok Sabha is declared void.

The Court further ruled that:

> In respondent No. 1, accordingly, stands disqualified for a period of six years from the date of this order, as provided in section 8A of the Representation of the People Act.

The Court further directed:

> The operation of the said order is accordingly stayed for a period of twenty days. On the expiry of the said period of 20 days or as soon as an appeal is filed in the Supreme Court, whichever takes place earlier, this order shall cease to carry effect.

5.2 Following the judgment of the Allahabad High Court setting aside the election of Smt. Indira Gandhi there was a spurt of political activity in Delhi in particular and in the rest of India in general.

5.3 Apparently, an effort was made by the followers of Smt. Indira Gandhi to create an atmosphere that she should, notwithstanding that she was unseated and disqualified to stand for election, continue to remain and function as Prime Minister of India regardless of the High Court verdict. With that object in view, a number of demonstrations, rallies and meetings were arranged by her supporters in Delhi and elsewhere....

5.6 The records of Delhi Transport Corporation show that 1761 DTC buses were requisitioned by the All India Congress Committee or the Delhi Pradesh Congress Committee for organising the rallies in support of Smt. Indira Gandhi between June 12, 1975 and June 25, 1975....

5.23 While Government bodies were vying with each other to show their support to or sympathy for the Prime Minister by misusing Government resources, there were Government employees, both highly and lowly placed, who were not willing to be a party to what they thought was wrong and improper in terms of employment of Government resources for a political party for partisan purposes. Shri R. N. Bhatnagar of the NDMC opposed the diversion of the NDMC trucks from the normal duties to proceed to the P.M.'s House, and lay in front of a truck of the NDMC, which was sought to be diverted to proceed to the P.M.'s House. He pleaded that if the employees and the authorities wanted to signify their support to Smt. Indira Gandhi, they were welcome to do so but not at the cost of the civic resources.

5.24 Certain employees of the DESU, who refused to participate in these rallies, were allegedly beaten up by the more enthusiastic amongst the supporters of the Prime Minister....

5.26 While the Government resources in Delhi and elsewhere were being utilised to demonstrate support in favour of the Prime Minister, the law was also discriminately applied to the Congress party as against the other parties. Enforcement of prohibition of meetings under section 144 of the Criminal Procedure Code, which had become a normal feature in the vicinity of the Prime Minister's House, was relaxed when it came to demonstrations and rallies arranged by the Congress party in support of the Prime Minister....

5.27 While these demonstrations of sympathy and support to the Prime Minister were going on apace, the Intelligence Bureau of the Government of India was being used to maintain surveillance on the activities of some of the important Congress leaders and Ministers. The Commission came across a Top Secret note dated June 18, 1975, sent by the then Director, Intelligence Bureau, to the Prime Minister's Secretariat. It contains matters which among other things could have been compiled only on the basis of a physical watch and telephone tappings of the persons concerned. This raises a very important issue which has relevance to the assault on the privacy of the individuals and even of Ministers of Government for purposes which are other than those strictly necessary for ensuring the security of the State....

5.61 As stated earlier, a notice under rule 5(2)(a) of the Commissions of Inquiry Rules was issued to Smt. Gandhi requesting her to file her statement in terms of rule 5(3). No such statement was filed by her. Smt. Gandhi was also issued a summons under section 8B of the Commissions of Inquiry Act. Though she responded to the summons under section 8B of the Act, she declined to take oath and give evidence on oath when the Commission desired to examine her under section 5(2) and according to the procedure analogous to the provisions of the Civil Procedure Code. But in one of the letters addressed by her to the Commission, dated November 21, 1977, in response to the invitation which was initially extended to her to assist the Commission, Smt. Gandhi had submitted a detailed reply to the Commission in regard to certain matters and, *inter alia*, raising certain objections to the procedure adopted by the Commission. In the course of her reply, she touched on the subject of declaration of Emergency and stated:

> I should further like to point out that the terms of reference on this Hon'ble Commission are one-sided and politically motivated. While they empower the Hon'ble Commission to enquire into the excesses committed during the emergency, they are silent about the circumstances which led to its declaration. This country is vast and beset with deep-rooted and wide-ranging problems. The administrative machinery is fragmented. Urgent measures have to be taken. Programmes are implemented at various levels and by different individuals and agencies. Some excesses in their implementation cannot always be avoided nor do they always come to notice at that time. I have publicly expressed regret for any unjust hardship caused to any individual. But if the professed purpose of the inquiry is to check abuse of power in the future, it is equally imperative that the circumstances which created chaotic conditions in the nation before the emergency should also be enquired into and not allowed to be repeated. For two years preceding the emergency the country was in the grip of grave crisis. The economic situation had deteriorated due mainly to internal and international causes beyond our control. Interested parties and groups wished deliberately to aggravate the situation for their own gain. Freedom of speech and expression were used to spread hatred and parochial regional sentiments. Noble institutions of learning were turned into hot-beds of political intrigue. Public property was destroyed at the slightest excuse. A Minister in the present cabinet is reported to have proudly claimed, "In November last (1975) in the Union State of Karnataka alone, we caused derailment of 52 trains". The attempt was to paralyse national life. The dissolution of the Gujrat Assembly was forced by undemocratic means. Duly elected legislators were beaten and intimidated into resigning from their seats in the Assembly.

> Relying upon the judgment of the Allahabad High Court, the demand for my resignation was made in the name of democracy and morality. But what was that morality and how did democracy come in? If at all, moral considerations were on my side as nothing had been found by the High Court against me which smacked of moral turpitude. I had lost on a legal technicality but law also gave

> me the right to reconsideration of the judgment by the highest
> court. And the act of seeking to remove a duly elected leader of the
> majority party through threats to gherao me and with a call to the
> Army and the Police to revolt could not be justified in the name of
> any known democratic principles. A chaotic state of affairs similar
> to that in India before July 1975 prevailed in France when de Gaulle
> came to power in 1958. His major response was constitutional
> reform and the introduction of Article 16 in the new Constitution
> which ... provided *inter alia* that "when the regular functioning of
> the constitutional governmental authorities is interrupted, the
> President of the Republic shall take the measures commended by
> the circumstances" to restore order.
>
> It must also be borne in mind that it would be impossible for a
> democratically elected government to function effectively if it is to
> live under the fear of politically inspired inquisitorial proceedings
> against its policies and decisions by a subsequent government.

5.62 Smt. Gandhi sent yet another reply dated December 2, 1977, in
response to another invitation, which was extended to her by the
Commission when the case dealing with the circumstances leading to the
declaration of Emergency was coming up for the First Stage of its hearing
before the Commission from December 5, 1977 and the following days. The
relevant portions of her reply are reproduced below:

> In fact, that the declaration of Emergency, according to this Hon'ble
> Commission, might be an excess and, therefore, calls for an inquiry,
> is a matter which does not fall within the purview of this Hon'ble
> Commission. The proclamation of Emergency by the President was
> a Constitutional step. It was approved by the Cabinet and duly
> ratified by both Houses of Parliament in terms of Article 352(2) of
> the Constitution. After the ratification, the proclamation which was
> political in character, became an Act of Parliament....
>
> No authority in this country, not excluding any commission
> appointed under the Commissions of Inquiry Act, can sit in
> judgment over such an Act of Parliament. For any political
> decision, the Government under our Constitution is answerable
> only to Parliament. If this Hon'ble Commission arrogates to itself
> the power to determine that the declaration of Emergency was an
> excess, this Hon'ble Commission will not only be stultifying the
> Constitutional Scheme, but also establishing a precedent which will
> make serious inroad into Parliamentary supremacy with disastrous
> consequences to Parliamentary freedom. Even the terms of
> reference of this Hon'ble Commission do not warrant such an
> inquiry. They are strictly confined to the determination of alleged
> excesses during the emergency or in the days immediately
> preceding it....
>
> During that period, ostensibly the attacks were concentrated upon
> me. In reality the political opposition had been using this strategy
> to weaken the Central Government and subvert its socialist and
> progressive programmes for quite some years. It was a question of
> change versus the status quo. Secular, democratic socialism on the
> one hand and retrograde, communal and capitalistic forces on the
> other had been struggling against each other to gain the upper
> hand. The split in the Congress in 1969 gave an edge to this
> confrontation. The nationalisation of banks and other measures
> which disturbed entrenched privileges and vested interests, and
> offered opportunity and help to the poor and weaker sections of
> our society, created such tremendous popular upsurge that

communal and capitalistic elements probably lost all hope of being able to successfully fight on an ideological plane. Hence they changed their methods. Similar such political phenomenon was not peculiar to India. Recent history is replete with such instances.

The vicious campaign of character assassination and denigration waged by political opponents denuded Indian politics of all ideological debates.... There was then a short interlude during which India faced one of the gravest challenges with which any nation has been confronted. The influx of ten million refugees from Bangladesh, aggression and the subsequent war, unprecedented country-wide drought and the global inflationary spiral aggravated by the oil crisis, and other factors would have upset the economic balance of any rich and developed country. India was fighting for her economic survival. It was during this period that the then Opposition resorted to extra-constitutional means to paralyse our democratic institutions. As I have explained in my previous statement, there was hardly any sphere of national life which was not sought to be disrupted.

The inevitable distress of many sections of our people was exploited to mount attacks on duly elected Governments and Assemblies of the day.... It was in this political atmosphere prevailing in the country that the judgment of the Allahabad High Court was delivered and was seized upon by the opposition to whip up political frenzy against me. Although I was in the immediate target, the real design was to dislodge the Congress Government and to capture power through extra-constitutional means. If a duly elected Government can be allowed to be pulled down by threats of violence and demonstrations in the streets and by incitement of the army and the police to revolt, the democratic structure of the nation would collapse. In 1958, while putting the case for constitutional reform the French Prime Minister, M. Gallard said, "Democracy is only in consequence an anarchy if those who hold power by the will of the majority do not also enjoy an authority corresponding to the responsibilities which they assume."

As Prime Minister of the country I could not abdicate my responsibility to stem the impending disaster merely for fear that my motive in proclaiming the emergency could be suspected. When the democratic institutions of a nation are held to ransom, and the Government of the day rises to the occasion to meet the challenge, certain freedoms of some individuals might be affected. That in fact is the rationale behind Article 352 of the Constitution which authorises the declaration of Emergency. Emergency was not intended to cause suffering and I have expressed deep sorrow for any hardship caused....

In these circumstances, the Hon'ble Commission's predetermination of certain dates while circumscribing the scope of its inquiry, belies reality. It has been repeatedly proclaimed by members of the present Union Government that it was allegedly because of the Allahabad High Court Judgment of the 12th June, 1975, and the qualified stay given by the Supreme Court on 22nd of June, that the Emergency was declared for personal reasons, namely, to stultify the judgment by extra-legal means and to maintain my position as Prime Minister by extra-constitutional methods. I have to point out, with utmost respect, that the Commission appears to have projected the theory propagated by my political opponents.

By putting the inquiry beforehand into a predetermined chronological matrix the evidence would naturally proceed under the conditioning of this predetermined matrix, and this untested material will be systematically publicised to make it appear as proof. This, in my humble opinion, directly defeats the ends of justice.

5.70 This was more in the nature of a shock treatment, than a legally permissible Emergency, which could be declared according to the law then in force.

5.71 If, however, an Internal Emergency could be declared apart from the External Emergency, the powers which were exercised before any Rules were framed, *i.e.* disconnecting the electricity connections of newspaper offices, were wholly unauthorised, since there was no law which conferred upon any authority such power. Again, the action taken by the authorities under the directions of the Prime Minister to arrest a number of political leaders was not supported by any law....

5.72 [T]he conclusions arrived at by the Intelligence Bureau after mounting surveillance upon political leaders and others, including tapping of their telephones, raise a grave issue of public interest. It has relevance to the assault on the liberty of an individual, which in a democratic country has very great importance and significance. Even the Ministers of the Government were not spared in the action taken by the Intelligence Bureau. They were subjected to the indignity of being shadowed and their telephones were tapped. Such a power, if at all, could be exercised only when authorised by statutory provisions and circumstances strictly necessary for ensuring the security of the State in grave times either of internal disturbance or external aggression or war and not at other times. On the materials placed before the Commission, there does not appear to be any statutory authority pursuant to which this action of the Intelligence Bureau was taken. In his statement to the Commission, Shri Atma Jaya Ram, the then Director, Intelligence Bureau, has stated that "it was the normal or usual practice to give such intelligence orally or in writing". Such action does not appear to be justified by the existence of any circumstance necessary for ensuring the security of the State against External aggression, war or internal Emergency.

5.73 As already submitted, it is for the Government to decide whether or not the Intelligence Bureau may be used for collecting information for purposes other than those strictly necessary for the security of the State. It would certainly be a travesty of the democratic institutions if the Government constituted by a political party is entitled to watch the activities of other political parties and even of members of its own party. If, however, such power is to be conferred on this institution, it must be by a statute or statutory Rules authorising it in that behalf. It is also to be ensured that this watch or surveillance does not degenerate into abuse and/or misuse of authority, which may well militate against individual freedom and liberty. A provision should, therefore, be made to see that it is resorted to only in extreme emergencies, when it is thought that it is appropriate to do so. In any event, this watch of the Intelligence agency on individuals and the materials collected thereby should be open to scrutiny to a Board or a Panel composed of officers or of public men before authorising the continuance of the watch. It should be possible to harmonise the demands of the security of the State with the democratic liberties....

It needs to be realised that the [Intelligence Bureau] as an institution plays a very important and vital role in the life and affairs of the nation. On its being able to function efficiently, effectively and yet impartially and objectively, depends not only the security of the State but also the liberty of its citizens. Considering, therefore, the stakes that are involved in the proper and purposeful functioning of the [Intelligence Bureau], it is imperative that it gets the benefit of advice, guidance and wisdom of a body of eminent, experienced and patriotic group of individuals drawn from different disciplines and whose loyalty and personal integrity cannot ever be called into question. This in turn will generate the requisite faith and confidence of the citizens of the country in this very important institution on the fair, correct and proper functioning of which alone would eventually depend the safety, the security and the liberty of the people of this country....

In a strict theoretical sense in a democratic country any secret operations of the nature conducted by the Intelligence Bureau, which have come to the notice of the Commission, would be contrary to the democratic norms. The Intelligence Bureau should not be its own judge of its operations with regard to the necessity or the propriety thereof, nor should it be allowed to act as an agency or an instrument of politicians or to degenerate into an institution of controlling the opponents of the political party in power or elements within the party in power with which the controlling authority of the party does not see eye to eye....

5.80 Attention may also be invited to the gross irregularities to which the provisions of the Maintenance of Internal Security Act [MISA] and provisions of the Defence of India Rules were misused to the detriment of political opponents.... [T]he minimum requirements of ... were not complied with, either at the behest of Smt. Indira Gandhi or her aides and orders were made without any grounds, without any satisfaction or maintenance of any record regarding the satisfaction of competent authorities; and personal liberty of many citizens was taken way and they continued to remain deprived of that liberty for substantial periods even in face of the safeguards which were ... disregarded with impunity.

5.81 In Delhi and in the States, which had advance information about the promulgation of Emergency, a large number of arrests/detentions followed under MISA in which the safeguards guaranteed against the misuse of the Act were ignored and grounds of detentions were not furnished in a large number of cases and in many cases grounds of detentions were prepared and even pre-dated and sent many days after the persons concerned had been arrested/detained in jails. In a number of cases grounds of detentions had no relevance to the factual positions and in a few cases grounds were fabricated by the police and the Magistrates did not hesitate to sign them. An era of collusion between the police and the Magistracy ensued. In many cases oral instructions were issued from the

State Headquarters for arrests of persons under MISA. In quite a few cases the persons were initially taken into custody under the preventive sections of law and thereafter detained under MISA. This was the device, which appears to have been resorted to in the Union Territory of Delhi shortly after the promulgation of Emergency. A number of persons were arrested on false charges under ... the Code of Criminal Procedure.... Such persons were produced before the Magistrates and the Magistrates in a number of cases either declined to grant bail or there was delay in effecting the orders of bail and in the meanwhile orders of detentions were procured from the Magistrates, which were passed not infrequently on non-existent or fabricated grounds. The manner in which the provisions of MISA were used was nothing short of perversion and mockery of its provisions and all the safeguards and guarantees that had been promised in the Parliament when the MISA Bill was enacted, were totally disregarded. Many apprehensions, which were expressed by the Members of Parliament, who spoke against conferment of such wide powers when the Bill was enacted, came true.

5.82 The safeguards enshrined in the enactment were rendered meaningless by the callous misapplication of this Act by the police and the Magistracy, in many cases with the full knowledge and concurrence of some of the State Governments. The use and/or the misuse of this Act raises issues, which require examination in the larger context. At no time, either normal or abnormal, should there be any possibility of misuse of the powers of arrest. It needs to be made clear to all those responsible for overseeing the correct application of the powers of arrest/detention by the junior officers, that the senior functionaries at the bureaucratic and political levels would be held directly accountable for any misuse or abuse of the powers of arrest and detention.

SIERRA LEONE: REPORT OF THE FORSTER COMMISSION OF INQUIRY ON ASSETS OF EX-MINISTERS AND EX-DEPUTY MINISTERS

(1968)

Final Report

The history of the sixties of this century will record one of the most turbulent epochs of the continent of Africa. There was a universal upsurge of nationalism, for good or ill, led by men who did not always see clearly where they were heading, and indeed, did not know how to achieve the sought for goal of political and economic freedom for those they professed to be leading.

Sierra Leone was no exception and, the political leaders who brought a politically rich-above-average country of this continent to a standstill and returned her welnigh [*sic*] to jungle-law times, were inexcusably guilty of grave moral lapses.

Between January, 1961 and April, 1964, Sierra Leone passed through a time of severe testing of its leaders. It was not possible to build a stable government because of primarily, a fundamental lack of basic educational qualification in many ministers, and secondly of a marked similarity with Dr. Faustus in their sense of values. Stealing from the government was as common as petty larceny of private property. This idea that one can take by way of gain from the government or other institutions without being guilty of theft is an all too prevalent and, we must say, utterly unmeritorious distinction of conscience these days, and is responsible for quite a lot of dishonesty. It is really to be hoped that the series of commissions of inquiry will make every citizen to see the lack of distinction more clearly.

The period commencing immediately with the death of the late Prime Minister, Sir Milton Margai, and culminating in the General Elections of March this year is one of which no self-respecting Sierra Leonean can be proud. Two characteristic assumptions marked this period, firstly that the government could do no wrong and secondly that the government would live forever. The danger attendant on all doctrines which are founded on assumptions, implications or fictions originally thought to be equitable is that they are apt to be extended by a process of logical development which loses sight of their origin and carries them far beyond the reach of any such justification as they may have originally possessed. There was such a widespread disregard of General Orders, Financial and Administrative Instructions that one is reminded of certain biblical times when there was no king in Israel and everyone did as he pleased, and might became right.

In submitting this report, which is complementary to our interim reports, we are conscious of our human limitations and fallibilities but we have tried to be as objective as possible within the confines of our laws, based on the Common Law and the provisions of *Magna Carta*.

If we appear to have been lenient in our judgments, it is because the evidence before us could not permit otherwise. Some may go to the other extreme and say that our findings are harsh; to them we say that our considered analysis of the evidence adduced before us, led us inexorably thither.

This report is a collation of individual interim reports we had submitted from time to time in the past months, and to which certain omissions therein indicated are now being made good.

This report relates to the following former Ministers and Deputy Ministers namely:...

Mr. R.G.O. King—Minister

The amount we find refundable by Mr. King as unlawfully obtained overseas subsistence allowances is Le 2,357.85 made up as follows:...

Summary: We find Mr. King unlawfully obtained the following:

(1) Le 2,357.85 from government as subsistence allowance for visits overseas;

(2) Le 247.80 from government as local allowance and cost he caused government to incur on his behalf while attending Party Rallies;

(3) Le 37,000 excess by government in purchasing various properties, obtained severally and jointly with three other ministers namely Messrs. A.J. Demby (*Mines, Lands and Labour*), M.J. Kamanda Bongay *Works*) and G. Dickson- Thomas (*Housing and Country Planning*);

(4) Sweets of office admitted by Mr. King to the tune of Le 86,920— inclusive of the Le 24,000 "fish money"....

Mr. Maigore Kallon-Minister

...(c) In July of this year (1966) Mr. Kallon was a special envoy of the ex-Prime Minister to the Ghana government, received full hospitality and should refund the Le 144.00 he received from government as subsistence allowance.

(d) Mr. Kallon visited Guinea twice, once from 13-17/6/66 and from 26-30/7/66, received full hospitality on that occasion and should refund the total of Le 310.00 received by him as subsistence allowance from that visit....

(e) Le 231.80 received as allowance and cost incurred by government in connection with Mr. Kallon's attendances at Party Rallies.

(f) Le 2,200 or the property at Murray Town bought by Mr. Kallon from Mr. Blell in 1964 from gifts received as sweets of office (*see* Exhibit 291)....

Report on Sir Albert Margai—Former Prime Minister

On the 1st January, 1961 Albert Michael Margai, then just turned 50 years of age was a Minister of the Government of Sierra Leone led by his late brother Sir Milton Margai, but between that date and the 28th of April, 1964 when he succeeded in becoming Prime Minister, following the death of Sir Milton, he had served in several Ministries, including Education and Finance. In his sworn declarations dated 16th May, 1967 (Exh. 104) and 31st May, 1967 (Exh. 105) respectively and evidence given before us, Sir Albert gave evidence that on the 28th April, 1964 he was worth Le 125,913.68 made up as follows:...

On the 23rd of March 1967, however, Sir Albert's wealth, according to his own sworn evidence before us had rocketed to Le 529,903.46, that is an addition of Le 403,989.78 in less than three years—that is in thirty-five months....

When Sir Albert's evidence on oath is considered, the total income proved amounts to Le 403,989.78 an excess of Le 398,731.45. Sir Albert could not explain how he came by this large sum excepting for Le 20,000 which he said he received as a gift from the Freedom Fighters of Rhodesia. This excess of Le 398,731.45 does not include the amount Sir Albert declared as the value of the former S.L.P.P. building at 19 Water Street, Freetown, i.e. Le 136,743.00. We are satisfied, and find that Sir Albert obtained this sum of Le 398,731.45 unlawfully....

Sir Albert admitted work was done by the Railway Department for him and for which he had not paid the department—making of garden seats and supplying cutting up old rails for fence posts, etc.—we have not been able to get details of this. We have, however, excluded the cost of improvement to the road outside Sir Albert's Lumley compound as though this work was carried out primarily for Sir Albert's benefit, yet the premises bordering the road were also thereby improved and the village itself consequently. We do not think it fair to lay the cost of this on Sir Albert. We also feel, most strongly that the payment of subsistence allowance to Sir Albert when in every instance of his overseas visits to Europe or America or other parts of Africa, he was in receipt of full hospitality while a Prime Minister, was unlawful and we find the total of such payments for the period May, 1964 to March, 1967 is Le 5,021.00. In addition the cost of passages and subsistence allowances paid his two private Secretaries Messrs. Brainard and During who were neither employed nor paid by Government, when accompanying Sir Albert overseas was unlawfully borne by Government; subsistence allowances alone for these two secretaries amounting to Le 3,506 during the said period; when it is remembered that other official secretaries from the Prime Minister's Office were in attendance, the need for the presence of Messrs. Brainard and During on these occasions we find purely personal to

Sir Albert and of no official value to Government. We find, in this connection that the same principle applies to passage fares and subsistence and transport allowances paid by Government to and in respect of Lady Margai's attendances on the same occasions, from the fact that she is the wife of the Prime Minister. Any other Minister in such missions would have had to bear the cost of his wife accompanying him even if that wife had to cook for members of the delegation. It is invidious to make any such distinction in the case of the Prime Minister. In her case, subsistence and transport allowances alone paid by Government to Lady Margai in June, 1965 amount to Le 2,106.18.

Sir Albert in his evidence on oath, assured us that he did not receive more than 50% of his due of night allowance for travelling within Sierra Leone, outside Freetown during his period of office as Prime Minister—his journeys within Sierra Leone for the earlier period 1st January, 1961 to 28th April, 1964, being negligible. The other sources from which Sir Albert said he derived some income were his commercial ventures and extensive landed properties which yielded substantial rents....

Lady Margai's total cash in Banks in March, 1967 was Le 13,458.70 about Le 5,000 of which was rent from her landed properties up to that date. Lady Margai ran a general provisions shop at Gbangbatoke, Sir Albert's home town, the net profit from which, at the best of times could not have been much....

Sir Albert has been leader of the S.L.P.P. since he became Prime Minister in April 1964 and had appointed himself Treasurer though there was an officially appointed National Treasurer, Mr. M.S. Mustapha, who remained thus till March, 1967. In his self-appointed capacity he garnered large sums of money for and on behalf of the S.L. Peoples' Party, keeping this fund privately responsible to nobody for its disbursement and accounting to nobody for any portion of it. It was from this fund he had the Party Building in Water Street erected on land he failed to satisfy us that he had leased to him or the Party by Government. Every former Minister or Deputy Minister who gave evidence before us was questioned about the said Party Building and each in turn avowed making no financial contribution thereto and knowing nothing about its construction saving what had been told them at various times by Sir Albert.... This property, 19 Water Street on which the Party Building was erected is found by us to belong to Government and the building was therefore ordered by us to be taken over by Government and this has since been done by an order of the Commission dated June 19, 1967....

We are satisfied, however, that Sir Albert has not told us the whole truth about the total amount he received, during his Prime Ministership for and on behalf of the Party he led; we believe he is still in possession of further Party Funds taking into consideration the circumstances leading to the debacle in March, 1967. Sir Albert initiated what has turned out to be a heavy drain on Government of public funds that is, Political Rallies, on a country-wide scale. Since their inception, after April, 1964, they have grown in size and importance. There is record of a dozen during the ensuing years ending March last and Sir Albert attended each with a fleet of motor vehicles and a large retinue of Government officials and private individuals. Sir Albert strongly denies that he attended these rallies per se. He asserts that the rallies were coincidental and took place while he was on official tours. We hasten to reject this assertion as untrue and are confidently satisfied that the camouflage of officialdom is patently weak. The repeated coincidences—if such they be, of official tours consistently overlapping with Party Rallies leads to only one sure conclusion and that we find to be that Sir Albert's attendances were made to that end howbeit, he may have done some official business to lend colour to his assertion. In three cases, he attended these rallies by chartered flight for which Government was debited and not the Party....

As a Prime Minister, Sir Albert was a modern Machiavelli. His use of his Ministers for his private material gain was clearly demonstrated in many financial transactions—

(a) We find he has not paid duty on his imported Cadillac Car which, we believe, the Hon. Finance Minister exempted only because he dared not offend his Prime Minister. The duty will have to be assessed and recovered from Sir Albert....

(c) We further find that Sir Albert had the Ministry of Lands and Mines farm out certain houses of his (2 in Brookfields, Freetown and 1 in Bo) to the S.L.P.M.B. at certainly high rent for which he was paid Le 5,760.00 in February, 1966 by the said Board....

(e) We find that Sir Albert in conjunction with his Secretary, Mr. G.S. Panda and Mr. A.J. Demby former Minister of Lands and Mines, trafficked extensively in diamonds; there is no evidence that any of them had licence so to do although, while Minister of Lands and Mines at this time, Mr. Demby was a partner in an active and profitable family Mining Company in Sierra Leone. Questioned about Ministers being engaged in commercial pursuits, Sir Albert said he thought it reasonable for his Minister of Lands and Mines to participate in the Demby Family Mining Company. Sir Albert's London account with S.B.W.A. (Exh. 347) shows that between June, 1961 and February, 1967 he had been credited with Le 24,419.15 in various sums which he said he knew nothing about. Some of these sums are recorded as having been paid into his bank account by his Secretary, Mr. G.S. Panda or by the latter's wife; a company recorded indifferently in (Exh. 311) as "S. Japhet and Company" and "Charlestone Japhet and Company" also paid large sums into this account and Sir Albert forswore all knowledge of any such company; a few other credits, paid in by other banks were equally not explicable to Sir Albert....

These items from each of these three bank statements do not exhaust the instances which confirm our finding of what seems perilously close to Illicit Diamond Trafficking by Sir Albert, his former Secretary and his former Minister of Mines. Sir Albert said to his sworn evidence before us that he had received £10,000 as a gift from Rhodesian Freedom Fighters and this sum appears in exhibit 347 as payment in on 29/6/65 from the Swiss Bank of

£6,000 and 14 months later on the 15/9/66, from the same Swiss Bank of £4,000. We are satisfied that these sums of money were sweets of office and unlawfully obtained by Sir Albert.

This is not a report on the conduct of Sir Albert as a Minister of Government, nay more as the former Prime Minister of Sierra Leone; enough has been publicised in the local press about this but the evidence heard by us when we inquired into Sir Albert's assets proved that he caused Government, without reasonable cause, to expend large sums of money on prestigious overseas delegations as when he led a delegation of 35 to the Prime Ministers' Conference in 1965. Sir Albert admitted that he controlled and settled the list of delegates and we find that he was solely liable for these unnecessarily large delegations which were never in the National interest and which were such a heavy drain on the slender Sierra Leone Exchequer....

There are yet other subject heads to be inquired into involving Sir Albert, in many instances, personally such as the 17 Statutory Corporations, one of which did not appear to have got off to a start, and 10 Pre-financed contract schemes. But the present state of Sir Albert's health which protracted the inquiry into his assets, may have some important bearing on the future course of the Commission's work....

Orders Finally Made by the National Reformation Council

1. The National Reformation Council, after reviewing the Orders of the Forster Commission of Inquiry, ordered on the 27th of February, 1968, that Sir Albert Margai, former Prime Minister, should pay to the State a total amount of Le 771,037.14 ... within thirty days from the 27th of February, 1968, failing which, action will be taken against Sir Albert in accordance with the provisions of the National Reformation Council (Forfeiture of Assets) (No. 2) Decree, 1967.

2. The National Reformation Council has also ordered that a Cadillac Saloon Car No. WU 838 in the possession of Sir Albert Margai should be confiscated to the State with immediate effect....

The National Reformation Council after reviewing the Orders of the Forster Commission of Inquiry ordered on the 15th of January, 1968 that the undermentioned Ex-Ministers and Ex-Deputy Ministers should pay within 30 days of the order, the amount shown against their respective names:

[The report then lists 21 former officials owing amounts ranging from 61 leones to 52,957 leones.]

UGANDA: LEGAL NOTICE CREATING THE COMMISSION OF INQUIRY INTO VIOLATIONS OF HUMAN RIGHTS

The Commissions of Inquiry Act
Legal Notice No. 5 (May 16, 1986)
(Cap. 56)

A Commission

Whereas for a period of nearly two decades the people of Uganda have experienced diverse forms of violation of human rights, breaches of the rule of law and excessive abuse of power, in contravention of the provisions of the Constitution of Uganda and of the Universal Declaration of Human Rights to which Uganda is party:

And Whereas in the interest of good Government, public security and welfare and constitutional supremacy it is deemed expedient that the causes of the circumstances surrounding and possible ways of preventing the recurrence of the matters aforesaid, be inquired into:

Now Therefore,

In Exercise of the powers conferred upon the Minister by section 2 of the Commissions of Inquiry Act, I, JOSEPH NYAMIHANA MULENGA, Do Hereby appoint,

    (i)   Hon. Mr. Justice Arthur O. Oder;
   (ii)   Mr. Edward Khiddu-Makubuya;
  (iii)   Mr. Jack Luyombya;
  (iv)   Mr. John Kawanga;
   (v)   Mr. John Nagenda;

to be Commissioners to inquire into all aspects of violation of human rights, breaches of the rule of law and excessive abuses of power, committed against persons in Uganda by the regimes in government, their servants, agents or agencies whatsoever called, during the period from the 9th day of October, 1962 to the 25th day of January, 1986 and possible ways of preventing the recurrence of the aforesaid matters, and in particular, but without limiting the generality of the foregoing, to inquire into,

    (a)   the causes and circumstances surrounding the mass murders and all acts or omissions resulting in the arbitrary deprivation of human life, committed in various parts of Uganda;

    (b)   the causes and circumstances surrounding the numerous arbitrary arrests, consequent detentions without trial, arbitrary imprisonment and abuse of the powers of detention and restriction under the Public Order and Security Act, 1967;

(c) the denial of any person of a fair and public trial before an independent and impartial court established by law;

(d) the subjection of any person to torture, cruel, inhuman and degrading treatment;

(e) the manner in which the law enforcement agents and the state security agencies executed their functions, the extent to which the practices and procedures employed in the execution of such functions may have violated the human rights of any person and the extent to which the state security agencies may have interfered with the functioning of the law-enforcement agents;

(f) the causes and circumstances surrounding the massive displacement of persons and expulsion of people including Uganda citizens from Uganda and the consequent disappearance or presumed death of some of them;

(g) the subjection of any person to discriminatory treatment by virtue of race, tribe, place of origin, political opinion, creed or sex, by any person acting under any written law or in the performance of the functions of any public office or public authority;

(h) the denial to any person of any other fundamental freedoms and rights prescribed under Chapter III of the Constitution of Uganda or the unlawful interference with the enjoyment by any person in Uganda of the said freedoms and rights;

(i) the protection by act or omission of any person that perpetrated any of the aforesaid things, from due process of law;

(j) any other matter connected with or incidental to the matters aforesaid which the Commission may wish to examine and recommend;

And I Do Hereby direct that Hon. Mr. Justice Arthur O. Oder be the Chairman of the Commission;

And I Do Hereby appoint Mr. Ben B. Oluka to be the Secretary to the Commission;

And I Do Hereby direct that in the proper discharge of its duty, the Commission may call such witnesses and ask for the production of such evidence as it may deem necessary and may receive such assistance from any person as it may think fit;

And I Do Hereby prescribe that the said Commission shall in the course of its inquiry, so far as is practicable, apply the law of evidence, and shall in particular conform with the following instructions, that is to say,

(a) that any person desiring to give evidence to the Commission shall do so in person;

(b) that hearsay evidence which adversely affects the reputation of any person or tends to reflect in any way upon the character or conduct of any person shall not be received;

(c)   that no expression of opinion on the character, conduct or motives of any person shall be received in evidence;

(d)   that any who in the opinion of the Commissioners is adversely affected by the evidence given before the Commission shall be given an opportunity to be heard and to cross-examine the person giving such evidence, and

except in so far as the Commissioners consider it essential for ascertaining the truth of the matter into which the Commissioners are commissioned to inquire, not to depart from such instructions;

And I Do Hereby direct that the said inquiry be held at places within Uganda as the said Commission may from time to time, determine, and may be held in public or in private or partly in public and partly in private as the Commission may from time to time determine;

And I Do Hereby direct that the Commission shall start as soon as possible and shall execute the said inquiry with all due diligence and speed and make their report to me with recommendations without undue delay and within the shortest possible time;

And I Do Hereby require all other persons, whom it may concern to take due notice hereby and to give their obedience accordingly.

Dated this 16th day of May, 1986.

JOSEPH NYAMIHANA MULENGA, S.C.,
Minister of Justice/Attorney-General.
Date of publication: 16th May, 1986.

2

PUBLIC ACCESS TO THE FILES OF THE FORMER SECRET POLICE

GERMANY: ACT CONCERNING THE RECORDS OF THE STATE SECURITY SERVICE OF THE FORMER GERMAN DEMOCRATIC REPUBLIC ("STASI RECORDS ACT")

(December 20, 1991)

Part One
General Provisions

§ 1. Purpose and Scope

(1) This Act regulates the custody, preparation, administration and use of the records of the Ministry for State Security of the former German Democratic Republic and its preceding and succeeding organizations (State Security Service) in order to

1. facilitate individual access to personal data which the State Security Service has stored regarding him, so that he can clarify what influence the State Security Service has had on his personal destiny,
2. protect the individual from impairment of his right to privacy being caused by use of the personal data stored by the State Security Service,
3. ensure and promote the historical, political, and juridical reappraisal of the activities of the State Security Service,
4. provide public and private bodies with access to the information required to achieve the purposes stated in this Act.

(2) This Act shall be applicable to the records of the State Security Service which can be found in the possession of public bodies of the Federal Republic or of the states [German "Länder"], of private individuals, or of other private bodies.

§ 2. Custody, Safekeeping, and Administration of the Records of the State Security Service

The Federal Commissioner for the Records of the State Security Service of the former German Democratic Republic shall take custody of, provide for the safekeeping of, administer, and use the records of the State Security Service as directed by this Act.

§ 3. Individual Rights

(1) Each individual shall have the right to enquire of the Federal Commissioner if the records contain personal data regarding him. If this is the case, the individual shall have the right to obtain information, to inspect the records, and to be provided with records as directed by this Act.

(2) Each individual shall have the right to use the information and records which he has obtained from the Federal Commissioner as provided by general law.

(3) It shall not be admissible to impair the legitimate interests of other individuals by disclosing information, permitting inspection of records or providing records.

§ 4. Admissibility of Use of Records of the State Security Service by Public and Private Bodies

(1) Public and private bodies shall have access to the records or use them only as provided by this Act. If data subjects, third parties, close relatives of missing or deceased persons, employees or beneficiaries of the State Security Service submit personal data of their own accord, this data may be used for the purpose for which it was submitted.

(2) If the Federal Commissioner establishes or is informed that personal data in the records is incorrect, or the data subject disputes that the data is correct, a separate remark to this effect shall be made in the records.

(3) If personal data is communicated pursuant to a request according to §§ 20-25, and after its communication it proves to be incorrect regarding the person about whom it was requested, it shall be corrected vis-a-vis the recipient unless it is irrelevant to the case under consideration.

(4) The overriding legitimate interests of other persons may not be impaired by use of the records.

§ 5. Specific Prohibited Use

(1) It is inadmissible to use personal data to the detriment of data subjects or third parties if it was collected about them in the course of deliberate, including secret, information-gathering or spying on these persons. This shall not be applicable to cases pursuant to § 21, paragraph (1), sentences 1 and 2 if statements made by the data subjects or third parties are proved to be partially or completely incorrect on the basis of this information.

(2) The use of records shall be inadmissible for a limited time period if the competent public prosecutor or the court declares to the Federal Commissioner that use of the records during this time period could affect the carrying out of criminal prosecution. This shall not apply if it would unreasonably impair individuals in obtaining their rights. In this case, use of the records shall occur in agreement with the public prosecutor or with the court.

§ 6. Definitions

(1) "Records of the State Security Service" means

　　1. all information-recording media, irrespective of the form of storage, in particular

a) files, data files, documents, cards, plans, films, visual material, audio material, and other recordings,
b) machine-produced or handwritten copies and other duplicates of the above,
c) evaluation aids, particularly programs for automated data processing to the extent that they came into the possession of or originated at the State Security Service or Department 1 of the Criminal Police Division of the Volkspolizei (People's Police) or were given to them for their use,

2. records submitted to the State Security Service by the courts and public prosecutors.

(2) The following shall not be deemed part of the records

1. written communications and their enclosures which the State Security Service sent to other public and private bodies, if these bodies were not legally or *de facto* authorized to issue directives vis-a-vis the State Security Service,
2. records which were returned or conveyed to other bodies for reasons of competence and in which no indication can be found that the State Security Service took measures or caused them to be taken,
3. records which were processed before 8 May 1945 and in which no indications can be found that the State Security Service took any other action than to prepare them for storage in its own archives,
4. objects and records which were unlawfully taken or kept from data subjects or third parties by the State Security Service; if this regards written communication, it is admissible for the Federal Commissioner to make copies for his records.

(3) "Data subjects" means persons about whom the State Security Service collected personal data by deliberate, including secret, information-gathering or spying. Sentence 1 shall not be applicable

1. to employees of the State Security Service, if collecting information served only to make contact with and recruit employees for the State Security Service or to monitor the activities of employees of the State Security Service, and
2. to beneficiaries, if collecting information only served to make contacts with them or to monitor their behaviour with regard to benefits received.

(4) "Employees of the State Security Service" means full-time employees and unofficial informers.

1. "Full-time employees" means persons who had an official employment or service relationship to the State Security Service. The term can also refer to "Special Task Officers."

2. "Unofficial informers" means persons who agreed to supply the State Security Service with information.

(5) The provisions regarding employees of the State Security Service shall be applicable *mutatis mutandis* to

1. persons who were legally or *de facto* authorized to issue directives to employees of the State Security Service with respect to their State Security Service-related activities,

2. unofficial informers of Department 1 of the Criminal Police Division of the Volkspolizei (People's Police).

(6) "Beneficiaries" means persons who

1. were substantially assisted by the State Security Service, in particular by being provided with economic advantages,

2. were protected by the State Security Service or at its behest from prosecution for a criminal act,

3. with the knowledge, connivance or assistance of the State Security Service, planned or committed criminal acts.

(7) "Third parties" means other persons about whom the State Security Service collected information.

(8) It shall be ascertained for each piece of information if the person involved was an employee of the State Security Service, a beneficiary, a data subject or a third party. The determining factor for ascertaining the above shall be the purpose for which the information was documented in the records.

(9) "Use of the records" means transmission of records, communication of information from the records, as well as other processing and use of the information. If it is not otherwise directed in this provision, the §§ 2 and 3 of the Federal Data Protection Act shall be applicable, except that religious societies shall be deemed to be private bodies.

Part Two
Taking Custody of Records

§ 7. Location of Records, Duty to Report

(1) All public bodies shall assist the Federal Commissioner in locating and taking custody of the State Security Service records. If they are aware or become aware in the course of their duties that such records are in their possession, they shall report this fact to the Federal Commissioner without delay.

(2) The Federal Commissioner, in agreement with a public body, is entitled to inspect the registers, archives, and other information collections of this public body, if there is sufficient indication that State Security Service records can be found therein.

(3) As soon as they become aware that they are in possession of State Security Service records, private individuals and other private bodies are obliged to report this to the Federal Commissioner without delay.

§ 8. Duties of Public Bodies to Relinquish Records

(1) At the request of the Federal Commissioner, each public body shall relinquish without delay State Security Service records, including written and machine-produced copies and other duplicates, which are in their possession.

(2) If the public body requires the records for the performance of its duties within the limitations of use pursuant to §§ 20-23 and 25, it shall be entitled to make duplicates of the records. Original records shall be kept only if they are indispensable for the performance of duties in an individual case. In such a case the Federal Commissioner, at his request, shall be provided with duplicates.

(3) The intelligence services of the Federal Republic and the states shall relinquish records regarding data subjects in their entirety and without retaining any part of the records or duplicates thereof.

§ 9. Duties of Private Bodies to Relinquish Records

(1) At the request of the Federal Commissioner, every private individual and every other private body shall relinquish State Security Service records without delay, if such records are not the personal property of the private individual or of the private body. Proof of ownership shall be incumbent upon the private individual or other private body. Personal ownership can be assumed to exist if the private individual or other private body personally compiled records as described in § 10, paragraph (4).

(2) If it is obligatory to relinquish records to the Federal Commissioner, then all copies and other duplicates shall also be relinquished to him.

(3) At the request of the Federal Commissioner, every private individual and every other private body shall relinquish records of the State Security Service which are their personal property to the Federal Commissioner, in order that written or machine-produced copies or other duplicates of these records can be made.

§ 10. Records of the German Socialist Unity Party and Other Organizations

(1) In order to perform his duties the Federal Commissioner shall be entitled to request information of the competent bodies regarding the nature, contents, and storage location of records of the German Socialist Unity Party (SED) and other related parties and mass organizations.

(2) The Federal Commissioner shall be entitled to request inspection of such records. He shall be assisted in locating such records.

(3) At his request the Federal Commissioner shall be provided with duplicates of records which are related to the activities of the State Security Service and which he requires to perform his duties. The duplicates shall become part of the records pursuant to § 6, paragraph (1).

(4) Paragraphs (1)-(3) shall be applicable *mutatis mutandis* to records which were recognizably established in cooperation between the State Security Service and other public or private bodies of the former German Democratic Republic, either at the behest of the former or in order to carry out its orders or directions.

§ 11. Relinquishment and Return of Records to other Authorities

(1) Records which belong to other authorities and contain no indications of measures taken or ordered by the State Security Service shall be returned to the competent bodies by the Federal Commissioner

> 1. at their request or
> 2. if he becomes aware of the existence of such records in the course of his duties.

(2) The Federal Commissioner shall relinquish records of the Federal Republic, the states, or their intelligence services with a classification of "Confidential" or higher to the Federal Minister of the Interior or the competent state authority. The Federal Commissioner shall be entitled to make duplicates for his records....

(5) If former full-time employees of the State Security Service are to be employed or to remain employed in public service, the necessary personnel records shall be relinquished to the competent body for personnel files. The Federal Commissioner shall be entitled to make duplicates for his records.

(6) If former full-time employees of the State Security Service receive pensions, the necessary personnel records shall be relinquished to the competent pension administration authority. The Federal Commissioner shall be entitled to make duplicates for his records.

Part Three
Use of the State Security Service Records

Sub-Part One
Rights of Data Subjects, Third Parties,
Employees of the State Security Service and Beneficiaries

§ 12. Procedural Provisions

(1) Requests for disclosure of information, for inspection of records or for obtaining records shall be filed in writing. The applicant shall be obliged to prove his identity by presenting a confirmation of it from the competent

State authority. If he is acting as an authorized representative, he shall be obliged to present a power of attorney. If the request is made by an authorized representative with power of attorney,

> 1. either the data subjects, third parties, employees or beneficiaries themselves or
> 2. their attorney, if he is expressly so authorized

shall be entitled to obtain information, to inspect the records, and to be provided with records.

(2) The Federal Commissioner shall disclose information in writing, unless circumstances warrant another form of disclosure. He shall exercise due discretion in this matter.

(3) If a request is to be handled with priority, it shall be required to justify the need for urgency. It can be assumed that the need for urgency is justified if the information is necessary for purposes of rehabilitation, compensation, to avert infringement of personal privacy or to exonerate the data subject from the accusation of cooperation with the State Security Service.

(4) Either the original records or duplicates shall be inspected. If, in addition to the personal data regarding the data subject, the records also contain information regarding other data subjects or third parties, inspection of original records shall be permitted only if

> 1. the other data subjects or third parties have given their consent or
> 2. separation of personal data regarding other data subjects or third parties is not possible or is possible only with unreasonable effort, and there is no reason to assume that the other data subjects or the third parties have an overriding legitimate interest in keeping them secret.

(5) Duplicates of records shall be provided only after the personal data regarding other data subjects and third parties has been depersonalized.

(6) The right to inspect and be provided with records shall not apply to evaluation aids (§ 6, paragraph (1), sentence 1, letter c). If the records cannot be found or can be found only with unreasonable effort, the right to inspect and be provided with records shall extend to duplicates of file cards which are used in the evaluation of the records and in which personal data regarding the applicant is contained.

§ 13. Data Subjects and Third Parties—Disclosure of Information, Inspection of Records and Providing Records

(1) At their request, data subjects shall be provided with information regarding their existing, prepared records. In their request, they shall supply particulars which make it possible to locate records. The purpose for which information is being requested need not be given.

(2) The information shall consist of a description of the existing prepared records regarding the data subject and their contents. Providing information can at first be limited to a communication that records exist and that the data subject may have the opportunity to inspect such records.

(3) At his request, the data subject shall be given the opportunity to inspect the prepared records which regard him.

(4) At his request, the data subject shall be provided with duplicates of his personal records. The personal data in the duplicates regarding other data subjects or third parties shall be depersonalized.

(5) If code names of employees of the State Security Service who gathered or evaluated personal data regarding the data subject, or names of their officers, together with particulars which make it possible to positively identify these employees, can be found in the existing prepared records which the data subject has inspected or for which he has obtained duplicates, the names of such employees shall be provided to the data subject at his request. Sentence 1 shall also apply to other persons who informed on the data subject in writing, if the contents of their reports were written in such a way as to be detrimental to the data subject. The interest of employees and informers in keeping their names secret shall not rule out disclosure of their names.

(6) Paragraph (5), sentences 1 and 2 shall not be applicable to employees of the State Security Service if they were not at least 18 years old at the time of the activities in question.

(7) Paragraphs (1)-(6) shall be applicable *mutatis mutandis* to third parties, except that the applicant shall supply particulars which make it possible to locate the information. The information shall be provided only if the necessary effort is not disproportionate to the interest of the applicant in obtaining information.

§ 14. Depersonalization and Erasure of Personal Data—Data Subjects and Third Parties

(1) At the request of data subjects or third parties, their personal data and the evaluation aids used to find records shall be depersonalized in the records of the State Security Service. Such requests shall be admissible after 1 January 1997.

(2) The depersonalization shall not be admissible,

1. if other persons have an obviously overriding interest in being permitted to use the information as evidence,

2. if the information is necessary for research related to the political and historical reappraisal,

3. as long as an access request is pending from a competent body, and

the interest of the applicant in depersonalization therefore must be subordinated. The personal data regarding the applicant contained in the records may only be communicated or used to the extent that this is indispensable to the purpose which rules out the depersonalization.

(3) Paragraphs (1) and (2) shall be applicable *mutatis mutandis* to personal data regarding an applicant which is contained in personnel records regarding an employee of the State Security Service.

(4) If depersonalization is not possible and if paragraph (2) is not applicable, the records shall be destroyed instead of depersonalized. If the records are automated, the information stored in them shall be erased instead of destroyed. Sentence 1 shall not be applicable if the records contain personal data of other data subjects or third parties and these do not give their consent to the destruction of the records.

§ 15. Rights of Close Relatives of Missing and Deceased Persons— Disclosure of Information, Inspection of Records and Providing Records

(1) At their request, close relatives shall be provided with information

1. for the rehabilitation of a missing or deceased person,
2. to protect the right to privacy of a missing or deceased person, particularly to clarify accusations of cooperation with the State Security Service,
3. to clarify the fate of missing or deceased persons. Persons requesting information shall substantiate the purpose for their request and provide proof of their relationship to the missing or deceased person.

(2) § 13, paragraph (1), sentence 2 and paragraphs (2)-(6) shall be applicable *mutatis mutandis*.

(3) Close relatives are spouses, children, grandchildren, parents, and siblings.

(4) Paragraph (1) shall not be applicable if the missing or deceased person has left another disposition or if his wishes to the contrary can clearly be inferred from other circumstances.

§ 16. Rights of Employees of the State Security Service Disclosure of Information, Inspection of Records and Providing Records

(1) At their request, employees of the State Security Service shall be provided with information regarding the personal data contained in their personnel records.

(2) The information can include a description of the nature and scope of their activities and of the group of persons who were the subjects of their reports, and also remarks about the frequency of their reports.

(3) At his request the employee shall be permitted to inspect his personnel records. § 12, paragraph (4), sentence 2, number 2 shall not be applicable.

(4) At his request the employee can be provided with information regarding reports which he prepared and can be permitted to inspect such

reports if he can substantiate a legitimate reason for doing so. This shall not be applicable if it is outweighed by the legitimate interests of data subjects or of third parties in maintaining secrecy.

(5) At his request the employee shall be provided with duplicates of his personnel records. Personal data in these records regarding data subjects or third parties shall be depersonalized.

§ 17. Rights of Beneficiaries

(1) § 16, paragraphs (1), (3), and (5) shall be applicable *mutatis mutandis* to the rights of beneficiaries to obtain information, to inspect the records, and to be provided with duplicates of records.

(2) The beneficiary shall supply particulars which make it possible to locate the records.

(3) Paragraph (1) shall not be applicable if the competent supreme federal authority or the competent State authority declares to the Federal Commissioner that disclosing information, permitting inspection of the records or providing records may not occur due to an overriding public interest.

§ 18. Right to Information—Files Submitted to the State Security Service by Courts and Public Prosecutors

With respect to files of courts and public prosecutors which are in the custody of the Federal Commissioner, the respective Orders of Legal Procedure shall be applicable instead of § 12, paragraphs (4)-(6) and §§ 13, 15-17, and 43.

Sub-Part Two
Use of Records by Public and Private Bodies
§ 19. Access to Records by Public and Private Bodies—Procedural Provisions

(1) The Federal Commissioner shall make declarations to public and private bodies, permit them to inspect records, and provide them with records, to the extent that their use is admissible pursuant to §§ 20-23, 25 and 26.

(2) It shall be admissible for a public body competent for the performance of its respective duty to direct a request to the Federal Commissioner. If a request is made by a private body, proof of entitlement shall be established in writing with reference to the legal basis for entitlement.

(3) The Federal Commissioner shall check if a request for disclosure of information, for inspection of records, or for obtaining records is related to an admissible purpose, if it lies within the remit of the recipient, and to what extent use of the records is necessary for the stated purpose. Regarding requests from courts, public prosecutors, and police authorities, to the extent

that they are acting as auxiliary bodies of the federal prosecutor, the Federal Commissioner shall check on admissibility only if due cause exists.

(4) The Federal Commissioner shall make declarations in writing, unless individual circumstances warrant another form of declaration. He shall exercise due discretion in this matter.

(5) If the request for a declaration is to be handled with priority, it must justify the need for urgency. It can be assumed that the need for urgency is justified,

1. if the information is necessary for purposes of rehabilitation, compensation, to avert infringement of personal privacy or to exonerate the data subject from the accusation of cooperation with the State Security Service,

2. for the clarification, taking custody of, and safekeeping of assets of the former German Democratic Republic and the former entities with headquarters within its territory, as well as the assets which were assigned to the Commercial Coordination sector,

3. for investigating persons in cases pursuant to § 20, paragraph (1), numbers 6 and 7 and § 21, paragraph (1), numbers 6 and 7,

4. for criminal prosecution and to avert harm in cases pursuant to § 23, paragraph (1), sentence 1, number 1, letters a and b and number 2.

(6) It shall be permitted to inspect records if declarations are not sufficient. § 12, paragraph (4) shall be applicable *mutatis mutandis* except that the person whom the request regards shall be substituted for the applicant.

(7) The records shall be provided if the requesting body can substantiate that declarations and inspection are not sufficient or that inspection would involve unjustifiable effort. Original sources shall be provided only if they are indispensable, particularly as evidence. They shall be returned to the Federal Commissioner without delay as soon as they are no longer required as evidence. § 12, paragraph (4), sentences 2 and 3 shall be applicable *mutatis mutandis* if the records also contain personal data regarding other data subjects and third parties in addition to the personal data regarding the involved person.

§ 20. Use of Records Containing No Personal Data—Public and Private Bodies

(1) If records contain no personal data regarding data subjects or third parties, they may be used as necessary by public and private bodies for the following purposes:

1. rehabilitation of data subjects and missing and deceased persons, compensation, payments pursuant to the Act on Prisoners,

2. protection of privacy,

3. clarification of the fate of missing persons and of unexplained deaths,

4. cessation or suspension of pension payments pursuant to the Pension Benefits Act or reduction or disallowance or cessation of payments in other cases for which the Pension Benefits Act is applicable,

5. clarification, taking custody, and safekeeping of assets of the former German Democratic Republic and the former entities within its territory, as well as the assets which were assigned to the Commercial Coordination sector,

6. investigations regarding the following persons and in accordance with the applicable provisions in order to establish if they were employed as full-time employees or as unofficial informers of the State Security Service, unless the person being investigated was not at least 18 years old at the time the activities occurred:

   a) members of the Federal Government or of a state government as well as other public-law officials,
   b) representatives and members of municipal representative bodies,
   c) members of the Advisory Committee pursuant to § 39,
   d) persons in federal or state public service, including municipalities and associations of municipalities, supranational and international organizations, of which the Federal Republic of Germany is a member, as well as persons employed or who are to continue to be employed by the churches,
   e) persons who are to continue practicing the profession of notary public or attorney,
   f) -   members of the managing board, managing directors, executives, or managers in concerns of a legal entity,
      -   persons who have been chosen by law, statute, or social contract to represent the majority, managing directors, executives, or managers in concerns of a majority-ruled organization,
   g) security clearance checks of persons
      -   who are entrusted with, have access to, or could acquire access to facts, objects, or knowledge which must be kept secret in the public interest, or
      -   who are employed or are to be employed in security-sensitive areas of installations of vital importance or of importance to defence;

The clearance check can also pertain to employment by a foreign intelligence service,

7. investigations regarding the following persons, with their consent, to establish if they were full-time employees or unofficial informers of the State Security Service, unless the person being investigated was not at least 18 years old at the time the activities occurred:

   a) political party executives down to district level,

b) persons who serve as jury members,
c) persons who hold honorary church offices,
d) persons who fill national or state-level executive positions in associations,
e) members of workers' councils,
f) persons who
 - in the above cases
 - in cases pursuant to number 6, letters a-f
 are applying for public office, for a position, for a professional license or for employment;

The investigation can also pertain to employment by a foreign intelligence service; if indications exist which warrant suspicion of activities for the State Security Service or for a foreign intelligence service, the person being investigated shall be informed but need not give his consent,

8. procedures pursuant to granting or denying permission to carry weapons pursuant to the Weapons Act, the Federal Hunting Act, the Explosives Act, the War Weapons Control Act, if indications regarding the personal reliability of the former State Security Service employee can be found in the records,

9. recognition of pensionable periods of service, payment and transfer of pensions of former employees of the State Security Service,

10. matters regarding decorations....

(3) The use for the purposes stated in paragraph (1), numbers 6 and 7 shall be inadmissible after a statutory period of 15 years. This statutory period shall begin on the day this Act comes into effect. After the expiration of this statutory period, it shall no longer be admissible to charge a person with activities for the State Security Service, nor to evaluate to his detriment the fact that such activities occurred.... The rights of other persons in connection with the activities of the employee, legal consequences of these activities and the decisions of courts or public administration authorities issued in relation to these activities shall remain unaffected.

§ 21. Use of Records Containing Personal Data—Public and Private Bodies

[The provisions of § 21 for use of records containing personal data are the same as those of § 20, with the omission of paragraph (1), numbers 8-10.]

§ 22. Use of the Records for the Purposes of Parliamentary Investigative Committees

(1) The right of parliamentary investigative committees to gather evidence, pursuant to § 44, paragraphs (1) and (2) of the Basic law, shall extend to the records of the State Security Service.

(2) Paragraph 1 shall be applicable *mutatis mutandis* to the parliamentary investigative committees of the states.

§ 23. Use of the Records for Criminal Prosecution and to Avert Harm

(1) If records contain personal data regarding data subjects or third parties, they may be used as necessary

1. for the prosecution of

a) criminal acts in connection with the regime of the former German Democratic Republic, particularly criminal acts in connection with employment by the State Security Service, or by other security, criminal-prosecution, or penal-system authorities, as well as by courts of the former German Democratic Republic,

b) crimes in cases pursuant to §§ ... of the Penal Code as well as criminal acts pursuant to

- § ... of the Weapons Act,
- § ... of the Act regarding the Control of War Weapons,
- § ... of the Controlled Substances Act,...

c) crimes in connection with the Nationalist Socialist regime,

d) crimes according to § 44 of this Act,

2. to avert an immediate substantial threat to public safety, in particular to avert threatened criminal acts.

§ 5, paragraph (1) shall not be applicable. Specific prohibited use pursuant to the provisions of the Rules of Criminal Procedure shall remain unaffected.

(2) Other records may be used, if necessary, for the prosecution of criminal acts, inclusive of providing legal counsel in criminal cases, or to avert a substantial threat to public safety, particularly threatened criminal acts.

§ 24. Use of Files Submitted to the State Security Service by Courts and Public Prosecutors

(1) With respect to the use of files from courts and public prosecutors in the custody of the Federal Commissioner, the respective legal procedures shall be applicable instead of §§ 19-21, 23, 25-30 and 43. § 5, paragraph (1) shall not be applicable if it is a matter regarding criminal acts pursuant to § 23, paragraph (1), number 1.

(2) The Federal Commissioner shall submit on request records pursuant to paragraph (1), sentence 1, to courts, public prosecutors and police authorities, if these are acting as auxiliary bodies of the public prosecutor. The records shall be returned without delay as soon as they are no longer required for the stated purpose.

§ 25. Use of the Records by Intelligence Services

(1) If the records contain personal data regarding data subjects or third parties, they may not be used by or for an intelligence service. Exceptions are records which contain personal data regarding

1. employees of the intelligence services of the Federal Republic, the states or their allies, if it is necessary to use the records to avert harm to these employees or to the intelligence services, or
2. employees of other intelligence services if use of the records is necessary for counter-espionage.

(2) Records, if they contain no personal data regarding data subjects or third parties, may be used by or for the intelligence services of the Federal Republic and the states within the framework of their duties as well as by or for intelligence services of allies if they contain information regarding

1. intelligence or counter-intelligence,
2. the areas of violent extremism or terrorism

pursuant to the Federal Constitutional Protection Act.

(3) In cases pursuant to paragraph (1), sentence 2, § 5, paragraph (1) shall remain unaffected.

(4) In cases pursuant to paragraph (1), sentence 2 and to paragraph (2), the Federal Minister of the Interior shall be empowered to order the Federal Commissioner to relinquish records without retaining any part or duplicates thereof, if leaving such records in the custody of the Federal Commissioner would be detrimental to the Federal Republic or a state. Such an order shall require the consent of the Parliamentary Control Commission pursuant to the Act regarding Parliamentary Control of the Intelligence Activities of the Federal Republic.

(5) In addition, records pursuant to § 26 may be used by or for intelligence services within the framework of their legal duties.

§ 26. Use of Service Regulations and Organizational Plans

Guidelines, service regulations, organizational plans and personnel plans of the State Security Service, if they contain no personal data regarding data subjects or third parties, may also be used for other purposes. The same shall be applicable to plans and drawings of property and other objects of the State Security Service, in particular ground plans and plans of plumbing and heating, electricity, and telephone installations.

§ 27. Unsolicited Reports to Public Bodies

(1) If in the course of his duties pursuant to § 37 the Federal Commissioner establishes that one of the following persons has been a full-time employee or unofficial informer of the State Security Service:

1. persons who hold a public-law office or a position pursuant to § 20, paragraph (1), number 6, letters a-c,
2. a civil servant who can be given leave of absence or an employee in a corresponding position,
3. a civil servant or employee who is the managing director of an authority,
4. an elected or honorary public official,
5. a judge or public prosecutor,
6. an attorney or notary public,
7. a person employed by a church,
8. a person who, because of his activities, may use records pursuant to § 20, paragraph (1), number 4 or § 21, paragraph (1), number 4,

he shall report this to the competent body.

(2) If the Federal Commissioner establishes in the course of his duties that there are indications in the records of

1. a criminal act in connection with activities of the State Security Service,
2. one of the criminal acts referred to in § 23, paragraph (1), number 1,
3. a substantial impairment of public safety,
4. the existence of assets pursuant to § 20, paragraph (1), number 5 and § 21, paragraph (1), number 5,

he shall report this to the competent body.

(3) If the Federal Commissioner establishes in the course of his duties pursuant to § 37 that there is information in the records regarding intelligence, counterintelligence, violent extremism, or terrorism pursuant to the Federal Constitutional Protection Act, he shall report this of his own accord to the Federal Minister of the Interior.

(4) Reports pursuant to paragraphs (1)-(3) shall only be admissible if they may also be made pursuant to a request.

§ 28. Unsolicited Reports to Private Bodies

(1) If the Federal Commissioner establishes in the course of his duties pursuant to § 37 that

1. political party executives down to the district level,
2. persons who fill national or state-level executive positions in associations,
3. members of the managing board, managing directors, executives, or managers in concerns of a legal entity,
4. persons who have been chosen by law, statute, or social contract to represent the majority, managing directors, executives or managers in concerns of a majority-ruled organization

have been full-time employees or unofficial informers of the State Security Service, he shall report this to the competent body.

(2) Reports pursuant to paragraph (1) shall only be admissible if they may also be made pursuant to a request.

§ 29. Limitations on Use

(1) Pursuant to §§ 19-23 and 25, and to §§ 27 and 28, personal data which has been conveyed may be processed or used only for the purpose for which it has been conveyed. It may be used for other purposes only if the requirements pursuant to §§ 20-23 and 25 have been met.

(2) Consent of the Federal Commissioner shall be required if, pursuant to paragraph (1), sentence 2, personal data regarding data subjects or third parties are to be processed or used for another purpose.

(3) Paragraphs (1) and (2) shall be applicable *mutatis mutandis* for personal data in the records which, pursuant to § 8, paragraph (2), remain with public bodies.

§ 30. Notification

(1) If the Federal Commissioner conveys personal data regarding a data subject pursuant to §§ 21, 27 paragraph (1) and § 28, the data subject shall be notified regarding the type of information provided and the recipient.

(2) Notification shall not be compulsory if the data subject has been otherwise informed of the conveyance or if notification would require unjustifiable effort.

(3) Notification shall not occur during a particular time period if the competent supreme Federal or state authority declares to the Federal Commissioner that notification of the conveyance would be detrimental to the Federal Republic or a state.

§ 31. Judicial Review of Decisions of the Federal Commissioner at the Request of Authorities

(1) If the Federal Commissioner refuses to honor the request of an authority for a declaration or for inspection or submission of records, the District Administrative Court shall, at the request of this authority, hold a hearing to decide on the legality of the refusal. The decision shall not be contestable. There shall be no pretrial hearing. The District Administrative Court of the district in which the Federal Commissioner has his headquarters shall have jurisdiction.

(2) It shall be admissible for the presiding judge to deny or limit inspection of the files or parts thereof, as well as to limit the preparation or distribution of excerpts or duplicates, if this is warranted by the particular circumstances. This decision and the decision of the District Administrative Court regarding the obligatory submission of documents ... shall not be

contestable. Furthermore, the participants shall maintain secrecy regarding the facts which have become known to them through inspection of the files.

Sub-Part Three
Use of the Records—Political and Historical
Reappraisal, Press and Broadcasting Sectors

§ 32. Use of the Records for Reappraisal
of the Activities of the State Security Service

(1) The Federal Commissioner shall provide the following records for research related to the political and historical reappraisal of the activities of the State Security Service and for political education:

1. records which contain no personal data,

2. duplicates of records in which the personal data has been depersonalized,

3. records containing personal data regarding
  - contemporary historical personages, political officeholders or public-law officials while in office, unless they are data subjects or third parties,
  - employees of the State Security Service, unless these were not at least 18 years old at the time of the activities described in the records,
  - beneficiaries of the State Security Service,

  unless publication of the records would impair the overriding legitimate interests of the persons involved,

4. records containing other personal data, if the data subjects have given their written consent, specifying both the intention and the persons who will carry it out.

(2) Records which, pursuant to § 37, paragraph (1), number 3, letters b–d are subject to special storage, may be used only with the consent of the Federal Minister of the Interior.

(3) It shall be admissible to publish personal data only if

1. the persons about whom the personal data is to be published have given their consent or

2. the personal data regards
  - contemporary historical personages, political officeholders or public-law officials while in office, unless they are data subjects or third parties,
  - employees of the State Security Service, unless these were not at least 18 years old at the time of the activities described in the records,
  - beneficiaries of the State Security Service,

  unless publication of such personal data would impair the overriding legitimate interests of these persons.

§ 33. Procedure

(1) Inspection of records for purposes of research or political education shall be permitted in the principal office or in one of the branch offices of the Federal Commissioner.

(2) The inspection may be limited to duplicates if this is warranted by the importance or the state of preservation of the records.

(3) If inspection of records is permitted, it shall be admissible to provide duplicates of records upon request.

(4) It shall be inadmissible to use duplicates which have been provided pursuant to paragraph (3) for other purposes or to pass them on to other bodies.

(5) It shall be inadmissible to inspect unprepared records.

§ 34. Use of Records by Press, Broadcasting, and Film

(1) §§ 32 and 33 shall be applicable *mutatis mutandis* to the use of records by the press, film, or broadcasting sectors or by their auxiliary enterprises or their journalistic-editorial personnel.

(2) If the publication of personal data by broadcasting corporations under federal law leads to the issue of counter-statements by the data subject, such counter-statements shall be added to and preserved with the stored data. The personal data may only be re-published together with the counter-statement.

Part Four
Federal Commissioner for the
Records of the State Security Service

§ 35. Federal Commissioner for the Records of the State Security Service of the former German Democratic Republic

(1) The Federal Commissioner for the Records of the State Security Service is a higher federal authority under the hierarchical supervision of the Federal Minister of the Interior. The principal office thereof is located in Berlin, and there are branch offices located in the States of Berlin, Brandenburg, Mecklenburg-West Pomerania, Saxonia, Saxonia-Anhalt, and Thuringia.

(2) On a proposal from the Federal Government, the *Bundestag* shall elect the Federal Commissioner for the Records of the State Security Service of the former German Democratic Republic. The Federal Commissioner must be at least 35 years old at the time of his election. The person elected shall use the name of the authority as his title of office. He shall be appointed by the Federal President.

(3) The Federal Commissioner shall swear the following oath in the presence of the Federal Minister of the Interior:

I swear to do everything in my power to further the well-being of the German people, to protect it from harm and to defend the Basic Law and the laws of the Federal Republic, to perform my duties conscientiously and to exercise justice in all my dealings, so help me God.

The reference to God may be omitted from the oath.

(4) The term of office of the Federal Commissioner shall be five years. It may be renewed once.

(5) The Federal Commissioner shall, as directed by this Act, have public-law official status with respect to the Federal Republic. He shall be independent in the performance of his duties and subject to the law only. He shall be subject to the legal supervision of the Federal Government. He shall be subject to the hierarchical supervision of the Federal Minister of the Interior.

§ 36. Legal Status of the Federal Commissioner

(1) The mandate of the Federal Commissioner for the Records of the State Security Service shall commence on delivery of the certificate of appointment. It shall end

    1. on expiration of his term of office;
    2. on his dismissal.

The Federal President shall dismiss the Federal Commissioner at the latter's request, or on a proposal by the Federal Government, when there are grounds which, in the case of an established judge, justify dismissal from service.... If the Federal Minister of the Interior so requests, the Federal Commissioner shall be obliged to continue his service until a successor has been appointed.

(2) The Federal Commissioner shall not hold any other paid office or pursue any gainful activity or occupation in addition to his official duties and shall not belong to the management, supervisory board or board of directors of a profit-making enterprise nor to a government or legislative body of the Federal Republic or a state.

(3) The Federal Commissioner shall inform the Federal Minister of the Interior of any gifts that he receives in the performance of his duties. The Federal Minister of the Interior shall decide how such gifts shall be used.

(4) The Federal Commissioner shall be obliged, even after termination of service, to maintain secrecy concerning information of which he has knowledge by reason of his duties. This shall not apply to communications made in the normal course of duties or regarding facts which are common knowledge or are not sufficiently important to warrant confidential treatment. The Federal Commissioner may not, even after leaving the service, make any pronouncements or statements either in or out of court regarding such matters without the consent of the Federal Minister of the Interior. This provision shall not, however, affect his duty by law to report

criminal offences and to take action to uphold the free democratic fundamental order whenever it is jeopardized.

(5) Consent to give testimony as a witness shall be refused only when such testimony would be to the detriment of the Federal Republic or a state or seriously jeopardize or impede the performance of public duties. Consent to deliver an opinion may be refused where it would be against the interest of the service....

§ 37. Duties and Authority of the Federal Commissioner

(1) The Federal Commissioner shall, as directed by this Act, have the following duties and authority:

1. he shall take custody of the records of the State Security Service,

2. he shall be responsible for the evaluation, organization, storage and administration of the records according to accepted principles for maintaining archives,

3. he shall administer the records in the central archives in the principal office and in the regional archives in the branch offices. The following records shall be stored separately

a) files of courts or of the public prosecutor which were submitted to the State Security Service,
b) duplicates pursuant to § 11, paragraph (2), sentence 2,
c) records regarding employees of intelligence services of the Federal Republic, the states, or their allies,
d) records
   - regarding employees of other intelligence services,
   - containing technical or other specialized instructions or descriptions regarding deployment of means and methods in the areas of intelligence, counter-intelligence, or terrorism
   if the Federal Minister of the Interior declares in an individual case that knowledge of the record contents would impair public safety or would otherwise be detrimental to the Federal Republic or a state;

For the separate storage according to letters b-d above, the regulations regarding the handling of classified information of the classification "Confidential" or higher shall be applicable,

4. he shall disclose information and make statements regarding the records, permit inspection of the records, and provide records,

5. he shall reappraise the activities of the State Security Service, informing the public about the structure, methods, and consequences of the activities of the State Security Service. § 32, paragraph (3) shall apply to the publication of personal data,

6. he shall promote research and political education during the historical and political reappraisal of the activities of the State Security

Service by permitting examination of the records and releasing duplicates of the records,

7. he shall inform and advise individuals, other private bodies, and public bodies. It shall also be admissible for the branch offices to give information and advice,

8. he shall establish and maintain documentation and exposition centers.

(2) The Federal Commissioner shall ensure that he will apply uniform principles in performing his duties.

(3) At the request of the *Bundestag*, otherwise at least every two years, and for the first time on 1 July 1993, the Federal Commissioner shall submit an activity report. Beginning with the second regular activity report, he shall report to what extent and within which period of time he will foreseeably no longer require the records for the performance of his duties. When so requested by the *Bundestag* or the Federal Government, the Federal Commissioner shall draw up opinions and reports. The Federal Commissioner can consult the *Bundestag*, at any time. In matters related to a legislative body, he shall report directly to this body.

§ 38. State Commissioner—Relationship to the Federal Commissioner

(1) To support the Federal Commissioner in performing his duties as directed by § 37 of this Act, the office of State Commissioner for the Records of the State Security Service of the Former German Democratic Republic can be established in the States of Berlin, Brandenburg, Mecklenburg-West Pomerania, Saxonia, Saxonia-Anhalt, and Thuringia. Particulars with respect to this office shall conform *mutatis mutandis* to the laws of the states.

(2) The Federal Commissioner shall give the state Commissioner the opportunity to comment on particulars specific to the respective state which may arise during the use of the records pursuant to § 3 of this Act.

(3) The laws of each state can provide that the State Commissioner shall advise individuals involved in obtaining their rights pursuant to §§ 13-17 of this Act. This activity can also include psychosocial counseling after the completion of procedures pursuant to § 12 of this Act.

§ 39. Advisory Committee

(1) An Advisory Committee to the Federal Commissioner shall be formed. This committee shall consist of

1. nine members to be named by the States of Berlin, Brandenburg, Mecklenburg-West Pomerania, Saxonia, Saxonia-Anhalt, and Thuringia, and

2. seven members to be named by the Federal Republic.

The members of the Advisory Committee shall be appointed by the Federal Minister of the Interior for a term of office of five years.

(2) The Federal Commissioner shall inform the Advisory Committee about all fundamental and otherwise important matters and shall discuss them with the committee. The Advisory Committee shall advise the Federal Commissioner in particular regarding the following matters:

1. taking complete custody of the records of the State Security Service and evaluating these records as directed by § 10 of this Act,

2. designating archive standards to be observed in the evaluation, organization, preparation, storage, and administration of the records,

3. establishing uniform standards for permitting inspection of records and providing records,

4. establishing evaluation criteria in cases pursuant to § 20, paragraph (1), numbers 6 and 7 and § 21, paragraph (1), numbers 6 and 7 of this Act,

5. establishing standards of priority with respect to individual requests to inspect records and to requests from public and private bodies,

6. establishing the duties of the branch offices with respect to their advisory functions,

7. planning programs for the reappraisal of the activities of the State Security Service and informing the public thereof,

8. supporting research and political education.

In addition, the Advisory Committee shall advise in the preparation of the activity report required pursuant to § 37, paragraph (3), sentence 1 of this Act.

(3) The Federal Commissioner shall chair the meetings of the Advisory Committee.

(4) The Advisory Committee shall establish its own rules of procedure, which shall require the approval of the Federal Republic.

(5) Members of the Advisory Committee shall be obliged to maintain secrecy regarding facts which become known to them in the course of their duties, unless such facts are public knowledge. Their obligation to maintain secrecy shall continue after their term of office has ended.

§ 40. Measures to Safeguard Records

(1) The Federal Commissioner shall take the organizational and technical measures necessary for his authority to safeguard the records against unauthorized access.

(2) It shall be particularly ensured that

1. the employees of the Federal Commissioner have access only to the records and data processing systems directly related to their duties. Each case of access to the records and the reason for access shall be documented,

2. no one shall establish unauthorized systems for locating data in the archives; no one shall enter, document, modify, or erase any stored data without authorization,

3. it shall be documented which records or data from records have been conveyed or transmitted to whom and at what time,

4. it shall be possible to check and establish which personal data have been entered into data processing systems by whom and at what time,

5. buildings in which the records of the State Security Service are stored shall be protected against unauthorized entry,

6. unauthorized persons shall not have access either to the records or to the data processing systems in which the records are stored,

7. unauthorized persons shall not have the possibility to read, copy, modify, or remove records,

8. records and data carriers shall be protected during transport against unauthorized reading, copying, modification, erasure or destruction,

9. the internal organization of the authority shall be arranged in such a way that it meets the specific requirements of data protection.

§ 41. Automated Retrieval Procedures Commissioned Data Processing

(1) The Federal Commissioner may store personal data in data files, modify or otherwise use, personal data from the records only as aids for performing his duties. The files shall contain only the information necessary for the location of records and the accompanying identification of persons. § 20 of the Federal Data Protection Act shall be applicable to these data files.

(2) The establishment of automated procedures for conveyance of information shall be inadmissible.

(3) Commissioned data processing of the records shall be admissible only if it is impossible or possible only with unreasonable effort for the Federal Commissioner to perform the data processing. Furthermore, it shall be admissible only if the contractor is carefully selected, with particular regard to his suitability for handling this data. The contractor may process the data only pursuant to the express directives of the Federal Commissioner.

Part Five
Final Provisions
§ 42. Costs

(1) Costs (fees and expenses) shall be charged for official actions pursuant to §§ 13-17 and *vis-à-vis* private bodies pursuant to §§ 20 and 21. No costs shall be charged to data subjects and third parties for information provided or for the opportunity to examine the records.

(2) The Federal Minister of the Interior shall be empowered to establish by decree what fees shall be charged for which official actions.

§ 43. Precedence of this Act

The regulations of this Act shall take precedence over provisions of other acts regarding the admissibility of conveying personal data. The Federal Data Protection Act shall not be applicable unless otherwise established in § 6, paragraph (9) and § 41, paragraph (1), sentence 3 of this Act.

§ 44. Criminal Offences

Anyone who publicly communicates personal data regarding data subjects or third parties from the original records protected by this Act or from duplicates thereof, shall be punished by imprisonment of up to three years or by a fine. This shall not be applicable if the data subject or third party has given his consent.

§ 45. Administrative Offences

(1) An administrative offence shall be deemed to have been committed by anyone who, either intentionally or through negligence

1. contrary to § 7, paragraph (3) of this Act does not report possession of records within the proper time,
2. contrary to § 9, paragraph (1), sentence 1 does not relinquish records to the Federal Commissioner or does not relinquish them within the proper time, or
3. contrary to § 9, paragraph (3) does not permit the Federal Commissioner to use records which are his personal property.

(2) Administrative offences shall be punishable by a fine of up to five hundred thousand Deutschmarks.

§ 46. Exemption from Punishment

Anyone who has gained possession of records of the State Security Service by unlawful means shall not be punished if he fulfills his obligation to report possession of records pursuant to § 7, paragraph (3) within a time period of three months after this Act comes into effect....

GERMANY: BROCHURE OF THE FEDERAL COMMISSIONER FOR THE STASI RECORDS

(1992)

Task, Structure and Work of This Authority

The Stasi Inheritance

Over a period of forty years the Ministry for State Security (MfS), under orders from the SED [East German Communist Party], collected information about millions of persons. Most of them were citizens of the GDR [German Democratic Republic], but a number were West Germans or foreigners. Millions of persons are registered in the MfS files; kilometres of file material form the Stasi bequest. At the end of the SED regime, the MfS payroll listed approximately 97,000 full-time employees.

The MfS was not simply an "ordinary" secret service: it intervened in the lives of countless numbers of persons. The MfS influenced professional success or failure, systematically exploited human weaknesses, and stopped at nothing, not even at the use of the most intimate information. Neither medical confidentiality nor bank or post secrecy were sacred to the Stasi. It had its own departments of investigations and its own special prisons.

The peaceful revolution in the autumn of 1989 brought an end to the activities of this gigantic apparatus of surveillance. Citizens' committees occupied the local and regional MfS offices. Under bizarre conditions, sometimes involving "cloak and dagger" operations, the destruction of files and the further destruction of card files could be hindered.

The unsorted written material from the numerous MfS departments was provisionally secured in bags and bundles in the various district administrative offices, which by now were under the control of the citizens' committees.

Under constantly increasing pressure from citizens, GDR Minister president Modrow appeared before the *Volkskammer* [GDR parliament] on 12 January 1990 and announced the decision to dissolve without replacement the State Security Service of the GDR. In the period of time that followed, East German citizens-rights activists and members of the GDR *Volkskammer* achieved special treatment for the Stasi records; affected individuals would have the possibility of finding out what information the MfS had collected about them. After German Unification, the Federal Government appointed Pastor Joachim Gauck, who had already been appointed by the democratically-elected *Volkskammer*, to the position of Special Commissioner for the Stasi Records. The then-existing legal status, however, permitted only a very limited use of the files.

The Stasi Records Act

On 29 December 1991 the Stasi Records Act came into effect; it had been passed with a great majority by the German *Bundestag*. Based on a law which had already been passed by the GDR *Volkskammer*, the Stasi Records Act regulates the use of the GDR secret-service material for the political, historical, and juridical reappraisal of Stasi activities. The Federal President appointed the then Special Commissioner to the position of Federal Commissioner.

The Authority of the Federal Commissioner has the following Responsibilities:

- To give the individual citizen the possibility of access to the personal data stored concerning him, so that he can clarify what influence the State Security Service has had on his personal destiny.
- To assist in rehabilitation of affected individuals, in the clarification of cases involving missing persons or unexplained deaths, and in the protection of privacy. To these ends, employees of the Federal Commissioner search for corresponding files and make them available to the courts or to relatives of the missing or deceased persons. In cases in which persons have been unjustifiably accused of activities for the State Security Service, the Federal Commissioner issues a declaration if no records with such content can be found, in order to protect these persons from further accusations.
- To investigate persons for possible past Stasi activities at the request of parliaments, public authorities, the, churches industry and commerce, and organizations. According to the Treaty of Unification, former Stasi employees are to be removed from positions of great trust. The Federal Commissioner makes no personal decisions in such matters; he merely communicates the findings of his investigations without adding a value judgment.
- Research into the structures, methods, and actions of the State Security Service for the purpose of historical and political reappraisal. Former employees of the State Security Service must be deprived of the possibility of dominating others through their knowledge of personal data. History must be reappraised on the basis of solid sources, and not, as has usually been the case due to statutory limitations, only after thirty years have passed. The public, especially the coming generation, is to be informed through publications, information programs, and exhibitions about the fatal effects of the activities of the State Security Service.
- Assistance with respect to criminal proceedings. All records which could serve to clarify a criminal act are to be made accessible to the investigative authorities. The Stasi's share of responsibility is to be uncovered, especially in cases involving

fatal shootings at the border, terrorism, arms trade, and criminal acts in the commercial sector (for example, in connection with the activities of the GDR hard-currency procurator Schalck-Golodkowski).

- Establishing Archives—this means custody, safekeeping, preparations, and administration of the records, as well as the return of records which were removed—in short, the expert processing of the records of the State Security Service as a basic prerequisite for carrying out the Stasi Records Act.

The Structure of This Authority

The principal office with four main departments is located in Berlin. Fourteen branch offices are located in the States of Berlin, Brandenburg, Mecklenburg-West Pomerania, Saxonia, Saxonia-Anhalt, and Thuringia.

The Work of This Authority

Whereas the Treaty of Unification provided for only very limited use of the Stasi records in the time period between October 1990 and December 1991, the Stasi Records Act of 29 December 1991 assigns extensive responsibilities to the employees of the Federal Commissioner. This called for and still calls for enormous efforts to be undertaken. By March 1993, more than 600,000 citizens had filed applications to inspect records, and approximately 1,250,000 applications for investigations had been filed. This means that by that point in time, the Federal Commissioner had already received a total of more than 1,850,000 requests.

The pressure generated by the understandable expectations of the citizens combines with the difficulty of setting up an entirely new federal authority and concurrently carrying out its assigned tasks. By March 1993 approximately 150,000 requests to inspect files had been filled and about 350,000 investigations had been completed. In addition, approximately seventy percent of the MfS records, which were largely unsorted, have since been organized according to archive principles. The laborious process of rebuilding functioning archives continues. In cases in which files were destroyed, a time-consuming search, for example, in copies of reports filed by unofficial informers in other records, has been necessary. Often the records are stored at completely different sites.

Even with the 3,406 employees who are planned for work in the main office and in the fourteen branch offices, the responsibilities of the Authority can only be carried out under great difficulty and through many years of constant effort. The MfS had nearly thirty times as many employees and was active for forty years. In the interests of all involved persons, the process of hiring and training employees who are responsible for the extraordinarily differentiated communication of information, requires a great deal of time. Since a small mistake can have serious consequences, it is necessary to use extreme care when analyzing the secret service files.

It is a known fact that the MfS could snoop around in anyone's private life. Each file must therefore be checked before it is released for reading to see if the legitimate interests of third parties could possibly be affected. No one may find out about his neighbour's extramarital affair by reading the Stasi files. The legal names or code names of full-time employees and unofficial informers are not covered by such protection.

Each document must first be carefully read by employees of the Authority, and, after it has been copied, it must be depersonalized; this means that names of third parties must be blackened out for their protection. This energy-consuming process makes long waiting periods inevitable. For this reason, the possibility of inspecting records should be granted first of all to older persons, persons who were imprisoned for political motives, and other persons who were severely harmed by the regime, for example, persons who were forcibly expatriated or forced to abandon their homes in border areas.

Detailed information about the organization and mode of operation of the Authority is contained in the Stasi Records Act. It can be obtained free of charge from the main office or any of the branch offices of the Federal Commissioner.

What Are Your Rights?

If you wish to file a request for information, for the possibility of inspecting records, or for obtaining copies of records of the State Security Service of the former German Democratic Republic, you require a special application form. This can be obtained at any of the offices of the Federal Commissioner. The law also requires you to bring a confirmation of identity from the registration authorities, to prevent unauthorized persons from inspecting your records—provided that personal records about you actually exist.

In addition to the possibility of inspecting records and obtaining copies thereof, it is possible in clear-cut cases to request the deciphering of the code names of MfS employees. The only costs which affected individuals have to pay are for copies which they may request after inspecting their records (5 pfennigs per 4 copy).

In addition to the above uses, the Stasi records are also available to historians and journalists. §§ 32 to 34 of the Stasi Records Act regulate the specific use of the records.

3

PURGE AND SCREENING

BULGARIA: LAW ON BANKS AND CREDIT ACTIVITY

(March 18, 1992)

Article 7

The bank shall be managed and represented jointly by at least two persons. They shall not delegate the entire management and representation of the bank to only one of them, but may authorize third persons to take individual actions....

Transitional and Concluding Provisions

...§ 9. Persons who, during the last fifteen years, have been elected to the central, regional, district, city and municipal leading bodies of the Bulgarian Communist Party, the Communist Youth League, the Fatherland Front, the Union of the Active Fighters against Fascism and Capitalism, the Bulgarian Trade Unions, and the Bulgarian Agrarian People's Union, or have been appointed to a managerial full-time position in the Central Committee of the Bulgarian Communist Party, as well as officers, and paid and unpaid associates of the State Security, shall not be elected to the managerial bodies of banks and shall not be appointed under Article 7. This restriction shall apply for a period of five years.

BULGARIA: CONSTITUTIONAL COURT DECISION ON THE LAW ON BANKS AND CREDIT ACTIVITY

Constitutional Case No. 7
Decision No. 8 (July 27, 1992)

Legal proceedings were instituted at the demand of 49 members of the 36th National Assembly, to establish the unconstitutionality of Article 9 of the Transitional and Concluding Provisions of the Law on Banks and Credit Activity. Article 9 says:

> Persons who, during the last fifteen years, have been elected to the central, regional, district, city and municipal leading bodies of the Bulgarian Communist Party, the Communist Youth League, the Fatherland Front, the Union of the Active Fighters against Fascism and Capitalism, the Bulgarian Trade Unions, and the Bulgarian Agrarian People's Union, or have been appointed to a managerial full-time position in the Central Committee of the Bulgarian Communist Party, as well as officers, and paid and unpaid associates of the State Security, shall not be elected to the managerial bodies of banks and shall not be appointed under Article 7. This restriction shall apply for a period of five years.

The claim is that Article 9 of the Transitional and Concluding Provisions of the Law on Banks and Credit Activity is in contradiction with Article 6, paragraph 2 of the Constitution and the international provisions and agreements constitutionally ratified by Bulgaria as parts of international human rights documents, in particular: Article 2, paragraph 2 and Article 25 of the International Covenant on Civil and Political Rights of 1966, as well as [ILO] Convention No. 111 of 1958.

In its decisions of April 21, 1992 and May 19, 1992 the Constitutional Court defined the Bulgarian Socialist Party, the Fatherland Union, the Bulgarian Democratic Youth, the Bulgarian Antifascist Union, the Confederation of Independent Trade Union, the Labor Confederation "Podkrepa," the National Assembly, the Minister of the Interior and the chairman of the Bulgarian National Bank as litigants in this case.

In its decision of June 2, 1992 the Constitutional Court acknowledged the demand [of the Members of Parliament] as lawful, based on Article 19, paragraph 1 of the Law on the Constitutional Court.

The Constitutional Court, having discussed the parties' arguments and reasons, decided:

According to Article 5 of the Constitution, the International Covenant on Civil and Political Rights, the International Covenant on Economic, Social and Cultural Rights, and the Vienna Convention on the Right of Contracts (State Newspaper, issue 87, 1987), which have been ratified by the constitutionally-established procedure, promulgated and come into force and are considered part of the domestic legislation of the country and hence supersede any domestic legislation stipulating otherwise.

On the other hand, the provisions of Article 6, paragraph 2 of the Constitution can bear no limitation, as they state that:

> All citizens shall be equal before the law. There shall be no privileges or restrictions of rights on the grounds of race, nationality, ethnicity, sex, origin, religion, education, opinion, political affiliation, personal and social status, or property status are allowed.

Also, Article 48 of the Constitution maintains the principle that "every citizen freely elects his profession and workplace."

The provisions of Article 9 of the Transitional and Concluding Provisions of the Law on Banks and Credit Activity speak of limiting the right to occupy an executive position in the executive bodies of banks, which in the sense of Article 1 of Convention No. 111 is discrimination in the accessibility of a specific profession. The text also contradicts Article 2, Paragraph 2 and Article 6, Paragraph 1 of the International Covenant on Economic, Social and Culture Rights, and Articles 2 and 25 of the International Covenant on Civil and Political Rights.

From all of the above, it follows that the provisions of Article 9 of the Law on Banks and Credit Activity are in contradiction both with Article 6, paragraph 2 of the Constitution and the aforementioned international Laws. The last are considered as part of domestic law and have priority over those provisions of the domestic legislation that Article 9 of the Transitional and Concluding Provisions of the Law on Banks and Credit Activity has been passed in violation of Article 6, paragraph 2 of the Constitution and the aforementioned international acts.

This is why, pursuant to Article 149, Paragraph 1, sections 2 and 4 of the Constitution, the Constitutional Court:

RULES:

The Court declares Article 9 of the Transitional and Concluding Provisions of the Law on Banks and Credit Activity unconstitutional and contradictory to the international conventions to which Bulgaria is a party.

The decision is final....

BULGARIA: LAW FOR TEMPORARY INTRODUCTION OF SOME ADDITIONAL REQUIREMENTS FOR THE MEMBERS OF THE EXECUTIVE BODIES OF SCIENTIFIC ORGANIZATIONS AND THE HIGHER CERTIFYING COMMISSION ("PANEV LAW")

(December 9, 1992)

Chapter One

General Principles

Article 1

This Law determines additional requirements for the members of the executive bodies of scientific organizations and the Higher Certifying Commission.

Article 2

(1) The provisions of this Law refer to:

   a. the members of the academic, faculty and scientific councils, the heads of the higher schools and faculties and their deputies;
   b. the members of the scientific councils, the heads of the academies and their independent units, and their deputies;
   c. the members of the scientific councils and the heads and their deputies in any scientific organizations other than those mentioned above which have the right to announce competitions and elect scientific or teaching staff;
   d. heads of Chairs;
   e. heads of Sections or their corresponding basic structural units in scientific institutions.

(2) The provisions of this Law refer to the members of the Higher Certifying Commission and its specialized scientific councils as well.

Chapter Two

Requirements for the Members of the Executive Bodies of Scientific Organizations and of the Higher Certifying Commission

Article 3

Members of the academic, faculty and scientific councils and of the executive bodies (heads and their deputies) of the higher schools, including and superior to Chair, members of scientific councils and the executive bodies (heads and their deputies) of scientific institutions and organizations, including and superior to the position of Head of Section or the corresponding basic structural unit, and members of the staff of the Higher Certifying Commission and its specialized councils, shall be limited to those persons who can show that they:

1. have not been members or candidate members of the Political Bureau, the Secretariat or the Central Committee of the former Bulgarian Communist Party;

2. have not been secretaries or members of regional, city, community, county or district committees of the Bulgarian Communist Party;

3. did not hold positions before November 10, 1989 which were directly accountable to the Political Bureau or the Secretariat of the Central Committee of the Bulgarian Communist Party and are defined in Section I and II of the "*Nomenklatura* of the staff accountable to the Central Committee of the Bulgarian Communist Party" (no. 1045 of July 19, 1978, approved by the Political Bureau of the Central Committee of the Bulgarian Communist Party in proceedings No. 280 of July 11, 1978);

4. have not been on the staff of or voluntary collaborators with the State Security or the Security and Guard Department;

5. have not compromised themselves through participation and involvement in the "revival process";

6. have not been on the teaching and research staff of, graduate from, or specialize in the Academy of Social Sciences and Social Management and its branches, the Higher Party School for leadership staff of the Bulgarian Communist Party, the Institute for History of the Bulgarian Communist Party, the Institute for Social Management or the schools of the KGB or State Security;

7. have not taught History of the Communist Party of the Soviet Union, History of the Bulgarian Communist Party, Marxist-Leninist Philosophy, Scientific Communism or Party Building;

8. have not been political officers or deputy commanding political officers and did not hold positions in the political headquarters of the Armed Forces;

9. have not been secretaries or members of party committees of the Bulgarian Communist Party in the higher schools and academies; secretaries of the party organizations of the Bulgarian Communist Party in the faculties, scientific institutes and other scientific organizations; or members of Personnel Commissions under the party committees of the higher schools, academies or other scientific organizations.

Article 4

(1) The facts pertaining to Article 3 shall be confirmed in a written declaration.

(2) Refusal to submit a written declaration shall be considered an admission that the person does not meet the requirements for membership in the executive bodies of organizations listed under Article 3.

Article 5

(1) Openings of competitions and elections to scientific and teaching staff, as well as openings of procedures for the defense of theses, shall be suspended until the requirements of Articles 3 and 4 have been met by the members of the corresponding academic, faculty and scientific councils.

(2) Opening of procedures for the defense of theses shall be suspended until the requirements under Articles 3 and 4 have been met by the members of the corresponding specialized scientific councils under the Higher Certifying Commission.

Chapter Three

Administrative Criminal Provisions

Article 6

The submission of the statements required in Article 4, Paragraph 1 with false contents shall be punished according to the Criminal Code.

Article 7

The heads of scientific organizations shall be fined from 8 to 12 regular monthly salaries if they neglect the dictates of one of the Transitory Provisions of this Law. The penalty shall be drawn up by the executive bodies of the Ministry of Education and Science, and the punitive measures shall be issued by the Minister of Education and Science or by a person authorized by him. The decrees of the Law for Administrative Offenses and Penalties shall be applied to these acts as well as to the drawing up and issue of penal decrees and to the appeals against them.

Transitory Provisions

§ 1.   The heads of all the organizations specified in Article 2, Paragraph 1 shall hold elections for new executive bodies and for new academic, faculty and scientific councils in accordance with Article 3, the Law for Academic Autonomy of Higher Schools and the Law for the Bulgarian Academy of Science within 4 (four) months of the effective date of this Law.

§ 2. Within the time limit in the preceding paragraph, the Higher Certifying Commission shall nominate and appoint new specialized scientific councils in accordance with the requirements of Article 3.

§ 3. (1) The members of the Presidium and of the scientific councils of the Higher Certifying Commission shall be dismissed the day this Law comes into effect.

(2) Within one month of the effective date of this Law, the Prime Minister shall appoint a new staff of the Presidium and of the scientific commissions of the Higher Certifying Commission, according to Article 33, Paragraph 2 of the Law for Scientific Degrees and Academic Ranks and in accordance with the requirements of Article 3 of this Law.

Final Provision

§ 4. The requirement of Article 3 of this law are to be applied for a period of 5 years from the day the Law comes into effect.

§ 5. The execution of the Law is assigned to the Council of Ministers.

BULGARIA: CONSTITUTIONAL COURT DECISION ON THE PANEV LAW

Constitutional Case No. 32
Decision No. 1 (February 11, 1993)

The legal proceedings are based on the grounds of Article 149(1), Paragraph 2 of the Bulgarian Constitution. They were initiated at the request of the President of Bulgaria for assertion of the unconstitutionality of the Law for Temporary Introduction of Some Additional Requirements for the Members of the Executive Bodies of Scientific Organizations and the Higher Certifying Commission....

Constitutional case #33/1993, initiated at the request of 102 Members of Parliament from the 36th National Assembly, for the assertion of the unconstitutionality of the same Law, has been attached to the procedure for a joint consideration and resolution, by a decision of January 7, 1993.

By a decision of January 12, 1993, the requests were accepted for consideration. The same decision constituted as parties to the case: the National Assembly; the Council of Ministers; the Ministry of Education, Science and Culture; the Bulgarian Academy of Science; St. Kliment Ohridski University of Sofia; the Council of Rectors; the Union of Scientists in Bulgaria; and the Higher Certifying Commission. In pursuance of the opportunity which they were given, the opinions on the requests have been expressed by the Chair of the National Assembly; the Council of Ministers; the Ministry of Education, Science and Culture; the Bulgarian Academy of Science; St. Kliment Ohridski University of Sofia; the Council of Rectors; the Union of Scientists in Bulgaria; and the Higher Certifying Commission. The following were accepted into evidence: the draft for first hearing, together with the motives of the introducers; the bill for second hearing; the opinion of the Legislative Commission, the Commission on Education and Science and the Human Rights Commission; written proposals of Members of Parliament concerning the bill; the protocols of the first and second hearings from the session of the Legislative Commission; the shorthand reports of first and second hearing from the plenary session of the National Assembly; and the *nomenklatura* list of the Central Committee of the Bulgarian Communist Party of July 11, 1978.

In order to make a decision on the requests, the Constitutional Court took into consideration the following:

Equality of all citizens before the law is a basic principle of every democratic society. In Article 6(2) of the Constitution, equality of all citizens before the law is stated as a constituting principle of civil society and the state. It was claimed that the Law for Introduction of Temporary Additional Requirements for the Members of the Boards of the Scientific Organizations and the Higher Certifying Commission contradicts this principle and the constitutional provisions which specify it in terms of concrete rights and freedoms: namely Article 4(2), Article 16, Article 38, Article 48(3) and Article 56. This is a groundless claim.

None of the additional requirements introduced by the Law defines any of the social criteria in Article 6(2) as ground for non-admission to the executive bodies of scientific organizations and the Higher Certifying Commission. It is a groundless claim that the requirements are aimed at the political opinion and political affiliations of these persons. Political opinions, as well as political affiliations, are irrelevant to the case. The Law is disinterested in past and present political opinions and political affiliations; it takes into consideration only the professionalism of those who participate in the realization of the national policy in science administration and development. That is why the criterion for a membership in administrative boards is the scientific commitment of the person, but not the activities which have served political or ideological party purposes.

Article 6(2) details the social criteria for non-restriction of rights and non-granting of privileges. Imposition of restrictions on the grounds of these criteria is a violation of the principle of equality of all citizens before the law. Professionalism is not among these criteria, and it is quite possible that professional skills are required for holding a certain position: restrictions are imposed where these skills are absent.

In this respect, the claim that the Law contradicts provisions of international agreements which impose equality and preclude all kinds of discrimination based on social criteria is unfounded. There is no violation of Articles 1, 2, 7, and 18 of the Universal Declaration of Human Rights; Articles 9 and 14 of the European Convention for Protection of Human Rights and Basic Freedoms; Article 2, Article 25-A, and Article 26 of the International Covenant on Civil and Political Rights; or Article 2, Paragraph 2 of the International Covenant on Economic, Social and Cultural Rights. The rights protected by these international agreements are not violated by the introduction of additional requirements for the members of the administrative boards in the scientific organizations and the High Certifying Commission. To the extent that these requirements might be considered restrictions on the basis of professionalism, this kind of restriction is admissible, according to Article 4 of the International Covenant on Economic, Social and Cultural Rights, and Article 1, Paragraph 2 of Convention #111/1958, on labor and professional discrimination. The creation of differences based on requirements for professionalism corresponds to the international instruments to which Bulgaria is a party, and does not violate the equality of citizens before the law.

The claim that the Law contradicts Articles 16, 38 and 48(3) of the Constitution is unfounded. The right to labor is guaranteed under the law, and all citizens are able to freely choose their profession and place of work. The additional requirements do not restrict the right to labor of the scientists. Their right of creative contribution and realization under equal conditions for acquiring a scientific degree, according to the principles of liberty, equality and justice, is not restricted. The chance of a scientist to become director or member of an administrative board is not a right, a choice of profession, or a choice of place of work.

The opportunity of citizens to become members of administrative boards is not treated as a right; it is not guaranteed and protected by the Constitution and Bulgarian laws. For this reason the Law for Temporary Introduction of Some Additional Requirements for the Members of the Executive Bodies of the Scientific Organizations and the Higher Certifying Commission does not violate Article 4(2) and Article 56 of the international instruments, which Bulgaria has [signed] and which has entered into force.

The claim that the Law contradicts the provisions of Article 53(4) of the Constitution is unfounded. According to this provision, the Institutions for higher education have academic autonomy. Neither the educational process and the scientific performance, nor other related activities in the Institutions for higher education, are violated by the introduction of some additional requirements for the members of the administrative boards of the scientific organizations. Their autonomy to set the organizational structure and organs of self administration is not violated. The Law only requires that the members of administrative boards be scientists with high professional qualities who have not deviated from scientific work, by involvement in organizational or ideological party work. The Law is also applicable to persons from the scientific communities who have combined party activity and administrative functions, while taking part in scientific councils or commissions in the administration of scientific organizations or their branches. Moreover, the combination of party and administrative power is denounced by the democratic principles of science administration. This is one of the main points of the Law, which does not contradict the Constitution.

On the basis of the above considerations, and on the grounds of Article 149(1), Paragraph 2 of the Constitution, the Constitutional Court:

DECIDED:

To reject the requests of the President of the Republic and 102 Members of Parliament of the 36th National Assembly for assertion of the unconstitutionality of the Law for Temporary Introduction of Some Additional Requirements to the Members of the Executive Bodies of Scientific Organization and the Higher Certifying Commission.

CAMBODIA: LAW ON THE OUTLAWING OF THE "DEMOCRATIC KAMPUCHEA" GROUP

"Anti-Khmer Rouge Law" (July 7, 1994)

The National Assembly of the Kingdom of Cambodia

Considering that the Agreements on a Comprehensive Political Settlement of the Cambodian Conflict of October 23, 1991 which the "Democratic Kampuchea" group had signed together with the three other Khmer signatories, required that the "Democratic Kampuchea" group, like the three other signatories, to implement all the provisions of the Agreements to bring peace and national reconciliation.

Considering the fact that the "Democratic Kampuchea" group has refused to implement the major provisions of the Agreements, and has especially violated those which require that:

- A cease fire be respected,
- The permission be granted to officials and staffs of UNTAC to enter into the Zones under its control,
- Regroupment, disarmament and demobilization of its armed forces be carried out,
- The human rights in Cambodia be respected.

Noting that in addition to the non-respect of the major provisions of the Agreements which it has signed, the "Democratic Kampuchea" group had committed armed aggression against officials and staff of the UN Transitional Authority, against the officials of the Royal Cambodian Government, and indiscriminately against the lives of the Cambodian people.

Considering that the "Democratic Kampuchea" group refused to register as a political party to participate in the elections according to the provisions of the UN Electoral Law for Cambodia dated August 12, 1992 and refused to cooperate in any matter as prescribed by this Law so that its group could become a legal political party.

Noting that from the period of the election of 1993 to the present, the "Democratic Kampuchea" group has continued to commit criminal, terrorist and genocidal acts which have been the hallmark of the group since it captured power in April 1975, of forcible movement of population, abduction, massacre and subsequently of robbery and banditry, laying mines indiscriminately throughout the plains and forests, destroying public and private property, murdering people, forcibly taking and illegally occupying national territory, and selling natural resources in violation of the sovereignty of the Kingdom of Cambodia.

Noting that [the] "Democratic Kampuchea" group has violated the Constitution of the Kingdom of Cambodia, in particular provisions of the following:

- Article 3 which states that "The Kingdom of Cambodia is one and indivisible."
- Article 49 which states that "Every Khmer citizen must respect the Constitution and the Law." Every Khmer citizen has the duty to take part in the national construction and to protect the country."
- Article 50 which states that "the Khmer citizen of both sexes must respect the principle of national sovereignty, liberal democracy and pluralism." "Every Khmer citizen of both sexes must respect public and legally acquired private properties."
- Article 52 which states that "the Royal Government of Cambodia is determined to protect the independence, sovereignty and territorial integrity of the Kingdom of Cambodia, must carry out the policy of national reconciliation in order to safeguard national unity, legitimacy and ensure public order and security."

Noting that the "Democratic Kampuchea" group has refused to heed the successive appeals to participate in the process of national reconciliation made by UNTAC, by leadership of the other Khmer parties, and later on by His Majesty the King and by the Royal Government emerging from the election held to solve the Cambodian problem.

Noting that the leadership of the "Democratic Kampuchea" group cannot use the Paris Peace Agreement on a Comprehensive Political Settlement of the Cambodia Conflict as a legal shield to conceal and to evade from its guilts of having committed criminal, terrorist and genocidal acts from 1975-1978 when the Pol Pot regime was in power. Crimes of genocide are not under the Statute of Limitations.

Hence, the National Assembly of the Kingdom of Cambodia hereby approves the Law which contains the following provisions:

Article 1

Outlaw the "Democratic Kampuchea" group and its armed forces.

Article 2

Upon entry into force of this Law, any person who is a member of the political organization and military forces of the "Democratic Kampuchea" group shall be considered as offenders of the Constitution and offenders of the Laws of the Kingdom of Cambodia.

Members of the political organization or military forces of the "Democratic Kampuchea" group are the ones who give orders, collaborate or engage directly in the armed conflict for the purpose of serving the policy of the "Democratic Kampuchea" group.

The category of people mentioned above does not apply to those who are or whose family members are living under the "Democratic Kampuchea" group's oppression.

Article 3

Members of the political organization and the military forces of the "Democratic Kampuchea" group or any person who commits crimes of murder, rape, robbery of people's property, the destruction of public and private property etc... shall be sentenced according to the existing criminal law.

Article 4

Members of the political organization and the military forces of the "Democratic Kampuchea" group or any person who is engaged in acts of:

- secession
- subversion against the Royal Government
- subversion against organs of the public authority
- public incitement to take up arms against the public authority

shall be regarded as criminals working against the national security and shall be sentenced to jail terms from 20 to 30 years or life.

Article 5

This Law shall allow for an amnesty period of six months after coming into effect to permit persons who are members of the political organization or military forces of the "Democratic Kampuchea" group to return to live under the authority of the Royal Government in the Kingdom of Cambodia without facing punishment for offenses they have committed.

Article 6

The amnesty prescribed above to not apply to the leaders of the "Democratic Kampuchea" group.

Article 7

His majesty the King shall have the right to grant partial or complete amnesty as stated in Article 27 of the Constitution.

Article 8

Once this Law has come into force, all assets in the hands of the "Democratic Kampuchea" group or other offenders and which generate from the illegal division of the territory of the Kingdom of Cambodia and from exploitation of the natural resources of the Khmer people, shall be confiscated and become national assets, be they in the Kingdom of Cambodia or any other country.

Article 9

Anyone who makes use of this Law to abuse the right of the population through the use of illegal threats, accusations, arrest, detention, torture or violation of the rights of dwelling shall be punished and jailed from two to five years.

Anyone who gives false information, acts as a fake witness and gives false evidence in the interest of using this Law to abuse the rights of people shall be punished and jailed from two to five years.

The victim of this injustice has the right to appeal for damages arising from the above mentioned of his rights violations.

Article 10

This Law is declared urgent.

CZECH AND SLOVAK FEDERAL REPUBLIC: REPORT OF THE PARLIAMENTARY COMMISSION ON StB COLLABORATORS IN PARLIAMENT*

The following is the text of the speech read by Petr Toman, spokesman of the Parliamentary Investigative Commission for the Clarification of the Events of November 17, 1989, to the Czechoslovak Federal Assembly on March 22, 1991.

Dear Mr. Chairman of the Federal Assembly, Dear Mr. President, Dear Representatives,

I have been charged by the investigative commission with the task of acquainting you with our commission's work: the findings of the *lustrace* [review, inspection]. But before I share with you the names of our colleagues who are registered collaborators with StB [State Security], I would like to apprise you of the procedures used by our commission, and of the evidence we gathered.

Our commission was constituted for the purpose of investigating the events of November 17, 1989. It consists of members of all the parties represented in parliament, with the exception of the *Együttélés* [Coexistence] party, which chose to be represented by another party. Since the parties were represented in proportion to their strength in parliament, it is impossible that the commission's findings have been directed against any particular party.

Resolution 94, passed by the Federal Assembly on January 11, 1991, charges us with the task of determining whether any of the representatives, ministers, their deputies, employees of the prime minister's office or of the Federal Assembly, are registered as collaborators in StB files. The resolution also charged us with the task of informing those who were positively identified with the results of our investigation. If they fail to voluntarily relinquish their posts within fifteen days of notification, Resolution 94 requires us to make their names public....

In view of the current state of the investigation, we will only report our findings concerning representatives to the Federal Assembly. The findings of our investigation concerning other persons who come under the purview of Resolution 94 will be given to the chairman of the Federal Assembly and the federal prime minister. Afterwards, the commission will apprise the Federal Assembly of the findings and their consequences in regard to these persons. [On May 22, fourteen members of the federal government and sixty other officials were declared to have been collaborators.]

We undertook the *lustrace* of the representatives with the knowledge that most of them, with the exception of those belonging to the Communist

---

* Excerpted from "Collaborators Revealed: The Parliamentary Commission's Report," *Uncaptive Minds*, vol. IV, no. 2(16) (Summer 1991), pp. 8-12.

Party of Czechoslovakia, had signed a declaration stating that they never cooperated with the StB and, we emphasize, that they assented to further investigation into these matters. In the course of its work, the commission made the surprising discovery that, with a single exception, its members were not the first since November 17, 1989 to look at the materials on the people it investigated. It follows that the commission is not the first to find out whether those under investigation are or are not registered in the files of the StB. Let us consider who had access to these files.

First, StB officers who managed agents and other StB employees who administered the files.

Second, members of screening committees, who had access to the materials during screenings.

Third, employees of the Office for the Defense of the Constitution and Democracy [the organization that replaced the StB], who, under the supervision of three successive directors, had access to these materials both at the Office's central location and in the individual districts.

Fourth, ministers of the interior at the republic and federal levels and the employees delegated by them.

Fifth, when the ministry of the interior was headed by three people—and therefore in fact by nobody—during the period following the establishment of the government of national accord, conditions at the ministry were such that nearly anyone was able to walk away with StB documents.

Thus it is safe to assume that documents pertaining to StB operatives are in the possession of a number of people. We have concrete proof that particular documents listed as destroyed still exist, and we have evidence that particular documents were photographed prior to their being destroyed.

The only way to prevent blackmail, the continued activity of StB collaborators, and a series of political scandals that could surface at crucial moments is to clear the government and legislative bodies of these collaborators.

From this perspective, the work of our commission does no harm and will not lead to political scandals. On the contrary, it will prevent them. The effects of unsubstantiated suspicions and misused information concerning StB collaborators can be seen in the development of the political situation in Moravia and Slovakia.

Dear colleagues, before beginning the *lustrace* we had to unambiguously define the criteria for determining who collaborated with the StB, and also decide whether Resolution 94 covers all types of collaborators. We decided to use the criteria set forth in the guidelines for agent operations issued by the StB in 1962 and the guidelines for work with secret collaborators of counterintelligence A-OPER-1-3 issued in 1972 and 1978—in other words, the regulations governing StB collaborators from 1962 to 1989. We were further guided by the directives on intelligence work issued by the first department of the SNB [regular police]. The main administration of the VKR [military counterintelligence] was established by Directive 66 of the minister of national security on May 29, 1952, and is therefore an integral part of the StB.

The official guidelines divide collaborators into two groups: secret collaborators and contacts. Secret collaborators were at different times undercover agents, agents, informers, occupants of apartments used in security operations, ideological collaborators, and secret collaborators with confidential contacts. From the wording of the directives one can determine the fundamental requirement for being considered a secret collaborator: awareness of the collaboration and agreement to engage in it. Those listed as contacts, however, did not always meet this requirement. There were contacts who were unaware that they were being used and contacts who received financial compensation, in some cases foreign currency, for their services. Therefore, in the case of contacts, we had to prove knowledge of collaboration.

Another category quite separate from the others is that of candidates for secret collaboration. In this case, we also had to prove knowledge of collaboration, because the majority of candidates for secret collaboration did not know they were being used, although there were some who were in fact experienced agents.

All the names of representatives which we make public are registered as agents of the counterintelligence service or are documented as secret collaborators of the intelligence service.... We did not find any contacts or candidates for secret collaboration who were aware that they were in contact with organs of the StB, were willing to maintain contact, and provided information or fulfilled the tasks with which they were charged.

What took place before someone was registered as an agent? An StB officer began the process by screening the person whom he believed was willing to collaborate. This consisted of preparing a proposal to establish a file for the person as a candidate for secret collaboration and drawing up a plan for the actual screening. If the person was already on record as having been screened or as hostile, there was no need for a new file, and the record of the screening was added to the existing file. After all the necessary materials had been collected, the StB officer prepared a "proposal for the recruitment of a prospective collaborator," which included an evaluation of the person in question, an evaluation of family members, documents testifying to his willingness to collaborate, and any materials that could be used to compromise him. Then the officer signed the proposal and gave it to the department head to sign. Within thirty days of approval, there took place the so-called binding action, or recruitment. Those who took part in the process besides the officer who initiated it included the prospective collaborator's case officer and the officer's superior. During the binding action, the person in question signed a document committing him to collaboration. This document was waived only in special cases, when the signature might endanger the good relations of the prospective secret collaborator in the course of his collaboration with the counterintelligence service. In such cases oral assent by the person in question was deemed sufficient. Then the prospective collaborator, after choosing a cover name, was instructed in the main principles of collaboration.... At the same time, he was assigned his first concrete task, instructed in the manner of its execution and the procedure for making contact, and given a password to be used for the duration of the binding action. In several cases the proceedings of the binding action were tape-recorded. At the end, minutes of the binding action were prepared and signed by the StB officers who were present and then forwarded for approval to the chief officer in charge of approving proposals for recruiting collaborators.

Only after such approval was the person in question registered as a collaborator of a given category. We emphasize that actual inclusion in the registry of files was not performed by an employee of the StB, but by a member of an autonomous department of the Federal Ministry of Internal Affairs. A case officer then signed a document confirming the validity of the addition of the new collaborator to the registry of files.

Esteemed delegates, in the course of the *lustrace* we asked a broad selection of StB employees whether they were familiar with the procedures mentioned above and whether they abided by them. All of them confirmed that a person registered as an agent knew he was in contact with an employee of the StB.... They excluded the possibility that a collaborator could be registered without his being aware that he was collaborating. They explained that the presence of the chief officer or his deputy was required during the binding action, and that meetings between StB officers and collaborators were supervised by superior organs. None of them knew of any case in which a person was registered who was not a collaborator.

When asked about specific representatives to the Federal Assembly, several StB officers reversed what they had said above. But their testimony was cast into doubt by the testimony of other StB officers. We have documentation of repeated meetings even after November 17, 1989. We have documentation that one of the representatives in the files offered his case officer the position of deputy if the representative became a minister. These occurrences are far too serious to ignore.

We consider the registry of files of the Federal Ministry of Internal Affairs to be the fundamental evidence on which we have based our conclusions. It is a directory of all persons of interest to the StB, that is, secret collaborators, persons who were screened, those who were considered hostile, and so on, with separate sections for every region of the country. Each registry is organized chronologically. Every entry is marked with a registration number and a date. In addition, the registry contains the real and cover names of the person in question, his category, his date of birth, the name of the officer who directed that the entry be made, the officer's department, section, the date when the entry was completed, and whether it should be eventually destroyed or kept in the archives. That is, all the facts that are of interest to us. Each change in the entry is explicitly documented, including the date it was made.

...All members of the commission rule out the possibility of falsification, that is, the possibility that falsification would not have been evident in the cases we investigated. Besides the fact that the individual entries were made line by line, numbered, and consecutively dated, it is possible to establish the age of the paper on which the entry was made, the age of the ink with which it was made, and the age of the ink with which it was stamped. In the case of an expunged entry it is possible to reconstruct the original. In conclusion, our commission considers the registry of files to be reliable.

Despite the registry's credibility, we sought to confirm the entries in it with further evidence, in particular, by questioning the StB case officers, their superiors, and their co-workers. Other persons were also questioned. We have photocopies of materials from the statistics and evidence department and printouts of computer files. We verified this information by examining other written materials. Only after cross-checking the evidence we had obtained did we conclude definitively that the person in question was registered as a collaborator of the StB....

CZECH AND SLOVAK FEDERAL REPUBLIC: SCREENING ("LUSTRATION") LAW

Act No. 451/1991 (October 4, 1991)

Article 1

1. This Act prescribes certain additional prerequisites for the exercise of the functions filled by election, appointment or assignment:

(a) in the State administration of the Czech and Slovak Federative Republic, Czech Republic and Slovak Republic;

(b) in the Czechoslovak Army;

(c) in the Federal Security Information Service, Federal Police Force and Palace Guard Police Force;

(d) in the Office of the President of the Czech and Slovak Federative Republic, the Office of the Federal Assembly, the Office of the Czech National Council, the Office of the Slovak National Council, the Office of the Government of the Czech and Slovak Federative Republic, the Office of the Government of the Slovak Republic, the Office of the Constitutional Court of the Czech and Slovak Federative Republic, the Office of the Constitutional Court of the Czech Republic, the Office of the Constitutional Court of the Slovak Republic, the Office of the Supreme Court of the Czech and Slovak Federative Republic, the Office of the Supreme Court of the Czech Republic, the Office of the Supreme Court of the Slovak Republic, the Presidium of the Czechoslovak Academy of Science and the Presidium of the Slovak Academy of Science;

(e) in the Czechoslovak Broadcasting Corporation, the Czech Broadcasting Corporation, the Slovak Broadcasting Corporation, the Czechoslovak Television, the Czech Television, the Slovak Television, the Czechoslovak Press Agency, the Czechoslovak Press Agency of the Czech Republic and the Czechoslovak Press Agency of the Slovak Republic;

(f) in State enterprises, State organizations, in the joint ventures where the majority-shareholder is the State, in international trade agencies, in the State organization of the Czechoslovak State Railways, in State funds, in State banking institutions and in the Czechoslovak State Bank, unless it is further provided otherwise.

2. The functions according to Article 1, paragraph 1, letter (b), are to be understood as functions in the Czechoslovak Army and at the Federal Ministry of Defence, for which the ranks of colonel and general are planned, as well as the functions of military attachés.

3. The functions according to Article 1, paragraph 1, letter (f), are to be understood as the functions of the head of an organization and of the leading executives within his direct management range. At high schools, these

functions are also to be understood as those of elected academic officers and those subject to approval by the academic senate.

4. This Act also prescribes certain other prerequisites for the exercise of office as a judge, an assessor, a prosecutor, an investigator at a prosecutor's office, a State notary, a State arbiter, as well as for persons carrying out the activities of a judiciary candidate, a legal-post candidate at a prosecutor's office, and a nominee for the post of a notary or of an arbiter.

5. This Act also lays down the conditions of reliability required for practicing certain concession-based trades.[1]

Article 2

1. For the exercise of any of the functions specified in Article 1, the prerequisite is that, during the period from 25 February 1948 to 17 November 1989, the citizen concerned was not:

(a) a member of the National Security Corps detailed to any State Security section;

(b) listed on the files of the State Security as a resident, an agent, a holder of a lent-out apartment, a holder of a conspiratorial apartment, an informer or an ideological collaborator of the State Security;

(c) a conscious collaborator of the State Security;

(d) a secretary of an organ/authority of the Communist Party of Czechoslovakia or of the Communist Party of Slovakia, from a district or higher-level committee, a member of the presidium of such committees, a member of the Central Committee of the Communist Party of Czechoslovakia or of the Central Committee of the Communist Party of Slovakia, a member of the Bureau for the Management of Party Work in the Czech Lands, or a member of the Committee for the Management of Party Work in the Czech Lands, with the exception of those who held these functions only during the period from 1 January 1968 to 1 May 1969;

(e) a member of the staff of any of the organs mentioned under letter (d) in the sector of political guidance of the National Security Corps;

(f) a member of the People's Militias;

(g) a member of an Action Committee of the National Front after 25 February 1948, of Screening Committees after 25 February 1948, or of Screening and Normalization Committees after 21 August 1968;

(h) a student at the Felix Edmundovich Dzerzhinsky High School under the aegis of the Council of Ministers of the Union of Soviet Socialist Republics for members of the State Security, at the High School of the Ministry of the Interior of the Union of Soviet Socialist Republics for members of the Public Security, or at the High Political School of the Ministry of the Interior of the Union of Soviet Socialist Republics, or a scientific assistant-professor, or a participant of training courses longer than three months, at any of these schools.

---

[1] Article 27, paragraph 2, of Act No. .../1991 of the *Official Gazette*, concerning professional trades and its Appendix No. 3.

2. Conscious collaboration with the State Security, according to paragraph 1, letter (c), for the purposes of this Act is to be understood in the sense that the citizen concerned has been listed on the files of the State Security as a confidant, a candidate of secret collaboration or as a secret collaborator of confidential contacts and knowledge, and he knew he was in contact with a member of the National Security Corps and was giving him information through the form of clandestine contacts, or was implementing tasks set by him.

3. In justifiable instances, the Minister of Defense of the Czech and Slovak Federative Republic may waive the condition prescribed according to paragraph 1, letter (a), if its application should interfere with an important security interest of the State and unless the purpose of this Act should be counteracted thereby.

Article 3

1. For the exercise of the functions specified in Article 1 in the Federal Ministry of the Interior, in the Federal Security Information Service, in the Federal Police Force and in the Palace Guard Police Force, the prerequisite is that, during the period from 25 February 1948 to 17 November 1989, the citizen concerned was not:

(a) a member of the National Security Corps detailed to a State Security section with counter-intelligence aims;

(b) appointed to the post of head of department or higher in any section of the State Security;

(c) a student at the Felix Edmundovich Dzerzhinsky High School under the aegis of the Council of Ministers of the Union of Soviet Socialist Republics for members of the State Security, at the High School of the Ministry of the Interior of the Union of Soviet Socialist Republics for members of the Public Security, or at the High Political School of the Ministry of the Interior of the Union of Soviet Socialist Republics, or a scientific assistant-professor, or a participant of training courses longer than three months, at any of these schools;

(d) in the National Security Corps in the function of secretary of the Central Committee of the Communist Party of Czechoslovakia or of the Central Committee of the Communist Party of Slovakia, a member of the Central Committee of the Communist Party of Czechoslovakia or of the Central Committee of the Communist Party of Slovakia, a member of the Plenary Committee of the Communist Party of Czechoslovakia or of the Plenary Committee of the Communist Party of Slovakia, or a member of the National Security Corps detailed to the Administration of Political, Educational, Cultural and Propaganda Activities of the Federal Ministry of the Interior;

(e) a person specified in Article 2, paragraph 1, letters (b) to (g).

2. In justified instances, the Minister of the Interior of the Czech and Slovak Federative Republic, the Director of the Federal Security Information Service and the Director of the Federal Police Force may waive the condition prescribed according to paragraph 1, letter (a), if its application should interfere with an important security interest of the State and unless the purpose of this Act should be counteracted thereby.

Article 4

1. The circumstances specified in Article 2, paragraph 1, letters (a) and (b), should be proved by the citizen concerned by means of a certificate issued by the Federal Ministry of the Interior.

2. The circumstances specified in Article 2, paragraph 1, letter (e), should be proved by the citizen concerned by means of a certificate issued by the Federal Ministry of the Interior or, alternatively, by means of a statement issued by the commission established according to Article 11.

3. The circumstances specified in Article 2, paragraph 1, letters (d) to (h), should be documented by the citizen concerned by means of an affidavit.

4. Before taking up any of the functions specified in Article 1, the citizen concerned must submit a declaration to the effect that he is not and has never been a collaborator of any foreign intelligence or espionage service.

Article 5

A citizen who is to exercise a function in any of the organs or organizations specified in Article 1, must submit the appropriate certificate, affidavit or statement to the head of the organ or organization concerned. The application for the issue of the certificate has to be submitted to the Federal Ministry of the Interior by the citizen himself, unless further provided otherwise.

Article 6

1. Instead of the citizen who is to exercise any of the functions specified in Article 1, or who has been exercising such a function by the date of enforcement of this Act, the application for the issue of the certificate has to be submitted to the Federal Ministry of the Interior;

(a) in the case of a citizen elected to the function concerned, by the organ relevant for this election;

(b) in the case of a citizen appointed to the function concerned, by the organ entitled to appoint him to this function;

(c) in the case of a citizen assigned to the function concerned, by the organ relevant for such an assignment.

The head of the organ or organization shall inform the citizen about his duty to submit the certificate within 30 days of its delivery.

2. The application for the issue of the certificate, submitted on behalf of a citizen who, by the day of enforcement of this Act, has been exercising a function specified in Article 1, must be sent to the Federal Ministry of the Interior within 30 days following the enforcement of this Act.

3. The Federal Ministry of the Interior shall send the certificate to the citizen whom it concerns, within 60 days following his application, and, simultaneously, notify the party that has applied for the issue of the certificate.

4. If a citizen exercising a function specified in Article 1 by the date of enforcement of this Act fails to produce, to the head of the organ or organization concerned, the required certificate within 30 days of having received it, the head of the organ or organization shall apply to the Federal Ministry of the Interior, within seven days, for a copy of the certificate issued.

Article 7

The President of the Czech and Slovak Federative Republic, the Presidium of the Federal Assembly, the Presidium of the Czech National Council, the Presidium of the Slovak National Council, the Government of the Czech and Slovak Federative Republic, the Government of the Czech Republic and the Government of the Slovak Republic, the Prosecutor-General of the Czech Republic and the Prosecutor-General of the Slovak Republic shall apply to the Federal Ministry of the Interior for the issue of certificates concerning persons in connection with the exercise of functions filled by appointment, to which they are entitled according to special regulations. The Federal Ministry of the Interior must comply with such an application without delay.

Article 8

1. Any citizen older than 18 years of age is entitled to apply to the Federal Ministry of the Interior for the issue of a certificate according to Article 2, paragraph 1, letters (a), (b) and (c), and, where appropriate, of a statement according to Article 13.

2. The application for the issue of a certificate must bear a revenue stamp in the value of 200 crowns, and the applicant's signature must be officially certified.

Article 9

1. The certificate is issued by the Federal Ministry of the Interior and must be delivered to the citizen himself; this provision shall not apply in the event of a certificate issued according to Article 7.

2. If the documentation needed for the issue of the certificate is in the possession of a different State organ, the latter must make available to the Federal Ministry of the Interior, on the basis of its request, within seven days,

all the documentation and other information needed for the issue of the certificate.

Article 10

For the purpose of this Act and for the purposes of judicial proceedings, the certificate, the statement and the information contained in them shall not be regarded as official secrets.

Article 11

1. For the purpose of ascertaining the circumstances specified in Article 2, paragraph 1, letters (c) to (h), an independent commission (hereinafter "the commission") shall be established under the auspices of the Federal Ministry of the Interior. The commission shall consist of a chairman, a vice-chairman and other members.

2. The chairman, the vice-chairman and one other member of the commission shall be appointed and recalled by the Presidium of the Federal Assembly, from among citizens who are blameless and are not members of the Federal Assembly. If the chairman of the commission is a citizen of the Czech Republic, the vice-chairman must be a citizen of the Slovak Republic, and vice versa.

3. Two members of the commission shall be appointed and recalled by the Minister of the Interior of the Czech and Slovak Federative Republic from amongst the staff of the Federal Ministry of the Interior, who shall simultaneously decide which of these nominees should function as the commission's secretary; one member of the commission shall be appointed and recalled by the Director of the Federal Security Information Service; one member of the commission shall be appointed and recalled by the Minister of Defence of the Czech and Slovak Federative Republic; three members of the commission shall be appointed and recalled by the Presidium of the Czech National Council, and another three by the Presidium of the Slovak National Council, from amongst citizens who are blameless and who are not members of the Czech National Council or of the Slovak National Council; one member of the commission shall be appointed and recalled by the Minister of the Interior of the Czech Republic; one member of the commission shall be appointed and recalled by the Minister of the Interior of the Slovak Republic, from among the staffs of these Ministries. The members of the commission appointed by the Ministers and by the Director of the Federal Security Information Service must have completed university-level legal education; for the purposes of this Act, the education acquired at the High School of the National Security Corps shall not be regarded as sufficient.

4. Membership of the commission is irreplaceable by any substitute. The exercise of functions as a member of the commission shall be recognized as an alternative act of general interest, for which the person concerned is entitled to compensation.

5. The functioning of the Commission shall be taken care of by the Federal Ministry of the Interior.

Article 12

1. The commission is capable of holding a session if the attending members include its chairman or vice-chairman, plus at least another seven members. The sessions of the commission are closed.

2. Before the beginning of the commission's deliberations, the citizen concerned must be enabled to become acquainted with all the evidence available, including written material relating to his person. In the course of the commission's deliberations, he must be given the opportunity of voicing his opinion on all the evidence considered.

3. Invited persons are obliged to turn up for the commission's session, to speak the truth and not to withhold any information.

4. The relevant provisions of Criminal Procedure shall apply to the duty to testify, as well as to the summons, the compulsory attendance, the prohibition of questioning, the right to refuse to denounce, the compensation for appearing as witness, the invitation of an expert and the duties of the latter.

Article 13

1. The commission commences the proceedings on the basis of a proposal which:

(a) may be submitted by a citizen who has received a certificate indicating that he is a person specified in Article 2, paragraph 1, letter (c);

(b) may be submitted by a citizen who claims that an affidavit made out by a person exercising a function specified in Article 1 is untrue. At the beginning of the proceedings, the citizen must deposit a security in the amount of 1,000 crowns, which is to be returned to him if it appears, in the course of the proceedings, that his proposal was justified;

(c) may be submitted by an organization in case it has any doubts about the truth of an affidavit by a citizen who is to exercise any of the functions specified in Article 1.

2. Within 60 days following the delivery of the application, the commission shall issue a statement as to whether the citizen concerned is a person specified in Article 2, paragraph 1, letters (c) to (h). The statement must contain a justification.

3. If a citizen who otherwise fails to fulfill the prerequisites for the exercise of a function specified in Article 2 proves that, after having ceased to be in the position of a person specified in Article 2, paragraph 1, letters (d) to (h), he has been penalized for acts specified in Article 2 of Act No. 119/1990 of the *Official Gazette*, concerning judicial rehabilitation, and that in accordance with that Act he has become rehabilitated, the commission shall

decide that he fulfills the prerequisites for the exercise of the functions specified in Article 1.

4. The commission shall send its statement to the citizen whom it concerns and, simultaneously, it shall notify the party that has submitted the proposal for the commencement of the proceedings.

5. If it is indicated in the statement that the citizen concerned is not a person specified in Article 2, paragraph 1, letter (c), this circumstance shall be recorded in all the files and documents, arguing that these records and documents cannot be used anymore.

Article 14

1. If a citizen fails to fulfil the prerequisites for the exercise of a function, as specified in Article 2, his employment shall terminate by notice given by the organization, within 15 days following the date when the organization came to know about it, unless the employment is terminated by mutual agreement or in another manner at an earlier date, or unless the citizen has been transferred to a function other than those specified in Article 1.

2. The provisions of paragraph 1 shall apply similarly to the termination of service by dismissal,[2] in case the citizen concerned fails to fulfil the prerequisites for the exercise of a function as specified in Article 3.

3. If a citizen has refused to issue an affidavit concerning the circumstances specified in Article 2, paragraph 1, letters (d) to (h), or in case his affidavit proves to be untrue, paragraph 1 or 2 becomes applicable.

Article 15

If a prosecutor or an investigator at a prosecutor's office fails to fulfil the prerequisites specified in Article 2, this circumstance shall provide grounds for the termination of his employment.

Article 16

Under the conditions specified in Article 14, paragraph 1, the appropriate organ shall submit a proposal for the judge or assessor concerned to be recalled from office.

Article 17

The provisions of the Labour Code to the effect that an organization can give notice of recall only after a previous consent of the appropriate trade union organ[3] shall not be applicable to the termination of employment according to Articles 14 and 15.

---

[2]Article 18, paragraph 1, letter (c), of Act No. 334/1991 of the *Official Gazette*, concerning the service of police officers of the Federal Police Force and of the Palace Guard Police Force.

[3]Article 59, paragraphs 2-4, of the Labour Code.

Article 18

1. If a citizen insists that the circumstances specified in the commission's statement are untrue, he may request the court to re-examine the contents of such a statement within two months following its delivery. Such proceedings fall within the jurisdiction of the district court of the citizen's permanent residence.

2. The invalidity of the termination of employment or service may be claimed by the citizen concerned, not later than within two months following the date when the employment or service was to be terminated. The proceedings fall within the jurisdiction of the district court of the citizen's permanent residence, in the capacity as a court of first degree.

Article 19

Without the previous written consent of the citizen concerned, it is forbidden to publicize the circumstances specified in the certificate, or to publicize the certificate, the statement itself, or any documentation serving as background material.

Article 20

Whoever, acting before the commission as a witness, an expert or an interpreter, is untruthful about a fact which is of substantial importance for the commission's statement, or whoever withholds information about such a fact, shall be punished by deprivation of personal liberty for up to three years, or by a pecuniary penalty.

Article 21

1. The publishers of periodical press, as well as the operators of radio and television, of agency newscasting and audiovisual programmes on the basis of a license, may request the Federal Ministry of the Interior, either on their own behalf or, following a previous written consent, on behalf of a member of their staff who takes part in the shaping of the intellectual contents of the communication media mentioned, to issue the necessary certificate, or they may request the commission for a statement under the provisions of Article 6, paragraph 3, of Article 9, paragraph 1, of Article 10, of Article 12, of Article 13, of Article 18 to 20 of this Act, which shall apply as previously stated.

2. The presidents or equivalent-level representatives of political parties, political movements and associations[4] may apply, on their own behalf or on behalf of a member of the leadership of the political party, political movement or association, subject to his previous written consent, to the Federal Ministry of the Interior for the issue of a certificate, or to the commission established according to Article 11, for the issue of its statement.

---

[4] Act No. 83/1990 of the *Official Gazette*, concerning the association of citizens, as amended by Act No. 300/1990 of the *Official Gazette*.

The provisions specified in paragraph 1 shall apply in such a case by analogy.

Article 22

1. If the laws of the National Councils authorize the Ministers of the Interior and the Ministers of Justice of the Czech Republic and of the Slovak Republic to investigate the circumstances specified in Article 2, paragraph 1, the Federal Ministry of the Interior and the commission must comply with their requests for the issue of the certificate or statement required.

2. The way of terminating the service of members of the Penitentiary Training Corps of the Czech Republic and of the Penitentiary Training Corps of the Slovak Republic and of the police officers serving in the Police Force of the Czech Republic and in the Police Force of the Slovak Republic shall be regulated by the laws of the National Councils.

Article 23

This Act becomes effective by the day of its promulgation and shall cease to be effective by 31 December 1996.

CZECH AND SLOVAK FEDERAL REPUBLIC: INTERNATIONAL LABOUR ORGANIZATION DECISION ON THE SCREENING LAW*

GB.252/16/19 (February 28, 1992)
252nd Session

Introduction

1. The Trade Union Association of Bohemia, Moravia and Slovakia (OS-CMS), by a letter dated 23 October 1991, and the Czech and Slovak Confederation of Trade Unions (CS-KOS), by a letter dated 11 November 1991, both referring to Article 24 of the Constitution of the International Labour Organisation, each made a representation alleging non-observance by the Czech and Slovak Federal Republic of the Discrimination (Employment and Occupation) Convention, 1958 (No. 111)....

11. Both complainant organisations based their respective representations on the adoption on 4 October 1991 and entry into force on 5 November 1991 of Act No. 451/1991 (the Screening Act) which they consider to be in violation of Convention No. 111....

The Committee's Conclusions

43. The Committee had available to it, for its assessment of Act No. 451/1991 and of the allegations of the complainant organisations, the comments of the Government but also the benefit of the views of the President of the CSFR, Mr. Vaclav Havel, as expressed in his letter of 17 October 1991 to the Federal Assembly to propose a revision of the Act. Reference is made also by one complainant organisation to the views of the President of the Federal Assembly of the CSFR, Mr. Alexander Dubcek, in a statement circulated by the CTK official news agency. The Committee wishes to stress the value it attaches to opinions from such eminent sources which testify to the exceptional importance of the debate involved.

44. From the information supplied by the complainants and the Government, the following main points have emerged regarding the circumstances of adoption of Act No. 451/1991, the objections made to its principles and provisions, and the legal and practical status of this "screening law".

1. There is concurrence of the views expressed that it was necessary and justified to remove from public institutions persons who

---

* Excerpted from International Labour Office, "Report of the Committee Set Up to Examine the Representations Made by the Trade Union of Bohemia, Moravia and Slovakia and by the Czech and Slovak Confederation (No. 111)," *Official Bulliten*, Vol. LXXV, 1992, Series B, Suppl. 1. Copyright © 1992, International Labour Organization, Geneva.

took part in suppressing human rights and that this should be done by due legal process. The Government consulted the ILO before putting forward the original draft. However, as a result of numerous amendments made in Parliament, Act No. 451/1991 differs substantially from the original draft submitted by the Government.

2. The central objection to Act No. 451/1991 is that it is based on a presumption of collective guilt, applied extensively in disregard of other principles of law such as non-retroactivity, burden of proof of guilt and presumption of innocence, right of appeal and of defence. Under the terms of the "screening law", from its entry into force until 31 December 1996, people are excluded from exercising a wide range of functions and occupations mostly in public institutions but also in the private sector, if they had been engaged in the past, in specified functions, activities, or in association with or membership of certain groups or bodies of the former political system, in a period of over 40 years from 25 February 1948 to 17 November 1989. Furthermore, the proof of such action or association may not be entirely reliable and may not even be refuted by the persons against whom it is directed, who incur the risk of being disproportionately penalised, without the possibility of any mitigating circumstances being entertained, including such situations as persons subjected to threat or pressure, persons having redeemed past failings or errors or persons acting on behalf of an opposition group who sought to obtain information by getting inside organs of the former system.

3. For these reasons, the complainant organisations hold that the "screening law" is in violation of the Constitution of the CSFR and of international obligations which are part of its legal order, and specifically, is in violation of Convention No. 111, in light of conclusions of the Committee of Experts to which they refer. The OS-CMS quotes a statement by the President of the Federal Assembly, Mr. Alexander Dubcek, on the discriminatory and unconstitutional nature of Act No. 451/1991. In his letter of 17 October 1991 forwarded with the Government's statement and to which the CS-KOS refers, President Vaclav Havel expresses the view that the legal provisions in question are contrary in their spirit to the established foundations of a democratic legal order. He refers therefore to the possibility of a ruling by the Constitutional Court of the CSFR when convened, or by a competent international institution, that Act No. 451/1991 is contrary to international standards accepted by the CSFR or to its Charter of Fundamental Rights and Freedoms which forms an integral part of its Constitution.

4. In this connection, Constitutional Act No. 23/1991 introducing the Charter of Fundamental Rights and Freedoms also provides for the precedence of ratified international human rights instruments over other national legislation (Article 2) and the harmonisation of all laws and regulations with the Charter, all contrary provisions ceasing to have effect by 31 December 1991 (Article 6)....

5.   In the meantime, according to the complainant organisations, Act No. 451/1991 is already being applied; persons have been dismissed in pursuance thereof, and it is estimated that the Act will concern more than one million Czechoslovak citizens....

Bearing of the Act No. 451/1991 on the Observance of Convention No. 111

52. The Committee notes that the issues raised in relation to Act No. 451/1991 involve many aspects and provisions of Convention No. 111.

53. The main substantive issue raised is that of determining whether Act No. 451/1991 establishes *discrimination on the basis of political opinion*, [under] Convention No. 111.... The relevant provisions of the Convention read as follows:

Article 1, Paragraph 1

For the purpose of this Convention the term "discrimination" includes—

(a)   any distinction, exclusion or preference made on the basis of race, colour, sex, religion, political opinion, national extraction or social origin, which has the effect of nullifying or impairing equality of opportunity or treatment in employment or occupation;

Article 1, Paragraph 3

For the purpose of this Convention the terms "employment" and "occupation" include access to vocational training, access to employment and to particular occupations, and terms and conditions of employment.

54. In determining the issue of discrimination, account must be taken of Article 1, paragraph 2, concerning the *inherent requirement of a particular job*, and of Article 4 concerning *measures regarding activities prejudicial to the security of State*. The relevant provisions of the Convention read as follows:

Article 1, Paragraph 2

2.   Any distinction, exclusion or preference in respect of a particular job based on the inherent requirements thereof shall not be deemed to be discrimination.

Article 4

Any measures affecting an individual who is justifiably suspected of, or engaged in, activities prejudicial to the security of the State shall not be deemed to be discrimination, provided that the individual concerned shall have the right to appeal to a competent body established in accordance with national practice....

The Requirements of Convention No. 111 as Regards Protection Against Discrimination on the Basis of Political Opinion

56. As noted earlier, the complainant organisations referred to the conclusions of the Committee of Experts on the Application of Conventions and Recommendations as regards the relevant requirements of Convention No. 111 and more especially as regards protection against discrimination on the basis of political opinion. The conclusions recalled below are drawn from the Committee of Experts' latest general survey of 1988 on discrimination and incorporate the Committee's earlier comments, either general or concerning individual countries, as well as comments of other ILO supervisory bodies, where appropriate.[1]...

57. As regards the contents and scope of the protection afforded by the Convention in this field, paragraph 57 of the above-mentioned general survey provides the following indications:

Nature and manifestation of opinions—

> ...the Convention implies [protection] in respect of activities expressing or demonstrating opposition to the established political principles—since the protection of opinions which are neither expressed nor demonstrated would be pointless.
> ...even if certain doctrines are aimed at fundamental changes in the institutions of the State, this does not constitute a reason for considering their propagation beyond the protection of the Convention in the absence of the use or advocacy of violent methods to bring about that result.

Collective advocacy of opinions—

> the protection of freedom of expression is aimed not merely at the individual's intellectual satisfaction at being able to speak his mind, but rather—and especially as regards the expression of political opinions—at giving him an opportunity to seek to influence decisions in the political, economic and social life of his society. For his political views to have an impact, the individual generally acts in conjunction with others. Political organisations and parties constitute a framework within which the members seek to secure wider acceptance of their opinions. To be meaningful, the protection of political opinions must therefore extend to their collective advocacy within such entities.

58. As regards the question of the inherent requirements of a particular job in relation to political opinion, the general survey of 1988 provides the following indications:

(paragraph 126)

Concept of "a particular job"—

---

[1] "*Equality in employment and occupation*; ILC, 75th Session, 1988, Report III (Part 4B). It may be noted that the essential points of these conclusions as regards the issue under consideration were given in the Office's reply of 6 September 1991 to the request of the Government of the CFSR for preliminary consultation on the original draft of the Act.

It appears from the preparatory work and the text of the Convention as ultimately adopted, that the concept of "a particular job" refers to a specific and definable job, function or task. Any limitation within the context of this exception must be required by the characteristics of the particular job, and be in proportion to its inherent requirements. Certain criteria may be brought to bear as inherent requirements of a particular job, but they may not be applied to all jobs in a given occupation or sector of activity, and especially in the public service, without coming into conflict with the principle of equality of opportunity and treatment in occupation and employment.

Consideration of political opinions—

although it may be admissible, in the case of certain higher posts which are directly concerned with implementing government policy, for the responsible authorities generally to bear in mind the political opinions of those concerned, the same is not true when conditions of a political nature are laid down for all kinds of public employment in general or for certain other professions: for example, when there is a provision that those concerned must make a formal declaration of loyalty and remain loyal to the political principles of the regime in power.

(paragraph 105)

Security checks—

the security measures adopted with respect to candidates for employment in the public service may also affect the observance of the principle laid down in the Convention.... [F]rom the information available it appears that in some countries such security checks are applicable without distinction to all posts in the administration. Such inquiries should not be permitted or carried out except where justified by the inherent occupational requirements of the post in question. Moreover, any person who is denied access to a particular post for security reasons ought to have the right to appeal against the decision. It is of the utmost importance that an appellate remedy should be available to persons who are wrongfully denied access to a post for security reasons that are based on unlawful grounds of discrimination, such as national extraction, social origin, religion or political opinion.

59. Concerning measures regarding activities prejudicial to the security of the State, paragraphs 135 to 137 of the General Survey of 1988 provide the following indications concerning the substantive conditions and the procedural guarantee laid down in Article 4 of the Convention:

Substantive Conditions

Activities covered—

Article 4 of the Convention excludes, first of all, any measures taken not because of individual activities but by reason of membership of a particular group or community; such measures could not be other than discriminatory. Secondly, the exception provided for in Article 4 refers to activities qualifiable as prejudicial to the security of the State, whether such activities are proved or whether concurring and precise presumptions justify suspecting such activities. Therefore, the expression of opinions or religious, philosophical or political beliefs is not a sufficient base for the application of the exception....

Measures within the meaning of Article 4—

...measures intended to safeguard the security of the State within the meaning of Article 4 of the Convention must be sufficiently well defined and delimited to ensure that they do not become discrimination based on political opinions or religion.

The application of measures intended to protect the security of the State must be examined in the light of the bearing which the activities concerned may have on the actual performance of the job, tasks or occupation of the person concerned. Otherwise, there is a danger, and even likelihood, that such measures entail distinctions and exclusions based on political opinion or religion, which would be contrary to the Convention.

Procedural Guarantee

In addition to these substantive conditions ... there is also a procedural guarantee: the right of the person affected by the measures described in Article 4 of the Convention, 'to appeal to a competent body established in accordance with national practice'. Existence of a right of appeal, while constituting a necessary condition for the application of the exception to the principle of the Convention, is however not sufficient in itself.... In a previous survey, the Committee already stated that 'enforcement through the courts will not suffice to guarantee the application of the standards embodied in the 1958 instruments in this respect if the provisions which the courts have to apply are themselves incompatible with these standards.'

Appeals may follow the normal procedural rules of judiciary or administrative courts. In certain cases, special procedures, often established under emergency legislation, are provided for the examination of measures taken. Compliance with Article 4 of the Convention must be examined on a case-by-case basis so as to ascertain that certain minimum conditions are met. There must be an appeals "body" which is separate from the administrative or governmental authority, and which offers a guarantee of objectivity and independence. This body must be "competent" to hear the reasons for the measures taken against the person in question, and to afford him or her the opportunity to present his or her case in full.

Assessment of Act No. 451/1991 in Relation to the Requirements of Convention No. 111

...61. The Committee has recorded earlier in this report, that the motivation at the origin of the Act was to remove from public institutions persons who took part in suppressing human rights, but that the Act as adopted has essentially diverged from its original intended purpose. The Committee considers that human rights violations, where amenable to law in a democratic legal system, should as criminal offences be dealt with by due process of law and that in any event, the effects of judicial convictions or administrative sanctions on that ground, in regard to employment and occupation, should not be deemed to fall outside the scope of Convention No. 111 if the definition and penalisation of such offences were to infringe in any way the protection that the Convention is intended to provide....

63. The Committee observes at the outset that the exclusions established by Act No. 451/1991 are based on past association or collaboration with organs and institutions of the State and party apparatus of the former political regime, with marked emphasis on questions of security and ideology. Such exclusions appear therefore to be based essentially on political or ideological opinions or on action linked thereto.

64. The Committee notes, however, that an exclusion may be deemed an inherent requirement of a particular job, pursuant to Article 1, paragraph 2, of the Convention, or a measure regarding activities prejudicial to the security of the State, pursuant to Article 4 of the Convention. The question as to whether or not the exclusions imposed by Act No. 451/1991 constitute discrimination by the terms of Convention No. 111 must therefore be examined in relation to these provisions of the Convention.

65. In endeavouring to determine the above issue the Committee is fully aware of the complexity of the task of evaluating such a wide range of situations as covered by Act No. 451/1991. The Committee intends in so doing to be guided by the conclusions of the ILO supervisory bodies. The Committee's own conclusions are not meant to be regarded as definitive pronouncements on each particular situation but rather as general comments concerning the principles to be observed in relation to the issues involved.

Inherent Requirements of a Particular Job

66. The following criteria may be drawn from the relevant conclusions of ILO supervisory bodies (see paragraph 58 above) regarding any exclusion made in pursuance of Article 1, paragraph 2, of Convention No. 111:

- Any exclusion based on the inherent requirements of a particular job should be in proportion to such requirements and should refer to a specific and definable job, function or task and not apply to an entire occupation or sector of activity, especially in the public service.
- Political opinions may accordingly constitute a condition laid down for certain higher posts directly concerned with implementing policy but not for all kinds of public employment in general or for certain other professions.
- Security checks should be limited to employment in confidential positions or in posts that are sensitive from the point of view of state security. An appellate remedy is of the utmost importance to persons who are wrongfully denied access to a post for security reasons that are based on unlawful grounds of discrimination.

67. To begin with the types of exclusions which would appear to be in line with the above criteria, it may be considered that among the functions

covered by Article 1 of Act No. 451/1991, those which entail particularly strict requirements of state security and of confidentiality may reasonably be subject to exclusions based on political opinion, given especially the context of recent and current events of history in Czechoslovakia. The exclusions imposed should nevertheless be in proportion to the inherent requirements of the particular jobs in question.

68. Accordingly, the exclusions established by Act No. 451/1991 may be considered on the whole to be justified as regards the military functions at the ranks of colonel and general in the Army and Ministry of Defence and military attachés, the Federal Security Intelligence Service, the Palace Guard Police Force and most functions in the Federal Ministry of the Interior (Article 1, paragraph l(b),(c), and paragraph 2; Article 3 of the Act). These exclusions may also be deemed acceptable as regards the Federal Police Force, although their application in this public service should be in proportion and be limited to particular functions, as in the case of the military functions mentioned above, and not as a blanket requirement for all functions in the service.

69. Regarding the functions in the Offices of the Federal President and of the federal and national assemblies and the Offices of the Constitutional and Supreme Courts covered by Article 1, paragraph l(d), of the Act, each ground for exclusion should be examined to ensure that it is in proportion to the requirements of security and confidentiality inherent to each particular job in the categories of functions concerned.

70. As regards functions in the Presidium of Academies of Science, covered by Article 1, paragraph 1(d), the principle of proportionality should be strictly observed in applying any of the exclusions laid down in the Act in relation to the inherent requirements of these functions which would appear in most cases to be of a different nature than the requirements of the other categories of functions dealt with above.

71. Regarding functions covered by Article 1, paragraph 1(f) and paragraph 3, of the Act, consideration of political opinions would appear to be justified for the exercise of functions of heads and leading executives in state industrial, commercial and financial undertakings and institutions when the functions in question involve the implementation of policies in important and sensitive fields, especially in the present circumstances of the country.

72. The Committee is not clear as to the nature and requirements of the functions of elected academic officers and of functions subject to approval by the academic senate in higher schools; nor is it clear as to the fields of learning covered by such schools. As a general rule, the Committee is of the view that consideration of political opinion is justified only where the opinions are in conflict with the obligations normally attached to teaching duties (e.g. objectivity and respect for the truth), or are in conflict with or prejudice the aims and principles professed by the schools to which the officers belong (e.g. the case of an institution for religious studies).

73. As regards functions in other "state organisations" that may be covered by the same provisions of Article 1, paragraph 1(f), of the Act, any exclusions should only be applied in strict observance of the relevant criteria

defined by the ILO supervisory bodies in accordance with the requirements of Convention No. 111.

74. The exclusions concerning functions in the state administration in general (Article 1, paragraph l(a), of the Act) are too extensive to be considered inherent requirements of particular jobs and such exclusions should be limited to senior or sensitive posts involving the implementation of government policies or confidentiality requirements.

75. The same restrictive approach should be followed regarding any exclusions for political reasons from the exercise of functions in the state media institutions (Article 1, paragraph 1(e), of the Act).

76. As regards the judicial and legal professions (Article 1, paragraph 4, of the Act), exclusions should be admissible under the Act only in cases where the past political record of the persons concerned is likely or is found to reflect upon their moral integrity and repute, or to endanger the confidentiality and impartiality of prosecution and adjudication and perhaps, the legal reliability of state notaries.

77. Finally, as regards the "conditions of reliability" required for practising certain concession-based trades (Article 1, paragraph 5, of the Act referring to Appendix 3 of Act No. 455/1991), any exclusions such as established under Article 2 of the Act should only apply to those trades listed in Act No. 455/1991, Appendix 3 (for example, in the arms and ammunition or explosive businesses, or in work on radiation sources or medical equipment) where requirements of public security and safety may be deemed to be put in jeopardy by the past political record of the persons concerned and not to trades, also listed under Act No. 455/1991, where such requirements are not involved (for example, auctioneers and antiques business).

Measures Regarding Activities Prejudicial to the Security of the State

78. In accordance with the substantive criteria elicited by ILO supervisory bodies (see paragraph 59 above), measures regarding activities prejudicial to the security of the State under Article 4 of the Convention should be directed at individual activities—proven or justifiably suspected— and not be motivated by membership of a particular group or community or by expression or demonstration of opinions opposed to established political principles and institutions without the use or advocacy of violent methods to change them. Such measures should be sufficiently well defined and delimited and should be applied in the light of the bearing of the activities in question on the performance of the job, task or occupation by the persons concerned.

79. By applying the above criteria to the exclusions laid down in Act No. 451/1991, the Committee has reached the view that these exclusions, which cover a very broad range of functions and are based on the past record—however reprehensible—of persons for their association or collaboration with the former political regime, cannot be regarded as measures within the meaning of Article 4 of the Convention. Such measures should be applied only to persons who are actually engaged in or justifiably

suspected of activities prejudicial to the security of the State, the definition of which must be consonant with the criteria recalled above (for example, collaboration with foreign intelligence or espionage service, as stipulated in Article 4, paragraph 4, of the Act).

Duration of Exclusion Measures

80. The Committee takes due note of the fact that the exclusions laid down by Act. No. 451/1991 will cease to apply after 31 December 1996 when the Act itself will lapse. In the view of the Committee, the duration of the exclusions would not have any decisive impact on the damages in respect of employment and occupation for the persons affected. The effects of such exclusions, whether or not justified by the terms of Convention No. 111, are likely to last long after their enforcement and perhaps permanently. The duration of the exclusions consequently does not constitute a significant element in the assessment of their conformity with the requirements of Convention No. 111.

General Conclusions on Exclusions

81. The preceding considerations have shown that in respect of Article 1, paragraph 2, of the Convention, the exclusions established by Act No. 451/1991 may be deemed inherent requirements of particular jobs only in a certain number of cases as referred to in paragraphs 67 to 77 above. These exclusions as such cannot be regarded as measures concerning activities prejudicial to the security of the State within the meaning of Article 4 of the Convention. The Committee is bound therefore to conclude that, to the extent indicated, the exclusions imposed by Act No. 451/1991 constitute discrimination on the basis of political opinion by the terms of Convention No. 111.

Appeals Procedure

82. The relevant conclusions of the ILO supervisory bodies (see paragraphs 58 and 59 above) have stressed the importance of appropriate appeals procedure to be made available to persons who have been the subject of exclusions as a result of security checks or of measures regarding activities prejudicial to the security of the State.

83. The Committee notes that under Article 11 of Act No. 451/1991, an independent commission of 15 members shall be established in order to ascertain the circumstances which constitute grounds for exclusion, as specified in Article 2, paragraph 1(c) to (h), of the Act. Of the 15 members of the commission, three each are appointed and revoked by the Presidium of the Federal Assembly (including the chairman and vice-chairman of the commission) and by the Presidiums of the two National Councils, from among blameless citizens not members of these assemblies. Of the six remaining members of the commission, who must have completed university-level legal education, two (including the commission's secretary)

are appointed and revoked by the Federal Minister of the Interior, one each by the Federal Minister of Defence and the Ministers of the Interior of the federated republics from among the staff of these ministries; and one member by the Director of the Federal Security Intelligence Service. The commission's procedure is set by Article 12 of the Act and includes hearing of persons concerned and of witnesses and experts, in accordance with relevant provisions of criminal procedure.

84. The Committee notes that of the 15 members of the commission, five members are government officials appointed and revoked by their responsible ministers and one member by the head of a federal security agency. While the nine members appointed by the legislative assemblies from among citizens thus outnumber the six government members, the Committee observes that by the terms of Article 11 of the Act, the commission is established under the auspices of the Federal Ministry of the Interior which is also responsible for its functioning. The Committee notes further that Article 12 of the Act provides that the commission can sit if attending members include the chairman and vice-chairman and seven other members and that government members may thus outnumber citizen members of the commission at sittings.

85. The Committee wishes to point out that according to the ILO supervisory bodies, the appeals body should be separate from the administrative or governmental authority and offer a guarantee of objectivity and independence. The committee considers that the composition and functioning of the commission established by Act No. 451/1991 do not fully meet the relevant requirements of the Convention....

87. The Committee further notes that under Article 13 of the Act, while affidavits submitted by the persons concerned regarding their own situation may be queried before the commission by other persons and organisations, the certificates issued by the Federal Ministry of the Interior may only be contested by the persons concerned in the case specified in Article 2, paragraph 1(c) of the Act (conscious collaborator of the State Security). It follows therefore that certificates concerning the cases specified in Article 2, paragraph l(a) and (b) of the Act (membership of National Security Corps and service in the State Security) and perhaps, although the Act is not clear, also the case specified in Article 2, paragraph 1(e) (official of the Communist Party in the political guidance sector of the National Security Corps) are not liable to appeal by the persons concerned.

88. The Committee considers that the absence of a right to appeal in the cases mentioned above is in breach of the relevant requirements of the Convention. It recalls that the complainant organisations have stressed the arbitrariness of these certificates which put irrefutable reliance on records kept by the State Security without any concern for circumstances of particular cases, including those of persons subject to threat and pressure. President Vaclav Havel himself gave attention to this question and suggested that a revised law should grant to the persons concerned the right of appeal to the court concerning certificates issued to them.

89. Finally, the Committee recalls that, as pointed out by the ILO supervisory bodies, the right of appeal cannot be considered a guarantee

unless the substantive conditions have been met. Consequently, appropriate appeals procedures can only contribute to the observance of the Convention in so far as the provisions for protection against discrimination are adequate or as the appellate body, for example a constitutional court, is empowered to overrule provisions that are in breach of such protection.

Other Matters

...93.   The Committee further notes that Article 21 of Act No. 451/1991 provides that publishers of periodical press and licensed operators of radio and television and newscasting programmes may apply for the necessary certificate or commission's statement, on their own behalf or following a previous written consent, on behalf of a member of their staff who takes part in the shaping of the intellectual contents of the communication media in question. The same possibility is granted to the presidents or equivalent level representatives of political parties, of political movements and those of associations (including professional organisations and governed by Law No. 83/1990 on the association of citizens) on their own behalf or on behalf of a member of the leadership of the organisation concerned, subject to that member's previous written consent.

94.   It would appear to the Committee that these provisions imply a possibility of indirectly imposing conditions of a political nature for the functions and positions in question in media organs and also in associations other than political parties and political movements. On that understanding, the Committee considers that such a possibility should be removed or made subject to the relevant requirements of the Convention, as examined above.

95.   Lastly, the Committee notes that, under Article 8 of the Act, any citizen over 18 years of age is entitled to apply for a certificate or statement regarding his/her situation in respect of Article 2, paragraph 1(a), (b) and (c), of the Act (member or collaborator of the state security). The Committee is concerned with the risk—pointed out by the CS-KOS—that this provision of the Act should lead to abuse and even more extensive discrimination on the basis of political opinion, by indirectly enabling employers to demand a certificate or statement from persons applying for or occupying a job not subject to the requirements of Act No. 451/1991. The Committee considers that appropriate provisions should be made to eliminate this possibility....

98.   On concluding its examination of the representations, the Committee feels confident that notwithstanding the difficulty and gravity of the problems involved, a satisfactory solution will eventually be reached. The Committee considers that the necessary elements conducive to such a solution already exist.

99.   In the first place, the exceptional quality of the democratic debate that is taking place on the issues raised by Act No. 451/1991 augurs well for future developments, given especially the weight of concurring views expressed from the highest sources in the land, on the need to remedy the situation.

100.   Furthermore, the Government itself points out in its statement that the Constitution of the CSFR requires laws and regulations to comply with

ratified international human rights instruments and with the Charter of Fundamental Rights and Freedoms, and that a solution to the current situation lies within the responsibility of the Constitutional Court. The Committee has subsequently been informed that the Constitutional Court has now been appointed by President Vaclav Havel from nominees proposed by the Federal Assembly.

101. The Committee notes that right of access to the Court is given in particular to the President of the CSFR and the Federal Government. The Committee trusts accordingly that the executive authorities which have responsibility for national compliance with international commitments will refer the matter to the Constitutional Court at the earliest date, for a ruling on the constitutionality of Act No. 451/1991 with due regard to the provisions of Convention No. 111. The Committee emphasises the need for prompt action in view of the fact that according to the complainant organisations Act No. 451/1991 is already in application and has caused dismissals....

The Committee's Recommendations

105. Having arrived at the conclusions laid out in this report on the issues raised in the representations, *the Committee recommends to the Governing Body*:

1. To approve the present report and in particular the conclusions and recommendations made in it.

2. To invite the Government of the CSFR, taking into account the conclusions made in the report:

    (i)   *to refer the matter to the Constitutional Court of the CSFR at the earliest date, for a ruling on Act No. 451/1991, with due regard to the provisions of Convention No. 111;*

    (ii)   *to take the necessary measures, in consultation with employers' and workers' organisations, to repeal or modify Act No. 451/1991, in conformity with the requirements of Convention No. 111;*

    (iii)   *to take the necessary measures to enable any person unjustly affected by the Act to obtain redress;...*

CZECH AND SLOVAK FEDERAL REPUBLIC: MEMORANDUM ON THE APPLICABILITY OF INTERNATIONAL AGREEMENTS TO THE SCREENING LAW

Submitted to the Constitutional Court of the Czech and Slovak Federal Republic in the Matter of the Constitutionality of Act No. 451/1991 (1992)

Submitted by:

Helsinki Watch (U.S.A.)
International Helsinki Federation for Human Rights
Project on Justice in Times of Transition, the Center for Human Rights and Humanitarian Law, Washington College of Law, The American University

[A summary of the memorandum, omitted here, precedes the detailed discussion below.]

Discussion

I. The Lustration Law Violates International Agreements Guaranteeing Rights to Work, to Associate, to Participate in Public Life, to Public Service, to Expression, and to Be Free From Discrimination Respecting These and Other Rights.

The CSFR has signed and ratified numerous international agreements by which it has agreed to honor the human rights of its people. These include the International Covenant on Civil and Political Rights, the International Covenant on Economic, Social and Cultural Rights, the Discrimination (Employment and Occupation) Covenant 1958 (No. 111), the European Convention for the Protection of Human Rights and Fundamental Freedoms, and the Treaty of the CSCE as elaborated by the Vienna and Copenhagen Concluding Documents. We believe all are violated by Act No. 451/1991 (Screening Law) with respect to the right to work, to associate, to participate in public life, to public service, to express one's political or other opinion, and to be free from discrimination with respect to the exercise of these and other rights.

Before setting forth the reasons why we have come to this conclusion, several prefatory comments may be helpful.

First, we present our views in this matter as friends of the CSFR. Many of us have worked for many years with those seeking a free, just, and prosperous society in Czechoslovakia and continue to do so today. It is thus in a spirit of friendship and cooperation that we offer these views.

Secondly, although we do not all agree on the best approach, we agree with the supporters of Act No. 451/1991 that it is appropriate to remove from sensitive positions those who threaten to sabotage an expeditious transition to democracy, or who will benefit from ill-gotten gains.

To achieve these purposes requires a carefully drawn law that focuses on individual responsibility. Unfortunately, and regardless of its good intentions, Act. No. 451/1991 is not carefully drawn. It strikes at people it should not and misses people such a law should perhaps include. In the process it violates rights that the CSFR has pledged itself to honor in the many international agreements discussed herein.

A. The Rights Violated by Act No. 451/1991.

1. The Right to Work

The International Bill of Rights includes two basic covenants: one on Civil and Political Rights and the other on Economic, Social and Cultural Rights. The two complement each other, and both have been ratified by the CSFR.

The very first substantive provision of the Economic Covenant, Article 6, recognizes the right to work, which includes the right of everyone to the opportunity to gain his living by work which he freely chooses or accepts, and will take appropriate steps to safeguard this right.

Paragraph 2 stresses the link with political freedom by requiring that states ensure that the right is exercised "under conditions safeguarding political and economic freedoms to the individual."

The right to work in Article 6 is implemented by Article 7c which guarantees an "equal opportunity for everyone to be promoted in his employment to an appropriate higher level, subject to no considerations other than those of seniority and competence."

This right to work recognized in Articles 6 and 7c is violated by the Lustration Law, which denies the categories of people in [Articles] 2 and 3 any opportunity to be elected, appointed, or designated, either initially or by promotion, to the offices listed in [Article] 1 because of their political views, associations, or backgrounds.

In addition, the Convention on Employment and Occupational Discrimination, No. 111, enforced by the International Labour Office, also guarantees the right to work and bans discrimination on the basis of political opinion or other illicit factors; the CSFR is a party to this as well. Because this matter is fully explored in the Report of the Governing Body of the International Labour Office (ILO), GB252/16/19 (2-6 March 1992), it will not be discussed here except to state that the undersigned organizations fully share the analysis and conclusions of the ILO.

2. The Right to Participate in Public Life and Access to the Public Service

Article 25 of the Civil and Political Covenant provides that:

> Every citizen shall have the right and the opportunity, without any of the distinctions mentioned in article 2 and without unreasonable restrictions:
>   a. To take part in the conduct of public affairs, directly or through freely chosen representatives;...
>   c. To have access, on general terms of equality, to public service in his country.

Since almost all the offices covered by Act No. 451/1991 are public, the Act denies the categories set forth in [Articles] 2 and 3 these rights as well. As the drafters of the Covenant repeatedly recognized, the rights set forth in this article are centrally important to the enjoyment of all other rights and thus deserve special protection against unwarranted restrictions.[2] While Article 25 permits "reasonable" restrictions on the right to public participation such as age, mental competency, and appropriate residency qualifications, it does not allow states to bar individuals from public life solely on the basis of political activities that were lawful when undertaken. The Human Rights Committee, which monitors compliance with the Covenant, has repeatedly found that restrictions barring certain individuals from public office violate Article 25.[3]

The Covenant provisions noted above do not refer to specific limitations on the rights involved; Article 6 of the Covenant on Economic, Social and Cultural Rights refers only to "appropriate steps to safeguard the right to work," and Article 25 of the Civil and Political Rights Covenant refers to "unreasonable restrictions" on those rights. In resolution 23 (XXXVI) of 29 February 1980, the United Nations Commission on Human Rights explained, however,

> that in the exercise of his rights and freedoms, everyone should be subject only to such limitations as were determined in the Charter of the United Nations, the Universal Declaration of Human Rights and the International Covenants on Human Rights and other relevant instruments....

These were described generally by the Commission as limited to "those which are provided by law, are necessary to protect national security, public order (*ordre public*), public health or morals or the rights and freedoms of others."

Act No. 451/1991 fails to meet these criteria because:

---

[2] *See, e.g.*, U.N. Doc. E/CN.4/SR.363 at 6, 11 (1953).

[3] *See, e.g., Mpandanjila et al v. Zaire*, Comm. No. 138/1983, U.N. GAOR Supp. (No. 40), U.N. Doc. A/41/40, Annex VIII (1986) (finding five-year ban on petitioners' ability to hold public office a breach of Article 25). Several of these cases involved a Uruguayan law that imposed a fifteen-year ban on public office on individuals who had been members of "Marxist or pro-Marxist Political Parties or Groups" that were legal at the time the affected individuals were active members. *E.g., Bazzano v. Uruguay*, Comm. No. R.1/5, U.N. GAOR Supp. (No. 40), U.N. Doc. A/34/40, Annex VII (1979); *Weinberger v. Uruguay*, Comm. No. R.7/28, U.N. GAOR Supp. (No. 40), U.N. Doc. A/36/40, Annex IX (1981), and *Pietraroia v. Uruguay*, Comm. No. R.10/44, U.N. GAOR Supp. (No. 40), U.N. Doc. A/36/40, Annex XVI (1981). *See also Stalla Costa v. Uruguay*, Comm. No. 198/1985, U.N. GAOR Supp. (No. 40), U.N. Doc. A/42/40, Annex VII (1987) (noting that "Uruguayan public officials dismissed on ideological, political or trade union grounds were victims of violations of article 25....").

(1) No law prescribes holding or expressing the opinions reflected in the actions performed by holders of the offices described in [Article] 1 of Act No. 451/1991. It was and is legal to believe and act on the Communist ideology that is the obvious target of the Act. This alone condemns Act No. 451/1991.

(2) The Act is not necessary to protect national security, public order, health or morals, or the rights or reputations of others. Only the possibility of infringing the rights of others to live in a free society could be involved, and there has been no showing that it is "necessary" to exclude the persons listed in [Articles] 2 and 3 from the offices listed in the Act to protect such rights.

Indeed, the Human Rights Committee has indicated that "reasonable restrictions" on public life permitted by Article 25 do not include general bans such as that imposed by the CSFR's Lustration Law. Instead, such a harsh measure as depriving individuals of political rights requires an individualized justification.[4]

Finally, both the drafting history of the Covenant and the Human Rights Committee's interpretations emphasize that no restriction is "reasonable" if it involves discrimination on the grounds enumerated in Article 2 of the Covenant, which include discrimination on the basis of "political opinion." As elaborated below in subsection (5), the CSFR's Lustration Law runs afoul of this prohibition.

3. The Right to Expression

Both the Civil and Political Covenant, Article 19, and the European Convention, Article 10, guarantee the right to hold and express one's opinion. It is well established, as the above-mentioned ILO opinion points out, that this extends to action manifesting such opinions. The ILO has explained how the Lustration Law impairs that right, and we share that judgment.

Both the Covenant and the Convention allow restrictions on this right, but only if "prescribed by law" and, under Article 19.3 of the Civil and Political Covenant, if necessary to protect the rights and reputations of others, national security, public order, public health, or morals.

For the reasons set forth above, the Act does not meet these criteria.

The European Convention, Article 10, has a similar provision, and though it contains a somewhat longer list of justifiable restrictions, none of these apply either. Here, too, the requirements of prescription by law and necessity are mandated but not met by Act No. 451/1991. In addition, Article 10 requires that the restriction be consistent with "a democratic society." A democratic society does not impose collective guilt or impose restrictions on

---

[4] *See Pietraria v. Uruguay, supra* note 3, at para. 16.

an individual's speech that cannot be justified by a showing of such necessity.[5]

4. The Right to Associate

...[Article] 21 of Act No. 451/1991 permits use of the Act for disqualifying people from the leadership of political parties, movements, and associations.... [B]ecause "leadership" is not defined, it will almost necessarily be defined by the chairman. It can be defined quite arbitrarily and can reach quite deeply into a group.... "In addition, the exclusion of persons described in [Article] 2(d) of the Act, those who held high-ranking positions in the Communist Party, also encroaches on the right to associate."

The Political and Civil Rights Covenant, Article 22, the European Convention Article 11, and Article 9.3 of the Copenhagen Document of the CSCE permit the same limits on the right to associate as are applicable to the right of expression. Such limits are inapplicable for the reasons set forth above.

5. The Right to Be Free From Discrimination

All the international human rights agreements that the CSFR has adopted condemn discrimination with respect to employment, ILO Convention No. 111; with respect to certain specified rights, European Convention 14 (rights in the Convention); Economic Social and Cultural Covenant, Article 2.2 (rights in the Covenant, including employment); or, generally, Civil and Political Rights Convention, Article 26, and the Copenhagen Document of the CSCE, ¶5.9. Act No. 451/1991, which mandates "exclusion [and] restriction" on the basis of "political or other opinion [such as communism] ... or other status [in this case, prior occupancy of any of the offices in Articles 2 and 3 of the Act]," is inconsistent with all of them.

That the Act produces discrimination is indisputable. Although the term is not specifically defined in these instruments, the Human Rights

---

[5] The European Court's rulings in the *Kosiek* (24.1, 1986), *Glasenapp* (28.8, 1986), and *Laender* cases (10/1985/96/144), are not to the contrary. In the first two cases, a German law required adherence to democratic values for jobs in the civil service. On a specific individual analysis of the views of the two job applicants, the German courts had found that they did not hold these views, and the European Court did not find it appropriate to overrule these individual conclusions. In the *Laender* case, the Court refused to override a judgment that the individual's views prevented his satisfying the necessarily stringent requirements for a job involving secret data and national security. None of these cases which focus on individual determinations bear on the validity of Act No. 451/1991, which is a broad disqualification based solely on holding a particular office at some time during a 41-year period, regardless of the individual person's own views or behavior. In addition, all three cases deal with access to the civil service, which the European Convention does not guarantee, though the Political and Civil Rights Convention does.

It should be noted that the dissenting opinion of Judge Spielmann in *Kosiek* and *Glasenappe* cases is generally considered to be more persuasive than the majority view. Moreover, the International Labour Office considers that the dismissals in *Glasenapp* and *Kosiek* violate Convention No. 111. *See* ILO Official Bull. LXXX, 1987, Series B, Supp. I.

Committee of the United Nations, in a recent comment on the Civil and Political Rights Covenant, declared

> the Committee believes that the term "discrimination" as used in the Covenant should be understood to imply any distinction, exclusion, restriction or preference which is based on any ground such as race, colour, sex, language, religion, political or other opinion, national or social origin, property, birth or other status, and which has the purpose or effect of nullifying or impairing the recognition, enjoyment or exercise by all persons on an equal footing, of all rights and freedoms.[6]

This definition is the same as that in the Discrimination (Employment and Occupation) Convention No. 111, Article 1, ¶1.

Differential treatment itself is not necessarily wrong. The question in every case, as the Human Rights Committee emphasized, is whether the criteria for the "distinction, exclusion, restriction or preference" on the basis of one of the stated grounds "are reasonable and objective and if the aim is to achieve a purpose which is legitimate under the Covenant" on Civil and Political Rights.[7]

Here that justification is lacking. The principal purpose of the Act, as stated by CSFR President Vaclav Havel and as appears in the press and elsewhere, is indeed legitimate: to prevent those who repressed freedom in the past from using the offices listed in [Articles] 2 and 3 for the purpose of "hindering, in many institutions, the formation of a true democratic order."[8] But to satisfy the "objective and reasonable criteria" standard, restrictions must be narrowly tailored to further a legitimate objective, restricting rights and covering individuals only to the extent strictly necessary to achieve that objective. Act No. 451/1991 fails to meet this test for the following reasons:

(1) Many of the people affected by the law have not held the offices or engaged in the activities in question for decades.

Absent evidence as to specific individuals, there is no reason to believe these people are any threat whatsoever to the development of democracy. (Compare the *Kosiek* and *Glasenapp* cases, where the views and conduct at issue were as of the time of the job application.) This is particularly true for those who were expelled from or were otherwise mistreated by the Communist Party in the aftermath of Prague Spring. The Act recognizes this latter point in the exception in [Article] 13(3), but this exception is too narrow. There are many persons other than those who meet the stringent criteria of [Article] 13(3) who were oppressed by the communist regime and who have long since repudiated and abandoned whatever views and behavior might be suggested by their meeting the criteria of [Articles] 2 and 3.

Indeed, Act No 451/1991 reaches so far into the past that it indicates very little, if anything, about whether someone is a threat to democracy

---

[6] UN Hum. Rts. Comm., CCPR/C/21/Rev.1/Add.1, 21 Nov. 1989 at pp. 2, 3.

[7] *Id.* at p. 4.

[8] *See* ILO Report ¶ 33 (letter from President Havel).

today, even if that person was not oppressed by the Communist regime after 1968. Only a case-by-case examination of what someone has done during the relatively recent past is a fair indicator.

(2) The past offices and activities listed in [Articles] 2 and 3 are too numerous and imply too little as to whether someone is likely to "hinder ... the formation of a true democratic order." Surely a young student who attended one of the security schools for a brief period many years ago and has done nothing since then is not such a threat; in the November 1989 resolution, some People's Militia members even aided students occupying university buildings by blocking the tram tracks against the regular police; membership of an 18-year-old in an Action Committee in 1948 indicates nothing about that 62-year-old person today. A recent American newspaper article reports on a cancer specialist who was induced to join the People's Militia and to teach first aid in order to be allowed to run a cancer institute in Chomolov, where such specialists are needed but hard to get.[9]

Indeed, many of the offices listed in [Article] 1 involve no threat whatsoever to democracy, especially those licensed occupations referred to in § 27, ¶ 2, of the Trade Act and Annex 3, which apparently can include taxi drivers, auctioneers, antique dealers, etc., as the ILO noted. This is also the case with respect to many of the state enterprises and organizations referred to in [Article] 1(f).

(3) The Act can be applied arbitrarily and haphazardly. On the one hand, exemptions from the Act are permitted under [Article] 2(3) and [Article] 3(2). On the other hand, under [Article] 21 the Act can be extended beyond the required areas of [Articles] 2 and 3 by private media, publishers and political leaders. In both cases, no criteria are set forth; instead, the matter is left to the complete discretion of the persons listed, providing an opportunity for capricious, whimsical, and preferential application.[10]

(4) The unfairness is compounded by the fact that many of the most serious threats to a "true democratic order" are not caught by this statute. The names of many current or recent high-level secret agents do not appear in these files at all.[11] Interior Minister Langos has also reported that many files are missing or destroyed, and in some cases "only fragments remain."[12] Several pages from the Slovak registers are known to be missing. Admittedly, the escape of some wrongdoers does not justify ignoring the existence of those who are available. Those who seek to reach the people who are available, however, must be especially careful not to perpetrate any injustice in addition to the unfairness resulting from the escape of many wrongdoers, many of whom may be much worse offenders than those who are available.

---

[9] Engelberg, "The Velvet Revolution Turns Rough," *The New York Times Magazine*, May 31, 1992, p. 31.

[10] This also raises the possibility of blackmail, corruption, and other misuse of this law.

[11] One estimate by Roman Zelenay of Slovakia is that "at least 16,000 top-level agents were not listed in any registers." Engelberg, *supra* note 9 at p. 49.

[12] Interview with *Mlada Fronta*, 20 February 1992.

(5) The absence of an individual case-by-case analysis of whether an individual is in fact a threat to the development of democracy in the CSFR is an imposition of collective guilt. It is based on the assumption that because a person has an attribute that is *sometimes* associated with a wrongful act, that person has in fact committed that act. That assumption may indeed be justified sometimes. But when large numbers of people are affected, involving numerous offices and activities, many of which were inevitably harmless, the assumption is quite unjustified, and widespread injustice is inevitable.

This is particularly true for the "conscious collaborators" referred to in [Article] 2(1)(c), (2). The criteria set forth in [Article] 2(2) include those who gave no information of any value at all, or provided information that harmed no one, or who performed the most harmless or meaningless tasks. Nor does it take into account the reasons why someone became a "conscious collaborator," or a member of any of the other groups listed in [Articles] 2 and 3. It is common knowledge that the Secret Police engaged in blackmail, threats, and many other coercive tactics to induce people to work with them, even if these people were deeply opposed to the Communist regime. To infer from a person's simply meeting the loose criteria of [Article] 2(2) that he or she is a current threat to "a true democratic order" is to risk the gravest injustice.

(6) No matter how often it may be formally denied, it is obvious that another purpose of Act No. 451/1991 is to punish those who have done wrong in the past by preventing them from benefiting from their wrongs by holding important state offices. That is the only possible explanation for this focus on the past and in many cases, the very distant past.[13] And the inclusion of "conscious collaborators," regardless of why they became "collaborators," and thus regardless of their actual views or conduct, manifests an intent to punish them for their agreeing to become "conscious collaborators."

This punitive purpose alone renders Act No. 451/1991 invalid under the "reasonable and objective criteria" test discussed above. Interpreting this test, the Human Rights committee has indicated that an otherwise legitimate distinction would be invalid under Article 26 of the Civil and Political Rights Covenant if it had a punitive purpose.[14]

Moreover, as an instrument of retribution, the Act perpetrates a grave injustice, for it punishes equally and heavily those whose "offenses," ranged from severe repression of human rights to totally harmless behavior. Surely someone who briefly attended a security school as a young student forty years ago or who became a "conscious collaborator" twenty-five years ago

---

[13] Indeed, the Act does not prohibit holding a § 1 office by *current* occupants of the positions in § 2(d) even though these current Communist Party officials would seem to be far more of a threat to "a true democratic order" than someone who held those positions forty or twenty-five years ago and was the subject of post-1968 repression. *See also* the letter from Pavel Bratinka, Daniel Kroupa, and, Vladimir Dlouhy, *The New York Review of Books*, June 11, 1992, p. 65....

[14] *See Jarvinen v. Finland* Comm. No. 295/1988, U.N. GAOR Supp. (No. 40), U.N. Doc. A./45/40, Annex IX (1990).

because of threats against his or her family or for fear of blackmail—surely such a person is very different from a high-ranking member of the state security police who persecuted opponents of the regime, especially if neither student nor the so-called "conscious collaborator" actually did anything to further such repression. Yet both they and the high-ranking members are denied the offices in [Article] 1 for five years with a possible loss of income, position, friendships, and reputation.

One of the most fundamental of all ethical principles is that it is unjust to treat similarly those who are unequal or dissimilar with respect to a particular matter. The widely diverse dissimilarities among the many different groups covered by [Articles] 2 and 3 with respect to the threat they pose to democracy in the CSFR are so great that it is grossly unjust to treat them similarly, as Act No. 451/1991 does.

(7) None of these objections can be overcome by the claim that, for reasons of administrative convenience, the CSFR government must utilize general categories to determine application of the Lustration Law.[15]

II. The Act Violates the Non-Retroactivity Principle.

Technically, Act No. 451/1991 is not subject to the principle *nulla poenae sine lege*, for it is not formally a criminal statute. The retrospective and retributive aspect discussed above makes it clear, however, that the justifications for the *nulla poenae* principle apply equally.

There are two reasons for this:

(1) *Fairness*. It is unfair to sanction someone today by today's standards for what was legitimate and even considered laudatory in the past. Insofar as the sanction is an unavoidable aspect of actions that must be taken in a good faith effort to guard against future harm, this concern can be overridden, but one must be sure of both the seriousness of the threat and the necessity of the action.

(2) *Truth*. For obvious reasons, the older the event, the more difficult it is to determine what really happened, in this case whether a person really fits the criteria of [Article] 2. Papers are lost, memories fade, witnesses die. Thus, both civil and criminal cases almost invariably have statutes of limitation that bar the initiation of proceedings against someone after a certain period of time except in unusual circumstances.

For these reasons, the backward-looking aspect of Act No. 451/1991 is a serious defect and is likely to do great and unjustified harm.

---

15 *See Gueye et al v. France*, Comm. No. 196/1985, U.N. GAOR Supp. (No. 40), U.N. Doc. A/44/40, Annex X (1989) (rejecting French government's claim that otherwise invalid distinction is necessary for administrative reasons).

III. The Procedures Do Not meet the Requirements for a Fair and Impartial Hearing.

International treaties adopted by the CSFR also require that anyone denied a civil right by official or administrative action "will have an effective means of redress." CSCE Copenhagen Document, para. 5.10, which includes "a fair and public hearing ... by an independent and impartial tribunal." European Convention Article 6. Act No. 451/1991 does not meet these criteria.

(1) The age of many of these matters and the admitted destruction of files and materials, together with the well-known propensity of secret police agents to falsify, all preclude a full airing of the relevant facts. A recent court hearing revealed a 1964 memorandum in Ministry of Interior files that reported "dozens of cases in which intelligence officers earned bonuses by entering false names in the file, or by attributing information from one person to three or four."[16]

(2) The Commission is likely to be controlled by the officials of the various executive branches, since nine out of fifteen will be appointed by federal and republic Interior, Defense, and Security Ministers. Since the Commission can sit when seven are present, it is possible that in many cases, *only* security officials will sit, especially if the National Council appointees are members of their respective National Councils and have other pressing responsibilities. The European Convention, Article 6, mandates such an impartial tribunal and the European Court of Human Rights has insisted on it.[17] Act No. 451/1991 does not satisfy this requirement, as both European Commission President Antonio LaPergola and Catherine Lalumiere, Secretary General of the Council of Europe, have concluded.[18]

(3) The Act does not require that the subject of a Commission hearing is entitled to the aid of counsel, to present his or her own evidence, or to refute the evidence against him.

(4) In fact, the procedures at such a hearing are left very indefinite. [Article] 12.4 of the Act provides that certain Criminal Procedure provisions will apply but only if "appropriate." The criteria for "appropriateness" are not stated.

Conclusion

In commenting on Act No. 451/1991, President Antonio LaPergola of the European Commission for Democracy Through Law observed that purges and other methods aimed at "cleansing" the system

---

[16] Engelberg, *The New York Times Magazine, supra* note 9 at p. 49.

[17] Laender, 10/1985/96/144 (26 March 1987).

[18] A. LaPergola, Opinion on the Lustration Law, 18 March 1992, p. 7; C. Lalumiere remarks, 7 April 1992 (the law does not protect people against unproven allegations and lacks "safety measures" to prevent mistakes).

are techniques borrowed from the totalitarian state ... [and] cannot become those of a democracy unless they are made subject to the aim of not obstructing the functioning of pluralism but, on the contrary, endowing it with solid means of defence. The ban on anti-democratic parties or methods must be implemented with a definite sense of moderation and, at any rate in a system of genuine constitutional rule, with careful concern to ensure that the exercise of authority is never divorced from a strict review of legality for each restriction on individual freedoms.[19]

We share these views. Although it is indeed necessary to guard against those who would undermine the development of democracy and to punish those who violated human rights, as presently written Act No. 451/1991 does not do so in a fair, just, and efficient way, and it is therefore inconsistent with the international human rights treaties signed and ratified by the CSFR.

Respectfully submitted,

Herman Schwartz
Lloyd Cutler
Diane Orentlicher
Attorneys

---

[19] Opinion, 18/3/92, p. 3.

CZECH AND SLOVAK FEDERAL REPUBLIC: CONSTITUTIONAL COURT DECISION ON THE SCREENING LAW*

(November 26, 1992)

...The provision of Article 2, paragraph 1, letter (c), Article 2, paragraph 2, Article 4, paragraphs 2 and 4 of Act No. 451/1991 *do not conform* with Article 2, paragraph 3, and Article 4, paragraphs 1 and 3 of the Bill of Basic Rights and Freedoms (hereinafter referred to as "the Bill [of Rights]") and Article 4 of the International Covenant on Economic, Social and Cultural Rights.....

The provisions of Article 2, paragraph 3, Article 3, paragraph 2, and Article 13, paragraph 3 of Act No. 451/1991 *do not conform* with Article 1 of the Bill [of Rights].

The provisions of Article 11, 12, Article 13, paragraphs 1, 2, 4 and 5, Article 18, paragraph 1 and Article 20 of Act No. 451/1991 *do not conform* with Article 37, paragraph 1 and Article 38 of the Bill [of Rights] and with Article 98, paragraph 1, of the Constitution of the Czech and Slovak Federal Republic [CSFR] No. 100/1960 as amended by Constitutional Act No. 326/1991.

The remainder of the proposal is rejected.

Substantiation

On March 10, 1992, a group of 99 deputies of the Federal Assembly of the Czech and Slovak Federal Republic submitted a proposal to the Constitutional Court of the [CSFR] that the Constitutional Court of the CSFR should declare that Act No. 451/1991, specifying some further prerequisites for the discharge of some functions in State organs and organizations of the Czech and Slovak Federal Republic, the Czech Republic and the Slovak Republic (hereinafter referred to as "the Act"), should lose force as of December 31, 1991 for its non-compliance with the Bill of Basic Rights and Freedoms, in accordance with Article 6, paragraph 1, of Constitutional Act No. 23/1991 introducing the Bill of Basic Rights and Freedoms....

Should the Constitutional Court of the CSFR ... arrive at the conclusion that the provisions of Article 6, paragraph 1, of Constitutional Act No. 23/1991 do not apply to Act No. 451/1991, the group of deputies proposes that the Constitutional Court of the CSFR issue a finding that Act No. 451/1991 does not conform with [several specified provisions of Constitutional Act No. 23/1991, the Bill of Basic Rights and Freedoms, the Constitution of the CSFR, Constitutional Act No 143/1968 on the Czechoslovak Federation], with the provisions of Article 2, 19, 22, 25 and 26

---

* Ref. No. Pl. US 1/92.

of the International Covenant on Civil and Political Rights..., with the provisions of Article 6 and 7 of the International Covenant on Economic, Social and Cultural Rights..., with the provisions of Article 1, 2, 3 and 4 of the Convention No. 111 on discrimination (profession and employment) of 1958,... and the provisions of Article 18, 26 and 28 of the Vienna Convention on Treaty Law.... Should the Federal Assembly of the CSFR fail to bring the Act into conformance with the above mentioned Constitutional Acts and international treaties, the Act would lose force six months following the promulgation of the ruling....

[The Court then provides a lengthy list of documents, obtained for its consideration of the present case, from the archives of the Ministry of the Interior, the archives of the Communist Party Central Committee, the legislature, and other sources, including the International Labor Organization reprinted above, as well as a list of witnesses.] Weighing this evidence, the Constitutional Court has come to the following conclusions:

In the period from 1948 to 1989, defined by Act No. 481/1991 as the period of bondage, the totalitarian power violated not only human rights, but also its own laws, which it had adopted for the usurpation and preservation of its power. In addition to the formally legitimate institutions of legislative and executive powers, the structure and operations of which had been adapted purposefully to suit its aim for power, the suppression of human rights and freedoms was also carried out by organs and organizations the activities of which were entirely devoid of legal support (People's Militia) or had been legalized in supplemental manner (Action Committees, screening commissions).

In accordance with the theory of permanent class struggle and the leading role of the Communist Party of Czechoslovakia, the totalitarian power deprived hundreds of thousands of persons not only of freedom, but in some cases also of life (Act No. 119/1991 on judicial rehabilitation alone concerns 245,000 people) as well as of their places of employment. These acts were arbitrary and were legalized only in supplemental manner, e.g., by Act No. 213/1948 qualifying the operations of the Action Committees as measures taken "in accordance with law, even in those cases which otherwise would not have been in conformity with the relevant regulations."

The analogous character of a mass purge was also reflected in the secret resolution of the Government of the CSR No. 256 of March 14, 1958, which connected the reorganization and wage restructuring to the "verification of the class and political reliability of the State and economic apparatus with the purpose of purging this apparatus of all politically unreliable elements and preventing them from obtaining other important posts." The directive enumerates the categories of persons who may not be employed in the State and economic apparatus. Their number includes, for example, wholesale merchants, owners of financial and legal agencies, former high-ranking State officials, military officials, managers of large enterprises and their close co-workers, as well as those whose close relatives lived in capitalist foreign countries or had been punished for anti-state activities. The measures applied not only to the specified categories of persons, but also to their close relatives. The severance of employment relations with these employees did not require the consent of the Labour Department of the appropriate District National Committee.

The so-called normalization process, which took place after the [1968] occupation of Czechoslovakia by the armies of the Warsaw Pact, was of the character of mass labour law repression. The executive organs of this normalization process were the screening and normalization commissions, the operation and decision-making of which were regulated by the directive of the Presidium of the Federal Assembly No. 9 of August 22, 1969, providing in Article 4: "He who disturbs the socialist social order by his activities and thus loses the trust required for the discharge of his function or his job, may be removed from his function or his employment relation may be severed instantaneously; in case of persons to whom the Labour Code provisions on the severance of employment relation do not apply, their employment, service or another analogous relation may be terminated instantaneously by dismissal. Students can be excluded from studies under the above-mentioned circumstances. College professors as well as teachers in other schools may be removed by the respective official, or their employment relation may be severed instantaneously if they educate the young people entrusted to them, at variance with their duties, in the spirit contrary to the principles of socialist society and its development. The possible disagreement of the Trade Union organ will not delay the decision."

The number of these repressive acts also includes the transfer of 77,500 administrative employees into production in the autumn of 1951 under the pretext of restricting a growing bureaucracy. In the same period, however, some 200,000 to 300,000 new employees, almost exclusively members of the Communist Party of Czechoslovakia, were recruited for jobs in State administration, security, judiciary and the military.

Ad hoc purges and inconsistent staffing of executive posts at all levels was successively replaced with the purposive and consistent personnel policy drafted by the Central Committee of the Communist Party of Czechoslovakia. Obligatory instructions (so-called "cadre orders") were issued for all levels which generally required candidates for all executive functions to comply with the condition of "political maturity, a creative Marx-Leninist approach to the solution of problems and the resolve to consistently bring to life the policy of the Party." Their professional ability was to be combined with the "skill to solve, in the region under their control, the issues of Party policy, ideology and moral quality, i.e., particularly the high responsibility before the Party and society."

By the end of 1989, the executive posts at all levels in the organs and organizations of the administrative and economic apparatus were staffed in accordance with these "cadre orders" (staffing instructions).

The abolition of the leading role of the Communist Party of Czechoslovakia in the Constitution and the legal directive of the Presidium of the Federal Assembly of the CSFR No. 362/1990, expanding the circle of leading functions staffed by appointment, which were intended to facilitate the recalling of compromised individuals from executing and leading functions, were not significant either with respect to importance or number of persons concerned.

The totalitarian regime based its power position primarily on a repressive apparatus, the decisive component of which was the State Security and its network of secret collaborators. According to the directive for the operative work of agents of the State Security of 1962, "the agency network forms an integral part of the operations of the State Security and is the principal instrument of the fulfillment of operative tasks. For this reason the most important object of the work of operative workers of State Security is the work with secret collaborators."

In accordance with these principles, the totalitarian power endeavoured to preserve to a maximum extent this mutually integrated apparatus which would enable it to influence democratic development and/or to overthrow it at a suitable opportunity. The justification of these fears can be documented *inter alia* by Directive No. CB-002040/03-89 for the operation of the counter-intelligence, issued on November 28, 1989, i.e., 11 days after November 17, 1989, which stipulated the following procedures in Part 3, letters (a) and (b):

Management, organization and collaboration:
- despite existing agency positions and official contacts in the respective bodies, for future objectives, maintain the conditions for the possible transfer of the State Security members into their structures.

Actual operative performance:
- increase substantially the conspirative character of operative activities in the whole scope of State Security;
- reassess the network of agents, ensure its stabilization and gradual expansion to genuinely high-quality positions. Emphasize agency in influential and leading positions. Activate maximally the work of agents, particularly through the use of influential agents;
- aim active measures at the misinformation of the opponent by compromising the most confrontation-minded representatives of these structures in the eyes of the public, and at the increase of ideological, personal and operational clashes;
- with maximum speed, acquire high-quality influential agents in mass media and among the students of higher-grade schools, capable of influencing the operative situation in these structures to the benefit of the Communist Party of Czechoslovakia.

To preserve the network of secret collaborators and/or to preclude their identification and individual assessment of the scope and contents of their activities, the former Vice-Minister of Interior of the CSFR, Lieutenant General Ing. Alojz Lorenc, issued on December 4, 1989, under ref. No. NZ-00671/89 to all heads of State Security administrations a directive for the destruction of the materials which "had lost their value to State Security."

The next to last paragraph of this document states: "It is necessary to proceed so that no materials which would be of a compromising character in light of the contemporary political order would remain." On December 8, 1989, the directive of the First Vice-Minister of Interior of the CSFR No. 00133/01-89 was issued with an annex containing an identical instruction with that of December 4, 1989, without however the paragraph on the removal of compromising materials. Simultaneously, the destruction of the initial directive of December 4, 1989, was ordered.

The expert standpoint of the Head of the Office of the Federal Ministry of the Interior for the Protection of the Constitution and Democracy, Col JUDr. Zdenck Formánek ... states that as a result of the first instruction, the operational files and documents of whole departments of interior intelligence were liquidated, including the files of secret collaborators. The report states that an almost "panicked" liquidation of files of secret collaborators, candidates of secret collaboration, confidants, and others took place. It has not been proved, however, whether they were destroyed or merely transferred to or concealed by some State Security officers who could use them subsequently for blackmail or extortion of former secret collaborators.

The statement of Dr. Zdenck Formánek before the Higher Military Court in Tábor on March 12, 1992 ... revealed that after his arrival at the Federal Ministry of the Interior (February 2, 1990) he ascertained that 90-95% of the vaults of the 2nd Administration (struggle against domestic enemies) were empty, and in other cases contained merely the file covers or some worthless papers.

According to the statement of the Statistical and Recording Department of the Ministry of the Interior, the number of files in the 2nd Administration (struggle against domestic enemies) dropped in the period from October 1, 1989 to January 31, 1990, from the initial number of 20,337 files to 2,189 files. Consequently, a total of 89.9% of all files were destroyed or transferred to an unknown destination. In the future, these files could serve for the restoration of the network of agents or for the blackmailing of individual agents.

The Constitutional Court reviewed the intentions of the legislator in the adoption of Act No. 451/1991, its substantiation and the consequences of its application. The decisive criterion was the assessment of whether the Act or some of its provisions contradict the Constitution of the CSFR or Constitutional Acts, or possibly international treaties on human rights and basic freedoms ratified and promulgated by the CSFR.... The Constitutional Court has come to the conclusion that the adoption of Act No. 451/1991 was substantiated.

A democratic State has not only the right, but also the duty to assert and protect the principles on which it is based. It cannot be inactive in the situation in which the leading posts on all levels were staffed on the basis of political criteria. A democratic State has the duty to endeavour to eliminate unjustified preference of a group of citizens, based on the principle of their membership in a certain political party, as well as to eliminate the discrimination against other citizens.

In democratic societies, the requirements imposed on the employees of State and public organs, and on the institutions which have some relation to the security of the State, include compliance with, and respect of, certain prerequisites of State citizenship which can be characterized as loyalty to democratic principles on which the State is based. Such restrictions may also extend to certain groups of persons without these persons being evaluated individually (for instance, in the Federal Republic of Germany, the enterprises producing high-tech products for the armament industry could not employ persons from the former German Democratic Republic or from the Eastern Bloc).

When compared with the fact that in the totalitarian regime, the executive posts on all levels were manned in contradiction to democratic principles and in contradiction to international standards, the Act concerns only a very limited circle of people in the power, administration and economic apparatus, possibly in licensed trades which are or could be a source of certain risks, from the viewpoint of the protection of the democratic system and its principles, state security or the protection of State secrets, or such functions as could influence, overtly or covertly, public opinion and the desired function of individual organs or organizations.

Moreover, the conditions specified by the Act for the discharge of these functions are limited in time to the period of assumed completion of the democratic process, i.e., until December 31, 1996....

In contrast to the totalitarian system, which was based on *ad hoc* purpose and was never based on legal principles, even less on the principle of constitutional law, the democratic State is based on entirely different values and criteria. These values also form the basis of Act No. 451/1991. It is not a retaliation against individual persons or groups of persons nor does it discriminate in their employment or profession against persons who in the past, in contradiction of generally recognized principles, and also of the norms then in force, violated fundamental human rights and freedoms, in collaboration with or through organs of repression. It merely specifies some further conditions for the discharge of certain decisive functions or the performance of licensed trades connected with the possession of or access to firearms, ammunition, particularly dangerous poisons or sources of radiation.

Conditions which are defined so generally are not at variance with any constitutional regulations or international covenants. Every State, especialy one which had been obliged to suffer the violation of basic rights and freedoms by the totalitarian power for more than forty years, has the right to apply such legislative measures which aim to foil the risk of subversion or the return of, or possible relapse into, the totalitarian regime, in order to establish a democratic system.

A rule-of-law State connected with democratic principles, established after the fall of the totalitarian system, cannot be considered amorphous with reference to values. The integration of the Bill of Basic Rights and Freedoms into our legal system has substantially changed the character and the system of values of the constitutional and legal system.

Constitutional Acts, other Statutes and legal rules, and their interpretation and application, must conform with the Bill of Basic Rights and Freedoms.... In this way, entirely new elements of the renaissance of natural human rights have been introduced into our legal system and a new basis of constitutional law and the rule-of-law State has been created.

The restoration of the rule-of-law State cannot be considered a continuity of the constitutional and legal consistency of the totalitarian regime; it must be understood as a transition from formally rational political legitimacy, the criterion of which was formal legality, to materially rational legitimacy. The previous legal positivism made it impossible to make any distinction between an unjust and a just law and to identify those political processes and legal norms the contents of which threatened the very substance of democracy, since they formally remained within the procedures and framework of legality.

The concept of a constitutional and rule-of-law State does not mean merely the observation of any law and any values which have originated by a procedurally legal manner, but the observation of such norms as are not at variance with the fundamental values of the human community as they are expressed primarily in the Bill of Basic Rights and Freedoms.

In this respect, even legal certainty cannot be considered in abstract terms; it must be measured by those values of the constitutional and rule-of-law State which are of system-constitutive character.

Legal certainty in a rule-of-law State must be the security of the intrinsic values of its contents. The rule-of-law State which is being formed at present and which is based on the discontinuity of values with the totalitarian regime cannot carry into the future those criteria of formally legal and materially legal continuity which are based on a different system of values, even in the situation which makes it possible by the formally normative continuity. Respecting the continuity of the old system of values would not guarantee legal certainty, but rather would cast into doubt the new values and the trust of the citizens in the credibility of the new system and would threaten legal certainty in society. Any incorporation of the alien values of the totalitarian regime into the newly established democratic system could disturb and threaten its intrinsic base of values.

With reference to the individual components of the proposal of the group of deputies, the Constitutional Court has come to the following conclusions:

By the reference to the provisions of Article 6, paragraph 1, of Constitutional Act No. 23/1991 introducing the Bill of Basic Rights and Freedoms, the proposal requests a judgment that Act No. 451/1991 has ceased to be valid as of December 31, 1991 due to its non-conformity with the Bill [of Rights].

The provisions of Article 6 of Introductory Act No. 23/1991 enjoin the legislator to make Acts and other legal regulations (to wit, those issued before January 9, 1991 when the Bill [of Rights] was promulgated) conform with the Bill [of Rights] by December 31, 1991.

As Act No. 451/1991 was adopted on October 4, 1991, e.g., after the adoption of the Bill [of Rights], the provisions of Article 6 of Act No. 23/1991 cannot be applied to it.

The proposal does not respect the specific character of the problems of Act No. 451/1991 and confuses its labour law character with the concepts and qualifications of criminal law (the introduction of responsibility, even collective responsibility, for unspecified "facts of the case," based on collective responsibility for membership in a vague, formally defined circle of persons). The contested Act, however, is not of a criminal law character either in contents or in its meaning, nor does it formulate any type of legal responsibility. Its substance is the adjustment, for a certain transition period, of the conditions for the discharge of certain closely defined functions or activities to the value criteria of a democratic State.

In the framework of its domestic norms and its accepted international obligations, the State has the right to define certain restrictions on basic civil rights and freedoms for the performance of specified occupations or activities (Article 26, paragraph 2, of the Bill [of Rights]). Unquestionably this applies also to the persons who are to discharge functions or perform activities which are decisive for the functioning of the State, its economy and security. For such legally defined conditions, the only decisive factors are the method and the extent of the restrictions, which are determined, on the one hand, by domestic norms, and on the other hand, by international obligations binding on the CSFR.

From domestic norms, the Bill of Basic Rights and Freedoms provides in Article 4, paragraph 2, that the bounds of basic rights and freedoms may be modified, under the conditions defined by the Bill [of Rights], only by law. In Article 26, paragraph 2, the Bill [of Rights] provides more narrowly that an Act may also specify conditions and limitations for the exercise of certain professions or activities. In Article 4, paragraph 3, the Bill [of Rights] provides that if such a legal restriction takes place, these legally stipulated conditions must apply equally to all cases meeting these conditions. Certain value conditions are defined in Article 2, paragraph 1 of the Bill [of Rights], according to which the State is based on democratic principles and must not be bound to either an exclusive ideology or an exclusive religious creed. Likewise Article 2, paragraph 1 of Constitutional Act No. 143/1968 on Czechoslovak Federation, in full wording promulgated under No. 103/1991, states the requirement that the State and both republics be based on the principles of democracy. These requirements applied to the State are binding unquestionably also for the persons representing this State or serving it.

The legislator justifiably based his considerations on the idea that it could not be assumed that the values of these constitutional principles would be automatically and unreservedly implemented by the members of the previous power structures of the totalitarian regime or by the persons appointed to important State, social or economic functions on the basis of contradictory value criteria to serve, as the representatives of an exclusive ideology, the preservation of the power monopoly of the ruling bureaucratic apparatus. The attempt to preserve these positions for the purpose of execution of anti-democratic activities and the likelihood of the threat to the democratic foundations of the State by these persons were proven, *inter alia*, by the instructions of one of the decisive components of the totalitarian regime, the State Security—see the Principles of the Operations of Counterintelligence of November 28, 1989.

When comparing the Act with international law obligations, it is necessary to investigate its conformity with the International Covenant on Civil and Political Rights and the International Covenant on Economic, Social and Cultural Rights...

The first of the above mentioned Covenants contains, in Article 2, the obligation of the State to ensure equal rights to all individuals without any distinction and in Article 26 the prohibition of any discrimination. With reference to the possibility of restriction of the discharge of functions or employment in public service, Article 25 of the Covenant provides generally three requirements:

1) no restrictions may be applied in respect of distinctions expressly specified in Article 2, first clause;
2) the restrictions must be reasonable and justifiable (Article 25, first clause); and
3) every citizen has the right to enter public service of his country on equal terms (Article 25, letter (c)) which means that the defined prerequisites for entering or staying in public service must apply to all persons.

The International Covenant on Economic, Social and Cultural Rights provides generally in Article 4 that the State may subject these rights only to such limitations as are determined by law and only insofar as this may be compatible with the nature of these rights and solely for the purpose of promoting the general welfare in a democratic society.

The right of everyone to the opportunity to earn his living by work which he freely chooses or accepts, formulated in Article 6 of the above-mentioned Covenant, respects the equality of both parties to the employment contract with reference to their decision and does not by any means establish any obligation to be employed and particularly to exercise decisive functions in such employment.

Article 7 concerns equality of opportunity in employment already performed, in particular equal opportunity for everyone to be promoted exclusively on the grounds of seniority and competence (Article 7, letter (c)). Consequently, it concerns the persons who are already performing their employment on the basis of specified prerequisites and conditions, and not the conditions and prerequisites for the exercise of the work itself.

The notion of discrimination in employment and profession is defined by the Discrimination Convention No. 111 of June 25, 1958.... Art 1, letter (b) defines discrimination as any distinction, exclusion or preference the purpose of which is to threaten or make impossible equal opportunity or equal treatment in matters of employment or profession. According to paragraph 2 of the same article, however, any distinction, exclusion or preference based on the qualification required for a certain profession is not considered as discrimination.

In stabilized democratic systems the requirements imposed on persons applying for employment in the service of the State (civil service), in public services and in the institutions considered sensitive with reference to the security and stability of the State, include the fulfillment of certain civic prerequisites signalling the consensus of opinions and loyalty with the interests of the State and the democratic principles on which the State is based. The absence of such prerequisites and the ensuing limitations may also apply to formally defined categories (groups) of persons without differentiation of these persons on the basis of their individual assessment.

Therefore, the State cannot be denied the right to specify certain requirements imposed on the persons employed in selected categories in the institutions, functions or activities significant for the protection of the democratic constitutional system, State security, its economic and political interests, protection of State secrets or the persons who can significantly interfere with public affairs in the discharge of their functions.

Such measures conform with Article 4 of the Convention No. 111, when they provide that all measures concerning the person who is justifiably suspected of activities harmful to State security are not considered as discrimination, as long as this person may appeal against these measures to the respective body established in accordance with the domestic practice of the State.

The Act respects the general requirement of the citizen's right to seek the protection of an independent court, specified in Article 36 of the bill, Article 6 of the Convention on the Protection of Human Rights and Freedoms, and Article 14, paragraph 1, first two clauses of the International Covenant on Civil and Political Rights. The citizen may appeal against the termination of his employment or service relation in accordance with Article 14 of the Act to the appropriate independent court. To emphasize the protection of citizens and to guarantee qualified decision-making in the cases concerning the invalidity of the termination of employment or service relation, the Act provides that the relevant court of first instance is the regional court in accordance with the citizen's domicile. Consequently, the citizen is granted higher judicial protection than the employees whose employment relation has been terminated by notice in accordance with the provisions of Article 44 of the Labour Code, for which the relevant court is a court of a lower tier (district court).

The judicial protection of citizens is guaranteed further also by the Civil Code, Articles 11 through 16.... Also the protection against the possible falsification of documents or perjury is guaranteed.

The specification of some further prerequisites for the discharge of some functions and activities, codified by Act No. 451/1991, is consequently, a permissible act in principle both on the basis of the norms of constitutional law and in conformity with the international law obligations. Measures of this type, which are also taken by other European States after the collapse of the totalitarian regime of monopoly power, are a legitimate means the objective of which is not to threaten the democratic character of the constitutional system and the system of values of a constitutional and rule-of-law State or the fundamental rights and freedoms of the citizens, but their protection and consolidation, as long as these measures respect and apply the provisions of Article 4 of the Bill of Basic Rights and Freedoms.

A comparison of the provisions of Act No. 451/1991 with Article 4 and Article 26 of the Bill [of Rights] reveals that the Act conforms both with Article 26 and with Article 4, paragraphs 1, 2 and 4 of the Bill of Basic Rights and Freedoms.

Article 4, paragraph 4 of the Bill [of Rights] provides the duty to respect the substance and the meaning of rights and freedoms when applying and limiting these basic rights and freedoms. Such limitations may not be used for other purposes than those for which they have been provided. The adequacy of such measures comprises both the selection of the means intended to achieve the intended objective and such balance of the measures as would exclude the prevalence of negative consequences over positive ones. The provisions of Article 4, paragraph 4 of the Bill [of Rights] may be so understood that the measures should be balanced adequately both with reference to the persons and functions concerned and the definition of the prerequisites themselves.

The system of measures adopted in European post-totalitarian States is diverse. The measures may concern whole fields of State activities regardless of functions (army, police, judicial system) and are either formulated unconditionally on the severance of employment or service relation is left to concrete assessment (absence of personal abilities required for the discharge of the function, non-existence of the need of employing the respective person for organizational reasons, etc.).

Act No. 451/1991 endeavours, to the maximum extent, to objectivize the cases concerned. By the enumeration of the functions in Article 1, it differentiates the functions and activities in the case of which it requires the compliance with further prerequisites beyond the customary framework. In doing so it selects certain functions and activities in proportion with the meaning and objective of the Act, differentiating them simultaneously also vertically (Article 1, paragraph 2 and paragraph 3); in the prevailing majority of cases it is limited only to higher or executive functions, while on lower levels it dispenses with the provision of further prerequisites.

The general objection of a violation of equality of basic rights and freedoms in the meaning of Article 3, paragraph 1 of the Bill [of Rights] must be assessed in relation to the meaning and contents of the contested Act. In principle, the specification of prerequisites and conditions for the discharge of certain functions or the performance of certain activities by the State is permissible from the constitutional law point of view, and with reference to the contemporary system of values and the character of the contemporary constitutional system, it is even necessary.

In the cases in which the Act violates this general principle of equality in Article 2, paragraph 3 (exceptions for the Minister of Defense of the CSFR), Article 3, paragraph 2 (exceptions for the Minister of Interior) and Article 13, paragraph 3 (exceptions for the persons rehabilitated under Act No. 119/1991), the Constitutional Court has complied with the proposal of the group of deputies and pronounced their non-compliance with Article 1 of the Bill [of Rights] in its finding.

The Constitutional Court further assessed the objection to the retroactivity contained in the proposal of the group of deputies. The proposal objects that the Act can be applied in retrospect to the situations and legal relations originated before its adoption only if it does not result in the violation of previously acquired rights. It is unquestionable that the citizen has the right to legal certainty including, i.e., also the guarantees that his previous acts will not be questioned if they were legally guaranteed at the time of their occurrence and if they were not at variance with the generally recognized norms of basic human rights and freedoms.

In the field of Criminal Law, the principle of retroactivity is accepted generally only in the cases in which it is more advantageous for the persons concerned.

The proposal changes the Act with retroactivity and points to the provisions of the Criminal Code and to the interpretation of Article 2, paragraph 2 of the Bill [of Rights] according to which everyone may do what is not forbidden by law. However, the principles valid in Criminal Law cannot be applied mechanically to other legal disciplines.

Similar to the Czechoslovak legal theory on the present rule-of-law State, the countries of the European Community (EC) also differentiate between the so-called real and apparent retroactivity. The real retroactivity of an act results in the fact that the legal consequences are effective also in the period preceding the date of promulgation of the legal norm concerned. Apparent retroactivity means that the law reassesses the legal criteria valid in the past, but with the effect only for the future, not for the past. The rule-of-law State does not exclude the apparent retroactivity of a law, but considers carefully its application from the viewpoint of whether the interest of society in legal certainty is in conformity with the interests of material justice and legal policy.

In the case of Act No. 451/1991, however, the principle of retroactivity does not apply at all. The Act does not declare the discharge of certain function in the past either unlawful or prosecutable or forming the facts of criminal acts (offenses) and does not connect them with any legal prosecution retroactively. It merely specifies some further prerequisites for the discharge of certain sensitive functions in the State administration and economic apparatus and simultaneously the remedy against the State based on an unjustified political preference on the one hand, and the discrimination of other citizens on the other hand. Above all, however, it should prevent destabilization of the democratic development of the State. Consequently, it does not involve even indirect retroactivity; it merely signifies the fact that legal relations are being changed with legal consequences for the future, beginning with the moment in which the Act enters into force (Article 14 of the Act).

The objection contained in the proposal, viz. that it involves a general application to certain categories of persons on the basis of a formal association must be rejected in all cases involving an association with the power apparatus and its repressive components in accordance with the policy of the totalitarian regime. This association could not have been neutral because of the character of the regime and the activities connected with it.

The enumeration of the categories of persons who do not comply with the prerequisites for the discharge of certain functions or activities for a limited period specifies, in parallel fashion, categories which are not fully comparable in significance. Also, the individual circumstances of the individual persons in the respective categories may be very different. It is pointed out that the Act does not include the persons whose participation in the functioning of the totalitarian State was not negligible. The proposals that the Act should be possibly extended to include these persons are within the competence of the legislator and not of the Constitutional Court....

The ideal equality of all categories, however, is not possible and not even necessary. The legislator tried to define the hazardous categories, the decisive factor for which was consideration of whether and to what extent persons in individual categories pose potential risks for the State and its democratic establishment in the near future particularly with reference to Instruction No. CB-002140/03/89 of November 28, 1989. The proportions in which these risks exist in the individual categories are not decisive if they do not exceed the scope justifiable in the present constitutional and rule-of-law State.

An analogous situation exists with respect to the definition of categories, functions and activities for the discharge and performance of which further conditions and prerequisites have been specified. An absolute comparability of the individual categories cannot be achieved here either. These differences and disproportions are balanced in Article 1, paragraphs 2 and 3 by the fact that in certain categories they concern only the functions of executive (managerial) character. However, in this case, too, the legislator may manoeuvre only within certain dimensions determined by the present constitutional and rule-of-law State.

The proposal of the group of deputies also points to the fact that the duration of the relationship of a person to the defined category lasted is without legal significance. The introduction of further criteria (not only the duration, but also, e.g., the age at which the citizen became associated with the defined category) would introduce further possible disparities into the Act, not to mention the problems of proof connected therewith.

These facts were considered comprehensively in connection with the objections of the disproportionate scope of the circle (number) of persons to which the Act applies. Although these quantitative criteria are not decisive for the legal assessment of the problem, the Constitutional Court has considered it necessary to deal with this quantification.

The report of the General Manager of the Board of Directors of the International Labour Office No. 6B 252/16/19, which, from March 2-6 1992 in Geneva, dealt with the complaint submitted by the Trade Union Association of Bohemia, Moravia and Silesia and the Czech and Slovak Confederation of Trade Unions against the violation of the Convention on Discrimination (employment and profession) No. 111 of 1958, is based, in its introduction, on the statement of the former Chairman of the Federal Assembly, A. Dubcek, that it is a discriminatory Act which will deprive about one million of Czechoslovak citizens of their basic human and Trade Union rights (paragraph II-12 of the Report).

The Constitutional Court has conducted investigations of the authorities concerned with the records of manpower and employment (Federal Ministry of Labour and Social Affairs, Federal Bureau of Statistics) as well as the authorities recording the issued certificates (Federal Ministry of the Interior). In accordance with the report of Division I of the Federal Ministry of the Interior of September 7, 1992, by that date, 168,928 [screening] certificates were issued, both upon the request of individuals and organizations (e.g. political parties), not all of which were connected with Act No. 451/1991. Out of the number of certificates issued, 153,504 certificates were negative[*] and 15,424 positive[†]. The number of positive certificates includes 4,061 persons filed in accordance with Article 2, paragraph 1, letter (c) of the Act, without which the total number of positive certificates concerns altogether 11,363 persons.

According to the records of the Federal Bureau of Statistics on the aforementioned date, there were 7,123,000 employed people in the CSFR. Consequently, the number of persons issued positive certificates (the persons filed under Article 2, paragraph 1, letter (c) excluded) amounted to 0.15% of employed people.

In respect to the objections which question the records in the files of the former Ministry of the Interior, the Constitutional Court, on the basis of the obtained orders and testimonies, has come to the following conclusions:

The cooperation of secret collaborators (agents), specified in Article 2, paragraph 1, letter (b) of the Act, with the State Security was formalized in considerable detail. A secret collaborator (agent) was acquainted in detail with his tasks and status and the cooperation was formally confirmed by the so-called binding act, in which the secret collaborator (agent) signed either a prepared commitment to collaboration or wrote it himself in a free form. Should the signature of the secret collaborator (agent) on such a document threaten the "good relation" of the recruited agent with the counter-intelligence, an oral consent was sufficient. The recruited secret collaborator (agent) chose his own cover name. Should he not do so, he was assigned one by the counter-intelligence officer.

The secret collaborator (agent) was not obliged to report in writing, and should he do so, he was not obliged to sign his reports. Oral reports, if not tape-recorded, were given written form by the counter-intelligence officer.

The statements of some publicized secret collaborators (agents) that they formally signed collaboration agreements, but subsequently did not perform any activities, is at variance with the system of recording and oversight explicitly provided for control of the network of agents and confirmed by testimonies.

In accordance with Article 78 of Directives No. A-oper-I.3 of January 25, 1978, on the oversight of activities of secret collaborators, the counter-intelligence officers entrusted with the oversight of secret collaborators (agents) were bound to regularly and consistently oversee the activities and the results of work of secret collaborators (agents), their behaviour in their work places and even in their private lives. The objective of this oversight was to obtain optimum guarantees that the secret collaborator (agent) was conscientiously fulfilling the tasks, submitting truthful information, not deceiving, not committing treachery and had been fulfilling his tasks in the

---

[*] [Editor's note: A negative certificate indicates that the State Security Records contain no evidence that the individual in question was ever an agent or collaborator with the State Security.]

[†] [Editor's note: This is the category of "conscious collaborators" with the State Security.]

way he had been ordered. Once a year a written assessment of all control measures and their results was made. The superior officers of the counter-intelligence participated in the oversight. The results of the oversight, particularly during the meetings with the secret collaborator (agent), were recorded and the document, with the appropriate conclusions, was included in the file of the collaborator (agent) (Article 81 of the Directive).

At least once a year, a comprehensive assessment of secret collaborators (agents) was made and their further instructions were outlined. This assessment was approved by the appropriate superior officer.

All these methods of exploitation and control of the network of agents did not differ in principle from those introduced after the take-over by the Communist Party of Czechoslovakia in 1948; they were merely specified with ever greater accuracy and supplemented with new data collected during the contact with the network of agents.

With reference to the recruitment of agents ("*verbovka*") and the contacts of secret collaborators (agents) with their control officers of the State Security, the Commission of the Federal Assembly of the CSFR for the Investigation of the Events of 17 November heard as witnesses, inter alia, Jan Roller, former head of Department 1 of the Division II of the State Security Administration in Brno, Josef Jecábek, senior officer of the Department 1 of Division II of the State Security Administration in Brno and subsequently the head of this Department, and Zdenck Kocuch, deputy head of Department 1 of Division II and since 1987 head of this Division. Their testimonies have confirmed identically that the instructions were strictly observed [with respect to] the "binding acts" of secret collaborators (agents) and the regular contacts with them, at least once every three months. This was recorded on a form with the entries of the date and place of meeting, which was overseen by the respective superior officer. If the meetings did not proceed as they should, the superior officer proposed discontinuing the collaboration or archiving of the file (Jan Roller, p. 2).

The Constitutional Court heard, apart from that, Mgr. Jan Frolík, head of the Archive and Statistical Department of the Federal Ministry of the Interior, and Dr. Jicí Setina, former head of the unit of the Federal Ministry of the Interior for the documentation and investigation of the operations of the State Security, who have confirmed these facts. The requirement of individual proof of the operations of secret collaborators, urged in the proposal of the group of deputies, was generally intentionally frustrated by the orders and actions of the leading officers of the State Security, i.e., by the intentional destruction of almost 90% of all files. The agency network formed an integral part of the operations of the State Security and was "the principal means of the fulfillment of operative tasks. Therefore, the most important part of the work of the operative officers of the State Security is their work with secret collaborators (agents)." (The ultra-secret instructions of particular significance to the Ministry of the Interior for the operative work of agents of the State Security from 1962). For this reason, the security authorities of the totalitarian regime did their utmost to keep the evidence of the operations of their secret collaborators (agents) secret also for the future....

The provisions of Article 1, paragraph 5 of the Act provide that the operation of certain licensed trades specified in Annex 3 of Act No. 455/1991 on Trades (the Trades Act) is subjected to essentially the same prerequisites as those for the discharge of functions specified in Article 1, paragraph 1 of the Act. These prerequisites are defined in Article 1, paragraph 5 as "the conditions of reliability." The scope of licensed trades, for which these conditions of reliability are required, is specifically enumerated in Annex 3 of the Trades Act and comprises such trades as are connected with the possession of or the handling of firearms, ammunition, explosives, particularly dangerous poisons, radiation sources, security and telecommunications facilities. Compliance with the conditions of reliability concerns not only the operator of the licensed trade (regardless of whether he is a natural person or a legal entity), but also his possible responsible representative...

The proposal points out that the notion of "reliability" is traditionally connected with the notion of "political unreliability" contained in the Decrees of the President of the Republic No. 137/1945 and No. 138/1945, and that the Act provides a stricter regime for licensed trades than is warrented by their character.

The reference of the proposal to the Decrees of the President of the Republic Nos. 137/1945 and 138/1945 is unsubstantiated. Both of these decrees are of Criminal Law character. Decree No. 137/1945 concerns the custody of persons considered "State-unreliable," and Decree No. 138/1945 provides the penalties of imprisonment or monetary fines for persons who aroused public indignation by improper behaviour offending national feelings during the period of intensive threat to the republic (1939-1945).

Like the whole Act, the provisions of Article 1, paragraph 5 of the Act, requiring compliance with the conditions of reliability for the performance of certain licensed trades are not of a Criminal Law normative character. They merely specify the conditions with which, in this particular case, the applicant for the license for certain licensed trades must comply in addition to general requirements.

The State, which is responsible for the preservation of democratic principles, stability of society and security of citizens, cannot be denied the right to provide certain strictly necessary measures aimed at the preservation of undisturbed development. It would be an irresponsible risk to permit the persons who participated in the violation or suppression of human rights and freedoms to possess the means which could be used to seriously destabilize democratic development and threaten the security of citizens.

The Constitutional Court has dealt extensively with the objections of the group of deputies to the incorporation of the group of persons specified in Article 2, paragraph 1, letter (c) in the Act, which points out that the inclusion of these persons in the records (of State Security) could have been made even without their signed commitment. In this part, the proposal is incomplete and inaccurate. According to Article 2, paragraph 2, this category of persons includes persons recorded as confidants, candidates of secret collaboration or secret collaborators of confidential contacts. The records of these persons were based on personal contacts with selected candidates, the purpose of which was "personal acquaintance, verification and deepening of the knowledge obtained about him by administrative methods and counter-intelligence methods, and also the ascertainment of the candidate's attitude towards State Security and his willingness to communicate information." Personal contacts were to be made in such a way as "would not impair in advance the conspiracy of the future secret collaborator (agent) and would not reveal to him the forms and methods of work ofcounter-intelligence or the actual reason of contacts" (Directive No. A-oper-I-3, Article 26 f.)

Consequently, the Instruction did not assume a signed commitment for cooperation in this category of persons. However, if the selected candidate of secret cooperation in this phase fulfilled concrete tasks or reported to the officers of State Security, whom he knew to be officers of State Security, then he belongs to the category to which the provisions of Article 2, paragraph 1, letter (c) apply.

On the basis of the testimonies of the witnesses,... as well as written documents, the Constitutional Court has come to the conclusion that the provisions of Article 2, paragraph 1, letter (c), Article 2, paragraph 2, and Article 4, paragraph 2, do not conform with Article 4, paragraph 3 of the Bill of Basic Rights and Freedoms.

While the certificate issued to the persons registered in accordance with Article 2, paragraph 1, letters (a) and (b) has an explicit character testifying either to conscious association with the repressive components of the totalitarian regime and the records connected therewith, or to the non-existence of such a record, the certificates based on the records in accordance with Article 2, paragraph 1, letter (c) are merely of a conditional character. It does not certify conscious collaboration, but merely expresses the intention of the State Security to recruit the recorded persons for conscious collaboration in the future.... [T]he records in accordance with Article 2, paragraph 1, letter (c) were made not only without the knowledge of registered persons, but also with the intention of State Security officers to feign their own service activities.

A citizen registered in this manner is obliged, under the provisions of Article 13, paragraph 1, letter (a), to apply to an Independent Commission under the Federal Ministry of the Interior, with the request that it verify whether he was or was not a conscious collaborator of the State Security, whether he knew that he had been in contact with an officer of the State Security and had reported to him in the form of secret contact or fulfilled the imposed tasks. Only such a determination, issued by the Independent Commission of the Federal Ministry of the Interior, represents the document decisive for the citizen under Act No. 451/1991. This differentiation of certificates as well as other facts reveal the unequal status of the persons registered in accordance with Article 22, paragraph 1, letter (c) of the Act in comparison with other categories, particularly those registered in accordance with Article 2, paragraph 1, letters (a) and (b).

In criminal proceedings against the former First Deputy Minister of the Interior of the CSFR, A. Lorenc, before the Higher Military Court in Tábor,... it was stated that on the basis of his instruction for the destruction of compromising documents deposited in the archives of the Ministry of the

Interior … between November 1989 and January 1990, 2,643 files out of the total number of 3,913 files of candidates of secret collaboration were destroyed. Also 9,176 files out of the total number of 13,346 files of confidants were destroyed in the same period….

Proof of conscious collaboration, together with often considerable passage of time in the records, death of witnesses, etc. results not only in the impossibility of observing the time limits stipulated for the issuance of a decision by the Independent Commission (Article 13, paragraph 2), but also in the impossibility of objective decision-making in the individual cases. According to the testimony of the Chairman of the Independent Commission, Jaroslav Basta, before the Constitutional Court of the CSFR, altogether 2,650 citizens filed a complaint that they had been registered unjustly as collaborators of the State Security (Article 2, paragraph 1, letter (c)). Only 300 of these complaints (i.e. 11%) have been dealt with so far; from this number the Commission came to the conclusion that they were conscious collaborators only in 13 cases. Two cases … submitted for a determination by the Independent Commission at the start of its activity have still not been decided.

Such a state of affairs does not only lead to an inequality of rights in the standing of individual citizens; non-adherence to the time limits for announcement of decisions also leads to doubts about the facts of the individual cases and results in legal uncertainty in labour law and civic relations. It is undesirable to allow such conditions, inter alia, because of the unfavourable consequences resulting from it for certain citizens during the period from submission of the application until a decision by the Commission (impossibility of application for the jobs specified in Article 1 of the Act, impossibility of success in a competition for such a job, etc.), the consequences of which cannot really be eliminated, even after a finding by the commission certifying the non-existence of conscious collaboration.

Therefore, taking into account all these circumstances and findings the Constitutional Court has come to the conclusion that Article 2, paragraph 1, letter (c) of the assessed Act and the provisions linked to it (the provisions on the Independent Commission of the Federal Ministry of the Interior and the proceedings before it) do not conform with the Bill of Basic Rights and Freedoms in the parts and extent specified in the Decision of this Finding.

Finally the character of the Independent Commission of the Federal Ministry of the Interior (Article 11 of the assessed Act) does not [withstand legal scrutiny]. The composition of the Commission (comprising, apart from the representative of the legislative bodies, also members appointed by the Minister of the Interior, Minister of Defense and the Director of the Federal Intelligence Service) testifies to the fact that the Commission is primarily an organ of State administration, the activities of which are ensured by the Federal Ministry of the Interior as the central State administration authority for the field of domestic order and security. The members delegated to the Commission by the Ministry of the Interior and the Ministry of Defense are bound by the vow of service which they have taken as the members of the police … and the army…. There is no doubt that they are bound by this vow also during their membership in the Independent Commission. Moreover, the situation is aggravated by the fact that the assessed Act does not require any vow either from these members or from other delegated members, although such a vow appears necessary [for an independent body] (Article 37 of Act No. 335/1991). Therefore, the establishment of such a Commission does not conform with the Constitutional Act (Article 98, paragraph 1 of the Constitution of the CSFR No. 100/1960 as amended by Constitutional Act No. 326/1991).

As the Commission is an administrative body, the provisions of the Code of Criminal Procedure (Article 12, paragraph 4) cannot be applied to the proceedings before it and it cannot combine these proceedings with criminal law consequences (Article 20 of the Act).... Article 39 of the Bill [of Rights] provides that only a law shall determine which act is a criminal offense and what penalty may be imposed for it. Such law is the Criminal Code. The provision of Article 20 of the Act is not characterized as a criminal act and without express reference [to a specific criminal law,] it supplements the criminal offense of false testimony and false expert opinion provided by Article 175 of the Criminal Code.... The provision of Article 20, moreover, is faulty in that it also includes the interpreter among the subjects of criminal responsibility, although he is not specified in Article 12, paragraph 2, of the Act.

Article 12, paragraph 3 of the Act provides that all summoned persons, i.e., including the persons to which the provisions of Article 2 of the Act apply, are obliged to speak the truth and to conceal nothing. In Article 40, paragraph 4, the Bill [of Rights] grants the accused the right to refuse testimony, of which [right] the citizen must not be deprived by any manner whatsoever. As the persons specified in Article 2, paragraph 1 of the Act do not appear in their own case as the accused in the sense of the criminal procedure, they cannot refuse to testify as provided by Article 40 of the Bill [of Rights], even if this testimony may be connected with labour law consequences for themselves or their near relatives under Article 1 of the Act.

In respect of these provisions, the Constitutional Court has come to the conclusion that the proposal is justified and pronounced their non-conformity with Article 37, paragraph 1, and Article 38 of the Bill [of Rights] and Article 98, paragraph 1 of the Constitution of the CSFR in the wording currently in force. Apart from that, after the abolition of the provisions of Article 2, paragraph 1, letter (c) of the Act, the Independent Commission of the Federal Ministry of the Interior loses its *raison d'être*.

The contested Act contains in Article 2, paragraph 3, and in Article 3, paragraph 2, the provisions according to which the Minister of Defense or the Minister of Interior of the CSFR, may waive the condition provided according to paragraph 1, letter (a) in substantiated cases, provided it does not impair an important security interest of the State and threaten the objective of the Act.

This provision, which assigns extraordinary possibilities and powers to the officials of two sectors only while not [likewise granting] the officials and the Ministers of other sectors, is at variance with Article 1 of the Bill [of

Rights] and the Constitutional Court has partly complied with the proposal in this section.

Also, the objection of the proposal that the provisions of Article 4, paragraph 4, are at variance with the principle of equality expressed in Article 4 of the Bill [of Rights], has been recognized, and the Constitutional Court has complied with the proposal of the group of deputies. According to Article 4, paragraph 4, citizens are obliged to submit, before entering a function specified in Article 1, a statement that they have not been and are not collaborators of any foreign intelligence or espionage service. In contradistinction to the category of citizens specified in Article 2, paragraph 1, letters (d) through (h) of the Act, who are obliged to document their possible association with the specified organizations by a sworn statement in accordance with Article 4, paragraph 3, in the category of collaborators of foreign intelligence or espionage services merely a civil statement is required. Because such a statement does not have the character of an act in the meaning of Article 39 of the Administrative Code, a false statement is not subject to any sanction. The fact that someone has been or is a collaborator of a foreign intelligence or espionage service is not connected with either any labour law or any other limitations because this fact is not specified in Article 2 of the Act. Consequently, it is a provision of a proclamative character which puts this category of persons into an unequal position relative to other groups not subjected to such limitations.

The proposal of the group of deputies in this part, therefore, is justified....

CZECH REPUBLIC: ACT ON THE ILLEGALITY OF THE COMMUNIST REGIME AND RESISTANCE TO IT

Act No. 198/1993 (July 9, 1993)

Aware of the obligation of the freely elected parliament to come to terms with the Communist regime, Parliament declares that the Communist Party of Czechoslovakia, its leadership and members, are responsible for the system of government in this country in the years 1948-1989, and particularly for the systematic destruction of the traditional values of European civilization, for the conscious violation of human rights and freedoms, for the moral and economic ruin combined with judicial crimes and terror against advocates of different opinions, the replacement of a prospering market economy with command management, the destruction of the traditional principles of ownership, the abuse of training, education, science and culture for political and ideological purposes, and the careless destruction of nature, and asserts that in its future work, it will use this Act as its point of departure.

Article 1

(1) The Communist regime and its active supporters,

    a) deprived citizens of any possibility of freely expressing their political will, forced them to conceal their opinion on the situation in the country and society, and forced them openly to express their agreement even with what they considered lies or crimes, and that by means of persecution or threats of persecution against the citizens themselves or their families and friends;

    b) systematically and constantly violated human rights, while oppressing certain political, social, and religious groups in a particularly sinister manner;

    c) violated the fundamental principles of a democratic State based on the rule of law, international treaties, and its own laws, in practice putting the will and interests of the Communist Party and its representatives above the law;

    d) used every means of exerting power to persecute citizens, and in particular:

        • executed them, murdered them, and imprisoned them in penitentiaries and forced labor camps, used brutal methods against them and exposed them to inhuman suffering—including physical and psychological torture—during investigation and incarceration,

- deliberately divested them of their property and violated their rights of ownership,
- deprived them of the opportunity to practice their professions or perform their duties, or attain higher education or specialized training,
- restricted their freedom to travel freely abroad and return freely,
- drafted them into Technical Support Battalions and Technical Battalions for unlimited periods of time;

e) did not hesitate to commit crimes to reach its objectives, facilitated the execution of these crimes with impunity, and provided unfair advantages for those who participated in these crimes and persecutions;

f) joined forces with a foreign power, and from 1968 maintained the aforementioned State by means of occupying troops.

(2) Those who implemented the Communist regime as officials, organizers, and agitators in the political and ideological sphere, are fully responsible for the crimes specified in paragraph (1).

Article 2

(1) It is particularly for the details specified in Article 1, paragraph (1) of this Act that the regime based on the communist ideology, which decided on the government of the State and the fate of the citizens of Czechoslovakia from 25 February 1948 to 17 November 1989, was criminal, illegal, and contemptible.

(2) As with other organizations based on the communist ideology, which oriented their operation toward the suppression of human rights and the democratic system, the Communist Party of Czechoslovakia was a criminal and contemptible organization.

Article 3

The aversion of citizens to this regime, expressed consciously and openly, individually or collectively, on the basis of democratic convictions of a political, religious, or ethical nature, by means of resistance or other activities on the territory of this State or abroad, even involving collaboration with a foreign democratic power, was legitimate, just, and morally defensible, and is commendable.

Article 4

All those who were unfairly harmed or persecuted by the Communist regime, and did not take part in the activities specified in Article 1, paragraph (1), of this act, deserve compassion and moral satisfaction.

Article 5

The period of time from 25 February 1948 until 29 December 1989 shall not be counted as part of the limitation period for criminal acts if, due to political reasons incompatible with the basic principles of the legal order of a democratic State, [a person] was not finally and validly convicted or the charges [against him] were dismissed.

Article 6

The court shall annul or reduce sentences for criminal acts that are not included in the exoneration under Act 119/1990 on judicial exoneration with respect to regulations of a later date, if it is proved during the proceedings and subsequent compensation that the objective of the defendant's actions was the protection of fundamental human and civic rights and freedoms and the means used were not obviously ill-suited. For the purpose of such proceedings, the stipulations of Article 4 and ff. of Act 119/1990 on judicial exoneration will be appropriately applied.

Article 7

The government restitution debentures issued to citizens with compensation claims under Article 23, paragraph 5 of Act 119/1990 on judicial exoneration are payable by the end of 1995.

Article 8

The government is authorized to rectify by decree some wrongs done to the adversaries of the Communist regime and to persons affected by persecution in the social, health, and financial spheres.

Article 9

This Act takes effect on 1 August 1993.

CZECH REPUBLIC: CONSTITUTIONAL COURT DECISION ON THE ACT ON THE ILLEGALITY OF THE COMMUNIST REGIME

(December 21, 1993)

...On 15 September 1993, a group of 41 Deputies of the Parliament of the Czech Republic submitted a petition requesting that the Constitutional Court, on the basis of Article 87, paragraph 1, letter (a) of the Constitution of the Czech Republic, annul Act No. 198/1993, regarding the Illegality of the Communist Regime and Resistance to It....

The overall conceptual approach to the problems of the contested Act are expressed primarily in points 2.1, 2.2 and 2.3 of the petition. In particular, it is stated in these points that Czech law is founded on the sovereignty of statutory law and on the principle of legality derived from it. From this point of view, the petitioners criticize the provisions of Article 2, paragraph 1 of the Act, according to which the political regime during the period from 1948-1989 was illegitimate, and label this statement as "unconstitutional."... The reasoning of the group's opinion makes reference to the fact that the Czech Republic is one of the legitimate successor States to the now defunct Czechoslovakia and that the inherited statutes and other legal regulations, as well as the legal obligations of the former Czechoslovakia remain in force in it. This "substantive continuity of domestic and international rights" is, according to the petitioners, an indication of the legitimacy of the governmental and political regime during the period from 1948-1989.

This perspective, which is obviously aimed at the provisions of Articles 1-4 of Act No. 198/1993, regarding the Illegality of the Communist Regime and Resistance to It, forms part of their general objections to the contested Act.

The petitioners object that a doctrinaire evaluation of a historical period of the former Czechoslovakia, introduced in the form of a statute, excludes other opinions and conclusions resulting from scholarly knowledge of historical facts, by which means the freedom of research is restricted (Article 15, paragraph 2 of the Czech Charter of Fundamental Rights and Basic Freedoms). Then in points three and four, they make arguments against the attempt—evidently presumed—on the part of the legislators to understand and interpret the provisions of Articles 1-4 of Act No. 198/1993 as the basis for sanctions in criminal law, employment law and in other areas of the law. According to the opinion of the petitioners, with the phrasing concerning crimes, persecution, murder and so forth, as well as the phrasing concerning the responsibility or joint responsibility of persons, the Act creates the impression that concepts bearing a direct relationship to substantive criminal law are involved, and that this responsibility or joint responsibility is borne by an entire group of persons for whom not even the declaratory nature of the provisions rules out collective or individual imposition of non-criminal sanctions....

In the Preamble and the whole first part of the Act (Articles 1 through 4), it is asserted that the Communist Party of Czechoslovakia, its leadership and its members are responsible for the manner of rule during the period from 1948-1989, then the characteristics of this manner of rule are mentioned, and § 1 describes the approach "...which the communist regime, its active supporters and those exercising power used in its decisionmaking about directing the government and about the fate of the citizens" (Explanatory Report). Thereafter, it expresses the joint responsibility of those who supported the communist regime for crimes committed and other arbitrary acts (Article 1, paragraph 2), a regime founded on the basis of communist ideology is declared to be criminal, illegitimate and abominable (Article 2, paragraph 1), as is likewise the Communist Party of Czechoslovakia, as well as other organizations founded upon the same ideology (Article 2, paragraph 2). Articles 3 and 4 express moral recognition of those citizens who put up resistance to this regime, as well as of its innocent victims.

The evaluation of individual objections stated in points 3 and 4 of the group of Deputies' petition depends on the determination—*a limine fori*—whether and to what extent these provisions are legal norms of an imperative or of a dispositive nature which bind the State or give it discretion to act in a certain way with this or some other legal consequences for persons, groups of persons or organizations.

It is possible to fully concur with the opinion of the group of Deputies that the sentences in the first part of the Act have only a general character, without at the same time conceding that they thereby become binding legal norms. It is also possible to agree, again without conceding them to be binding legal norms, that they are provisions which are worded "axiomatically and broadly", and that they do not make use of precisely and specifically defined concepts, that established legal concepts with precise contents have not been used, as well as with the designation of the sentences as declaratory norms.

Contrary to the assertion of the petitioners, however, neither the text of the Act itself nor the Explanatory Report give any grounds at all for inferring that the first part of Act No. 198/1993, regarding the Illegality of the Communist Regime and Resistance to It, might have created, in the area of substantive criminal law or in some other area of the law, a legal duty or a statutory power of the State to prosecute certain persons, or to inflict non-criminal sanctions upon them. The precondition for a criminal act is the definition of its elements. Nothing in Articles 1 through 4 can be understood as the designation of the material of a criminal act.

The first part of the Act represents the moral-political viewpoint of the Czech Parliament, the purpose of and the grounds for which are explained in the above-mentioned quotation from the Explanatory Report. The first four paragraphs of the Act are concerned with the nature of the regime, its specific aims and methods and its structural characteristics, not at all with the nature of individuals who, out of some motive or another, were members of organizations upon which the regime relied.

The Act discusses the "joint responsibility" of individuals on two levels: the joint responsibility of the members of the Communist Party of Czechoslovakia (KSC) for the manner of rule in the years 1948-1989 and further the joint responsibility of those ... who actively supported the communist regime ... (Article 1, paragraphs 1 and 2 of Act No. 198/1993)—in this instance for the crimes committed by the regime. In both cases, the differentiation of the levels of political and moral, and not of criminal, responsibility of individuals is concerned, and is characteristic of Parliament's initiative to reflect upon the past.

The joint responsibility of members of the KSC for the manner of rule is expressed only in the Preamble to the Act and should be understood as an effort to instigate reflection on the part of those who were, or from then on continue to be, members of an organization, the leadership and political activities of which over and over again departed markedly, not only from the basic values of humanity and of a democratic law-based State, but also from its own programs and laws....

We cannot criticize the Parliament for the fact that, in its moral-political, juridical-political proclamation, it did not make use of customary legal terminology. In this respect, this portion differs from Articles 5 and 6 of the Act, in which—and in which alone—crimes are not spoken of, but which use the precise terminology of criminal law: "criminal act." At the same time, the Explanatory Report gives no evidence of any effort to introduce a new definition of the material elements of a crime into the criminal law, when it explains § 2 with the words: "With the exception of cases involving the infringement of the provisions of the criminal law then in force, the words abomination and criminality must be considered rather as terminology from the domains of politics and morals."

If the declaratory character of the provisions of the first part of Act No. 198/1993 is undeniable, it is not necessary to scrutinize the petitioners' particular arguments stated in points 3 and 4 of the petition—with the exception of three of them.

The first of these objections states that a declaratory provision does not exclude the possibility of making use of non-penal sanctions contained in other legal norms, for example, in statutes governing the rights and duties of educational employees and research assistants, journalists, writers and artists. This objection must be rejected because it does not relate to the contested Act itself but to other legal norms not more specifically designated, none of the legal substance of which is changed by Act No. 198/1993. Also, the term "non-criminal sanctions" is vague. The so-called Lustration Law, for example, does not impose sanctions, rather it sets the prerequisites for holding certain offices which, in consideration of their nature and political significance, have a constitutional stature in those countries founded on the principle of the law-based act.

Likewise the petitioners make the further objection that the "joint responsibility" or "collective responsibility" dealt with in the first part of the contested Act is "firstly ... joint responsibility under criminal law", but this objection is of a moral-political, and not a juridical, character. This means that the appraisal of an historical period of the former Czechoslovakia in no way excludes opinions and conclusions other than those expressed in the text of Parliament's statute. The freedom of research guaranteed by Article 15, paragraph 2 of the Charter as well as by international legal instruments is not affected thereby. From the point of view of scholarly and journalistic activities, the evaluation contained in the contested Act does not represent a binding opinion....

The petitioners find a further element of anti-constitutionality in the intention "...that the Act serve an interpretive function in relation to court decisions"—an intention which the legislators never expressed in the text of the Act. A relevant intention is one that is expressed in a legally relevant manner. An objection to the wording of an Explanatory Report cannot be the subject of review or a decision of the Constitutional Court. Moreover, the conditional nature of the Explanatory Report's expression ("should serve ... if need be also for a decision of the court in this field") does not show a clear intention.

Also the introductory declaration of Parliament, "...that in its future work, it will use this Act as its point of departure," cannot be considered a legal norm which would bind Parliament. It concerns an expression of political will of a programmatic character, a will established at a certain time and with a certain line-up of forces in Parliament, a fact which may not be interpreted inconsistently with the right of Parliament, in the area and within the bounds of its competence, to adjust the matter differently at another time, nor inconsistently with the principle of the free exchange of views on the floor of the Parliament.

The constitutional foundation of a democratic State does not deny the Parliament the right to express its will as well as its moral and political viewpoint by means which it considers suitable and reasonable within the confines of general legal principles—and passably in the form of a statute, if it considers it suitable and expedient to stress its significance in the society and the scope of its declaration in the legal form of a statute. Such an example was the statute issued under the First Republic which stated that T. G. Masaryk deserves credit for the building of the State.

On the whole, it is evident that the Act under attack does not define the material elements of any new criminal act and that nothing analogous can [be] deduced from the text of the first part of it. In addition, Article 40, paragraph 6 of the Charter of Fundamental Rights and Basic Freedoms applies as a general norm for judging any sort of act from the perspective of its criminal nature, and according to it "criminal liability for an act shall be considered and punishment shall be imposed in accordance with the law in force when the act was committed. A later law shall be applied only if it is more favorable to the defendant."

However, the objections of the petitioners, contained in points 2.1 and 2.2 of the petition, are directed at certain general issues of the fundamentals of Czech law and the nature of the governmental and political systems during the period from 1948 to 1989. Above all, the group of Deputies objects that the provisions of Article 2, paragraph 1 of Act No. 198/1993 contain "the unconstitutional statement that the political system during the period 1948 to 1989 was illegitimate." Its assertion concerning the legitimacy of this regime rests upon the principle of the continuity of law, the given reception of the domestic legal acts and the continuity of the international legal obligations form the period of the "old regime"; on page 3 of its petition, it concluded: "If the statutory statement concerning the illegitimacy of the governmental political systems during the period 1948 to 1989 were correct and remained in effect, then the other legal acts adopted during the stated period would no longer have been valid as of 1 August 1993; naturally, this did not occur, for legal certainty is one of the basic characteristics of a State based upon law, and that certainty depends upon the constancy of legally expressed principles in particular areas of the law, on constancy of legal relations" and so on (point 2.3 of the petition).

It is necessary to evaluate an objection of such a fundamental nature in relation to the basic outline of the Constitution and the constitutional foundation of the Czech Republic....

[I]n Germany, the National Socialist domination was accepted as legal, even though it gnawed out the substance and in the end destroyed the basic foundations of the Weimar democracy. After the war, this legalistic conception of political legitimacy made it possible for Klement Gottwald to "fill up old casks with new wine." Then in 1948 he was able, by the formal observance of constitutional procedures, to "legitimate" the February Putsch. In the face of injustice, the principle that "law is law" revealed itself to be powerless. Consciousness of the fact that injustice is still injustice, even though it is wrapped in the cloak of law, was reflected in the post-war German Constitution and, at the present time, in the Constitution of the Czech Republic.

Our new Constitution is not founded on neutrality with regard to values, it is not simply a mere demarcation of institutions and processes, rather it incorporates into its text also certain governing ideas, expressing the fundamental, inviolable values of a democratic society. The Czech Constitution accepts and respects the principle of legality as a part of the overall basic outline of a law-based State; positive law does not, however, bind it merely to formal legality, rather the interpretation and application of legal norms are subordinated to their substantive purpose, law is qualified by respect for the basic enacted values of a democratic society and also measures the application of legal norms by these values. This means that even while there is continuity of "old laws," there is a discontinuity in values from the "old regime."

This conception of the constitutional State rejects the formal-rational legitimacy of a regime and the formal law-based State. Whatever the laws of a State are, in a State which is designated as democratic and which proclaims the principle of the sovereignty of the people, no regime other than a democratic regime may be considered as legitimate. Any sort of monopoly on power, in and of itself, rules out the possibility of democratic legitimacy. The starting point of our Constitution is the substantive-rational conception of legitimacy and the law-based State. In the overall structure of a democratic constitutional State and of a functioning democracy, legality *mutatis mutandis* undoubtedly embodies a part of the legitimacy of the regime, however, these concepts are not quite interchangeable. In a regime, in which hardly anybody was unaware that the elections were not elections, that the parties were not parties, that democracy was not democracy and that law was not law (at least not in the sense of a law-based State, since the application of the law was politically schizophrenic and everywhere discarded when the interests of those governing entered into the picture) it is even less possible to reduce the concept of legitimacy to that of the formal legality of normative legal regulation.

A political regime is legitimate if, on the whole, it is accepted by the majority of citizens. Political regimes which lack democratic substance avoid empirical verifications of legitimacy in favor of ideological arguments, primarily from the perspective of formal-rational legality. In this they are facilitated by the fact that consolidated governmental power is not just a fact of political power, but at the same time of legally organized power. However, it is precisely in such a regime that politics most differs from law and legality from legitimacy. For this reason, not even the continuity of law signifies recognition of the legitimacy of the communist regime. It cannot be asserted that every act or all conduct, so long as it does not cross over the line given by law, is legitimate, because, in this way, legality becomes a convenient substitute for an absolute legitimacy.

The legitimacy of a political regime cannot rest solely upon the formal legal component because the values and principles upon which a regime is built are not just of a legal, but first of all of a political nature. Those principles of the Czech Constitution, such as the sovereignty of the people, representative democracy, and a law-based State, are principles of the political organization of society, which are not entirely normatively definable. Positive law proceeds from them, however, normative regulation does not make up the full contents of these principles—something apart from it remains.

For these reason, on the basis of the substantive rational starting point of the Czech Constitution, the petitioners' concept, that the political regime from 1948 to 1989 was legitimate, must be rejected. The phrasing of Article 2, paragraph 1 of the contested Act concerning the illegitimate nature of that regime cannot be considered unconstitutional....

DENMARK: PURGE LAWS

Law Concerning Addenda to Civil Penal Code Regarding Treason and Other Crimes Against the State
Law No. 259/45 (June 1, 1945)

Chapter I.

§ 1.

¶ 1. The provisions of this Law are applicable with respect to acts committed during the period after, and including, April 9, 1940 and up to 2 years following the date on which this Law goes into effect. The general provisions of the civil penal code concerning the relationship between new and older laws offer no impediment to the rendering of a decision in accordance with the regulations set forth in this Law.

¶ 2. Those Acts to which this Law is applicable which were committed prior to August 29, 1943 are exempt from punishment, given the assumption that the perpetrator acted in accordance with laws or orders or instructions issued by the lawful Danish authorities within their areas of jurisdiction. If the act was committed on or after the aforementioned date, prosecution may be forborne or the sentence reduced or, under special mitigating circumstances, withheld under said given assumption....

§ 2.

¶ 1. This Law shall be applicable with respect to acts committed by persons who, at the time of the Commitment of the Act, were Danish citizens by Right of Birth or who were residents of the Danish State, without taking into Consideration whether the Act was committed within or outside thereof and, in the latter instance, without taking into consideration whether it is punishable pursuant to the laws of the place of its perpetration. The Law is correspondingly applicable to Danish citizens who have acquired the rights of German citizenship after April 9, 1940.

¶ 2. Charges for violations of this Law may be brought even if the perpetrator has previously been tried or acquitted for the act in question, whether here or abroad. Sentences previously served will be deducted from the sentence imposed pursuant to this Law. If a sentence has previously been imposed, but not served for the same act, a concurrent sentence shall be imposed.

§ 3.

¶ 1. The following punishments are applicable for acts covered by this Law: capital punishment or imprisonment. Sentencing to a workhouse, preventive detention or detention in a mental institution may not be imposed pursuant to this Law. Suspended sentences are not applicable.

¶ 2. Capital punishment is carried out by firing squad in accordance with specific regulations set forth by Royal Decree. Persons who were under 18 years of age at the time of the commission of the criminal act may not be executed.

¶ 3. Prison sentences ranging from 2 years to life may be imposed. Under mitigating circumstances, including:

1) if the perpetrator brought the criminal activity to an end prior to or shortly after August 29, 1943,
2) if the perpetrator has committed the criminal act under the duress of extraordinary pressure or under the influence of his education or as the result of a lack of maturity attributable to being of a young age, or if there are any other extenuating factors with respect to the conditions under which he has grown up,
3) if the criminal activity was of short duration,
4) if the criminal act consists in that the party in question enlisted in the German Armed Services, and said Enlistment took place prior to August 29, 1943, and
5) if the criminal Act consists in that the party in question enlisted in the German armed services or security services, and said enlistment took place abroad,

the sentence may be reduced to 1 year in prison. If a sentence reduction is otherwise warranted, the sentence may be reduced to 30 days in prison.

¶ 4. ...Release on parole may occur in accordance with the regulations of the Civil Penal Code, although such parole may not occur until 1 year of the sentence has been served, at the earliest....

§ 4.

¶ 1. When anyone is found guilty of a crime which is punishable pursuant to this Law, it may be determined by the court that his property and interest and income assets belonging to him shall be seized entirely or in part and deposited in the National Treasury.

¶ 2. Dispositions which have been made by anyone aware of impending Confiscation in an effort which is capable of recognition by the transferee as having been for the purpose of securing his assets against such confiscation are invalid.

§ 5.

¶ 1. Assets which belong to the Danish National Socialist Labor Party, the Hipo-, Sommer- or Schalburg Corps, the Danish Folkeværn [People's Defense] or similar organizations which have been associated with or otherwise acted on behalf of the German Wehrmacht, shall be seized and deposited in the National Treasury....

§ 6.

¶ 1. Anyone who is found guilty of any of the Crimes which are punishable pursuant to this Law shall forfeit the Rights enumerated below:

1) The right to vote, and eligibility for public office.
2) Public service and commissions, and the opportunity to be advanced to public service and commissions. This forfeiture does not prevent the party in question from discharging civil duties which do not involve any relationship of trust.
3) The right to perform military service. Determinations concerning forced labor in compensation for discontinued military service may be set forth by Royal Decree.
4) The right to work as a physician, as a lawyer, or in any other position which requires official certification.
5) The right to work as a minister for any religious community, or to engage in teaching activities in any public or private schools or classes of any type, or to act as a leader in any youth organization.
6) The right to participate in the leadership of or have a financial interest in any theatrical enterprise, film production or the operation of movie theaters.
7) The right to act as director, chairman, board member or to hold any other leadership position or position of trust in any commercial corporation or association.
8) The Right to be involved in the daily press or political publications as a publisher or editor, or to have a financial interest in any newspaper or political publication.

¶ 2. If the sentence is withheld pursuant to § 1, ¶ 2, or if withholding of the sentence is otherwise justified, the court may determine that only those rights enumerated under items 1-3 above shall be forfeited or, depending upon the relevant circumstances, that no forfeiture of rights shall occur.

¶ 3. The forfeiture of rights shall last for 5 years, if the sentence imposed by the court is less than 4 years in prison. If the sentence is 4 years in prison or more, the court shall determine the extent to which the forfeiture shall last in perpetuity, or for a specified number of years not less than 5 years. The rights are forfeited as of the day on which the decision of the court becomes final. The decision shall indicate which rights have been forfeited, and the duration of said forfeiture.

¶ 4. If a term of forfeiture is set, said term shall run from the day on which the sentence is served to its conclusion or commutation. In case of release on parole, the term shall run from the day on which the sentence would have been served to its conclusion, had the release on parole not occurred.

¶ 5. If the forfeiture of rights occurs in connection with a decision in which the sentence is considered to be withheld, the term shall run from the day on which the decision became final....

¶ 7. Restitution may be granted under the Law to the extent justified by the particular circumstances of each individual case....

§ 7.

Criminal liability and other legal consequences pursuant to this Law, and the opportunity to execute decisions handed down in accordance with the same are not subject to the statute of limitations.

Chapter II.

§ 8.

¶ 1. Anyone who, in order to advance German interests, or with an objective which is similarly harmful to the State, or for purposes of terrorism, has committed an act which is punishable pursuant to the Civil Penal Code, shall be punished by imprisonment. However, the sentence imposed may not be less than the minimum sentence prescribed in the Civil Penal Code for the crime in question.

¶ 2. However, capital punishment may be imposed:

1) if the crimes per §§ 98, 99 and 111, ¶ 1 of the Civil Penal Code were committed under aggravated circumstances,
2) if the act described per § 180 or § 183, ¶ 2 of the Civil Penal Code has led to any loss of life or caused anyone to be threatened by impending loss of life,...
4) if the Acts described per §§ 245-246 and 250 of the Civil Penal Code have been committed to compel explanations or confessions.

§ 10.

¶ 1. Anyone who has enlisted in or allowed themselves to be enlisted in the German Armed Services shall be punished by imprisonment. The imposed sentence may be reduced if special considerations are applicable, and the charges may be dismissed under extraordinary circumstances.

¶ 2. Anyone who has performed service in a Corps which acted in association with the Occupying Forces against the lawful organs of the Danish State or against its citizens, or who otherwise has engaged here in Denmark in activities of a constabulary nature in the service of the Germans shall be sentenced to not less than 4 years in prison. The sentence may be reduced to 1 year in prison under mitigating circumstances.

¶ 3. The sentence imposed upon anyone who, after September 19, 1944, engaged in constabulary activities in the service of the Hipo-Corps or any other similar organization shall be capital punishment or imprisonment for not less than 10 years.

§ 11.

Any public servant who has rendered unrequired and not inconsiderable aid to the Occupying Forces above and beyond that followed as a consequence of the invariable instructions for the post in question shall be punished by imprisonment.

§ 12.

¶ 1. Anyone who, by acting as an informer or in any other manner, has contributed to anyone being arrested or subject to arrest by the German authorities or any organization or individual person in collaboration therewith, or to anyone being imprisoned or punished pursuant to the interim Danish Emergency Wartime Laws, which were established in the German interest, shall be punished by imprisonment.

¶ 2. If the Act has led to any loss of life, serious injury to body or health, or to anyone being expatriated or deprived of their freedom for an extended period, or if such consequences have been intended, capital punishment may be imposed.

§ 13.

Anyone who has acted in association with the Occupying Forces or any organization or person collaborating therewith to enable the German authorities to interfere with the Danish Government or other Danish authorities, or who has engaged in negotiations with the occupying forces with respect to interests which were the province of the Danish authorities, shall be punished by imprisonment.

§ 14.

Anyone who, by making application to the German authorities or organizations or persons in collaboration therewith, has sought to achieve financial or any other advantage from the special conditions attributable to German intervention in the affairs of Danish citizens, persons residing in Denmark or persons or organizations engaged in activities in Denmark on behalf of the United Nations, shall be punished by imprisonment.

§ 15.

Anyone who, by recourse to membership in Germanophilic organizations or on the basis of their own national or political orientation has, through a particularly objectionable Initiative or in a similarly improper manner, collaborated with the Occupying Forces as a purchaser, supplier or contractor or acted as an intermediary in the procurement of Danish workers to work in Germany or in countries occupied by Germany without having been under prior contract for the work in question, shall be punished by imprisonment.

§16.

¶ 1. The following persons are punishable by imprisonment:

1) anyone who has been a member of the top leadership of the Danish National Socialist Labor Party or any other Nazi organization in improper collaboration with the Occupying Forces, and who in that capacity has contributed to or failed to oppose the collaboration of these organizations with the Occupying Forces and any assistance rendered to said forces via propaganda or in any other manner;

2) anyone who has acted as publisher, editor or business manager of any newspaper or publication which was known by the party in question to be involved in work contributing to the advancement of German propaganda, or who otherwise in writing or speech, whether in public or for a larger circle, has acted in the service of German propaganda;

3) anyone who has provided significant financial support to press organs or organizations which have, in an improper manner, collaborated with or supported the Occupying Forces;

4) anyone who has, in an effort to advance German interests, otherwise opposed the war efforts of the United Nations or in an improper manner acted in opposition to the Danish Resistance Movement or its organs;

5) anyone who—without having engaged in such constabulary activities as are encompassed in § 10, ¶¶ 2 and 3—has been employed by the German police or the German prison administration and has in that capacity participated in

   a) the interrogation of prisoners or
   b) the guarding or inspection of the imprisoned or interned;

6) anyone who has, after September 19, 1944, agreed to serve or for an extended period thereafter has continued to serve as an armed anti-sabotage guard at any business which was known to the party in question to have been particularly liable to attack in the fight against the Occupying Forces and maintained an anti-sabotage watch for the purpose of combating such attacks by force of arms;

7) anyone who—assuming that the conditions are not encompassed by item 5 above or § 10, ¶¶ 2 and 3—has been employed by the German Security Police or in the Hipo Corps in a capacity which bears a relation to the activities of the organization in question;

8) anyone who has, in an effort to advance German interests or obtain for himself financial gain or any other advantage in any manner other than through civilian salaried work, normal company operations or some other normal commercial activity, otherwise rendered assistance by word or deed to the Occupying Forces, or to organizations or persons in collaboration therewith.

¶ 2. In the cases encompassed in ¶ 1, Items 4-8, the provisions as per § 10, ¶ 1, 2nd point find corresponding application.

Chapter III.

§ 17.

By agreement with foreign nations, and on the condition of reciprocity, Danish citizens who have committed acts while in a country occupied by Germany which constitute criminal acts in the country in question may be extradited to said country at the request of its government....

Law Concerning Addenda to Law No. 259 of June 1, 1945 Concerning Addenda to Civil Penal Code Regarding Treason and Other Crimes Against the State

Law No. 260/45 (August 28, 1945)

§ 1.

The Provisions of this Law are Applicable with respect to acts committed after April 9, 1940.

§ 2.

¶ 1. Anyone who has, in an improper manner, collaborated with the Occupying Forces in a commercial sense, but under circumstances which are not encompassed in the Penal Provisions of Law No. 259 of June 1, 1945 regarding Treason and other Crimes against the State, shall be punished by up to 4 years in prison.

¶ 2. Corporations and other legal entities which are guilty of committing a crime pursuant to ¶ 1 may be punished by fine. In such cases, the provisions of §§ 6 and 8 are correspondingly applicable. Specific regulations concerning liability for such fines may otherwise be set forth by Royal Decree.

¶ 3. The provisions set forth in ¶¶ 1 and 2 are correspondingly applicable when the collaboration has not taken place directly with the Occupying Forces, but rather with one or more individual persons or businesses serving in an intermediary capacity, if the party in question perceived or should have perceived that German interests were being advanced by the activity in which he was engaged.

¶ 4. "Occupying Forces" shall be considered hereinafter to encompass foreign citizens or foreign businesses which have engaged in business activities in the interests of the Occupying Forces, whether abroad or here in Denmark.

§3.

Criminal liability pursuant to § 2, ¶ 1 may be ascribed to anyone who has held a leadership position or had an essential financial interest in the business in question. Pursuant to the same provision, criminal liability may similarly be ascribed to other persons employed by the business, if particularly aggravating circumstances are present, by virtue of which the demonstrated activities must be deemed to constitute improper collaboration as encompassed by the Law.

§ 4.

In determining whether and to what degree the activity must be deemed improper, consideration must be given in particular to the extent to which the party in question:

1) has personally been active in seeing that the business relationship was established, continued or expanded, unless it was thereby possible, in the Danish interest, to achieve essential advantages with respect to obtaining provisions for Denmark, or to avoid the implementation by the Occupying Forces of measures intended to cause essential harm to Danish interests,

2) has, in the German interest, undertaken a reorganization of the business, or offered or sought to offer increased or more rapid production than required by the circumstances,

3) has called upon the Occupying Forces for assistance in securing the business—unless the activities fall within the scope of Law No. 259 of June 1, 1945, §§ 13 and 14—in order to achieve higher prices or increased deliveries than the Danish authorities wished to sanction, or to otherwise protect his interests,

4) has prevented or sought to prevent the Danish authorities from having full access to knowledge concerning the circumstances surrounding the business,

5) has gained or sought to gain unreasonable profits or other advantages which were without reasonable commercial grounds, except for cases in which it has been demonstrated that the unreasonable demands had as their sole purpose the prevention of the transfer of the delivery, etc., to the party in question.

§ 5.

¶ 1. Additional punishment in the form of fines may be imposed for violations of the provisions of this Law. Such additional fines shall generally be imposed when the crime is of a gross nature.

¶ 2. If the convicted party has willfully failed to pay such a fine, a prison sentence of up to 2 years may be imposed.

§6.

¶ 1. Confiscation of the assets of a suspected or convicted party may occur in order to secure fines pursuant to the same regulations as are set forth in Chapter 68 of the Law concerning the Administration of Justice.

¶ 2. If, in order to secure the fine for which the suspected or convicted party is liable, it is deemed necessary that his assets or business be temporarily placed under administration, the court may, at the request of the prosecuting authorities, render a decision with respect thereto and appoint an administrator....

§ 7.

If the accused is considered unable to pay an imposed fine, it may be determined that the fine may be legally discharged with reference to a life insurance policy or annuity subscribed by him.

§ 8.

¶ 1. If the accused is considered unable to pay an imposed fine, gifts given by him, including such gifts as are in the form of irrevocable bestowals upon a favored party in connection with the subscription of a life insurance policy or annuity, may be invalidated, if the gift was conferred after the criminal act had been committed.

¶ 2. Under the same conditions, other dispositions may be invalidated if they were known to the transferee to have been made with the intent of protecting assets from legal prosecution in connection with the criminal act.

¶ 3. If the transferred assets have been further conveyed, such invalidation may apply to the acquiring party, if he has had knowledge of the aforementioned intent behind the conveyance.

§ 9.

¶ 1. Decisions concerning invalidation, etc., per §§ 7-8 shall, to the greatest extent possible, be made in connection with the disposition of the criminal case, but they may, depending upon the circumstances, be reached in a subsequent verdict by the court which tried the case in the first instance, although without the involvement of assessors. In the latter case, in order to protect the interests of the convicted party, he shall have defense counsel appointed for him, unless he is handling his own defense.

¶ 2. The third party against whom claims are valid pursuant to § 8 shall be summoned and given an opportunity to protect his interests before a decision or verdict is pronounced, and he shall have an opportunity to appeal the decision to a higher court through the customary administration of the criminal justice appeal process.

§ 10.

If the party upon whom a fine is imposed should die before said fine is paid, the fine may be levied against the estate of the deceased.

§ 11.

¶ 1. If a violation of § 2 of the Law has occurred, the net earnings derived from the criminal act shall be deposited in the National Treasury.

¶ 2. Under very special circumstances, the amount which is to be confiscated and deposited in the National Treasury may be reduced or even dismissed entirely.

¶ 3. A pronouncement may be obtained by order of the prosecuting authorities or the court from the committee established pursuant to § 2 of Law No. 330 of July 12, 1945 concerning the investigation of certain German payments to serve as a guideline in the determination of the amount of the confiscation claim.

¶ 4. If the amount of the earnings cannot be ascertained with sufficient certainty, for example, in cases wherein the party in question has simultaneously engaged in businesses for other than German interests, or in cases involving missing or incomplete financial records, an estimated amount may be confiscated for deposit in the National Treasury....

¶ 6. If new information of significance with respect to resolution of a confiscation matter should come to light after a decision has been pronounced, a new confiscation action may be brought.

§ 12.

Anyone who is found guilty of any criminal act pursuant to this Law may be declared by the court to be unworthy of public trust pursuant to the regulations set forth in Law No. 259 of June 1, 1945, § 6, or may forfeit certain rights as set forth in the provisions of said Law.

§ 13.

Regardless of any obligation to maintain secrecy concerning their experiences in the course of their activities as are imposed under the law or by any other regulations, public institutions and private persons or concerns are entitled to provide the police and the prosecuting authorities with any information which is deemed to be of significance with respect to the prosecution of criminal cases under this Law....

§ 14.

Public institutions and private persons or businesses which are in possession of or have in some other manner gained control of assets belonging to persons whom they know have been accused or convicted of violation of this Law are obligated to provide information concerning such assets to the police or prosecuting authorities. Failure to do so or the provision of incorrect information is punishable by up to 2 years in prison, and by fine or light imprisonment under mitigating circumstances.

§ 15.

Criminal liability and other legal consequences pursuant to this Law are limited in accordance with the statutes set forth in the Civil Penal Code, except that the statute of limitation first begins to run from the date on which this Law goes into effect....

§ 18.

¶ 1. The provisions set forth in this Law concerning fines and confiscation claims and the provisions of §§ 13 and 14 are correspondingly applicable in criminal cases involving prosecution of violations of §§ 15 and 16 of Law No. 259 of June 1, 1945 concerning Addenda to the Civil Penal Code regarding Treason and other Crimes against the State.

¶ 2. The provisions of § 3, ¶ 4 of Law No. 259 of June 1, 1945 are not applicable in cases which are prosecuted under this Law.

§ 19.

This Law goes into effect immediately.

EL SALVADOR: MEXICO PEACE AGREEMENTS— PROVISIONS ON PURGING OF THE ARMED FORCES

(Mexico City, January 16, 1992)

The Government of El Salvador and the Farabundo Marti National Liberation Front [FMLN] (hereinafter known as "the Parties"),

Reaffirming that their purpose, as set forth in the Geneva Agreement of 4 April 1990, is to "end the armed conflict by political means as speedily as possible, promote the democratization of the country, guarantee unrestricted respect for human rights, and reunify Salvadoran society",

Bearing in mind the San Jose, Mexico, and New York Agreements of 26 July 1990, 27 April 1991 and 25 September 1991 respectively, arrived at by them in the course of the negotiating process conducted with the active participation of the Secretary-General of the United Nations and of his Representative, which Agreements form a whole with the Agreement signed today,

Having concluded negotiations on all the substantive items of the Caracas Agenda of 21 May 1990 and of the New York Compressed Negotiations of 25 September 1991,

Have arrived at the following political agreements that follow, whose implementation, together with that of the earlier Agreements mentioned above, will put a definitive end to the Salvadorian armed conflict:

Chapter I

Armed Forces

3. Purification

...The Parties agree to a process of purification of the armed forces, within the framework of the peace process and with a view to the supreme objective of national reconciliation, based on evaluation of all members of the armed forces by an ad hoc Commission.

A. The evaluation shall take into account the past performance of each officer, including, in particular: (1) his record of observance of the legal order, with particular emphasis on respect for human rights, both in his personal conduct and in the rigor with which he has ordered the redress and punishment of unlawful acts, excesses or human rights violations committed under his command, especially if serious or systematic omissions are observed in the latter respect; (2) his professional competence; (3) his capacity to function in the new situation of peace, within the context of a democratic society, and to promote the democratization of the country, guarantee unrestricted respect for human rights and reunify Salvadorian society, which is the common purpose agreed upon by the Parties in the Geneva Agreement. The existence of serious deficiencies in any one of the above-mentioned areas could be sufficient grounds for the ad hoc Commission to take decisions required under Paragraph "G" of this section.

B. The evaluation shall be carried out by a rigorously impartial ad hoc Commission composed of three Salvadorians of recognized independence and unimpeachable democratic credentials. It shall also include two officers of the armed forces with impeccable professional records, who shall have access only to the deliberations of the Commission; they shall not have access to the investigation phase to be carried out by the ad hoc Commission, nor be involved in the final phase of the investigation, but they may have access to its conclusions.

The selection of the three civilian members of the ad hoc Commission is the result of a process of consultations carried out by the Secretary-General of the United Nations, the outcome of which has already been communicated to both Parties. The President of the Republic shall issue, within five days from the signing of this Agreement, his endorsement giving legal form and force to the Commission. If necessary, the same procedure shall be used to replace any member of the Commission who is permanently unable to serve. The two officers of the armed forces who are to participate in the ad hoc Commission on the conditions indicated above shall be appointed by the President of the Republic.

C. The Commission on the Truth established by the Mexico Agreements of 26 April 1991 (hereinafter referred to as "the Commission on the Truth") may appoint an observer to the ad hoc Commission.

D. The ad hoc Commission shall be provided with such civilian support staff as it considers necessary.

E. The Ministry of Defence and Public Security (see footnote 1[*]), as well as any public entity, shall supply the ad hoc Commission with any information it requests, including information on the service record of each officer. In any case, the ad hoc Commission may avail itself of information from any source which it considers reliable.

F. The ad hoc Commission shall adopt and, where necessary, request the adoption of any measure which, in its view, is necessary for its own safety and to ensure that safety and physical and moral integrity of persons who, in any form or manner, cooperate with it in the fulfillment of its mission.

G. The ad hoc Commission shall adopt its conclusions, after hearing the parties concerned, on the basis of the provisions of paragraph (A) of this section. Its conclusions may include a change of duty station and, where necessary, the discharge of the staff evaluated.

H. The ad hoc Commission shall endeavour to adopt its decisions unanimously, but if this is not possible a vote by the majority of its members shall suffice.

I. The evaluation will be extended to non-commissioned officers when, in the judgment of the ad hoc Commission, there is justification for doing so.

J. The ad hoc Commission will conclude its evaluation within a maximum period of three months from the date of its establishment. The

---

[*] Footnote 1: The results of the constitutional reform will be taken into account.

corresponding administrative decisions shall be taken within 30 days from the date on which the conclusions are communicated to the Government by the ad hoc Commission and shall be implemented within 60 days from that date.

K. The results of the evaluation shall not prevent the implementation of such recommendations as the Commission on the Truth may make at the appropriate time....

5. End to Impunity

The Parties recognize the need to clarify and put an end to any indication of impunity on the part of officers of the armed forces, particularly in cases where respect for human rights is jeopardized. To that end, the Parties refer this issue to the Commission on the Truth for consideration and resolution. All of this shall be without prejudice to the principle, which the Parties also recognize, that acts of this nature, regardless of the sector to which their perpetrators belong, must be the object of exemplary action by the law courts so that the punishment prescribed by law is meted out to those found responsible....

7. Intelligence Services

...The National Intelligence Department shall be abolished and State intelligence services shall be entrusted to a new entity to be called the State Intelligence Agency, which shall be subordinated to civilian authority and come under the direct authority of the President of the Republic. During the transitional period, the Director of the State Intelligence Agency shall be a civilian appointed by the President of the Republic on the basis of his ability to attract broad acceptance. He may be dismissed by resolution of the Legislative Assembly on grounds of serious human rights violations....

The incorporation into the State Intelligence Agency of staff of the National Intelligence Department who so request shall be permitted only after rigorous evaluation of their past performance, abilities and capacity to adapt to the new doctrine. Such evaluation shall be made by the Director of the Agency, under the authority of the President of the Republic, with the support of international advisory services and United Nations verification....

13. Redeployment and Discharge

A. Troops belonging to units that are to be abolished or disbanded shall be redeployed within the armed forces where such redeployment is compatible with the armed forces troop strength required by the objectives of this Agreement, and with the conclusions and recommendations of the ad hoc Commission provided for in section 3 of this chapter.

B. All troops discharged as a result of these agreements shall be given compensation equivalent to one year's pay at their wage level and the Government shall promote projects permitting the integration of such individuals into civilian life.

ETHIOPIA: VOTING RESTRICTIONS

Directive on the Election of Interim Administrative Committee Members for Districts and Neighborhoods

Directive No. 1/1992 (March 1992)
Issued by the Electoral Commission of
the Transitional Government of Ethiopia

16. Restrictions: Any person who was a member of the Workers' Party of Ethiopia ... does not have the right to elect or be elected....

GERMANY: ACT FOR LIBERATION FROM NATIONAL SOCIALISM AND MILITARISM

Act for Liberation from National Socialism and Militarism (March 5, 1946)

1. For 12 years National Socialism and Militarism ruled Germany with terror and violence, committed most serious crimes against the German people and the world, plunged Germany into distress and misery and destroyed the German Reich. The liberation from National Socialism and Militarism is an indispensable prerequisite to political, economic and cultural reconstruction.

2. American Military Government has, during the past months following the surrender carried out the removal and exclusion of National Socialists and Militarists from public administration and other positions.

3. On January 12, 1946, the Control Council has, in Directive No. 24, issued regulations for all Germany for removal and exclusion which are binding upon the German Governments and the German people.

4. Law No. 8 of Military Government and Regulation No. 1 thereunder extended the liberation to the field of trade and industry and introduced the appeal procedure through German investigation Boards.

5. American Military Government has now decided that the German people may share the responsibility for liberation from National Socialism and Militarism in all fields. The discharge of the task thus entrusted to the German people will be accomplished by this law, within the framework of Control Council Directive No. 24.

6. For a uniform and just execution of the task the following law is hereby simultaneously enacted and promulgated for Bavaria, Greater-Hesse and Wuerttemberg-Baden:

Chapter I.

Principles.

Article 1.

1. To liberate our people from National Socialism and Militarism and to secure a lasting base for German democratic national life in peace with the world, all those who have actively supported the National Socialist tyranny, or are guilty of having violated the principles of justice and humanity, or of having selfishly exploited the conditions thus created, shall be excluded from influence in public, economic and cultural life and shall be bound to make reparations.

2. Everyone who is responsible shall be called to account. At the same time he shall be afforded opportunity to vindicate himself.

Article 2.

1. The individual shall be judged by a just consideration of his individual responsibility and his actual conduct, taken as a whole. In accordance therewith there shall be determined in just gradation the extent of sanctions and of exclusion from participation in the public, economic and cultural life of the people in order to eliminate permanently the influence of National Socialistic and Militaristic conduct and ideas.

2. External criteria, such as membership of the NSDAP [the Nazi Party], any of its formations or other organizations, shall not be decisive by themselves alone for the degree of responsibility under this law. They may be taken as important evidence as to a person's conduct as a whole, but may be overcome, wholly or partly, by evidence to the contrary. Conversely, non-membership by itself is not decisive to absolve one of responsibility.

Registration.

Article 3.

1. In order to seek out all persons responsible and to carry out this law, a registration procedure is hereby established.

2. Every German above the age of 18 will fill out and submit a registration form....

Groups of Persons Responsible.

Article 4.

In order to make a just determination of responsibility and to provide for imposition of sanctions, the following groups of persons shall be formed:

1. Major Offenders,
2. Offenders (activists, militarists and profiteers),
3. Lesser Offenders (probationers),
4. Followers,
5. Persons exonerated.

Major Offenders.

Article 5.

Major Offenders are:

1. Persons who, out of political motives, committed crimes against victims or opponents of National Socialism;

2. Persons who, in Germany or in the occupied areas, treated foreign civilians or prisoners of war contrary to International Law;

3. Persons who are responsible for excesses, plundering, deportations, or other acts of violence, even if committed in fighting against resistance movements;

4. Persons who were active in leading positions in the NSDAP, one of its formations, or affiliated organizations, or in any other Nazi or Militaristic organizations;

5. Persons who in the government of the Reich, of a *Land* [State], or in the public administration of formerly occupied areas, were active in leading positions which could have been held only by leading Nazis or supporters of the National Socialistic tyranny;

6. Persons who otherwise gave major political, economic, propagandistic or other support to the National Socialist tyranny or who, by reason of their relations with the National Socialist tyranny, received very substantial profits for themselves or others;

7. Persons who were actively engaged for the National Socialist tyranny in the Gestapo, the SD, the SS, or the Geheime Feldpolizei or Grenzpolizei;

8. Persons who, in any form whatsoever, participated in killings, tortures, or other acts of cruelty in a concentration camp, a labor camp, an internment camp, or a medical institution or asylum;

9. Persons who, for personal profit or advantage, actively collaborated with the Gestapo, SD, SS or similar organizations by denouncing or otherwise aiding in the persecution of the opponents of the National Socialistic tyranny.

Article 6.

Until rebuttal anyone who is listed in Class I* of the list attached to this law is deemed to a Major Offender.

Activists.
Article 7.

I.   Activists are:

1. Persons who, by reason of their position or activity, substantially assisted in the tyranny of the NSDAP.

2. Persons who exploited their position, their influence or their connections to impose force and utter threats, to act with violence and to carry out oppressions or other unjust measures.

3. Persons who manifested themselves as avowed believers in the National Socialistic tyranny and especially in racial creeds.

II.   Activists are, in particular, the following persons insofar as they are not Major Offenders:

1. Anyone who substantially contributed to the establishment, consolidation or maintenance of the National Socialistic tyranny, by word or

---

* [Editor's note: The list referred to, not reprinted here, includes 259 categories of people subject to investigation under the Denazification law.]

deed, especially in public through speeches or writings or through voluntary donations out of his own or another's property or through using his personal reputation or his position of influence in political, economic or cultural life;

2. Anyone who by teaching National Socialist doctrines or as educator poisoned the spirit and soul of the youth;

3. Anyone who, to strengthen the National Socialistic tyranny, undermined family and marital life by this contemptuous disregard of recognized moral principles;

4. Anyone who, in the service of National Socialism, illegally interfered in the administration of justice or abused politically his office as judge or prosecutor;

5. Anyone who, in the service of National Socialism, agitated with incitement or violence against churches, religious communities or ideological groups;

6. Anyone who, in the service of National Socialism, derided, damaged or destroyed artistic or scientific values;

7. Anyone who took a leading or active part in destroying trade unions, suppressing labor, and squandering trade union property;

8. Anyone who as a provocateur, agent or informer caused or attempted to cause the initiation of proceedings to the detriment of others because of their race, religion, or political opposition to National Socialism, or because of violations of National Socialistic regulations;

9. Anyone who exploited his position of influence under the National Socialistic tyranny to commit offenses, in particular, extortions, embezzlements or frauds;

10. Anyone who, by word or deed, took an attitude of hatred towards opponents of the NSDAP at home or abroad, towards prisoners of war, the population of formerly occupied territories, foreign civilian workers, internees or similar persons;

11. Anyone who favored the exemption from military service (UK-Stellung) or from combat service of individuals because of their National Socialist attitude, or who effected or attempted to effect their induction into military service or their transfer to the front because of their opposition to National Socialism.

III. Activists will also include persons who after 8 May 1945 have endangered the peace of the German people or of the world by advocating National Socialism or Militarism.

Militarists.

Article 8.

I. Militarists are:

1. Persons who attempted to bring the life of the German people in line with a policy of militaristic force;

2. Persons who advocated or are responsible for the domination of foreign peoples, their exploitation or deportation; or

3. Persons who promoted armament for these purposes.

II. Militarists are in particular the following persons, insofar as they are not Major Offenders:

1. Persons who, by word or in writings, formulated or disseminated militaristic doctrines or programs or who were active outside the *Wehrmacht* in any organization which served to promote militaristic ideas;
2. Persons who before 1935 organized or participated in the organization of the systematic training of youth for war;
3. Persons who, exercising power of command, are responsible for the wanton devastation of cities and rural areas after the invasion of Germany;
4. Persons who, as members of the Armed Forces (*Wehrmacht*), the Reich Labor Service (*Reichsarbeitsdienst*), the Organization Todt (OT), or the Transport Group Speer, without regard to their rank, abused their authority to obtain special personal advantages or to mistreat subordinates brutally.

Profiteers.

Article 9.

I. Profiteers are:

Persons who, selfishly and by reason of their political position or their connections, extracted personal or economic advantages for themselves or for others from the tyranny of the NSDAP, the rearmament, or the war.

II. Profiteers are in particular the following persons, insofar as they are not Major Offenders:

1. Anyone who, solely on account of his membership in the NSDAP, obtained an office or a position or was preferentially prompted therein;
2. Anyone who received substantial donations from the NSDAP, its formations or affiliated organizations;
3. Anyone who, at the expense of those persecuted for political, religious or racial reasons, directly or indirectly gained or strove for excessive advantages for himself or others especially in connection with expropriations, forced sales or similar dealings;
4. Anyone who in armament or war transactions made profits which were manifestly disproportionate to the services rendered;
5. Anyone who unjustly enriched himself in connection with the administration of formerly occupied territories;
6. Anyone who, an adherent to National Socialism, escaped from military service or combat duty by exploiting his personal or political connections or by joining the NSDAP.

Article 10.

Until rebuttal, anyone who is listed under Class II of the list attached to this law is deemed to be an Offender (Activist, Militarist or Profiteer).

Lesser Offenders (Probationers).
Article 11.

I.   A Lesser Offender is:

1.   Anyone who would otherwise belong to the group of Offenders who, however, because of special circumstances (Article 39-II) merits milder consideration and who, because of his character may be expected, after he has proved himself in a period of probation, to fulfill his duties as a citizen of a peaceful, democratic state.
2.   Anyone who would otherwise belong to the group of Followers but who, because of his conduct and character, should first have to prove himself.

II.   The probationary period should be at least two years and, as a rule, not more than three years. The group to which the person concerned will be finally assigned will depend upon his conduct during the period of probation (Article 42).

III.   A Lesser Offender in particular is:

1.   Anyone born after 1 January 1919 who is not a Major Offender but appears to be an Offender, without, however, having manifested despicable or brutal conduct and who because of his character may be expected to prove himself.
2.   Anyone not a Major Offender who appears to be an offender but who, at an early stage, turned away from National Socialism and its methods unqualifiedly and clearly.

Followers.
Article 12.

I.   A Follower is:

Any person who was not more than a nominal participant or an insignificant supporter of National Socialism and who did not manifest himself as a Militarist.

II.   Subject to this test, a Follower is in particular:

1.   Anyone who as a member of the NSDAP or of any of its formations, except HJ and BDM [youth divisions] did no more than pay his membership dues, participate in meetings where attendance was obligatory, or fulfilled

unimportant or purely routine duties which were prescribed for all members.

2. Anyone who was a candidate for membership in the Party and who was not finally admitted as a member.

Persons Exonerated.

Article 13.

Exonerated are:

Persons who in spite of their formal membership, candidacy or other external indications, not only showed a passive attitude but also actively resisted the National Socialistic tyranny to the extent of their powers and thereby suffered disadvantages.

Sanctions.

Article 14.

In accordance with the extent of responsibility, the following sanctions shall be imposed in just selection and gradations, to accomplish the exclusion of National Socialism and Militarism from the life of our people, and reparation of the damage caused.

Major Offenders.

Article 15.

The following sanctions must be imposed upon Major Offenders:

1. They shall be assigned to a labor camp for a period of not less than two and not more than ten years in order to perform reparations and reconstruction work. Political internment after 8 May 1945 can be taken into account. Disabled persons shall be required to perform special work according to their physical capacity.

2. Their property shall be confiscated as a contribution to reparations. There shall be left to them only an amount necessary to cover the bare existence after family conditions and earning capacity have been taken into consideration. They shall be subject to current special taxes for a reparation fund, insofar as they have an income.

3. They shall be permanently ineligible to hold a public office, including that of a notary or attorney.

4. They shall lose any legal claims to a pension or allowance payable from public funds.

5. They shall lose the right to vote and to be elected, to be politically active in any way, or to be members of a political party.

6. They shall not be allowed to be members of a trade union or a business or vocational association.

7. The shall be prohibited for a period of not less than 10 years:

a) To be active in a profession or, independently, in an enterprise or economic undertaking of any kind, to own a share therein or to supervise or control it;

b) to be employed in any dependent position other than ordinary labor;

c) to be active as teacher, preacher, editor, author, radio commentator.

8. They shall be subject to restrictions with regard to housing and residence, and may be conscripted for public works service.

9. They shall lose all licenses, concession and other privileges granted to them, as well as the right to keep a motor vehicle.

Offenders.

Article 16.

Sanctions against Offenders:

1. They may be assigned to a labor camp for a period up to five years in order to perform reparations and reconstruction work. Political internment after 8 May 1945 can be taken into account.

2. If they are not assigned to a labor camp, they are to be conscripted for special work for the benefit of the community.

3. Their property will be confiscated in whole or in part as a contribution to reparations. In case of complete confiscation, Article 15, par. 2, second sentence will apply. In case of partial confiscation, capital goods shall be confiscated preferentially. The most necessary items for daily use are to be left to them.

4. They shall be permanently ineligible to hold a public office, including that of notary or attorney.

5. They shall lose their legal claims to a pension or allowance payable from public funds.

6. They shall lose the right to vote or to be elected, to be politically active in any way, or to be members of a political party.

7. They shall not be allowed to be members of a trade union or a business or vocational association.

8. They shall be prohibited for a period of not less than 5 years:

a) to be active in a profession or, independently, in an enterprise or economic undertaking of any kind, to own a share therein or to supervise or control it;

b) to be employed in any dependent position other than ordinary labor;

c) to be active as a teacher, preacher, editor, author or radio commentator.

9. They shall be subject to restrictions with regard to housing and residence.

10. They shall lose all licenses, concessions and other privileges granted to them, as well as the right to keep a motor vehicle.

Lesser Offenders (Probationers).

Article 17.

Sanctions against Lesser Offenders:

I.   During the period of probation they are not allowed:

a)   To direct an enterprise as owner, partner, manager or executive; to supervise or control an enterprise; or to acquire an enterprise in whole or in part, or any interest or share therein in whole or in part;

b)   to be employed in any dependent position other than ordinary labor;

c)   to be active as teacher, preacher, editor, author or radio commentator.

II.   In case the Lesser Offender is the owner of an enterprise or of any interest therein at the time of his classification, his interest in such enterprise will be blocked during the period of his probation and a trustee appointed therefor. The Tribunal will decide what part of the business income received by the trustee will be paid over to the Lesser Offender. The ultimate disposition of the property so blocked will be determined at the time of final classification of the Lesser Offender.

III.   The term "enterprise" as used in Paras I, (a) and II of this Article shall not include small undertakings, especially manual trade enterprises, retail stores, farms and like undertakings, with less than ten employees.

IV.   Property values, acquisition of which resulted from exploitation of political connections or special National Socialistic measures such as "Aryanization" and armament, shall be confiscated.

V.   Single or recurrent special contributions to a reparation fund shall be ordered.

VI.   During the period of probation, certain additional sanctions, as specified in Article 16, may be imposed in just selection and modification, in particular:

a)   Restrictions in the exercise of a free profession, and prohibition to train apprentices;

b)   With regard to civil servants: reduction of retirement pay, transfer to retirement or to a position of inferior rank or to another office with reduced pay, rescission of promotion, transfer from civil service status to contractual employment;

c) With regard to trade and industry, including agriculture and forestry: prohibition to carry on an enterprise, duty to sell an interest, increase in delivery of agricultural or other products, and requirement to perform special services.

VII. Assignment to a labor camp and complete confiscation of property may not be ordered.

Followers.

Article 18.

Sanctions against Followers:

1. They shall be ordered to pay single or recurrent contributions to funds for reparations. There shall be taken into account the length of membership, the amount of dues and other contributions, the property, income, and family conditions, and similar circumstances.

2. In addition, in the case of civil servants, transfer to retirement or to an office with inferior rank or to another agency, possibly with reduction in pay, or the rescission of a promotion received while the person belonged to the NSDAP, may be ordered. With regard to persons in trade and industry, including agriculture and forestry, similar measures may be ordered.

Extenuating Circumstances.

Article 19.

With respect to the imposition of discretionary sanctions, the following extenuating circumstances may especially be taken into consideration:

1. Youth or immaturity;
2. Serious bodily disability resulting from the impact of the war;
3. Heavy and permanent strain upon the earning power of a person because of invalidity of relatives, especially as a result of impact of the war.

Article 20.

1. With regard to persons born after 1 January 1919, sanctions can be imposed under this law only if they are Major Offenders or Offenders.

2. In accordance with special regulations, sanctions against such persons may be reduced if they are not Major Offenders.

Article 21.

In case confiscation of property values is ordered, all dispositions and other transactions, which have been or will be made with the intent to defeat or to render more difficult the application of the property for reparations, are void.

Relation to Criminal Law.

Article 22.

1. Criminal offenses by National Socialists or Militarists may be criminally prosecuted independently of this law. This applies especially to war crimes and other offenses which have remained unatoned under the National Socialistic tyranny.

2. Proceedings under this law shall not bar prosecution under criminal law for the same offence. However, in imposing sanctions under this law penalties for the same act imposed in criminal proceedings may be taken into account.

Chapter II.

The Minister.

Article 23.

The Minister President shall appoint a Minister for Political Liberation who shall be responsible for carrying out this law. He must be an opponent of long standing of National Socialistic tyranny and Militarism, actively pro-democratic, and an avowed supporter of the principles of this law.

The Tribunals.

Article 24.

1. The Tribunals shall decide the classification of the responsible persons and the sanctions to be imposed.

2. Trial Tribunals shall be established in urban and rural districts.

3. Appellate Tribunals shall be established for the review of decisions.

4. A Public Prosecutor will be assigned to each of the Tribunals.

Article 25.

1. The Tribunals shall be composed of one chairman and at least two assessors.

2. The members of the Tribunals must be at least thirty years of age.

3. The chairman of the Trial Tribunal should, and the chairman of the Appellate Tribunals shall, be qualified for the office of judge or for the higher administrative service.

4. The members of the Trial Tribunals shall be familiar with local conditions within their area of jurisdiction. The occupational group to which the respondent belongs, or a related group, shall be represented, to the extent possible, among the assessors. However, such persons may not constitute a majority and may not be business competitors of the respondent.

Article 26.

1. The chairmen, their deputies, the assessors of the Tribunals (Trial and Appellate Tribunals) and the public prosecutors shall be appointed by the Minister for Political Liberation. The appointment of the chairmen and their deputies shall be made after consultation with the Minister of Justice.

2. The democratic parties authorized at *Land* level are to be invited to submit proposals concerning appointment of assessors. A one-sided political combination of Tribunals shall be avoided.

3. The selection of assessors for individual sittings is to be made by the chairmen, in a pre-determined sequence.

Article 27.

1. The members of the Tribunals shall be independent and subject only to the law.

2. They shall take an oath in public session that they will administer justice in no one's favor and to no one's harm, to the best of their knowledge and conscience, and without bias or prejudice. It is permissible to add formal words of religious affirmation.

3. The Minister for Political Liberation shall exercise administrative supervision over the Tribunals.

Article 28.

All persons entrusted with the execution of this law must be known as opponents of National Socialism and Militarism. They must be personally beyond reproach and be fair and just.

Venue.

Article 29.

The venue of the Tribunals is determined by:

a) the present or last domicile or residence of the respondent;
b) the place where the respondent is detained by order of the authorities;
c) the place where the respondent has been active at any time;
d) the place where property of the respondent is located.

In case of doubt, the Minister for Political Liberation will decide as to the venue....

Substantive Jurisdiction.

Article 31.

1. The Tribunals shall be authorized and obligated under this law to decide on all cases without being bound by previous decisions of other agencies.

2. No other proceedings for the purpose of political liberation shall take place apart from the proceedings before the Tribunals.

Persons Eligible to Apply For Institution of Proceedings.

Article 32.

1. The following shall be eligible to apply for institution of proceedings:

The Minister for Political Liberation and his authorized representatives.
The public prosecutor.
The mayor of the present and former residence.
The supreme administrative authority of the *Land*, with regard to civil servants and employees of the public administration.
The injured person, provided he was directly harmed by the respondent in the particular case.
The trade unions, the vocational or business associations, and the political parties authorized at *Land* level, as well as any other authorized organization.
The respondent himself or his legal representative.

2. The application must designate the respondent, and contain brief reasons. It may be filed with any Tribunal.

The Public Prosecutor.

Article 33.

1. The Public Prosecutor shall ascertain all responsible persons (Article 4). He shall receive and examine all registration forms (*Meldebogen*) (Article 3), applications (Article 32), denunciations and other data referring to responsible persons, and institute the investigations *ex officio*. He shall carry out the investigation, prefer the charges and prosecute the case before the Tribunal.

The charge must contain:

    a)   the group of responsible persons to which the respondent shall be assigned;
    b)   the basis for the charge;
    c)   essential evidence;

d) the motion as to whether the decision shall be taken in summary proceedings or on the basis of oral trial.

2. Insofar as the list attached to this law or directives of the Minister for Political Liberation designate groups of persons or individuals as specially requiring investigation, such investigation shall be conducted with particular care.

3. If the respondent falls within Class I of the attached list, his investigation shall be given priority and the charge filed shall contain a motion to allocate him to the group of major offenders. In such a case an oral hearing is obligatory.

4. If the respondent falls within Class II of the attached list, the charge filed by the public prosecutor shall contain a motion to allocate him to the group of major offenders or offenders, or if it seems to the public prosecutor warranted by the result of his investigation, to the group of probationers. In such a case, also, an oral hearing is obligatory if requested by the public prosecutor, the person who applied for institution of the proceedings, or the respondent.

5. If the respondent does not fall within any of the categories enumerated in the list, the public prosecutor shall move to allocate him into such group of persons responsible as is warranted by the result of his investigation.

If the respondent falls within the class of major offenders or offenders, the public prosecutor shall proceed in accordance with paragraphs 3 and 4. If the respondent belongs to the group of lesser offenders or that of followers, the public prosecutor shall move for a decision in summary proceedings. If such a respondent appears to be exonerated or not incriminated at all, the public prosecutor shall quash the proceeding.

6. The charge, any motion for a decision in summary proceedings, or any order quashing the proceedings, must be served upon the respondent and the person who applied for institution of the proceedings....

Burden of Proof.

Article 34.

If the respondent falls within Class I or II of the list attached to this law, he has to show in a clear and convincing manner that he falls within a group more favorable to him. He shall immediately submit his evidence to the Tribunal. If the respondent falls within Class I, any defense offered by him shall be judged by particularly rigid standards. Whoever claims to be a follower or exonerated has the burden of proof if this should be questioned.

Procedure Before the Tribunal.

Article 35.

1. The Tribunals shall regulate their procedure according to their unfettered discretion. On their own motion they shall do everything necessary to ascertain the truth.

2. They may hear witnesses and experts under oath and receive affidavits; they may, by subpoena and fines, compel the respondent, a witness, or an expert to appear personally.

3. The date of trial shall be published in advance in a suitable manner.

4. The respondent is entitled to a fair hearing. He may have the assistance of an attorney at law or any other licensed counsellor.

5. If the respondent fails to appear without excuse or cannot be reached, the case may be tried and decided in his absence.

Article 36.

In the case of an absent person, whose whereabouts are unknown or who stays outside of the *Land* or whose appearance before the competent Tribunal appears not to be feasible, an oral hearing shall take place only if the public prosecutor so moves. The absent person shall be summoned in an appropriate manner by service by publication. A representative must be appointed for him.

Article 37.

If the respondent is dead, a proceeding for the purpose of confiscating his estate in whole or in part, situated within the *Land* may be carried out upon the order of the Minister for Political Liberation, without regard to statutory inheritance or testamentary dispositions. Such a proceeding may be ordered only if the respondent is considered to have been a major offender or offender within the meaning of this law.

Article 38.

1. Without being bound by any motions, the Tribunal shall decide on the basis of the evidence according to its free conviction formed from the whole trial.

2. The Tribunal shall decide by a majority vote in secret deliberation.

Article 39.

In determining the group of persons responsible to which the respondent shall be allocated, the Tribunal shall take into consideration, in particular, the following circumstances:

I. Against the Respondent:

1. That he personally gave eager support to Nazi ideas and measures;

2. That he exploited his position as superior for political purposes; for example, that he exercised pressure upon subordinates for the purpose of causing them to join the NSDAP or its formations;

3. That he employed political pressure to achieve private aims;

4. That he physically mistreated or menaced political opponents;

5. That he showed an unsocial or brutal attitude towards political opponents, persons who were economically weaker, in particular, against persons in dependent positions, for instance, against foreign workers, or against racial or religious minorities;

6. That he used threats against public servants to enforce or suppress official acts.

II. In favor of the Respondent:

1. That he resigned from the NSDAP and its formations prior to 30 January 1933, or if he resigned thereafter, by a personal declaration made under circumstances requiring courage; that he was expelled from the NSDAP and its formations, provided such expulsion was based on his resistance against party demands and not upon dishonorable conduct, subsequent rejoining cancels the effect of such a declaration of resignation or such expulsion;

2. That it is proved that he cooperated with a resistance movement or with any other movement directed against the Nazi tyranny, if such resistance was based upon anti-Nazi and anti-militaristic motives;

3. That it is proved that he regularly and publicly attended the services of any recognized religious sect, if there is clear evidence that such participation signified rejection of Nazism;

4. That it is proved that he repeatedly supported and assisted victims and opponents of Nazism, if this was done for anti-Nazi motives;

5. That it is proved that, despite his membership in the NSDAP or one of its formations, he was subject to political persecution or suppression by the Nazi tyranny on account of his anti-Nazi activities or attitude.

III. The fact that a respondent was compelled by orders to be active in the Health Service shall not be considered against him even though he held a rank in connection with such activity.

Article 40.

1. The Tribunals, and in case of urgency the chairmen, may issue interlocutory orders at any stage of the proceedings.

2. They can, in particular, order the arrest and confinement of the respondent; they can prohibit his continued employment; and they can order blocking of his property.

Article 41.

The decision of the Tribunal shall state whether the respondent is a major offender, an offender, a lesser offender (probationer), follower, or is exonerated, and shall impose the appropriate sanctions.

Article 42.

1. In allocating a respondent to the group of lesser offenders (probationers) the Tribunal shall fix a period of probation. At the same time it shall determine the sanctions to be applied during the period of probation.

2. Upon expiration of the period of probation, the public prosecutor shall make a motion, based upon the results of his investigation, to allocate the respondent to a group of persons responsible. Together with its decision upon this motion, the Tribunal shall finally determine the sanctions to be imposed. If the respondent does not prove himself, he shall be allocated, upon application of the public prosecutor, even before the end of the probationary period, in a new proceeding, to the class of offenders. At that time sanctions shall be determined.

Article 43.

If the decision is made in summary proceedings, the respondent shall be afforded adequate opportunity for his defense and for submitting his evidence.

Article 44.

The decision of the Tribunal shall be in writing, with brief reasons emphasizing any circumstances in favor of and against the respondent; it shall be signed by the members of the Tribunal....

Appeal.

Article 46.

From the decision of the Tribunal the persons designated in Article 45 may file an appeal to the Appellate Tribunal. The appeal shall be filed with the Trial or Appellate Tribunal within one month after service of the decision and shall contain in writing the grounds for appeal.

Article 47.

1. The appeal may challenge both the allocation into a certain group and the imposition of sanctions insofar as they are within the discretion of the Tribunal.

2. The appeal can be based only upon the ground that the facts as found did not warrant the decision of the Trial Tribunal, or that the proceedings were conducted in an arbitrary or partial manner. The Appellate Tribunal may dismiss appeals which are manifestly unmeritorious. It may itself take new evidence if, in its discretion, this appears to be necessary for a just decision of the case. This applies, in particular, if essential facts or evidence could not previously have been presented.

3. The Appellate Tribunal may in its decision affirm or modify the decision appealed from, or may remand the case for a new trial to the same or another Trial Tribunal.

4. In all other respects, the provisions governing procedure before the Trial Tribunals shall apply to the Appellate Tribunals so far as practicable.

Reopening of Proceedings.

Article 48.

1. The proceedings may, upon motion, be reopened on the ground of new essential facts or evidence.

2. The Trial Tribunal shall decide without oral hearing whether reopening of the proceedings shall be permitted. A decision rejecting the reopening of a proceeding may be appealed from.

Exclusion of Other Remedies.

Article 49.

Remedies other than appeals shall not be permissible. In particular, interlocutory orders are not subject to any review.

Enforcement of Decisions.

Article 50.

The Minister for Political Liberation shall issue the necessary regulations for enforcement of any measures which may be ordered.

Group Register.

Article 51.

1. After final decision by the Tribunals, the classification of the respondent and the sanctions imposed upon him shall be entered on his identification card and in a register established for this purpose.

2. The register shall be open for public inspection.

Review.

Article 52.

1. The Minister for Political Liberation may request that any decision be submitted to him for review.

2. If the public prosecutor believes that a final decision of the Tribunal is obviously wrong or inconsistent with the purposes of this law, he must submit the case to the Minister for Political Liberation for review.

3. The Minister may vacate the decision, order a new trial, and in such event he may remand the case to a different Trial Tribunal.

Article 53.

If during a substantial period of time after the final decision, a respondent has manifested by his whole conduct that he has completely turned away from Nazism, and that he is fit and willing hereafter to participate in reconstructing Germany on a peaceful and democratic basis, the public prosecutor, may, after a thorough examination of the case, propose to the Minister for Political Liberation to mitigate or vacate the decision against the respondent. The Minister shall decide fairly and equitably, taking into consideration the policies and aims of this law.

Pardon.

Article 54.

The power of pardon shall be exercised by the Minister President acting on the recommendation of the Minister for Political Liberation.

Assistance from Other Agencies.

Article 55.

The public prosecutor and the Tribunals are authorized to exercise official functions outside of their districts, without the consent of the local competent authorities.

Article 56.

1. All agencies of the state, the communities and the police administration, as well as the self-governing and special administrative authorities, shall cooperate with the agencies entrusted with the administration and enforcement of this law. It is not permissible to reject any such request for cooperation. Costs and expenses resulting from such cooperation will not be refunded to the agencies thus requested.

2. No stamps, fees, and public imposts, which by the law of the *Land* are payable in connection with a request for official cooperation, shall be levied.

3. The above provisions are applicable also where a request for official assistance on the basis of this law is made by the authorities of another German *Land*....

Chapter III.

Statutory Prohibition of Activities and Employment.

Article 58.

1. From the effective date of this law persons who are enumerated in Class I or II of the list attached to this law, or who were otherwise members of the NSDAP or one of its formations except the Hitler Youth (HJ and

BDM), shall not be employed or active in all public and private enterprise, non-profit and welfare organizations, as well as in professions, except in ordinary labor. If such persons are still active or employed in any way other than in ordinary labor, they shall be removed and excluded from their positions on the effective date of this law. They shall no longer be active in the same agency or in the same business. In other places they may be employed only in ordinary labor.

2. Removal and exclusion applies not only to persons who work in dependent positions, but also to entrepreneurs, owners of a business, and persons owning an interest therein.

3. The provisions of this Article do not apply to owners and employees of small enterprises, particularly manual trade enterprises, retail stores, farms, and similar enterprises, employing less than ten persons. These provisions also do not apply to persons engaged in independent professions provided they do not employ more than two assistants, such as clerks, nurses, and similar personnel.

4. The prohibition of employment and activities is effective until a final decision by the Tribunal. After decision of the Tribunal, restrictions upon employment or activities will be governed by the sanctions imposed.

Article 59.

1. Persons whose employment or activities have been temporarily approved by Military Government or Pursuant to Military Government Law No. 8 may, until final decision by the Tribunal, continue in their activities or employment unless prior to such decision Military Government has revoked such approval.

2. Any person who pursuant to an order of Military Government or Military Government Law No. 8 has been removed or excluded from public office or any other position, shall not be re-employed therein until the Tribunal has made a final decision in his favor.

Temporary Exemptions.

Article 60.

The Minister for Political Liberation may, temporarily and revocable, authorize continued activities or employment under the following conditions:

a) Continued employment or activities must be absolutely indispensable for maintaining public health or safety because of the special qualifications of the person concerned;

b) There must not be available any qualified, politically unincriminated person;

c) The person concerned must not fall within the group of major offenders;

d) He must not owe his position exclusively to the NSDAP;

e) He must not have an influence on the management and business policies of the enterprise nor upon the hiring, and discharging, of others;

f) His income from his work must not exceed in any case the amount of RM 500 per month;

g) He must be replaced by a politically unincriminated person as soon as possible.

Statutory Blocking of Property.

Article 61.

1. The property of persons removed and excluded pursuant to Article 58 is subject to blocking.

2. For administering and safeguarding property blocked under this law, the Minister for Political Liberation, or an agency designated by him, shall appoint a trustee.

Chapter IV.

Transitory Provisions.

Article 62.

Proceedings under this law need not be initiated by the public prosecutor against persons who, after investigation, have received final approval of Military Government for their employment or activities, unless they were members of the NSDAP or one of its formations (excluding HJ or BDM). Persons whose activities or employment, after investigation, have received final approval of Military Government shall be classified in a group not higher than followers, unless there is evidence against them.

Chapter V.

Final Provisions.

Article 63.

Ordinary labor within the meaning of this law is deemed to be any activity in skilled or unskilled labor, or as employee in a position of subordinate importance, in which the employee is not active in any way in a supervisory, managerial, or organizing capacity, and does not participate in any way in hiring or discharging personnel or in any other personnel policies.

Article 64.

The respondent cannot derive any claim for reinstatement or damages from a decision of a Tribunal declaring him to be a lesser offender, follower, or exonerated person.

Article 65.

1. The following are punishable by imprisonment or fine:

    a) Any person who gives a false or misleading certificate or declaration or who obscures facts which are relevant to the application of this law;
    b) Any person who after 1 June 1946 violates any prohibition of employment or who continues any activities prohibited under this law;
    c) Any person who fails to give information required under this law;
    d) Any person who fails to perform his duty of registration;
    e) Any person who, for the purposes of evading this law or any orders made under this law, undertakes to remove or conceal property or assists any other person in so doing.

In the cases of (a) and (e), loss of civil rights may be imposed in addition to imprisonment.

2. In other respects, the provisions of the Criminal Code remain applicable.

Article 66.

The Minister for Political Liberation shall issue regulations to carry out this law....

GERMANY: SCREENING QUESTIONNAIRE ("*FRAGEBOGEN*")

Allied Military Government of Germany (1945)

WARNING: Read the entire *Fragebogen* carefully before you start to fill it out. The English language will prevail if discrepancies exist between it and the German translation. Answers must be typewritten or printed clearly in block letters. Every question must be answered precisely and conscientiously and no space is to be left blank.... If the question is inapplicable, so indicate by some appropriate word or phrase such as "none" or "not applicable." Add supplementary sheets if there is not enough space in the questionnaire. Omissions or false or incomplete statements are offences against Military Government and will result in prosecution and punishment.

A. Personal

1. List position for which you are under consideration (include agency of firm):
2. Name: Surname: Fore Names:
3. Other names which you have used or by which you have been known:
4. Date of birth:
5. Place of birth:
6. Height:
7. Weight:
8. Colour of Hair:
9. Colour of Eyes:
10. Scars, marks or deformities:
11. Present address (City, street and house number):
12. Permanent address (City, street and house number):
13. Identity card, type and number:
14. *Wehrpass* No.:
15. Passport No.:
16. Nationality:
17. If a naturalized citizen, give date and place of naturalization:
18. List any titles of nobility ever held by you or your wife or by the parents or grandparents of either of you:
19. Religion:
20. With what church are you affiliated?
21. Have you ever severed your connection with any church, officially or unofficially?
22. If so, give particulars and reasons:
23. What religious preference did you give in the census of 1933?
24. List any crimes of which you have been convicted, giving dates, location and nature of the crimes:

B. Secondary and Higher Education

Name and Type of School (If a special Nazi school or military academy, so specify): Location:
Dates of Attendance: Certificate, Diploma or Degree:
Did Abitur Permit University Matriculation? Date:

25. List any German University Student Corps to which you have ever belonged:

26. List (giving locations and dates) any Adolf Hitler school, Nazi Leaders College or military academy in which you have ever been a teacher:

27. Have any of your children ever attended any such schools? Which ones, where and when?...

C. Professional or Trade Examinations

Name of Examination	Place Taken	Result	Date

D. Chronological Record of Full Time Employment and Military Service

29. Give a chronological history of your employment and military service beginning with 1st of January 1931, accounting for all promotions or demotions, transfers, periods of unemployment, attendance at educational institutions (other than those covered in Section B) or training schools and full-time service with para-military organizations. (Part time employment is to be recorded in Section F.) Use a separate line for each change in your position or rank or to indicate periods of unemployment or attendance at training schools or transfer from one military or para-military organisation to another.

From	To	Employer and Address or Military Unit	Name and Title of Immediate Supervisor or C.O.	Position or Rank	Duties and Responsibilities	Reason for Change of Status or Cessation of Service

30. Were you deferred from Military Service?
31. If so, explain circumstances completely:
32. Have you ever been a member of the General Staff Corps?
33. When?
34. Have you ever been a Nazi Military Leadership Officer?
35. When and in what unit?
36. Did you serve as part of the Military Government or *Wehrkreis*-administration in any country occupied by Germany including Austria and Sudetenland?

37.   If so, give particulars of offices held, duties performed, location and period of service:

38.   Do you have any military orders or military honours?

39.   If so, state what was awarded you, the date, reasons and occasions for its bestowal:

E. Membership in Organisations

40.   Indicate on the following chart whether or not you were a member of and any offices you have held in the organizations listed below. Use lines 96 to 98 to specify any other fraternity, union, syndicate, chamber, institute, group, corporation, club or other organisation of any kind, whether social, political, professional, educational, cultural, industrial, commercial or honorary, with which you have ever been connected or associated....

				Highest	
Yes				Office	Date
or No	From	To	Number	Rank Held	Appointed

[Lines 41-95 list a variety of organizations, ranging from the Nazi Party and the military to the National-Socialist Nurses' League, the German Family League, German Music Chamber, German Faith Movement, German Red Cross, and Comrades League USA]

99.   Have you ever sworn an oath of secrecy to any organization?

100.   If so, list the organizations and give particulars:

101.   Have you any relatives who have held office, rank or post of authority in any of the organisations listed from 41 to 95 above?

102.   If so, give their names and addresses, their relationship to you and a description of the position and organization:

103.   With the exception of minor contributions to the *Winterhilfe* and regular membership dues, list and give details of any contributions of money or property which you have made directly or indirectly to the NSDAP or any of the other organizations listed above, including any contributions made by any natural or juridical person or legal entity through your solicitation of influence:

104.   Have you ever been the recipient of any titles, ranks, medals, testimonials or other honours from any of the above organizations?

105.   If so state the nature of the honour, the date conferred, and the reason and occasion for its bestowal:

106.   Were you a member of a political party before 1933?

107.   If so, which one?

108.   For what political party did you vote in the election of November 1932?

109.   In March 1933?

110.   Have you ever been a member of any anti-Nazi underground party or groups since 1933?

111.   Which one?

112. Since when?
113. Have you ever been a member of any trade union or professional or business organization which was dissolved or forbidden since 1933?
114. Have you ever been dismissed from the civil service, the teaching profession or ecclesiastical positions or any other employment for active or passive resistance to the Nazis or their ideology?
115. Have you ever been imprisoned, or have restrictions of movement, residence or freedom to practise your trade or profession been imposed on you for racial or religious reasons or because of active or passive resistance to the Nazis?
116. If you answered yes to any of the questions from 110 to 115, give particulars and the names and addresses of two persons who can confirm the truth of your statements:

F. Part Time Service with Organizations

117. With the exception of those you have specially mentioned in Sections D and E above, list: (a) Any part time, unpaid or honorary position of authority or trust you have held as a representative of any *Reich* Ministry or the Office of the Four Year Plan or similar central control agency; (b) Any office, rank or post of authority you have held with any economic self-administration organization…, as well as their subordinate or affiliated organizations and field offices; (c) Any service of any kind you have rendered in any military, paramilitary, police, law enforcement, protection, intelligence or civil defence organizations….

From	To	Name and Type of Organization	Highest Office or Rank you Held	Date of Your Appointment	Duties

G. Writings and Speeches

118. List on a separate sheet the titles and publishers of all publications from 1923 to the present which were written in whole or in part, led or edited by you, and all public addresses made by you, giving subject, date and circulation or audience. If they were sponsored by any organization, give its name. If no speeches or publications write "none" in this space.

H. Income and Assets

119. Show the sources and amount of your annual income from January 1 1931 to date. If records are not available, give approximate amounts.

Year	Source of Income	Amount

120.   List any land or buildings owned by you or any immediate members of your family, giving locations, dates of acquisition, from whom acquired, nature and description of buildings, the number of hectares and the use to which the property is commonly put:

121.   Have you or any immediate members of your family ever acquired property which had been seized from others for political, religious or racial reasons or expropriated from others in the course of occupation of foreign countries or in furtherance of the settling of Germans or *Volksdeutsche* in countries occupied by Germany?

122.   If so, give particulars, including dates and locations, and the names and whereabouts of the original title holders:

123.   Have you ever acted as an administrator or trustee of Jewish property in furtherance of Aryanization decrees or of ordinances?

124.   If so, give particulars:

I. Travel or Residence Abroad

125.   List all journeys or residence outside of Germany including military campaigns:

126.   Was the journey made at your expense?

127.   If not, at whose expense was the journey made?

128.   Persons or organizations visited:

129.   Did you ever serve in any capacity as part of the civil administration of any territory annexed to or occupied by the *Reich*?

130.   If so, give particulars of office held, duties performed, location and period of service:

131.   List foreign languages you speak indicating degree of fluency:

Remarks

The statements on this form are true and I understand that any omissions or false or incomplete statements are offences against Military Government and will subject me to prosecution and punishment.

Signed: *Date:*

Certification of Immediate Superior

(Verify that the above is the true name and signature of the individual concerned and that, with the exceptions noted below, the answers made on the questionnaire are true to the best of my knowledge and belief and the information available to me. Exceptions—if no exceptions, write "none")

Signed: *Official Position:*   *Date:*

HAITI: 1987 CONSTITUTION

Article 291

...For ten years following publication of this Constitution, and without prejudice to any criminal action or civil suit for damages, none of the following may be candidates for any public office:

a) Any person well known for having been by his excess zeal one of the architects of the dictatorship and of its maintenance during the last twenty-nine years;
b) Any accountant of public funds during the years of the dictatorship concerning whom there is presumptive evidence of unjustified gain;
c) Any person denounced by public outcry for having inflicted torture on political prisoners in connection with arrests and investigations or for having committed political assassinations.

Article 292

The Provisional Electoral Council charged with receiving the registration of candidates, shall see to the strict enforcement of this provision.

Article 293

All decrees expropriating real property in urban and rural areas of the Republic of the last two Haitian governments for the benefit of the State or companies in the course of incorporation shall be annulled if the purpose for which such actions were taken has not been attained during the last 10 years....

HUNGARY: LAW ON BACKGROUND CHECKS TO BE CONDUCTED ON INDIVIDUALS HOLDING CERTAIN IMPORTANT POSITIONS

Law No. 23 (March 8, 1994)

In order to promote the integrity of government business of a democratic State the Parliament has adopted the following Law:

§ 1

It is to be verified whether the persons, described in § 2,

a) classified as career officers, were assigned "open" (unclassified) or "top secret" duties and served with Division 3/3 of the Department of the Interior, with Department 3/3 of the Budapest Police Headquarters or any of the County Police Headquarters, and/or with the predecessors of these organizations (Division of Political Security at the Budapest Headquarters of the Hungarian State Police, the organizational units specialized in counterintelligence activities targeting "Internal Reactionaries" under the control of the Department of State Security of the Hungarian State Police, the State Security Organization of the Department of the Interior, and of the State Security Organization, Department 4, also called the Internal Reaction Counterintelligence Unit of the Department of the Interior, Department 5, also called the Department for the Fight Against Internal Reactionaries, which was under control of the Division of Political Investigations of the Department of the Interior) according to the final version, dated February 14, 1990, of the relevant Register on file with the Department of the Interior; or

(b) provided to the agencies listed in item (a) statements related to the acceptance of network assignments and bearing their own signatures, and submitted any reports or received any kind of commission, bonus or benefit for their activities; or

(c) served in the State security units of the armed forces during 1956 through 1957; or

(d) held any political or government office in which they received information on data falling under the authority of agencies described in item (a) in order to facilitate their decision making activities; or

(e) were members of the Hungarian Nazi Party.

§ 2

The verification described in § 1 shall include the data on

1. members of the Parliament;
2. all individuals elected by the Parliament and required to take an oath;
3. members of the Government;

4. the president of the Hungarian National Bank;
5. the political, honorary and administrative assistant secretaries of state, and the government officials of identical legal status;
6. the mayor of the capital;
7. ambassadors;
8. deputy assistant secretaries of state and the directors of national public agencies, and other public service officials of identical legal status;
9. the commanding officer and the chief of staff of the Hungarian Army, the national commanding officer of the Frontier Patrol Corps, and the national chief commissioner of police;
10. the presidents of the Hungarian Radio, the Hungarian Television and the general director of the Hungarian News Service;
11. individuals assigned to permanent positions by rank of a general, and the chief commissioners of police;
12. vice presidents of the Hungarian National Bank;
13. deputies of the commanding officer and the chief of staff of the Hungarian Army, the national commanding officer of the Frontier Patrol Corps, and the national chief commissioner of police;
14. division heads of the Departments, and the government officials of identical legal status;
15. chairpersons of the general assemblies of each county, the mayors of the cities and the districts of the capital, and the deputies of the mayor of the capital;
16. vice presidents of the Hungarian Radio, the Hungarian Television and the deputy general directors of the Hungarian News Service;
17. chiefs of police;
18. presidents, deans and general directors of the universities and colleges with majority State ownership (control);
19. career judges;
20. district attorneys;
21. the editors, and employees holding positions higher than the editors, of the Hungarian Radio, the Hungarian Television or the Hungarian News Service;
22. editors, and employees holding positions higher than the editors, at daily newspapers and weekly magazines averaging over 30,000 copies per edition;
23. department heads, and the officials with higher positions, at universities and colleges with majority State ownership (control);
24. directors of economic agencies with full State or majority State ownership (control);
25. managers of banks, specialized financial institutions and insurance agencies with majority State ownership.

§ 3

The verification shall be performed in the order specified in § 2, with reference to positions described under the same item, in alphabetical order of the names of the individuals concerned, and on the basis of a list of names which is suitable for the purpose of identification and compiled by the committee described in § 5.

§ 4

Upon the request of ecclesiastical officials or organs with proper authorization, the verification in accordance with § 1, regarding individuals holding ecclesiastical positions specified by those making the request, will be performed by the Secretary of the Interior, or the Secretary of Defense, who will also inform the solicitor about his findings.

§ 5

(1) The verification shall be performed by two or more committees, each consisting of three judges. The committees shall consist of judges nominated by the National Security Committee of the Parliament and appointed by the Parliament for a specified term, and approved by the Chief Justice of the Supreme Court.

(2) In case of the incapacity of a member of the committee a new member shall be appointed by the Parliament according to the procedure described in paragraph (1). The appointment of the new committee member shall cease upon the termination of the incapacity.

(3) The nomination to be a member of the committee requires the consent of the judge concerned.

(4) The judge appointed as a member of the committee may not administer justice, and his service relations shall be suspended from the date of the appointment until the termination of his membership in the committee. The period of suspension shall be considered time of service.

(5) With reference to the legal status of employment of the members of the committee, with the exception of remuneration, Law No. 23 (*sic*) of 1992 on the legal status of public officials shall be applicable. Remuneration to the members of the committee shall be provided by the Government.

(6) The members of the committee act independently, but within the confines of the laws. The members of the committee shall not be held responsible for facts or opinions stated in the course of their performing these duties, but are not released from their obligation to follow the provisions of the statutes on secrecy.

§ 6

(1) Judges may be nominated as members of the committee only if they were never involved in activities specified in § 1, nor participated in passing judgements which were vacated by virtue of Law No. 36 of 1989 on the remedy of convictions related to the public uprising of 1956, of Law No. 26 of 1990 on the voiding of convictions resulting from judgements passed unlawfully between 1945 and 1963, and of Law No. 11 of 1992 on the voiding of convictions resulting from judgements passed for certain crimes committed against the State and the public order between 1963 and 1989.

(2) Before the nomination each judge is required to sign a written statement whether or not he/she was ever involved in activities specified in § 1, or participated in passing judgements described in paragraph (1).

§ 7

The background checks on the judges appointed to the committee shall be performed by the National Security Committee of the Parliament on the basis of the information provided by the Secretary of the Interior and the Secretary of Defense with reference to the individuals concerned. If no information is available to the Secretary of the Interior or the Secretary of Defense regarding the individuals concerned, the National Security Committee of the Parliament shall be informed by such secretaries about this matter.

§ 8

The committee, and, during the background verification process set forth in § 7, the National Security Committee of the Parliament, may examine—in compliance with the statutes on secrecy and without any other restriction—the documents related to activities specified in § 1(hereinafter: Register), with respect to the individuals checked, and may request information contained in the Register from the Secretary of the Interior, or—with reference to service in the State security units of the Armed Forces—from the Secretary of the Interior and the Secretary of Defense.

§ 9

The Secretary of the Interior, jointly with the Secretary of Defense with reference to service in the State security units of the Armed Forces, shall provide the conditions necessary for the National Security Committee of the Parliament and the committee to examine the Register.

§ 10

(1) Upon the commencement of a background verification procedure, the committee will send a timely written notification to the individual whose background is being checked, and at the same time inform him/her that he/she may appear before the committee on the date specified in the notification to state his/her position, or submit it in writing by a certain date. At least 15 days before the date specified in the notification, the committee shall inform the individual under background investigation about the data referring to his/her activities described in § 1, or about the fact that no such information was found.

(2) Before the date specified in the notification from the committee, the individual subjected to checking may request the committee to set another date not exceeding 15 more days than the previously set date for him/her to appear in person, or to submit his/her position in writing.

(3) If the individual under background investigation does not appear before the committee, nor does he/she submit his/her position in writing until the date specified in paragraph (2), the committee will make its decision described in § 14 on the basis of the available information.

§ 11

(1) If the individual under background investigation proves that he/she does not hold a position specified in § 2, or resigned from that position, or has initiated his/her own discharge, the verification procedure must be terminated immediately. The committee shall inform the individual under background investigation about the termination of the verification procedure without delay.

(2) If the individual concerned requests the investigation on the basis of § 22, it must be performed accordingly.

§ 12

Besides examining the Register, the committee may use any lawful means of evidence during the procedure in order to verify the data found in the Register.

§ 13

The procedure must be conducted by the committee behind closed doors, in the course of which only individuals invited and, on the date specified in paragraphs (1) and (2) of § 10, the individual under background investigation, may be present. Information used and/or developed during the proceedings of the committee is to be handled in accordance with the regulations pertaining to State secrets.

§ 14

As a result of the background verification procedure, the committee may establish in its decision whether or not the individual under background investigation was involved in activities described in § 1.

§ 15

In its decision, the committee shall present the information on which the decision is based and disclose it to the individual under background investigation without delay.

§ 16

The committee shall make its decision by a secret vote, by majority.

§ 17

All other rules and regulations of the operation of the committee shall be established by the committee.

§ 18

(1) If, according to the decision of the committee, the individual under background investigation was involved in activities described in § 1, the committee will request that he/she resign from his position within 30 days, or initiate his/her own discharge, and at the same time inform the individual that otherwise the decision of the committee will be made public after the 15th day following the said 30 days. The committee furthermore notifies the individual under background investigation that he/she may appeal the

decision in court and request the annulment of the decision. No court proceedings are allowed for reasons of violation of privacy rights with respect to the statements as stated in the decision.

(2) The committee shall announce its decision in the personal section of the Hungarian Journal, and at the same time forward it to the Hungarian News Service for the purpose of release.

§ 19

(1) The individual under background investigation may take legal action against the decision by filing a claim with the Municipal Court within 15 days of the public announcement of the same.

(2) The regulations governing the judicial review of administrative decisions (Civil Code, Chapter 20) shall be applicable in these legal proceedings.

(3) The court shall inform the committee without delay if a claim has been filed.

(4) The filing of a claim has a delaying force regarding the public release of the decision of the committee.

(5) The action shall be brought against the Department of the Interior, or in case information relevant to service in the State security units of the Armed Forces is challenged—if the records are not kept by the Department of the Interior—against the Department of Defense.

(6) The court shall inform the committee of its final decree.

(7) The legal proceedings shall be conducted by the court in a closed hearing.

§ 20

(1) If the individual under background investigation is requested by the committee to resign his/her position or to initiate his/her own discharge, but the individual resigns or initiates his/her discharge within 30 days of the announcement of the decision, or in case of legal proceedings described in § 19 within 30 days of the release of the final decision regarding the dismissal of the claim, and informs the committee about the completion of the same in a credible manner within 15 days following the said 30 days, the committee will not disclose the decision.

(2) The committee will not disclose its decision if it was abrogated by a final decree issued in the course of legal proceedings described in § 19.

§ 21

If an individual is requested by the committee to resign his/her position or to initiate his/her own discharge, and the individual does not resign or initiate his/her own discharge within 30 days of the announcement of the decision, further, in case of legal proceedings described in § 19, within 30 days of the issuance of the final decision regarding the dismissal of the claim, the committee shall disclose its decision within 15 days following the said 30 days, and at the same time, based on the request of the committee, the Secretary of the Interior shall declassify the "secret" information.

§ 22

(1) Those who resign their positions listed in § 2 while this Law is in effect, or hold elected positions which shall be affected by new elections during that time, but decide not to run for office, may request the committee to certify that they were not members or agents of the organizations specified in § 1.

(2) Upon filing their application, the persons described in paragraph (1) are required to prove that they have resigned or have withdrawn from candidature.

(3) If the applicant is not found in the Register, the committee will issue a certificate about the same within 30 days.

§ 23

A copy of the decision and of the final court decree, the certificate proving that the individual under background investigation does not hold the position described in § 2, as well as the documents attesting to the fact that the individual under background investigation has resigned his/her position or initiated his/her own discharge, shall be attached to the records related to the individual under background investigation and kept on file in accordance with the regulations on secrecy.

§ 24

The funds necessary for the operation of the committee and payment for the expenses incurred by the Department of the Interior and by the Department of Defense in connection with the examination of the records in the Register shall be provided for in the appropriation bill.

§ 25

Unless otherwise provided by the Law, the records related to the individual under background investigation may not be reviewed for 30 years starting from the announcement of the decision or the final decree, or with respect to other individuals, for 30 years starting from the 6th year after the Law has taken effect. The Secretary of the Interior is responsible for the safeguarding of the Register, or with reference to service in the State security units of the Armed Forces, the Secretary of the Interior and the Secretary of Defense.

§ 26

No supplemental payment may be made to staff members assigned to perform "top secret" duties serving in Division 3/3 (State Security) of the Department of the Interior and/or at its predecessors, for which they would be entitled on their past service time. This provision does not affect pension eligibility based on the length of employment.

§ 27

(1) With the exception set forth in paragraph (2), this Law will take effect on July 1, 1994, and, with the exception of §§ 23, 25 and 26; it will cease to have effect on June 30, 2000.

(2) §§ 5 through 9, and, with respect to the verification of the information on a member of the committee described in § 5, § 1 of the Law, shall take effect on the day it is made public.

(3) The background checks of individuals holding positions listed in § 2 as of July 1, 1994 are to be completed no later than June 30, 1995, and in case of those accepting such positions later, within one year of taking office.

(4) In case of those holding offices listed in § 2 repeatedly during the period this Law is in effect, the background verification procedure—provided it was completed previously—does not have to be performed again, even if a request, as described in paragraph (3), is received. In this case, the committee shall request the individual under background investigation to resign his/her position or to initiate his/her own discharge by virtue of its previous decision. Regarding the announcement of the decision, the committee shall take steps by reasonable application of the provisions of §§ 20 and 21 for setting a date reckoned from the date of notification.

ITALY: CONSTITUTION—
TRANSITORY AND FINAL PROVISIONS

(1947)

XII

Reorganization of the former Fascist Party, under any form whatsoever, is prohibited.

Notwithstanding Article 48, temporary limitations are established by law, for a period of not over five years from the effective date of the Constitution, on the suffrage and eligibility of the responsible heads of the Fascist regime.

LITHUANIA: DECREE BANNING KGB EMPLOYEES AND INFORMERS FROM GOVERNMENT POSITIONS

Decree No. 418 (October 12, 1991)

Concerning Those Who Worked for the Committee for State Security of the Former USSR

In view of the crimes and anti-State activities of the Committee for State Security [KGB] of the USSR and their activities in the Republic of Lithuania, it is decreed:

(1) It is ordered that former employees of the Committee for State Security, including informers (agents), may not serve in the ministerial departments of the Republic of Lithuania, other State services and inspectorates, the basic structures of ministries and their sub-divisions (departments), or as leading employees of cities and districts (as administrators and their deputies) for a period of 5 years.

Former employees of the Committee for State Security of the USSR, as well as informers (agents), presently serving in such capacities must resign their positions no later than October 1, 1992.

(2) We would like to point attention to the fact that all who collaborate with the Committee for State Security of the USSR and its structures will be considered to be criminals against the State and will be brought to criminal responsibility according to the procedure established by law.

LITHUANIA: LAW ON THE VERIFICATION OF MANDATES OF THOSE DEPUTIES ACCUSED OF CONSCIOUSLY COLLABORATING WITH SPECIAL SERVICES OF OTHER STATES

Law No. I-2115 (December 17, 1991)

The Soviet State security agencies, in an effort to organize divisive activities against the Lithuanian State and its institutions, created a wide net of secret collaborators into which deputies of various levels may have been taken. It is the opinion of the Supreme Council that, should the secret collaboration by deputies with the KGB (MVD) and other special services become clear, it would be the basis for questioning good faith in them by the voters. In view of this, the Supreme Council has set down the following verification mechanism of their mandates (that is, confirmation or nullification).

Article 1

If it is alleged after the elections that a deputy was a conscious collaborator with the special agencies of the USSR or agencies of other governments (security, intelligence or counter-intelligence), a special commission of deputies will be established to investigate the facts, and, when necessary, will seek the assistance of procurators and the officials of internal affairs and the national security service.

Article 2

The commission of deputies will question the accused deputy, familiarizing him with the facts indicating his collaboration, will listen to his explanations and, evaluating the facts which would show his innocence, inform him of the conclusions of the commission. If the deputy does not show any essential contradictions in the conclusions of the commission, he will sign the conclusions and then these conclusions will be forwarded without delay to the appropriate council and deputy.

Article 3

In those instances in which the accused deputy does not admit collaboration with the special agencies of other States and the charges against him, the commission of deputies will forward to the courts the accumulated facts as well as other evidence, testifying to the collaboration of the individual with special agencies, that is to say, to the affirmation or negation of such facts.

As soon as the commission of deputies receives the decision of the court regarding facts which confirm such collaboration, it shall be forwarded to the appropriate council.

Article 4

Whether or not the commission of deputies has properly and juridically evaluated the accumulated evidence will be analyzed by:

1) for a deputy of the Supreme Council of the Republic of Lithuania—the chamber of first instance of the civil division of the Supreme Court;
2) for local government deputies—the district or city court.

Such evidence shall be examined by the court according to the procedure of the court and without delay.

Article 5

Throughout this Law, the term "collaboration" is to be understood as including the following:

1) Inclusion of an individual in the lists of the KGB/MVD or other special services as a resident, agent, administrator or informer and if evidence exists of his specific activities;
2) The providing of facilities to the KGB (special services) to organize or implement subversive activities;
3) Any other systematic, conscious (and repeated) efforts to provide the KGB or other special services with information, the receiving or implementing of assignments from them;
4) Official activities in the service of such security services.

Article 6

The Council, having received the commission's conclusions supported by the fact of the collaboration of a deputy with the KGB or other special services, or an appropriate decision of a court to this effect, direct the electoral commissions of the Republic or the relevant district, city or county to organize a vote for the specific purpose of confirming or nullifying the deputy's mandate, and this will suspend the mandate for such period of time until the deputy's mandate is verified.

Article 7

The electoral commission of the Republic, district or city, having received specific instructions of the Council to verify the mandate of the deputy, shall organize a vote and conduct it according to this Law and the laws of the Supreme Council of the Republic of Lithuania and local councils.

Article 8

The electoral commission of the Republic, district or city, having received the appropriate instructions of the Council, will assign an election date within 5 days for the verification of a deputy's mandate and will notify the deputy as well as the voters.

The election date cannot be set any later than 30 days from receipt of the notice.

Article 9

The electoral commissions of the Republic, district or city, within 7 days from the receipt of the notice, shall organize electoral regions and committees.

Article 10

Persons are empowered to vote in the districts in accordance with verified voter registration lists.

The ballot for verification of a deputy's mandate include the name of the deputy, his surname, the election district and the following text:

> In view of the fact that deputy ___ collaborated with the KGB (or other special services), as shown in the facts which have become clear, I am in favor of the mandate of this deputy being
> "Confirmed"
> "Declared null"
> (Cross out the unnecessary word)

The publication of the electoral ballot as well as the commissions concerned with them and their order is set by the Republic, district or city electoral commissions....

Article 11

The mandate of a deputy is confirmed if he has received more than one half of the votes of voters listed in the electoral list of the election district.

If less than one half of the voters have confirmed the mandate of a deputy, or if less than one half of voters listed in the electoral list of the electoral district participate in the election, his mandate is considered to be annulled, i.e. not in force effective the day of the vote.

The results of the voting are forwarded by the electoral commission to the appropriate Council for verification.

Article 12

Repeated votes for the verification of the mandate of a deputy are not permitted, with the exception of those instances in which the electoral commission establishes that, during the counting of votes or the determination of results, a law has been violated which had an essential impact on the results of the election. In such cases, the electoral commission of the Republic, district or city shall conduct a second vote for verification of the deputy's mandate.

Complaints and announcements concerning the organization of the election and its implementation are to be examined by the electoral commission of the Republic.

Article 13

A deputy under investigation for collaboration with special services has the right to resign at any stage of the development of the investigation by submitting his notice to the appropriate council for which he withdraws as deputy.

Such a request must be accepted by the council without further debate, with the exception of those cases in which there is evidence that the deputy was not acting according to his free will.

Article 14

This Law is effective from the date of adoption and applies to activities committed after June 15, 1940.

RUSSIA: DECREES BANNING THE COMMUNIST PARTY

Decree on Suspending the Activity of the Communist Party of the Russian Soviet Federated Socialist Republic
Decree No. 79 (August 25, 1991)

The Communist Party [CP] of the Russian Soviet Federated Socialist Republic [RSFSR], operating on the territory of the RSFSR and not registered by the stipulated procedure, supported the so-called State Committee for the State of Emergency in the USSR, which carried out a coup d'état and removed the USSR President from his post by violent means. Emergency committees (commissions) were set up in a number of regions of the RSFSR with the direct participation of republican, kray, and oblast organs of the CP of the RSFSR, which is a gross violation of the USSR law on "public associations."

The organs of the CP of the RSFSR in the republics, krays, and oblasts have on several occasions, in spite of the RSFSR Constitution, interfered in judicial activity, and are obstructing the execution of the RSFSR President's Decree of 20 July 1991 "On Discontinuing the Activity of the Organizational Structures of Political Parties and Mass Public Movements in State Organs, Establishments, and Organizations in the RSFSR."

On the basis of the above, I decree:

1. The RSFSR Ministry of Internal Affairs and the RSFSR Procuracy are to carry out an investigation into cases of anti-constitutional activity by organs of the CP of the RSFSR. The relevant materials are to be sent for examination by judicial organs.
2. Until the question of the unconstitutionality of the actions of the CP of the RSFSR have been resolved by judicial procedures, the activity of the organs and organizations of the CP of the RSFSR is to be suspended.
3. The Ministry of Internal Affairs of the RSFSR is to guarantee that the property and monetary resources of the bodies and organizations of the CP of the RSFSR are to be kept safe until the adoption of a final decision by the judicial bodies.
4. The central bank of the RSFSR is to guarantee that operations to suspend resources from the accounts of the bodies and organizations of the CP of the RSFSR are to be suspended until special instructions are issued.
5. The proposal is to be made to the procuracy's office of the RSFSR that it guarantee supervision of the execution of the above Decree.
6. This Decree comes into force when it is signed.

———— ⣿⬧⣿ ————

Decree on the Property of the Communist Party of the Soviet Union and the Communist Party of the Russian Soviet Federated Socialist Republic

Decree No. 90 (August 25, 1991)

In connection with the dismissal of the Central Committee of the Communist Party of the Soviet Union [CPSU] and suspension of operating activities by the Communist Party [CP] of the Russian Soviet Federated Socialist Republic [RSFSR] the following was decided:

1. To declare all real and movable property of the CPSU and the CP of the RSFSR as government property of the RSFSR, including monetary assets denominated in rubles or foreign currency, held by banks, insurance agencies, joint-stock companies, joint ventures and other establishments and organizations in the territory of the RSFSR and abroad.
   The assets of the CPSU located abroad shall be distributed among the republics in accordance with the terms of an agreement to be reached after they sign a Federal Treaty.
2. The Central Bank of the RSFSR, the Bank of External Trade of the RSFSR, and the Ministry of Finance of the RSFSR must strictly monitor all monetary assets denominated in rubles or foreign currency of the CPSU and the CP of the RSFSR, held by the State National Bank of the USSR (Gosbank), the Bank of the External Trade of the USSR, the Ministry of Finance of the USSR and other organizations and establishments of the USSR in the territory of the RSFSR, and suspend their use until released by a special order of the President of the RSFSR or the Chairman of the Ministry Council of the RSFSR.
3. To transfer the usage rights within the territory of the RSFSR of the real and movable property of the CPSU and the CP of the RSFSR, being the property of the Central Committee of the CPSU and of the Central Committee of the CP of the RSFSR, to the Ministry Council of the RSFSR. The usage rights of the property of the republican, kray, oblast, district, city and rayon committees of the CPSU and the CP of the RSFSR shall be turned over to the appropriate organizations with executive power in the RSFSR in the territory where they are located.

Several buildings of the Central Committee of the CPSU in Moscow shall be turned over to the Ministry Council of the RSFSR and the Federal Republics which are members of the USSR.

4. To transfer the Public-Political Center of the Moscow State Committee and the Moscow Committee of the CP of the Soviet Union located at 2 Tsvetnoy Blvd. to the Presidium of the Supreme Soviet of the RSFSR.

5. To charge all organizations with executive power at the RSFSR, the Ministry Council of the RSFSR, the Ministry of Internal Affairs of the RSFSR, the Committee of State Security (KGB) of the RSFSR with the responsibility of preventing any attempts to damage or embezzle the real or movable property of the CPSU and the CP of the RSFSR as well as attempts to use this property for mercenary purposes by individuals or organizations.

   To charge all organizations with executive power with the responsibility to provide broad public notification of the populace regarding their decisions on the use of the above-indicated property.

6. The Ministry of Foreign Affairs of the RSFSR shall immediately appeal to the governments of all countries to freeze funds of the CPSU held by banks and other organizations of these countries and shall also notify the Ministry Council of the RSFSR regarding the amount of these funds and the corresponding bank information.

7. This Decree becomes effective from the moment of its signing.

Decree on the Activities of the Communist Party of the Soviet Union and the Communist Party of the Russian Soviet Federated Republic

Decree No. 169 (November 6, 1991)

The events of 19-21 August made it very obvious that the Communist Party of the Soviet Union [CPSU] has never been a party. It was a special mechanism to form and implement political power by integrating it with State structures or subordinating them directly to the CPSU.

The leading CPSU structures were implementing their own dictatorship and were setting up, at the expense of the State, a property basis for unlimited power.

This was confirmed in the course of open hearings at the Russian Soviet Federated Socialist Republic [RSFSR] Supreme Soviet dedicated to the role of the CPSU in the coup d'état of 19-21 August.

The CPSU leading structures, which have basically absorbed the State and which have been using it as their own instrument, are responsible for a historical impasse into which the peoples of the Soviet Union were pushed and for the disarray in which we found ourselves.

The activity of these structures were manifestly against people and against the Constitution. They were directly connected with stirring up religious, social, and national strife among the peoples of the country. They were encroaching upon fundamental human and citizens' rights and freedoms recognized by the entire international community.

The anti-constitutional coup of 19-21 August that was supported by the CPSU leadership served as the natural end of its political activities.

In spite of the measures adopted in relation to these structures, they did not stop their unlawful activities aimed at further worsening the crisis and creating conditions for a new coup against the people.

It has become clear that while the CPSU structures exist there can be no guarantees against another putsch or coup taking place.

Attempts to blacken the names of millions of ordinary members of the party who have nothing to do with the arbitrary rule of force carried out in their names or to introduce a ban on them in the professions is not to be tolerated, but attempts to reanimate the gigantic mechanisms of the Communist Party [CP] machinery and to give it the opportunity to trample the shoots of Russian democracy are likewise not to be tolerated.

Taking into account that the CP of the RSFSR has not been registered properly and that the earlier registration of the CPSU by the USSR State bodies that were directly in charge of the CPSU Central Committee was carried out with blatant violations of the law and therefore, in the RSFSR, does not have legal force, and on the basis of the implementation of Articles 7 and 124-4 of the RSFSR Constitution, I resolve:

1. To put a stop to the activities in the RSFSR of the CPSU, the CP of the RSFSR, and to dissolve their organizational structures.
2. To eliminate the possibility of the State bodies of the RSFSR executive authority in krays, oblasts, autonomous oblasts, autonomous okrugs, and in the cities of Moscow and St. Petersburg as well as the procuracy bodies from persecuting RSFSR citizens for belonging to the CPSU or the CP of the RSFSR.
3. The property of the CPSU and the CP of the RSFSR in the RSFSR is to be handed over to State ownership. The RSFSR Council of Ministers is to supervise the handover of the property in the RSFSR belonging to the CPSU and the CP of the RSFSR as well as its coming under the jurisdiction of the bodies of State administration in the RSFSR and in the republics within the RSFSR.
4. The RSFSR Council of Ministers, the RSFSR ministries and departments, the relevant RSFSR executive bodies in the republics, krays, oblasts, autonomous oblasts, autonomous okrugs, and the cities of Moscow and St. Petersburg are to adopt the necessary measures to ensure the immediate and thorough implementation of this Decree.

RUSSIA: CONSTITUTIONAL COURT DECISION ON THE BANNING OF THE COMMUNIST PARTY

(November 30, 1992)

In the matter of examining the constitutionality of the following decrees by the President of the Russian Federation was considered in open session: No. 79 "On Suspending the Activity of the Communist Party of the Russian Soviet Federated Socialist Republic [CP RSFSR] dated 23 August 1991, No 90 "On the Property of the Communist Party of the Soviet Union [CPSU] and the Communist Party of the RSFSR" dated 25 August 1991, and No 169 "On the Activity of the CPSU and the CP RSFSR" dated 6 November 1991; and also of examining the constitutionality of the CPSU and the CP RSFSR.

...The grounds for considering the matter, in accordance with Article 58 Section 4 of the Law on the Constitutional Court of the Russian Federation, was a petition from a group of Russian Federation people's deputies to examine the constitutionality of these decrees, including the demand to recognize that they are not in accordance with the 24 May and 1 November 1991 versions of the Constitution of the Russian Federation since, in the opinion of the petitioners, in issuing these decrees, the President of the Russian Federation encroached into the sphere of the legislative and judicial authorities.

1....The need to examine the constitutionality of the aforementioned decrees in a single procedure resulted from the direct link between these enactments, namely, that they have the same subject of regulation and they touch upon a single set of legal relationships. The decrees concern the activity on the territory of the Russian Federation of a single organization—the CPSU and the CP RSFSR as an integral part thereof; and property that the CPSU possessed, enjoyed, and disposed of on the territory of the Russian Federation, and they also include an assessment of the activity of organizational structures of the Communist Party.

The decree of the President of the Russian Federation dated 23 August 1991 suspended the activity of the CP RSFSR, and the decree dated 6 November 1991 halted the activity of the CPSU and the CP RSFSR on the territory of the Russian Federation; the decree dated 23 August 1991 entrusted the RSFSR Ministry of Internal Affairs with the task of ensuring the safekeeping of the property of the CP RSFSR, and the RSFSR Central Bank with the task of freezing accounts belonging to organs and organizations of the CP RSFSR, while the decrees of 25 August and 6 November 1991 made provision for a number of custodial measures with respect to the property of the CPSU and the CP RSFSR on the territory of the Russian Federation, which was pronounced to be State property, and in this connection the right to enjoy this property was transferred to State bodies. The measures envisaged with respect to the CPSU and CP RSFSR in the decrees of 23 and 25 August 1991 were enlarged upon in the decree of 6

November 1991, which in terms of its legal consequences largely cancels out the two preceding decrees....

2. During the period of preparation for consideration of this petition, petitions from a number of people's deputies of the Russian Federation were filed with the Constitutional Court between 12 and 25 May 1992 regarding an examination of the constitutionality of the CPSU and the CP RSFSR. The petitions ... contain demands to recognize the CPSU and the CP RSFSR as unconstitutional organizations, while recognizing the above-mentioned decrees as constitutional.... Article 165-1, included in the Constitution of the Russian Federation of 21 April 1992 and entering into force on 16 May 1992, empowers the Constitutional Court to examine matters concerning the constitutionality of political parties and other public associations....

The preamble to the decree of the President of the Russian Federation "On the Activity of the CPSU and the CP RSFSR" dated 6 November 1991 controverts the nature of the CPSU as a political party. At the same time the question of the constitutionality of the CPSU and the CP RSFSR is closely linked with the question of their legal nature, which is the point of departure in assessing the constitutionality of measures adopted with respect to them in accordance with the decrees being examined. Thus, there is an obvious commonality between the subject of the petitions filed with the Constitutional Court by various groups of people's deputies of the Russian Federation.

On this basis, ... the Constitutional Court has consolidated the petition to examine the constitutionality of the three above-named decrees by the President of the Russian Federation and the petitions to examine the constitutionality of the CPSU and the CP RSFSR....

3. The decrees in question were issued by the President of the Russian Federation under conditions of contradiction and gaps in the legislative regulation of the activity of political parties in the Russian Federation.

The only republic-level enactment regulating the status of public associations that existed in the Russian Federation was the Statute on Voluntary Societies and Unions dated 10 July 1932, which contained, in particular, provisions on administrative procedure for liquidating these public associations. The Statute on Voluntary Societies and Unions, however, defined the legal status not of parties, trade unions and other mass public associations, but "organizations for public self-initiated activity by the working masses in cities and the countryside," and supervision and control of them was entrusted to the central and local bodies of executive power. Therefore this statute cannot serve as a legal basis for defining the constitutionality of political parties and the competence of State bodies relating to parties during the period when the decrees in question were issued.

With respect to the 9 October 1990 USSR Law "On Public Associations," in practice this law was in fact declared to be in force and was applied on the territory of the Russian Federation. It can be seen from the content of the 23 August 1991 decree "On Suspending the Activity of the CP RSFSR" that the President of the Russian Federation also proceeded on that basis.

After having examined the decrees in question and having heard statements from the parties involved, and the conclusions of experts and testimony of witnesses, and having studied the documents presented, and being guided in this case by Article 1 Section 4 and Article 32 of the Law on the Russian Federation Constitutional Court, the Russian Federation Constitutional Court has ruled as follows:

I

It is claimed in the petition of the group of people's deputies of the Russian Federation that the 23 August 1991 decree of the President of the Russian Federation "On Suspending the Activity of the CP RSFSR" is anticonstitutional since suspension of the activity of a public association is possible only in a state of emergency, which did not exist at the time when the decree was issued, and thus the President of the Russian Federation exceeded his powers.

Representatives of the President of the Russian Federation have asserted that the President's decision to suspend the activity of the CP RSFSR on the territory of the Russian Federation was in accordance with his constitutional powers established in ... the Constitution of the Russian Federation by the delineation of competence among the highest bodies of government and control in the Russian Federation.

It follows from what is contained in the 23 August 1991 decree that when the President of the Russian Federation issued it, he proceeded on the basis of the status of the Communist Party as a public association. In particular, it was noted in the decree that the CP RSFSR was not registered in accordance with established procedure, and that organs of the Communist Party supported the State Committee for the State of Emergency and were directly involved in the creation of emergency committees in a number of regions, which was in gross violation of the Constitution and laws of the Russian Federation and the USSR Law "On Public Associations," and also hindered compliance with the President of the Russian Federation's decree "On Suspending the Activity of Organizational Structures of Political Parties and Mass Public Movements in State Bodies, Institutions, and Organs of the RSFSR" dated 20 July 1991.

It was stated in the Declaration on the State Sovereignty of the Russian Federation, adopted on 12 June 1990 by the First Congress of People's Deputies of the Russian Federation, that the Russian Federation guarantees to all citizens, political parties, and other public associations operating within the framework of the Constitution of the Russian Federation equal legal opportunities to participate in the management of State and public affairs. Article 7 of the Constitution of the Russian Federation in the wording of 16 June 1990 established that all political parties, public associations, and mass movements carrying out the functions envisaged in their programs and charters should operate within the framework of the Constitution of the USSR, the Constitution of the Russian Federation, and the constitutions of the republics making up the Russian Federation, and the laws of the USSR, the Russian Federation, and the republics making up the Russian Federation.

The CP RSFSR was founded in 1990. It was created as part of the CPSU. Paragraph 2 of the resolution of the CP RSFSR Constituent Congress stated as follows: "It is established that the Communist Party of the RSFSR unites party organizations located on the territory of the republic, is an integral part of the CPSU, is guided by its program documents and charter, and has a single party card with it." (*Pravda* 22 June 1990). It was stated in the declaration adopted by the Constituent Congress that the CP RSFSR was formed as part of a unified and renewed CPSU. These provisions were reproduced in the Appeal of the Constituent Congress to the communist parties of the union republics, the Appeal to the Communists and Peoples of Russia, and the Resolution on the Present Time and the Priority Tasks of the Communist Party of the RSFSR (*Pravda* 24 June 1990).

This position was not subsequently officially revised. All documents of the CP RSFSR testify that it considered itself a structural part of the CPSU. In accordance with the CPSU Statutes [by-laws], the CP RSFSR ... was obliged to follow its line in the sphere of state building and socioeconomic and cultural development in the republic (paragraph 22). Consequently, no provision was made for registration of the CP RSFSR. Neither did the CP RSFSR enjoy the rights of a legal entity.

The purpose of the CP RSFSR was to unite party organizations of the CPSU located on the territory of the RSFSR, coordinate and direct their activity, and represent them in mutual relations with CPSU organs and also other parties and movements.

The following circumstances also prove that the CP RSFSR was not an independent party:

a) The CP RSFSR came into being on the initiative of the CPSU Central Committee Politburo as an integral part of the CPSU. The corresponding decision was adopted on 3 May 1990. It was subsequently confirmed in a CPSU Central Committee Politburo decision of 8 June 1990. However, in accordance with the USSR Law "On Public Associations," the initiators in the creation of a party can only be citizens, not a party (Article 8 sections 1 and 2);

b) According to the CPSU Statutes, the communist parties of the union republics were declared to be independent within the CPSU system and likewise, membership in any of them at the same time meant membership in the CPSU. Here, paragraph 2 of the Statutes banned a member of the CPSU from being a member of other parties. Hence, the formation of the CP RSFSR as an integral part of the CPSU did not alter the status of communists on the territory of the Russian Federation: They remained members of the CPSU but became members through the CP RSFSR;

c) In accordance with the above-mentioned law, a voluntary formation that has come into being as the result of the free will of citizens banding together on the basis of commonality of interests is deemed to be a public association. No attention was paid to this in the formation of the CP RSFSR. The Constituent Congress received that status during the course of the work of the Russian Party

Conference; its participants were elected to the 28th CPSU Congress as delegates for the communists of Russia, who were not granted powers to create an independent party. The will of the communist CPSU members from Russia with respect to the creation of a new communist party, and with respect to each of them joining it and leaving the CPSU, was not made known. This is permissible if the formation of the CP RSFSR is regarded as a structural re-arrangement of the CPSU. But if the status of the CP RSFSR is analyzed from the standpoint of its claims to be called an independent party, independent of the CPSU, then ignoring the demands with respect to voluntariness and the free will of citizens becomes an additional and weighty basis for refusal to recognize the CP RSFSR as a new party independent of the CPSU. Moreover, the law excludes collective membership in a party; it can be only individual;

d) The CP RSFSR did not have its own Statutes or its own Program.

Thus, the CP RSFSR was not an independent party and there was no need to register it. Therefore, the charge made against it with respect to non-registration as contained in the preambles of the decrees of the President of the Russian Federation "On Suspending the Activity of the CP RSFSR" dated 23 August 1991, and "On the Activity of the CPSU and the CP RSFSR" dated 6 November 1991 should be deemed to be of no legal value....

Since it was an integral part of the CPSU, the CP RSFSR could not become an independent owner of property separate from the CPSU.

In the resolution of the First Congress of People's Deputies of the Russian Federation "On the Mechanism for Government by the People in the RSFSR" and in the "Decree on Power" in the Russian Federation adopted by the Congress as a basis, the equality of citizens was proclaimed, regardless, in particular, of political or other convictions or affiliation with parties or other public associations operating within the law (which was secured in Article 34 of the Constitution of the RSFSR); the holding of any position by leaders in the organs of government and control while simultaneously holding any other position was banned, including in political or sociopolitical organizations; and it was established that "any unlawful interference by political parties, party-political organs or other public organizations in the activity of the organs of government and control or in the economic and sociocultural activity of State enterprises, institutions, and organizations should be stopped immediately and decisively." In the implementation of these decisions of the Congress, on 20 July 1991 the President of the Russian Federation issued the decree "On Suspending the Activity of Organizational Structures of Political Parties and Mass Public Movements in State Organs, Institutions, and Organizations in the RSFSR."...

On 19 August 1991, in a statement from the Soviet leadership, a state of emergency was declared in particular localities of the USSR (which were not defined), and in order to manage the country and effectively handle the regime of a state of emergency, the State Committee for the State of

Emergency (GKChP) in the USSR was formed, that is, an unconstitutional State body.

The leadership of the CPSU and the CP RSFSR and many area [oblast] and territorial [kray] party committees directly or indirectly supported the actions of the unconstitutional GKChP, and this is confirmed in particular by the following:...

[The Court then lists several documents demonstrating the relationship of the CPSU and the CP RSFSR with the GKChP.]

Under conditions of virtual inaction by the highest State organs in the USSR, the President of the Russian Federation issued a number of decrees aimed at safeguarding the Constitution and the rule of law, and at ensuring State and public safety. Here, the President exercised the powers afforded to him by the Constitution and the 21 August 1991 resolution of the Russian Federation Supreme Soviet "On Additional Powers for the President of the Russian Federation To Ensure Legality in the Activity of the Councils of People's Deputies in the Conditions Prevailing in the Liquidation of the Attempt To Carry Out a State Coup in the USSR."

The actions of the President of the Russian Federation and of other republic organs of government and control in protecting the constitutional order were approved in the 22 August 1991 decree of the Russian Federation Supreme Soviet "On the Political Situation in the Republic Resulting From the Anticonstitutional State Coup in the USSR."

The position and actions of the leadership in Russia, which enabled the restoration of constitutional power in the country, was approved in the USSR President's decree of 22 August 1991 "On Repealing the Anticonstitutional Enactments of the Organizers of the State Coup," and also in decrees of the USSR Supreme Soviet "On the Situation That Has Arisen in the Country in Connection with the State Coup That Has Taken Place" dated 29 August 1991, and "On Priority Measures To Prevent Attempts To Carry Out a State Coup" dated 30 August 1991.

The unlawful decision of the GKChP to declare a state of emergency, like all its other enactments, was repealed on 22 August 1991 by decree of the President of the USSR. No state of emergency was declared by the President of the Republic on the territory of the Russian Federation, and at the time when the 23 August 1991 decree was issued there was no state of emergency. On this basis it is claimed in the petition of the group of people's deputies of the Russian Federation that suspending the activity of the CP RSFSR by this decree was unlawful since such suspension is possible only under conditions of a state of emergency.

In the law in force in this period, and operating now on the territory of the Russian Federation, there are no general standards that provide directly for a basis and procedure for suspending the activity of political parties and other public associations or their leading structures. At the same time the possibility of such suspension has been secured not only in paragraph "c" of Article 23 of the Russian Federation law "On States of Emergency" and a similar Union law in connection with the declaration of a state of emergency, but also in the 2 April 1990 law of the USSR "On Strengthening

Responsibility for Encroachment on the National Equality of Citizens and Violation by Force of the Territorial Unity of the USSR."...

[B]oth the Russian and the Union legislator proceeded on the basis of the principle whereby suspension by competent State bodies of the activity of political parties and other public associations, apart from cases of a state of emergency, is possible on the same grounds—that their activity is inadmissible. In accordance with Article 7 Section 2 of the Russian Federation Constitution, the latter is permissible and necessary in order to suppress the unlawful acts enumerated in this standard.

Suspending the activity of public associations should thus be carried out in the interests of ensuring the safety of citizens and State and public safety and the normal activity of State institutions. In all such cases the activity of public associations is suspended pending a ruling by the court. Suspending the activity of a public association, when grounds for so doing suggest that it has been involved in anticonstitutional acts which are the subject of investigation, serves precisely these aims. At the same time, its procedure has not been regulated....

Suspending the activity of the CP RSFSR for the reasons listed above by decree of the President of the Russian Federation was done in the situation that had taken shape in August 1991. It was in accordance with the provisions of Article 4 of the 24 May 1991 version of the Russian Federation Constitution, which obliges State organs to ensure the maintenance of law and order, the interests of society, and the rights and freedoms of citizens, and to comply with existing legislation, and it was also in line with the constitutional status of the President of the Russian Federation, first and foremost as envisaged by Article 121-5 Section 11 Paragraph 1 in the 24 May 1991 version of the Russian Federation Constitution, with respect to his powers to take steps to ensure State and public safety in the Russian Federation, and on its behalf to be involved in ensuring the State and public safety of the USSR. Adoption of such measures is not necessarily linked to the declaration of a state of emergency on the territory of the Russian Federation. The powers indicated include the right of the President of Russia to recognize the presence of a threat to State and public safety in the country and, depending on the degree of reality of the threat, to adopt decisions in accordance with his competence.

In this case the President of the Russian Federation acted as the highest official of the republic and the head of its executive power (Article 121-1 Section 1 of the 24 May 1991 version of the Russian Federation Constitution) in accordance with his own oath, in which he pledged himself, in particular, to protect the sovereignty of the Russian Federation (Article 121-4 of the 24 May 1991 version of the Russian Federation Constitution).

In promulgating the 23 August 1991 decree, the President of the Russian Federation proceeded on the basis of the status of the CP RSFSR as a public association.... The decree was aimed at direct application of Article 7 Section 2 of the 24 May 1991 version of the Russian Federation Constitution, which prohibits activity by parties, organizations, and movements having the aim or method of action, in particular, of forcible change to the constitutional order and undermining State security. Here, no legal procedure had been secured in the Russian Federation Constitution for abridging the right of association. But the decree made provision for an appeal to the organs of the judicial power following completion of investigation to resolve the question of the unconstitutionality of the actions of the CP RSFSR, which was in accordance with the principles for examining similar issues as established by the USSR law "On Strengthening Responsibility for Encroachment on the National Equality of Citizens and Violation by Force of the Territorial Unity of the USSR." The Constitutional Court does take into account the fact that the activity of the CPSU on all territory of the USSR was suspended by the 29 August 1991 USSR Supreme Soviet decree "On the Situation That Has Arisen in the Country in Connection with the State Coup That Has Taken Place"; in accordance with this decree, a decision on its subsequent fate was to depend on the results of an investigation by the organs of the prosecutor's office according to the facts concerning the involvement of leading organs of the CPSU in the actions in regard to forcible change of the constitutional order, and in the event that such actions were confirmed, it envisaged their examination at the highest judicial level.

Suspending the activity of the CP RSFSR required the adoption of measures to safeguard its property. On the basis of the above-named provisions in the 24 May 1991 version of the Russian Federation Constitution, and also Article 10 of that Constitution, which provides for an obligation on the part of the State to protect the right of ownership and ensure equal protection for all forms of ownership, and taking into account the need to prevent the unlawful removal and use of party property and assets, steps were taken as enumerated in subsections 3 and 4 of the 23 August 1991 decree of the President of the Russian Federation, namely the following: The RSFSR Ministry of Internal Affairs was assigned to ensure the safekeeping of the property and monetary assets of the organs and organizations of the CP RSFSR pending a final ruling by the court, while the RSFSR Central Bank was assigned to ensure suspension of operations involving the use of assets in accounts of organs and organizations of the CP RSFSR pending a special order.

These actions were supported by the President of the USSR, who in his own 24 August 1991 decree "On the Property of the CPSU" made it incumbent upon the councils of people's deputies to take over the safekeeping of CPSU property, and determined that matters concerning its subsequent use should be decided strictly in accordance with the laws of the USSR and the republics on property and public associations.

On 16 September 1991, the Russian Federation Supreme Soviet Presidium announced that "any dealings with respect to property, valuables, bank deposits abroad, or other objects belonging to the CPSU and the organizations, institutions, or enterprises that make up the CPSU, located both in the USSR and abroad, shall be null and void, with all the consequences stemming from this in accordance with legislation of the RSFSR."

The measures envisaged by Subsection 3 of the 23 August 1991 decree of the President of the Russian Federation have as their aim protecting the interests of the State, safeguarding State and public property, and ensuring the security and defense capability of the country, which is in line with the provisions in Article 125 Section 2 paragraphs 3 and 4 of the 24 May 1991 Russian Federation Constitution.

At the same time, the Constitutional Court notes that the order contained in paragraph 1 of the decree for the RSFSR prosecutor's office to conduct an investigation of ... the anticonstitutional activity of organs of the CP RSFSR, and the proposal set forth in paragraph 5 of the decree for the RSFSR prosecutor's office to exercise supervision over compliance with this decree, have no legal standing since the corresponding obligation of the prosecutor's office stems from Articles 176, 177, and 179 of the 24 May 1991 Russian Federation Constitution.

It does not accord with the principle of the delineation of competence between State organs as contained in paragraph 1 of the assignment for the RSFSR Ministry of Internal Affairs to conduct an investigation of the ... anticonstitutional activity of organs of the CP RSFSR, since in accordance with Article 126 of the republic's Penal and Procedural Code, organs of internal affairs do not enjoy a right to conduct a preliminary investigation in these kinds of matters.

It was established in paragraph 6 of the decree that it would enter into force from the moment that it was signed. However, in accordance with the general principle of law, any legal enactment of a generally binding nature and affecting the rights, freedoms, and obligations of the individual, must enter into force no earlier than its publication or its notification to the general public by other means. No procedure had been established for publishing decrees of the President of the Russian Federation in this period, but existing practice made it possible to consider it analogous to the procedure for publishing laws, and this was subsequently confirmed in the 26 March 1992 decree of the President of the Russian Federation "On Procedure for Publishing and the Entry into Force of Enactments of the President of the Russian Federation and the Government of the Russian Federation."

At the same time the Constitutional Court takes under advisement the fact that the 23 August 1991 decree of the President was brought to general attention on radio and television simultaneously with its signing.

II

In the petition of the people's deputies to examine the constitutionality of decrees of the President of the Russian Federation, the announcement on State ownership of property of the CPSU and the CP RSFSR is called "nationalization," and it is claimed that this removal was done by the President in contradiction of the Russian Federation Constitution (Articles 10 and 49) and existing laws in the Russian Federation, in particular the RSFSR law "On Property in the RSFSR" (Articles 1, 2, 17, 30, 31, and 32) and the USSR law "On Public Associations" (Articles 18 and 22), which contain guarantees of the right of ownership by public associations.

During the course of the judicial hearing, the Constitutional Court has established that property of the CPSU and CP RSFSR shown on balance sheets included objects that could belong to various owners, including the

State. This was proven by the documents attached to the case (instructions from the USSR Council of Ministers on the allocation of currencies, decisions on gratis transfer of buildings belonging to the State, and so forth), and by witness's testimony (V.V. Ivanenko).

Accurate determination of the subject with respect to right of ownership to any particular object under the control of organs and institutions of the CPSU was hampered as the result of the statization of the main part of the national wealth.

The 1977 USSR Constitution established in Article 10 that together with State (national) and kolkhoz-cooperative ownership of socialist property, there is also property belonging to trade unions and other public organizations essential for them to carry out their statutory tasks. Systematic interpretation of the standards of the USSR Constitution and the Constitution of the Russian Federation, and also the Fundamentals of Civil Law in the USSR and the Union republics and the Civil Code of the Russian Federation lead the court to the conclusion that the concept of "public organizations" in this context did not include the CPSU.... In the Constitution, it talked about the CPSU in Article 6, while the role of the trade unions, the Komsomol, and cooperative and other public organizations was covered in Article 7.... At that time, the legislator could not include the CPSU in the concept of "other public organizations" since this would have been in radical contradiction of the CPSU's actual position as "the leading and guiding force in society." In Article 6 of the USSR Constitution the CPSU was defined as "the nucleus of the political system in Soviet society and State and public organizations." And the CPSU is not named among the public organizations in Article 7 of the USSR Constitution. The reluctance of the CPSU to identify itself with the public organizations is thus confirmed by the text of the USSR Constitution.

The CPSU was outside the civil-legal regulation of relations in terms of its property. This thesis is proved by the materials of the case since it has been established that no financial control was exercised by the State with respect to CPSU property. Nor did the general supervision of the prosecutor's office touch upon the sphere of CPSU activity. Even bookkeeping in the CPSU was not done in accordance with established procedure. Organs and officials of the CPSU would frequently give subjects of the right of ownership binding instructions to dispose of property without posting it to its own balance sheet. There were cases here of unfounded enrichment of the CPSU at the expense of the State in violation of Article 133 of the Fundamentals of Civil Law in the USSR and republics.

The indeterminate nature of the right of ownership of property found under the control of the CPSU and CP RSFSR does not make it possible to recognize its owners unambiguously. Property was easily transformed from one form of socialist property to another by the will of organs of the CPSU managing property but not being the formal owner....

In declaring the impossibility in this judicial case of clarifying the true will of the owner during the transfer of property from the State to the CPSU, the Constitutional Court considers that the property controlled by the CPSU was at its disposal without legal basis. This statement does not exclude the possibility in principle that part of the property controlled by the CPSU did legally belong to it by right of ownership.

Thus, in assessing the constitutionality of the 25 August 1991 decree of the President "On the Property of the CPSU and the CP RSFSR," the Constitutional Court proceeds on the basis that the property controlled by the CPSU and the CP RSFSR respectively belonged to three categories of owner: a) the State, b) the CPSU, c) other owners. However, in respect of where the ownership of one subject ends and the ownership of another begins, and in some cases even with respect to who the owner is, there is legal indeterminacy that can be eliminated only by civil or arbitral judicial proceedings. The Constitutional Court has been unable to enter into discussion of the question of which part of CPSU property is State property since in accordance with Article 1 Section 4 of the Law on the Constitutional Court, the Court is restrained from establishing and investigating actual circumstances [where] this falls within the competence of other courts.

In connection with the disintegration of the CPSU as an all-union party, the question of its property cannot be resolved on the basis of Article 14, nor on the basis of Article 22 of the USSR law "On Public Associations." It states in Article 6 of this law that those associations whose activity, in accordance with statutory tasks, takes place across the territory of all or the majority of the union republics, are all-union. And if this condition is not met and the all-union association disintegrates, the consequences were not envisaged by the law. Thus, a situation arose of legal indeterminacy with respect to a significant part of the property of the former CPSU on the territory of the Russian Federation. Under conditions in which the principle of the separation of powers was not consistently developed in the legislation of the Russian Federation on property, and in which many legal standards were at variance with that principle, a constitutional solution to the question of the fate of the property that used to be under the control of CPSU organs could be reached only if the highest legislative, executive, and judicial organs of the Russian Federation were to participate in resolving the entire set of problems....

In respect of the State property under the control of the CPSU and the CP RSFSR, the decree of the President of the Russian Federation meets the provisions of Article 10 of the Russian Federation Constitution, according to which the State in particular recognizes and protects the right of ownership and ensures equal protection for all its forms. In this section the decree also meets the provisions of Article 11-1 of the Constitution, which regulates the bases of the status of State ownership in the Russian Federation.... The instructions on the use of State property contained in the decree fall within the sphere of his competence:... in accordance with Article 125 Section 2 paragraph 3 of the Constitution, he takes steps, in particular, to safeguard the interests of the State and preserve socialist property.... The President's instructions in this connection, directed to the organs of executive power, are consonant with his competence also by dint of Article 121-5 paragraph 11 of the Constitution, which establishes an obligation on the part of the President to take steps to ensure State and public safety.

Unconditional declaration of State ownership of a particular part of the property under the control of the CPSU, to which right of ownership belonged as a public association (members' dues, income from publishing activity) cannot be recognized, nor likewise that part of the property whose ownership is unknown. Under existing law, conversion of such property to State property cannot be done by enactment of the executive power because it is at variance with the provisions of Article 10, Article 49 Section 2, Article 109 Section 1 paragraph 6, Article 121-5, and Article 121-8 of the Russian Federation Constitution.

Declaration of State ownership of property that was not in State ownership cannot fall within the competence of the executive power if it is not empowered so to do by special enactment of the legislative power. In this case there was no such empowering enactment.

<h2 style="text-align:center">III</h2>

For a long time, an unlimited regime that relied on confining power to a narrow group of communist functionaries, joined together in the CPSU Central Committee Politburo led by the CPSU Central Committee General Secretary, dominated within the country.

The materials of the case testify that the leading organs and highest officials of the CPSU in an overwhelming majority of cases acted secretly from the rank-and-file members of the CPSU, and frequently even in secret from responsible party functionaries. At the lower levels of control, down to regional [rayon] level, real power was vested with the first secretaries of the corresponding party committees. Only at the level of the primary organizations of the CPSU were the features of a public association to be found, although ... these organizations made the members of the CPSU dependent on their leadership, which was closely connected with administration. The materials of the case, including the testimony of witnesses, confirm that the leading structures of the CPSU were the initiators, while structures at the local level were often the conductors of a policy of repression against millions of Soviet people, including against deported peoples. This went on for decades.

After the change was made to Article 6 of the USSR Constitution, just as in preceding years, the organizational structures of the CPSU resolved many of the issues falling within the competence of the corresponding [State] organs of power and control. Thus, on 10 May 1990 at a meeting of the CPSU Central Committee Politburo, the question of selling gold and diamonds was considered (document 67). During 1990, questions concerning the transformation of diplomatic missions of the USSR, the texts of reports of the USSR State Committee for Statistics, the use of foreign currency earnings by institutions of the arts and culture, the production of fire-fighting equipment, the activity of the military-industrial complex and the Ministry of Foreign Economic Relations, the transfer to the USSR State Committee for Material and Technical Supply of material assets from the State Reserves, personal awards of USSR Lenin and State prizes, eavesdropping on service telephone conversations, the withdrawal of Soviet troops from Hungary, the composition of Soviet troops in Germany in 1991 and the subsequent period, measures connected with anti-army demonstrations, the thrust of work in the USSR Ministry of Foreign Affairs, invitations to the leaders of fraternal parties for vacations, work on nuclear power engineering, the debts of Soviet organizations to "firms of friends," and safeguards for certain factories (documents 64-72) were discussed in the CPSU Central Committee.

In 1991 questions concerning reserves of material resources, the poor supplies of raw materials to enterprises, the unstable situation in Abkhazia, a trip by a corresponding member of the USSR Academy of Sciences to a session of the UN University in Macao, and the USSR's foreign debt were considered in the CPSU Central Committee. In 1991 union departments sent the CPSU Central Committee materials on the work of the defense complex, the partial change in the RSFSR Supreme Soviet decree on bringing into force the RSFSR law "On Property in the RSFSR," the reception of foreign citizens for training in the USSR, and so forth.

The appointment of top officials and conferment of the rank of general were done only with the agreement of the CPSU Central Committee (documents 10, 11, 12, 21, and others).

The CPSU Central Committee Secretariat's resolution dated 12 April 1990, "On Changes in the Defense Councils of Certain Autonomous Republics and Areas [Oblasts] of the RSFSR," (document 15); a list of members of military councils from among the party leadership in the republics, territories, and areas as of 1991 (document 203); and the memorandum from CPSU Central Committee secretaries O.S. Shenin and O.D. Baklanov dated 9 January 1991 "On Party Leadership in Questions of Defense Building" (document 433) testify to the direct merging of military and party organs.

Before passage of the USSR law on the organs of State security, the Provision on the USSR Council of Ministers Committee for State Security [KGB] and Its Local Organs, dated 9 January 1959 and confirmed by the CPSU Central Committee Presidium, was still in force. It was stressed in this provision that organs of the KGB are political, carry out measures of the CPSU Central Committee and operate under its direct leadership, that leading workers in the KGB are on the party *nomenklatura*,* and that orders issued by the chairman of the KGB are issued with the approval of the CPSU Central Committee.

In 1990, the chairman of the USSR KGB certified that his department remained under the control of the CPSU. The corresponding reports and memoranda continued to arrive in the CPSU Central Committee, and associates of the KGB were recruited to carry out political (party) measures.

Virtually until the end of its activity, the CPSU retained the *nomenklatura*. The last list of the *nomenklatura* was confirmed by the CPSU Central Committee on 7 August 1991. It included 7,000 persons occupying key positions in the State—presidents of republics, chairmen of councils, chairmen of councils of ministers, and so forth.... The procedure continued

---

* [Translator's note: the *nomenklatura* is the official schedule of appointments reserved for party members.]

to operate whereby no major appointment could be made without preliminary approval from the CPSU Central Committee.

The CPSU also tried to further control the mass media. In 1990 the party leadership assigned the USSR State Committee for Television and Radio Broadcasting to create a regular television program devoted to problems of the CPSU and its role and place in modern society; the ideological department commented to the State Committee for Cinematography about a movie in which shots of the Nuremberg trials were shown....

The use by the CPSU of State assets also continued in 1990-1991. Thus, an audit conducted by the Main Military Prosecutor's Office confirmed instances of uncompensated use by CPSU Central Committee secretaries of aircraft, and the use of dozens of teletype machines in the building of the CPSU Central Committee and in the courier service of party structures on the country's territory were not paid for; trips abroad were posted to the State account; ministries and departments were assigned to create a press center for a conference of the Russian Communist Party and for the 28th CPSU Congress.

Party workers were still being paid using State assets. In 1991 State dachas were transferred free of charge to the CPSU Central Committee, and republic and area newspapers maintained at State expense were put on the party budget. In 1990 and 1991, maintenance of the political organs of the KGB, the MVD [Ministry of Internal Affairs], and the Ministry of Defense cost the State 691 million rubles. In the interests of keeping the party budget inviolate, the CPSU Central Committee took steps to pay the debts of the so-called "firms of friends" using the State budget and unconnected currency credits.

All of the above relates to the leading structures of the CPSU and the CP RSFSR, first and foremost their committees, from the central committees to the regional committees with secretariats and buros (the politburos in the central committees), and also to the apparatuses of these committees. The mass of rank-and-file members, including the members of the primary organizations, were unable to participate in a practical way in State activity. Even the right of party control over the activity of administrations at enterprises and in institutions, provided for prior to 1990 by the CPSU Statutes, more often than not were empty formalities because representatives of the *nomenklatura* of these CPSU (or CP RSFSR) committees were the heads of administrations.

At their own meetings, the rank-and-file members of the CPSU (and CP RSFSR) approved the political actions of central and other committees and their apparatuses. Only recently has criticism started to be seen from them, but they have still been unable to achieve any decisive influence by rank-and-file members of the CPSU (CP RSFSR) in their own organizations.

The leading structures of the CPSU and CP RSFSR appropriated State-power authority and actively exercised it, preventing the normal activity of constitutional organs of power. This served as the legal basis for liquidating the structures by decree of the top official in the Russian Federation. The actions of the President were dictated by the objective need to prevent a return to the earlier situation, and to liquidate structures whose daily practice was based on the fact that the CPSU occupied within the State mechanism a position that was at variance with the bases of the constitutional order.

The grounds set forth by paragraph 1 of the decree dated 6 November 1991 banning the activity and dissolving the regional structures of the CPSU and the CP RSFSR are first and foremost the provision in Article 4 Section 1 of the 1 November 1991 version of the Russian Federation Constitution, which lays upon the State and its organs an obligation to ensure the safeguarding of law and order, the interests of society, and the rights and freedoms of citizens. The President of the Russian Federation acted here in compliance with his oath, as set forth in Article 121-4 of the Constitution and obliging him to defend the sovereignty of the Russian Federation and respect and safeguard the rights and freedoms of the individual and the citizen. The steps taken by the President form the essence of the measures to ensure State and public safety in the Russian Federation that the President is obliged to take in accordance with Article 121-5 Section 11 Paragraph 1 first part of the 1 November 1991 version of the Russian Federation Constitution.

The anticonstitutional nature of the activity by leading structures of the CPSU and CP RSFSR that existed at the time of publication of the decree by the President of the Russian Federation dated 6 November 1991 "On the Activity of the CPSU and CP RSFSR" excludes the possibility of restoring them in the earlier form. Members of the Russian Federation Communist Party do have the right to create any new leading structures fully in accordance with the requirements of the existing Constitution and the laws of the Russian Federation and on an equal footing with other parties.

However, too broad a formulation of Section 1 of the decree envisaging cessation of the activity and dissolution of the organizational structures of the CPSU and the CP RSFSR does not take into account the difference noted above between the leading structures and primary organizations of the CPSU and the CP RSFSR formed on the territorial principle.

A limited interpretation of Section 1 prevailed in the practical implementation of the decree: communist deputies retained their mandates and factions in the representative organs, and their membership in the Communist Party, and previous work in it does not provide grounds for any kind of discrimination, and new parties with a communist orientation were created without hindrance. However, the existing text of this paragraph in the decree in its literal interpretation can be used both for inadmissible discrimination against communists, the provisions contained in Section 2 of this same decree notwithstanding, and for equally inadmissible failure to apply measures of legal liability against specific persons guilty of anticonstitutional actions by leading structures of the CPSU and CP RSFSR.

Paragraph 2 of the decree, banning organs of executive power in the Russian Federation and in the territories, areas, autonomous areas, and autonomous districts [okrug], and in the cities of Moscow and St. Petersburg, and also organs of the prosecutor's office, from persecuting Russian citizens for the fact of affiliation with the CPSU or CP RSFSR, offers a guarantee for compliance with a number of constitutional provisions ensuring observance of the rights and freedoms of citizens.

What is set forth above as applied to the 25 August 1991 decree of the President of the Russian Federation "On the Property of the CPSU and the CP RSFSR" also applies fully to paragraph 3 of the decree. This paragraph in the decree is constitutional with respect to that part of the property of the CPSU and CP RSFSR for which right of ownership belongs to the State, and is unconstitutional with respect to the remainder of this property.

With respect to paragraph 4 of the decree, it is directed toward ensuring compliance with its paragraphs 1 through 3. From what has been stated above it follows that the obligation laid upon the State organs listed in this section as applied to compliance with the orders contained in sections 1 and 3 of the decree is constitutional only to the extent that these sections of the decree are constitutional.... In issuing the decree the President was guided by Article 121-4 and also by Article 121-8 Section 1 of the Constitution, which endows him with the right to issue decrees that are binding for compliance on all territory of the Russian Federation, and to check compliance with them....

As far as the lower organs of executive power are concerned, Article 132-1 Section 2, Article 134, and Article 146 Section 1 of the Constitution serve as the basis for the right of the President to issue instructions to these organs within the limits of his powers.

IV

In considering the concomitant issue during the course of the hearing, the Constitutional Court has checked on whether the CPSU meets the attributes of a public association as envisaged in particular in the USSR law "On Public Associations."

In connection with the events of 19-21 August 1991, on 25 August 1991 the CPSU Central Committee General Secretary M.S. Gorbachev called on the CPSU Central Committee "to make the difficult but honorable decision to dissolve itself," and he stated the following: "The fate of the republic communist parties and local party organizations is to be decided by them themselves.... For myself I do not think it is possible to carry out any further the functions of CPSU Central Committee General Secretary, and I relinquish the corresponding powers."

This was the start of the collapse of the CPSU as an all-union political organization. In August the Secretary of the Communist Party of Kazakhstan Central Committee, CPSU Central Committee Politburo member N.A. Nazarbayev, relinquished his powers. At the same time Secretary of the Communist Party of Azerbaijan A.N. Mutalibov and Secretary of the Communist Party of Uzbekistan I.A. Karimov announced their resignation from the CPSU Central Committee Politburo. It was also reported that members of the CPSU Central Committee and Central Control Commission had resigned from those organs.

Subsequently the following decisions were taken: to halt the activity of the Communist Party of Georgia (by decree of the President of Republic of Georgia dated 26 August), of Belorussia (by decree of the Belorussian Supreme Soviet dated 25 August), of Tajikistan (by decree of the Supreme

Soviet of the Republic of Tajikistan dated 2 October), of Kyrgyzstan (by resolution of the Supreme Soviet of the Republic of Kyrgyzstan dated 31 August); to dissolve the Communist Party of Kazakhstan (by decision of the Communist Party of Kazakhstan Extraordinary 18th Congress dated 7 September); to dissolve the Communist Party of Azerbaijan (by decision of the Communist Party of Azerbaijan Extraordinary 23rd Congress dated 14 September); to suspend the activity of the Communist Party of Armenia (by decision of the 29th Communist Party of Armenia Congress dated 7 September), and of organizations of the CPSU Communist Party of Estonia (by decree of the Government of Estonia dated 22 August); to withdraw the communist parties of Turkmenistan and Uzbekistan from the CPSU (by decision of a plenum of the Turkmen Communist Party Central Committee dated 26 August and by decision of the Uzbek Communist Party 23rd Congress dated 14 September respectively) with subsequent liquidation of the communist parties on the territories of these republics; to ban the activity of the Communist Party of Moldova (by decree of the Moldovan Supreme Soviet Presidium dated 24 August), of Ukraine (by decree of the Ukrainian Supreme Soviet Presidium dated 30 August), of Latvia (by decree of the Latvian Republic Supreme Soviet dated 10 September), and of Lithuania (by decree of the Lithuanian Republic Supreme Soviet dated 23 August).

Thus, by November 1991 as a result of the dissolution, cessation, banning, and other transformation, the communist parties in the republics had ceased to exist. This meant that the CPSU no longer possessed the attributes of an all-union political party as envisaged by Article 6 Section 2 of the USSR law "On Public Associations."

With respect to the CP RSFSR, as noted above, right up to the moment that the decrees of the President of the Russian Federation in question were issued, it remained an integral part of the CPSU and no independent political party had been formed.

The CP RSFSR was independent only as a structure of the CPSU system and within the limits defined by the CPSU Statutes. In this sense the status of the CP RSFSR and of the territorial party organization almost matched, and CP RSFSR Central Committee former First Secretary I.K. Polozkov confirmed this (the shorthand report of 7 October 1992, pages 93-100) when he addressed the Court.

Establishing the fact that the leading structures of the CPSU and the CP RSFSR carried out State-power functions in practice despite existing constitutions means that their dissolution was lawful and their restoration impermissible....

Thus, since it has been established that for more than a year, neither the CPSU nor the CP RSFSR has existed, it must be recognized that the petition from people's deputies of the Russian Federation to consider the unconstitutionality of the CPSU lacks a subject.

With respect to the request contained in the petition to consider the decrees of the President of the Russian Federation constitutional, the Constitutional Court notes that no provision is made in the Russian Federation Law on the Constitutional Court for petitions to consider the enactments of State organs constitutional, and essentially they have no meaning since any enactment by a State organ is considered to be constitutional until the opposite is established by a Constitution or law.

On the basis of the above and guided by Article 6 Section 4 and Article 64 of the Law on the Russian Federation Constitutional Court, the Russian Federation Constitutional Court has ruled as follows:

> I. On the question of examining the constitutionality of the decree of the President of the Russian Federation of 23 August 1991, No. 79, "On Suspending the Activity of the Communist Party of the RSFSR":

1. Finds that the instruction in paragraph 1 of the decree, from the President of the Russian Federation to the Ministry of Internal Affairs, to conduct an investigation is not in accordance with the Constitution of the Russian Federation ... in ... that this instruction violates the rules of prosecution established by law.

2. Finds that paragraph 2 of the decree is in accordance with the Constitution of the Russian Federation....

3. Finds that paragraph 3 of the decree is in accordance with the Constitution of the Russian Federation....

4. Finds that paragraph 4 of the decree is in accordance with the Constitution of the Russian Federation....

5. Finds the instructions of the President of the Russian Federation to the prosecutor's office, in paragraphs 1 and 5 of the decree, to have no legal consequence since the corresponding responsibility of the prosecutor flows directly from Articles 176 and 177 of the Constitution of the Russian Federation....

6. Finds that paragraph 6 of the decree is not in accordance with the general principle of law under which a law or any other normative act that provides for restricting the rights of citizens takes effect only after its publication in accordance with official procedure.

> II. On the question of examining the constitutionality of the decree of the President of the Russian Federation of 25 August 1991, No. 90 "On the Property of the CPSU and the Communist Party of the RSFSR":

1. Finds that paragraph 1 of the decree is in accordance with the Constitution of the Russian Federation ... with respect to that portion of the property owned by the State but which, at the time the decree was issued, was actually in the possession, use and at the disposal of the organs and organizations of the CPSU and the CP RSFSR.

Finds that paragraph 1 of the decree is not in accordance with the Constitution of the Russian Federation ... with respect to that portion of the property owned by the CPSU, as well as that portion of the property which, at the time the decree was issued, was actually in the possession, use and at the disposal of the organs and organizations of the CPSU and the CP RSFSR, but the owner of which was not determined.

2. Finds that paragraph 2 of the decree is in accordance with the Constitution of the Russian Federation....

3. Finds that paragraphs 3 and 4 of the decree are in accordance with the Constitution of the Russian Federation ... with respect to that portion of the property owned by the State but which, at the time the decree was issued, was actually in the possession, use and at the disposal of the organs and organizations of the CPSU and the CP RSFSR.

Finds that paragraphs 3 and 4 of the decree are not in accordance with the Constitution of the Russian Federation ... with respect to the remaining property in that part in which the decree makes an unjustifiable connection between the transfer of the right to use the given property and the legal power of the State to use this property in the capacity of owner.

4. Finds that paragraphs 5 and 6 of the decree are in accordance with the Constitution of the Russian Federation....

5. Finds that paragraph 7 of the decree is not in accordance with the general principle of law under which a law or any other normative act that provides for restricting the rights of citizens takes effect only after its publication in accordance with official procedure.

6. Proposes that the President of the Russian Federation, in execution of paragraph 5 of the decree, ensure that the public is given complete information about the decisions made with respect to the property of the CPSU and the CP RSFSR and about the actual use of this property.

> III. On the question of examining the constitutionality of the decree of the President of the Russian Federation of 6 November 1991, No. 169, "On the Activity of the CPSU and the CP RSFSR":

1. Finds that paragraph 1 of the decree is in accordance with the Constitution of the Russian Federation ... with respect to the dissolution on the territory of the Russian Federation of the leading organizational bodies of the CPSU and of the CP RSFSR insofar as it was a component part of the CPSU.

Finds that paragraph 1 of the decree on the dissolution of the organizational bodies of the CPSU and of the CP RSFSR is not in accordance with the Constitution of the Russian Federation ... with respect to the primary organizations of the CP RSFSR, formed on the territorial principle, insofar as these organizations retained their social nature and were not changed into State structures, and also on the condition that, in the event of their official organization as a political party on an equal basis with other parties, the requirements of the Constitution and laws of the Russian Federation shall be observed.

2. Finds that paragraph 2 of the decree is in accordance with the Constitution of the Russian Federation....

3. Finds that paragraph 3 of the decree is in accordance with the Constitution of the Russian Federation ... with respect to that portion of the property owned by the State but which, at the time the decree was issued,

was actually in the possession, use and at the disposal of the organs and organizations of the CPSU and the CP RSFSR.

Finds that paragraph 3 of the decree is not in accordance with the Constitution of the Russian Federation ... with respect to that portion of the property owned by the CPSU, as well as that portion of the property which, at the time the decree was issued, was actually in the possession, use and at the disposal of the organs and organizations of the CPSU and the CP RSFSR, but the owner of which was not determined.

4. Finds that paragraph 4 of the decree is in accordance with the Constitution of the Russian Federation ... with respect to the execution of the provisions of the decree, the constitutionality of which was acknowledged by the present ruling....

4

PROSECUTION AND AMNESTY

NUREMBERG: CHARTER OF THE INTERNATIONAL MILITARY TRIBUNAL

(1945)

I. Constitution of the International Military Tribunal

Article 1.

In pursuance of the Agreement signed on the 8th day of August 1945 by the Government of the United States of America, the Provisional Government of the French Republic, the Government of the United Kingdom of Great Britain and Northern Ireland and the Government of the Union of Soviet Socialist Republics, there shall be established an International Military Tribunal (hereinafter called "the Tribunal") for the just and prompt trial and punishment of the major war criminals of the European Axis....

Article 6.

The Tribunal established by the Agreement referred to in Article 1 hereof for the trial and punishment of the major war criminals of the European Axis countries shall have the power to try and punish persons who, acting in the interests of the European Axis countries, whether as individuals or as members of organizations, committed any of the following crimes.

The following acts, or any of them, are crimes coming within the jurisdiction of the Tribunal for which there shall be individual responsibility:

(a) Crimes Against Peace: namely, planning, preparation, initiation or waging of a war of aggression, or a war in violation of international treaties, agreements or assurances, or participation in a common plan or conspiracy for the accomplishment of any of the foregoing;

(b) War Crimes: namely, violation of the laws or customs of war. Such violations shall include, but not be limited to, murder, ill-treatment or deportation to slave labor or for any other purpose of civilian population of or in occupied territory, murder or ill-treatment of prisoners of war or persons on the seas, killing of hostages, plunder of public or private property, wanton destruction of cities, towns or villages, or devastation not justified by military necessity;

(c) Crimes Against Humanity: namely, murder, extermination, enslavement, deportation, and other inhuman acts committed against any civilian population, before or during the war; or persecutions on political, racial or religious grounds in execution of or in connection with any crime within the jurisdiction of the

Tribunal whether or not in violation of the domestic law of the country where perpetrated.

Leaders, organizers, instigators and accomplices participating in the formulation or execution of a common plan or conspiracy to commit any of the foregoing crimes are responsible for all acts performed by any persons in execution of such plans.

Article 7. *No immunity for Heads of States!*

The official position of defendants, whether as Heads of State or responsible officials in Government Departments, shall not be considered as freeing them from responsibility or mitigating punishment.

Article 8. *"Due Obedience" cannot be a justification!*

The fact that the Defendant acted pursuant to order of his Government or of a superior shall not free him from responsibility, but may be considered in mitigation of punishment, if the Tribunal determines that justice so requires.

Article 9.

At the trial of any individual member of any group or organization the Tribunal may declare (in connection with any act of which the individual may be convicted) that the group or organization of which the individual was a member was a criminal organization.

After receipt of the Indictment the Tribunal shall give such notices as it thinks fit that the prosecution intends to ask the Tribunal to make such declaration and any member of the organization will be entitled to apply to the Tribunal for leave to be heard by the Tribunal upon the question of the criminal character of the organization. The Tribunal shall have power to allow or reject the application. If the application is allowed, the Tribunal may direct in what manner the applicants shall be represented and heard....

NUREMBERG: EXCERPTS FROM TRIBUNAL DECISIONS

(October 1946-April 1949)

Reason for Prosecution: The Milch Case (No. 2)[*]

In a civilized state which recognizes the sanctity of human lives and human rights, no man—no group of men—should be endowed with omnipotence. The history of human relations, from Herod to Hitler, has repeatedly demonstrated this to be true. Omnipotence is only for God. Be a man ever so wise, ever so benevolent, ever so trustworthy, there still exists in him the frailty, the fallibility, the susceptibility to temptation that is inherent in every man. If the only protection against the tyranny of an autocrat is his own self-restraint, that is not enough, for power feeds on power, and the temptation to stretch authority to its limit is irresistible.

What, then, of the responsibility of those who bask in the reflected radiance of omnipotence, who get their sustenance from it and who arrogantly carry out its mandates and crush any resistance to it? Are they not the hands and limbs of the monster carrying out the orders of the head? Surely, they cannot be allowed to detach themselves from the corpus by saying, "These arms and legs are innocent—only the head is guilty?"

Sentence

This Tribunal takes no pleasures in performing the duty which confronts it, but the deliberate enslavement of millions must not go unexpiated. The barbarous acts which have been revealed here originated in the lust and ambition of comparatively few men, but all Germans are paying and will pay for the degradation of their souls and the debasement of the German honor, caused by following the false prophets who led them to disaster.

It would be a travesty on justice to permit those false leaders, including this defendant, to escape responsibility for the deception and betrayal of their people. It would be even a greater injustice to view with complacence the mass graves of millions of men, women, and children whose only crime was that they stood in Hitler's way. Retribution for such crimes against humanity must be swift and certain. Future would-be dictators and their subservient satellites must know what follows their defilement of international law and of every type of decency and fair dealing with their fellow men. Civilization will be satisfied with nothing less.

The purpose of these postwar trials obviously is not vengeance. The object aimed at (as in the criminal jurisprudence of all civilized nations) is

---

[*] Excerpted from "The Milch Case (No. 2)," *Trials of War Criminals Before the Nuernberg Military Tribunals Under Control Council Law* No. 10, Vol. II (1950), pp. 794, 796, 859.

the ascertainment of truth. When guilt is established, the penalty imposed is to serve as a deterrent to all others who might be similarly minded. Albert Speer, convicted in the first trial, stated here in this courtroom that had trials such as these followed the First World War, the Second World War might have been averted. Erhard Milch may obtain some comfort from the realization that by the publication of the evidence of this trial he is definitely contributing to the education and well-being of Germany's future, as indeed a precise contribution is being made to the cause of world justice itself.

Defenses of Act of State and Superior Orders[*]

The principle of international law, which under certain circumstances, protects the representatives of a state, cannot be applied to acts which are condemned as criminal by international law. The authors of these acts cannot shelter themselves behind their official position in order to be freed from punishment in appropriate proceedings. Article 7 of the Charter expressly declares:

> The official position of Defendants, whether as heads of State, or responsible officials in Government departments, shall not be considered as freeing them from responsibility, or mitigating punishment.

On the other hand the very essence of the Charter is that individuals have international duties which transcend the national obligations of obedience imposed by the individual state. He who violates the laws of war cannot obtain immunity while acting in pursuance of the authority of the state if the state in authorizing action moves outside its competence under international law.

It was also submitted on behalf of most of these defendants that in doing what they did they were acting under the orders of Hitler, and therefore cannot be held responsible for the acts committed by them in carrying out these orders. The Charter specifically provides in Article 8:

> The fact that the Defendant acted pursuant to order of his Government or of a superior shall not free him from responsibility, but may be considered in mitigation of punishment.

The provisions of this article are in conformity with the law of all nations. That a soldier was ordered to kill or torture in violation of the international law of war has never been recognized as a defense to such acts of brutality, though, as the Charter here provides, the order may be urged in mitigation

---

[*] Excerpted from "Excerpts from Nuernberg: Act of State Defense," *Trial of the Major War Criminals before the International Military Tribunal* (1947), pp. 223-224.

of the punishment. The true test, which is found in varying degrees in the criminal law of most nations, is not the existence of the order, but whether moral choice was in fact possible.

⊷ ⊱≼◆≽⊰ ⊶

The High Command Case (No. 12)[*]

Superior Orders

Control Council Law No. 10, Article II, paragraphs 4 (*a*) and (*b*), provides:

> 1 (*a*) The official position of any person, whether as Head of State or as a responsible official in a Government Department, does not free him from responsibility for a crime or entitle him to mitigation of punishment.
>
> (*b*) The fact that any person acted pursuant to the order of his Government or of a superior does not free him from responsibility for a crime, but may be considered in mitigation.

These two paragraphs are clear and definite. They relate to the crimes defined in Control Council Law No. 10, Article II, paragraphs 1(*a*), (*b*), and (*c*). All of the defendants in this case held official positions in the armed forces of the Third Reich. Hitler from 1938 on was Commander in Chief of the Armed Forces and was the supreme civil and military authority in the Third Reich, whose personal decrees had the force and effect of law. Under such circumstances to recognize as a defense to the crimes set forth in Control Council 10 that a defendant acted pursuant to the order of his government or of a superior would be in practical effect to say that all the guilt charged in the indictment was the guilt of Hitler alone because he alone possessed the law-making power of the state and the supreme authority to issue civil and military directives. To recognize such a contention would be to recognize an absurdity.

It is not necessary to support the provision of Control Council Law No. 10, Article II, paragraphs 4(*a*) and (*b*), by reason, for we are bound by it as one of the basic authorities under which we function as a judicial tribunal. Reason is not lacking.

In as much as one of the reiterated arguments advanced is the injustice of even charging these defendants with being guilty of the crimes set forth in the indictment, when they were, it is said, merely soldiers and acted under governmental directives and superior orders which they were bound to

---

[*] Excerpted from "Official Transcript of the American Military Tribunal [Tribunal V] in the matter of the *United States of America, vs. Wilhelm von Leeb, et al.*, defendants, sitting at Nuernberg, Germany, on 27 October 1948" in *Trials of War Criminals Before the Nuernberg Military Tribunals Under Control Council Law No. 10*, vol. XI (1950), pp. 507-513, 525.

obey, we shall briefly note what we consider sound reasons for the rejection of such a defense.

The rejection of the defense of superior orders without its being incorporated in Control Council Law No. 10 that such defense shall not exculpate would follow of necessity from our holding that the acts set forth in Control Council Law No. 10 are criminal not because they are therein set forth as crimes but because they then were crimes under international common law. International common law must be superior to and, where it conflicts with, take precedence over national law or directives issued by any national governmental authority. A directive to violate international criminal common law is therefore void and can afford no protection to one who violates such law in reliance on such a directive.

The purpose and effect of all law, national or international, is to restrict or channelize the action of the citizen or subject. International law has for its purpose and effect the restricting and channelizing of the action of nations. Since nations are corporate entities, a composite of a multitude of human beings, and since a nation can plan and act only through its agents and representatives, there can be no effective restriction or channelizing of national action except through control of the agents and representatives of the nation, who form its policies and carry them out in action.

The state being but an inanimate corporate entity or concept, it cannot as such make plans, determine policies, exercise judgment, experience fear, or be restrained or deterred from action except through its animate agents and representatives. It would be an utter disregard of reality and but legal shadow-boxing to say that only the state, the inanimate entity, can have guilt, and that no guilt can be attributed to its animate agents who devise and execute its policies. Nor can it be permitted even in a dictatorship that the dictator, absolute though he may be, shall be the scapegoat on whom the sins of all his governmental and military subordinates are wished; and that, when he is driven into a bunker and presumably destroyed, all the sins and guilt of his subordinates shall be considered to have been destroyed with him.

The defendants in this case who received obviously criminal orders were placed in a difficult position, but servile compliance with orders clearly criminal for fear of some disadvantage or punishment not immediately threatened cannot be recognized as a defense. To establish the defense of coercion or necessity in the face of danger there must be a showing of circumstances such that a reasonable man would apprehend that he was in such imminent physical peril as to deprive him of freedom to choose the right and refrain from the wrong. No such situation has been shown in this case.

Furthermore, it is not a new concept that superior orders are no defense for criminal action. Article 47 of the German Military Penal Code, adopted in 1872, was as follows:

> If through the execution of an order pertaining to the service [Dienstsachen], a penal law is violated, then the superior giving the order is alone responsible. However, the obeying subordinate shall be punished as accomplice [Teilnehmer]: (1) if he went beyond the

order given to him, or (2) if he knew that the order of the superior concerned an act which aimed at a civil or military crime or offense.

The amendment of this in 1940 omitted the last two words "to him" in paragraph (1) above, and in paragraph (2) changed the words "civil or military crime or offense" to "general or military crime or offense." If this amendment had any effect, it extended rather than restricted the scope of the preceding act.

It is interesting to note that an article by Goebbels, the Reich Propaganda Minister, which appeared in the "Voelkischer Beobachter", the official Nazi publication, on 28 May 1944, contained the following correct statement of the law:

> It is not provided in any military law that a soldier in the case of a despicable crime is exempt from punishment because he passes the responsibility to his superior, especially if the orders of the latter are in evident contradiction to all human morality and every international usage of warfare.

Orders

A question of general interest to the various defendants in this case involves the criminal responsibility for drafting, transmitting, and implementing illegal orders of their superiors.

For the first time in history individuals are called upon to answer criminally for certain violations of international law. Individual criminal responsibility has been known, accepted, and applied heretofore as to certain offenses against international law, but the Nuernberg trials have extended that individual responsibility beyond those specific and somewhat limited fields.`

This Tribunal is therefore charged not only to determine whether certain acts infringe international law, but also whether criminal responsibility attaches to an individual for such infringement, and we must look not only to the international law itself but to fundamental principles of criminal law as generally accepted by the civilized nations of the world for determination of that question. Such has been the principle applied by the Tribunals which have preceded us and we conform to that standard. For a defendant to be held criminally responsible, there must be a breach of some moral obligation fixed by international law, a personal act voluntarily done with knowledge of its inherent criminality under international law.

Control Council Law No. 10 [Article II, Paragraph 4(*b*)] provides that:

> The fact that any person acted pursuant to the order of his government or of a superior does not free him from responsibility of a crime, but may be considered in mitigation.

It is urged that a commander becomes responsible for the transmittal in any manner whatsoever of a criminal order. Such a conclusion this Tribunal considers too far-reaching. The transmittal through the chain of command constitutes an implementation of an order. Such orders carry the authoritative weight of the superior who issues them and of the subordinate commanders who pass them on for compliance. The mere intermediate administrative function of transmitting an order directed by a superior authority to subordinate units, however, is not considered to amount to such implementation by the commander through whose headquarters such orders pass. Such transmittal is a routine function which in many instances would be handled by the staff of the commander without being called to his attention. The commander is not in a position to screen orders so transmitted. His headquarters, as an implementing agency, has been bypassed by the superior command.

Furthermore, a distinction must be drawn as to the nature of a criminal order itself. Orders are the basis upon which any army operates. It is basic to the discipline of an army that orders are issued to be carried out. Its discipline is built upon this principle. Without it, no army can be effective and it is certainly not incumbent upon a soldier in a subordinate position to screen the orders of superiors for questionable points of legality. Within certain limitations, he has the right to assume that the orders of his superiors and the state which he serves and which are issued to him are in conformity with international law.

Many of the defendants here were field commanders and were charged with heavy responsibilities in active combat. Their legal facilities were limited. They were soldiers—not lawyers. Military commanders in the field with far-reaching military responsibilities cannot be charged under international law with criminal participation in issuing orders which are not obviously criminal or which they are not shown to have known to be criminal under international law. Such a commander cannot be expected to draw fine distinctions and conclusions as to legality in connection with orders posted by his superiors. He has the right to presume, in the absence of specific knowledge to the contrary, that the legality of such orders has been properly determined before their issuance. He cannot be held criminally responsible for a mere error in judgment as to disputable legal questions.

It is therefore considered that to find a field commander criminally responsible for the transmittal of such an order, he must have passed the order to the chain of command and the order must be one that is criminal upon its face, or one which he is shown to have known was criminal.

While, as stated, a commanding officer can be criminally responsible for implementing an illegal order of his superiors, the question arises as to whether or not he becomes responsible for actions committed within his command pursuant to criminal orders passed down independent of him. The choices which he has for opposition in this case are few: (1) he can issue an order countermanding the order; (2) he can resign; (3) he can sabotage the enforcement of the order within a somewhat limited sphere.

As to countermanding the order of his superiors, he has no legal status or power. A countermanding order would not only subject him to the severest punishment, but would be utterly futile and in Germany, it would undoubtedly have focused the eyes of Hitler on its rigorous enforcement.

②   His second choice—resignation—was not much better. Resignation in wartime is not a privilege generally accorded to officers in an army. This is true in the Army of the United States. Disagreement with a state policy as expressed by an order affords slight grounds for resignation. In Germany, under Hitler, to assert such a ground for resignation probably would have entailed the most serious consequences for an officer.

③   Another field of opposition was to sabotage the order. This he could do only verbally by personal contacts. Such verbal repudiation could never be of sufficient scope to annul its enforcement.

④   A fourth decision he could make was to do nothing.

Control Council Law No. 10, Article II, paragraph 2, provides in pertinent part as follows:

> Any person without regard to nationality or the capacity in which he acted, is deemed to have committed a crime as defined in paragraph 1 of this article, if he... (*b*) was an accessory to the commission of any such crime or ordered or abetted the same or (*c*) *took a consenting part therein* or (*d*) *was connected with* plans or enterprises involving its commission.... [Emphasis supplied.]

As heretofore stated, his "connection" is construed as requiring a personal breach of moral obligation. Viewed from an international standpoint, such has been the interpretation of preceding Tribunals. This connection may however be negative. Under basic principles of command authority and responsibility, an officer who merely stands by while his subordinates execute a criminal order of his superiors which he knows is criminal violates a moral obligation under international law. By doing nothing he cannot wash his hands of international responsibility. His only defense lies in the fact that the order was from a superior which Control Council Law No. 10 declares constitutes only a mitigating circumstance.

In any event in determining the criminal responsibility of the defendants in this case, it becomes necessary to determine not only the criminality of an order in itself but also as to whether or not such an order was criminal on its face. Certain orders of the Wehrmacht and the German army were obviously criminal. No legal opinion was necessary to determine the illegality of such orders. By any standard of civilized nations they were contrary to the customs of war and accepted standard of humanity. Any commanding officer of normal intelligence must see and understand their criminal nature. Any participation in implementing such orders tacit or otherwise, any silent acquiescence in their enforcement by his subordinates, constitutes a criminal act on his part.

There has also been much evidence and discussion in this case concerning the duties and responsibilities of staff officers in connection with the preparation and transmittal of illegal orders. In regard to the responsibility of the chief of staff of a field command, the finding of Tribunal V in Case No. 7 as to certain defendants has been brought to the attention of the Tribunal. It is pointed out that the decision as to chiefs of staff in that case was a factual determination and constitutes a legal determination only insofar as it pertains to the particular facts therein involved. We adopt as sound law the finding therein made, but we do not give that finding the scope that is urged by defense counsel in this case to the effect that all criminal acts within a command are the sole responsibility of the commanding general and that his chief of staff is absolved from all criminal responsibility merely by reason of the fact that his commanding general may be charged with responsibility therefor. It is further pointed out that the facts in that case are not applicable to any defendant on trial in this case.

The testimony of various defendants in this case as to the functions of staff officers and chiefs of staff has not been entirely consistent. Commanding generals on trial have pointed out that there were certain functions which they necessarily left to the chiefs of staff and that at times they did not know of orders which might be issued under authority of their command. Staff officers on trial have urged that a commanding officer was solely responsible for what was done in his name. Both contentions are subject to some scrutiny.

In regard to the functions of staff officers in general as derived from various documents and the testimony of witnesses, it is established that the duties and functions of such officers in the German Army did not differ widely from the duties and functions in other armies of the world. Ideas and general directives must be translated into properly prepared orders if they are to become effective in a military organization. To prepare orders is the function of staff officers. Staff officers are an indispensable link in the chain of their final execution. If the basic idea is criminal under international law, the staff officer who puts that idea into the form of a military order, either himself or through subordinates under him, or takes personal action to see that it is properly distributed to those units where it becomes effective, commits a criminal act under international law....

This Tribunal does not hold field commanders guilty for a failure to properly appraise the fine distinctions of international law, nor for failure to execute courts martial jurisdiction which had been taken away from them, but it does consider them criminally responsible for the transmission of an order that could, and from its terms would, be illegally applied where they have transmitted such an order without proper safeguards as to its application. For that failure on their part they must accept criminal responsibility for its misapplication within subordinate units to which they transmitted it....

Criminal Organizations[*]

The Accused Organizations

Article 9 of the Charter provides:

> At the trial of any individual member of any group or organization the Tribunal may declare (in connection with any act of which the individual may be convicted) that the group or organization of which the individual was a member was a criminal organization.
>
> After receipt of the Indictment the Tribunal shall give such notice as it thinks fit that the prosecution intends to ask the Tribunal to make such declaration and any member of the organization will be entitled to apply to the Tribunal for leave to be heard upon the question of the criminal character of the organization. The Tribunal shall have power to allow or reject the application. If the application is allowed, the Tribunal may direct in what manner the applicants shall be represented and heard.

Article 10 of the Charter makes clear that the declaration of criminality against an accused organization is final, and cannot be challenged in any subsequent criminal proceeding against a member of the organization. Article 10 is as follows:

> In cases where a group or organization is declared criminal by the Tribunal, the competent national authority of any Signatory shall have the right to bring individuals to trial for membership therein before the national, military or occupation courts. In any such case the criminal nature of the group or organization is considered proved and shall not be questioned.

The effect of the declaration of criminality by the Tribunal is well illustrated by Law Number 10 of the Control Council of Germany passed on 20 December 1945, which provides:

> Each of the following acts is recognized as a crime:....
> (d) Membership in categories of a criminal group or organization declared criminal by the International Military Tribunal....
> (3) Any person found guilty of any of the crimes above mentioned may upon conviction be punished as shall be determined by the Tribunal to be just. Such punishment may consist of one or more of the following:
> (a) Death.
> (b) Imprisonment for life or a term of years, with or without hard labor.
> (c) Fine, and imprisonment with or without hard labor, in lieu thereof.

In effect, therefore, a member of an organization which the Tribunal has declared to be criminal may be subsequently convicted of the crime of membership and be punished for that crime by death. This is not to assume

---

[*] Excerpted from "Criminal Organizations," *Trial of the Major War Criminals before the International Military Tribunal* (1947), pp. 255-257, 262, 267-268, 273, 275.

that international or military courts which will try these individuals will not exercise appropriate standards of justice. This is a far reaching and novel procedure. Its application, unless properly safeguarded, may produce great injustice.

Article 9, it should be noted, uses the words "The Tribunal may declare", so that the Tribunal is vested with discretion as to whether it will declare any organization criminal. This discretion is a judicial one and does not permit arbitrary action, but should be exercised in accordance with well-settled legal principles, one of the most important of which is that criminal guilt is personal, and that mass punishments should be avoided. If satisfied of the criminal guilt of any organization or group, this Tribunal should not hesitate to declare it to be criminal because the theory of "group criminality" is new, or because it might be unjustly applied by some subsequent tribunals. On the other hand, the Tribunal should make such declaration of criminality so far as possible in a manner to insure that innocent persons will not be punished.

A criminal organization is analogous to a criminal conspiracy in that the essence of both is cooperation for criminal purposes. There must be a group bound together and organized for a common purpose. The group must be formed or used in connection with the commission of crimes denounced by the Charter. Since the declaration with respect to the organizations and groups will, as has been pointed out, fix the criminality of its members, that definition should exclude persons who had no knowledge of the criminal purposes or acts of the organization and those who were drafted by the State for membership, unless they were personally implicated in the commission of acts declared criminal by Article 6 of the Charter as members of the organization. Membership alone is not enough to come within the scope of these declarations....

The Indictment asks that the Tribunal declare to be criminal the following organizations: The Leadership Corps of the Nazi Party; the Gestapo; the SD; the SS; the SA; the Reich Cabinet, and the General Staff and High Command of the German Armed Forces.

The Leadership Corps of the Nazi Party

...The Tribunal declares to be criminal within the meaning of the Charter the group composed of those members of the Leadership Corps holding the positions enumerated in the preceding paragraph who became or remained members of the organization with knowledge that it was being used for the commission of acts declared criminal by Article 6 of the Charter, or who were personally implicated as members of the organization in the commission of such crimes. The basis of this finding is the participation of the organization in War Crimes and Crimes against Humanity connected with the war, the group declared criminal cannot include, therefore, persons who had ceased to hold the positions enumerated in the preceding paragraph prior to 1 September 1939.

Gestapo and SD

...Conclusion

The Gestapo and SD were used for purposes which were criminal under the Charter involving the persecution and extermination of the Jews, brutalities, and killings in concentration camps, excesses in the administration of occupied territories, the administration of the slave labor program, and the mistreatment and murder of prisoners of war. The Defendant Kaltenbrunner, who was a member of this organization, was among those who used it for these purposes. In dealing with the Gestapo the Tribunal includes all executive and administrative officials of Amt IV of the RSHA or concerned with Gestapo administration in other departments of the RSHA and all local Gestapo officials serving both inside and outside of Germany, including the members of the Frontier Police, but not including the members of the Border and Customs Protection or the Secret Field Police, except such members as have been specified above. At the suggestion of the Prosecution the Tribunal does not include persons employed by the Gestapo for purely clerical, stenographic, janitorial, or similar unofficial routine tasks. In dealing with the SD the Tribunal includes Ämter III, VI, and VII of the RSHA and all other members of the SD, including all local representatives and agents, honorary or otherwise, whether they were technically members of the SS or not, but not including honorary informers who were not members of the SS, and members of the Abwehr who were transferred to the SD.

The Tribunal declares to be criminal within the meaning of the Charter the group composed of those members of the Gestapo and SD holding the positions enumerated in the preceding paragraph who became or remained members of the organization with knowledge that it was being used for the commission of acts declared criminal by Article 6 of the Charter, or who were personally implicated as members of the organization in the commission of such crimes. The basis of this finding is the participation of the organization in War Crimes and Crimes against Humanity connected with the war; this group declared criminal cannot include, therefore, persons who had ceased to hold the positions enumerated in the preceding paragraph prior to 1 September 1939....

Conclusions: The SS was utilized for purposes which were criminal under the Charter involving the persecution and extermination of the Jews, brutalities and killings in concentration camps, excesses in the administration of occupied territories, the administration of the slave labor program and the mistreatment and murder of prisoners of war. The Defendant Kaltenbrunner was a member of the SS implicated in these activities. In dealing with the SS the Tribunal includes all persons who had been officially accepted as members of the SS including the members of the Allgemeine SS, members of the Waffen SS, members of the SS Totenkopf Verbände, and the members of any of the different police forces who were members of the SS. The Tribunal does not include the so-called SS riding units. Der Sicherheitsdienst des Reichsfürer SS (commonly known as the SD) is dealt with in the Tribunal's Judgment on the Gestapo and SD.

The Tribunal declares to be criminal within the meaning of the Charter the group composed of those persons who had been officially accepted as members of the SS as enumerated in the preceding paragraph who became or remained members of the organization with knowledge that it was being used for the commission of acts declared criminal by Article 6 of the Charter, or who were personally implicated as members of the organization in the commission of such crimes, excluding, however, those who were drafted into membership by the State in such a way as to give them no choice in the matter, and who had committed no such crimes. The basis of this finding is the participation of the organization in War Crimes and Crimes against Humanity connected with the war; this group declared criminal cannot include, therefore, persons who had ceased to belong to the organizations enumerated in the preceding paragraph prior to 1 September 1939.

The SA

...Conclusion

Until the purge beginning on 30 June 1934, the SA was a group composed in large part of ruffians and bullies who participated in the Nazi outrages of that period. It has not been shown, however, that these atrocities were part of a specific plan to wage aggressive war, and the Tribunal therefore cannot hold that these activities were criminal under the Charter. After the purge, the SA was reduced to the status of a group of unimportant Nazi hangers-on. Although in specific instances some units of the SA were used for the commission of War Crimes and Crimes against Humanity, it cannot be said that its members generally participated in or even knew of the criminal acts. For these reasons the Tribunal does not declare the SA to be a criminal organization within the meaning of Article 9 of the Charter.

The Reich Cabinet

The Prosecution has named as a criminal organization the Reich Cabinet (Die Reichsregierung) consisting of members of the ordinary cabinet after 30 January 1933, members of the Council of Ministers for the Defense of the Reich and members of the Secret Cabinet Council. The Tribunal is of [the] opinion that no declaration of criminality should be made with respect to the Reich Cabinet for two reasons: (1) because it is not shown that after 1937 it ever really acted as a group or organization; (2) because the group of persons here charged is so small that members could be conveniently tried in proper cases without resort to a declaration that the Cabinet of which they were members was criminal.

UNITED NATIONS COMMISSION ON HUMAN RIGHTS: REPORT ON THE CONSEQUENCES OF IMPUNITY*

Question of the Human Rights of All Persons Subjected to Any Form of Detention or Imprisonment— Question of Enforced or Involuntary Disappearances

Forty-sixth session (January 24, 1990)

Report of the Working Group on Enforced or Involuntary Disappearances

18. Local, regional and international non-governmental organizations ... submitted reports about the general framework within which enforced or involuntary disappearances took place in each country. As in the past, one of the most serious problems set forth concerned the *de facto* impunity enjoyed by those responsible for disappearances in countries under review. That the culprits would be exempt from punishment for their actions contributed, in the estimation of these reports, to the continuing occurrence of disappearances.

19. The most important phenomenon relating to the problem of impunity was set forth as the *de facto* non-functioning of established judicial procedures charged with human rights concerns. Judicial procedures in many countries where disappearances had allegedly occurred often proved incapable of protecting the rights of detainees in military or police custody.

Habeas corpus proceedings, for example, only infrequently resulted in the reappearance of the missing person. Furthermore, it was alleged that official inquiries into human rights violations very seldom led to the prosecution and conviction of military or police personnel. Paramilitary groups allegedly often enjoyed similar degrees of impunity.

20. According to non-governmental organizations, the non-effectiveness of judicial procedures, in most cases, was not a result of constitutional shortcomings or insufficient *de jure* powers of these bodies. On the contrary, many of the Governments concerned, especially civilian democracies elected after periods of military rule, had reportedly strengthened powers and widened the scope of institutions and procedures concerned with disappearances. For various reasons, however, such mechanisms had allegedly demonstrated shortcomings when implementing this authority. Judges and other responsible authorities had allegedly often failed to investigate human rights violations thoroughly. Those that had attempted to do so were reportedly confronted with intransigence on the part of military and police officials, who allegedly often restricted or refused access to detention centres, and failed to appear when summoned to court

---

*United Nations Doc. E/CN.4/1990/13.

proceedings. Those leading investigations into disappearances were reportedly sometimes subject to death threats or murdered.

21. Communications received from non-governmental organizations, associations of relatives of missing persons and family members also revealed threats, harassment and violence directed at persons directly involved in the search for disappeared persons, at human rights activists defending or promoting cases of disappeared persons in judicial proceedings, and at witnesses capable of providing information on disappearances. These problems were reportedly accentuated by too strict an interpretation of rules of procedure on the part of official judicial organs which often rejected appeals by relatives searching for disappeared persons when the information they could provide had been *prima facie* too vague. Together, these factors allegedly helped to breed an attitude of mistrust among the general population towards official bodies, and a perception that judicial institutions and procedures were unable or unwilling to protect or promote human rights concerns....

23. The Working Group also received reports that, in several countries where large numbers of disappearances had occurred, amnesty laws granting impunity from legal sanctions to alleged violators of human rights, including those responsible for disappearances, had been promulgated and implemented. The Working Group has consistently expressed its concern about such amnesties, which prevent families of disappeared persons both from continuing the search for their missing relatives, through official judicial proceedings, and from obtaining an effective remedy for the violation committed. More generally, these measures, in maintaining structures responsible for enforced or involuntary disappearances, may leave the impression in the society that such crimes can recur in the future....

344. Perhaps the single most important factor contributing to the phenomenon of disappearances may be that of impunity. The Working Group's experience over the past 10 years has confirmed the age-old adage that impunity breeds contempt for the law. Perpetrators of human rights violations, whether civilian or military, will become all the more brazen when they are not held to account before a court of law. Impunity can also induce victims of these practices to resort to a form of self-help and take the law into their own hands, which in turn exacerbates the spiral of violence.

345. Military courts contribute significantly to impunity, in the Working Group's experience. A recurrent theme in times of internal crisis or under the doctrine of national security is that military personnel attested to have engaged in gross misconduct, are almost invariably acquitted or given sentences that are disproportionate to the crime committed. Subsequent promotions are even commonplace.

346. One other cause of impunity, apart from the conduct induced by the State, is often institutional paralysis of the judicial system. In particular, the virtual or total lack of implementation of *habeas corpus*. Paralysis may be due either to overburdening of the judicial system on top of a longstanding lack of resources, or to assassination or systematic intimidation of judicial officers and other magistrates. Paralysis may also occur through lack of co-operation by the executive branch. *Habeas corpus*, for instance, is

potentially one of the most powerful legal tools for unearthing the fate or whereabouts of a disappeared person. The most sophisticated rules governing this institution, however, are rendered inoperative in a situation where co-operation stops at the barrack's gate. In certain countries, *habeas corpus* laws have purposefully been subjected to severe restrictions.

347. On the question of impunity and responsibility, the Working Group's position, though clear and consistent from the very beginning, seems worth restating.... [T]hose responsible for disappearances should be prosecuted to the full extent of the law, a task that falls on the State. This concern was shared very early on by the General Assembly in resolution 33/173, which is one of the bases for the Group's mandate.

UNITED NATIONS GENERAL ASSEMBLY: RESOLUTION ON DISAPPEARED PERSONS

General Assembly Resolution 33/173
(December 20, 1978)

The General Assembly,

Recalling the provisions of the Universal Declaration of Human Rights, in particular articles 3, 5, 9, 10, and 11 concerning, *inter alia*, the right to life, liberty and security of person, freedom from torture, freedom from arbitrary arrest and detention, and the right to a fair and public trial, and the provisions of articles 6, 7, 9 and 10 of the International Covenant on Civil and Political Rights, which define and establish safeguards for certain of these rights,...

1. *Calls upon* Governments:

(a) In the event of reports of enforced or involuntary disappearances, to devote appropriate resources to searching for such persons and to undertake speedy and impartial investigations;

(b) To ensure that law enforcement and security authorities or organizations are fully accountable, especially in law, in the discharge of their duties, such accountability to include legal responsibility for unjustifiable excesses which might lead to enforced or involuntary disappearances and to other violations of human rights....

ARGENTINA: AMNESTY LAW ("LAW OF NATIONAL PACIFICATION")

Law No. 22.924 (September 22, 1983)

Article 1

The penal actions arising from crimes committed with terrorist or subversive motivation or objective between May 25, 1973 and June 17, 1982 shall be declared annulled. The benefits granted by this Law extend, in the same way, to all criminal activities resulting from or motivated by the development of actions directed at the avoidance, prevention or termination of the terrorist or subversive activities mentioned, whatever may have been their nature or the legal tenet violated. The effects of this Law extend to the authors, participants, instigators, accomplices and accessories, and include related common crimes and related military crimes.

Article 2

Excluded from the benefits provided in the preceding Article are members of illicit terrorist or subversive organizations who, on the date until which the benefits of the Law remain effective, do not reside legally and openly in the territory of the Argentine Nation or in places subject to its jurisdiction, or who have demonstrated by their conduct an intention to continue their connection with these organizations.

Article 3

Also excluded are unconditional sentences resulting from the crimes and actions of a penal nature mentioned in Article 1, without prejudice to the powers that, in conformity with paragraph 6 of Article 36 of the National Constitution, the National Executive Power may exercise in matters of pardon or commutation of penalties imposed by these sentences in order to complement the pacifying purpose of this Law.

Article 4

Not included in the benefits of this Law are the crimes of economic subversion characterized in Articles 6, 7, 8 and 9 of Law No. 20.340.

Article 5

No one can be interrogated, investigated, summoned to appear or enjoined in an manner because of imputations or suspicions of having committed the crimes or participated in the actions referred to in Article 1 of this Law, or on suspicion of knowledge of them, or of their circumstances, their authors, participants, instigators, accomplices, or accessories.

Article 6

Under the force of the present Law, civil actions arising from the crimes and acts comprised in Article 1 are also nullified. A special Law will determine compensatory regulations on the part of the State.

Article 7

The present Law will function with full rights from the time of its proclamation and will apply at the Government's initiative or by request.

Article 8

The Common Court, Federal Court, Military Court or military organization before which cases are being tried, and to which this Law may be applicable, *prima facie*, will, without further procedures and within forty-eight (48) hours, refer them to the corresponding court of appeals or to the Supreme Council of the Armed Forces. It will be understood that within the scope of the present Law are those cases in process or temporarily stayed in which acts are being investigated whose perpetrators may not yet have been singled out but are thought to be members of the Armed Forces, Security Forces or Police, or in which it is said that they appealed to some of these organizations.

The provisions expressed previously also apply when conditions of terrorism have been alleged or it has been shown to involve an apparently irresistible force.

By order of the corresponding court, all cases dealing with the same acts which have not been tried at the present time will be tried jointly.

Article 9

Once the cases have been received by the courts of appeal indicated in the preceding Article the Public Ministry or Federal Prosecutor and the plaintiff, if any, will be given a hearing for three (3) working days and at the end of this period, a decision will be rendered within a period of five (5) days.

Article 10

The only evidence that will be admitted is that which has been added to the case and the official reports that are essential for the assessment of the facts or the behavior being judged. In these reports, no reference will be made other than those that are indispensable for the pertinent assessment. The assembled evidence will be appraised in conformity with the system of free convictions.

Article 11

When the benefits of this Law are to be accorded to pending cases, the dismissal will be prescribed by annulment of the action.

Article 12

The Common, Federal, or Military Judges or military organizations before which indictments or complaints based on the imputation of crimes and acts covered in Article 1 are brought will reject them without any trial.

Article 13

The present Law will apply even though a prescribed action or penalty may have intervened.

Article 14

In case of doubt the ruling should be in favor of the recognition of the benefits established by the preceding provisions.

Article 15

For the purpose of the present Law, those norms that contradict it will not apply....

ARGENTINA: AMNESTY NULLIFICATION

Law No. 23.040 (December 27, 1983)

Article 1

The *de facto* Law No. 22.924 shall be revoked as unconstitutional and declared irrevocably null.

Article 2

The *de facto* Law No. 22.924 has no legal effect in the judgment of penal, civil, administrative or military responsibilities arising from the acts it pretends to cover, the principle of the more benign penal law established in Article 2 of the Penal Code being in particular inapplicable in this instance.

The provision of the preceding paragraph will not be altered by the existence of final judicial decisions that may have applied the *de facto* Law No. 22.924.

Article 3

Any person who may have recovered his freedom through the application of the *de facto* Law No. 22.924 must present himself before the court where the case was filed by the fifth (5th) day of the effectiveness of the present Law. Otherwise, he will be declared a fugitive and his capture will be ordered without the requirement of previous summons.

If a civilian subjected to military jurisdiction is involved, the appearance referred to in the preceding paragraph can be effected simultaneously with the objection to this judgment, and in the court where this objection is filed.

Article 4

In the cases described in Article 3, an exemption from prison and a release from confinement will take effect without the necessity of meeting the requirements established in Article 379 of the Code of Criminal Procedure, unless there exist reasons to presume that the accused will try to evade the course of justice.

The intervening court, if it grants freedom under bail, can impose on the accused, in addition to the obligations referred to in Article 336 of the Code of Criminal Procedure, that of having to present himself periodically before the court or the police station nearest to his actual residence.

The resolution that establishes the freedom under bail and that which imposes the obligations mentioned in the preceding paragraph cannot be appealed. That which denies the freedom under bail can be appealed through a statement submitted within a period of three (3) days....

ARGENTINA: TRIAL OF MEMBERS OF THE FORMER MILITARY JUNTA

Federal Criminal and Correctional Court of Appeals, Federal District of Buenos Aires[*]

(Cámara Nacional de Apelacionesen lo Criminal y Correccional de la Capital Federal) Judgment of December 9, 1985

These proceedings were commenced pursuant to Decree No. 158 issued by the National Executive Power on December 13, 1983, ordering those named therein [nine members of the former Military Juntas that ruled Argentina from 1976-1983] be brought to justice before the Supreme Council of the Armed Forces, on charges of homicide, unlawful deprivation of freedom, and torture. Trial on those charges shall in no way prejudice later trials for other crimes which the above mentioned superior officers may have perpetrated as primary or secondary parties, instigators or accomplices....

[T]he measures which were ... taken were radically different than those authorized by the law. The operating structure of the armed forces continued to function in the same manner as before, but those subordinated to the defendants detained a large number of people, lodged them clandestinely in military units or in places controlled by the armed forces, subjected them to interrogation under torture, kept them in captivity under inhumane conditions, and, finally, either submitted those persons to the courts or to the National Executive Power, released them, or killed them. These proceedings, which assume the secret derogation of the laws in force, were carried out in accordance with plans approved and implemented by the military commanders.

In order to ascertain the reasons that prompted the defendants to take those measures, it should be recalled that the defendants assigned top priority to the objective of obtaining all possible information considered useful in the struggle against terrorist organizations.... Military directives emphasized that the success of the struggle against subversion greatly depended on the scope and quality of the intelligence services.... The defendants did not hesitate in downgrading the law in order to obtain political power, the use of torture, inhumane treatment, the imposition of

---

[*] Excerpted from "Conviction of Former Military Commanders (Federal Criminal and Correctional Court of Appeals; Buenos Aires)," *Human Rights Law Journal*, vol. 8, no. 2-4 (1987), pp. 368-369, 372-374, 378-379, 383, 386-388, 390-393, 395-397, 400-401, 404-406, 410-418, 421-424. Case reported and translated by: Henry Dahl and Alejandro M. Garro. [Editor's note: To clarify their choice of English words and phrases, the translators of this appellate court decision and the four selections which follow inserted the original Spanish-language terms of the documents in brackets at several points in the translation. These insertions have been omitted in the present volume.]

work and the imposition of the belief that no one was able to help the captives. For them, those were the most effective means of obtaining information....

Lack of confidence in civilized methods to prevent the repetition of terrorist acts or to punish the instigators, the certainty that national and international public opinion would not tolerate a massive application of the death penalty, and the desire to avoid the public scrutiny that such a course of action would have entailed, prompted the defendants to take the steps that were subsequently followed in the campaign against subversion. In essence, those steps consisted of kidnapping and then physically eliminating those who were identified—according to the judgment of those who executed the orders—as subversive criminals. That the system chosen to fight subversion departed from the rule-of-law—even from those laws of exception which are designed for times of emergency—is reflected not only in the violence characterizing the operations, but also in the measures which were taken for the purpose of concealing the arrests and the fate of the detainees, submitting them to unacceptable conditions of captivity. All the evidence which has been produced and evaluated in the preceding chapters confirms this assertion.

On the basis of evidence, it can be concluded that the defendants deliberately concealed the facts from the courts, from the families of the victims, from national and foreign institutions and organizations, from the Church, from governments of foreign countries, and from society at large.

The system put into practice guaranteed immunity to those primarily responsible for the illegal acts. The immunity was granted by concealing evidence, by not reporting the crimes, and by providing erroneous or insufficient information to the courts. Only this immunity made possible this criminal method. The immunity was also assured by the lack of intervention on the part of those authorities who were in charge of preventing crimes.

In sum, the commanders secretly established a criminal method for fighting terrorism. Low-ranking officers of the armed forces were granted broad discretion to deprive of freedom whoever appeared to be, according to intelligence information, an agent of subversion. It was decided that the investigations were to be conducted under torture and that the detainees were to be subjected to inhuman treatment while being held in clandestine captivity. The broadest discretion was conferred on those officers to decide how to proceed with the victim.... Had the victims been placed under the jurisdiction of the courts or at the disposal of the National Executive Power, the legal system would have taken care of them. However, their captors enjoyed absolute discretion to decide whether to set them free or to kill them.

This discretionary power granted to subordinate officers for choosing their targets led more often than not to the detention of people who had no connections with the struggle against subversion or were involved with it in a very indirect manner....

Limits of the Judgment

The Court must consider the 700 cases that the prosecutor has selected in formulating the charges. The factual and legal issues raised by those formal charges and the corresponding defenses mark the boundaries of the competence of this Court. Those issues constitute the so-called *thema decidendum* of this judgment. This does not in any way imply—and this has been expressly clarified by the prosecutor—that the illicit acts perpetrated with the motive of repression, and carried out by the armed forces in order to combat terrorism, are limited to 700 cases.

As the proceedings have shown, there is sufficient evidence indicating that the actual number of victims ranged in the thousands of people: some disappeared (a euphemism which designated death) and some regained their liberty only after being deprived of it clandestinely and after suffering financial and spiritual losses, torture and seizure of their property.

Thus it remains clear that the particular cases considered in this chapter do not exhaust in any manner the quantity of injustices committed. The limited number of cases does, however, reduce the task of the Court to reasonably manageable terms. This task would otherwise be virtually impossible given the magnitude of the criminal events. To do otherwise may dangerously delay the duration of these proceedings and impair the defendants' right of due process. One manifestation of the right to due process is to obtain a judicial pronouncement that puts an end, as soon as possible, to a situation of uncertainty and to the restriction of liberty imposed by the criminal proceedings (Supreme Court, [*Decisions*], 272:188; 301:197)....

Weight Given to the Findings of the National Commission on the Disappearances of Persons

In connection with what has been said regarding evidence, the report made by the National Commission on the Disappearances of Persons (CONADEP) has been incorporated together with the other records using the information provided by victims of repression. A file was made out of each case, and some of those files had been submitted as evidence by the prosecution.

[CONADEP was created by Decree No. 187 of December 15, 1983 (Official Gazette, December 19, 1983). The purpose of this commission, as explained in Article 1 of the decree, was to clarify the circumstances surrounding the disappearance of persons.] According to its purpose, the tasks assigned to it, and its budget (Article 9, Decree No. 187), CONADEP was an entity of public law (Article 3 of the Civil Code). Members of CONADEP were appointed by the government and had the status of public officials (Decree No. 187, Article 5), and the documents drafted by them have the status of public instruments (Civil Code, Article 979(2)). The information contained in the reports drafted by members of CONADEP on the basis of the statements made by victims (Article 2(a) of Decree No. 187) do not amount to testimonial evidence, because those statements do not meet the requirements established by military law for the declaration of witnesses. It is therefore unnecessary to question the fact that they had not taken the oath required by law.

However, the fact that these statements were not made under oath does not deprive them of their value as evidence, nor does the law prohibit their consideration. If appropriately introduced as evidence (C.M.J. [Code of Military Justice], Articles 201, 202, 305 et seq.), the influence of those statements in the outcome of the case, its potential for creating a sense of certainty in the judge, will depend on a careful weighing of these statements within an entire set of factors of different and diverse natures. Furthermore, it should be pointed out that the Court is not going to consider a fact as proven on the exclusive basis of the evidence furnished by CONADEP....

Having made these considerations, we now turn to an examination of the cases....

The Cases: Factual Circumstances...

1.   The unlawful deprivations of freedom that have been proven correspond to the definition of the crime found in Article 144 bis (1) of the Argentine Criminal Code[2]...

2.   It has been found that a large number of the captives were subjected to physical tortures, in some cases in order to obtain information from them and in other cases, when no information could be extracted from them, in order to break their will.

We have already referred to the nature of the torture inflicted, the motivations behind such actions, and the state of total helplessness in which the victims were found. The victims were continually reminded that they were completely deprived of protection and subject to the whim of their captors (see Section two of this decision, Chapter XIII).

These tortious acts constitute a crime defined as infliction of torture ... by the Law which was in force at the time the acts were committed (Law No. 14.616). This provision is to be applied because it is more lenient than the one presently in force embodied in Article 2 of Law No. 23.077....

5.   It has been verified that in many cases those persons who carried out the detentions took illegal possession of things of value belonging to the victims or their families. This occurred during and after the acts of violence. This constitutes the crime of robbery, defined in Article 164 of the Criminal Code.... [T]hat the personnel sent to detain people might steal property for their own benefit was necessarily contemplated and consented by those who gave the orders. The fact that the defendants were able to foresee the results of their actions and consented to it evidences recklessness on their part. The

---

2 Article 144 bis of the Argentine Criminal Code provides: "Jailing or imprisonment from one to five years and special disqualification for twice that period of time shall be imposed on: (1) Any public official who, misusing his powers, or without acting according to the formalities prescribed by law, deprives anybody of his personal liberty."

criminal acts will be imputed to the defendants taking into account this subjective feature....

Concealment: In the opinion of the prosecutor, the defendants who succeeded the original members of the Military Junta who took power on March 24, 1976, must have learned of the crimes of homicide, illegal deprivation of liberty, and torture for which their predecessors were responsible. The prosecutor asserts that the defendants failed to inform the judicial authorities of those crimes, in spite of their obligation to do so as public officers (Criminal Code, Article 277(6)).

In the opinion of this Court, an essential element of this crime is that the official had knowledge of the commission of the criminal acts which he was obliged to report to the competent authorities. It is therefore necessary to demonstrate in a specific manner whether the defendants had actual knowledge of each and every crime, because only under such circumstances it can be charged that one failed to give notice of known facts. This is why the Court has pointed out the lack of evidence regarding the defendants' actual knowledge of the crimes the existence of which they were accused of having concealed....

Grounds of Justification Alleged by the Defendants

Legal Background

Having examined the legal significance of the criminal behavior on the basis of which the prosecutor brought formal charges against the defendants, we will now examine whether that behavior fits the criminal definitions or whether there are valid defensive arguments that may justify the criminal behavior.

While considering this issue, it is necessary to examine the political and institutional situation in Argentina at the time the defendants decided to launch the campaign against terrorist subversion.

The Terrorist Phenomenon in Argentina before March 24, 1976

It has been sufficiently proven that the terrorist phenomenon went as far back as 1960. This situation brought about a general sense of fear on the part of the population and serious concern on the part of the authorities. It is also beyond discussion that by the beginning of the 1970's terrorist activities increased significantly. This increase became evident in the methods resorted to by the insurgents, the amount of terrorist acts, the military structure of the operations, the offensive acts, the capabilities of the terrorist groups, the financial resources acquired through theft; kidnappings and other crimes; the operational infrastructure and means of communication used by the commandos, the organization which provided those groups with immunity from prosecution, the indiscriminate and irrational terrorist attacks perpetrated by surprise, the insurgents' capabilities to intercept the mass media, and their capacity to take over police stations and military units.

In brief, it has been proven that terrorist subversion became a condition without which the criminal acts under examination probably would not have taken place. Moreover, the Court acknowledges that those terrorist acts amounted to an illegal act of aggression against Argentine society and the State. It is also acknowledged by this Court that Argentine society was compelled to react. This reaction was necessary in order to prevent that further increase of terrorism which would endanger the stability of institutions whose philosophical foundations are found in the Federal Constitution....

Legal Response to Terrorism Prior to 1976

From 1970 on the federal government began to enact special legislation in order to strengthen the defense of the State against terrorism....

Legal Response to Terrorism after March, 1976

On March 24, 1976, the commanders of the armed forces took administration of the country. A military *junta* terminated the powers of the President of the Argentine Nation as well as the mandates of the governors and vice-governors of the provinces. Congress was dissolved and the members of the Supreme Court of Justice were removed from office (Act for the Process of National Reorganization, March 24, 1976, Official Gazette of March 29, 1976).

The basic goal set by the Military Junta was the following: "To restore the essential values which are fundamental for governing the State, emphasizing the sense of morality, capability and efficiency. These values are paramount in order to rebuild the content and image of the Nation, eradicate subversion, and promote national economic development. These goals will assure the subsequent reestablishment of a democracy—republican, representative, and federal—that is appropriate to the requirements for progress of the Argentine people." (Law Explaining the Purpose and Basic Objectives of the Process of National Reorganization, Official Gazette, March 29, 1976).

The Military Junta granted broad powers to itself and their appointees. Between March 29, 1976 and 1979, when the terrorist groups were militarily defeated, the *junta* issued numerous enactments regulating the fight against terrorism. These enactments include the so-called institutional acts issued in 1976....

Grounds of Justification

Having examined the legal background and the legal means which were available, we must now determine whether the means chosen by the former commanders to fight subversion were in accordance with the law. More specifically, we must ascertain whether such methods were illegal, or whether their actions are excused by any of the causes of justification provided by the Criminal Code....

[handwritten margin note: Goal of the Military Junta (March 24, 1976 – 1979)]

We must therefore ascertain whether any of the following causes of justification are found: a) the defense of state of necessity; b) obedience to the law; or c) self-defense....

The state of necessity may be defined as a situation in which a person believes it necessary to commit a criminal offense in order to avoid a greater harm or evil than that sought to be prevented by the criminal offense (Ricardo C. Nuñez, *Derecho Penal Argentino*, ed. Bibliográfica Argentina, Buenos Aires, 1964, vol, I., p. 316). The state of necessity justification for committing a crime is recognized by the Argentine Criminal Code. The Criminal Code exempts from punishment those persons who commit a crime in order to avoid a greater and imminent harm or evil for which they are not responsible.

The criminal offense must be defined in the Criminal Code, and the evil sought to be avoided must be greater than that sought to be prevented by the law defining the offense. The comparison between the evils or harm to be avoided must be carried out on a case-by-case basis. The assessment of those evils must be made considering the liberal nature of our legal system and in light of a systematic interpretation of the different penalties for those criminal offenses. Human life and the preservation of that life are at the apex of the scale of legal values. Also the evil to be avoided must be imminent. There can be no state of necessity if the danger that the harm will occur is not immediate....

It is evident that the incriminating conduct which prompted the bringing of the criminal charges (illegal deprivation of freedom, torture, robbery, homicide) produced great harm, and that such harm was produced by those who were in command of the forces of the State. It is also clear that such a harm was connected with another harm sought to be avoided, that is, the acts of terror carried out by subversive groups.

The evils brought by the subversive groups presented two principal evils: (a) the actual killings, robberies, and bombs thrown by those groups; and (b) the danger that such a harm posed to the very existence of the State. The main problem to be resolved was how to avoid the first evil and how to preclude the subversive groups from taking over the government. In spite of the existence of this difficult problem, it is the opinion of this Court that the defense of necessity does not apply to this case....

If the idea was to kill and kidnap in order to prevent the subversive groups from continuing to kill and kidnap, then this would not be a situation where a "lesser" evil is being resorted to in order to avoid a "greater" evil. Both evils would have produced, at best, equal damage. Therefore, the defense of necessity does not apply.

Furthermore, if the defendants perpetrated those crimes in order to preclude the subversive groups from overthrowing the government and establishing a totalitarian and oppressive regime, this evil—albeit perhaps greater than the one sought to be avoided—was not imminent. Although this Court agrees with the arguments raised by counsels for the defense with regard to the gravity of the situation and the perverse objectives of the terrorists, those objectives were far from ever being achieved.

The subversives had not occupied or overtaken any portion of the national territory. Their acts had not been acknowledged in this country or abroad as producing a state of war. Their acts were not manifestly supported by a foreign power. And, the subversives lacked the support of the population. In brief, the terrorists were far from being able to take over the government of the country, an evil which could have eventually justified the reaction of the *junta*…. Moreover, the defense based on an existing state of necessity must be rejected for the reason that the defendants failed to exhaust less damaging means to control the subversive activities.

In view of the stage of the struggle against subversion at the time the Military Junta took command of that fight, and taking into account the broad legislative and executive powers of the *junta*, the defendants could have resorted to methods which were less harmful than those of which they actually availed themselves. Among many other means, the defendants could have provided for the enactment of new criminal and procedural laws in order to speed up the proceedings against subversives, issued military regulations; established summary proceedings pursuant to the Code of Military Justice for the prosecution of ordinary criminal offenses, military crimes, and violations of military regulations perpetrated by subversives; arrested at the disposition of the Executive Branch all those terrorists against whom no sufficient evidence was gathered to bring formal charges; provided for an expanded fight to emigrate while establishing the most severe punishment for those who returned to the country, given immunity and other privileges to those who became informants; and pursued international agreements with neighboring countries for the purpose of avoiding the escape of subversives or the plotting of subversive activities in those countries. In sum, there were many options the government could have pursued before they established in Argentina a state of *faida* or collective vengeance….

Let us see … whether there existed an unlawful aggression and the means used by the defendant to prevent the aggression were reasonable…. The heart of the issue is whether the government was justified in the methods it used to fight aggression. Or, in the words of the law, whether there was a "rational need of the means employed to prevent or avert the aggression…."

Of course several acts taken individually may have been justified. For example, when a police station or garrison was stormed, those who defended them were fully justified—even if the attackers were killed. The justification for that reaction is two-fold: the police forces acted pursuant to their legal duties (Criminal code, Article 34(4) and in self-defense (Article 34(6) and (7). The same can be said if during the legitimate action the police or the soldiers shot back. The overpowering and arrest of a person who bears arms without authorization is also justified on grounds of both the authority's duty and of self-defense. The same reasoning applies to the capture of a member of an illegal subversive group when he is carrying the message.

Still, even in these cases, once the criminal is apprehended, torture, homicide and illegal deprivation of freedom are impermissible. And, once the aggression is neutralized the persistence of violence and deprivation of freedom ceases to be a legitimate defense and becomes an unnecessary revenge....

It then follows that the acts in question were not committed as self-defense. Neither the illegal deprivations of freedom, the tortures, the homicides, the robberies, the damage nor any other illegal action—even if an illegal aggression prompted their reaction—can be deemed a necessary reaction....

The illegal deprivations of freedom, the tortures, the forced confessions, the homicides and the robberies with which the defendants have been charged are acts of obvious illegality. These criminal offenses violated legal rights of vital importance. They were also acts against society inasmuch as they attacked fundamental aspects of the legal order that rules society as a whole. The acts in question cannot be considered the justified means to a justified end. These proceedings have already established that the tactics deployed against terrorism did not conform with the law in force, with Argentine tradition, or with the custom of civilized nations. It was also made clear that the State had many alternative means at its disposal which were entirely suitable.

Because the means used were atrocious and inhuman and because society was—and still is—shocked by such acts, these illegal acts fall outside the cultural behavioral patterns of this Nation. The Republic's interest, shown through its most diverse activities, is not in seeking war but peace, is not in the rejection of law but in its enforcement. The Nation's interest is not, and never has been, in the regression to a primitive state of nature. It should be noticed, for instance, that although the death penalty had been considered for adoption by the Criminal Code, and it is still a penalty under the C.M.J., it has never been applied in recent decades.

Although terrorist subversion threatened the root of society, the behavior of the accused—far from re-establishing order—threatened the very fabric of society.... The discrepancy between the acts that were carried out and what is admissible to a civilized society appears to have been recognized by the commanders themselves. For this reason, they chose to cover the procedures they had employed, even after the fight was over....

The defendants contend that terrorist aggression unleashed a war in which the Armed Forces had the duty to intervene. Such war was won and it left no room for law, moderation, ethics, religion or humanitarian principles. Everything is valid during a war. A war cannot be tried in court. And if it were, only the defeated side could be brought to justice. In no way can this court accept such a theory, which obviously disregards a legal and cultural tradition that also pertains to the armed forces.

To follow this theory would amount to the negation of a cardinal principle of our legal system: the notion that the legal order is a closed system and that there can be no law if some people or acts remain outside its reach. Legally all behavior is either lawful or unlawful. Raising the existence of a third position only tries to justify what lacks juridical justification. It is not admissible to say that the end justifies the means, and that all means are noble if the end is noble.

The court can only resolve the present case by resorting to legal rules. In so doing, we are not denying the gravity of a revolutionary war or the state of necessity that such a war entails. The cultural progress of the people, however, has incorporated notions such as state of necessity, emergency situations, internal commotion, sedition, and war itself into the legal system. Thus all those concepts must be examined in the light of the rule of law. The rule of law can not be ignored for the sake of destroying an evil enemy, nor can it be set aside by winners or losers in a war. No one who wants to keep alive the permanent values of society—which is the ultimate goal of the rule of law—may ignore the rule of law.

Perhaps methods chosen by the defendants to fight subversion accelerated the victory. However, it was not the victory of law or civilization. Only force won....

The acts under examination cannot be justified on the grounds that the country was under a state of siege. A state of siege allows the arrest and detention of persons by order of the Executive Branch. It does not allow the armed forces or the people to arrest without a trial, to indiscriminately steal and ruin other people's property, to torture prisoners, to treat them inhumanely, or to kill....

Conclusion

We have examined the incriminating conduct in light of the grounds for justification listed in Criminal Code, the substantial illegality of that conduct and excessive use of defensive force. We have also analyzed the notions of war, civil war, international war, and revolutionary or subversive war....

We have examined the applicability of the positive rules of municipal law and the written rules of the *jus gentium*. We have studied the opinions of legal scholars on constitutional law and public international law, as well as different theories concerning conventional warfare and revolutionary war. We have taken into account the usages of civilized nations in regard to war....

Not even one rule has been found that could justify, or pardon at least, those authorizing the acts in question. We have not found in written or customary laws or in the opinion of legal scholars a single note of justification or exculpation of homicide, torture, robbery, indiscriminate injury, and illegal deprivation of freedom. The acts in question are illegal under Argentine municipal law and they violate international law; they find no justification in our cultural patterns; they contradict ethical and religious principles.

Criminal Participation

Facts Which Have Been Proven

It has been demonstrated that on a date close to March 24, 1976,—the day when the Armed Forces overthrew the constitutional authorities and took over the government—some of the defendants, acting as Commanders of their respective units, ordered a way to combat terrorist subversion which basically consisted of: a) capturing those who might be suspected of having some link to subversion according to intelligence reports; b) sending them to places located in military units or under military control; c) once there, interrogating them, under torture, in order to extract from them as much information as possible about other people; d) subjecting them to subhuman treatment to break their will; e) carrying out all which was described above in the most absolute secrecy. The kidnappers did not reveal their names and performed their tasks usually at night while the victims remained absolutely incommunicado, blindfolded, and their existence was to be denied to any authority, relative or friend of the prisoner, as well as the places of detention. And f) the commanders gave ample freedom to subordinates to determine the victim's fate, such as who could later be freed, handed over to the Executive Power, subjected to a military or a civilian trial, or killed.

These activities were to be carried out according to the existing rules on fighting subversion, but not abiding by those rules which contradicted the above methods. In this system, the military was assured complete impunity. This was achieved by preventing the interference of the courts, denying ... or hiding the truth of the facts from judicial inquiries, organizations, relatives and foreign government, and using governmental means to persuade local and foreign public opinion that the accusations were false. Also the defendants defended themselves against charges of human rights violations by referring to an orchestrated campaign of terror against the Argentine government.

It has been proven that the orders that were given caused a great number of crimes of illegal deprivation of freedom, torture and homicide. It has also been shown that in carrying out these acts, the subordinates committed other crimes not directly ordered, but which could be considered as a natural consequence of the chosen system.

Defenses Raised

It should now be established whether or not the accused who gave such orders are criminally liable for the charges brought against them, and, if so, in what manner, considering that none of them personally performed any of the crimes.

The prosecution has claimed that the orders given were to kidnap, torture, and physically eliminate a great number of people vaguely defined under the generic category of "subversive". Also, such orders implied that while performing those acts other crimes could be committed, such as robbery, abortions, rape, and suppression of the civil status of minors.

Based on the above, the prosecution considered that the accused are indirect perpetrators of the crimes committed by the staff under their command, since they controlled the events through a system which allowed them to determine the consequences and to make sure that the crimes would be committed....

The defenses raised by the defendants, in essence, were the following:

a) That the Argentine Criminal Code does not accept the theory of control of the acts as a fundamental criterium of criminal responsibility, but rather the formal objective theory, under which only the principal or direct perpetrator of the crime, can be considered criminally responsible.

b) That the legality of the crime and its punishment would lose validity if responsibility could be defined outside the typical criminal actions.

c) That indirect responsibility becomes inapplicable when the individual who is the direct perpetrator is a person with legal capacity and therefore subject to criminal liability. In such a case it cannot be argued that the individual directly responsible is believed to control the situation.

d) That the theory of criminal responsibility based on an organized system of power refers to a different situation from the one involved in this case. The defense argues that such a theory has been greatly opposed by legal scholars, mostly on grounds related to the many problems involved in finding criminally liable all those persons who are in between the direct and the indirect perpetrators of the crime.

e) That none of the defendants can be considered instigators, since the elements of accessory participation are not present here....

Applicable Law

...The applicable law should now be examined. The acts judged in these proceedings fall under military jurisdiction (Article 108 C.M.J. and Article 10 of Law 23,049). Accordingly, the criminal liability of the accused should be determined following the rules of the Code of Military Justice.... Article 514 of the C.M.J. ... provides that "when a crime is committed through the execution of a service-connected order, the superior officer who gave the order shall be the only responsible party. The subordinate officer shall be considered an accomplice only when he exceeds compliance with such order." Under this provision, therefore, the only responsible party is the superior officer who gives the order.

This notion of criminal responsibility found in military law does not follow the criteria of the so-called "formal-objective theory," since the superior officer does not personally commit the crime. Rather, the basis of criminal responsibility in Article 514 of the C.M.J. is founded on the special relationship of subordination between superior and subordinate military officers. Strict obedience to orders is essential to military institutions, whose structure and well-functioning depend on the unquestionable obedience of the subordinate personnel and the maintenance of discipline as a fundamental value.

Article 7 of Law No. 19.101 establishes commanding powers and disciplinary duties for each military rank. Article 12 of that Law provides for military superiority based on position, rank or seniority. Article 1 of the Military Justice Regulations (R.V. 110/10) declares that ... superiority of command calls for respect and obedience on the part of subordinates (paragraph 2). To ensure that orders are obeyed, disobedience is punished, and Articles 667 and 674 of the C.M.J. respectively establish the crimes of subordination and of disobedience. Article 675 provides in turn that "no complaint excuses from obedience nor suspends compliance with a military order".

If the duty to obey could be stalled by a claim, command would be inefficient and would depend on the inferior's will.... Because orders must be strictly obeyed, the only person who may be found criminally responsible is the one who gave the orders. Therefore, the provision found in Article 514 of the C.M.J., which has not been constitutionally challenged, amounts to a statutory acceptance of indirect criminal responsibility.

Article 514 also assumes the adoption of the theory of control of acts in order to distinguish between perpetrator and participant. The superior who gives an order that shall be obeyed is in control of the causal course of events, because the commission of the crime—the execution of which has been entrusted to a subordinate—depends on his will.... Attributing responsibility to a commanding officer for a crime committed by a subordinate following a military order is not an invention of Argentine law. On the contrary, it has been adopted by many other legal systems and it has become a uniformly accepted rule....

Indirect Responsibility

As stated before, Article 514 of the C.M.J. establishes a case of indirect responsibility for those who order a subordinate to commit a crime.

a) Legal commentators generally agree in ascribing the term "indirect perpetrator" to the individual who orders another to commit a crime. Except in certain cases, no one today challenges the need to resort to such a characterization.... The idea is that the indirect perpetrator is criminally responsible because he is in control of the perpetration of the crime. The indirect perpetrator controls the criminal act by controlling the will of the person who actually perpetrates the crime. In contrast to the basic features of criminal coresponsibility—based on the "control of the action" or "functional control" of the criminal act—the indirect perpetrator controls the will of the perpetrator....

The different circumstances in which the indirect perpetrator actually controls the criminal act, and the cases in which such control is transferred to the exclusive domain of the person who performs the criminal act are issues of great controversy. These controversial issues have produced a variety of opinions by legal commentators on the different hypotheses of indirect responsibility. The crucial issue is whether the individual who plays the role of an instrument used by the indirect perpetrator commits a crime by a justifiable mistake (hence not being responsible on grounds of mistake), or whether he is not guilty because of some grounds of justification other than mistake.

The greater freedom enjoyed by the direct perpetrator, the less control the person behind the scene will have over the act. Thus, there can be no indirect perpetrator unless the direct perpetrator's will is controlled by the former....

b) It is now pertinent to focus again on the oft-cited Article 514 of the C.M.J.... The reason such a rule makes the subordinate not liable for crimes committed under orders received while on duty is none other than the principle of due obedience to orders.

Few topics in criminal law have created such intense debate as that of obedience to orders. This may be because it encompasses a conflict between different values held by society. Regardless of the label used for this ground of impunity (e.g., absence of a statutory definition of the criminal offense, justification, culpability by reason of mistake or violence), we are dealing with a situation where the perpetrator of a crime is not criminally responsible....

If the notion of indirect responsibility is to be excluded whenever the person who acted as an instrument is criminally responsible, one must determine the circumstances in which obedience to orders is to be discarded as a defense. According to Article 11 of Law No. 23.049, which was enacted in order to construe Article 514 of the C.M.J., the subordinate is liable for the crime he committed if he exercised decision-making powers, knew that the order was illegal, or if the order required the commission of atrocious or aberrant acts.

As it has been demonstrated, the illegal orders were part of the scheme devised for the defendants to fight subversion. These orders were given in the context of heavy indoctrination about the non-conventional character of the war against subversion and the need to curb terrorism. [I]t is conceivable that many subordinates may raise the defense of following orders or "invincible error" (error incapable of being overcome) concerning the legality of the orders received. There is no doubt, however, that some officers (especially those of high military rank) knew of the illegality of the system, while others performed atrocious acts without the slightest hesitation. It follows that certain subordinates shall not be able to raise the defense of obedience to orders and that they are liable for the acts they committed as are those who gave the orders.

This raises the issue of whether it is possible to attribute indirect responsibility to the accused, or if, according to the theory expressed above, they are liable as instigators (whose degree of responsibility differs from that of the indirect responsible perpetrator).

Analysis of the Defendants' Criminal Responsibility

In the opinion of this court, the defendants are responsible for the crimes committed by their subordinates independently of the criminal responsibility of the latter. The criminal acts perpetrated by the subordinate officers were always under control of the defendants, hence they must answer as indirect perpetrators even if some of the direct perpetrators can be exempt from criminal responsibility on the bases of some grounds of justification. The expression "control of the acts" becomes meaningful when it is examined in the light of a specific empirical hypothesis. Therefore, a close examination of the facts is necessary in order to ascertain whether the defendants were actually "in control" of criminal acts that were perpetrated by military personnel and members of the police forces. The defendants decided to fight terrorist guerrillas unlawfully and with atrocious means. This decision was taken at a time when the armed forces were already in charge of the fight against subversion, a struggle which was subject to laws and regulations. The unlawful acts were perpetrated through a regular chain of command, the effect of which was to overrule the applicable legislation which was in conflict with the given orders (place of detention, treatment of prisoners, immediate intervention of civil or military justice, or handing over to the national Executive Power). In all other respects the directives continued to be in force.

All the military structure set up to fight subversion functioned normally under the command of the defendants. Only the "means" employed in the fighting changed as a result of the decision taken by the defendants.

The assurances of impunity given to the direct or actual perpetrators of the crimes were also part of the plan approved by the defendants. The acts were to be carried out with no interference and in absolute secrecy. To that effect, concrete measures were taken in order to preclude the operation of the regular system of criminal justice (for example, the regional commanders would request a "green light" from the local police forces in order to proceed freely). It was also part of the strategy devised by the defendants to deny the existence of the facts to any request from the authorities or relatives of the victims. They gave false answers to judicial requests, prevented publication by the news media of facts related to disappearances or the finding of bodies, simulated investigations to clarify the facts, set up important administrative centers for the purpose of tracing people who had disappeared while being well aware that the efforts made by those centers were useless, attributed the phenomenon of the disappearances to vague motives, and characterized the whole situation as a campaign instigated abroad by the guerrilla....

The defendants were in control of those acts because the machinery of people and property that made possible the commission of the crimes was under their command. The events in question are not the result of the erratic, solitary and individual decision of those who carried them out; they were part of an overall strategy devised by the commanders-in-chief of the armed forces in order to fight subversion. The acts were performed throughout a complex group of elements (men, orders, places, arms, vehicles, food, etc.) that took part in every military operation.

The criminal acts could not have taken place without all those elements. After the coup or March 24, 1976, the armed forces continued the struggle against subversion under the orders of the defendants. Such a struggle was carried out in an obviously unlawful manner, although the rules of law governing the limits of that struggle had not changed.

It must equally be borne in mind that the defendants not only commanded their own forces, but also the security forces which were in charge of preventing crimes. The defendants had installed themselves, through an act of force, as the only source of power in the Republic, so that there was no authority capable of exercising an effective control over what went on....

Under these circumstances, who actually perpetrated the crimes is not so important. The control of those who headed the system was absolute. Even if a subordinate refused to obey, he would be automatically replaced by another who would conform to the directives. Thus the plan conceived by the defendants could not have been upset by the will of the actual and direct perpetrator of the crimes, who simply performed a minor function within a gigantic machine.

This case does not concern the usual case of control of the will through participation. The instrument operated by the man behind the scenes is the system itself, which he manipulates at his discretion, a system composed of interchangeable men.... Regardless of who the subordinate officers (i.e., the directly responsible parties) happen to be, the criminal acts would have taken place anyway. The actual or direct perpetrator loses significance, since he plays only a secondary role in committing the crime. Who controls the systems, controls the will of the men who are part of that system.

The defendants' lack of knowledge of the existence of each criminal act in particular and of the victims' identities is not relevant in determining their criminal responsibility. The orders referred generally to all "subversive people" allowing ample freedom for the subordinates to determine who fell in that category and to act accordingly. The commanders, however, always retained the power to stop the crimes that were being committed. There is ample evidence showing that when the defendants deemed it necessary, they suddenly stopped all irregular operations and announced to the population that "the war had ended". After that time, there was no further kidnapping, torture, or disappearances.

Furthermore, the intervention of the defendants from the very top of the power structure was not limited to ordering an unlawful activity. They also contributed actively to the commission of the crimes. As previously noted, the direct perpetrators of the crimes would have not been able to commit those crimes unless they had the necessary means. These means were made available to them by the order of the commanders: clothes, vehicles, fuel, weapons and ammunition, detention centers, food, etc., were indispensable factors.

There was still another circumstance which made possible the success of the illegal plans and which only the defendants could have made available: impunity.

While this criminal system was implemented, society was still governed by the traditional legal order. The constitution (with the limitations imposed by a *de facto* government) was still in force, the police continued to arrest criminals and courts continued to render judgments. Such a system was incompatible with the one applied to the fight against the guerrillas. The stunning co-existence of a legal and extra-legal system during such a prolonged time was only possible with the presence of the defendants at the summit of power. From there, an attempt was made to hide the facts by lying to judges, to the victims' relatives, to national and foreign organizations, to foreign governments. They orchestrated fake investigations, gave misleading assurances of hope and childish explanations. The harmful consequences of this psychotic behaviour aimed at deceiving the community at large cannot be predicted .

Because the defendants aided and abetted the direct perpetrators in the commission of the crimes, they could also be considered accomplices. This categorization, however, does not affect their criminal liability as indirect perpetrators, because it is well known that if a party to a crime participates as principal and as an accessory, his criminal responsibility as a principal party displaces his eventual liability as a secondary party. It could be reasonably argued that the defendants should answer as co-participants according to their functions. Considering that this categorization of the defendants' criminal liability is of little consequence, the Court deems it appropriate to convict them as indirect perpetrators.

Attribution of Criminal Liability to the Defendants

...Now its time to determine specifically the criminal behavior of each of the defendants. We must decide whether it is possible to attribute to each defendant the commission of crimes which have been described in other parts of this judgment, or whether they must be acquitted from the charges brought against them by the prosecutor.

It has been established in these proceedings that the orders in question did not originate with the Military Junta, but that each of the defendants retained the exclusive and effective command of his respective force. Accordingly, the charges brought by the prosecutor against a commander for crimes committed by subordinates belonging to another force must be rejected....

Case of (Retired) Lieutenant General Jorge Rafael Videla[11]

a)   As commander-in-chief of the Army, since March 24, 1976, Videla gave orders to fight subversion pursuant to the methods previously described in this judgment. Accordingly, he is responsible for all criminal activities which followed the pattern that he devised and were committed directly by his subordinates during his tenure as commander of the army. He is also responsible for those crimes which, though not necessarily part of the system ordered by him, were committed and consented to as a result of that pattern.

The measure of attributing such responsibility is made in accordance with the facts of each case.... [T]he Court decides that Jorge Rafael Videla is responsible for the following crimes committed with specific intent.

1)   Sixteen counts of homicide aggravated by cruelty—Articles 55 and 80(2) of the Criminal Code—(Cases 181, 183, 186, 242, 243, 244, 426, 427, 428, 429, 434, 435, 436, 663, 664 and 683).*

---

[11]The Videla case is translated as an example of the examination of the criminal liability attributed to all the other defendants in this case.

* [Editor's note: Each of the subsequent charges follow the same pattern of citation to specific provisions of the Criminal Code of Argentina and to individual cases from the 700 reviewed by the court. These citations are omitted in this excerpt.]

2) Fifty counts of homicide aggravated by cruelty and with the assistance of at least three people....

3) Three hundred and six counts of unlawful deprivation of freedom aggravated by violent threats....

4) Ninety-three counts of torture....

5) Four counts of torture followed by death....

6) Twenty-six counts of robbery....

These crimes were committed in conjunction with each other....

b) The Court has acquitted Videla of the other acts that he has been charged with. This is so either because they are criminal acts committed by personnel of a different branch of the armed forces, their existence was not proven, they did not correspond with the orders establishing the repressive system, or because it is not proven that Videla consented to the commission of those crimes, or because the acts do not fit the statutory definitions of the crimes.

The acquittals apply to the following charges:

1) Nineteen counts of aggravated homicide....

2) One hundred and four counts of aggravated unlawful deprivation of freedom....

3) One hundred and seventy counts of torture....

4) Seventy-six counts of robbery....

5) Six counts of abduction of a minor....

6) Twenty-three counts of illegal serfdom....

7) Five counts of criminal detainer of real property....

8) Kidnapping for ransom....

9) Two counts of extortion....

10) One hundred and twenty counts of insertion of falsehood into a public document....

11) Withholding of a public document....

Sentence

This act is declared open order to pronounce the dispositive part of the judgment to be rendered ... against the following persons pursuant to Decree No. 158/83 of the National Executive Power:

General Jorge R. Videla
Admiral Eduardo Emilio Massera
Brigadier Orlando Ramon Agosti
General Roberto Eduardo Viola
Admiral Armando Lambruschini
Brigadier Omar Rubens Graffigna
General Leopoldo Fortunato Galtieri
Admiral Jorge Isaac Anaya
Brigadier Basilio Arturo Lami Dozo

in connection with crimes committed during the repression of subversive terrorism....

In the preceding analysis we have examined all the issues raised by the parties and addressed each one of them.

We have examined the situation ... that existed prior to March 1976, characterized by terrorist activity which, because of its duration, gravity and intensity, has been referred to as a revolutionary war.

It has been shown that the commanders of the Armed Forces who seized power on March 24, 1976, despite having at their disposal the legal means and instruments to carry out the repression in a lawful manner, chose to establish a system of clandestine and illegal operations. Those operations were based on orders given by the defendants within the chain of command of their respective forces.

It has been shown that there was no joint command and that none of the commanders was subordinated to any person or organization.

It has been established that said orders produced damage against a great number of people who may or may not have belonged to subversive organizations. These acts consisted of violent seizures, clandestine detention, interrogation under torture, and in many cases the physical elimination of the victims accompanied in a great number of instances by the looting of the victims' dwellings.

It has also been shown that the criminal acts were of a different magnitude within each of the armed forces. In the case of the army, which had primary responsibility in the struggle against subversion, those acts were more widespread and greater in number. In the case of the navy, the criminal acts were limited to certain naval bases.... [In] the air force, they were limited to only three districts of the Buenos Aires province.

The justifications alleged by the defendants have been rejected, since, without ignoring the need to curb and fight the bands of terrorists, such repression should never have violated the law....

The incriminating behavior of the defendants has been examined in the light of the grounds for justifications found in the Criminal Code dealing with material unlawfulness and excess. Legal doctrines dealing with the laws of war, civil war, international war, revolutionary or subversive war have been considered.

We have studied the rules of municipal and international law, consulted the opinions of scholars in constitutional and public international law, as well as examining different theories of conventional warfare and revolutionary war. The teachings of the Catholic Church have been taken into consideration. And we have found not even a single rule that justifies or forgives the commission of acts such as those that were brought to the attention of this Court.

The responsibility of each of the commanders has been established with regard to the orders effectively imparted within their respective branch of the military. Based on the rules of the Code of Military Justice and the Penal Code the defendants have been found criminally responsible for the acts that their subordinates, in following those orders, carried out in a criminal manner....

⊷⊷ ⊠◊⊟ ⊷⊷

Supreme Court of Argentina, Buenos Aires*
(Corte Suprema de Justicia de la Nación)
Judgment of December 30, 1986

Conviction of Former Commanders Affirmed on Different Grounds of Criminal Responsibility

...14. The interpretation of Article 514 of the C.M.J. followed by the Appeals Court is not in accordance with law. Said Article 514 establishes that when a crime derived from an order is committed, the only responsible party will be the superior who imparted such order. The subordinate shall be considered an accomplice insofar as he exceeded the scope of the order. The text of Article 514 suggests three possible interpretations. The first one looks exclusively at the superior officer and shifts the responsibility for the act to him. This is either because the subordinate officer is presumed to have acted in error, or because the criminal act implies an excess directly and immediately linked to the order and related to specific military activities. However, this interpretation cannot be adopted when, during times of peace, the order implies the commission of an act against life or freedom, as in the case of homicide, unlawful deprivation of freedom and torture, where people who are not related to military life or under military jurisdiction happen to be the victims. This is so because orders connected with military service are not to be challenged pursuant to Article 675 of the C.M.J.,... and the subordinate officer must follow the order, once imparted, except in certain cases. However, in cases where a crime is committed, Article 514 of the C.M.J. establishes that criminal responsibility must be transferred to the superior officer. The responsibility is based on the different areas of competence of military officers and the purpose of the rule, which is to ensure the strictest military discipline. That is to say, Article 514 of the C.M.J. does not establish transfer of authorship but of the ensuing criminal responsibility for the sake of maintaining discipline.

The second possible interpretation of Article 514 relates to the subordinate officer, who is considered an accomplice if he exceeded the order, that is, if he did something different from what he was ordered to do.

---

* Excerpted from Judicial Proceedings against Jorge R. Videla *et al.* originally brought before the Supreme Council of the Armed Forces pursuant to Decree No. 158 of December 13, 1983. Published in *Revista de Jurisprudencia Argentina*, No. 5513, April 29, 1987, and *Revista La Ley*, Volume 1987-A, pp. 531-597 in "Conviction of Former Commanders Affirmed on Different Grounds of Criminal Responsibility and Dissenting Opinion (Supreme Court of Argentina, Buenos Aires)," *Human Rights Law Journal*, vol. 8, no. 2-4 (1987), pp. 430, 433-440. Case reported and translated by: Henry Dahl and Alejandro M. Garro.

This interpretation includes those cases where the illegality of the order rendered it more likely to be abused or where the excess in following the order was contemplated by the superior while giving the order. Finally, Article 514 can also be understood as shifting criminal responsibility to the superior officer who gave the order, in order to punish the lack of diligence on the part of the superior while discharging his military duties. Under this view, the superior is supposed to verify the way in which the subordinate carries out the order. Accordingly, the superior officer is bound to supervise the execution of the order and is deemed responsible for the acts of the subordinate which do not conform to that order. Whether the order is legitimate or not, its execution must be confined to its normal or regular limits.

15. In order to construe Article 514 of the C.M.J. it is necessary to ascertain the formal and substantive meaning of the expression "service-connected order." Crimes committed while following service-connected orders are those acts related to specific military duties, to the exclusion of acts carried out in times of peace and directed against the life or freedom of people, such as the crimes we are presently investigating—homicides, unlawful deprivations of freedom, torture. Consequently, the only crimes envisioned by Article 514 are those intimately connected with the specific area of the military activity, when the victim or the things in question are within the scope of that activity. Actually, the commission of crimes, such as those mentioned above, would amount to a departure from the specific scope of military duties. Even if we were to accept that Article 514 adopts the doctrine of control of the act, the said doctrine could not be applied to common crimes such as those imputed to the defendants affecting people who are complete strangers to military life....

17. In the opinion of this Court the scope of application of Article 514 of the C.M.J. in times of peace, such as those during which the crimes were committed, is limited to activities and service-connected orders. Within a military context some exceptional circumstances may justify disobedience or warrant the mitigation of the crime of insubordination, when disobedience is the result of a reaction to the abuses committed by a superior officer. But out of a military context the arbitrary use of military command is a crime subject to military jurisdiction and which must be reported to the authorities. Failure to report such a crime amounts to harboring a criminal. It then becomes obvious that the Appeals Court should have considered the applicability of Article 45 of the Cr.C. [Criminal Code], referred to by Article 513 of the C.M.J. Article 45 of the Cr.C. determines the degree of criminal intervention in ordinary crimes committed by military personnel during times of peace, such as the criminal offenses now under consideration....

24. The judgment of the Appeals Court errs twice in its extensive application of the notion of criminal authorship. The first mistake is due to an interpretation of Article 514 of the C.M.J. which creates a logical contradiction by merging the responsibility of an indirect perpetrator—in

"control of the act"—and a direct perpetrator—the one who actually carries out the crime. The simultaneous existence of both levels of criminal responsibility is unfounded, because if somebody actually performs the crime and is responsible for it, such person would have the "control of the act", leaving no room for a so-called "indirect perpetrator." To accept the coexistence of both kinds of perpetrator it is necessary to resort to an extensive notion of criminal authorship.... The broadening of the concept of authorship can only take place under Article 45 of the Cr.C., which characterizes the perpetrator or perpetrators as those who have taken part in the execution of the crime and characterizes as accomplices all other persons who performed any other act before or after the commission of the crime. In the light of Article 45 of the Cr.C., which requires a perpetrator to "take part in the performance of the act," any other activity linked to the crime should be treated as an act of cooperation, help or assistance.

25. The second mistake made by the Appeals Court refers to the inclusion of the characterization of "indirect authorship" in the last part of the Article 45 of the Cr.C. as a form of direct participation in a crime which is beyond the notion of instigation. This is an elliptic way of accepting the coexistence of an indirect perpetrator by extending the notion of instigator beyond the permissible boundaries of Article 45 of the Cr.C. If the expression "directly caused another person to commit such act" incorporated into Article 45 of the Cr.C. amounts to the simultaneous acceptance of instigation and authorship, it follows that the indirect perpetrator would be subject to the same degree of culpability as the instigator of a crime. According to this interpretation, the party who controls the act would be in the double position of instigator and perpetrator. Such an obvious contradiction cannot be avoided by the simple procedure of classifying indirect authorship as an extensive form of instigation. This is inadmissible, since the concept of instigation implies a psychic participation by which the instigator tries to obtain from another the free, voluntary and conscious decision to commit a crime. Such intellectual activity deployed by the instigator ceases when the decision to commit the crime is actually taken, so that the perpetration of the crime depends on the acts of the person who has been instigated to commit it. If the crime is actually carried out, then the person who was instigated to commit it becomes its only perpetrator. If the instigator supplies any material help, he then becomes a perpetrator who assists, helps or cooperates in the commission of a crime. Whether the acts of the instigator necessarily make him a perpetrator depends on the significance of the acts of cooperation or assistance.

26. That the Cr.C. does not accept the notion of indirect perpetrator in the sense used by the Appeals Court may be demonstrated by referring to Article 80(3) of the Cr.C., dealing with homicide for a price or for a promise of remuneration, a criminal offense which has been specifically defined by our Criminal Code since 1921. According to Article 80(3) he who pays or promises to pay another person for the commission of a crime, and simultaneously performs certain acts in the preliminary stages of the crime is

not considered a perpetrator or a co-perpetrator. His responsibility can only be established through Article 45 of the Cr.C., so that if the payment, the promised supply of weapons, or the protection afforded to the perpetrator are decisive for the commission of the crime, the payor or promisor is deemed to be a "necessary assistant" to the crime....

28. Taking into account the findings of the Appeals Court, we conclude that when the defendants gave secret and illegal orders to combat terrorism, and when they supplied the direct perpetrators with the necessary means to obey such orders, assuring them that later they would not have to answer for their crimes and hence guaranteeing their impunity, the defendants provided the assistance which was needed for the commission of the crimes. During the preliminary stages the acts of the defendants helped the commission of the crime. The fact that the criminal responsibility of the defendants may be the same as that of the perpetrators does not mean that their structural behavior is the same. Necessary assistance to the commission of a crime is not the same as the actual perpetration of the crime, therefore the legal characterization of the degree of criminal intervention of the defendants must be modified....

Having heard the opinion of the Procurator General, the judgment on appeal is affirmed in general, and the characterization of the level of criminal intervention of the defendants as indirect perpetrators is modified to parties who provided necessary assistance for the commission of the crimes. The sentences are confirmed pursuant to Article 45 of the Cr.C....

Dissenting Opinion*...

14. We now consider the applicability of Article 514 of the C.M.J., the constitutionality of which has not been challenged by the appellants. This provision is included in the chapter of the C.M.J. dealing with complicity. The provisions contained in the C.M.J. are applicable to this case inasmuch as the crimes for which the defendants are being tried fall under military jurisdiction.

According to Article 513 of the C.M.J., the rules on criminal intervention and authorship contained in the Cr.C. are applicable to these crimes. Article 514 of the C.M.J. provides for an exception to this general principle. If a crime is committed following orders, the only responsible party is the one who imparted the order. However, if the subordinate acts beyond the scope of the given order, or makes his own decisions or follows orders directed to the commission of atrocious or aberrant acts, such subordinate officer also becomes criminally responsible....

A careful analysis of these rules shows that military laws attribute criminal responsibility as principal perpetrator only to the superior who gave the order in those cases where the subordinate is exempt from punishment by virtue of Article 34 (5) of the Cr.C. In cases where the subordinate officer is not in a position to be protected by that cause of

---

* [Editor's note: The dissenting opinion was translated by the *Human Rights Law Journal*.]

justification, criminal responsibility is shared by the superior and subordinate officers.

The preservation of the military structure requires the strengthening of discipline. Strict obedience to orders is a necessity in this area. The possibility of challenging orders given by competent authority is limited (C.M.J., Article 675) and failure to obey is punishable (C.M.J., Articles 667 and 674). This should suffice to justify the attribution of responsibility to the one imparting the order, in those hypotheses where the actual perpetrator acts under the shield of due obedience....

15. Even if the person who carries out a general criminal scheme is fully responsible for his acts, we are of the opinion that the interpretation made by the Appeals Court allows a reasonable application of Article 514 of the C.M.J. Superior officers retained the control of the acts through the machinery of the State, so they become indirect perpetrators of the crimes committed by their subordinates. One of the main features of this level of intervention in the perpetration of a crime is the control discretely exercised over those who are part of the machinery of the State. This control is not exercised over the will of one specific person or persons, but rather over the general will of the officials who are part of the system. The criminal acts would take place anyhow, regardless of the identity of the particular person who carries out the orders.

The main feature of this system of criminal responsibility is the interchangeability of the direct perpetrator, who does not act as an individual but as a mere instrument of a machinery. It suffices that the indirect perpetrator controls the buttons of the whole machine; even if some of the would-be perpetrators refuse to carry out the plan, they will be immediately replaced by others who would perform the criminal acts. This notion of indirect authorship is suitable to the facts of this case, because the vertical structure of military institutions makes it possible for whoever is at the top to resort to all or part of the forces under his control in order to perpetrate crimes.

This is why, in my opinion, Article 514 of the C.M.J. makes the superior officers criminally liable even in those cases where the actual perpetrators are also fully responsible.

ARGENTINA: FULL STOP LAW*

Law No. 23492 (December 23, 1986)
Anales de Legislación de Jurisprudencia, Argentina No. 324

Article 1

Criminal prosecutions against any person, based on his alleged participation, of any nature, in the crimes referred to in Article 10 of Law [No.] 23049 are extinguished by operation of law, unless such person is a fugitive, or has been pronounced in default, or is indicted by a court of competent jurisdiction within sixty calendar days as of the date of promulgation of this Law.

Under the same conditions shall be extinguished all criminal prosecutions against any person who has participated, on or before December 10, 1983, in the commission of crimes related to the use of violent means of political action.

Article 2

Within the period established in the previous Article, the Federal Courts of Appeal may examine the cases pending before the Supreme Council of the Armed Forces for the purpose established in the last paragraph of Article 10 of Law No. 23049.†

All criminal complaints filed within said period before the Supreme Council of the Armed Forces must be reported within forty-eight hours by the Supreme Council of the Armed Forces to the competent Federal Appeals Court. The Federal Appeals Court shall examine the complaint and assume jurisdiction over the case if appropriate.

Article 3

If in a case pending before a court summons are issued for the arrest or preventive detention (Articles 363-375, Code of Criminal Procedure; Articles 309-318, C.M.J.) of members of any rank in active duty belonging to the armed, security, police, or prison forces, such measures shall be carried out pursuant to Article ⌐15, second paragraph, of the C.M.J., provided that so is requested by the commanding officer of the unit where the person in question serves or by any other superior officer in the chain of command. In such case the requesting superior officer shall be responsible for the

---

* Reprinted from "Law No. 23492" (Law of "Full Stop") (Argentine Legislation), in *Human Rights Law Journal*, vol. 8, no. 2-4 (1987), p. 476. Translated by Alejandro M. Garro and Henry Dahl.

† [Editor's note: Law No. 23049, adopted in February 1984, modified the Code of Military Justice and established jurisdiction for the prosecution of military and security personnel for crimes committed during military rule, from March 1976 to September 1983.]

immediate appearance of the accused before the court which issued the summons.

Article 4

The period of time established in Article 1 shall be suspended in case of jurisdictional conflicts between the Supreme Council of the Armed Forces and Federal Courts of Appeal or among the latter courts. This time period shall also be suspended in case of pending of appeals precluding a competent court from deciding on an indictment.

The period running between the date of notification to the Supreme Council of the Armed Forces of the requirement made by the Federal Appeals Court pursuant to Article 2 and the date when the record of the proceedings is received by such Court shall not be counted for the purpose of the time period established in Article 1.

The last paragraph of Article 252 bis of the C.M.J. shall not be applied for the purpose of Article 1 of this law.

Article 5

The law does not apply to criminal prosecutions for the crimes of change of civil status and kidnapping and hiding of minors.

Article 6

The exemption established in Article 1 does not preclude filing a civil claim.

ARGENTINA: DUE OBEDIENCE LAW*

Law No. 23521 (June 4, 1987)
Anales de Legislación de Jurisprudencia, Argentina No. 335

[handwritten: ☆ Hierarchy — Status Based Limit]

Article 1

It is presumed, without proof to the contrary being admitted, that those who at the time of the perpetration of the acts had the rank of chief officers, subordinate officers, officials, and soldiers of the armed, security, police, and prison forces are exempt from punishment for the crimes referred to in Article 10, first paragraph, of Law No. 23049 by virtue of having followed orders. In those cases it shall be deemed by operation of law that those persons acted under duress, in subordination to a superior authority and following orders, without having the possibility of resisting or refusing to follow those orders and of examining their lawfulness.

The same presumption applies to officers of higher rank, excepting those occupying the position of Commander in Chief, Chief of Zone, Chief of Sub-zone, or Chief of Security, Police, or Prison Forces, unless the competent judicial authorities rule within thirty days of the passage of this Law that those officers of higher rank made decisions of their own or took part in the formulation of the orders.

Article 2

The presumption established in the previous article shall not apply to crimes of rape, kidnapping and hiding of minors, change of civil status, and appropriation of immovables through extortion.

Article 3

Within five days of coming into effect, this law shall be applied by the courts on their own initiative to all pending cases, regardless of the stage of the proceedings. As to the personnel referred to in the first paragraph of Article 1, the intervening court shall issue an order pursuant to Article 212 bis of the C.M.J. or shall revoke any summons, as the case may be.

The court's inactivity during this period or the one established in the second paragraph of Article 1 shall have the effects referred to in the preceding paragraph with the force of *res judicata*.

If in the course of the proceedings it has not yet been possible to ascertain the rank or function performed at that time by the person who has been summoned, the time period shall start to run as from the time when

---

* Reprinted from "Law No. 23521" (Law of "Due Obedience") (Argentine Legislation), in *Human Rights Law Journal*, vol.8, no. 2-4 (1987), p. 477. Translated by Alejandro M. Garro and Henry Dahl.

such rank or function is established by the submission of a certificate or report issued by competent authorities.

Article 4

Without prejudice to what is provided in Law No. 23492, in those cases where the time period established by Article 1 of the same law has not yet lapsed, no summons shall be issued against those persons referred to in Article 1 of this law.

Article 5

Decisions relating to the application of this law are subject to an ordinary appeal before the National Supreme Court. The appeal shall be filed within five days of the notification of the decision. If the decision takes place by operation of law, the period shall start running as from the date it is deemed to have been rendered pursuant to this law.

Article 6

Article 11 of Law No. 23049 shall not apply to those personnel mentioned in Article 1 of this law.

ARGENTINA: SUPREME COURT
DECISION ON THE DUE OBEDIENCE LAW*

Judgment of June 22, 1987
(Causa No. 547 incoada en virtud del
Decreto No. 280/84 del Poder Ejecutivo Nacional)

...This Law established an irrebuttable presumption of impunity for those crimes mentioned in the first paragraph of Article 10 of Law No. 23049. The law presumes, without admitting proof to the contrary, that those who held the military ranks specified by Article 1 of Law 23521 at the time the crimes were committed, acted following orders. Also included within the benefits of the law are superior military officers who have not acted as Commander-in-Chief, Chief of Zone, Chief of Sub-Zone, or Chief of Security, Police or Penitentiary Forces, provided that they did not have capacity to decide or that they did not participate in the elaboration of the orders....

We cannot accept the argument that this Law prevents courts from examining issues which are of their exclusive competence. Neither can we accept the argument that this Law disregards or alters the decisions rendered by the courts of law. Congress has the power, as explained above, to seek its policy objectives in a reasonable manner through the enactment of laws. In this particular case, the purpose of the law is to exempt from punishment and prosecution those persons who held the indicated military rank and discharged the duties described by law at the time such law was enacted. This provision does not contradict the principle of equal protection, because this Court has repeatedly held that the legislator may treat different situations in different ways, provided that the discrimination is not unfair or invidious, and that it does not imply hostility against, or undue privileges in favor of, certain persons. The right to equal protection of the law does not require that all laws treat everybody in the same way; it simply establishes a prohibition to enact laws reflecting hostile purposes towards people or groups of people....

Concurring Opinion of Justice Carlos S. Fayt

...13) The statement of legislative intent accompanying this Law refers to very serious circumstances prompting its enactment. The virtual collapse of our constitutional system must be added to such circumstances. Amid a reprehensible social indifference, the National Constitution was regarded as a third-rate code of laws, and the powers conferred on the executive and legislative branches of government were concentrated in one head. Now this

---

* Reprinted from "Constitutionality of the Law of 'Due Obedience' and Dissenting Opinion (Supreme Court of Argentina, Buenos Aires)," in *Human Rights Law Journal*, vol. 8, no. 2-4, (1987), pp. 441-443, 446-460, 463, 465-470. Translated by Alejandro M. Garro and Henry Dahl.

administration is trying to deal adequately with the consequences of such historical period.

14) In light of the gravity of this situation, the Supreme Court cannot disregard the reasons which motivated the enactment of the Law.... It becomes necessary to recall that our Constitution is the result of a long history of sacrifice and glory..., and this historical process has not terminated with the enactment of the Constitution. Consequently, constitutional interpretation as well as the Court's efforts to insure its survival cannot be divorced from the realities of the present time..., no matter how bitter such reality proves to be.

This result-oriented approach does not disregard the noble principles on which the Constitution is based. The purpose of this method of constitutional interpretation is to preserve the higher value of safeguarding its own survival.... Whereas other values and solutions may be preferable to the one embodied in this Law, it is not the province of this Court but of Congress to decide on the path to take under the present circumstances....

In principle, within the administrative hierarchy of civil servants, an employee is not bound to obey an order which is illegal. Article 248 of the Cr.C. expressly sanctions the subordinate who follows illegitimate orders, and he cannot invoke the justification established in Article 34 (5) of said code....

20) Things are different in military life. The subordinate's duty to obey stems from Article 7 of Law No. 19101, defining the incidence of command and discipline pertaining to each military rank. Article 12 of the same Law determines the military hierarchy in regard to the position, rank and seniority of each military officer. Article 1 of the Regulations of Military Justice establishes that superiority of command requires respect and obedience on the part of subordinate officers. A military structure requires, as an essential condition, that subordinate officers strictly follow service-connected orders. Thus, the possibility of questioning orders is limited and disobedience is punished under the C.M.J. Article 667 of the C.J.M. punishes the military officer who ostensibly resists or expressly refuses to obey a service-connected order. Article 674 of the same code also punishes those who do not follow a service-connected order without a justified cause. Article 675 of such code provides in turn that no claim may dispense from the duty to obey or may suspend the execution of a service-connected order. All these rules are aimed at insuring strict compliance with service-connected orders despite the subordinate's ability to discern the legal or illegal nature of the order.

This Court has already decided that the illegal orders imparted were connected with acts of military service. It has been thus held that typical acts that may constitute illegal orders given in the regular chain of command are deemed to be ordinary crimes perpetrated in connection with acts of military service. Even though such acts may have been illegal, they are related to activities which were entrusted by law to the military authority, such as the duty to combat terrorism....

21) This does not mean that the duty to obey is blind. This would not make sense, because those who participate in the relationship of subordination are human beings endowed with an ample margin of freedom. Subordinate officers have the legal capacity to verify the extrinsic characteristics of the act for the purpose of establishing whether or not it is actually an order. The faculty to verify relates to the determination as to whether the order has been imparted by a superior officer and whether it is connected to an act of military service. But such capacity to verify does not extend to examination of the legal or illegal nature of the order, for in this area the C.M.J. has imposed the limitations which have been mentioned above.

22) Criminal legal scholarship has analyzed *ad nauseam* the place of "due obedience" within the theory of crime. Thus, the duty to obey has been characterized as a cause of justification for a crime and as a ground for exemption from guilt. Within the latter category, due obedience has been considered as a variation of duress or as a species of mistake. Yet the courts must decide each case on its own facts, weighing the facts which have been found and considering the historical circumstances under which the acts took place.

23) The duty to obey orders only applies to service-connected acts. Article 878 of the C.M.J. defines what is to be understood as a service-connected order, requiring it to be related to the specific activities of military authority, i.e., whether the order is necessarily connected with the specific functions pertaining to the armed forces. There is no doubt in this particular case that the orders in question were service-connected. The orders derived from the duties assigned to the armed forces by the Executive through Decrees 2770, 2771 and 2772, of 1975....

[First] Dissenting Opinion

Justice Enrique Santiago Petracchi dissented in part....

3) Law No. 23521 was challenged at a time the case at bar was being examined by this Court.

4) The issue of the applicability of Law 23521 to this case makes it necessary to examine the legal situation at the time when the acts in question were committed. Such examination calls for the analysis of the defense of due obedience, as established in Article 514 of the C.M.J.

This Court faces a tremendous responsibility and must bear in mind the commitment undertaken by the members of the Supreme Court to the Argentine people and to Argentine ethical and cultural traditions. We must take into account the special times that our society is going through. At long last, the people of Argentina have decided to build a political community based on the freedom and dignity of all men pursuant to the ideas of our founding fathers.... The mission of this Court is to serve the legal conscience of our people. This mission is accomplished by enforcing the values of the humanist tradition on which our Nation was based....

Recalling the tragedy of Nazism a distinguished legal philosopher wrote:

> ...During several centuries we have been taught a philosophy and a theology of order, that obedience due to superiors ... was the most important of all virtues, and that those who obey are entirely blameless for the carrying out the orders they were given. Accordingly citizens have followed reprehensible rules, soldiers have followed criminal orders, and judges have applied unjust laws ... without remorse, and all this not only during dictatorships. It was not their business to resist, this was up to those in higher positions who had a broader perspective. (Arthur Kaufmann, prologue to *Widerstandsrecht*, Darmstadt, 1972, page XIV).

In contrast with this view, the ideas that base order on freedom have claimed that obedience must be guarded by civic responsibility and a humanitarian sense. Already medieval commentators, developing Roman legal principles, determined that the limit of all obedience was that of atrocious crimes, as distinguished from crimes. The liberalism of the XIX Century emphasized the role of one's own liability while obeying, even within a military context, declaring as punishable those crimes committed following orders as long as the illegality of the order was manifest. The former view of due obedience was espoused by feudal systems, and the second the democracies based on the rule of law.... It is appropriate to examine it at this point the legal tradition on which our notions of due obedience are based and later to examine the historical background of the due obedience defense in Argentina.

5) At Roman law, atrocious acts were excluded from any possible justification based on due obedience. In the Pandects, the only passage related to due obedience during classical times is found in a controversial comment made by Ulpianus to the Edict (Digest, Book 9, Title IV, Law 2, paragraph 1). *See* Giuseppe Bettiol, *L'Ordine dell'Autorita nel Diritto Penale*, Milano, 1934, pages 11-13. But during post-classical times many Roman texts stated that the duty to obey only applies with regard to crimes *quae non habent atrocitatem facinoris*. These acts may be translated, approximately, as those lacking the atrocity which is characteristic of a serious crime (Digest, Book 24, Title II, Law 43, paragraph 7; Digest, Book 44, Title VII, paragraph 20; Digest, Book 50, Title XVII, paragraph 157; Digest, Book 25, Title XXI, paragraph 1; Digest, Book 47, Title XVII, Law 10, paragraph 7; *see also* Theodosian Code, Book 9, 10, 4). Based on these Roman sources the glossators and post-glossators stated that there is no duty on the part of the subordinates to obey orders when those orders pointed to the commission of very serious crimes (*see* Bettiol, *op. cit. supra*, reviewing the opinions of Baldo, Decio, Accursio, Bartolus, Godofred, Prospero Farinaccio, Jason de Magno, pages 23-27)....

The atrocity of the act operates as an indicator of the knowledge that the subordinate must have had about the illegality of the act. Thus we reach the opinion of Gandino, who is not so much concerned about the atrocity of the act but rather whether the order is manifestly illegitimate, overtly legitimate, or of a dubious legality. According to Gandino, punishment of the subordinate is appropriate only in the first case (*see* Bettiol, *op. cit. supra*, at 26). Odofredo and Alberico share a similar opinion, in the sense that all atrocious crimes are deemed to have been committed with malice (Bettiol, *op. cit. supra*, at 24-25, note 4).

The issue concerning the doubtful legality of the order deserves a separate paragraph. In this regard,... Grotius ... refutes the widespread opinion of medieval legal scholars that the doubtful legality of an order exempts the subordinate from punishment. Following the tenets of classical philosophy, Grotius is of the opinion that in case of doubt it is necessary to choose the lesser evil. In case of war, Grotius considers that disobedience is a lesser evil vis-á-vis homicide, especially if many innocent lives are at stake (*see* H. Grotius, *Droit de la guerre et de la paix*, Chapter XXIII, p. 546 *et seg.*, and Chapter VI, No. 4, p. 607-613, transl. by M.P. Pradier-Fodere, Paris, 1867).

6) The foregoing survey on due obedience includes military obedience, as shown by the principles of Canon law which were in force at the time. Counsel for the defendants refers to a famous passage of Saint Augustin (*1 City of God*, Chapter 26), in support of his argument favoring blind obedience to orders. A full reading of this chapter, however, clearly shows that such conclusion can only be reached by reading the passage out of context, as it was actually done by the defense attorneys. In fact, the vocabulary and images used by Saint Augustin have been taken by Gracian's Decree to advance a conclusion which is precisely the opposite of that proposed by the defense, that is, that a soldier who obeys the order to kill is justified as long as his acts are in accordance with the law.... The father of the Church has made clear that the ecclesiastical doctrine on due obedience also applies in a military context. According to said doctrine, orders against the divine law must be disobeyed (*see* F. Blasco Fernández de Moreda, *El valor exculpatorio de la ignorancia, el error y la obediencia debida en el pensamiento jurídico-penal español*, 74 La Ley 848, 958; Bettiol, *op. cit. supra*, at 21, note 4). The only qualification made with regard to the justification of due obedience in military life is the acknowledgement that a subordinate is to be punished only if he was certain that the order was illegal. Although in most cases a state of doubt indicates guilt, within a military context doubt exempts from punishment. This idea originating in Canon law resulted in long-lasting consequences in matters of due obedience.

The principle that one must obey God rather than men has been expounded in the *Hechos de los Apostoles* (chapter V, paragraph 29), and it has been very well developed by Christian ethical writings of all times. This philosophical approach is reflected in thoughts such as the following one from Pio XII: "There is no excuse for the perpetration of an act which is immoral, and there is no right, no obligation, no license to perform an act that is intrinsically immoral. This is so even if the act is ordered and refusal to obey triggers the worst personal consequences...." (Speech addressing the participants to the VI International Congress of Penal Law, October 3, 1953). Similarly, John XXIII in *Pacem in Terris* states the following: "Those magistrates who fail to recognize or who violate human rights not only fail to fulfill their duty, but also their orders and directives have no binding force...."

7) Liberal theory of criminal law follows the traditional legal principles inspired by scholastic Christianity. Underscoring the importance of personal responsibility, liberal criminal theory is not concerned with the distinction between atrocious crimes (not justifiable for reason of obedience) and lesser crimes (which are justifiable), but rather focuses on whether the subordinate knew that the act ordered by the superior was illegal. This issue has been already pointed out, as shown in paragraph 5 of this opinion, by early legal scholarship on the subject. In a passage cited in the explanatory note to Article 4, title III, of the Penal Code drafted by Tejedor, Chaveau states the following:

> Early legal commentators, following Roman law, distinguished between atrocious and lesser crimes. An order from the prince did not justify the commission of the former kind of crimes but exempted those who committed the latter kind of crimes from punishment. Livingston reproduced the same distinction in Louisiana's code: Mere soldiers who commit a misdemeanor following an order imparted from an officer will not be punished; but if they commit a felony the order is not a cause for justification (Articles 36 and 37). This distinction appears to be based on the fact that low ranking military officers are less likely to recognize the illegality of an order pointing to the perpetration of a misdemeanor since its immorality is less piercing. But the greater or lesser immorality is irrelevant as to the intention of the perpetrator. Did the subordinate believe in the legitimacy of the order or not? Did he detect the criminality of the order? This is the crucial issue. If he knowingly commits a misdemeanor, he is liable. The fact that the crime committed is not so serious is not enough to remove criminal responsibility from its perpetrator. The not-so-serious nature of the crime may create at best a presumption that the subordinate officer did not know about the illegality of the order. (*See* Rodolfo Moreno, 2 *El Código Penal y sus Antecedentes* 268-269, Buenos Aires, 1922.) The passage cited by Tejedor was taken from Adolphe Chaveau & Helie Faustin, *Théorie du Code Penal* 577-579, 4th ed., Paris, 1861).

A clear example of this trend can be seen in the now repealed Penal Military Code of 1872 for the German Empire. This code prescribed that if the performance of a service-connected order violated a penal law, only the superior would be responsible. The subordinate officer, however, was to be punished as a party to the crime when he exceeded the scope of the order or when he knew that the order pointed to the commission of an act involving a crime or a civil wrong (*see* Paul Herz and Georg Ernst, *Código de Justicia Militar para el Imperio Alemán* 85, Berlin, 1908). This rule has been applied by the courts of the German Federal Republic to denote that, at any rate, military obedience receives a privileged treatment. Whereas under the general principles of criminal law, doubts about the illegal nature of an act do not provide a justification for its commission, according to Section 47 of the Penal Military Code the subordinate is to be punished only if he knew for sure that the order was illegal (Federal Supreme Court of Germany, case reported in *Entscheidungen des Bundesgerichtshofes in Strafsachen*, 5. Band, page 239, 241, Colonia-Berlin, 1954).

During the Weimar Republic the German Supreme Court made an interesting application of Section 47 of the Criminal Code of Military Justice. The Court stated:

> Although it can be argued in favor of military subordinates that they were precluded from questioning the orders given by their superiors, and that the validity of said orders might have been assumed, this is not the case in those exceptional instances where the illegality of the order is universally recognized by everyone, even by the defendants. This happens only in rare and exceptional circumstances, but the case at bar presents precisely one of those circumstances. It was perfectly clear to the defendants that killing defenseless people in lifeboats cannot be anything else than a violation of the law. The defendants should have realized that the order given by Patzig was a means which he resorted so as to violate the law. Consequently, the defendants should have refused to obey such order. Because they did not refuse to obey, they must be punished. (*See* Luis Jiménez de Asúa, 6 *Tratado de Derecho Penal* 856, Buenos Aires, 1962.)

8) The horrors of World War Two and of the Vietnam War also gave rise to significant judicial developments on the issue of military due obedience. We now turn to review some of those developments.

a) United States Military Tribunal Sitting in Nuremberg.

Case of the German Supreme Command (1948). This case arose at the trial of members of the German Supreme Command during World War Two, for charges involving their participation in "atrocities and crimes" against prisoners of war and civilian population in general. Among the specific charges, the following were included: "homicide, genocide, inhuman treatments, torture, murder of hostages, devastation not required by military need. Defendants raised the defense of due obedience. The military tribunal started to analyze this argument citing Law No. 10 of the Control Council, Article 11, paragraphs 4 (a) and (b):

> ...The fact that someone has acted obeying an order imparted by his government or superior does not relieve him from responsibility for the commission of a crime, but it can be an attenuating circumstance....

The defense argued that only the State or its leader were responsible for the atrocities that took place, to which the court answered:

> ...To maintain that only the State, an inanimate entity, is guilty for the crimes, and that the criminal liability does not extend to its agents, living persons, who have planned and carried out their policies is to disregard reality and to follow an unacceptable fiction. Neither can we accept, not even under a dictatorship, that a

dictator—no matter how absolute—becomes a scapegoat through whom all the sins of the subordinates are expiated, and that when this dictator takes refuge in a "Bunker", where he is to be presumably destroyed, all the responsibility of his subordinates are purged. The defendants found themselves in the difficult position of receiving orders which were obviously criminal. But servile obedience to clearly criminal orders is not justified on account of fear of some inconvenience or punishment that was not presented as an immediate threat. In order to establish a defense of duress or state of necessity, a defendant must prove that a reasonable man would have realized that he was exposed to direct physical danger preventing him from choosing between good and evil. Such circumstance was not proven in the case at bar. Moreover, the notion that due obedience does not justify a criminal act is not a novel theory. Section 47 of the German Military Penal Code, enacted in 1872, read as follows: "If while carrying out a service-connected order a penal law is violated, only the superior who gave the order is to be held accountable. The subordinate officer, however, shall be punished as a party to the crime when (1) he exceeded the scope of the order or (2) when he knew that the order pointed to the commission of an act involving a crime or a civil wrong." It is interesting to point out that and article by Goebbels, the Reich's Minister of Propaganda, published on May 28, 1944, in the *Voelkischer Beobachter*, the Nazi official newspaper, contained the following accurate interpretation of the law: "No military law provides that a soldier, who commits a despicable crime, is to be exempted from punishment just because the criminal responsibility is shifted to his superior officer, especially if the order received is patently in contradiction of human morality and international customs during times of war...."

The Court also recognized that in spite of the fact that many of the soldiers were not in a position to ascertain the legitimacy of the orders, it was nonetheless true that

> ...At least some of the orders given to the *Wehrmacht* and of the German army were obviously criminal. The expert opinion of legal counsel was unnecessary to determine the illegality of such orders. By any civilized standard the orders went against customs of war and humanitarian principles. Any commanding officer of average intelligence is capable of understanding their criminal nature. Any participation in the implementation of such orders, tacit or otherwise, any silent acceptance while abiding by them, constitutes a criminal act by the subordinate....

b) Military Commission of the United States.

Case of Atolon of Jaluit (1945): In this particular case certain Japanese military officers were charged with killing some American prisoners of war. Following precedent, the military commission held that

> ...A soldier is bound to obey only the superior's legitimate orders. If he is ordered to commit an illegal act, he is not bound, neither by virtue of a legal duty nor by his pledge of allegiance, to carry it out. Such order, far from being an excuse, turns the one who imparted it in an accomplice of the crime....

Citing a case where an American soldier had murdered a Nicaraguan citizen, the military commission said:

...An order which is illegal *per se*, not condoned by the rules and usages of war, of such nature that an average person could determine without hesitation that it is illegal cannot justify homicide, provided that the act meets all the tests to be considered a crime according to law....

c) District Court of Jerusalem (1961)

The Eichman Case. On the issue under discussion, the Court referred to past cases and stated the following.

...The distinctive feature of an order which is manifestly illegal flies as a red flag on top of the order as a warning reading "forbidden". Here we are not concerned with formal illegality, hidden or half hidden, nor with the illegality that only a legal expert can detect, but rather with an obvious breach of the law, a well-defined illegality that is readily apparent; an illegality that is so strong that cannot be overlooked, disregarded or unnoticed, except for those of blind sensitivity, of a heart made of stone or completely corrupted. Such is the standard of "manifest illegality" which is required to free the soldier from his duty to follow orders and to make him accountable for his acts....

The Court noticed further what has been mentioned in the past by other tribunals, that is, that not even the Nazis had repealed Section 47, paragraph 2 of the German Code of Military Justice, providing for the subordinate's criminal responsibility when he knew about the illegality of the order. Finally, the Court rejected the defense that Eichman had acted under coercion from his superiors:

...Although the defendant displayed the obedience of a good Nazi and S.S. member, into whom an absolute and rigid sense of obedience had been inculcated, that does not mean he committed reprehensible acts only because he was so ordered. To the contrary, he complied with his duty in every case with internal conviction, willingly and happily....

d) Supreme Court of Israel (1962).

In a case on appeal, the Supreme Court struggled with the difficult problem faced by a soldier who must choose between committing a crime or being court martialled for disobedience. The Court said:

...It is not easy for anyone, and more so for a soldier who is poorly educated, to decide whether an order addressed to him is reasonably necessary for the purpose of ending a disturbance ... to make things worse he is subject to two different jurisdictions (Glanville Williams, *The Criminal Law, etc.* 297, 2d. ed).... The intermediate solution favored by is general principles of criminal law in this country—following English legal tradition—that obedience to orders serves as an excuse only if the order was not manifestly illegal....

Regarding the issue of duress, the Court referred to a decision of an American court which had stated:

> ...The threat must be direct, real and inevitable.... The test to be applied is whether the subordinate acted under duress or he had accepted the principle underlying the order. In the latter case there can be no justification on grounds of following orders.... When the will of the executioner merges with the will of the one who imparted the order, there is no room for a defense of having acted under the duress of superior orders....

e) Instructions of the Military Judge in re "Calley" (1971).

*Maylai Massacre Vietnam

Lieutenant Calley was tried by an American military court for the massacre of civilians in the village of May-Lai, Vietnam. On the subject of due obedience, the following was said:

> Soldiers are taught to obey orders, particularly orders given in the battlefield. Military efficiency depends on obedience to orders. On the other hand, a soldier's obedience is not that of a robot. A soldier is a rational human being, who is not supposed to answer like a machine but as a person. The legal system takes these elements into account in order to determine criminal responsibility for acts undertaken pursuant to illegal orders. Those acts are excused unless the order was such that a person of average understanding and common sense would have realized, under the circumstances, that the order was illegal, or unless the defendant knew perfectly well that the order was illegal... (all of the foregoing decisions can be found in 2 *The Law of War. A Documental History*, edited by Leon Friedman).

f) German Supreme Court, Criminal Division (BGHSt 2,234) (1952).

This case was about two senior Nazi officers who collaborated in the transport of thousands of people to extermination camps, where most of them were murdered. The defendants raised the argument of due obedience, alleging that they merely followed the rules ordering them to arrest "enemies of the state". [The Court rejected the argument.] In a later judgment rendered in 1964 the same court rejected the defense of mistake on the legality of orders to kill defenseless civilians on the following terms:

> ...Despite his long brainwashing at the S.S., aimed at obtaining blind obedience from the subordinates, he knew that not all orders were "sacred" and that not all orders from a Nazi leader triggered unconditional compliance. The defendant was aware that the duty to obey had its limitations, even if the orders were coming from Hitler, Himmler, or any other Nazi chief. The boundaries are fixed by law and morality, and the orders were so much in conflict with human morality and legality that obedience should have been refused to avoid conscious collaboration in the commission of a crime....

Further on the court rejected the defense of duress on the ground that "the overall behavior of the defendants clearly implies an intimate

immeadite fear of injury

willingness to execute the orders that were received from above..." (*2 Justiz und NS Verbrechen 23 et seq.*).

g) German Supreme Court, November 22, 1952 (BGHSt 2,251).

The defendants, members of the S.S., had followed orders to murder four defenseless civilians. The tribunal rejected the argument of due obedience on the following terms (pages 257-258):

> Criminal law does not recognize a cause of justification based on blind obedience. This defense cannot be recognized, for that would imply a waiver of the very basis of responsibility as human beings. Even the Nazi pledge of allegiance to the flag, binding soldiers to unconditional obedience to Hitler, did not eliminate Section 47 of the Criminal Code of Military Justice ... so even the oath of allegiance to the S.S. was legally irrelevant with regard to the defense of due obedience. Those who subject themselves to the will of another remain criminally responsible. The criminal military codes of most countries do not eliminate but rather limit the responsibility of the subordinate officer. Section 47 of the German Criminal Code of Military Justice applied to the subordinate officer the same punishment as a principal party to a crime. In recent times, Anglo-American law does not recognize any excuse other than not having been able to determine the illegality of the order. The defendants argue in their favor a special status for having belonged to the S.S., invoking the application of Section 52 of the Criminal Code rather than Section 47 of the Criminal Code of Military Justice. But according to the findings of the lower court the defendants are not in a position to invoke a state of necessity, for they were not in danger of losing their lives or under any other physical threat in case they refused to obey. At least such feat was not expressed among them or to third persons. Their participation in the crime was not given as a result of fear. They carried out the orders with actual knowledge of its illegality and prompted by their convictions as members of the S.S. and the Nazi party. This does not amount to a state of necessity, but rather to a responsible action motivated in their willingness to follow the order.

9) In the context of our legal tradition, liberal trends on the issue of due obedience were expounded during the last century by Carlos Tejedor, who found support in the writings of Chaveau and Pellegrino Rossi. Thus, Tejedor states:

> The notion of passive obedience has been advanced in connection with the duty to follow orders by the military. It is generally asserted that the military must not pass judgment on the orders received, but it is bound to see through the eyes of the superior in command, who is solely responsible for a criminal order. This doctrine appears to us as too rigid. All obedience must cease when the order is clearly criminal. It is not true either that military officers are to be regarded as blind instruments. In fact, many times they are compelled to examine the legality of the orders they receive... (Carlos Tejedor, *Curso de Derecho Criminal*, First Part, pages 49-50, 2nd ed., Buenos Aires, 1871)....

10) Similar ideas were present at the time when we were debating the fundamental principles of our legal institutions. Those ideas are reflected in

the parliamentary discussions concerning the enactment of Law No. 1982 of the Confederate Congress, concerning the punishment to be imposed on those who arrested or jailed someone without a written order. Senator Palma opposed the punishment of the subordinates who carried out such orders in the following terms:

> ...If the perpetrators were to understand the law, let them be punished. But crimes committed out of legal ignorance should not be punished. I am against the idea of punishing an ignorant agent who obeys out of a habit or submission, prompted perhaps by the educational system prevailing within the military. The day we are able to civilize the masses, then it will be an appropriate time to demand from the common man the complete fulfillment of his social duties.

The rebuttal of Senator Vega also deserves to be quoted, because it is a clear and courageous statement which still holds true today:

> ...Let us assume that a chief of police orders a citizen to be killed. I wonder whether those who follow such order are guilty of homicide. Of course they are. Because they must know that their superior, the chief of police, does not have the power to issue such an order... I do not believe one needs to be a legal expert to appreciate this. It suffices to understand which are the duties inherent to the post one holds. It suffices for the subordinate to know that he is not supposed to obey blindly and for policemen to understand that they are not mere pawns of uncontrolled power. It is necessary that the perpetrators be punished in order to inculcate an ethical standard to the administration and protect citizens from governmental abuses. (*Diario de Sesiones de la Cámara de Senadores del Congreso Nacional*, No. 25, July 2, 1863, at 231, 1st and 2d columns).

Argentine precedents on this matter are condensed in the eloquent brief of the Procurator General, Doctor Francisco Pico, which was fully endorsed by the Supreme Court in the case reported in 5 [*Decisions*] 181, 188-192):

> An order from a superior officer does not suffice to shield the subordinate who has followed such order. He must still face full criminal responsibility if his act violates the law. Why? Because man is an entity endowed with a will and with discernment, not a blind and insensible instrument. He only owes obedience to orders of his superiors imparted within the sphere of their competence, and even within such sphere no obedience is due if the order points to the commission of a crime. This is the case, for example, of an officer ordering to open fire on defenseless civilians who just stroll by the street; of a chief accountant of a business firm who orders his subordinates to forge documents; of a military commandant who orders his soldiers to attack the government. In these cases and in similar ones, obedience is not due. It is obvious that such acts are crimes punished by law. Anyone who commits those crimes must be punished, without being able to take refuge in the excuse that he was following orders which actually he was not bound to follow. This is the doctrine expounded by the jurisconsults pursuant to the *Siete Partidas* (Partida I, Title XV, Law 5). The underlying principle is quite clear, except in those cases where it is not easy to ascertain the legality of the act or whether the order is given within the sphere of authority of the superior. If the subordinate is to be acquitted in this case, the acquittal is not

due to the fact that the order relieves him from responsibility, but rather on account of his lack of knowledge or intention to commit a crime....

11) Blind obedience is absolutely incompatible with a republican system of government, and the philosophical underpinnings of such doctrine are in conflict even with the basic tenets of different political regimes.... It is clear that blind obedience is anathema to our constitutional system, and it is the duty of the Supreme Court to apply the Constitution. The way in which laws on obedience are to be interpreted cannot be divorced from our republican and democratic principles or from our legal traditions, compelling us to acknowledge that the subordinate is a thinking individual who is expected to behave as such. Subordinate military officers should not be excused from their acts with arguments that denigrate the citizen status granted to those who have chosen the honorable profession in a republic.

12) This Court is bound to adopt a doctrine on due obedience which is consistent with the international commitments contracted by the Republic of Argentine. Law No. 23338, enacted on July 30, 1986, promulgated on August 19 of the same year and published in the Official Gazette of February 26, 1987, has approved the Convention Against Torture and Other Cruel, Inhuman or Degrading Treatment or Punishment [hereinafter "U.N. Convention Against Torture"], adopted by the United Nations General Assembly on December 1984 and signed by the Argentine government on February 4, 1985. According to a report filed with this Court, the U.N. Convention Against Torture was signed and ratified by the President with the consent of the Senate on September 2, 1986, and the instrument of ratification was deposited at the United Nations headquarters on the 24th of the same month and year.

This convention does not seem to be part yet of our municipal law, because the Ministry of Foreign Affairs reports that only 19 ratifications have been received to this date, out of the 20 ratifications which are needed under Article 27 for the convention to enter into force. However, the convention engenders the international responsibility of Argentina according to Article 18 of the Vienna Convention on the Law of Treaties of May 23, 1969 [hereinafter referred to as the Vienna Convention].

Article 18 of the Vienna Convention reads as follows.

A State is obliged to refrain from acts which would defeat the object and purpose of a treaty when:

(a) it has signed the treaty or has exchanged instruments constituting acceptance or approval, until it shall have made its intention clear not to become a party to the treaty; or
(b) it has expressed its consent to be bound by the treaty, pending the entry into force of the treaty and provided that such entry into force is not unduly delayed.

Article 2 of the U.N. Convention Against Torture provides:

1. Each State Party shall take effective legislative, administrative, judicial or other measures to prevent acts of torture in any territory under its jurisdiction.
2. No exceptional circumstances whatsoever, whether a state of war or a threat of war, internal political instability or any other public emergency, may be invoked as a justification of torture....
3. An order from a superior officer or a public authority may not be invoked as a justification of torture....

13) The heinousness of the criminal offense has been always taken into account by Congress while enacting amnesty laws....

14) The distinction between political offenses and ordinary offenses connected with political motives has been consistently followed in our judicial precedents for the purpose of precluding the amnesty of barbarous crimes.... Thus, the Supreme Court held that the indiscriminate pardon of atrocious crimes, carried out inhumanly and lacking a justifiable connection with the political motivations alleged by the perpetrators, "borders on arbitrariness in the exercise of legislative powers"(254 [*Decisions*] 315). This statement, however, was only one of many other guidelines used by the Court for the purpose of excluding the possibility that atrocious crimes be covered by an amnesty by virtue of judicial interpretation. Moreover, it was clearly stated by the Court on that occasion that "the basic hierarchy of values at stake while granting an amnesty strictly binds us to respect the legislative will" (245 [*Decisions*] 455). It was also pointed out that an eventual arbitrariness on part of the legislator may be "exempted from judicial review."...

Finally, we can recall the extradition case of the German citizen Gerhard Bohne, charged with heading an organization for the massive and systematical elimination of mental patients, using gas chambers disguised as shower rooms. In this case the Supreme Court of Argentina handed down a judgment of significance in connection with this issue, whose paragraphs 14), 15), and 16) deserve to be quoted:

14) Neither political justifications nor the alleged military need can be admitted as a ground for refusing to extradite the defendant, especially when we are facing criminal acts which are clearly inconsistent with the common feeling of civilized nations on account of their cruelty and immorality. Moreover, the alleged resort to euthanasia does not bare any ostensible relationship with political or military violations.
15) According to precedents reported in 21 [*Decisions*] 121; 54:464, and 115:312, this Supreme Court has refused to treat as political offenses acts which are repugnant because of their heinous and barbaric nature.
16) That in the case at bar it is obvious that the charges against the defendant involve acts which are repugnant to basic humanitarian feelings....

It is now necessary to proceed with a technical analysis of Article 514 of the C.M.J. and related rules in light of the principles stated above.

15) The simple grammatical analysis of Article 514 reveals, without any doubt, that in the same way that the lack of responsibility of the one who carried out the order never shelters he who gave the order, conversely, the responsibility of the one who imparted the order does not shield, in every case, the one who followed such order.

This Court has held in Case No. C.895.XX, "Proceedings originally brought before the Supreme Council of the Armed Forces pursuant to Decree No. 158," dated December 30, 1986, that

> A careful analysis of these rules shows that military laws attribute criminal responsibility as principal perpetrator only to the superior who gave the order in those cases where the subordinate is exempt from punishment by virtue of Article 34(5) of the Cr.C. In cases where the subordinate officer is not in a position to be protected by that cause of justification, criminal responsibility is shared by the superior and subordinate officers. (Opinions of Justices Enrique S. Petracchi and Jorge A. Bacqué, paragraph 14....

16) The limits of due obedience set forth in Article 514 of the C.M.J. must be now analyzed for the purpose of ascertaining when the superior and subordinate officers are to be considered jointly liable. We must point out at the outset that, as acknowledged in paragraph 15) of the minority opinion in the case cited above, military discipline is essential for the maintenance of a military structure. Thus service-connected orders are to be strictly followed, with a very limited possibility of questioning such order (C.M.J., Article 675) and sanctions are imposed in case of disobedience (C.M.J. 667 and 674). Military discipline has a bearing, of course, on the way in which obedience is to be exercised. This is the difference with other areas of the administration, such as public service. However, the different role played by discipline in a military context is irrelevant with regard to the nature and limits imposed on the duty to obey.

It does not follow from the premise that the subordinate's power to scrutinize orders is more limited in a military context than in others that the subordinate will escape responsibility regardless of the content of the order. If the order is manifestly illegal the subordinate officer need not enjoy the power to question the order. Because the illegality is so obvious, there is no need to examine the nature of the order in order to detect its unlawful character.

17) Therefore, the case for impunity established by Article 514 of the C.M.J. operates only within the limits established by that code. This exceptional case takes place when the order is not patently illegal, it is given by a superior officer within the sphere of his authority (service-connected), and as long as it points to the execution of an act which is also within the sphere of competence of the subordinate officer. Beyond those limitations, as evidenced by the facts of the case at bar, the order contradicts principles and convictions of the general legal conscience. The subordinate who abides by such order would have exceeded the sphere where due obedience operates as a justification. Consequently the subordinate is responsible, together with the superior officer who gave the order.

Because all of the acts of which the defendants have been convicted clearly exceed the said limitations and hence are not sheltered by the justification of due obedience, it is actually unnecessary to decide which is the precise systematical place occupied by due obedience within the general theory of crime. Indeed, those legal scholars who acknowledge that due obedience is a cause for justification of crimes limit its scope to cases where the order does not manifestly breach the legal system, or does not impose a behavior beneath human dignity or against the general rules of international law, etc....

18) The brief outline set forth in the previous paragraph centers on the classification of due obedience within the more general theory of crime. This is a different issue than the one focusing on the limits within which this cause for justification is admissible. Because of the seriousness and manifest illegality of the crimes of which the defendants in this case have been convicted, it would be against the most basic ethical legal principles to leave them unpunished on account of due obedience....

The sphere of competence of the judiciary focuses on ascertaining whether past events submitted to its judgment are subject to the laws to be applied in each particular case. In order to perform their function, judges must interpret the law and the facts, for it is only through this procedure that it is possible to verify whether the factual circumstances fit a particular hypothesis envisioned by the law. In contrast, the sphere of competence of the legislative branch centers on the elaboration of general and abstract rules of law which in principle are to be applied to future events....

26) It follows from the principle of separation of powers that those powers vested in each of the three branches of government are to be exclusively exercised. The concurrent use of said powers would necessarily entail the disappearance of the line of separation among the three political branches, hence destroying the basis of our system of government....

29) In the same way that the courts are limited in their jurisdictional powers, the Constitution has limited the powers of the legislative branch. In contrast with the judiciary, the purpose of congressional powers is to elaborate and abstract rules to govern the conduct of individuals in the future....

[T]his Law forces upon judges a particular finding of facts in each particular case submitted to the courts, establishing an irrefutable presumption about those facts. It has been frequently said in this regard that such presumptions are inadmissible in criminal law, especially in cases involving the proof of guilt or innocence of the defendant....

The "presumptions" set forth by this Law are not linguistic constructions aimed at advancing a particular interpretation of a rule of law. They present a bold finding of facts, thus replacing the independent fact-finding process carried out by the judges for the arbitrary assessment of the legislator....

34) However, the interpretation of laws cannot be undertaken without considering the particular political context in which they are enacted, nor may such interpretation be indifferent to the possible effects ensuing from a declaration of unconstitutionality.... Consequently, in spite of the serious flaws of this Law this Court cannot ignore that beyond the letter of the law there is a clear political decision made by the legislator, the wisdom of which it is not for the judicial branch to assess.

It must be recalled that the intention of the legislator cannot be frustrated as a result of technical imperfections (271 [*Decisions*] 7; 280:307), and that the mission of judges is not exhausted with reviewing the letter of the law. It is the unavoidable duty of judges to fix the meaning of the law applicable to a particular case (249 [*Decisions*] 37). This is particularly true under circumstances in which both the executive and legislative powers have decided, in the face of the serious conflict of interests afflicting Argentine society on this issue, to preserve social peace by channeling the popular will along a course that avoids confrontation, in pursuit of achieving the indispensable union of all Argentines....

35) Judges are not in a position to substitute the authority of other powers charged with the responsibility of preserving the peace, nor may judges assume the competence given to that authority.... Since it is obvious that Congress has decided to block the criminal prosecutions of those persons mentioned in Article 1 of Law 23521, it must be concluded that Congress has actually exercised the amnesty powers conferred by Article 67(17) of the Constitution....

39) ...This Court must therefore apply this amnesty law in spite of its formal flaws. This does not mean that the Court shares the view that such legislative measure can attain its purpose, i.e., the preservation of social peace and the reconciliation of the Argentine people within a democratic system. This Court fulfills its fundamental duty not to interfere with the political decisions of the other branches of government, but it is also the obligation of the Court to take a stand for the record as to the relationship between the measure under consideration and the goals that it seeks to achieve. This Law affects the legal consequences but not the causes of the behavior subject to amnesty. This Law deals with conduct which has had a destructive influence on social relations, and the amnesty has placed a full stop on judicial review for the purpose of pacification. But this amnesty does not necessarily amount to a first step towards a lasting peace where stable institutions and harmonious coexistence can take root. The will of the Argentine people to consolidate democracy requires not only the elimination of the penal consequences of the acts which took place, but also the definite removal of the circumstances that made those acts possible.

While upholding the constitutionality of this Law, it is the duty of this court to urge the other branches of government to take complementary measures for the purpose of establishing a new frame of reference in military-civilian relations, modernizing the armed forces and incorporating them into a democratic system subject to the Constitution. Only in this way, which a mere amnesty law cannot specify, will the Argentine attain the dream of our founding fathers—so often postponed yet so clearly expressed in the Constitution....

[Second] Dissenting Opinion

Justice Jorge Antonio Bacqué filed a dissenting opinion:...

According to Law 23521, those favored by its terms are presumed *jure et de jure* to have acted under duress and without being able to review the orders. This rule prevents judges appointed pursuant to the Constitution from ascertaining whether duress and impossibility of reviewing the orders actually existed. Arguably, it is a congressional prerogative to create legal presumptions (*see* Article 1113 of the Civil Code). However, irrebuttable presumptions in criminal law have been traditionally stigmatized by legal scholars....

12) For the above reasons, Article 1 of Law 23521 contravenes the principle separation of powers (Articles 1, 94, 95 and 100 of the Constitution)....

Admitting, arguendo, that Law 23521 is actually an amnesty law in spite of the name given to it by Congress, such amnesty could extinguish the legal consequences of the crime of torture. On the one hand, a settled legal tradition, which has been extensively discussed in paragraphs 39 and 40 of this opinion, sustains that the primary goal of an amnesty is to cover only political crimes or common crimes reasonably connected with the alleged political purpose it seeks to attain. Consequently, it has been always understood that atrocious or aberrant crimes could not be subject to amnesty, for no political goals may justify that sort of criminal offense. On the other hand, Article 18 of the Constitution clearly provides in its pertinent part that "all kinds of torture and lashing ... are abolished for ever...." This constitutional provision presents an insurmountable obstacle to the constitutionality of Law 23521. It is also part of the ethical framework of all civilized communities, which cannot allow impunity for atrocious and aberrant acts such as torture....

30) Before examining the arguments raised by defendant Berges it should be pointed out that the criminal offenses he is charged with are those within the category of "atrocious and aberrant."... As to the charges brought against the defendant Etchecolatz, the lower court has established ... his participation as indirect perpetrator ... in ninety one counts ... of torture....

31) The impunity for those crimes established by Law 23521 seriously engages the responsibility of the members of this Court. This responsibility must take account of the Court's duty towards the Argentine people and their ethical and legal traditions. We must also take into account the particular circumstances through which Argentine society is currently living. There are times of unprecedented collective experience, highly emotional

and intense, in the history of a people. Those times lead to great decisions with a potential for opening a new historical path. It is clear that the Argentine people has decided to build a political community based on freedom and dignity of all men and women, thus crystallizing at long last the mandate of the founding fathers....

In the face of the perverse pressures exerted on our modern lives, it seems almost ridiculous to reach out for the old principles of ethical humanism in order to proclaim their effective compliance. However, nothing is more practical and realistic than to do so, and without concessions. It has become obvious that technical idiocy, unbridled fanaticism and Realpolitik have pushed humanity, for the first time in its history, to the brink of a precipice where the mode and conditions of life are at risk. This danger may be averted only by paying unconditional respect to human dignity. This is the point of departure for addressing the issue of due obedience in a military context. It is appropriate to review first the legal tradition referred to above and to deal later with the way in which the principle of due obedience was adopted by the Argentine legal system....

40) Since the early days of our country it has been firmly settled that brutal and inhuman acts should not be decriminalized....

ARGENTINA: PRESIDENTIAL PARDONS

Decree 1002/89

(October 6, 1989)

CONSIDERING the consequences of confrontations between Argentinean citizens that have been taking place over the past two decades have been a constant factor in destroying social harmony and preventing us from achieving agreement and union, which should be the first priority of the National Government; and

WHEREAS:

That in spite of the time that has passed since the complete restoration of constitutional institutions, the measures that have been taken so far (notwithstanding the large number of defendants that have been involved) have not been sufficient to overcome the deep divisions that still remain in the heart of our society, the responsibility for which must be assumed by everyone, as integral members and participants in a society organized on legal principles.

That in light of the situation that has resulted from these divisions, the social conduct required is not to ignore them or cynically to pretend that they do not exist. But it also should not be—at the other extreme—an attitude that submits community life to the ordinary, depressing, and frustrating influence of these divisions and keeps open the wounds they have caused, keeping all of us locked within a divisive and fatalistic reality. What is required is a loftiness of spirit that can overcome rancor—however understandable it may be—and replace it with magnanimity, without which we shall never be able to achieve internal peace and the national unity called for by our Constitution.

That leaving behind these gloomy events is not an act of irresponsible condescension. It is rather the prerequisite that we must fulfill in order to become united in solidarity, as a single people, without the division into two factions, which our past wants to drag us into. Only after we rebuild this united front can we regain the vital energy we need to be a true nation with a true destiny. The central idea of this time is national reconciliation. We Argentineans must reconcile with one another, and in doing so, achieve the spiritual peace that can bring us back to brotherhood. We shall never achieve this by holding on to the tragic events of yesterday, the sole memory of which is enough to unnerve and weaken us.

That this national reconciliation "aims, above all, at the heart of the People, which has been torn apart, for which purpose it is necessary that each person pacify his own spirit, removing from it all hate; each person must have the courage to look at himself sincerely and admit his own faults;

to make a sincere commitment not to exclude anyone arbitrarily and unjustly from the right to participate in determining the course to be taken by society; to encourage rational and sincere dialogue as the only acceptable weapon in political struggles, and instead of trying to defeat the opponent, attempts to achieve a harmony of thoughts and desires; to adopt an attitude of brotherly understanding towards those who are in error or who have caused us harm, attempting to take the initiative for meeting them half-way; to exercise justice with honor and truth without a spirit of vengeance; to promote feelings of lenience in applying the penalties for crimes committed, until a spirit of sincere forgiveness is achieved, which is applicable not only to individual relationships but also to social relationships." (Argentinean Bishops' Conference, August 11, 1982).

That in order to achieve the above, it is necessary, beyond every consideration of the truth or falseness of various doctrinaire and ideological positions, to adopt the measures that can create the conditions under which we—with the invaluable support of the spiritual greatness of the men and women of this Nation—can achieve a permanent reconciliation among all Argentineans, which is the only possible solution for the wounds that still remain to be healed, and to build a true Nation of brothers and sisters.

That it is the responsibility of the NATIONAL EXECUTIVE AUTHORITY, not to be delegated, to place the supreme interest of the Nation before any other interest, and thereby to meet the historical challenge that this highly political decision entails.

That it must be stated, nevertheless, that this measure is only a political mechanism, provided for by the constitution in order to create the conditions necessary for national pacification. It does not imply in any manner whatsoever that these objectives have been obtained or that there is any guarantee that they will be obtained. It is merely one more of the many measures that the National Government, sacrificing obvious legitimate and historical convictions, is prepared to carry out in order to achieve the pacification of the Country.

That the NATIONAL EXECUTIVE AUTHORITY is attempting in this manner to create the conditions and scenario necessary for national reconciliation, mutual pardon, and national unity. But the principal actors in the Argentinean drama, among whom are also those people who are now running the government, those who with humility, beginning with the acknowledgement of their own errors and the positive points of their adversaries, bring a sincere disposition and desire to achieve reconciliation and unity. Only an attitude free of partiality and prejudice can make the pain suffered by Argentineans over the past decades bear fruit, as was the case with the blood of our ancestors in the struggle for independence. May those who died in the struggle for their ideals rest in peace, and may their memory serve not to divide the Argentinean people; rather, may their blood serve to unite us even more; to create for us, our children, and our grandchildren, a climate of peace, progress, well-being, and the realization of dreams.

That this decision is also an attempt to consolidate democracy in Argentina, as its objective is on the same level and of equal importance as the goals of pacification and reconciliation. Only the people, by means of voting and the free exercise of constitutional mechanisms, should be responsible for electing their rulers and replacing them when necessary. The future that we want to bring about must also prevent those of any persuasion who attempt to seize power by any means other than the will of the people.

That with respect to the legal context in which the present decree is dictated, in accordance with the general terms used in Article 86, par. 6 of the National Constitution, it must comply with the interpretation which states that when authority is expressly granted in general terms, it cannot be restricted unless such interpretation is based on a specific text, either expressly stated or inferred by implication. (C.S.J.N. [National Supreme Court of Justice], *Decisions*, 136:258).

That it is also a guiding rule in this matter that the Constitution must be interpreted in such a way that its limitations do not interfere with the efficient and just exercise of the authority attributed to the State, and permit the fulfillment of its goals in the manner most beneficial to the community. (C.S.J.N., *Decisions*, 214:425).

That, for this reason, this comports with the docrined established by the Supreme Court of Justice, in the case of "IBANEZ J." (*Decisions*, k136:258), according to which, for the purpose of carrying out the authority to grant pardons, the Constitution requires that there be an ongoing case against the proposed benefactor of the pardon, but not that the case must have necessarily have reached a certain stage in the legal proceedings, that is, the executory sentence.

That as a consequence, the pardon may be granted both to persons who have been convicted and to those who are in the legal process.

That in addition, the measures that are to be taken, inasmuch as they affect the decision not to impose a penalty or to terminate the proceedings against the person receiving the pardon, do not in any way constitute the execution of judicial functions, nor are they considered to be revisions of legal decisions or actions concerning ongoing cases, in contradiction of the principle laid down in Article 95 of the National Constitution. These measures do not serve to resolve controversies or render decisions with respect to legal matters; rather, they constitute the execution of EXECUTIVE AUTHORITY, based on high juridical reasoning, with the intent of leading to a true national reconciliation and pacification.

That the present measure is decreed in accordance with the authority granted by Article 86, paragraph 6 of the National Constitution.

Therefore,

THE PRESIDENT OF THE REPUBLIC OF ARGENTINA DECREES:

Article 1

The granting of a pardon to the persons whose names appear in the attached Annex, which is an integral part of this document, with respect to the cases in which each party is involved.

Article 2

To be announced, published, transmitted to the NATIONAL HEADQUARTERS OF THE OFFICIAL REGISTRY, and filed.

Decree 2741/90

(December 29, 1990)

CONSIDERING the measures imposed by the National Government to create conditions that permit the definitive reconciliation among Argentinians, and

WHEREAS:

That a profound reflection on the situation prevailing in the Republic leads to the conclusion that it is necessary that the NATIONAL EXECUTIVE POWER carry out, in regard to the acts of violence and the clashes that have occurred in the recent past, a final contribution to assure the process of pacification in which the sectors that are truly representative of the Nation are involved.

That on the basis of this conviction and the experience gained over more than one year of the acts initiated with the issuance of Decrees No. 1002 and No. 1003 of October 6, 1989, it is resolved that the moment has arrived to finish them with the same finality and purpose that inspired these decisions.

That the fundamental ideas expressed in the WHEREAS clauses of the decrees alluded to are completely applicable to the present, provided that the same social, political and judicial assumptions are valid in the case.

[The Decree then repeats most of the language of the 1989 pardon.]

Therefore,

THE PRESIDENT OF THE ARGENTINE NATION DECREES:

Article 1

Those persons included in the Attachment shall be pardoned from the proceedings and penalties of deprivation of freedom imposed by the cases indicated therein.

Article 2

Let it be known, transmitted, published, submitted to the NATIONAL DIRECTOR OF THE OFFICIAL REGISTRY, and archived.

ATTACHMENT TO DECREE No. 2741

[The attachment lists the various members of the military junta who had been previously convicted.]

ARGENTINA: ORGANIZATION OF AMERICAN STATES, INTER-AMERICAN COMMISSION ON HUMAN RIGHTS— DECISION ON FULL STOP AND DUE OBEDIENCE LAWS

Report No. 28/92
Cases 10.147, 10.181, 10.240, 10.262, 10.309, 10.311

(October 2, 1992)

Introduction

1. In late 1987, the Commission began to receive petitions against the Government of the Argentine Republic (hereinafter "the Government"), which denounced the Legislature's passage of Laws No. 23,492, enacted on December 24, 1986, and No. 23,521, enacted on June 8, 1987, and their enforcement by the Judiciary; the petitioners alleged that this violated, *inter alia*, their right to judicial protection (Article 25) and their right to a fair trial (Article 8) recognized by the [American Convention on Human Rights]....

2. Law 23,492 set a 60-day deadline for terminating all criminal proceedings involving crimes committed as part of the so-called "dirty war". Law 23,521 established the irrefutable presumption that military personnel who committed crimes during the "dirty war" were acting in the line of duty, thereby acquitting them of any criminal liability. The Law even extended that protection to high-ranking officers who did not have decision making authority or any role in drawing up orders. Unless otherwise indicated, the instruments in question will be referred to as "the Laws."

3. Starting in November 1989, some of the petitioners, alleging the same violations, elaborated upon their petitions by protesting the effects of the Presidential Decree of Pardon No. 1002, of October 7, 1989 (hereinafter the "Decree"), which ordered that any proceedings against persons indicted for human rights violations who had not benefitted from the earlier laws be discontinued....

6. [T]he petitioners alleged that the criminal proceedings for human rights violations—disappearances, summary executions, torture, kidnapping—committed by members of the Armed Forces were canceled, encumbered or obstructed by the Laws and the Decree, and that this constituted a violation of rights guaranteed to them under the Convention.

7. [T]he Government maintained that the alleged violations occurred before the Argentine State's ratification of the Convention and therefore were inadmissible *ratione temporis*. The Government also argued that some of the cases had already been heard in other international fora. As for the merits, the Government stated that an exhaustive official investigation was conducted and former military leaders convicted, so that there was no breach of the Convention. As for the OAS Charter and the American Declaration of the Rights and Duties of Man, Argentina insisted that while

534 • *Laws, Rulings, and Reports*

these instruments do recognize rights, they reserve enforcement of those rights for the national courts....

13. The bulk of the human rights violations ... occurred in the 1970s. The military government took over in Argentina in 1976, and democratic institutions were only restored with the inauguration of the civilian government on December 10, 1983.

14. For Argentina, the Convention entered into force on September 5, 1984, with deposit of the instrument of ratification of the Convention.

15. Law No. 23,492 was enacted on December 24, 1986, Law No. 23,521 on June 8, 1987, and Presidential Decree No. 1002 on October 7, 1989.

16. The violation at issue in the instant case is the denial of the right to judicial protection and of the right to a fair trial, since the Laws and Decrees in question paralyzed the judicial inquiry. Therefore, the disputed measures were adopted at a time when *the Convention was already in force*, for the Argentine State.

17. Argentina alleges that the present government is being blamed for "events that occurred prior to ratification of the Convention." In this regard, it invokes Article 28 of the Vienna Convention on the Law of Treaties (1969), the jurisprudence on the subject and the body of international practice concerning the nonretroactivity of treaties. It therefore asks that the petitions be declared inadmissible *ratione temporis*.

18. The petitioners argue that the violations being denounced did not predate the Convention's entry into force, but came after, upon approval of the Laws and the Decree being challenged, which had the effect of denying them their rights to judicial protection and to a fair trial (Articles 25 and 8, in relation to Article 1.1 of the Convention). Article 8.1 of the Convention states the following:

> Every person has the right to a hearing, with due guarantees and within a reasonable time, by a competent, independent, and impartial tribunal, previously established by law, in the substantiation of any accusation of a criminal nature made against him or for the determination of his rights and obligations of a civil, labor, fiscal, or any other nature.

Article 25.1 of the Convention reads as follows:

> Everyone has the right to simple and prompt recourse, or any other effective recourse, to a competent court or tribunal for protection against acts that violate his fundamental rights recognized by the constitution or laws of the state concerned or by this Convention, even though such violation may have been committed by persons acting in the course of their official duties.

19. The articles of the Convention that the petitioners invoke concern events that occurred after Argentina became a State Party to the Convention. Therefore, the petitions are admissible *ratione temporis*....

The Government's Observations on the Report Prepared Pursuant to Article 50

25. The Argentine Government contends that the Argentine State has been the one that has best dealt with the "difficult problem" of finding a solution to past human rights violations through a response that came from the "very sectors of the nation that were affected" and that Laws No. 23,492 and No. 23,521 and Decree 1002/89 were approved by "only the appropriate democratic institutions" (IACHR Report 1985-1986). It underscores the fact that these were actions taken by democratic bodies because of the compelling need for national reconciliation and consolidation of the democratic system.

26. The Government points out that the Argentine State has said "never again" and has enacted Laws that benefit the victims of the National Reorganization Process....

27. The Government notes that the violations denounced in the report were the result of acts of State terrorism in Argentina in the period from 1976 to 1983, but that once the rule of law was restored, the State assumed responsibility and paid fair compensation for the violations committed.

28. The Government believes that there was redress because of the laws and decrees enacted for that express purpose; because of the international commitments honored and because of its resolve to instill the notion "never again" in the national consciousness and to mirror it in this Government's every action. Consequently, it asks that the Commission find that the appropriate measures have been taken.

The Merits

...30. [T]he question the Commission has before it is whether or not the Laws and the Decree are compatible with the Convention.

A. As to the Convention's Interpretation

> Article 29 of the Convention reads as follows:
>
> No provision of this Convention shall be interpreted as:
>
> a. permitting any State Party, group, or person to suppress the enjoyment or exercise of the rights and freedoms recognized in this convention or to restrict them to a greater extent than is provided for herein;
> b. restricting the enjoyment or exercise of any right or freedom recognized by virtue of the laws of the State Party or by virtue of another convention to which one of the said states is a party;
> c. precluding other rights or guarantees that are inherent in the human personality or derived from representative democracy as a form of government; or
> d. excluding or limiting the effect that the American Declaration of the Rights and Duties of Man and other international acts of the same nature may have.

31. The Commission notes that any interpretation of the Convention must be rendered in accordance with this provision.

B. As to the Right to a Fair Trial

32. The effect of passage of the Laws and the Decree was to cancel all proceedings pending against those responsible for past human rights violations. These measures closed off any judicial possibility of continuing the criminal trials intended to establish the crimes denounced; identify their authors, accomplices and accessories after the fact, and impose the corresponding punishments. The petitioners, relatives or those injured by the human rights violations have been denied their right to a recourse, to a thorough and impartial judicial investigation to ascertain the facts.

33. What is denounced as incompatible with the Convention are the legal consequences of the Laws and the Decree with respect to the victims' right to a fair trial. One of the effects of the disputed measures was to weaken the victim's right to bring a criminal action in a court of law against those responsible for these human rights violations.

34. In a good number of the criminal law systems in Latin America, the victim or his or her attorney has the right to be the party making the charge in a criminal proceeding. In systems that allow it—such as Argentina's—the victim of a crime has a fundamental civil right to go to the courts. That right plays an important role in propelling the criminal process and moving it forward.

35. The question of whether the rights of the victim or his or her relatives, guaranteed by the domestic laws, are protected by the international human rights law, means determining: a) whether those rights recognized in the constitution and laws of that State at the time the violations occurred acquired international protection through ratification of the Convention, and then b) whether those rights can be abrogated through subsequent enactment of a special law, without violating the Convention or the American Declaration.

36. Under Article 1.1 of the Convention, the State Parties are obliged "to respect the rights and freedoms recognized herein and to ensure to all persons subject to their jurisdiction the free and full exercise of those rights and freedoms...."

37. The Laws and the Decree sought to, and effectively did obstruct, the exercise of the petitioners' right under Article 8.1 cited earlier. With enactment and enforcement of the Laws and the Decree, Argentina has failed to comply with its duty to guarantee the rights to which Article 8.1 refers, has abused those rights and has violated the Convention.

C. As to the Right to Judicial Protection

38. Article 25.2 reads as follows:

2. The States Parties undertake:

a. to ensure that any person claiming such remedy shall have his rights determined by the competent authority provided by the legal system of the state;
b. to develop the possibilities of judicial remedy; and
c. to ensure that the competent authorities shall enforce such remedies when granted.

39. With passage of the Laws and the Decree, Argentina has failed in its obligation to guarantee the rights recognized in Article 25.1 and has violated the Convention.

D. As to the Obligation to Investigate

40. When interpreting the scope of Article 1.1, the Inter-American Court of Human Rights stated that "The second obligation of the States Parties is to 'ensure' the free and full exercise of the rights recognized by the Convention to every person subject to its jurisdiction.... As a consequence of this obligation, the States must *prevent*, investigate and punish any violation of the rights recognized by the Convention...."[2] The Court elaborates upon this concept in several paragraphs that follow: "What is decisive is whether a violation of the rights recognized by the Convention has occurred with the *support or the acquiescence of the government*, or whether the State has allowed the act to take place without taking measures to prevent it or to punish those responsible...;"[3] "The State has a *legal duty* to take reasonable steps to prevent human rights violations and to use the means at its disposal to *carry out a serious investigation* of violations committed within its jurisdiction, *to identify those responsible, to impose the appropriate punishment* and to ensure the victim adequate compensation;"[4] "...If the *State apparatus* acts in such a way that the *violation goes unpunished* and the victim's full enjoyment of such rights is not restored as soon as possible, *the State has failed to comply with its duty to ensure the free and full exercise of those rights to the persons* within its jurisdiction."[5] As for the obligation to investigate, it states that the investigation "must have an objective and be *assumed by the State as its own legal duty, not as a step taken by private interests* that depends upon the initiative of the victim or his family or upon their offer of proof without an *effective search for the truth by the government*."[6] (Emphasis added by the Commission).

41. By its enactment of these Laws and Decree, Argentina has failed to comply with its duty under Article 1.1 and has violated rights that the Convention accords to the petitioners.

---

[2] Inter-American Court of Human Rights, Velásquez Rodríguez Case, Judgment of July 29, 1988. Series C, No. 4, paragraph 166.

[3] Ib. paragraph 173.

[4] Ib. paragraph 174.

[5] Ib. paragraph 176.

[6] Ib. paragraph 177.

The Commission's Opinion and Conclusions

42. The Commission is aware of the exemplary measure taken by the Argentine State when it established the official national commission (CONADEP) that investigated and documented the disappearances that occurred during the so-called "dirty war" in its historic report *Nunca Más*.

43. The commission was also pleased to observe the historic precedent the Argentine Government set when it put on trial high-ranking officials of the *de facto* government and convicted them of human rights violations.

44. The Government argues that it has taken adequate measures by enacting provisions to benefit the victims of the National Reorganization Process.

45. Among those measures, the Government cites enactment of Law 23,466, of October 30, 1986, which grants a pension equal to 75% of the minimum lifetime salary to the next-of-kin of the disappeared, which pension can also be claimed by minors under the age of 21 who demonstrate that one or both parents were the victim of forced disappearance prior to December 10, 1983.... A surviving spouse and children under the age of 21, parents and/or siblings, and orphaned sibling minors with whom the victim lived prior to the disappearance can also qualify to receive the pension. The Law stipulates that its beneficiaries may claim the coverage provided by the National Social Services Institute for Retirees and Pensioners.

46. The Government also mentions Law 24,043, of December 23, 1991, which awarded a pension to persons who, during the previous dictatorship, were arrested on orders from the National Executive Power during the state of siege or who, as civilians, were arrested by virtue of warrants issued by military tribunals. The benefit consists of one thirtieth of the monthly remuneration at the highest category on the civil service scale. This Law stipulates that the indemnizations are to be paid in the form of bonds, in accordance with Law 23,982 on Public Debt and Consolidation of Economic Securities. According to the Government's estimates, this Law will benefit some 8,500 people.

47. Reference is also made to Decrees 70/91 and 2151/91, executive decrees similar to the previous Law but that benefitted only a certain number of victims who, after having filed an action for economic compensation— without success—in the domestic courts, filed a complaint with the Commission.

48. The Commission is pleased with the measures adopted by the Government to redress and compensate the victims of the "dirty war." It refers here not only to the celebrated trials of the principal guilty parties under the previous dictatorship, but also to CONADEP's investigation, and the various measures adopted to compensate victims of human rights violations under the *de facto* government.

49. Nevertheless, the Commission must make clear that the issue in the instant cases is not only economic compensation for damages and injuries caused by the State.

50. In this report, one of the facts denounced is the legal consequence of the passage of the Laws and the Decree, in that it denied the victims their

right to obtain a judicial investigation in a court of criminal law to determine those responsible for the crimes committed and punish them accordingly. Therefore, the violation of the right to a fair trial (Article 8) and of the right to judicial protection (Article 25) in relation to the obligation of the States to guarantee the full and free exercise of the rights recognized in the Convention (Article 1.1) is denounced as incompatible with the Convention. These violations occurred with enactment of the disputed legal measures in 1986, 1987 and 1989, after the Convention had entered into force for Argentina in 1984.

51. On the other hand, the question of economic compensation—to which the petitioners have a right—concerns the reparation for the *original or substantive violations*, most of which took place during the 1970s, before Argentina's ratification of the Convention and before enactment of the Laws and Decree denounced. It is a question of the right to be compensated by the State for its failure to ensure the right to life, humane treatment and freedom, but not the denial of justice that was the legal consequence of the Laws and the Decree at issue in the instant case. Compensation was not the only purpose of the petitions and not the only issue in this report.

52. While both questions (denial of justice upon cancellation of the criminal proceedings and the compensation for violations of the rights to life, humane treatment and liberty) are intimately related, they must not be confused. Each question materially differs and moreover concerns events that occurred at different times; the rights or provisions of the Convention affected also differ.

Given the foregoing, the ***Inter-American Commission on Human Rights***:

1) Concludes that Law Nos. 23,492 and 23,521 and Decree No. 1002/89 are incompatible with Article XVIII (right to a fair trial) of the American Declaration of the Rights and Duties of Man and Articles 1, 8 and 15 of the American Convention on Human Rights.

2) Recommends that the Argentine Government pay the petitioners just compensation for the violations referred to in the preceding paragraph.

3) Recommends to the Argentine Government that it adopt the measures necessary to clarify the facts and identify those responsible for the human rights violations that occurred during the past military dictatorship....

BANGLADESH: COLLABORATORS (SPECIAL TRIBUNAL) ORDER

President's Order No. 8 of 1972
(as amended February 1972)

WHEREAS certain persons, individually or as members of organizations, directly or indirectly; have been collaborators of the Pakistan Armed forces, which had illegally occupied Bangladesh by brute force, and have aided or abetted the Pakistan Armed forces of occupation in committing genocide and crimes against humanity and in committing atrocities against men, women and children and against the person, property and honour of the civilian population of Bangladesh and have otherwise aided or cooperated with or acted in the interest of the Pakistan Armed Forces of Occupation or contributed by any act, word or sign towards maintaining, sustaining strengthening, supporting or furthering the illegal occupation of Bangladesh by the Pakistan Armed forces or have waged war or aided or abetted in waging war against ... Bangladesh;

AND WHEREAS such collaboration contributed towards the perpetration of a reign of terror and the commission of crimes against humanity on a scale which has horrified the moral conscience of the people of Bangladesh and of right–thinking people throughout the world;

AND WHEREAS it is imperative that such persons should be dealt with effectively and be adequately punished in accordance with the due process of law.

AND WHEREAS it is expedient to provide for the setting up of SPECIAL TRIBUNALS for expeditious and fair trial of the offenses committed by such persons:

NOW, THEREFORE, in pursuance of the Proclamation of Independence of Bangladesh, read with the Provisional Constitution of Bangladesh Order, 1972 and in exercise of powers enabling him in that behalf the President is pleased to make the following Order:

1. (1) This Order may be called the Bangladesh Collaborators (Special Tribunals) Order, 1972.
   (2) It extends to the whole of Bangladesh.
   (3) It shall come into force at once and shall be deemed to have taken effect on the 26th day of March, 1971,

2. In this Order, —

   (a) "Code" means the Code of Criminal Procedure, 1898 (Act V of 1898):
   (b) "Collaborator" means a person who has—

     (i)   participated with or aided, or abetted the occupation army in maintaining, sustaining, strengthening, supporting or furthering the illegal occupation of Bangladesh by such army;

    (ii)   rendered material assistance in any way whatsoever to the occupation army by any act, whether by words, signs or conduct;

   (iii)   waged war or abetted in waging war against the People's Republic of Bangladesh;

   (iv)   actively resisted or sabotaged the efforts of the people and the liberation forces of Bangladesh in their liberation struggle against the occupation army;

    (v)   by a public statement or by voluntary participation in propagandas within and outside Bangladesh or by association in any delegation or committee or by participation in purported bye–elections attempted to aid or aided the occupation army in furthering its design of perpetrating its forcible occupation of Bangladesh.

Explanation

A person who has performed in good faith functions which he was required by any purported law in force at the material time to do shall not be deemed to be a collaborator:

Provided that a person who has performed functions the direct object or result of which was the killing of any member of the civil population or the liberation forces of Bangladesh or the destruction of their property or the rape of or criminal assault on their women–folk, even if done under any purported law passed by the occupation army, shall be deemed to be a collaborator.

    (c)   "Government" means the Government of the People's Republic of Bangladesh;

    (d)   "Liberation forces" includes all forces of the People's Republic of Bangladesh engaged in the liberation of Bangladesh;

    (e)   "Occupation army" means the Pakistan Armed Forces engaged in the occupation of Bangladesh;

    (f)   "Special Tribunal" means a Tribunal set up under this Order.

3. (1)   Any police officer or any person empowered by the Government in that behalf may, without a warrant, arrest any person who may reasonably be suspected of having been a collaborator.

    (2)   Any police officer or person making an arrest under clause (1) shall forthwith report such arrest to the "Sub–divisional Magistrate" together with a precis of the information or materials on the basis of which the arrest has been made, and, pending receipt of the order of the "Sub–divisional Magistrate" may, by order in writing, commit any person so arrested to

such custody as the Government may by general or special order specify.

(3) On receipt of a report under clause (2), the "Sub–divisional Magistrate" may by order in writing direct such person to be detained for an initial period of six months for the purpose of inquiry into the case.

(4) The Government may extend the period of detention if, in the opinion of the Government, further time is required for completion of the inquiry.

(5) Any person arrested and detained before the commencement of this Order who is alleged to be a collaborator, shall be deemed to be arrested and detained under this Order and an order in writing authorising such detention shall be made by the Government;

Provided that the initial period of detention of six months in the case of such person shall be computed from the date of his arrest.

4. Notwithstanding anything contained in the Code or in any other law for the time being in force, any collaborator, who has committed any offence specified in the Schedule shall be tried and punished by a Special Tribunal set up under this Order and no other Court shall have any jurisdiction to take cognizance of any such offence.

5. (1) The Government may set up as many Special Tribunals as it may deem necessary to try and punish offences under this Order for each district or for such area as may be determined by it.

(2) A Special Tribunal shall consist of one member.

(3) No person shall be qualified to be appointed a member of a Special Tribunal unless he is or has been a Sessions Judge or as Additional Sessions Judge or an Assistant Sessions Judge.

6. (1) A Special Tribunal consisting of a Sessions Judge or an Additional Sessions Judge shall try and punish offences enumerated in parts I and II of the Schedule.

(2) A Special Tribunal consisting of an Assistant Sessions Judge shall try and punish offences enumerated in Parts III and IV of the Schedule.

7. A Special Tribunal shall not take cognizance of any offence punishable under this Order except upon a report in writing by an officer–in–charge of a police station.

8. (1) The provisions of the Code in so far as they are not inconsistent with the provisions of this Order, shall apply to all matters connected with, arising from or consequent upon a trial by a Special Tribunal.

(2) A Special Tribunal shall, for the purpose of the provisions of the Code, be deemed to be a Court of Sessions trying cases without the aid of assessors or jury and without the accused being committed to it by a Magistrate for trial and shall follow the procedure prescribed by the Code for the trial of summons cases by Magistrate.

(3) A person conducting prosecution before a Special Tribunal shall be deemed to be a Public Prosecutor.

9. (1) A Special Tribunal shall not be bound to adjourn a trial for any purpose unless such adjournment is, in its opinion, necessary in the interests or justice.

(2) No trial shall be adjourned by reason of the absence of any accused person, if such accused person is represented by counsel, or if the absence of the accused person or his counsel has been brought about by the accused person himself, and the Special Tribunal shall proceed with the trial after taking necessary steps to pinpoint an advocate to defend and an accused person who is not represented by counsel.

10. A Special Tribunal may, with a view to obtaining the evidence of any person supposed to have been directly or indirectly concerned in, or privy to the offence, tender a pardon to such person on condition of his making a full and true disclosure of the whole circumstances within his knowledge relative to the offence and to every other person concerned, whether as principal or abettor, in the commission thereof....

11. Notwithstanding anything contained in any other law for the time being in force,—

(a) any collaborator who is convicted for any of the offences specified in Part I of the Schedule shall be punished with death or transportation for life and shall also be liable to a fine;

(b) any collaborator who is convicted for any of the offences specified in Part II of the Schedule shall be punished with rigorous imprisonment for a term not exceeding ten years and shall also be liable to a fine;

(c) any collaborator who is convicted for any of the offences specified in Part III of the Schedule shall be punished with rigorous imprisonment for a term not exceeding five years and shall also be liable to a fine;

(d) any collaborator who is convicted for any of the offences specified in Part IV of the Schedule shall be punished with rigorous imprisonment for a term not exceeding two years and shall also be liable to a fine;

12. Without prejudice to any sentence passed by the Special Tribunal the property, immovable, movable, or any portion thereof, of a collaborator

may, on his conviction, be forfeited to the Government, upon an order in writing made in this behalf by the Government.

13. If any accused is convicted of and sentenced for more than one offence, the sentences of imprisonment shall run concurrently or consecutively, as determined by the Special Tribunal.

14. Notwithstanding anything contained in the Code, no person who is in custody, accused or convicted of an offence punishable under this Order shall be released on bail....

16. (1) A person convicted of any offence by a Tribunal may appeal to the High Court.

(2) The Government may direct a Public Prosecutor to present appeal to the High Court from an order of acquittal passed by a Special Tribunal; upon intimation to the Special Tribunal by the Public Prosecutor that such an appeal is being filed, the person in respect of whom the order of acquittal was passed shall continue to remain in custody.

(3) The period of limitation for an appeal under clause (1) shall be 30 days from the date of sentence and for an appeal under clause (2) shall be 30 days from the date of the order of acquittal.

(4) The appeal may lie on matters of fact as well as of law.

17. (1) If the Government has reasons to believe that a person who, in the opinion of the Government, is required for the purpose of any investigation enquiry or other proceedings connected with an offence punishable under this Order, is absconding or is otherwise concealing himself or remaining abroad to avoid appearance, the Government, may, by a written proclamation published in the official Gazette or in such other manner as may [be] considered suitable to make it widely known:—

(a) direct the person named in the proclamation to appear at a specified place at a specified time;

(b) direct attachment of any property, movable or immovable, or both, belonging to the proclaimed person.

Explanation

"Property belonging to the proclaimed person" shall include property, movable and immovable, standing in the name of the proclaimed person or in the name of his wife, children, parents, minor brothers, sisters or dependents or any benamdar.

...(6) If any claim is preferred to, or objection made to the attachment of, any property attached under, this Article, within seven days from the date of such attachment, by any person other than the proclaimed person, on the ground that the claimant or objector has an interest in such property, and that such interest is not liable to attachment under this Article, the claim or objection shall be inquired into, and may be allowed or disallowed in whole or in part:

Provided that any claim preferred or objection made within the period allowed by this clause may, in the event of the death of the claimant or objector, be continued by his legal representative.

(7) A claim or an objection under clause (6) may be preferred or made before such person or authority as is appointed by the Government.

(8) Any person whose claim or objection has been disallowed in whole or in part by an order under clause (6) may, within a period of one month from the date of such order, appeal against such order to an appellate authority, constituted by the Government, for such purpose, but subject to the order of such appellate authority, the order shall be conclusive.

(9) If the proclaimed person appears within the time specified in the proclamation, the Government may make an order releasing the property from the attachment.

(10) If the proclaimed person does not appear within the time specified in the proclamation, the Government may pass an order forfeiting to the Government the property under attachment.

(11) When the property has been forfeited to the Government under clause (10), it may be disposed of in such manners as the Government directs.

18. Notwithstanding the provisions of the Code or of any other law for the time being in force, no action or proceeding taken or purporting to be taken under this Order shall be called in question by any Court, and there shall be no appeal from any order or sentence of a Special Tribunal save as provided in Article 16.

19. The Government may, by order published in the official Gazette, direct that any power or duty which is conferred or imposed by this Order upon the Government shall, in such circumstances and under such conditions, if any, as may be specified in the direction, be exercised or discharged by any officer or authority subordinate to it.

EL SALVADOR: LAW ON GENERAL AMNESTY FOR THE CONSOLIDATION OF PEACE

Decree No. 486 (March 20, 1993)

The Legislative Assembly of the Republic of El Salvador,

Considering:

I. That the peace consolidation process in our country requires the creation of confidence amongst our society in order to attain the reconciliation and reunification of the Salvadorian family. This is to be achieved by means of legal provisions to be enforced immediately which will guarantee to all inhabitants of the Republic of El Salvador, from all sections of society, a climate of harmony, respect and confidence.

II. That on January 23rd 1992, the Legislative Assembly approved the Law of National Reconciliation, contained in the Legislative Decree #147, published in the Official Journal #14, Volume 314. Through this decree, a restricted amnesty was declared to all responsible in any way for political crimes, or any deeds with political ramification, and for those who participated in common crimes committed by no less than twenty people, before January 1st, 1992.

III. That the above mentioned restriction did not permit the Law of National Reconciliation to be applied generally, regardless of the sector to which they belonged during the armed conflict, to those who participated in acts of violence which left a mark on society, and situations in which justice needs to be applied, in order to be consistent with the development of the democratic process and the reunification of the Salvadorian society.

IV. That in order to drive toward and to achieve national reconciliation, it is [advisable] to bestow the pardon of a broad, absolute and unconditional amnesty, in favor of all those who participated, in any way, in criminal acts which occurred before January 1, 1992. Such acts include political crimes or any crime with political ramification, or common crimes committed by no less than twenty people, including those people who would have received a sentence, or against whom legal proceedings have begun for their crimes, or those whom as yet have no proceedings against them. The amnesty will cover those not included in the Law of National Reconciliation, who participated as direct or indirect perpetrators of those crimes, or as accomplices.

Therefore:

Using the power granted to the Legislative Assembly by the constitution, and through the initiative of the following representatives … decrees the following:

Law of General Amnesty for the Consolidation of Peace

Article 1

A broad, absolute and unconditional amnesty is granted in favor of all those who in one way or another participated in political crimes, crimes with political ramifications, or common crimes committed by no less than twenty people, before January 1st 1992, regardless of whether proceedings against them for the perpetration of these crime have commence or not, or whether they have received a sentence as a consequence. This amnesty will cover all those who participated as direct or indirect perpetrators or as accomplices in the above mentioned crimes. The pardon will extend to those referred to in Article 6 of the Law of National Reconciliation.…

Article 2

For the purpose of this Law, apart from those specified in Article 161 of the Penal Code, also considered as political crimes are those mentioned in Articles 400-411 and 460-479 of the same code, and those committed as a consequence of or resulting from the armed conflict, without having to take into consideration the political condition, militancy, affiliation or ideology.

Article 3

Those who will not be favored by the amnesty are:

(a) Those who individually or collectively participated in the crimes typified in the second item of Article 400 of the penal code, and carried out these crimes with a view to profit, whether or not the person is serving time in prison as a consequence; and

(b) Those who individually or collectively participated in the crime of kidnapping and extortion typified in Articles 220 and 257 of the penal code and those included in the law regulating drug related activities, whether or not legal proceedings have begun against them, or whether or not the person is serving a prison sentence for on of these crimes, regardless of whether they have political connotations.

Article 4

The amnesty pardon granted by this Law will function in the following manner:

(a) For those convicted of a crime which deprives them of liberty, the judge or court carrying out the sentence will officially decree the release of those condemned, without having to pay bail. The same procedure will apply to the court taking up the case, even if the sentence has not been executed;

(b) For those absentees convicted of a crime for which they are to be deprived of liberty, the competent judge or court shall immediately cancel the order of arrest against them, without restriction, the discontinuance of the case, in favor of those prosecuted, by annulling the punitive act, and ordering the immediate release of those involved;

(c) In the case of those who as yet have not entered into legal proceedings, when the process begins against them for crimes committed (crimes mentioned in this amnesty), those accused can oppose the case by petitioning a dismissal in their favor, if captured they would be placed under the jurisdiction of the appointed judge who would decree their release;

(d) Those who are not included in the above, and through their own initiative or for any other reason wish to be favored by the amnesty, should present themselves to the respective first instance judges, who will issue a document outlining the reasons why those making the petition cannot be deprived of their rights as citizens; and

(e) The amnesty granted by this Law extinguishes all civil responsibilities.

Article 5

Without going against the contents of the previous Article, those who have been prosecuted, and wish to acquire the benefits of this Law, should make their petition in writing, either personally or though a proxy, or should direct themselves to the first instance judges, petition a corresponding dismissal in their favor; if this is admissible, the appointed judge will dictate the nonsuit, without restrictions and bail having to be paid. The petition can also be presented to the peace judges, departmental governors, town mayors and consuls accredited abroad, who on receiving them, should send them immediately to the respective first instance judges, in order for the corresponding procedures to be followed. The functionaries mentioned in this article who do not comply with their obligation will be issued a fine by the corresponding judge, of between one thousand and five thousand colones, according to the procedure established in Article 718 of the Code of Penal Procedure.

Article 6

All dispositions contrary to the present Law shall be repealed, especially Article 6 and the last subsection of Article 7, both taken from the Law of National Reconciliation....

EL SALVADOR: SUPREME COURT OF
JUSTICE DECISION ON THE AMNESTY LAW*

Proceedings No. 10-93 (May 20, 1993)

In relation to the ... arguments of the petitioner, inasmuch as they refer to the substance of the contested bill of law, the following considerations are made:

(I) Prior to the examination of the merits of the problem, it is essential to determine precisely if the pretension, in what refers to the substance of the law considered unconstitutional, is comprehended within the scope of competence of this Tribunal.

To that respect, it is convenient to point out that the fundamental mission of the competence of the Judicial Organ, is that of being a severe guardian of the acts of the public powers, thus deterring the invasion of the space reserved to liberty by the arbitrary and abusive exercise of power; for if governmental ordainment and the individual liberties contained in the institutional system organized by the Constitution, were to be transgressed with impunity, constitutional precepts would be no more than theoretical or ethical enunciations....

[B]oth the legislative and executive branches require a certain margin of arbitrary power to conduct the affairs of the State; we must therefore conclude that the Judicial Organ lacks competence to deal with affairs purely political, the nature of which are completely different to the essence of the jurisdictional function; and, therefore, their elucidation is exclusively of the competence of the political powers; the legislative and executive branches. Samuel Weaver expresses that "the term political is used in its broadest sense. It encompasses affairs which, under the Constitution, are to be decided by the people in its sovereign capacity or which have been delegated to the complete discretion of the executive or legislative departments". There is no doubt that this is a logical consequence of the application of the principle of the division of powers—the backbone of our institutional system—insofar as the judiciary is not to deal with affairs that the Constitution itself has not assigned to it; the contradiction of which would perturb the separation of functions, giving way to the possibility that the judges become government; and, consequently, the necessary tripartite equilibrium would be broken inasmuch as the remaining powers would lose their independence.

The Magna Carta has carefully and thoroughly assigned to the different organs created by her their respective competencies, in such a way as to warrant the collaboration and reciprocal control of the performance of the State apparatus. Of what has been said in the preceding paragraphs, it is to

---

* Reprinted from "Unconstitutionality Judgement Proceedings No. 10-93," in *Special Edition N°1* (Legal Studies Institute of El Salvador, 1993), pp. 63-78.

be inferred that affairs of purely political nature are not of the domain of the tribunals of justice, insofar as dealing with them would constitute an interference which undoubtedly would affect the principle of equilibrium and independence wisely established by the Constitution.

Affairs of a purely political nature are also known as non-judicial affairs, for they are not, in principle, of the competence of the judicial organ; an idea which finds its explanation and justification as a natural consequence of the principle to which we have been referring to: that of the separation of governmental organs. Therefore, tribunals lack in certain cases, the faculty to review the form and opportunity with which political powers exercise the attributions that pertain to them in a privative manner.

(II) When the political powers of the State exercise the attributions that have been constitutionally bestowed to them, they act as representatives of the Sovereign. It is therefore convenient to make a short reference to the concept of sovereignty....

[M]odern doctrines view sovereignty as the supreme power that rests in the people, the essence of which lies in the capacity of self-determination, of granting its own laws, of organizing itself politically and of self-government.

Sovereignty as a concept has two aspects, one political and the other juridical. To that respect, Carlos Sánchez Viamonte, an Argentine, has successfully explained that, clearly "from a political point of view, sovereignty is the will of the majority, even though the expression, "will of the majority", must be understood as binded and in accordance to a judicial ordainment, precisely because democracy is the State organized in accordance to law, to which it is subjected in the totality of its existence and manifestation; thus political sovereignty remains subordinated to juridical sovereignty.... Sovereignty is a will, but it is also a channel through which that will must circulate.... Thus, in a political sense, sovereignty is the will of the majority of the people; and, in a juridical sense, it is the subjection of its activity to the postulates of juridical ordainment, specifically the Constitution.

Sovereignty as the political will of the people, reunites the following characteristics:

a)   it is inalienable, inasmuch as it is, in itself, the personality of people, and being a personality it cannot be alienated, ceded or renounced;

b)   it is indivisible, inasmuch as sovereignty contains the idea of a supreme hierarchical power; and as such, it cannot recognize another; consequently, all possibility of sharing, is excluded;

c)   it is limited, for it supposes a *potestas* or faculty ruled by juridical principle, from which it derives its validity and legitimacy; which means, that sovereignty is a force limited by law; and

d)   it cannot be delegated, for even [though the people entrust the government to functionaries], they are mere representatives of the people and executors of its will.

Our Fundamental Law, following constitutional doctrine of American origin, rules under Article 83: "El Salvador is a sovereign State. Sovereignty resides in the people, who exercise it in the prescribed form and within the limits of this Constitution". This disposition indicates that the people itself is the sovereign; and therefore it is for [the people] to exercise that sovereign will of self-determination, to choose the form of government that best accommodates its needs, and to designate the governmental organs....

Now, having pointed out that the people deposits sovereignty in the Constitution at the moment it dictates and, consequently, rests subordinated to her, that circumstance does not signify that the people renounce sovereignty, which by nature continues pertaining to it. To that effect, the people in a given moment, can manifest that sovereignty through certain acts.

(III) With relation to the petition of unconstitutionality in point, it is indispensable to analyze the [concept] of amnesty, pointing with precision [to] its origin, justification and juridical nature, for that will allow us to determine the limits of the competence of this Tribunal with relation to its capacity to hear and decide over that [concept].

The word amnesty comes from the Greek word *amnestía* or *amnesis*, which means to forgive, to lose memory; and it has been defined as the "act of the legislative power that orders official forgiveness of one or many categories of crimes, thus ending proceedings already initiated or that are to be initiated, or verdicts that have already been pronounced" also as "the discretional attribution of Congress in the rest of the commonwealth to forgive, in a general form, determined crimes"; and, in our country it has been expressed that amnesty "consists in the pardon or forgiveness of a crime granted by the Public Power—by virtue of the right of grace—in determined cases prescribed by law, which extinguishes completely the action and the penalty, and eliminates the quality of condemned in favor of whom or whose it is decreed".

Historically the right of grace was initially an act of individual clemency of theocratic origin. The divine nature of grace was linked to the sacred character of the king, as a divinity or as an intermediary between divinity and mankind.

From the moment constitutional proceedings were born, the idea of the power of clemency as an attribute of the sovereign power of the people also took place, and it is [the people] who has the faculty to grant clemency throughout its different manifestations. Thus, individual grace develops in a parallel form with collective grace, the real predecessor of modern amnesty.

In modern times, the right of grace is a manifestation of society to recognize to all citizens the right of forgiveness, and what is pursued is [the facilitation of] social rehabilitation. Within this evolution, the broadest manifestation of the right of grace supposes forgiveness of a crime that has been committed, for it extinguishes the corresponding penalty and all its effects, all of which constitutes the institution of amnesty. This [concept] is considered a collective grace that seeks to warrant social and political peace, inasmuch as it constitutes the juridical expression of a political act that allows for the opening of a democratic process that favors national consensus, the primordial objective of which is the neutralization of an internal crisis—a noninternational armed conflict—or the consolidation of the termination of an armed international conflict.

On the justification or motivation of this [concept], it has been unanimously recognized by jurists that it is an act of State, the objective of which is to maintain social peace. Thus, Eduardo Novoa Monreal, enunciates that the [concept] of amnesty "deals with an institution born to solve difficulties that originate in cases of profound social or political changes, specially in cases of revolutionary or abnormal situations"; Carlos Fontán Balestra assures that "amnesty is a politically prevailing measure of a general character, which signifies the forgiveness of a crime in order to reestablish peace and social harmony"; Ricardo C. Nuñez expresses that amnesty is justified by "virtue of urgent requirements of the public interest, more so in causes of political character that allow for a call to collective harmony and appeasement". Ihering stated that the faculty to grant amnesties is "a security valve of the law, a correction of the generality of *jus strictum* in the face of the needs of equity"; and in a very expressive manner, José E. Sobremonte Martínez affirms that "amnesty is the instrument of peace".

In the well known work, "Reasoned Dictionary of Legislation and Jurisprudence", of Joaquín Escriche, the thoughts of the Count of Peyronnet, Minister of Charles X, King of France, contained in very expressive maxims, have been transcribed as follows:

> Amnesty is abolition, forgiveness. Pardon is indulgency, piety.... When Thrasybulus overturned the thirty tyrants, he established a law that the Athenians christened with the title of Amnesty, which means forgiveness. It was ordered in it that nobody should feel uneasy for his past actions and it is from there that we have inherited the act and even the name. Amnesty does not restore, it erases. Pardon does not erase, it abandons and restores. Amnesty turns to the past and destroys even the first trace of the sea. Pardon turns to the future, and preserves the past and everything it has produced. Amnesty, with the exception of accusation, does not suppose anything. Pardon supposes crime.... In political accusations the contrary is more often seen; for if the State does not forgive, neither will individuals; and if he remains an enemy, individuals will also remain enemies. Pardon is more judicial than political. Amnesty is more political than judicial. Pardon is an isolated favor more convenient to individual acts: amnesty is a general absolution more convenient to collective acts. Amnesty is sometimes an act of justice; and sometimes an act of prudence and ability. There is more to be found in amnesty than in pardon, a certain seal of generosity and of force imposed by the people, which gains fame to the Prince, when applied. Amnesty surpasses pardon in that it does not leave behind any legitimate motive of resentment.

On the juridical nature of the institution we are examining, there is consensus in recognizing that amnesty presents two dimensions: manifestation or prerogative grace and legislative competence or repeal form of legislation with retroactive and temporal effects.

In relation to the first aspect, since ancient times amnesty has been considered—as indicated lines above—a grace of the Sovereign, that is, a manifestation of sovereign clemency.

In that sense, it is said—rightly—that amnesty finds foundation in sovereignty itself, arguing that the faculty of clemency is an attribute of sovereignty; for as has been stated by José María Rodríguez Devesa in his "Spanish Penal Law", "the right of clemency is the right of the State, as the sole guardian of the right to punish, to renounce the imposition of penalty, partially or completely, or to demand fulfillment if already imposed by tribunals." In similar terms Eugenio Cuello Calón states that the faculty of grace has been defended as a manifestation of the monarchs' prerogatives—that is to say the Sovereign—as a means to attain public tranquillity after profound internal commotions.

The exposed idea—as indicated before—is not recent, for J. Story in his "Commentary on the Federal Constitution of the United States", declared that the power of pardon is an indispensable consequence of the power of punishment itself, upholding both figures in sovereignty itself, and Pessina states in his "Elements of Penal Law", that the "faculty of clemency, whatever the form it adopts, is an attribute of sovereignty".

With respect to the second dimension of amnesty, even though some jurists had already announced partially that aspect—Puig Peña stated that amnesty supposes the derogation of a penal law or of the efficiency of the law with relation to particular cases to which it is applied; and already Luis Silvela, at the end of the XIXth century, stated that it was a real transitory derogation of the laws—it is not until the last decades that insistence has been made on that characteristic of amnesty; and it has been [pointed] out, that the institution is not to be examined from a limited perspective of the right of grace, and that it can be conceived as a reason to repeal a law and its knotted and linked effects. Gustavo Zagrebeisky points out that amnesty must be appreciated, more as a manifestation of the faculty of grace as an exception to legal ordainment, than as a corrective instrument of law; adding that inasmuch as amnesty constitutes a temporal derogation with retroactive effects of some rules of law, it can be likened to the retroactivity of penal laws when they favor a convict of a determined crime.

(IV) If we link what was expressed in the preceding paragraph with what had already been said pages before, we arrive at the following conclusions:

a) the Tribunal charged with constitutional control within our juridical system, the Constitutional Chamber, cannot have hearings on purely political questions;

b) sovereignty resides in the people, even though deposited in the Constitution;

c) the faculty of granting grace or clemency is a manifestation of sovereignty; and that, consequently, it is an eminently political act;

d) amnesty constitutes a form of grace;

e) amnesty is also a derogation with retroactive effects of a penal norm. Amnesty appears thus, as a measure of character, in order to appease rancours and resentments inseparable from social and political struggles.

Applying the preceding conclusions to the *sub judice* case, we have to recognize that when the faculty to grant amnesty, constitutionally conferred upon the Legislative Assembly, has been exercised—Article 131, attribution 26 of the Magna Carta—a purely political function has been executed, and therefore, of the exclusive incumbency of the political power of the State to which it has been conferred: the legislative organ.

Amnesty is, as has been so recognized in Latin America by Alfonso Reyes Echandía, a Colombian penalist, an exceptional measure destined to procure in a given moment of a nation's life, social tranquillity and political appeasement, and that its application depends on the political branches of public power and not on the jurisdictional branch, is understandable for otherwise it would be contradictory and dissolvent within a juridical organization to charge judges with such a function. Manzini, in Europe, after stating that amnesty is an attribute of sovereignty, adds that inasmuch as amnesty functions in the penal sphere as a supreme moderator of the forces of the law and judicial sentence, "the political opportunity and equity are the motives, not submitted to judicial appraisal or supervision".

As a manifestation of sovereignty, amnesty constitutes an eminently political act, to the degree it expresses itself through a legislative act, with all the characteristics inherent in this type of act, with the difference that it manifests itself as a repeal act with retroactive effects.

But what has been said, must not be [assessed] in absolute terms, that is to say, that amnesty does not, in any case, avoid being subjected to jurisdictional control in relation to its constitutionality; and it must be understood that the faculty to grant amnesty, in what refers to its essence and on account of it being a purely political act, corresponds to the Legislative Assembly, which can make use of this faculty in a discretional form, without being the object of judicial qualification on the [advisability or inadvisability] of the act. It is evident that there are cases where there is constitutional jurisdictional control over amnesty, and it is of the competence of the Constitutional Chamber to pronounce itself over its [merits or lack of merits] *ab initio* , or to initiate proceedings, in accordance [with] the case, [inasmuch] they are filed before the Chamber. This depends, of course, on the reasons that the citizen invokes in his petition, and if they are able to provoke in the Tribunal charged with constitutional control, a reasonable doubt over its constitutionality; and if, in any case, the admission and handling of petitions is a medium toward the upholding of constitutional institutions, and not, on the contrary, a perturbation of social peace.

It must be concluded in the present case, that the Constitutional Chamber is not authorized to examine and decide over the unconstitutionality of the impugned law, for that situation would surpass the orbit of competence that has been delimited to it by the Fundamental Charter, and would invade the sphere of other powers of the State.

The preceding considerations motivate this declaration of inadmissibility of the petition that is being examined, and it must so be declared.

Finally, this Chamber estimates it is [advisable] to make reference to three very important aspects:

In the first place, the seriousness of the tragedy in which the Nation has been immersed during the last twelve years is not something strange to this Tribunal, nor are the efforts realized by the totality of the Salvadorian people to find a way out of it through civilized channels and of common acceptance, that should allow for the obtainment of social peace, of which political sovereignty, now being considered by us, is one of them, thus making effective the values of justice, juridical security and commonwealth established by the Constitution.

The purely political nature of amnesty is further confirmed by the circumstance that when dealing with the problem of granting pardons, a prior favorable opinion of the Supreme Court of Justice is mandatory, an element which does not exist in the case of amnesty. From this it must be inferred that in the case of [pardon], although formally a legislative act, there are material jurisdictional consequences, inasmuch as the participation of the Judicial Organ is indispensable; an assumption that is not demanded ... in the case of amnesty, in accordance [with] its purely political nature.

On the other side, and as an exclusively teleological [assessment, that] which has been established by the Additional Protocol of the Geneva Accords of August twelfth of nineteen-hundred forty-nine related to the Protection of Victims of Armed Conflicts of Noninternational Character, or Protocol II, must be remembered; and which in Article 6.5 rules: "5. At the cessation of hostilities, authorities in power shall procure granting the broadest possible amnesty to persons that have taken part in the armed conflict or that are deprived of their liberty, interned or detained by motives related with the armed conflict".

[Based] on the exposed considerations, this Chamber decrees: The petition of unconstitutionality ... is hereby declared inadmissible.

ETHIOPIA: PROCLAMATION ESTABLISHING THE OFFICE OF THE SPECIAL PROSECUTOR

Proclamation No. 22/1992 (August 8, 1992)

WHEREAS, the people of Ethiopia have been deprived of their human and political rights and subjected to gross oppression under the yoke of the fascistic rules of the Dergue-WPE regime for the last seventeen years;

WHEREAS, heinous and horrendous criminal acts which occupy a special chapter in the history of the peoples of Ethiopia have been perpetrated against the people of Ethiopia by officials, members and auxiliaries of the security and armed forces of the Dergue-WPE regime;

WHEREAS, officials and auxiliaries of the Dergue-WPE dictatorial regime have impoverished the economy of the Country by plundering illegally confiscating and destroying the property of the people as well as by misappropriating public and state property;

WHEREAS, in view of the fact that the historical mission of the Ethiopian People's Revolutionary Democratic Front (EPRDF) has been accomplished, it is essential that higher officials of the WPE and members of the security and armed forces who have been detained at the time of the EPRDF assumed control of the Country and thereafter and who are suspected of having committed offenses, as well as representatives of urban dwellers associations and peasant associations, and other persons who have associated with the commission of said offenses, must be brought to trial;

WHEREAS, it is in the interest of a just historical obligation to record for posterity the brutal offences the embezzlement of property perpetrated against the people of Ethiopia and to educate the people and make them aware of these offenses in order to prevent the recurrence of such a system of government;

WHEREAS, it is necessary to provide for the establishment of a Special Public Prosecutor's Office that shall conduct prompt investigation and bring to trial detainees as well as those persons who are responsible for having committed offences and are at large both within and without the Country;

NOW THEREFORE, in accordance with Article 9(d) of the Transitional Period Charter of Ethiopia, it is hereby proclaimed as follows:

1. Short Title

This Proclamation may be cited as the "Special Public Prosecutor's Office Establishment Proclamation No. 22/1992."

2. Establishment

1. The Special Prosecutor's Office (hereinafter the "Office") is hereby established.

2. The Office shall be accountable to the Prime Minister of the Transitional Government.

3. The Office shall have a Chief of the Special Public Prosecutors, Deputy and Assistant Chiefs of the Special Public Prosecutors, other Special Public Prosecutors and the necessary staff.

3. Appointment

1. The appointment of the Chief and the Deputy Chief of the Special Public Prosecutors shall be approved by the Council of Representatives upon recommendation by the Prime Minister and presentation by the President.

2. Assistant Chiefs of the Special Prosecutors and other Special Public Prosecutors shall be appointed by the Prime Minister upon presentation by the Chief of the Special Public Prosecutors.

4. Term of Office

The term of the Office shall terminate upon the accomplishment of its task.

5. Qualifications for the Appointment of Special Public Prosecutors

Any Ethiopian citizen who:

1. is faithful to the Transitional Period Charter of Ethiopia;
2. is either trained in law or has acquired broad legal skill through experience and capable of rendering proper decision based on law;
3. has distinguished himself by his diligence, integrity and good conduct and has not, in any way, participated in the offences to be prosecuted by the Special Public Prosecutors; and
4. was not a member of the WPE or of the security force;

may be appointed as a Special Public Prosecutor.

6. Powers of the Office

The Office shall, in accordance with the law, have the power to conduct investigation and institute proceedings in respect of any person having committed or responsible for the commission of an offence by abusing his position in the party, the government or mass organization under the Dergue-WPE regime.

7. Applicability of Existing Laws

1. Laws concerning criminal investigation and instituting criminal proceedings as well as laws applicable to the ordinary prosecutors shall also apply to the activities undertaken by the Office.

2. Notwithstanding the provisions of sub-article (1) of this Article, the provisions concerning limitations of criminal action and the time limit concerning the submission of charges, evidence and pleading to charges shall not be applicable to proceedings instituted by the Office.

3. The provisions of habeas corpus under Article 117 of the Civil Procedure Code shall not apply to persons detained prior to the coming into force of this Proclamation for a period of six months starting from the effective date of this Proclamation in matters under the jurisdiction of the Special Prosecutor as indicated in Article 6 hereof.

8. Decisions of the Special Public Prosecutors

A superior Special Public Prosecutor may amend, suspend, alter, revoke, or confirm decisions made or measures taken by a Special Public Prosecutor subordinate to him.

9. Transfer of Cases

Where, in the process of investigation, the Office discovers cases which are outside its jurisdiction, it shall transfer such cases to the regular public prosecutor's office.

10. Delegation

1. The Office, may, whenever necessary, delegate its powers under Article 6 of this Proclamation to the regular public prosecutor in respect of offences not punishable by rigorous imprisonment.
2. A delegation given [under] sub-article (1) of this Article shall be decided jointly by the Chief of the Special Public Prosecutors and his Deputies.

11. Miscellaneous Provisions

1. The Chief of the Special Public Prosecutors may, with respect to a person suspected or one whose case is under investigation, apply to a court for an order prohibiting such persons from leaving the Country or requiring the attachment of the property of such person for a period not exceeding three months where it has reason to believe that such property is the fruit of the crime. The court shall give an appropriate ruling; provided, however, that the Chief of the Special Public Prosecutors shall, without prejudice to the foregoing provision, have the power to detain any person or seize any property in the event of urgency. Such cases shall be brought to the court as soon as possible.
2. Unless the Chief of the Special Public Prosecutors decides otherwise, offences that fall under Article 6 hereof and with respect to which criminal proceedings have been instituted in the ordinary courts before the coming into force of this Proclamation shall continue to be tried in the same courts.

12. Inconsistency with other Laws

Any law inconsistent with this Proclamation shall not be applicable to matters covered by this Proclamation....

ETHIOPIA: REPORT OF THE OFFICE OF THE SPECIAL PROSECUTOR

The Special Prosecution Process of War Criminals and Human Rights Violators in Ethiopia

(February 1994)

Background

By Proclamation 22/1992, the Transitional Government of Ethiopia (TGE) established the Office of the Special Prosecutor [SPO]. Its mandate is twofold:

1. To establish for public knowledge and for posterity a historical record of the abuses of the Mengistu regime.
2. To bring those criminally responsible for human rights violations and/or corruption to justice.

The mandate is broad and ambitious. Implicit in this mandate is the acceptance by the TGE of their international legal obligations to investigate and bring to justice those involved in human rights crimes. Furthermore, the mandate is also a policy choice regarding how a society can productively deal with past abuses to create a more democratic future. The policy choice made is to expose those involved in abuses and to sanction them. This is [a] rarely available choice to a successor government to an abusive regime, because of political limitations (recent examples include El Salvador, Haiti, Chile and Argentina).

From an international human rights law perspective, the policy decision taken by the TGE is the most desirable and theoretically the most beneficial to the construction of a society based on the rule of law.

The ambitious nature of the decision has both risks and benefits. It is easier to say one is going to do something, than to do something novel and precedent setting well. The mandate has created expectations in the international human rights community, the donor community, and in the Ethiopian community.

The SPO must be juxtaposed with the recently formed UN War Crimes Tribunal. This Tribunal will pull together the most well-respected scholars and practitioners throughout the globe. Their estimated annual operating budget is over 30 million USD. The task facing the SPO and the UN Tribunal are similar in scope and complexity, the financial resources available are not. This does not mean the SPO's task is impossible without a 30 million USD annual budget. It means that efficiency, pragmatism and the involvement of the international community will be necessary for this project to work. The need for the SPO to [draw] upon international scholars and practitioners to the degree possible, to ensure this, is evident.

The Crimes

The regime of Mengistu Haile Mariam was one of the most notorious in recent history. He constructed a highly centralized government, where he presided over every major policy decision made from 1974-1991.

In reality, the SPO has tens times more evidence than needed to successfully prosecute several of the detained and many of the exiles for serious criminal offenses.

The following are cases and areas of repression where the detained are criminally implicated in one or more of the actions:

In November of 1974 the Dergue [the Mengistu government] sat in a General Assembly and discussed the fate of the high government officials from the regime of Haile Selassie. Most of the exofficials of the emperor's government were detained starting in June of 1974. The SPO has the minutes of this meeting. The minutes include information about [which] Dergue members were present at the meeting and the comments they made during the discussions. Each former official's case was brought to the General Assembly for discussion. Each official was discussed separately and an order given on each individual. The decisions were unanimous regarding the 60 ex-officials that were ordered to be executed.

In the days preceeding May Day 1976, the EPRP [Ethiopian People's Revolutionary Party] youth committees were planning a nation-wide protest against the Dergue regime. The day before May Day, the Dergue Campaign Department issued a directive to the Dergue Special Forces to eliminate all those who were planning to participate in the EPRP demonstration. It is important to note that the Dergue Campaign Department was under the direct command of the Dergue Standing Committee[—a] committee chaired by Mengistu Haile Mariam.

On April 30, 1976 hundreds of youths were executed throughout the country. For example, Addis Ababa was divided into 28 zones. On average 15-30 youths were killed in each zone. Hundreds more were killed outside of Addis. In zone (higher) 18, for example, the SPO has proof of 21 youths being executed.

The SPO has proof that all the youths that were killed in this massacre in the Addis Ababa area were taken to the morgue at Menelik Hospital. The government authorities would not allow the victims' families to take their corpse without first paying for the bullets used to kill the victim.

You will all remember the Red Terror was authorized by Proclamation 121 of 1977. It was the largest and best known campaign of systematic violations of fundamental human rights carried out by the Dergue. It resulted in thousands of summary executions, disappearances, and cases of torture between 1976 and 1979.

The SPO has literally hundreds of orders, directives, and reports of summary executions carried out during the Red Terror.

The forced resettlement programme consisted of moving hundreds of thousands of peasants from the north of the country to the south. Originally dubbed a famine relief programme, we have evidence of the political nature of the relocation. According to non-governmental relief organizations, between 15-20% of those resettled died either in transport or upon arrival in the resettlement camps. Given that 600,000 people were resettled between 1984-1986, about 100,000 people lost their lives due to this governmental policy.

On a Wednesday in June 1988, government Air Forces systematically attacked the market town of Hawzen i Tigray. The bombardment by Mig fighters lasted from dawn to dusk and approximately 2,500 civilian market goers where killed. To prevent anyone from fleeing, Air Force helicopters circled the market town.

The Detained

There are presently 1,200 prisoners suspected for gross human rights violations of whom the majority were detained shortly after the fall of the Mengistu regime in May 1991. The detained are located in three different prisons in and outside Addis Ababa and receive treatment according to international standards.

Understanding that the individuals have been detained for almost 18 months without charge by the time the SPO staff was hired, the SPO immediately began a process to determine the legitimacy of the detention and to release those detainees that may have been detained unjustly or who are implicated in less serious crimes.

The SPO has released on bail approximately 900 of those originally detained by the [Ethiopian People's Revolutionary Democratic Front]. The courts, through *habeas corpus* proceedings, have released another 200 on bail. These first actions of the SPO support the idea that the Office is interested in serving justice with the aim of true national reconciliation. The actions of the courts indicate that the new judiciary is acting with a degree of independence which is unfortunately unfamiliar in Ethiopia.

The SPO has also arrested approximately 220 individuals in the last months. The current detained population is 1,200 people. All detainees presently being held are suspected of serious crimes (e.g. multiple murders).

Even given the rigorous demands of the *habeas corpus* proceedings, the SPO has been attempting extensive planning on how it will successfully fulfill its mandate. Teams have been created, work divided, detailed work-plans created, and needed resources defined.

The Time Schedule

According to one worst case scenario, if we were to try all individuals that we could for murder, given the present capacity, it would take over 20 years! This is true given the myriad of defenses available (e.g. superior order and suspension of existing laws by the previous regime). Certainly, such an extended period is wholly intolerable and unthinkable (a clear violation of the right to a fair and speedy trial).

Our research shows that crimes such as summary executions, forced disappearances, and torture carried out systematically on a wide scale as a matter of state policy constituted flagrant violations of international law, and specially crimes against humanity. These types of violations were clearly established as crimes and in force during the previous regime.

It took the Transitional Government time to begin the process of establishing an independent judiciary and the SPO. Frankly, while both have made progress, neither are where they should be. In August of 1992 the SPO was established by Proclamation. It is important to note that the officials of the SPO were not named until the end of 1992 and most of the Special Prosecutors were not appointed until January of 1993.

November 1993 - February 1994:

Identification of criminals living outside Ethiopia, assemble supporting documents, prepare and submit extradition requests. Where necessary, the SPO will facilitate the creation of extradition treaties with the countries where the potential defendants are living.

Funds for computerization secured from SIDA, the Swedish Aid Agency, SPO staff computer training began during the first week of October (all attorneys and most investigators are already being trained). Computer/database designer has been working on revising the database used in El Salvador for a couple of months and document registration and coding started in the beginning of February.

September - November:

Negotiations with regional administrations regarding the creation of SPO regional offices is ongoing. Recruitment of personnel and deployment is awaiting approval of SPO budget.

Supplemental personnel identify and collect relevant documents. This work is now 80 percent completed.

January - April 1994:

Relevant documents coded for the computer.

February - April 1994:

Coded information entered into computer.

February - April 1994:

Forensic teams have arrived and will do important exhumations (chosen in accord with SPO's priorities) and laboratory work.

Ongoing:

Reception of reports and memorandums from NGO's (e.g. American Bar Association and American law firms, International Human Rights Law Group's research on extradition of human rights criminals when no treaty exists) and academics. Amnesty International, Africa Watch and the International Committee of the Red Cross have all contributed to the work of the SPO.

April 1994:

Computer reports are generated and policy-level decisions can be considered. Ongoing training of SPO staff and judges [who] will try cases on the special nature of these types of cases.

March 1994:

Three top UN experts arrive to work with SPO and TGE policy-makers to analyze computer generated reports, other evidence, the capacity of the courts and prisons, and the relevant political factors to make recommendations regarding what type of charges and against whom should be brought. Also the French Attorney General is scheduled for a working visit with the SPO.

April - May 1994:

[Drawing] on all inputs, SPO will finalize the legal strategy which has been in development since the creation of the Office. Charges will be filed that, according to our best effort and judgment, will bring justice to the victims, promote the respect for international law and firmly establish the rule of law in Ethiopia.

May:

Trials begin.[*] Estimated duration of trials: one year.

It Took Time Elsewhere

Ethiopia is not the first country to undertake an extensive investigation in abuses of past regimes. To give an idea of the time-consuming work this represents, we have compiled some experiences from other countries as well as comparative comments.

a. El Salvador

As you will recall under UN mediation and supervision the FMLN rebels and the Salvadoran government entered into a peace accord to end over ten years of fighting. The peace accord included one aspect related to the SPO: the UN Truth Commission. Notably only part of the SPO's mandate.

The Truth Commission was given a mandate to create a definitive historical record of the human rights violations which transpired during the period of the civil war.

This Commission was given six months to complete its work and well over 3 million dollars as well as the support of the UN logistics (as many vehicles as were needed and quick access to relevant UN agencies for support). Note: [The] El Salvador civil war was about 10 years long, it has only about 5 million people, and its land mass is similar to that of Eritrea.

---

[*] [Editor's note: The trials actually began in December 1994.]

After the three people to head the Commission were named (which included a leading human rights scholar who was President of the Inter-American Court on Human Rights, the former President of Colombia, and one of Venezuelas leading lawyers/diplomats), they took almost one year to begin their work.

In this time, internationally renowned lawyers, investigators, scientists, and computer experts were recruited and briefed. They were completely oriented before the six months began.

In fact the Commission's extensive infrastructure, including computers, vehicles, and office space, was in place[, as] well as a plan of action. And most importantly, support from the human rights NGO community was discussed and clarified.

Once they officially began to work, everything was in place. Nonetheless, the Commission took nine months and ran well over its $3 million budget.

The biggest difference between Ethiopia and El Salvador was not the budget (200,000 USD vs. over 3 million [plus] all necessary infrastructure— even though this is definitely a difference worth noting), nor was it the difference in staff (recruited locally v. recruited internationally), but the support of the NGO sector.

The Truth Commission received over 15 volumes of computer generated reports from the NGO's. These reports were a computerized compilation of all the human rights testimonies collected by the leading 2 human rights groups in El Salvador over the past decade. At least 6 local and 3 international NGO's provided vast amounts of support to the Truth Commission. Each had done extensive investigations for over a decade.

In comparison to the type of support received by the SPO from the Ministry of Interior and the Anti-Red Terror Committee, the SPO is very lonely. It has a great burden and little assistance.

Regardless of this vast difference, the SPO will go further. In El Salvador, once the Truth Commission's report was released it blamed over 80% of the human rights violations on the government. The government, which still controlled the Legislative Assembly, immediately passed an amnesty law. Thus, while an official record of the past exists, no one was brought to justice because of the Truth Commission's investigations, even though they had recommended prosecutions be brought in a number of cases.

b. Chile

After more than 16 years of military rule by Pinochet, democracy was restored when Patricio Aylwin was elected president in March 1990. In May of 1990 the President established the Commission on Truth and National Reconciliation.

The Commission's task was to investigate the abuses of the Pinochet regime. Here again, the Commission received extensive support from national and international human rights organizations. The Commission interviewed more than 4,000 people regarding 3,400 cases. Note: the Commission had no power to compel testimony or initiate prosecutions.

The report was made public in March of 1991. It called for further investigation in 641 cases and the opening of judicial procedures in 230 cases. Given that the military still has a great deal of power in Chile, no successful prosecutions have been made.

The Commission took 11 months. It had resources of the State available for use. It had enormous support from the NGO sector. It, as opposed to the SPO, could focus on its investigations. It had more support from its government and NGO sector than the SPO. Nonetheless, its investigations were partial and did not include government documents. Importantly, no prosecutions came out of their work.

c. Argentina

Within months of the fall of the military junta and the election of Raul Alfonsin as President, he established the National Commission on Disappeared Persons (CONADEP) (early 1984).

The Commission's mandate was limited to investigating abuses of the past, focusing on disappearances. [Ten] prominent Argentines served on the Commission; it had an ample staff, and all sectors of the government were ordered to co-operate with it (e.g. even diplomats serving in foreign countries were ordered to take declarations regarding human rights abuses of the past regime).

Importantly in Argentina, like El Salvador, throughout the investigation, the Commission received invaluable assistance from human rights organizations which provided it with personnel assistance, technical resources, extensive documentation, and experience acquired from working under the difficult conditions of military rule.

CONADEP's report was released at the end of November 1984. It documented 8,960 disappearances. CONADEP then submitted over 1,800 cases to the judicial system to investigate the possibility of bringing criminal charges against the military and security forces for human rights violations.

By April of 1985 preliminary jurisdictional issues were resolved and only nine members of the junta were charged in the civilian court with many counts of homicide, torture, and false arrest.

By December of 1985, 5 of the 9 had been convicted. The appeals related to these cases finally ended with a decision from the Supreme Court in December of 1986.

Following the trial of the junta, the public turned its attention to the over 2,000 remaining criminal complaints (filed by individuals). While importantly few were detained, 100s of military personnel faced prosecution.

There were some cases brought to trial in 1986 and 1987 (some were commenced 3 years after the formation of CONADEP), but in the end most prosecutions were prevented by the passage in December 1986 of the "full stop law," (a sort of statute of limitations passed for political reasons/pressure from the military) and in June 1987 of the "due obedience law" (a law limiting the prosecutions to higher officials passed due to military pressure).

The Argentine case is most similar to that of Ethiopia, in that both investigations and prosecutions were carried out. The dissimilarity is evidenced by the differences in limitations: in Argentina it was political in that the military still had a great deal of power, in Ethiopia the limitations relate more closely to resources.

In Argentina, with huge amounts of NGO support, its investigation period was 11 months. It took 6 months to three years to begin the few prosecutions that were brought after the investigations were completed.

Nonetheless, it is worth quoting from an America's Watch report on the Argentine experience:

> For good and for ill, the Argentine experience is an example to the world. The exposure of past abuses in Argentina, and the trials that have taken place, have played a major part in bringing to an end what began some two decades ago in which systematic torture and disappearances characterized military rule in many countries.... The setbacks to the effort to subordinate the armed forces to the rule of law in Argentina have also been felt throughout the region, and elsewhere in the world where Argentina was a beacon of hope following the restoration of democratic government in 1983. Despite these setbacks, we consider that Argentina's example will have a positive impact if its government [will proceed with prosecutions and gradually strengthen its democratic institutions.]

d. Republic of Chad

From 1982-1990, the government of Chad, led by President Hissein Habre, was responsible for gross human rights violations, including arbitrary arrests, secret detention, long-term detention without charge or trial, torture, and extra-judicial executions. In fact, President Hissein ordered the execution of 300 detainees right before he fled the country.

One month following the military victory of the [Patriotic Movement of Salvation] in December, 1990, the Commission of Inquiry was established.

The Commission worked for almost 2 1/2 years, before issuing its report. Its main source of evidence was the interviews of thousands of people. It worked with few resources, and its work was slowed by a lack of vehicles.

While an extensive report was published, no one was brought to trial in Chad, and many human rights reporters have complained the investigations did not go far enough to institutionalize the rule of law.

e. Uganda

Human rights organizations estimate over 800,000 people were killed or disappeared between 1966-1986. In January 1986 the [National Resistance Movement] came to power. Shortly thereafter, the government created the Human Rights Commission.

In May of 1986 the Commission was formed with a mandate to investigate the governmental abuses of the past.

After 5 years, as of May 1991, the Commission had received 1,600 complaints and had interviewed 500 witnesses in 39 of Uganda's 41 districts.

After 7 years, the Commission has conducted a few important public hearings regarding the human rights violations, [but] it has not yet issued its report and no one has been prosecuted because of its work.

While the Ford Foundation has provided a good amount of funding to the Commission, the lack of vehicles and resources has greatly slowed their process.

[T]he scope of investigation in Uganda is similar [to Ethiopia]. Further, [the Commission does] not have a dual mandate. It is not also responsible for bringing gross human rights violators to trial.

f. UN Tribunal on Yugoslavia

War crimes and gross human rights violations have been taking place in former Yugoslavia for the last few years. Thus, it is noteworthy that the Security Council has established a body to investigate and bring to justice those implicated in gross violations of international law.

Many of the complex legal issues this tribunal is struggling with are similar if not the same to those the SPO is dealing with. The UN has pulled together experts from throughout the world to work on this project. Many international and national human rights groups are working to support it's work. Further, it is utilizing the extensive UN infrastructure and the expertise of many of its agencies. Beyond that, its first year operating budget is 31 million USD. In terms of resources and support, the difference between the SPO and the Yugoslav tribunal is vast.

It should be noted, that with all the work and money spent to this point by the UN, the SPO is much closer to prosecuting human rights violators.

War Criminals in Exile

Some 300 military officers and civil leaders from the Mengistu regime fled the country when it became clear that the Transitional Government would charge the people responsible for 17 years of abuses and gross human rights violations. The fugitives reside in a variety of countries. Kenya and the United States of America [have] the highest number of fugitive Ethiopian war criminals.

The SPO has investigated the whereabouts of a total of 60 fugitives and started the process of demanding extradition. The most notorious exile is Colonel Mengistu Haile Mariam who was granted political asylum on humanitarian grounds in Zimbabwe in May 1991. Mr. Mengistu's recent political statements to the independent "Sunday Gazette" in Harare has caused strong reactions both from the Zimbabwean and Ethiopian governments. The Zimbabwean Ministry of Foreign Affairs writes in a statement that it "is deeply disturbed by (Mengistu's) political statement to 'The Sunday Gazette' which 'goes against the grain and tenet of his status in Zimbabwe'". The Daily Gazette writes in an editorial that "it's time to send him home".

Three former officers and ministers have sought refuge on the compound of the Italian Embassy in Addis Ababa where they have camped for two years and eight months. A fourth colleague on the compound committed suicide.

Ethiopia is currently in the process of negotiating an extradition treaty with the United States where a total of 14 fugitives have been identified and located.

In one case, three Ethiopian women who were tortured in jail during the Mengistu regime were awarded 500,000 dollars each and punitive damages in a landmark verdict in an Atlanta (US) court in August 1993. The judge said in the verdict that each woman "clearly established her claims of torture" against the defendant, Kelbesse Negewo, who was granted political asylum in the United States in 1987. Mr. Negewo is wanted for several crimes in Ethiopia where he is suspected of overseeing torture and execution of several prisoners during the 1977/78 "Red Terror" campaign.

The SPO is expecting positive support from governments and NGO's in the work with the extraditions.

In the draft extradition requests the SPO has identified some applicable legal principles for the extraditions.

The surrender of fugitives from justice by one independent nation to another on request is based on international comity or reciprocity, or the provisions of an existing treaty of extradition between the two nations or on the duty to extradite for international crimes under conventional international criminal law (a multilateral treaty containing an extradition clause) or under the rules of customary international law.

In the instance of international comity, a government's sense of justice and regard for what is due other states obtains, rather than any absolute rule. In the second instance, the obligation is discharged by the surrender of fugitives charged with the offenses prescribed in the treaty. In the third instance, a number of multilateral conventions on international criminal law establish explicitly the duty to prosecute or extradite (extradition clause). In the last case the duty to extradite stems from customary international law.

Extradition Based on Comity of Nations or Reciprocity

A government may, as a matter of comity, voluntarily exercise the power to surrender a fugitive from justice to the country from which he has fled. And it is said that a nation is under a moral duty to do so if such action is consistent with its own constitution and laws. In some instances a state can request extradition with the assurance that it would reciprocate, even in the absence of an extradition treaty or an extradition clause. On the other hand particular rules of comity, maintained over a long period, may develop into rules of customary law (Ian Brownlie, *Principles of Public International Law*, Clarendon Press, Oxford, 1990, p. 30).

The Duty to Extradite for International Crimes under Conventional and Customary International Criminal Law

A number of conventions on international criminal law establish explicitly the duty to prosecute or extradite. These multilateral conventions also establish that they can be relied upon by states who require a treaty for extradition, and serve as a basis for states who do not require a treaty as a legal basis for extradition. The number of such conventions and the number of signatories therefore warrant the conclusion that the duty to prosecute or extradite for international crimes has become part of *jus cogens*.

It can also be said that although this duty arises under conventional international law, its acceptance by a significant number of states raises it to the level of a general duty under customary international law (M. Cherif Bassiouni, *International Extradition*, Second Revised Edition, Oceana Publications, Inc./London Rome New York, 1987, p. 22).

In this sense, in spite of the fact that the Convention against Torture and Other Cruel, Inhuman or Degrading Treatment or Punishment has not been yet ratified by Ethiopia and Zimbabwe, the obligation to extradite established in Article 8 of this Convention, must be considered as a principle of customary international law.

The obligation to extradite persons suspected to be guilty of war crimes and crimes against humanity is clearly stated as a principle of customary international law in General Assembly Resolution 3074 (XXVIII) of 3 December 1973, "Principles of international co-operation in the detection, arrest, extradition and punishment of persons guilty of war crimes and crimes against humanity". According to this resolution:

> 5. Persons against whom there is evidence that they have committed war crimes and crimes against humanity shall be subject to trial and, if found guilty, to punishment, as a general rule in the countries in which they committed those crimes. In that connection, States shall co-operate on questions of extraditing such persons....
>
> 8. States shall not take any legislative or other measures which may be prejudicial to the international obligations they have assumed in regard to the detection, arrest, extradition and punishment of persons guilty of war crimes and crimes against humanity.
>
> 9. In co-operating with a view to the detection, arrest and extradition of persons against whom there is evidence that they have committed war crimes and crimes against humanity and, if found guilty, their punishment, States shall act in conformity with the provisions of the Charter of the United Nations and of the Declaration on Principles of International Law concerning Friendly Relations and Co-operation among States in accordance with the Charter of the United Nations.

The following is a listing of the major conventions ratified both by Ethiopia and Zimbabwe that apply to cases related with Mengistu's criminal liability, containing the duty to prosecute or extradite:

Humanitarian Law of Armed Conflict

- Geneva Convention for the Amelioration of the Condition of the Wounded and Sick; in the Armed Forces in the field, 12 August 1949
    Article 49 (duty to search for and prosecute or extradite)
    Article 50 (recognition as a crime)

- Geneva Convention Relative to the Treatment of Prisoners of War, 12 August 1949
    Article 129 (duty to search for and prosecute or extradite)
    Article 130 (recognition as a crime)

- Geneva Convention Relative to the Protection of Civilian Persons in Time of War, 12 August 1949
    Article 146 (duty to search for and prosecute or extradite)
    Article 147 (recognition as a crime)

- Protocol I Additional to the 1949 Geneva Conventions, 12 December 1977, has been ratified by Zimbabwe (Ethiopia has not yet ratified this treaty)
    Article 88 (duty to cooperate with other states in the matter of extradition)[1]

Prohibition against Genocide

- Convention on the Prevention and Punishment of the Crime of Genocide, 9 December 1948
    Articles VI and VII (duty to extradite)
    Article VII (duty not to apply political offense exception for the purpose of extradition)

Persons Subject to Extradition

For purposes of extradition, a fugitive from justice has been broadly defined as one who commits a crime within a state and then withdraws from its jurisdiction. It has also been defined as one who commits a crime in one state and thereafter leaves it and is found in another. To be a fugitive from justice the accused need only be absent from the demanding state when it seeks to have him answer for the crime, and be found within the jurisdiction of another state. It is not necessary to establish that the accused was indicted before leaving the state, or that he fled in order to avoid prosecution. The mission, motive, or purpose inducing a person accused of being a fugitive from justice to leave the demanding state is immaterial in an extradition proceeding.

---

[1] N.B. The fight between the Dergue's forces and the Eritrean liberation movements must be assimilated to international armed conflicts, according to Protocol Additional I, Article 1 (4), that applies to armed conflicts in which peoples are fighting against colonial domination and alien occupation and against racist regimes in the exercise of their right of self-determination. And that is why beyond any doubt the cases related to this conflict are governed by the provisions of the Geneva Conventions cited above. The fact that Protocol Additional has not yet been ratified by Ethiopia is irrelevant concerning the international character of the Eritrean armed conflict against the Dergue's forces. The recognition of the international character of the liberation wars ... is not only related to this Protocol. The international character of these conflicts has been affirmed by several Resolutions from the General Assembly of the United Nations (specially resolutions 2105 (XX), 2621 (XXV) and 3103 (XXVIII). A supplementary confirmation of this principle is afforded by Article 7 of the United Nations Convention of 10 October 1980.... These principles apply both in Ethiopia and Zimbabwe. On the other hand the Ethiopian Penal Code has incorporated the grave breaches of the Geneva Conventions without any distinction between international and internal armed conflicts (article 282 ff.).

Foreign Support

The international community has been convinced that the SPO can work as an important catalyst for the creation of a just justice system in Ethiopia. Most important donors presently view the SPO as the best opportunity to improve the judicial system. Most are contemplating or have recently committed to provide financial and technical assistance. About 6/8 of the SPO's financial proposal has been covered and a possibility exists that it will be completely funded.

The following is a list of secured donations to this point:

- Sweden — 403,000 USD (computerization, both equipment and necessary supplemental personnel)

- U.S./Carter Center — 200,000 USD (two phases of the forensic experts, resident international legal consultant, and money for Argentine prosecutor)

- Norway — 100,000 USD and two Norwegian experts

- The Netherlands — 50,000 USD

- Canada — 40,000 USD and assistance toward one public relations consultant/expert

- Denmark — In-kind experts for 1-4 months

The reputation of the SPO among the donor community has greatly improved over the last 5 months. The donors are still concerned that the detainees remain in jail without charge, but their focus is now on how they can contribute positively to the process, so that the SPO can reach its potential and truly contribute to the transition.

The process of requesting and receiving international assistance will, and has, augmented the donors' expectations that the process meet international standards. They will not accept proceedings that do not meet international standards after having waited so long and provided financial resources. They are committing financial resources because they believe the plan included in the proposal is viable and workable.

Even if donor countries confirmed their support several months ago, funds have only recently become available because of foreign exchange restrictions and internal, bureaucratic problems. Such problems have severely delayed the prosecution process.

NGO Support

The expectation of the international human rights community is twofold. On one hand, they believe the SPO presents a unique opportunity for the development of human rights law; a project worth supporting. On the other hand, they are watchdog organizations which bring to light violations of a government. The fact that a week after the detainees were picked up by the EPRDF forces, the TGE was violating the rights of the detainees by failing to charge them, has created a difficult contradiction for the human rights community.... Most have resolved this contradiction—as did the International Human Rights Law Group in its recent report—by stating that the TGE has already clearly and excessively violated the rights of the detainees (e.g. the SPO was not even established for a year and half after they were originally detained), but the verdict is not yet out on the process.

Basically, the delay has made the international community skeptical about the desire and the ability of the TGE/SPO to meet international standards. A half-baked process that contains many defects will not be tolerated. Less than full and complete compliance with international standards will not be tolerated given the delay.

This means that when proceedings begin, there will be extensive scrutiny. For example, if proceedings were to begin today, the result would be far from the international standards expected. The SPO and the courts are wholly unprepared to withstand the type of scrutiny that will accompany the proceedings.

To this point, the international human rights community participation has been limited. Presently, the SPO is poised to integrate respected members of this community in the process.

The Ethiopian Legal System

Ethiopia follows the continental legal system. Most of the codes in use today were influenced by French, Swiss and other followers of that legal system. [These codes] (Civil code, Criminal Code, Commercial Code,...) were produced with the intent of following an international trend. Nevertheless, customary and religious rules were given great importance in the process of codification. The *Fetha Neguest* (Law of Kings), a law based on religion and used by kings before the reign of Haile Selassie I had great influence on the present legal instruments.

Attempts to incorporate international laws were also made....

Organization of Judicial System

With the recent establishment of National/Regional self-government (in accordance with the National/Regional Self-government Establishment Proclamation No 7/1992), Ethiopia has: Three levels of courts in each Nation/Region (courts of the National/Regional self-government) and three levels of courts of the central government (central courts).

According to Article 7 of Proclamation No. 40/1993, "central courts" means the central supreme court, the central high court or the central first instance court established under Article 3 of the Proclamation.

To each of the three levels of central courts, we find "parallel" courts of National/Regional self-government.

Position of SPO

When "jurisdiction of criminal cases" is concerned and in particular to those cases related with the SPO, Article 6 of Proclamation No. 40/1993 states that "the central courts shall have penal jurisdiction over the following on the basis of the provisions of penal laws," among which sub-article 27 provides for "offences falling under the competence of the SPO as indicated under the Special Prosecutor's Office Establishment Proclamation No 22/1992."

Sentencing System

It should be noted that the Ethiopian Penal Code allows for consecutive sentencing,

• First Degree Homicide:	Life imprisonment or death
• Second Degree Homicide:	5-25 years imprisonment
• Homicide by Negligence:	Not to exceed 5 years
• Grave Willful Injury:	1-10 years
• Common Willful Injury:	Not less than 6 months
• Exposure of Life of Another:	3 months to 3 years
• Failure to Lend Aid:	Not to exceed 6 months
• Unlawful Arrest or Detention:	Not to exceed 5 years
• Abuse of Power:	Not to exceed 5 years
• Genocide; Crimes against Humanity	5 years to life, or death
• War Crimes against the Civilian Population:	5 years to life, or death
• War Crimes against Wounded:	5 years to life, or death
• War Crimes against Prisoners and Interned Persons:	5 years to life, or death
• Use of Illegal Means of Combat:	Not less than 3 months; in grave cases, 3 years to life or death

And under the "Special Penal Code" of Mengistu:

• Abuse of Authority:	3 - 15 years
• Failure to Supervise:	Not to exceed 3 years
• Unlawful Arrest or Detention:	Not to exceed 5 years
• Jeopardizing Defence/Famine:	10 years to life

The Courts and Public Defence

The Special Prosecutor's Office has, together with the courts, taken an initiative to establish a Public Defender Office in Ethiopia. It is estimated that at least half of the detained have no economic resources to hire a defence lawyer. The details related to an eventual Public Defender Office (PDO) are not clear yet, but a Danish expert is working with the courts and Ethiopian lawyers to establish a system giving each defendant the right to his or her own legal council. The expert is hired by the International Commission of Jurists and financed by the Danish Aid Agency DANIDA.

None of the former regimes have had a public defence system. During the reign of Emperor Haile Selassie, lawyers who happened to be present in the courts were asked to take on the defence of some defendants without a fee.

To establish a system which will not only work during the [tenure of the SPO] but also function after the trials, the PDO is dependent on international, financial support. In this connection, a proposal for financing of the PDO over a period of two years is presented to the donors.

At the same time, an extensive training programme is carried out for the courts. Also the courts have received international, financial support to make them able to take on the immense workload expected when trials start in May. Two international consultants are hired to do both training and organizational work together with the Central Supreme Court.

The Computerization Process

The SPO computerization process consists of the following 4 phases:

1. Government document collection
2. Analysis of detainee interviews, victim and witness testimonies, and government documents
3a. Entry of the documents' analysis into the database
3b. Scanning (creating an electronic image) selected documents, both for security and for the historical record
4a. Reports to help prosecutors to prepare their cases
4b. Reports for the historical record

The first phase of the work is almost complete. We have organized the paper archives so that the second phase, analysis, will be possible while maintaining a strict control over the 250,000 plus pages of government documents now in the SPO. The prosecutors themselves will do the data analysis, possibly with assistance from others whom they will train.

Analysis consists of reducing the documents to their structural elements, for example, by enumerating all the individuals mentioned in a given document according to the ways they are mentioned. These analyses will be passed to the data entry staff, who will enter the enumerated information into the database. Particularly important documents (as so judged by the prosecutors) will be scanned. Since scanned images require a great deal of computer space, we will archive the scanned images to compact disks....

The most important aspect of any database system, of course, is the reports that can be generated from it. The fourth phase of the SPO computerization project involves designing reports. The priority will be to generate reports that will support the prosecutors' work....

It should be noted that the computerization will:

1. Create a good historical record of the *documentable* abuses of the Mengistu regime.
2. In regard to the higher officials, demonstrate systematic (pattern and practices) abuses linked to them through the political or military structure. This information will be extremely helpful—perhaps

essential—to support charges against high officials who were responsible for creating and implementing the system of repression.

3. Define according to the documents available who the most notorious violators are. This will allow the SPO [to] rationally classify offenders and thereby to focus murder (where the burden of proof is the highest) charges on those most culpable and lesser charges on the others.

4. And last but certainly not least, it will create the first group of prosecutors and investigators that are computer literate in the country. Computer training is an essential component of our plan and is already being implemented. Training will provide our SPO staff members functional skills with Amharic and English word processing (e.g. using the computer to create court documents and memorandums) and in the use of our specialized database of human rights violations. This will be a clear contribution to the infrastructure of our justice system.

GERMANY: TRIAL OF BORDER GUARDS

Berlin State Court, Docket No. (523) 2 Js 48/90 (9/91)

[*Editor's note: On February 5, 1989, two East Germans, Chris Gueffroy and Christian Gaudian, attempted to escape across the border from the German Democratic Republic into the Federal Republic of Germany. During the course of their attempt, they were spotted by members of the East German Border Guard. Although the pair successfully crossed several of the barriers constructed by the East German government, they were shot by Border Guard soldiers as they attempted to scale the last border fence. Gueffroy was killed by a bullet to the chest; Gaudian was wounded and arrested. Similar shootings had occurred repeatedly over the years against those trying to flee across the border of the German Democratic Republic. This was the last such incident prior to the tearing down of the Berlin Wall and the reunification of East and West Germany. In 1991, four members of the Border Guard involved in the Gueffroy-Gaudian incident—identified as defendants K, S, Sch, and H—were brought to trial before a German court. Excerpts from the ruling, dealing primarily with defendant H, follow.*]

The 23rd Grand Criminal Court—Court of Assizes—of the Berlin State Court, on the basis of the main trial on 2, 4, 9, 11, 16, 19, 25, 30 September, 2, 7, 9, 16, 24 October, 4, 11, 13, 25, 27 November, 2, 4, 9, 11, 16, 20, 30 December 1991, 6, 8, 13, and 20 January 1992,... ruled as follows during the Court Session of 20 January 1992:

The following are hereby sentenced:

Defendant H for homicide to a prison sentence of 3 (three) years and six months,

Defendant K for two crimes, committed as combined act, involving attempted homicide, to a prison sentence of 2 (two) years, whose enforcement is suspended for probation.

Defendants Sch and S are acquitted, Defendant H is also acquitted in as much as he was charged with another offense of attempted homicide....

Legal Assessment

...The punishability of the defendants is to be judged primarily according to the law of the scene of the act as it applied in the former GDR (Article 2, Paragraph 1, Criminal Code). According to Articles 3, 8 and 9 of the Unification Treaty of 6 September 1990, in combination with Appendix I, Chapter III, Subject Field C, Section II, No. 1 b and Section III, Nos. 1 and 2 (see BGBl. [Federal Legal Gazette, II, 28 September 1990, pages 890, 892, 954-956)—apart from a few exceptions—the Criminal Code of the Federal Republic of Germany took effect on 3 October 1990 in the former territory of the GDR with the measures specified in Articles 315-315 c, New Series, EGStGB [Introductory Act to the Criminal Code]; at the same time, the Criminal Code of the GDR—apart from some exceptions that are not significant here—has been invalidated. According to Article 315 EGStGB, in the version of the Unification Treaty, Article 2, Criminal Code, with the measures regulated in Article 315, Paragraphs 1-3, EGStGB is applicable to acts committed in the GDR prior to the date of effectiveness of the entry of the GDR in the Federal Republic, in other words, prior to 3 October 1990.

The acts committed by the defendants therefore are to be judged first of all according to GDR criminal law which was applicable at the scene of the action at the time of the action (Article 2, Paragraph 1, Criminal Code) and they are thus to be gauged in favor of the defendants in the light of the criminal law of the Federal Republic which has taken its place since....

In the case at hand ... the punishment threatened under the Criminal Code [of the Federal Republic] is less and therefore ... this is to be applicable.

The following applies to the individual defendants:

[Defendant H]

a) With the aimed round fired, single-shot, from the Kalashnikov submachine gun, from a range of less than 40 m, in the manner described above, at the upper part of the body of Chris Gueffroy, who was standing at the border fence, facing toward him, Defendant H killed a human being without being a murderer (Article 212, Criminal Code). Chris Gueffroy died on the spot within a few minutes as a consequence of the round which passed through the heart. Even immediate medical assistance could not have prevented the occurrence of death.

b) Chris Gueffroy's killing was unlawful; the defendant did not have any legally justifying grounds on his side....

According to Article 27, Paragraph 2, Clause 1, Border Protection Act, the use of firearms while on Border Guard duty was justified if it served the purpose of preventing the immediately impending execution or continuation of a criminal act which, according to the circumstances, looked like a crime or for the apprehension of persons who were compellingly suspected of a crime. Unlawful border crossing (Article 213, Criminal Code/GDR), however, was to be classified as a crime only in serious cases.... In the case at hand, according to GDR law, there was a serious case of attempted border crossing because the act was committed together with others (Article 213, Paragraph 3, Subparagraph 5, Criminal Code/GDR, OGH [Supreme Court]/GDR 10/222) and because the act was accomplished along with the use of dangerous means or methods, that is to say, with the use of the grappling hook (Article 213, Paragraph 3, Subparagraph 2, Criminal Code/GDR).

...In contrast to GDR law, only really grave offenses are qualified as crimes in the Federal Republic. In the then GDR, however, a mere act of "unlawful border crossing" could already become a "crime" if—as in this case—it was committed by at least two persons simultaneously or, to mention another provision that is particularly flexible, "with particular intensity" (Article 213, Paragraph 3, Subparagraph 3, Criminal Code/GDR). Firing was permitted in all of these cases; just as to how this was to be done, the law only says: "The life of persons is to be spared to the extent possible" (Article 27, Paragraph 5, Clause 1, Border Protection Act).

Within the practice of law, such as it was in effect at the time of the action in what then was the GDR,... the soldiers however repeatedly were given the general suggestion during "guard mount"—according to witness Fabian—that no escapee was allowed to slip through and that a "breach of the border" would have to be prevented at all costs. In this way, many soldiers were bound to get the impression and indeed could get the impression that a dead escapee was always better than an escaped escapee with the consequence that their inhibition threshold—when it came to firing their submachine guns at unarmed people—was lowered.

That this is something the superiors wanted in this way is documented particularly clearly by the testimony of witness Fabian according to which soldiers were praised even if they had fired only at a single escapee although, even according to GDR law applicable at that time, it would not have been permitted to fire on him. In such cases, the soldiers were given to understand from the very beginning that they probably just saw a shadow and that nothing would happen to them as a result of unjustified use of firearms.

The case at hand also confirms that the use of firearms in the final analysis was always considered to be justified; there was no investigation at all as to the legality of firearm use; instead, the defendants were praised and rewarded with special leave and monetary bonuses. But if one wished to accept the reality, which corresponded to the legal situation at that time and to what the law was really like in the GDR,... then one would indeed have to note that, in Article 30, the GDR Constitution granted its citizens protection of life, physical integrity, and health.... From this, one can deduce that government interference in these assets within the context of a legally permissible use of firearms, was bound to be guided strictly by the principle of proportionality, such as it is also spelled out in the Border Protection Act , although inadequately, at that....

In looking into the question as to whether it may be permissible to threaten with death the person who does not want to abide by the exit prohibition and, disregarding it, wants to cross the border, and whether it may if necessary also be permissible to kill him, we run into the question as to whether everything that is formal and that was considered as a right by virtue of interpretation is indeed rightful.

On this score, it has been recognized in Supreme Court jurisprudence, that there is a certain core area of law which no law and no sovereign act may touch according to the legal consciousness of the general public.

On that point, it says the following in a ruling handed down by the Federal Court in 1952 (BGH St 2, 234, 237):

"The freedom of a State to determine, for its area, what is lawful and what is unlawful, no matter how widely it is determined, however, is not unlimited. In the consciousness of all civilized nations, with all of their differences revealed by the various national bodies of law, there is a certain nucleus of the law which, according to general legal concepts, must not be violated by any law and by any other sovereign State measure. It encompasses certain basic principles of human behavior that are considered untouchable and that have taken shape with the passage of time among all cultured nations on the fertile ground of coincident basic moral views and which are considered to be legally binding, regardless of whether individual regulations in national bodies of law seem to allow that they be disregarded."

Similar statements can be found in the other rulings of the Federal Court from the years 1952 and 1960 (BGH St 3, 347; 14, 104 and 15, 60).

The last-mentioned ruling comments as follows on this point:

"Particularly strict requirements must be established when attacks against human life are involved. It is in keeping with jurisprudence such as it prevails among all cultured nations, later on also expressed in the Convention for the Protection of Human Rights, that the individual's right to life must be protected to a greater degree. Killings without a court verdict accordingly are permissible only if they result from an absolutely required use of force."

The Federal Constitutional Court also recognizes the basic principle that laws, which interfere in the described core area of the law, are null and void. A 1953 decision (BVerfG [Federal Constitutional Court] 3, 232), whose presently applicable content, by the way, the court confirmed in 1957 (BVerfG 6, 199) states the following:

"It was especially the time of the National Socialist regime in Germany that taught us that the legislator can also legislate injustice, in other words, if practical legal usage is not to stand defenseless against such historically thinkable developments, there must be a possibility, in extreme cases, to evaluate the basic principle of material justice more highly than the principle of legal certainty, such as it is expressed in the applicability of positive law for routine cases."

As a criterion for the existence of such a special case, the Federal Constitutional Court points to the formulation by Gustav Radbruch (cf., Radbruch, SUEDDEUTSCHE JURISTENZEITUNG [South German Jurists' Journal], 1946, 105), according to which such a case does exist when the contradiction between positive law and justice has reached such an unbearable degree that the law must yield to justice since it is "incorrect law." The rule of law includes not only certainty and safety under the law but also material justice (BVerfG 25, 284 with further references).

These legal principles, to be sure, were developed on the occasion of the crimes of the National Socialist regime of injustice in Germany which, in the monstrosity of their scope, cannot be compared to the situation under discussion here. Nevertheless, the court has no objection in following this jurisdiction also in the case at hand; this is because the protection of human life applies quite generally and cannot depend on the materialization of a certain number of killings. The permission given to Border Guard soldiers and, moreover, the idea subconsciously suggested by their superiors, to shoot persons who wanted to leave the country without permission, if necessary, if this could not be prevented by other methods, was a minor matter in legal terms because the occasion for shooting, that is to say, the mere act of crossing the border without official permission, is in such an unbearable disproportion to the possibly occurring consequence, that is, the death of a human being, that such a regulation does not deserve any respect and that one may refuse to obey it.

...Accordingly, at any rate, such exemptions from punishment which are provided for under scene-of-the-crime law and which are in crass contradiction to generally recognized principles of the rule of law, cannot prevent punishment of the most serious legal violations—in this case, offenses involving killings—according to German law.... The regulation on unlawful border crossing (Article 213, Criminal Code/GDR), which threatened many years of imprisonment, was designed to prevent the population from leaving the socialist power sphere of the GDR and thus ensuring the continued existence of the totalitarian system of rule; anyone who for such political reasons intentionally kills a person is violating the fundamental principles of law and of humaneness.

This legal concept has been criticized essentially by Gruenwald (cf., JZ 1966, 638, and Strafverteidiger 1991, 37) and by Rittstieg in the latter's expert opinion handed over to the court by the defense and presented by the defense; the international-law expert report by Pepper, presented by the defense, also contains statements on the question of unlawfulness. The arguments cited here however do not hold water in the view of the court....

Pepper in his expert report ... deals primarily with international-law issues. He even comments that the practices and procedures of the Border Guard soldiers correspond on a worldwide basis to conditions prevailing along the boundaries of other States. In this connection, he cites the circumstance that, in response to corresponding inquiries at the national missions assigned to the UN, he essentially received positive answers to his questions as to whether the border security agencies of the particular countries are carrying arms or have access to arms and whether they are permitted to use these weapons in agreement with fixed rules or procedures.

Gruenwald (loc. cit.) recognizes that regulations on the use of firearms could be null and void on account of violation of super-positive law but arrives at the result that this is not the case because West German law of the Federal Republic of Germany contains similar regulations.

In the opinion of the court, these views are untenable.

To the extent that Pepper thinks that he can conclude from the answers to his questions that there is identical international usage, one cannot figure out how he could arrive at this conclusion because he did not at all ask the crucial question, that is to say, the question as to the prerequisites for the use of firearms.

To document their views, Rittstieg and Gruenwald claim that the law of the Federal Republic of Germany contains similar provisions, in other words, the regulation applicable to enforcement officers of the Federal Government, in other words, Federal Border Guard and Customs, according to which a firearm may be used on Border Guard duty also against persons who refuse to obey the repeated instruction to stop or who refuse to tolerate an examination of their person or any means of transportation or objects taken along (Article 11, Paragraph 1 of the Act on Direct Compulsion in the Exercise of Public Authority by Enforcement Officers of the Federal Government—UZwG; Article 15, Paragraph 1, Subparagraph 2 of the on the Use and Exercise of Special Authority by Soldiers of the West German Armed Forces and Civilian Guards—UZwGBw).

These regulations, however, only govern the conditions under which there may be any kind of shooting at all; they have nothing to say as to the way in which the weapon is to be used. This is regulated in Article 12, Paragraph 2, UZWG or Article 16, Paragraph 2, UZwGBw, which the authors do not mention and where it says:

"The purpose of using firearms may only be to render [a person] incapable of attacking or fleeing."

It is rather difficult to see how one can consider—as one of the defense attorneys did—"that this constitutes authorization for intentional killing actions." On the contrary, there can be no doubt that the mentioned provisions do not allow a direct or conditionally intentional lethal shot....

The basic principle to the effect that an act can be punished only if punishability was determined by law before the act was committed (Article 103, Paragraph 2, Constitution, Article 7 EMRK), does not hinder punishment in this case.... The Federal Constitutional Court expressly emphasized that, in the cases, at hand, the principle of material justice must be evaluated more highly than the principle of certainty under the law (BVerfG 3/232, see also BVerfG 25/284)....

Defendant H knowingly and willingly fired at Gueffroy and also wanted to hit the upper part of his body. To that extent, his determination—which was to make a hit—was unconditional. Of course, it was not possible to prove that he absolutely wanted to kill Gueffroy in doing this; the only thing he was concerned with was to prevent Gueffroy's and Gaudian's escape. Nevertheless, he acted at least with a conditional intention to kill. When he aimed at Gueffroy's upper body from a short range, he knew only too well that his round under certain circumstances could hit in a deadly manner and that it was impossible to rule out this possibility in case of an aimed round fired at the upper body of a person, where vital organs are located.... Conditional intention exists according to continuing jurisdiction of the Federal Court when the culprit recognizes and approves the materialization of the factual outcome and recognizes and approves that it is not entirely remote. The assumption as to approval is obvious when the culprit carries out his intention in spite of extreme dangerousness without being able to have confidence in a happy outcome and when he leaves it to accident as to whether the danger, recognized by him, will or will not materialize. That is what the situation was here.... Anyone who in the manner described aims at the upper part of the body of a person cannot seriously have confidence that the lethal outcome, which is considered possible, will not materialize. If he fires nevertheless, then he is acting on a conditional killing intention and not perhaps only negligently. H also had an understandable motive for such a grave deed, as the killing of a human being, where the inhibition threshold is particularly high. He wanted at all costs to prevent the flight, following the wish of his superiors. When he noted that shots fired at the feet did not produce any effect, he aimed at the upper part of the body because it had been suggested to him that a dead escapee is always better than an escaped escapee.

It follows from Article 6, Paragraph 2, Criminal Code/GDR, that action based on conditional intention was punishable also according to GDR law such as it was applicable at that time....

Defendant cannot claim Article 258, Criminal Code/GDR.

According to this regulation, a solider was not liable under criminal law for an action which he carried out by way of execution of an order given by a superior, unless the execution of the order obviously clashed with recognized standards of international law or if it violated criminal laws. The application of this regulation cannot be considered in this case already because there was no specific killing order. Only the command, given by patrol leader S: "Go ahead, shoot!" can be considered an "order" here within the meaning of this regulation. There was no talk here of "shooting down." The firearms use regulations known to the defendant did not contain any direct official order; instead, by way of legal standards or administrative regulations, they only supplied the formal basis for the issue of a military order. All defendants and the above-mentioned members of the Border Forces stated that, according to official instructions, they were to fire only at the feet or so that the escaping person would be disabled in terms of the attempt to escape. Along with that, to be sure, it was suggested that no escapee must be allowed to get through. But this cannot be considered an order to shoot somebody down. But even if one were to construe—as "order" within the meaning of Article 258, Criminal Code/GDR—the generally stated requirement that none must be allowed to get through, the results still would not be any different. Such an order would be unlawful and would not have deserved any obedience because this would have been an invitation to commit crimes, that is to say, the unlawful and intentional killing of people, and the execution of the order would have violated criminal laws (Arts. 112, 113, Criminal Code/GDR)....

Shooting at people, which may lead to killing, that is to say, people who merely wanted to leave the territory of the then GDR, constitutes such a violation of the standards of ethics and human coexistence that—even considering indoctrination, education, and training in the former GDR—one really cannot visualize that the defendant, considering his origin, his schooling, and his personality, as regards the action against the escapees with which he is charged, was in a state of prohibition misinterpretation that would rule out any guilt on his part. In the case of the defendant, one cannot assume that he was unable to recognize the few basic principles that are indispensable for human coexistence and that belong to the untouchable basic assets and core of the law, such as it lives in the legal consciousness of all cultured nations—perhaps because he had not been educated in a knowledge of these principles. Justice and humanity were explained and pictured as ideals also in the then GDR. To that extent, generally adequate ideas as to the basis of natural justice were indeed disseminated. That this is so is pointed up also by the circumstance that a considerable multitude of inhabitants of the former GDR considered action against so-called border violators along the Berlin Wall and along the inner-German boundary to be unjust. The background of the accused, his schooling, and his comment on the motives and assessments of the conflicts, in which so-called border violators were enmeshed, show that he did have and could have available the fundamentals of a normal legal consciousness. He had every reason to think deeply as to whether it was permitted to happen that people may, if necessary, be shot down along the border only because they wanted to leave the GDR without official permission. He had sufficient references and if he had thought about them carefully, he could have figured out for himself that an event, such as it is to be judged here, was not compatible with the set of values prevailing in his environment. In making this examination, one of course cannot consider as representatives of the environment—as the defense argues—those pillars of the system of justice of the then GDR, such as members of the State Security Ministry, judges, or prosecutors; instead, what is important here is to find out whether the "people of the State" of the GDR did or did not approve the procedures under discussion here. The defendant did not engage in these considerations at the moment he acted; instead, he should have tried to figure this out beforehand; this is so because conscience must be examined at the right time, especially since the defendant, in intellectual terms, was able to come to grips with and did concern himself with the possible factual situation long before the act, as one can see from the view —generally advocated in discussions among Border Guard soldiers—that one must disable the escaping person in practice by firing at the legs, along with the widespread endeavor among soldiers to get out of Border Guard duty with their hands clean.

The realization that deadly shots along the border were a crass injustice and that they were in crying contradiction to the generally recognized basic principles of law and justice should and could have been a matter of general knowledge and usage if the Border Guard soldiers and their superiors had developed the proper conscience. This emerges already from the fact that, on high national holidays and visits by foreign official guests, they were not allowed to shoot, except in cases of desertion and self-defense. Here there was every reason to think deeply as to why the use of firearms was restricted in these cases; after all, what kind of State would reduce its fight against crime and would forget about catching criminals and, if necessary, shoot them down, merely because there was a foreign official guest visiting the country? That could only be a hint that the then GDR leadership was afraid of being challenged in case an escapee was shot down at the border before the very eyes of an official guest of State and that the worldwide public could pillory these incidents as crimes.

In addition, there is the fact that Defendant H—like the other defendants, by the way—made sure not to wear in public his subsequently awarded medal of merit and also his previously earned marksmanship badge because all of them were afraid that they would thus be exposing themselves in public at least to unfriendly verbal attacks from the population and that they would be insulted as "snipers."

That even the then rulers of the GDR did not have a clean conscience also springs from the fact that—as was customary in such cases and as the Border Guard soldiers and Defendant H also knew before the act—there was a general news blackout about the event, that the soldiers were sworn to silence, that their weapons were taken from them, that the soldiers were transferred from Border Guard duty, and that their names were erased in the documents of the Border Forces in order to wipe out all traces.

The name of the killing victim was also subsequently eliminated in the hospital's records. This, to be sure, was done after the fact but it proves that they wanted to hush up the deadly shots fired at the escapees because they knew that the population would not approve such action if it became known. Naturally, these measures were also intended to prevent the Western media from reporting such incidents and this effort was made precisely so that the East German population would, if at all possible, not learn about these events either. The generally widespread wish of the Border Guard soldiers to be discharged from the Border Forces with "clean hands," that is to say, without getting into a situation in which they would have to take action against an escapee, also proves that most Border Guard soldiers did not really like their assignment although they were exposed to constant political indoctrination.... That the defendant would also intellectually have been in a position to get the correct picture as to the injustice of the use of firearms against unarmed escapees from the circumstances he obviously was fully familiar with is furthermore made clear by the fact that he himself stated that, until his induction into the Border Forces, he was convinced that shooting people along the border was unlawful and that he considered this a crime against humanity because this, so to speak, was equivalent to a death sentence; he claims that he changed his opinion only in the course of military training and indoctrination during political education. When it comes to killing people for the sake of preserving the power of the rulers, then one must not so quickly turn off one's conscience in this last quarter of the 20th Century. Defendant H had every reason to try to find out, outside the Army, whether the legal community of the then GDR citizens did or did not approve the shooting down of persons along the border in 1989, half a year before the so-called big change....

Defendant H accordingly was to be punished for homicide committed at least with conditional intention to kill....

Apportionment of Punishment

...It follows from the considerations given below that we are dealing here with an "otherwise less grave case" within the meaning of Art. 213, Criminal Code:

The acts carried out by the defendants must be viewed against the background of the inhuman system of compulsion prevailing in the then GDR which educated the defendants, with all means of mass psychology, to blind onesidedness and imparted a restricted image of the world which the defendants, in terms of their personality and education, had little to counter with.

Here again, one had to keep in mind that all those who contributed to the distortion of the legal consciousness of the Border Guard soldiers—be it in school, in the so-called mass organizations, or in political indoctrination sessions in the military—cannot be made liable for this under criminal law because the law does not know any criminal action facts in this context. Furthermore, it was to be considered here by way of mitigation that the defendants acted in an extraordinary life situation that would never be repeated for them. In the view of the court, that alone, to be sure, would not justify the application of the provision of Article 213, Criminal Code. But one must add that the defendants acted in the context of an avoidable error as to prohibition. An overall assessment of all of these circumstances therefore justifies the grading of these acts as less grave cases within the meaning of Article 213, Criminal Code, so that the penalty was to be taken from the punishment criteria of this regulation....

In the case of Defendant H, there was an aggravating factor in that his shot, fired at the upper part of the body of Chris Gueffroy, with conditional killing intention, from the previously described short range, reveals a particularly strong measure of cold bloodedness and reprehensibility. When it comes to the content of guilt, it makes a big difference whether a Border Guard soldier, imagining that he must act this way, decides to fire several short bursts at escapees with conditional killing intention from a range of 125 m and more or whether, from a range of at most 39 m, he aims at the chest of a person standing upright at the border fence. The penalty to be meted out against Defendant H therefore was to be taken from the upper half of the penalty criterion spelled out in Article 213, Criminal Code....

Weighing all of the circumstances that speak for and against the defendants, the administration of the following penalties was quite in keeping with the guilt but it was also required in order impressively to make them aware of the injustice of their actions:

In the case of Defendant H, a prison sentence of 3 years and 6 months.

HONDURAS: ORGANIZATION OF AMERICAN STATES, INTER-AMERICAN COURT OF HUMAN RIGHTS: VELÁSQUEZ RODRÍGUEZ CASE

Judgment of July 29, 1988, Series C No. 4

1. The Inter-American Commission on Human Rights (hereinafter "the Commission") submitted the instant case of the Inter-American Court of Human Rights (hereinafter the "Court") on April 24, 1986. It originated in a petition (No. 7920) against the State of Honduras (hereinafter "Honduras" or "the Government"), which the Secretariat of the Commission received on October 7, 1981....

3. According to the petition filed with the Commission, and the supplementary information received subsequently, Manfredo Velásquez, a student at the National Autonomous University of Honduras, "was violently detained without a warrant for his arrest by members of the National Office of Investigations (DNI) and G-2 of the Armed Forces of Honduras." The detention took place in Tegucigalpa on the afternoon of September 12, 1981. According to the petitioners, several witnesses reported that Manfredo Velásquez and others were detained and taken to the cells of the Public Security Forces Station No. 2 located in the Barrio El Menchén of Tegucigalpa, where he was "accused of alleged political crimes and subjected to harsh interrogation and cruel torture." The petition added that on September 17, 1981, Manfredo Velásquez was moved to the First Infantry Battalion, where the interrogation continued, but that the police and security forces denied that he had been detained....

148. [T]he Court finds that the following facts have been proven in this proceeding: (1) a practice of disappearances carried out or tolerated by Honduran officials existed between 1981 and 1984; (2) Manfredo Velásquez disappeared at the hands of or with the acquiescence of those officials within the framework of that practice; and (3) the Government of Honduras failed to guarantee the human rights affected by that practice.

149. Disappearances are not new in the history of human rights violations. However, their systematic and repeated nature and their use not only for causing certain individuals to disappear, either briefly or permanently, but also as a means of creating a general state of anguish, insecurity and fear, is a recent phenomenon. Although this practice exists virtually worldwide, it has occurred with exceptional intensity in Latin America in the last few years....

155. The forced disappearance of human beings is a multiple and continuous violation of many rights under the Convention that the States Parties are obligated to respect and guarantee.... The existence of this practice, moreover, evinces a disregard of the duty to organize the State in such a manner as to guarantee the rights recognized in the Convention, as set out below.

159. The Commission has asked the Court to find that Honduras has violated the rights guaranteed to Manfredo Velásquez by Articles 4, 5 and 7 of the Convention. The Government has denied the charges and seeks to be absolved.

160. This requires the Court to examine the conditions under which a particular act, which violates one of the rights recognized by the Convention, can be imputed to the State Party thereby establishing its international responsibility.

161. Article 1(1) of the Convention provides:

> Article 1. Obligation to Respect Rights
>
> 1. The States Parties to this Convention undertake to respect the rights and freedoms recognized herein and to ensure to all persons subject to their jurisdiction the free and full exercise of those rights and freedoms, without any discrimination for reasons of race, color, sex, language, religion, political or other opinion, national or social origin, economic status, birth, or any other social condition.

162. This article specifies the obligation assumed by the States Parties in relation to each of the rights protected. Each claim alleging that one of those rights has been infringed necessarily implies that Article 1(1) of the Convention has also been violated....

164. Article 1(1) is essential in determining whether a violation of human rights recognized by the Convention can be imputed to a State Party. In effect, that article charges the States Parties with the fundamental duty to respect and guarantee the rights recognized in the Convention. Any impairment of those rights which can be attributed under the rules of international law to the action or omission of any public authority constitutes an act imputable to the State, which assumes responsibility in the terms provided by the Convention....

166. The second obligation of the States Parties is to "ensure" the free and full exercise of the rights recognized by the Convention to every person subject to its jurisdiction. This obligation implies the duty of the States Parties to organize the governmental apparatus and, in general, all the structures through which public power is exercised, so that they are capable of juridically ensuring the free and full enjoyment of human rights. As a consequence of this obligation, the States must prevent, investigate and punish any violation of the rights recognized by the Convention and, moreover, if possible attempt to restore the right violated and provide compensation as warranted for damages resulting from the violation.

167. The obligation to ensure the free and full exercise of human rights is not fulfilled by the existence of a legal system designed to make it possible to comply with this obligation—it also requires the government to conduct itself so as to effectively ensure the free and full exercise of human rights....

169. According to Article 1(1), any exercise of public power that violates the rights recognized by the Convention is illegal. Whenever a State organ, official or public entity violates one of those rights, this constitutes a failure of the duty to respect the rights and freedoms set forth in the Convention.

170. This conclusion is independent of whether the organ or official has contravened provisions of internal law or overstepped the limits of his authority: under international law a State is responsible for the acts of its agents undertaken in their official capacity and for their omissions, even when those agents act outside the sphere of their authority or violate internal law....

172. Thus, in principle, any violation of rights recognized by the Convention carried out by an act of public authority or by persons who use their position of authority, is imputable to the State. However, this does not define all the circumstances in which a State is obligated to prevent, investigate and punish human rights violations, nor all the cases in which the State might be found responsible for an infringement of those rights. An illegal act which violates human rights and which is initially not directly imputable to a State (for example, because it is the act of a private person or because the person responsible has not been identified) can lead to international responsibility of the State, not because of the act itself, but because of the lack of due diligence to prevent the violation or to respond to it as required by the Convention....

174. The State has a legal duty to take reasonable steps to prevent human rights violations and to use the means at its disposal to carry out a serious investigation of violations committed within its jurisdiction, to identify those responsible, to impose the appropriate punishment and to ensure the victim adequate compensation.

175. This duty to prevent includes all those means of a legal, political, administrative and cultural nature that promote the protection of human rights and ensure that any violations are considered and treated as illegal acts, which, as such, may lead to the punishment of those responsible and the obligation to indemnify the victims for damages. It is not possible to make a detailed list of all such measures, since they vary with the law and the conditions of each State Party....

176. The State is obligated to investigate every situation involving a violation of the rights protected by the Convention. If the State apparatus acts in such a way that the violation goes unpunished and the victim's full enjoyment of such rights is not restored as soon as possible, the State has failed to comply with its duty to ensure the free and full exercise of those rights to the persons within its jurisdiction. The same is true when the State allows private persons or groups to act freely and with impunity to the detriment of the rights recognized by the Convention.

177. In certain circumstances, it may be difficult to investigate acts that violate an individual's rights. The duty to investigate, like the duty to prevent, is not breached merely because the investigation does not produce a satisfactory result. Nevertheless, it must be undertaken in a serious manner and not as a mere formality preordained to be ineffective. An investigation must have an objective and be assumed by the State as its own legal duty, not as a step taken by private interests that depends upon the initiative of the victim or his family or upon their offer of proof, without an effective search for the truth by the government. This is true regardless of what agent is eventually found responsible for the violation. Where the acts of private

parties that violate the Convention are not seriously investigated, those parties are aided in a sense by the government, thereby making the State responsible on the international plane.

178. In the instant case, the evidence shows a complete inability of the procedures of the State of Honduras, which were theoretically adequate, to carry out an investigation into the disappearance of Manfredo Velásquez, and of the fulfillment of its duties to pay compensation and punish those responsible, as set out in Article 1(1) of the Convention.

179. As the Court has verified above, the failure of the judicial system to act upon the writs brought before the various tribunals in the instant case has been proven. Not one writ of habeas corpus was processed. No judge had access to the places where Manfredo Velásquez might have been detained. The criminal complaint was dismissed.

180. Nor did the organs of the Executive Branch carry out a serious investigation to establish the fate of Manfredo Velásquez.... The offer of an investigation in accord with Resolution 30/83 of the Commission resulted in an investigation by the Armed Forces, the same body accused of direct responsibility for the disappearances. This raises grave questions regarding the seriousness of the investigation. The Government often resorted to asking relatives of the victims to present conclusive proof of their allegations even though those allegations, because they involved crimes against the person, should have been investigated on the Government's own initiative in fulfillment of the State's duty to ensure public order. This is especially true when the allegations refer to a practice carried out within the Armed Forces, which, because of its nature, is not subject to private investigations. No proceeding was initiated to establish responsibility for the disappearance of Manfredo Velásquez and apply punishment under internal law. All of the above leads to the conclusion that the Honduran authorities did not take effective action to ensure respect for human rights within the jurisdiction of that State as required by Article 1(1) of the Convention.

181. The duty to investigate facts of this type continues as long as there is uncertainty about the fate of the person who has disappeared. Even in the hypothetical case that those individually responsible for crimes of this type cannot be legally punished under certain circumstances, the State is obligated to use the means at its disposal to inform the relatives of the fate of the victims and, if they have been killed, the location of their remains.

182. The Court is convinced, and has so found, that the disappearance of Manfredo Velásquez was carried out by agents who acted under cover of public authority. However, even had that fact not been proven, the failure of the State apparatus to act, which is clearly proven, is a failure on the part of Honduras to fulfill the duties it assumed under Article 1(1) of the Convention, which obligated it to ensure Manfredo Velásquez the free and full exercise of his human rights.

183. The Court notes that the legal order of Honduras does not authorize such acts and that internal law defines them as crimes. The Court also recognizes that not all levels of the Government of Honduras were necessarily aware of those acts, nor is there any evidence that such acts were the result of official orders. Nevertheless, those circumstances are irrelevant

for the purposes of establishing whether Honduras is responsible under international law for the violations of human rights perpetrated within the practice of disappearances.

184. According to the principle of the continuity of the State in international law, responsibility exists both independently of changes of government over a period of time and continuously from the time of the act that creates responsibility to the time when the act is declared illegal. The foregoing is also valid in the area of human rights although, from an ethical or political point of view, the attitude of the new government may be much more respectful of those rights than that of the government in power when the violations occurred.

185. The Court, therefore, concludes that the facts found in this proceeding show that the State of Honduras is responsible for the involuntary disappearance of Angel Manfredo Velásquez Rodríguez. Thus, Honduras has violated Articles 7, 5 and 4 of the Convention....

189. Article 63(1) of the Convention provides:

> If the Court finds that there has been a violation of a right or freedom protected by this Convention, the Court shall rule that the injured party be ensured the enjoyment of his right or freedom that was violated. It shall also rule, if appropriate, that the consequences of the measure or situation that constituted the breach of such right or freedom be remedied and that fair compensation be paid to the injured party.

Clearly, in the instant case the Court cannot order that the victim be guaranteed the enjoyment of the rights or freedoms violated. The Court, however, can rule that the consequences of the breach of the rights be remedied and that just compensation be paid.

190. During this proceeding the Commission requested the payment of compensation, but did not offer evidence regarding the amount of damages or the manner of payment. Neither did the parties discuss these matters.

191. The Court believes that the parties can agree on the damages. If an agreement cannot be reached, the Court shall award an amount. The case shall, therefore, remain open for that purpose. The Court reserves the right to approve the agreement and, in the event no agreement is reached, to set the amount and order the manner of payment....

NICARAGUA: LAW ON GENERAL AMNESTY AND NATIONAL RECONCILIATION

Law No. 81 on General Amnesty and National Reconciliation (1990)

The President of the Republic of Nicaragua...

Considering:

I. That the Government of the Republic of Nicaragua has promoted peace, democracy, and economic and social development for the peoples of Central America, by signing and complying with all the Agreements reached by the Presidents of the Central American countries, beginning with the Agreement signed in Esquipulas in August 1987, up to the present.

II. That in order to comply with these Agreements, the Government of Nicaragua signed a series of accords with all the political forces of the country in August 1989, which have been completely adhered to.

III. That in addition, wide sectors of our society have identified the need for an authentic national reconciliation to facilitate peace and internal stability, and the reconstruction of the country.

IV. That the reconciliation of the Nicaraguan family requires us to pardon and forget those events that brought unrest to the nation, in order to create a climate of peace, which up to the present time has been denied us, and in which all of us together can build a new society based on justice and brotherhood.

V. That in compliance with the Agreements signed by the Presidents of the Central American countries and the accords reached with the political forces of Nicaragua in order to achieve a national reconciliation, we have decided to enact a general and unconditional Amnesty Law for all Nicaraguans, with no distinctions made for any particular class.

In accordance with the authority granted to him, decrees the following:

LAW ON GENERAL AMNESTY
AND NATIONAL RECONCILIATION

Article 1

General and unconditional amnesty is hereby granted to:

1. All Nicaraguans, whether or not currently residing in the country, who committed crimes against the public order and the internal and external security of the State, and other related acts.

2. All civilian and military Nicaraguans who may have committed infractions in the course of carrying out or investigating the criminal acts described in the preceding paragraph.

3. All officials and public employees who may have committed the criminal acts described in Volume Two of the Penal Code and its Revisions, in particular Law No. 217 dated Nov. 12, 1985, who have not been officially charged. The pardon granted includes both civil and administrative responsibility.

Article 2

The amnesty referred to in the preceding paragraph includes the period from June 19, 1979 up to the date on which the current Law goes into effect.

Article 3

The present Law shall go into effect beginning on the date of its publication by any medium of public communication, without this affecting its subsequent publication in "The Gazette," the Official Journal.

SOUTH AFRICA: INDEMNITY ACT

*Act No. 35 (May 18, 1990) as amended by
Indemnity Amendment Act, No. 124 of 1992*

To Provide for the Grant of Temporary Immunity or Permanent Indemnity; and for Incidental Matters.

Preamble.

WHEREAS recent world events and domestic realities have created opportunities for reconciliation and a joint search for common goals and peaceful solutions in South Africa;

AND WHEREAS the course of events has resulted in criminal charges against and the arrest of a number of persons being possible or pending;

AND WHEREAS for the sake of reconciliation and for the finding of peaceful solutions it has now become necessary from time to time to grant temporary immunity or permanent indemnity against arrest, prosecution, detention and legal process to such persons:

1. State President may Grant Temporary Immunity.

(1) The State President may, if he is of the opinion that it is necessary for the promotion of peaceful constitutional solutions in South Africa or the unimpeded and efficient administration of justice, by notice in the *Gazette* grant to any person the immunity referred to in subsection (2), either unconditionally or on the conditions he may deem fit.

(2) No proceedings, either civil or criminal, shall be instituted or continued in any court of law against any person to whom has been granted such immunity, during the period stipulated in such notice in respect of him, in respect of anything done or omitted by him on any date prior to the commencement of that period, and such person shall not be detained during such period in terms of any law in respect of an act or omission at any time prior to the commencement of that period.

2. State President may Grant Indemnity.

(1) The State President may by notice in the *Gazette* grant indemnity to any person or category of persons, either unconditionally or on the conditions he may deem fit, in respect of any event or category of events specified in the notice.

(2) No proceedings, either civil or criminal, shall be instituted or continued in any court of law against any person who has been granted

indemnity in terms of subsection (1), in respect of the events specified in the said notice, and such person shall not be detained in terms of any law in respect of those events.

2A. Disposal of Articles Seized.

(1)(a) Notwithstanding anything to the contrary contained in any law, any article seized in accordance with the provisions of Chapter 2 of the Criminal Procedure Act, 1977 (Act No. 51 of 1977), in connection with any event or category of events in respect of which indemnity has, in terms of section 2 of this Act, been granted to any person or category of persons, is or shall be forfeited to the State as from the time at which it was or is so seized.

(b) If the Minister of Law and Order or an officer in the South African Police designated by the said Minister is satisfied, on the ground of any written proof submitted to him by any person within 30 days after the granting of any relevant Indemnity referred to in paragraph (a) or after the coming into operation of this section, whichever occurs last, that any article so forfeited to the State was not unlawfully possessed, or was not possessed or used for unlawful purposes, by any person and that he is entitled to the possession thereof, the said Minister or the officer concerned, as the case may be, shall order that such article be handed over to the first-mentioned person.

(2) Any article forfeited to the State in terms of subsection (1)(a) shall be dealt with in accordance with the directions of the Minister of Law and Order or the directions of any person authorized by the said Minister in writing to issue such directions.

(3) The provisions of subsections (1) and (2) shall not affect the rights which any person, other than the person or the category of persons to whom indemnity was granted under section 2, may have in respect of the article forfeited to the State in terms of subsection (1)(a), if the Minister of Law and Order or an officer in the South African Police designated by the said Minister, is satisfied, on the ground of written proof submitted to him by such person within 30 days after the granting of the said indemnity or after the coming into operation of this section, whichever occurs last, that he did not know or could not reasonably have known that such article was being or would be used in connection with the events in question or that he could not prevent such use, and that he is entitled to the possession thereof.

(4) The provisions of subsections (1), (2) and (3) shall also apply to any articles seized as is contemplated in subsection (1) which on the date of coming into operation of this section is still in the possession of the South African Police, irrespective of when any relevant indemnity was granted.

(5) Section 4 shall not apply in respect of this section.
[S. 2A inserted by s. 1 of Act No. 124 of 1992.]

3. Regulations.

(1) The State President may make regulations regarding any matter to which this Act relates if he considers it necessary or expedient so as to achieve the objects of this Act.

(2) Any regulation which results in expenditure from the State Revenue Fund shall be made after consultation by the Minister of Justice with the Minister of Finance.

4. Saving.

(1) Any section of this Act shall, subject to the provisions of subsection (2), cease to have effect after the expiry of one year from the commencement of that section, but it shall not affect the previous operation of that section or any immunity or indemnity granted in terms thereof.

(2) The period referred to in subsection (1) may be extended by the State President by proclamation in the *Gazette* for one year at a time: Provided that a second or subsequent extension shall only take place with the concurrence of all three Houses of Parliament.

5. Short Title and Commencement.

(1) This Act shall be called the Indemnity Act, 1990, and shall come into operation on a date fixed by the State President by proclamation in the *Gazette*.

(2) Different dates may be so fixed in respect of different provisions of this Act.

[Following the transfer of power in South Africa, the Indemnity Act, 1990 was confirmed and extended by the post-transition government as follows:]

Presidential Proclamation Extending the Indemnity Act

No. 101 (May 16, 1994)

Indemnity Act, 1990
Extension of Period of Operation

Under subsection (2) of section 4 of the Indemnity Act, 1990 (Act No. 35 of 1990), and with the concurrence of Parliament, I hereby, in relation to the said Act as a whole, extend the period referred to in subsection (1) of that section for a future period of one year ending on May 17, 1995....

Notice of Temporary Immunity Under the Indemnity Act

No. 986 (May 17, 1994)

Notice by the President of the Republic of South Africa

Under section 1 (1) of the Indemnity Act, 1990 (Act No. 35 of 1990), I hereby, for the period from 18 May, 1994 up to and including 17 May, 1995, unconditionally grant immunity referred to in section 1 (2) of the aforementioned Act to the persons to whom temporary immunity was granted by Government Notices Nos. 882 of 17 May 1993, 366 of 19 February 1994 and 458 of 244 March 24, 1994.

SOUTH AFRICA: 1993 CONSTITUTION

(Entry into force, April 27, 1994)

National Unity and Reconciliation

...This Constitution provides a historic bridge between the past of a deeply divided society characterized by strife, conflict, untold suffering and injustice, and a future founded on the recognition of human rights, democracy and peaceful co-existence and development opportunities for all South Africans, irrespective of color, race, class, belief or sex.

The pursuit of national unity, the well-being of all South African citizens and peace require reconciliation between the people of South Africa and the reconstruction of society.

The adoption of this Constitution lays the secure foundation for the people of South Africa to transcend the divisions and strife of the past, which generated gross violations of human rights, the transgression of humanitarian principles in violent conflicts and a legacy of hatred, fear, guilt and revenge.

These can now be addressed on the basis that there is a need for understanding but not for vengeance, a need for reparation but not for retaliation, a need for *ubuntu* but not for victimization.

In order to advance such reconciliation and reconstruction, amnesty shall be granted in respect of acts, omissions and offenses associated with political objectives and committed in the course of the conflicts of the past. To this end, Parliament under this Constitution shall adopt a law determining a firm cut-off date, which shall be a date after 8 October 1990 and before 6 December 1993, and providing for the mechanisms, criteria and procedures, including tribunals, if any, through which such amnesty shall be dealt with at any time after the law has been passed....

URUGUAY: LAW NULLIFYING THE STATE'S CLAIM TO PUNISH CERTAIN CRIMES (*"LEY DE CADUCIDAD DE LA PRETENSIÓN PÚNTIVA DEL ESTADO"*)*

Law No. 15,848 (December 22, 1986)

Article 1

It is recognized that, as a consequence of the logic of the events stemming from the agreement between the political parties and the Armed Forces signed in August, 1984, and in order to complete the transition to full constitutional order, the State relinquishes the exercise of penal actions with respect to crimes committed until March 1, 1985, by military and police officials either for political reasons or in fulfillment of their functions and in obeying orders from superiors during the *de facto* period.

Article 2

The above Article does not cover:

a) judicial proceedings in which indictments have been issued at the time this Law goes into effect;
b) crimes that may have been committed for personal economic gain or to benefit a third party.

Article 3

For the purposes contemplated in the above Articles, the court in pending cases will request the Executive branch to submit, within a period of thirty days of receiving such request, an opinion as to whether or not it considers the case to fall within the scope of Article 1 of this Law.

If the Executive branch considers the Law to be applicable, the court will dismiss the case. If, on the other hand, the Executive branch does not consider the case to fall under this Law, the court will order judicial proceedings to continue.

From the time this Law is promulgated until the date the court receives a response from the Executive branch, all pretrial proceedings in cases described in the first paragraph of this Article will be suspended.

Article 4

Notwithstanding the above, the court will remit to the Executive branch all testimony offered until the date this Law is approved, regarding persons

---

* Reprinted from "The Ley de Caducidad," in *Challenging Impunity: The Ley de Caducidad and the Referendum Campaign in Uruguay, An Americas Watch Report* (Americas Watch Committee, 1989), pp. 15-16.

allegedly detained in military or police operations who later disappeared, including minors allegedly kidnapped in similar circumstances.

The Executive branch will immediately order the investigation of such incidents.

Within a 120-day period from the date of receipt of the judicial communication of the denunciation, the Executive branch will inform the plaintiffs of the results of these investigations and place at their disposal all information gathered.

Uruguay: Letter from President Sanguinetti to Amnesty International Regarding the *Ley de Caducidad*[*]

(March 31, 1987)

Dear Secretary General,

1. I am writing in reply to your letter dated 29 January 1987, in which you conveyed to me some comments on Law 15,848 of 22 December 1986 which concerns the nullification of the State's claim to take punitive action....

2. I understand Amnesty International's concerns in sending me this letter and I fully appreciate the efforts undertaken by your organization for the defence of human rights, without any kind of discrimination, all over the world. The aims of Amnesty International in this regard coincide with those of the Government of Uruguay which, on taking office on 1 March 1985 as a result of entirely free elections, made it a priority to ensure full and absolute enjoyment of human rights within a framework of democratic institutions.

3. In my letter of 17 September 1986, I explained to the then Secretary General of Amnesty International, Thomas Hammarberg, my Government's reasons for submitting the amnesty bill that was under consideration at the time.

I think some of the remarks made then seem particularly pertinent at this time and should be reproduced here:

> The problem of punishment of military and police personnel who committed crimes against the person has been made more complicated because of the progressive politicization of the issue. In the opinion of the Executive Power, while there are persons and organizations driven by a sincere desire for justice (Amnesty International is one of them, even though it may err in its interpretations), the banner of "justice and punishment for the culprits" is being used to open a breach between the armed forces and the rest of the country. An aggressive campaign is being unleashed, based on denunciations and accusations with the aim— there can be no doubt—of influencing the minds of the judges.
>
> Faced with this panorama, it seems obvious that the Executive Power should act in order to preserve public peace, cutting off a poisonous plant at the root.... [T]here are other arguments which can be brought to bear. Amnesty International itself sets them out when in the letter sent to me it says: "Amnesty International recognizes that governments elected to power following periods of civil strife or political polarization or other serious social disturbance, must favor the adoption of measures to bring lasting reconciliation and unity to their country, and that the inheritance of a recent past continues to weigh, sometimes heavily, on national

---

[*] Reprinted from "Letter from President Sanguinetti to Amnesty International," in Amnesty International Publication: *Uruguay: Legislation Dealing with Past Human Rights Abuses* (1987), pp. 11-16. AI Index: AMR 52/02/87.

occurrences, limiting the field of action of the authorities with respect to the investigation of past abuses and the judging of those responsible."

The Uruguayan government has decided to take measures of "magnanimity or clemency" utilizing a mechanism provided for in the Constitution of the Republic (the amnesty). The 12 years of dictatorship have left scars which will need a long time to heal and it is good to begin to do so. The country needs reconciliation to face a difficult but promising future.

Looking backwards to find culprits—which without doubt there were—will not revive the dead nor relieve the pain of those who suffered torture. Looking forward, we can build a better country that will have banished for ever terror and violence.

The country pardoned the subversives, it must now pardon those who confronted them. And while forgiveness reaches the hearts of the people, the amnesty accomplishes it formally as an expression of the legal will of the State.

4.... In view of events and circumstances in the country, the significance of which is beyond reasonable doubt, and which might have had a detrimental effect on the development of normal democratic processes in Uruguay—a necessary prerequisite and framework for human rights to be real and effective for all—the amnesty bill was sent by the Executive to Parliament and was rejected by the Senate.

The presentation of the bill was preceded by political discussions and negotiations aimed at dealing constructively with the institutional issues involved at the time and at seeking agreement on commonly held views so that the situation could be faced with the support of a broad political front, based on scrupulous respect for democratic principles and strict adherence to the Constitution.

The Senate of the Republic shelved the bill sent to it by the Executive and debated and passed a bill submitted by senators of the *Partido Nacional*, the main opposition party, which was passed by a huge majority in both Chambers and promulgated by the Executive on 22 December 1986. All the procedures followed were in accordance with Articles 133, 134 and 136 of the Constitution.

5. It is not the case that Law 15,848 grants "immunity from prosecution to all police and military personnel alleged responsible for human rights violations committed in exercise of their official duties or on superior orders, prior to March 1985," as incorrectly stated in the letter which I am answering.

The device used by the law to solve the problem that had been posed is distinct from a declaration of "impunity" or "immunity from prosecution." Article 1 of the Law says as follows:

[It is recognized that, as a consequence of the logic of the events stemming from the agreement between the political parties and the Armed Forces signed in August, 1984, and in order to complete the transition to full constitutional order, the State relinquishes the exercise of penal actions with respect to crimes committed until March 1, 1985, by military and police officials either for political

reasons or in fulfillment of their functions and in obeying orders
from superiors during the *de facto* period.]

Furthermore, the aforementioned Law, whose exceptional nature should be interpreted restrictively, does not affect the principle of "*res judicata*" or alter the competencies and independence of the branches of Government nor does it in any way limit—such a thing would have been impossible—the powers of the Supreme Court of Justice, as the supreme body responsible for the defence of the Constitution (articles 239, 256, 261 and 330 of the Constitution). Of all the legal effects of the criminal act, only the State's claim to take punitive action has been nullified.

6. It is inappropriate in this letter to enter into an exhaustive legal analysis of the meaning of the expression used in the Law "nullity of the State's claim to take punitive action" in order to tackle the problem that required a solution. But, in answering your letter, it is pertinent to point out that some of the effects of this nullification are, in a sense, analogous or similar to those of an amnesty. However, in order to avoid any misunderstanding it should be clearly understood that no amnesty, in the strict sense of the word, has been granted. Although this is evidently the case from a legal standpoint, with all that this implies, it should be pointed out that there are in point of fact, some similarities with the situation that results from an amnesty, which is precisely what our Government proposed, believing this to be the best solution.

Now, paragraph 14 of Article 85 of the Constitution empowers the Legislature to grant "amnesties" "in exceptional circumstances," "by an absolute majority of votes out of the total number or members in each Chamber." In the political history of our country, the amnesty has been the crucial legal instrument for concluding the most distressing periods in the life of the nation, for healing wounds, for overcoming hatred and for getting down to the rebuilding of democracy and proclaiming freedom for everyone, founded on a reconciliation of all citizens. The present law, which is different and is a product of the different circumstances the nation has faced, is an attempt to achieve the same historical result.

7. The amnesty, the pardon and the commutation of sentence are institutions whose existence has been recognized by International Human Rights Law, not only as the natural expression of the sovereign power of the State in organizing its criminal and procedural system, but also as a safeguard of the human rights which are recognized and safeguarded in international law (for example, article 6, paragraph 4 of the International Covenant on Civil and Political Rights and article 4, paragraph 6 of the American Convention on Human Rights).

These forms of clemency are among the remedies that governments have traditionally used when exceptional circumstances have made it advisable to modify the full force of criminal law, or refrain from using it, for the purpose of avoiding social upheavals or other consequences that would upset the normal course of national life. As a means of social pacification, they are essentially political acts.

The State's obligation to administer justice cannot be performed in the abstract without taking into account other State functions, of which the most important are to ensure that its citizens live together in peace and to foster the development of the community within this framework of peace and security. The severity of the law in prescribing a penalty must be attenuated when its application would result in a greater social ill than that of allowing a crime to go unpunished. And this ability of the greater benefit (namely, social peace) is an essential aspect of holding political office. In a word, the renunciation of the power of punishment is merely another way of administering justice, since the political basis of the amnesty is the same as that on which the exercise of punitive power is based: the intention underlying both of these elements, amnesty and punitive authority, is, ultimately, to bring peace and tranquility to all members of the community.

8. There may, of course, be laws in which amnesties or pardons are granted, sentences are commuted, or analogous instruments, whatever name they may be given, are enacted, which do violate the domestic or international legal system for the recognition and protection of human rights. In particular, a law providing for amnesty or some similar instrument, that was discriminatory and flouted egalitarian or anti-Constitution; article 2, paragraph 1 and article 26 of the Covenant on Civil and Political Rights; articles 1 and 24 of the American Convention of Human Rights).

Law 15,737 of 8 March 1985 (Official Gazette of 22 March 1985) granted an amnesty in respect of all political offences and common and military offenses related thereto committed after 1 January 1962. In line with the process of national reconciliation and the restoration and strengthening of democracy, by means of law 15,848, the process of bringing the law to bear on situations arising from the abnormal and regrettable situation that affected the county until recently, was made complete. Law 15,737 was one of the first acts of the new government and benefited all who had committed crimes of subversion, whether they had been sentenced or brought to trial or had gone into exile or had never been arrested.

Another act was the reinstatement of thousands of former public employees, who have been restored to their former duties. By 31 December 1986, 9,000 public employees who had been persecuted and suffered wrongly at the hands of the dictatorship had been returned to their jobs or had received some other form of compensation.

9. In all honesty and reasonableness, it cannot be said that the law with which this letter is concerned is in violation of human rights. No textual reference to the constitution can be made in this regard, nor can any international, covenantal, or common law legal provision be invoked to claim that violations have taken place....

I would point out straight away that it was precisely to make human rights violations such as involuntary disappearances impossible that law 15,848 was passed. In a constitutional and democratic system such as that of Uruguay, where all individual and procedural safeguards are fully operational and untrammelled and where the legislative, executive and judicial branches have freedom of action, reprehensible incidents of this kind should not occur.

10. To interpret or, rather, to understand the meaning of Law 15,848, one must take account of the aim and intention of the law, that is, the teleological aspect.

This law had and has the aim of ensuring the permanence, development and reinforcement of the democratic system. It is therefore a law to safeguard human rights, since without democracy there can be no respect for human rights and without respect for human rights there can be no democracy.

If democracy ceased to exist, all human rights would disappear. Consequently this law, which was born of an exceptional situation has to be considered as a law to enable democracy and human rights to exist as a genuine reality, as the present and future expression of something that comes from the everlasting aspiration of the Uruguayan people to live in freedom and justice under a government created by the legitimate expression of its political will and with the capability to impose the rule of law....

12. One final word. The Government that I have the honor to lead recognizes that Amnesty International is worthy of respect and accords it this respect.... It would be very regrettable were Amnesty International involuntarily to associate itself, whether through error, oversight or ingenuousness, with an anti-government campaign which, with a few exceptions, is waged by those who defend human rights on a selective basis and only when it suits their partisan ends and many of whom, moreover, do not believe in human rights by virtue of belonging to organizations dedicated to violence and subversion in times of democracy.

Yours sincerely,

Julio Maria Sanguinetti

URUGUAY: ORGANIZATION OF AMERICAN STATES, INTER-AMERICAN COMMISSION ON HUMAN RIGHTS— DECISION ON THE *LEY DE CADUCIDAD*

Report No. 29/92
Cases 10.029, 10.036, 10.145, 10.305,
10.372, 10.373, 10.374 and 10.375

(October 2, 1992)

I. Introduction

1. Between June 16, 1987 and April 7, 1989, the Inter-American Commission on Human Rights, (hereinafter "the Commission") received a total of eight petitions, filed against the Uruguayan State:...

2. The petitions denounced the legal effects of Law No. 15,848 (hereinafter "the Law") and its application by the Judiciary, which they allege violated rights upheld in the American Convention (hereinafter "the Convention"): the right to judicial protection (Article 25) and the right to a fair trial (Article 8), among others....

6. Since the Executive Branch entrusted the investigation to military judges, doubts were raised as to the seriousness and impartiality of the investigative proceeding, and as to whether the duty to provide the essential judicial guarantees has been observed (Articles 8 and 27 of the Convention).

7. The law was declared constitutional by the Uruguayan Supreme Court and was approved by a national referendum called for that purpose pursuant to the provisions of Article 79 of the Uruguayan Constitution.

II. Summary of the Petitions and the Government's Reply

...9. All the petitions ... cite the effects of the law as a fundamental violation of the Convention. The petitioners contend that inasmuch as the law denies them their right to turn to the courts as a last resort, a thorough and impartial investigation of the human rights violations that occurred during the past *de facto* government is being obstructed.

10. Consequently, the petitioners allege that the law violates Articles 25 and 8 of the Convention in relation to Article 1.1 thereof, in that its judicial effect has been to deny them their right to judicial protection from the courts and to dismiss proceedings against those responsible for past human rights violations.

11. The basic position of the Government of Uruguay (hereinafter "the Government") has been that this legislative measure, which constitutes an exercise of its sovereign right to grant clemency, violates neither the Convention nor any other rule of international law. The Government alleged that the petitions were inadmissible because the domestic remedies had not

been exhausted. It argued that the petitioners could have filed suit for civil damages and that some of the petitioners took their cases as far as the Supreme Court. As for the merits of the case, it argued that the law was the result of a democratic decision and was found to be constitutional. It further alleged that the Convention provides for the suspension of the rights recognized therein and that this law was an integral part of a national reconciliation process.

III. The Processing in the Commission

...13. [T]he Commission held hearings during which it received the petitioners and government representatives.

14. Because the question that each petition raises is basically the same in all the petitions, the Commission has decided to join the cases and regard them as a single case....

IV. Observations of the Government on the Report Adopted in Accordance with Article 50

21. Essentially, the Government contends that the Commission has failed to consider the "democratic juridical-political context" inasmuch as it has not taken into account the domestic legitimacy of the law and has failed to consider important aspects of the present political situation, as well as the higher ethical ends of the Caducity Law [the *Ley de Caducidad*]. What follows is a summary of the principal arguments in the Government's reply.

22. The Government avers that the amnesty question should be viewed in the political context of the reconciliation, as part of a legislative program for national pacification that covered all actors involved in past human rights violations, i.e., "political crimes and related common and military crimes;" that the Caducity Law was adopted for "the sake of legal symmetry and for very justified and serious reasons of the utmost political importance," with "unqualified adherence to its constitutional system and its international commitments." Uruguay emphasizes the fact that this law, approved by the necessary parliamentary majority, was also "the subject of a plebiscite" by the electorate; that it cannot accept the Commission's finding that while the domestic legitimacy of the law is not within the Commission's purview, the legal effects denounced by the petitioners are; "the express will of the Uruguayan people to close a painful chapter in their history in order to put an end, as is their sovereign right, to division among Uruguayans, is not subject to international condemnation."

23. The Government pointed out that as with any treaty, the Convention must be interpreted in accordance with the principles embodied in the Vienna Convention on the Law of Treaties, in good faith and in the light of its object and purposes. Accordingly, it pointed out that Articles 8.1 and 25.1 of the Convention should be interpreted in the light of Articles 30 and 32 of the Convention, whereby the enjoyment and exercise of the rights recognized in the Convention can be restricted when such restrictions are the product of laws enacted for reasons of general interest or when those rights

are limited by the rights of others, by the security of all and by the just demands of the general welfare in a democratic society. The Government pointed out that the Caducity Law was enacted in exercise of an authority recognized in international law (Articles 6.4 and 14.6 of the International Covenant of Civil and Political Rights and Article 4.6 of the Convention).

24. The Government contends that Article 8.1 of the Convention refers to the rights of the accused in a criminal proceeding and not to someone filing a criminal action. The Government contends, further that the right to bring a criminal action, independently of the case brought by the public prosecutor, does not exist in Uruguayan procedural law; it further asserted that this right is not protected by international human rights law. It stated that private parties are not the owners of a criminal action and that only in exceptional cases is a private interest allowed to intervene. Criminal proceedings are public and only the State has the authority to waive the exercise of that right. The only thing that the law declared expired was the power of the public prosecutor to bring charges in a court of criminal law.

25. As for Article 25.1 of the Convention, the Government argued that its purpose was to "redress the injured right and, if not, secure reparation for the damage suffered"; that since, in the cases being denounced, it is impossible to redress rights injured during the *de facto* regime, all that remains is the right to damages, which the Caducity Law has in no way impaired.

26. The Government alleges that it did not violate its obligation to investigate and punish violations of human rights in accordance with the interpretation of Article 1.1 of the Convention as rendered by the Inter-American Court of Human Rights. It asserted that the Caducity Law "waived exercise of the State's punitive power and regulated the duty to investigate in the spirit of and in keeping with the objectives of that legislative act of sovereign clemency." Therefore "the law had not in any way affected the individual human right in question, since criminal law is confined to the denunciation of the crime." Consequently the duty to investigate and the question of an amnesty law must be analyzed as a whole. In this case, the expiry of the State's punitive intention is for the sake of the common good, since "investigating facts that occurred in the past could rekindle the animosity between persons and groups, and obstruct the reconciliation, pacification and strengthening of democratic institutions. Knowledge of the truth is a legitimate aspiration on anyone's part and the legal system should make available to the interested party the procedural means to that end; but, for those same reasons, the State may opt "not to make available to the interested party the means necessary for a formal and official inquiry into the facts in a court of law."

27. The Government further contended that the Commission had failed to note that the Caducity Law does not prevent the injured party from seeking damages in a civil court; hence, the recommendation made to the Government that the victims be awarded just compensation for past human rights violations was out of order.

V. The Opinion and Conclusions of the Commission

30. The question in these cases is not the domestic legitimacy of the legislation and other measures adopted by the Government to achieve the effect herein denounced. Under long-standing principles of international law and under specific provisions contained in the Convention, the Commission is obliged to determine whether certain of its effects constitute a violation of the obligation undertaken by the Government under the Convention (Article 27 of the Vienna Convention on the Law of Treaties).

31. As for the domestic legitimacy and the "approval of the Caducity Law by a popular referendum," it should be noted that it is not up to the Commission to rule on the domestic legality or constitutionality of national laws. However, application of the Convention and examination of the legal effects of a legislative measure, either judicial or of any other nature, insofar as it has effects incompatible with the rights and guarantees embodied in the Convention or the American Declaration, are within the Commission's competence....

A. As to the Interpretation of the Convention

33. Article 29 of the Convention stipulates the following:

> No provision of this Convention shall be interpreted as:
> a.   permitting any State Party, group, or person to suppress the enjoyment or exercise of the rights and freedoms recognized in this Convention or to restrict them to a greater extent than is provided for herein;
> b.   restricting the enjoyment or exercise of any right or freedom recognized by virtue of the laws of any State Party or by virtue of another Convention to which one of the said States is a party;
> c.   precluding other rights or guarantees that are inherent in the human personality or derived from representative democracy as a form of government; or
> d.   excluding or limiting the effect that the American Declaration of the Rights and Duties of Man and other international acts of the same nature may have.

34. The Commission notes that any interpretation of the Convention must be rendered in accordance with this provision.

B. As to the Right to a Fair Trial

35. The law in question has the intended effect of dismissing all criminal proceedings involving past human rights violations. With that, the law eliminates any judicial possibility of a serious and impartial investigation designed to establish the crimes denounced and to identify their authors, accomplices, and accessories after the fact.

36. The Commission must also consider the fact that in Uruguay, no national investigatory commission was ever set up nor was there any official report on the very grave human rights violations committed during the previous *de facto* government.

37. It is fitting, in this, regard, to cite the Commission's general position on the subject, as set forth in its Annual Report of 1985-1986:

> ...one of the few matters that the Commission feels obliged to give its opinion in this regard is the need to investigate the human rights violations committed prior to the establishment of the democratic government. Every society has the inalienable right to know the truth about past events, as well as the motive and circumstances in which aberrant crimes came to be committed, in order to prevent a repetition of such acts in the future. Moreover, the family members of the victims are entitled to information as to what happened to their relatives. Such access to the truth presupposes freedom of speech, which of course should be exercised responsibly; the establishment of *investigating committees* whose membership and authority must be determined in accordance with the internal legislation of each country, or the provision of the necessary resources so that the *judiciary* itself may undertake whatever investigations may be necessary.[2] (Emphasis added)

38. The Commission must also weigh the nature and gravity of the events with which the law concerns itself; alleged disappearances of persons and the abduction of minors, among others, have been widely condemned as a particularly grave violation of human rights. The social imperative of their clarification and investigation cannot be equated with that of a mere common crime.

39. The law under examination had various effects and adversely affected any number of parties or legal interests. Specifically the victims, next-of-kin or parties injured by human rights violations have been denied their right to legal redress, to an impartial and exhaustive judicial investigation that clarifies the facts, ascertains those responsible and imposes the corresponding criminal punishment.

40. What is denounced as being incompatible with the Convention are the legal consequences of the law with respect to the right to a fair trial. One of the law's effects was to deny the victim or his rightful claimant the opportunity to participate in the criminal proceedings, which is the appropriate means to investigate the commission of the crimes denounced, determine criminal liability and impose punishment on the those responsible, their accomplices and accessories after the fact.

41. The Commission is not taking issue with the public and official nature of criminal proceedings. However, in Uruguay the victim or injured party does have a right to participate in the criminal proceeding beyond the indictment. The Uruguayan Code of Criminal Procedure authorizes the injured party to request, during the summary proceedings, all measures that may be useful in ascertaining the crime and determining those responsible (Article 80). Consequently, in systems that allow it, the victim of the crime has access to the courts because of a citizen's fundamental right, which becomes particularly important as a dynamic of the criminal process.

---

2 Annual Report of the Inter-American Commission on Human Rights, 1985-1986, page 205.

42. To answer the question of whether the rights of the victim or his next-of-kin, guaranteed under domestic law, are protected by international human rights law, one must determine: a) whether the rights embodied in the constitution and the laws of that State at the time the violations occurred became subject to international protection through subsequent ratification of the Convention, and b) whether those rights can be abrogated absolutely through subsequent enactment of a special law, without violating the Convention or the American Declaration.

43. Article 1.1 of the Convention makes it the duty of the States Parties "to respect the rights and freedoms recognized herein and to ensure to all persons subject to their jurisdiction the free and full exercise of those rights and freedoms.... "

44. Article 8.1 of the Convention states the following:

> Every person has the right to a hearing with due guarantees and within a reasonable time, by a competent, independent, and impartial tribunal, previously established by law, in the substantiation of any accusation of a criminal nature made against him or for the determination of his rights and obligations of a civil, labor, fiscal or any other nature.

45. The intended effect of the law, and the effect that was in fact achieved, was to prevent the petitioners from exercising the rights upheld in Article 8.1.

46. By enacting and applying the Law the Uruguayan Government failed to abide by the obligation to guarantee observance of the rights recognized in Article 8.1, and thereby infringed those rights and violated the convention.

C. With Respect to the Right to Judicial Protection

47. Article 25.1 of the Convention stipulates the following:

> Everyone has the right to simple and prompt recourse, or any other effective recourse, to a competent court or tribunal for protection against acts that violate his fundamental rights recognized by the constitution or laws of the State concerned or by this Convention, even though such violation may have been committed by persons acting in the course of their official duties.

48. Article 25.2 stipulates the following:

> The States parties undertake:
> a. To ensure that any person claiming such remedy shall have his right determined by the competent authority provided for by the legal system of the State;
> b. To develop the possibilities of judicial remedy; and
> c. To ensure that the competent authorities shall enforce such remedies when granted.

49. When it enacted the law, Uruguay ceased to guarantee the rights stipulated in Article 25.1 and violated the Convention.

D. With Respect to the Obligation to Investigate

50. When interpreting the scope of Article 1.1, the Inter-American Court of Human Rights stated that "the second obligation of the States Parties is to 'ensure' the free and full exercise of the rights recognized by the Convention to every person subject to its jurisdiction.... As a consequence of this obligation, the States must *prevent, investigate and punish any violation* of the rights recognized by the Convention...."[3] The Court elaborates upon that concept in several paragraphs that follow: "What is decisive is whether a violation of the rights recognized by the Convention has occurred with the *support or the acquiescence of the government,* or whether the State has allowed the act to take place without taking measures to prevent it or to punish those responsible;"[4] "The State has a *legal duty* to take reasonable steps to prevent human rights violations, and to use the means at its disposal to carry out a *serious investigation* of violations committed within its jurisdiction, *to identify those responsible, to impose the appropriate punishment* and to ensure the victim adequate compensation;[5] "If the *State apparatus* acts in such a way that the *violation goes unpunished* and the victim's full enjoyment of such rights is not restored as soon as possible, *the State has failed to comply with its duty to ensure the free and full exercise of those rights to the persons* within its jurisdiction".[6] As for the obligation to investigate, the Court notes that "An investigation must have an objective and be *assumed by the State as its own legal duty, not as a step taken by private interests* that depends upon the initiative of the victim or his family or upon their offer of proof, without *an effective search for the truth by the Government....*"[7] (Emphasis added by the Commission).

51. When it enacted this law, Uruguay ceased to comply fully with the obligation stipulated in Article 1.1 and violated the petitioners' rights upheld in the Convention.

52. As for the interpretation of Article 1.1, Article 8.1 and Article 25.1, and the possible restrictions on those rights as set forth in Articles 30 and 32, the Commission respects but nevertheless disagrees with the Uruguayan Government's" interpretation of those provisions.

53. As for compensatory damages, the Commission points out that while it is true that the text of the law did not affect the possibility of filing a suit for such damages, the ability to establish the crime in a civil court has been considerably curtailed since vital testimony from the moral and material authors, military and police personnel of the State, cannot be adduced or used. The Commission also noted that four years after the fact, the State invoked the caducity exception, even though at the time the crimes were committed a dictatorial government was in power whose judiciary

---

[3] Inter-American Court of Human Rights, Velásquez Rodríguez Case, Judgment of July 29, 1988. Series C, No. 4, paragraph 166.

[4] *Ibid*, paragraph 173.

[5] *Ibid*, paragraph 174.

[6] *Ibid*, paragraph 176.

[7] *Ibid*, paragraph 177.

lacked any independence, especially in matters of this nature. In the past year, the Commission has noted, with satisfaction, a number of important damages agreements that the Uruguayan State and certain victims of past human rights violations have reached, including three petitioners in these cases. Nevertheless, the Commission must make clear that the purpose of these petitions is to object to the denial of justice (Articles 8 and 25 in relation to Article 1 of the Convention) with enactment and application of the 1986 Law, and not to the violations of the rights to life (Article 4), humane treatment (Article 5) and liberty (Article 7), among others, which triggered the right to a fair trial and the right to judicial protection, but that occurred before the Convention entered into force for Uruguay on April 19, 1985, and therefore were not a subject of these complaints.

54. The Commission has carefully weighed the political and ethical dimensions of the measure adopted by the Uruguayan Government and reached a conclusion different from that of the Government as to whether, with the law, the Government's highest mission according to the obligations of the American Convention, which is to defend and promote human rights, is being served.

Given the foregoing considerations, the *Inter-American Commission on Human Rights*:

1. Concludes that Law 15,848 of December 22, 1986, is incompatible with Article XVIII (Right to a Fair Trial) of the American Declaration of the Rights and Duties of Man, and Articles 1, 8 and 25 of the American Convention on Human Rights.

2. Recommends to the Government of Uruguay that it give the applicant victims or their rightful claimants just compensation for the violations to which the preceding paragraph refers.

3. Recommends to the Government of Uruguay that it adopt the measures necessary to clarify the facts and identify those responsible for the human rights violations that occurred during the *de facto* period....

5

STATUTES OF LIMITATIONS

CONVENTION ON THE NON-APPLICABILITY OF STATUTORY LIMITATIONS TO WAR CRIMES AND CRIMES AGAINST HUMANITY

Adopted and opened for signature, ratification and accession by United Nations General Assembly Resolution 2391 (XXIII) of 26 November 1968 Entry Into Force: 11 November 1970, in accordance with Article VIII.

Preamble

The States Parties to the present Convention,

Recalling resolutions of the General Assembly of the United Nations 3 (I) of 13 February 1946 and 170 (II) of 31 October 1947 on the extradition and punishment of war criminals, resolution 95 (I) of 11 December 1946 affirming the principles of international law recognized by the Charter of the International Military Tribunal, Nürnberg, and the judgment of the Tribunal, and resolutions 2184 (XXI) of 12 December 1966 and 2202 (XXI) of 16 December 1966 which expressly condemned as crimes against humanity the violation of the economic and political rights of the indigenous population on the one hand and the policies of *apartheid* on the other,

Recalling resolutions of the Economic and Social Council of the United Nations 1074 D (XXXIX) of 28 July 1965 and 1158 (XLI) of 5 August 1966 on the punishment or war criminals and of persons who have committed crimes against humanity.

Noting that none of the solemn declarations, instruments or conventions relating to the prosecution and punishment of war crimes and crimes against humanity made provision for a period of limitation,

Considering that war crimes and crimes against humanity are among the gravest crimes in international law,

Convinced that the effective punishment of war crimes and crimes against humanity is an important element in the prevention of such crimes, the protection of human rights and fundamental freedoms, the encouragement of confidence, the furtherance of cooperation among peoples and the promotion of international peace and security,

Noting that the application to war crimes and crimes against humanity of the rules of municipal law relating to the period of limitation for ordinary crimes is a matter of serious concern to world public opinion, since it prevents the prosecution and punishment of persons responsible for those crimes,

Recognizing that it is necessary and timely to affirm in international law, through this Convention, the principle that there is no period of limitation for war crimes and crimes against humanity, and to secure its universal application,

Have agreed as follows:

Article I

No statutory limitation shall apply to the following crimes, irrespective of the date of their commission:

(a) War crimes as they are defined in the Charter of the International Military Tribunal, Nürnberg, of 8 August 1945 and confirmed by resolutions 3 (I) of 13 February 1946 and 95 (I) of 11 December 1946 of the General Assembly of the United Nations, particularly the "grave breaches" enumerated in the Geneva Conventions of 12 August 1949 for the protection of war victims;

(b) Crimes against humanity whether committed in time of war or in time of peace as they are defined in the Charter of the International Military Tribunal, Nürnberg, of 8 August 1945 and confirmed by resolutions 3 (I) of 13 February 1946 and 95 (I) of 11 December 1946 of the General Assembly of the United Nations, eviction by armed attack or occupation and inhuman acts resulting from the policy of *apartheid*, and the crime of genocide as defined in the 1948 Convention on the Prevention and Punishment of the Crime of Genocide, even if such acts do not constitute a violation of the domestic law of the country in which they were committed.

Article II

If any of the crimes mentioned in Article I is committed, the provisions of this Convention shall apply to representatives of the State authority and private individuals who, as principals or accomplices, participate in or who directly incite others to the commission of any of those crimes, or who conspire to commit them, irrespective of the degree of completion, and to representatives of the State authority who tolerate their commission.

Article III

The States Parties to the present Convention undertake to adopt all necessary domestic measures, legislative or otherwise, with a view to making possible the extradition, in accordance with international law, of the persons referred to in Article II of this Convention.

Article IV

The States Parties to the present Convention undertake to adopt, in accordance with their respective constitutional processes, any legislative or other measures necessary to ensure that statutory or other limitations shall not apply to the prosecution and punishment of the crimes referred to in Articles I and II of this Convention and that, where they exist, such limitations shall be abolished....

European Convention on the Non-Applicability of Statutory Limitations to Crimes Against Humanity and War Crimes

Council of Europe
(January 25, 1974)

The member States of the Council of Europe, signatory hereto,

Considering the necessity to safeguard human dignity in time of war and in time of peace;

Considering that crimes against humanity and the most serious violations of the laws and customs of war constitute a serious infraction of human dignity;

Concerned in consequence to ensure that the punishment of those crimes is not prevented by statutory limitations whether in relation to prosecution or to the enforcement of the punishment;

Considering the essential interest in promoting a common criminal policy in this field, the aim of the Council of Europe being to achieve a greater unity between its members;

Have agreed as follows:

Article 1

Each Contracting State undertakes to adopt any necessary measures to secure that statutory limitation shall not apply to the prosecution of the following offences, or to the enforcement of the sentences imposed for such offences, in so far as they are punishable under its domestic law:

1. the crimes against humanity specified in the Convention on the Prevention and Punishment of the Crime of Genocide adopted on 9 December 1948 by the General Assembly of the United Nations;

2. (a) the violations specified in Article 50 of the 1949 Geneva Convention for the Amelioration of the Condition of the Wounded and Sick in Armed Forces in the Field, Article 51 of the 1949 Geneva Convention for the Amelioration of the Condition of Wounded, Sick and Shipwrecked Members of Armed Forces at Sea, Article 130 of the 1949 Geneva Convention relative to the Treatment of Prisoners of War and Article 147 of the 1949 Geneva Convention relative to the Protection of Civilian Persons in Time of War;

(b) any comparable violations of the laws of war having effect at the time when this Convention enters into force and of customs of war existing at that time, which are not already provided for in the above-mentioned provisions of the Geneva Conventions, when the specific violation under consideration is of a particularly grave character by reason either of its factual and intentional elements or of the extent of its foreseeable consequences;

3. any other violation of a rule or custom of international law which may hereafter be established and which the Contracting State concerned considers according to a declaration under Article 6 as being of a comparable nature to those referred to in paragraph 1 or 2 of this Article.

Article 2

1. The present Convention applies to offences committed after its entry into force in respect of the Contracting State concerned.

2. It applies also to offences committed before such entry into force in those cases where the statutory limitation period had not expired at that time.

Article 3

1. This Convention shall be open to signature by the member States of the Council of Europe. It shall be subject to ratification or acceptance. Instruments of ratification or acceptance shall be deposited with the Secretary General of the Council of Europe.

2. The Convention shall enter into force three months after the date of deposit of the third instrument of ratification or acceptance.

3. In respect of a signatory State ratifying or accepting subsequently, the Convention shall come into force three months after the date of the deposit of its instrument of ratification or acceptance.

Article 4

1. After the entry into force of this Convention, the Committee of Ministers of the Council of Europe may invite any non-member State to accede thereto, provided that the resolution containing such invitation receives the unanimous agreement of the Members of the Council who have ratified the Convention.

2. Such accession shall be effected by depositing with the Secretary General of the Council of Europe an instrument of accession which shall take effect three months after the date of its deposit.

Article 5

1. Any State may, at the time of signature or when depositing its instrument of ratification, acceptance or accession, specify the territory or territories to which this Convention shall apply.

2. Any State may, when depositing its instrument of ratification, acceptance or accession or at any later date, by declaration addressed to the Secretary General of the Council of Europe, extend this Convention to any other territory or territories specified in the declaration and for whose

international relations it is responsible or on whose behalf it is authorised to give undertakings.

3. Any declaration made in pursuance of the preceding paragraph may, in respect of any territory mentioned in such declaration, be withdrawn according to the procedure laid down in Article 7 of this Convention.

Article 6

1. Any Contracting State may, at any time, by declaration addressed to the Secretary General of the Council of Europe, extend this Convention to any violations provided for in Article 1, paragraph 3 of this Convention.

2. Any declaration made in pursuance of the preceding paragraph may be withdrawn according to the procedure laid down in Article 7 of this Convention.

Article 7

1. This Convention shall remain in force indefinitely.

2. Any Contracting State may, insofar as it is concerned, denounce this Convention by means of a notification addressed to the Secretary General of the Council of Europe.

3. Such denunciation shall take effect six months after the date of receipt by the Secretary General of such notification.

Article 8

The Secretary General of the Council of Europe shall notify the member States of the Council and any State which has acceded to this Convention of:

(a) any signature;

(b) any deposit of an instrument of ratification, acceptance or accession;

(c) any date of entry into force of this Convention in accordance with Article 3 thereof;

(d) any declaration received in pursuance of the provisions of Article 5 or Article 6;

(e) any notification received in pursuance of the provisions of Article 7 and the date on which the denunciation takes effect.

CZECH REPUBLIC: CONSTITUTIONAL COURT DECISION ON THE ACT ON THE ILLEGALITY OF THE COMMUNIST REGIME

(December 21, 1993)

On 21 December 1993, the Plenum of the Constitutional Court of the Czech Republic ... concerning the petition of submitted by a group of Deputies to the Parliament of the Czech Republic seeking the annulment of Act No. 198/1993, on the Illegality of the Communist Regime and Resistance to It,[*] decided thusly:

The petition is rejected.

Reasoning

On 15 September 1993, a group of 41 Deputies of the Parliament of the Czech Republic submitted a petition requesting that the Constitutional Court, on the basis of Article 87, paragraph 1, letter (a) of the Constitution of the Czech Republic, annul Act No. 198/1993, on the Illegality of the Communist Regime and Resistance to It....

The main object of the group of Deputies' criticism is Article 5 of Act No. 198/1993, according to which "the period of time from 25 February 1948 until 29 December 1989 shall not be counted as part of the limitation period for criminal acts if, due to political reasons incompatible with the basic principles of the legal order of a democratic State, [a person] was not finally and validly convicted or the charges [against him] were dismissed."

According to the petitioners' view "...the fact that State bodies, which no longer exist and formerly had competence over criminal matters, were, *for whatever reason*, inactive or ineffectual and brought on the termination of criminal liability for certain acts by virtue of the expiration of the limitations period, was not and is not a component of the subjective element [the *mens rea* or culpability requirement] of a criminal act, came about independently of the will of the offender, and therefore may not be to his detriment."

Thus, the Constitutional Court is, in the first place, concerned with the question why the "formerly competent State bodies [were] inactive and ineffectual," and further with the question whether the reasons for their failure to criminally prosecute politically shielded offenses, by their significance, their extent and their consequences to society, justify the measures in Article 5 of Act No. 198/1993.

At the same time, the Constitutional Court proceeds from the recognition that the constitutional law texts of the communist regime merely formulated a principle of legality that was general and equally applicable to

---

[*] [Editor's note: The Act, together with another portion of this Constitutional Court decision, appears in Chapter 3 of the present volume.]

all (or the so-called socialist legality). As early as the Constitution of 9 May (No. 150/1948), the duty to uphold the constitution and laws (Article 30) was imposed on every citizen regardless of office or official position.... However, these legal norms became fictional and hollow whenever the party recognized such to be advantageous for its political interests. Its monopoly on political and governmental power and the bureaucratically centralized organization of them were constructed upon this simple expedient.... The authorities in charge of the protection of legality thus became instruments of the central monopoly power.

In the period from 1948 to 1989, the regime of illegality that went unprosecuted attained a massive scope: starting with the purges in 1948, through the illegal way in which agriculture was collectivized, the transfer of 77,500 employees of administrative bodies to manufacturing work in 1951, the arrests and executions in the context of the so-called fight against agents of imperialism, to the preparations for invasion of the Warsaw Pact armies, the illegality of the so-called normalization process and the firings and prosecutions of political dissidents on a massive scale....

Although the Deputies' petition seeking the annulment of the Act regarding the Illegality of the Communist Regime and Resistance to It does not generally dispute that, during the given period, illegal activities occurred and that the State did not prosecute them, even though it knew about them; however, it is clear from the type of arguments they make that, as regards the extent and implications of these cases, they do not consider them worthy of special attention or special resolution. Rather, the group of Deputies bases its arguments on juristically worded objections which can be summarized as follows:

(1) ...By excluding the period from 25 February 1948 until 29 December 1989 from the running of the limitation period, [the Act] considerably extends the limitation period, leading to the destabilization of rights and an infringement of citizens' legal certainty;

(2) Paragraph 5 infringes a principle of law-based States, that criminal liability many not be revived once it has been extinguished by the expiration of the limitation period, and it introduces retroactive effect ... of statutes, otherwise permissible only in instances where the subsequent statute is more favorable to the offender. According to the petitioners, this situation violates Article 40, paragraph 6 of the Charter of Fundamental Rights and Basic Freedoms, as well as the Czech Republic's international legal obligations;

(3) Alongside the preceding argument on the anti-constitutionality of retroactivity, the petition also raises its incompatibility with Article 1 of the Charter concerning the equality of all persons before the law and Article 40, paragraph 6 of the Charter, according to which the criminal liability of an act should be judged in accordance with the laws in force when the act was committed....

The introduction of new legal impediments to the running of the statutory period limiting the right to bring a criminal prosecution is not, in and of itself, unconstitutional, which means that the Constitutional Court would not be required to deal with the matter at all. However, this claim relates to issues which affect the evaluation of the other objections raised against Article 5 of Act No. 198/1993, so that we can not pass over it.

Act No. 198/1993 itself does not alter the regulation of the legal institution of the limitation of criminal prosecutions. According to Article 67, paragraph 2 of the Criminal Act No. 140/1961, as subsequently amended, periods of time when it was not possible to bring an offender before a court due to legal impediments, as well as periods when he remained abroad, are not counted as part of the limitation period. Nor does the length of the limitation period set down in Article 67, paragraph 1 of the Criminal Act change: it is twenty years when the act permits the imposition of an exceptional punishment, ten years if the upper limit of the sentencing scale is likewise ten years, five years if the punishment could be as long as three years, and three years for other criminal acts.

Paragraph five of Act No. 198/1993 neither modifies the scale of the limitation period nor creates any further (new) legal impediments to the running of the limitation period beyond those which, on the basis of Article 67, paragraph 2 of the Criminal Act, already exist....

Therefore, in assessing Article 5 of Act No. 198/1993, we are not concerned either generally with the institution of the limitation of actions as such, or with the introduction of a new statutory impediment to the running of the limitation period, rather with the question whether the institution of the limitation of actions should be viewed as real or as fictional for a period when the infringement of legality in the entire sphere of legal life became a component of the politically as well as governmentally protected regime of illegality. Paragraph five of Act 198/1993 is not a constitutive norm, rather a declaratory norm. It is merely a declaration that during a certain stretch of time and for a certain type of criminal act the limitation period could not run, as well as the reason therefor. It is well-known that, apart from those areas of societal and individual life where the legal order from 1948 to 1989 retained a certain real significance and was based on legality, there were also spheres of the ruling class' political interest in which a condition of legal uncertainty existed and which the regime maintained as a measure of preventive self-defense and as an instrument for the manipulation of society.

The criminal behavior of person in political and governmental positions, inspired or tolerated by the political regime when, in consideration of its actual or supposed interests, the governing class found it expedient to contravene even its own laws. The group of Deputies is not at all credible in its arguments that the limitation period was running during that era even for this category of governmental and political criminal behavior, that carried out entirely by the State.... The State became much rather a guarantor of their non-sanctionability and their actual criminal law immunity....

An indispensable component of the concept of the limitation of the right to bring a criminal prosecution is the intention, efforts and readiness on the part of the State to prosecute a criminal act. Without these prerequisites, the content of the concept is not complete, nor can the purpose of this legal institution be fulfilled. That happens only if there has been a long-term interaction of two elements: the intention and the efforts of the State to punish an offender and the ongoing danger to the offender that he may be punished, both giving a real meaning to the institution of the limitation of actions. If the State does not want to prosecute certain criminal acts or certain offenders, then the limitation of actions is pointless: in such cases, the running of the limitation period does not take place in reality and the limitation of actions, in and of itself, is fictitious. Written law is deprived of the possibility of being applied. In order for a criminal act to become statute-barred, it would be necessary for the process involved in the running of the limitation period to proceed, that is, a period of time during which the State makes efforts to criminally prosecute the offender is necessary. An action is barred at the end of the limitation period, only if at the time the ongoing efforts of the State to prosecute a criminal act remain futile. This prerequisite cannot be met for the category of politically protected offenses from 1948 until 1989. The condition of mass, State-protected illegal activities was not the consequence of individual errors, blunders, negligence or misdeeds, which would have left open some possibility for criminal prosecution, rather it was the consequence of the purposeful and collective behavior of the political and State authorities *as a whole*, which ruled out criminal prosecution in advance. By these means, the protection of offenders became as universal as the system of power.

Therefore, we cannot agree with the petitioners' position that an *a priori* awareness of the non-prosecutability of certain offenses was not a part of the subjective element of these criminal acts and that this "quasi limitation of actions" ran independently of the intent of the offender. The situation is different for the offenders under the political protection of the State. Their criminal act was *de facto* "statute-barred," even before it was committed. This fact sometimes functioned precisely as an incentive to additional criminal acts.... There was a type of "legal certainty" which the perpetrators of such criminal acts already had when they began their activities and which consists of State-assured immunity from criminal liability.

This "legal certainty" of offenders is, however, a source of legal uncertainty to citizens (and vice versa). In a contest of these two types of certainty, the Constitutional Court gives priority to the certainty of civil society, which is in keeping with the idea of a law-based State. Some other solution would mean conferring upon a totalitarian dictatorship a stamp of approval as a law-based State, a dangerous portent for the future: a sign that crime may become non-criminal, so long as it is organized on a massive scale and carried out over a long period of time under the protection of an organization empowered by the State. That would mean the loss of credibility of the present law-based State, as well as the current infringement of Article 9, paragraph 3 of the Constitution of the Czech Republic "...legal norms may not be interpreted so as to justify eliminating or jeopardizing the foundations of a democratic State."...

A requirement for a law-based State is the maintenance of a state of trust in the durability of legal rules. The perpetrators of this type of criminal activity do not have the continuity of written law in mind, rather that of unwritten practices. It would be an infringement of the continuity of written law, if the violation of law, which was committed under the protection of the State, could not even now be criminally prosecuted.

All of these individual points of view gain significance in direct proportion to the considerable extent of which this form of State-protected or tolerated political criminal behavior was committed. In forced labor camps and in the so-called auxiliary technical battalions alone, over 200,000 persons were held during this period of time. As is known, nearly a quarter of a million persons have already been rehabilitated on the basis of the Act on Legal Rehabilitation. In many of these cases of rehabilitation, the power apparatus' violation of its own legal principles was an important, if not the principal factor....

[I]t is necessary to assess to what extent the provision of Article 40, paragraph 6 of the Charter of Fundamental Rights and Basic Freedoms or Article 15 of the International Convention on Civil and Political Rights (No. 120/1976) prevents a subsequent amendment to the procedural rules, making possible the subsequent running of the limitation period in those special cases when the prior political regime prevented it from running.

Under Article 40, paragraph 6 of the Charter, criminal liability for an act should be judged and punishment imposed in accordance with the laws in effect when the act took place. A subsequent statute shall be applied if it is more favorable to the offender. Article 15 of the Convention is worded according to the same sense and, in addition, paragraph 2 makes it possible to punish acts in accordance with "the general principles of law recognized by the community of nations."

Article 40, paragraph 6 the Charter of Fundamental Rights and Basic Freedoms defines and restricts the prohibition on the retroactive effect of statutes in two respects, namely:

(a) if a "criminal act" is concerned, or
(b) if the "imposition of punishment" is concerned....

Article 40, paragraph 6 of the Charter manifestly does not permit the retroactivity of a statute where the definition of criminality or the severity of punishment is concerned.... Nothing more was intended by Article 40, paragraph 6 than what is stated, namely that the definition of individual criminal acts and of their criminal nature, which is effected under the Criminal Act by the designation of their specific characteristic features and the degree of danger which the individual acts pose to society; it may not be *ex post*, an amendment to the detriment of the offender adopted subsequently to the commission of an act. The same requirements are also set for the definition and setting of the length of punishment. The second sentence of paragraph 6 defines the prohibition of the retroactivity of law only in this sense and to this extent....

Neither in the Czech Republic, nor in other democratic States does the issue of the procedural requirements for a criminal prosecution in general, and that of the limitation of actions in particular, rank among the principal fundamental rights and basic freedoms which, under Article 3 of the Constitution, form a part of the constitutional order of the Czech Republic and, thus take the place of the usual chapter in a constitution on fundamental rights and basic freedoms found in other constitutions.

The argument that the limitation of actions is an institution of substantive criminal law is not crucial to judgment in this matter, not only due to the fact that the issue is an ongoing subject of dispute in criminal law doctrine and that in several other democratic States it is considered, for the most part, as a procedural law institution, but first and foremost due to the fact that neither the Constitution nor the Charter of Fundamental (and not of other) Rights and Basic Freedoms resolve detailed issues of criminal law, but set down, in the first place, uncontested and basic constitutive principles of the State and of law. Article 40, paragraph 6 of the Charter of Fundamental Rights and Basic Freedoms deals with the issue of *which* criminal acts may in principle be prosecuted (namely those which were defined by law at the time the act was committed) and does not govern the issue of *for how long* these acts may be prosecuted. As a consequence, the regulations on the limitation of actions and on the limitation period, especially those setting the period during which an act which is declared to be criminal may be prosecuted, cannot be understood to be an area governed by Article 40, paragraph 6 of the Charter.... The procedural requirements for prosecution are not the subject of this reservation.

From among the European judicature, we can refer to the same point of view of the Federal Constitutional Court of the [Federal Republic of Germany], which in 1969 ruled that the prohibition on the retroactivity of statutes did not apply to the statute of limitations: the subsequent designation of criminality or of a higher possible punishment fall under this prohibition, but not the limitation of actions, governing the period of time during which an act which is declared to be criminal may be prosecuted and leaving the criminality of an act unaffected....[1]

The group of Deputies also detect in 5 of Act No. 198/1993 a violation of Article 1 of the Charter of Fundamental Rights and Basic Freedoms concerning the equality of all persons before the law because—as they assert—it involves discrimination against one segment of the citizenry because those who were not put on trial, for reasons that were not political, will still enjoy the right not to be prosecuted, while this right is denied to others, if the political reasons they were not convicted or the charges against them were dropped.

---

[1] The statute on the "tolling" of the limitation period for the unlawful acts of the SED (the Socialist Unity Party of East Germany) of March 1993 proceeds from the same point of view. Under this statute, in calculating the period of limitation for the prosecution of acts which were committed during the rule of the unlawful regime of the SED, but on the basis of the explicit or presumed wishes of the State or party leadership of the former GDR (German Democratic Republic), such acts were not prosecuted on political or other grounds incompatible with the free order of a law-based State, the period from 11 October 1949 until 2 October 1990 shall not be counted. Thus, a criminal prosecution may be instituted for acts which are already "statute-barred" before then. Later, a second statute regulated more precisely the running of the limitation period and excluded the criminal prosecution of acts which were statute-barred by a later deadline of 27 September 1993.

Equality before the law must always be judged in relation with the nature of the matter at issue. When assessing matters that are apparently, or even only in certain formal respects, identical, legislators must make efforts that they do not contradict the ideas of justice and reasonableness, which belong among the conceptual requirements of a law-based State.... In the case of Article 5 of Act No. 198/1993, it seems reasonable and just to extend the possibility of criminal prosecution for those criminal acts which, by the will of the political and State leadership, were earlier exempted from that possibility. In contrast to what the Deputies contend, this is the way to rectify the inequality with those who had already faced the possibility of being put on trial because, not only were they not under special political protection, but it was the State's wish and in its interest to prosecute them for the criminal acts which they committed.

Even under the law then in force, the principle of the equality of citizens before the law required a general investigation of criminal acts and a consistent and just application of the criminal law without regard to the identity of the offender.

With regard to the principle of the equality of citizens before the law, Article 5 of Act No. 198/1993 does not establish any special or extraordinary criminal law regime: Article 5 does not permit the principle of collective guilt or collective responsibility, nor does it alter the principle of the presumption of innocence or the prohibition of the retroactivity of statutes, which means that criminal prosecution is only possible for acts which were criminal at the time of their commission, and only on the basis of the law then in force, unless the subsequent statute is more favorable for the offender. Article 5 of Act No. 198/1993 merely alters the period of time during which a criminal prosecution may take place and defines only a certain category of such criminal acts for which this may be done, meaning those that the principle of the equality of citizens before the law makes necessary in order for a law-based State to maintain its credibility.

It follows from the definition of the criminal acts in Article 5 of Act No. 198/1993, that criminal prosecution on the basis of this provision is ruled out:

1. in the case of criminal acts the period of limitation for which has already expired since the start of the limitation period, that is since 30 December 1989;

2. in the case of criminal acts, when the former regime, as an exception, considered it expedient to show an effort to punish violations of legality by its agents; for these exceptional cases, the internationally recognized principle "*ne bis in idem*" applies, even if the final judgment of the former regime was extraordinary lenient;

3. in the case of criminal acts which did not result in a final, valid conviction or where the charges were dropped, not on political grounds incompatible with basic principles of a law-based State, but on grounds other than exactly political ones.

From the perspective of the equality of citizens before the law, comparability of treatment is maintained even in the respect that similarly to other—earlier punishable—criminal acts, it can be presumed that in this category of previous criminal acts, for which the limitation period has had the chance to run only afterwards, far from all these criminal acts will be tracked down, discovered and proven, so that obviously only a small part of this category of crimes is concerned. In reality, this category of criminal acts is not at all less favorably treated; it has actually enjoyed an advantage because the punishment of these acts is made more difficult due to the additional time, a long period, which has passed since the commission of the act, as well as the offenders' interest in the speeding removal of evidence and the difficulty of proving things after a long time interval....

GERMANY: ACT REPEALING THE STATUTE OF LIMITATIONS FOR THE CRIMES OF GENOCIDE AND MURDER

Sixteenth Act for the Amendment of Criminal Law (July 16, 1979)

Article 1
Amendment of the Criminal Code

§ 78 of the Criminal Code is amended as follows:

§ 78

(1) The statute of limitations excludes the imposition of sanctions for an act as well as the imposition of measures[1] (Article 11, Paragraph 1, No. 8).

(2) Crimes pursuant to Article 220a (genocide) and to Article 211 (murder) are not subject to the statute of limitations.[2]...

---

[1] [Translator's note: The so-called measures include in particular the commitment to a mental institution.]

[2] [Translator's note: The statute of limitations for murder was originally 20 years. In the case of Nazi crimes, this period was computed as starting from 1949. In the 1960s, the statute of limitations for murder was extended to 30 years. It was essential for the prosecution of Nazi criminals to lift the statute for murder in general, since only a prosecution for murder does not present ex post facto problems.]

HUNGARY: CONSTITUTIONAL COURT DECISION ON THE STATUTE OF LIMITATIONS

No. 2086/A/1991/14 (March 5, 1992)

Pursuant to the petition submitted by the President of the Republic seeking a constitutional review of the Law passed by Parliament but not yet signed into law, the Constitutional Court has made the following resolution:

The Constitutional Court holds that the Law passed during the November 4, 1991 session of Parliament concerning "the prosecutability of serious criminal offenses committed between December 21, 1944 and May 2, 1990 and not prosecuted for political reasons" is unconstitutional.

The vagueness and indeterminacy of the statutory language violates the requirement of the security of the law.

The Law violates the requirement of constitutional criminal law that statutes of limitation—including their tolling and re-commencement—must apply the Law in effect at the time of the commission of the offense except if during the running of a statute regulations more favorable to the defendant are introduced.

Concerning the question of the constitutionality of specific provisions of the Law, the Constitutional Court's opinion is the following:

1. Reimposition of criminal culpability for offenses for which the statutes of limitation had run is unconstitutional.
2. Extension of the statutes of limitation for criminal offenses for which the statutes have not yet run is unconstitutional.
3. Enactment of a law to recommence the running of the statutes of limitations for criminal offenses for which the statutes have not yet fully run is unconstitutional.
4. Tolling of the statutes of limitation by retroactive law is unconstitutional.
5. There is no constitutional basis for differentiating between the State's foregoing of its claim to punish for political or other reasons.
6. The vagueness of the declaration that the "State's foregoing of its claim to punish was based on political reasons" violates the security of the law and its invocation to toll the statutes of limitation is therefore deemed unconstitutional.
7. It is unconstitutional for a law to incorporate the crime of treason within its scope without consideration of the fact that the subject-matter subsumed by this category of criminal offense has undergone numerous modifications under different political systems.
8. Restriction of the right of clemency, in order to permit a partial or total mitigation of the lawfully prescribed punishment is unconstitutional.

Reasoning

I.

1. During the November 4, 1991 session of Parliament, the following Law was passed:

> 1. § (1) On May 2, 1990 the statute of limitation recommences for the prosecutability of criminal offenses committed between December 21, 1944 and May 2, 1990 which, constituting offenses by the Law in effect at their commission, are defined by the 1978 Law IV as treason (144 § (2)), voluntary manslaughter (166 § (1) and (2)), and infliction of bodily harm resulting in death (170 § (5)), provided that the State's foregoing of its claim to punish was based on political reasons.
>   (2) The punishment prescribed under Paragraph (1) can be mitigated without any restriction.
>
> 2. § This Law becomes effective on the day it is signed into law.

2. The President of the Republic did not sign it into law but on November 16, 1991 petitioned for the review of its constitutionality....

II

The Constitutional Court holds that the provisions of the Law are not unambiguous.

1. The vagueness of the statutory text allows the following deductions:

- that the statutes of limitation are recommenced for crimes for which the statutes had already run their courses;
- that, as of May 2, 1990, the statutes of limitation for crimes for which the statutes have not yet run are uniformly extended—irrespective of the time which had already lapsed; and likewise
- that with respect to some criminal offenses, the statutes of limitation had been tolled and their running would continue on the basis of this Law.

2. This Law defines the criminal offenses falling within its scope on the basis of the 1978 IV Law, thus ignoring that the legal definition of these offenses has changed on a number of occasions and in a variety of ways not only between 1944 and 1978 but also since 1978.

The overall ambiguity and vagueness of the Law offends the principle of the security of the Law and hence is unconstitutional.

III

The Law under review illustrates with unusual sharpness the relationship between the law of the preceding political system and the new Constitution-based on a State under the rule of law. For this reason, a separate summary of the Constitutional Court's viewpoint on this matter is warranted.

1. The October 23, 1989 enactment of the constitutional amendment in effect gave rise to a new Constitution which, with its declaration that "the Hungarian Republic is an independent, democratic State under the rule of law, conferred on the State, its law and the political system a new quality, fundamentally different from that of the previous era." In the context of constitutional law, this is the substance of the political category of the "change of system" (*rendszerváltás*).[3] Accordingly, an evaluation of the State measures necessitated by the "change of system" cannot be understood separate from the requirements of a State under the rule of law, as crystallized by the histories of constitutional democracies and also posited by the 1989 Hungarian constitutional revision. The Constitution defines the basic institutions of the the State under the rule of law's organization and their most important operative laws and delineates human and citizenship rights together with their basic guarantees.

That Hungary is a State under the rule of law is both a statement of fact and a statement of policy. A State under the rule of law becomes a reality when the Constitution is truly and unconditionally given effect. For the law the "change of system" means, and a change of legal systems can be possible only in this sense, that the Constitution of the State under the rule of law must be brought into harmony—and so maintained given new legislative activity—with the whole system of laws. Not only the regulations and the operation of the State organs must comport strictly with the Constitution but the Constitution's values and its "conceptual culture" must imbue the whole of society. This is the rule of law, this is how the Constitution becomes a reality. The realization of the State under the rule of law is an ongoing process. For the organs of the State, participation in this process is a constitutional duty.

2. ...The Constitutional Court was the first new organ of the State under the rule of law to commence operation. Already with its first resolution (1/1990(II.12)AB—concerning the effect of the November 26, 1989 referendum on the possibility of constitutional amendment) and with respect to other matters of political significance prior to the convocation of the new Parliament (such as the legal status of the temporary presidency of the Republic and matters pertaining to voting rights) the Constitutional Court made it clear that political endeavors of any kind must be realized within the constitutional framework, and that everyday political considerations are precluded from the adjudication of the constitutionality of the laws. From the beginning, the Constitutional Court has not differentiated in its constitutional reviews between pre- and post-constitutionally enacted laws.

3. The "change of system" proceeded on the basis of legality. The principle of legality imposes on the State under the rule of law the requirement that the regulations governing the legal system be given full

---

[3] [Translator's note: *Rendszerváltás* in the ordinary sense of the word designates any change of systems. However as a political category it designates Hungary's transition during 1898 and 1990 from a one-party state to a democratic one.]

effect. The politically revolutionary changes ushered in by the Constitution and the pivotal laws following on its heels were all effected in a procedurally impeccable manner, fully in accordance with the old legal system's regulations of the power to legislate, thereby gaining their binding force. The old law retained its validity. With respect to its validity, there is no distinction between "pre-Constitution" and "post-Constitution" law. The legitimacy of the different (political) systems during the past half-century is a matter of indifference from this perspective, that is, from the viewpoint of the constitutionality of laws it does not comprise a meaningful category. Irrespective of its date of enactment, each and every valid law must comport with the new Constitution. Likewise, constitutional review does not admit two different scales for the evaluation of laws. The date of enactment can be important insofar that older laws may have become unconstitutional when the renewed Constitution became effective.

Special treatment accorded to the law of the preceding systems—even with legality and legal continuity recognized—can arise in two contexts. The first question is: what could be done with the legal relationships created by the old, and now proven unconstitutional, laws—could they be harmonized with the Constitution? The second question is whether, in adjudicating the constitutionality of new laws seeking to replace the unconstitutional provisions of the bygone systems, one should consider the unique historical circumstances constituting the "change of systems." These questions, too, must be answered in a manner which comports with the requirements of the State under the rule of law.

4. The State under the rule of law's basic element is the security of the law. Security of the law demands, among other things, the protection of rights previously conferred, non-interference with the creation or termination of legal relations and limiting the ability to modify existing legal relations to constitutionally mandated provisions. As the Constitutional Court held in its resolution of 10/1992 (II.25.)AB, the consequences of the unconstitutionality of a law must be primarily evaluated with reference to the impact on the security of the law. This is the guiding principle for determining the date of invalidation for an unconstitutional law, and especially for the invalidation of the legal relations arising therefrom. This is so, for the individual legal relations and legal facts become independent of the sources whence they emerge and do not automatically share their fate. Were this otherwise, a change in the law would necessitate in every instance a review of the whole body of legal relations. Thus, from the principle of the security of the law, it follows that established legal relations cannot be constitutionally altered either by enactments or by invalidation of existing law, neither by the legislature nor by the Constitutional Court.

Exception to this principle is permissible only if a constitutional principle competing with the security of the law renders this outcome unavoidable, and provided that in light of its objectives it does not impose a disproportionate burden. Acquittal of a defendant based on the review of a lawfully completed criminal process subsequently struck down as unconstitutional is an example of such an exception. Constitutional criminal justice system demands this exception. However, the unjust outcome of legal relations does not constitute an argument against the principle of the security of the law. As the Constitutional Court's (9/1992(I.30.)AB) resolution stated, in part, "the constitutional State's demand for social justice may be effected subject to remaining within the institutional safeguards for the security of the law." The attainment of social justice "…does not amount (cannot amount) to a constitutionally recognized legal subject-right…."

…Retroactive modification of the law and legal relations is permitted only within very narrow confines. Problems created by declaring extant laws unconstitutional can be constitutionally rectified by the enactment of new, prospective laws.

5. One question is the extent to which the unique historical circumstances of the "change of systems" should be considered in reviewing the constitutionality of new laws pertaining to the unconstitutional regulations of the defunct (political) systems.

Within the framework of the State under the rule of law, and in order to further its development, the given historical situation can be taken into consideration. However, the basic guarantees of the State under the rule of law cannot be brushed aside by reference to historical situations and the State under the rule of law's demand for justice. A State under the rule of law cannot be created by undermining the rule of law. The security of the law based on formal and objective principles is more important than the necessarily partial and subjective justice. In its precedents, the Constitutional Court has already given effect to this principle.

The Constitutional Court cannot ignore history, since it, too, has a historical purpose. The Constitutional Court is the repository of the paradox of the "revolution of the rule of law": in the process of achieving the rule of law, beginning with the Constitution and manifesting itself in the peaceful "change of system," the Constitutional Court within its competence must unconditionally guarantee the comportment of the legislative power with the Constitution….

[T]he law ordering the recommencement of the statute of limitation oversteps the bounds of the State's criminal powers; these are guaranteed rights, whose restriction Paragraph 8 § (4) of the Constitution does not permit, even when other basic rights can be constitutionally suspended or restricted. In contrast with the restriction of property rights, the basic institutions of the constitutional criminal law cannot even be theoretically relativized, nor is it imaginable to balance them against some other constitutional right or duty. This is so, for the guarantees of the criminal law already contain the outcome of a balancing act, namely that the risk of unsuccessful criminal prosecution is borne by the State. (V.ö 9/1992/(I.30.)AB resolution). Hence, the presumption of innocence cannot be restricted on account of some other constitutional right, nor is it conceptually possible not to give it full effect; pursuant to the State's inaction, once the statute of limitations runs out, the non-indictability acquired at the moment the statute expires is complete, amenable neither to subsequent "reduction" nor resuscitation; nor can the condition of *crimen sine lege* be substituted by, for instance, the pursuit of some other constitutional task seeking the protection of the rights of others. Simply put, historical situations, justice, etc. are of no consideration in this matter. Even conceptually, exemption from the guarantees of the criminal law is only possible with their overt disregard, an outcome precluded by the principle of the rule of law.

IV

...In the Constitutional Court's opinion, in a constitutional State under the rule of law, the violation of rights can only be responded to by upholding the rule of the law. The legal system of a State under the rule of law, cannot deprive anyone of legal guarantees. These guarantees are basic rights appertaining to all. Wherever the value of the rule of law is entrenched, not even a just demand can justify the disregard of the State under the rule of law's legal guarantees. Justice and moral argument may, of course, motivate penal sanction but its legal foundation must be constitutional.

1. The Constitutional Court's resolution of 9/1992(I.30.)AB pointed out that the Constitution declared "State under the rule of law" to be the basic value of the Republic. The provisions of the Basic Law describe in detail the fundamental value of the State under the rule of law but they do not fully account for its content. Accordingly, interpretation of the concept of the State under the rule of law is one of the Constitutional Court's important duties. In reviewing laws, the principles which constitute the basic values of the State under the rule of law are evaluated by the Constitutional Court on the basis of their comportment with specific Constitutional provisions. But the principle of the State under the rule of law, in comparison with these specific constitutional provisions is not a mere auxiliary regulation, nor a mere declaration, but an independent constitutional value, whose violation per se is accordingly grounds for declaring a law unconstitutional. In the Constitutional Court's precedents, the security of the law is closely intertwined with the constitutional law's doctrine of the State under the rule of law.

According to the Constitutional Court's interpretation, security of the law demands of the State, and primarily the legislature, that the whole of the law, its specific parts and individual provisions be clear, unambiguous, their impact predictable and their consequences foreseeable by those whom the laws address, including the penal code. From the principle of predictability and foreseeability, the criminal law's prohibition of the use of retroactive legislation, especially *ex post facto* legislation and reasoning by analogy directly follows....

2. In a State under the rule of law, the State does not and cannot have unlimited punitive powers. This is especially so because the sovereign power itself is not limitless. Given constitutional basic rights and constitutionally protected liberties, the sovereign power can interfere with individuals' rights

and freedoms only on the basis of constitutional authorization and constitutional reasons.

Paragraph 8 §§ (1) and (2) of the Constitution is also authoritative with respect to the constitutional requirements imposed on the criminal law. Accordingly, the Hungarian Republic recognizes the inviolable and inalienable basic rights of human beings, their respect and protection being the State's primary duty. The Constitution's important prescription is that "regulation of basic rights and duties is to be determined by law, but the substantial content of basic rights cannot be restricted." According to the Constitutional Court's holdings, restriction of basic right and the content of freedom can be restricted by law only when unavoidably called for in order to protect some other basic right or constitutional value, and only in a manner which is strictly necessary and proportional to the objective. The criminal law's prescriptions and prohibitions, and especially its penalties, touch upon every basic right or constitutionally protected right and values. Lawful restrictions where unavoidable, necessary and proportional is the basis and constitutional meaning of those explanations of criminal law's punishment (as legal intervention) which perceive it as the final instrument of legal recourse.

The Constitutional Court points out emphatically that the reviewed Law is unconstitutional not simply because it violates the constitutional penal code's prohibition of retroactive punishment (Penal Code § 2), thus contradicting the principle of the security of the law (its predictability and foreseeability) as contained in Paragraph 2 § (1) of the Constitution, but also as this Law does not comport with the constitutional requirements of unavoidability, necessity and proportionality for the intervention of criminal punishment. Not even in an extraordinary situation, state of emergency, or grave danger does the Constitution permit the restriction or suspension of the criminal law's constitutional basic principles (Paragraphs 54-56. §, 57. §§ (2)-(4)).

3. The criminal system of a liberal, democratic State construes the principles of *nullum crimem* and *nulla poena sine lege* (prohibition of retroactivity)—pillars of classical criminal law—as a (constitutional) duty imposed on the State: the conditions of the exercise of its punitive powers must be fixed by law. In the process of exercising these punitive powers, this principle had taken on an ever-growing importance. This trend is exemplified by the expansion of the requirements of criminal liability going beyond the prescriptions contained in parts of the Law under review....

In a constitutional State under the rule of law, the criminal law is not merely an instrument but it protects and embodies values: the principles and guarantees of the constitutional criminal law. Criminal law is the legal basis for the exercise of punitive powers as well as a warranty of freedom for the protection of individual rights. Though criminal law protects values, as a warranty of freedom it cannot become an instrument for moral purges in the process of protecting moral values.

Nullum crimen sine lege and *nulla poena sine lege* are constitutional basic principles whose legal content is determined by a number of criminal law provisions.... The individual's constitutional human rights and freedoms are impacted not only by the select provisions and specific punitive sections of the criminal law, but especially by the interconnected and closed system of regulations of criminal liability, culpability and sentencing guidelines. Modification of every regulation of criminal liability fundamentally and directly impacts the individual's freedom and constitutional position. Modification of the statutes of limitation can thus only proceed if they remain consonant with the basic constitutional requirement of criminal liability.

4. Summing up: the principles of *nullum crimen sine lege* and *nulla poena sine lege* are part of the constitutional principle of criminal law's legality, but do not comprise the sole criterion for a constitutional review of criminal liability. In the Constitutional Court's view, the constitutional principle of legality incorporates the following....

• Conviction (declaration of guilt) and the meting out of punishment can only proceed pursuant to the law that was in effect at the time of the commission of the offense. This requirement is imposed by Paragraph 57 § (4) of the Constitution, echoed by the Penal Code's prohibition of retroactivity. The court adjudicates (determines criminal liability, convicts and passes sentence) the offense in accordance with the law that was in effect at the time of its commission and the punishment, too, is determined accordingly, except if a new law passed subsequently prescribes a more lenient punishment, or no longer designates the offense as criminal, thus making the action non-punishable by criminal law. This is the necessary outcome of the prohibition of retroactivity embodied in the principle of the security of the law (foreseeability and predictability) which, in turn, stems from the principle of a State under the rule of law whose logical precondition is the knowability of the law at the time of the commission of an act (Penal Code § 2). In addition to the express prohibition of retroactivity, the requirement of the application of the more lenient sentencing guidelines also springs from the constitutional requirement of the State under the rule of law: the Constitution cannot permit the application of norms which are alien to its basic principles (such as the imposition of the death penalty), even when at the time of the commission of the offense that penalty was the basic rule.

On the basis of the foregoing, the Constitutional Court holds that the law under review is unconstitutional because it does not comport with the constitutional criminal law's requisite of legitimacy.

V

The constitutional problems presented by the law under review were examined separately and without consideration of the possibility that adoption of a viewpoint regarding one issue may render the resolution of another superfluous or outright impossible. The Constitutional Court desires to address every conceivable interpretation of the law under review and examine some of its conceptual components in light of the fact that the law will necessarily be re-introduced in Parliament.

From the conclusion reached in Part IV of this resolution concerning the legality of criminal law as a constitutional requirement, it follows that the statute of limitation, too, must be determined in accordance with the law that was in effect at the time of the commission of the offense. The Constitutional Court concluded that those constitutional requirements imposed on the criminal law which relate to the rule of law and especially the security of the law cannot be confined to select provisions and specific punitive sections. The same constitutional requirements are imposed on every aspect of criminal liability—from the conditions governing criminal culpability to the regulation of sentencing.

There is no constitutional basis for the selective application of the prohibition of retroactivity, or the retroactive imposition of a harsher sentence, onto specific elements of the criminal process. For this reason, the Constitutional Court examined the problem of the statute of limitations on the basis of the legality of the criminal law, without consideration of the theoretical disputes concerning the procedural nature of the statute of limitation or its status as a legal-subject right.

The constitutionality of penal laws are not to be evaluated merely by reference to the criminal law guarantees expressly detailed in the Constitution. The criminal law is influenced by many other basic principles and basic rights. Thus, there is no specific provision in the Constitution prohibiting the imposition of strict liability in criminal cases, and yet the right to human dignity dictates that *mens rea* be a constitutional requirement for holding a person criminally liable. Another constitutional principle giving content to a State under the rule of law is that the lawfully imposed conditions and restrictions on the State's punitive powers cannot be modified at the expense of the individual whose act is being judged. No additional burden can be imposed on the criminal tortfeasor on account of a change in public policy pertaining to criminal punishment, or due to a mistake or dereliction of duty by the designated authorities....

The running of a statute of limitation is a matter of fact, but the statute itself is a matter of legal determination. Only a court can determine lawfully, that is in a manner that is dispositive of the case and binding on all, whether the statute of limitation for a specific criminal offense has run its course. In computing the length of the requisite time and reckoning the period remaining, the law in effect at the time of the commission of the offense controls, except if at the time of judgment a law more favorable to the defendant is available. The legislature's sole constitutionally mandated discretion to interfere with the statute of limitation is to enact a more lenient standard. In contrast, regulations seeking the contrary goal are unconstitutional for a variety of reasons, discussed below, depending on whether or not the statute of limitations had already run.

1. The re-imposition of criminal liability for a crime whose statute of limitation had already expired violates the Constitution.

With the running of the statute of limitation, the criminal liability of the offender is irrevocably extinguished. The primary reason for the State's termination of criminal culpability is the restriction of its own punitive powers. These reasons are not related to the determination of criminal liability and guilt, as are, for instance, excuses which justify a conduct thus precluding culpability; these reasons do not alter the nature of the act as the criminal offense remains criminal. The reasons for the termination of criminal liability are independent of the offender's volition and their impact, anyhow uncertain, are in no way dependent on the offender's conduct. The perpetrator of a crime may hope—for clemency, a change in the evaluation of the societal threat posed by his/her actions or that the statute of limitation has already run its course—but he/she cannot expect to partake of these saving graces. (There is one exception: death is a certainty). The commissioner of an offense acquires the right to be free of accountability only if the conditions for extinguishing culpability materialize.

Hence, if the statute of limitation had run its course, the offender acquires the right as a legal subject not to be punished. This legal subject right ripens when the State's claim for punishment ceases to exist due to its inability to apprehend and punish the offender during the time allocated for the exercise of its punitive powers. Faith in the law unconditionally demands that once a requirement for extinguishing culpability is met there be no new law making the same offense punishable once again. What legal technicality is employed to reimpose criminal culpability—whether the statute of limitations is restarted or *ex post facto* legislation is imposed to toll the statute—is a matter of indifference, their constitutionality judged in the same light as a law retroactively imposing punishment on a conduct which, at the time, did not constitute a criminal offense. From the perspective of culpability, an offense whose statute of limitation had run its course must be treated—given that the State's claim for punishment had vanished—as never having been punishable.

The statute of limitation cannot be restarted for an offense whose statute had already run its course. This comports with the Constitution's express criminal law provisions which keep in check the State's punitive powers and never permit the shifting of the burden onto the offender due to the State's failure to prosecute lawfully. Just as the presumption of innocence protects others than the innocent, the statute of limitation, too, extinguishes culpability irrespective of the reasons for not prosecuting the offender; the offender cannot be burdened by the State's dereliction of its duty..... That a person is evidently guilty matters not, and he/she remains innocent, if the guilt cannot be legally established; that all the evidence is available and society demands punishment matters not—and the statute of limitation continues to runs—if the State does not prosecute.

Hence, the law making offenses punishable whose statutes of limitation had already run is contrary to Paragraph 2 § (1) of the Constitution because it offends the security of the law, violates the principle of placing checks and balances on the State's punitive powers and, furthermore, it is also contrary to Paragraph 57 § (4) by retroactively imposing criminal liability....

4. The obstacles presented by retroactive legislation for the extension of the statute of limitation cannot be side-stepped by the explanation that the statute has been "tolled." For if the statute had indeed been tolled by the law prevailing at the time of the commission of the offense then declaration of this fact in a new law is unnecessary. Determination of whether or not the statute had run—by application of the law pertaining to the specific offense—is left exclusively to the prosecutor and, in the last instance, to the courts. The legislature cannot retroactively decide this question. According to the statute of limitation in effect at the time of the offense, or those subsequent regulations prescribing a more lenient standard, no law can retroactively declare that the statute was tolled for reasons which the law in effect at the time of the commission of the offence and during its running did not acknowledge as applicable to that criminal offense. Running of the statute of limitation is a matter of legal facts, that is, the natural fact—the passing of time—must be transformed by the application of the law into a legal fact. The legal facts determining the commencement and duration of the statute of limitation must exist during the running of the statute and they either do or do not exist. What did not then constitute a legal fact warranting the tolling of the statute cannot be so declared retroactively. For that would constitute an extension of the statute of limitation which, on the basis of the aforenoted discussion, is unconstitutional.

5. and 6. The statute of limitation for the criminal offenses singled out by the law under review recommences "if the State's foregoing its claim to punish was based on political reasons." This condition per se is unconstitutional.

Security of the law demands the clear and unambiguous formulation of legal rules in order that everyone affected by them could understand their own legal situation, adjust accordingly their decisions and behavior and could predict the legal ramifications of their actions. Pertinent to this requirement is the predictability of the behavior of other legal subjects, as well as that of the authorities themselves. The incorporation of the condition that "if the State's foregoing its claim to punish was based on political reasons" into the criminal law does not meet this aforementioned requirement. Not even with an awareness of the special purpose of this law can the meaning of "foregoing its claim to punish" be determined with sufficient certainty. Failure to initiate proceedings, suspension of criminal proceedings in the absence of legal justifications fall within the ambit of this concept, but so does, for instance, the closing of a proceeding with unlawfully lenient punishment, such as a warning. Likewise, what constitutes "political reasons" and what criteria are to be applied cannot be determined with the necessary unambiguity—especially in light of the many political changes which had taken place during the long interval covered by this law.

The choice of politically motivated failure to prosecute as the criterion for extending the duration of criminal culpability also violates the basic principle of constitutional criminal law expounded herein—as well as in the Court's resolution of 9/1992(I.30.)AB. According to this principle, an offender cannot be burdened by the criminal justice system's inability, brought about by the State's failure to prosecute, to achieve its designated purpose of delivering a just sentence. From the perspective of this constitutionally allocated burden, it makes no difference whether the State exercised its prosecutorial powers improperly or simply failed to exercise them all together; likewise, the reasons for acting one way or another are of no importance. Whether the prosecutorial authorities are poorly equipped, or their investigators are negligent, corrupt or willful accessories after the fact, the burden is equally borne by the State in every case. An era's policy of criminal sanctions can be retroactively classified as unconstitutional; but then, it is not possible to maintain that the exercise of punitive powers putatively in violation of the principles of rule of law did not extend to select provisions of the criminal law, and to conclude on the basis of this retroactive assessment of the non-existence of such that the statutes of limitation could not even had begun to run for those offenses subsumed under these select provisions.

With regards to the Law under review, the statutes of limitation for the criminal offenses committed between December 21, 1941 and May 2, 1990 could have run only on the basis of reasons which were recognized by the law in effect at the time the offenses were committed. That "the State's foregoing of its claim to punish was based on political reasons" did not exist as a justification for tolling the running of the statute. Although Law VII § 9. of the people's tribunal of 1945 tolled retroactively the statute of limitation for all criminal offenses committed in 1919 and thereafter, "whose prosecution was prevented by the ruling power," and decreed its date of commencement with December 21, 1944, the designated duration of that law and the law under review are different....

7. Treason is a crime against the State. The subject matter subsumed under this category changes with the change in political systems, acquiring different meanings. Conceptual convergence of agreements notwithstanding, treason is treated differently in different political systems. Failure to prosecute an act of treason for "political reasons" is typically an *ex post facto* classification, constituting a retroactive determination of the legal fact. Certain aspects of what constitutes treason today were not so considered at the time of their commission and weren't prosecuted accordingly. The law under review does not consider this change. Deciding what constitutes treason in one era, by applying the value judgments of a subsequent political period, clashes with Paragraph 57 § (4) of the Constitution: the criminal offense defined by the new order is retroactively applied to the previous era and is punished accordingly, even though at the time of its occurrence it did not constitute a crime.

What has been said about the statute of limitation is also applicable in principle to treason. However, the constitutional law issue raised by the "change of systems" (*rendszerváltás*) concerning this offence is not related to the statute of limitation....

NETHERLANDS: CONSTITUTION

(1983)

Article 16

No offence shall be punishable unless it was an offence under the law at the time it was committed....

Additional Articles

Article IX

Article 16 shall not apply to offences made punishable under the Wartime Offences Decree (*Besluit Buitengewoon Strafrecht*)....

6

COMPENSATION AND
REHABILITATION

UNITED NATIONS: DECLARATION OF BASIC PRINCIPLES OF JUSTICE FOR VICTIMS OF CRIME AND ABUSE OF POWER[*]

General Assembly Resolution 40/34 (November 29, 1985)

The General Assembly,

Recalling that the Sixth United Nations Congress on the Prevention of Crime and the Treatment of Offenders recommended that the United Nations should continue its present work on the development of guidelines and standards regarding abuse of economic and political power,

Cognizant that millions of people throughout the world suffer harm as a result of crime and the abuse of power and that the rights of these victims have not been adequately recognized,

Recognizing that the victims of crime and the victims of abuse of power, and also frequently their families, witnesses and others who aid them, are unjustly subjected to loss, damage or injury and that they may, in addition, suffer hardship when assisting in the prosecution of offenders,

1. *Affirms* the necessity of adopting national and international measures in order to secure the universal and effective recognition of, and respect for, the rights of victims of crime and of abuse of power;

2. *Stresses* the need to promote progress by all States in their efforts to that end, without prejudice to the rights of suspects or offenders;

3. *Adopts* the Declaration of Basic Principles of Justice for Victims of Crime and Abuse of Power, annexed to the present resolution, which is designed to assist Governments and the international community in their efforts to secure justice and assistance for victims of crime and victims of abuse of power;

4. *Calls upon* Member States to take the necessary steps to give effect to the provisions contained in the Declaration and, in order to curtail victimization as referred to hereinafter, endeavour:

(a) To implement social, health, including mental health, educational, economic and specific crime prevention policies to reduce victimization and encourage assistance to victims in distress;...

(d) To establish and strengthen the means of detecting, prosecuting and sentencing those guilty of crimes;...

---

[*] Report No. A/40/881.

(f) To promote the observance of codes of conduct and ethical norms, in particular international standards, by public servants, including law enforcement, correctional, medical, social service and military personnel, as well as the staff of economic enterprises;

(g) To prohibit practices and procedures conducive to abuse, such as secret places of detention and incommunicado detention;

(h) To co-operate with other States, through mutual judicial and administrative assistance, in such matters as the detection and pursuit of offenders, their extradition and the seizure of their assets, to be used for restitution to the victims;...

Annex

Declaration of Basic Principles of Justice for Victims of Crime and Abuse of Power

A. Victims of Crime

1. "Victims" means persons who, individually or collectively, have suffered harm, including physical or mental injury, emotional suffering, economic loss or substantial impairment of their fundamental rights, through acts or omissions that are in violation of criminal laws operative within Member States, including those laws proscribing criminal abuse of power.

2. A person may be considered a victim, under this Declaration, regardless of whether the perpetrator is identified, apprehended, prosecuted or convicted and regardless of the familial relationship between the perpetrator and the victim. The term "victim" also includes, where appropriate, the immediate family or dependents of the direct victim and persons who have suffered harm in intervening to assist victims in distress or to prevent victimization.

3. The provisions contained herein shall be applicable to all, without distinction of any kind, such as race, colour, sex, age, language, religion, nationality, political or other opinion, cultural beliefs or practices, property, birth or family status, ethnic or social origin, and disability.

Access to Justice and Fair Treatment

4. Victims should be treated with compassion and respect for their dignity. They are entitled to access to the mechanisms of justice and to prompt redress, as provided for by national legislation, for the harm that they have suffered.

5. Judicial and administrative mechanisms should be established and strengthened where necessary to enable victims to obtain redress through formal or informal procedures that are expeditious, fair, inexpensive and accessible. Victims should be informed of their rights in seeking redress through such mechanisms.

6. The responsiveness of judicial and administrative processes to the needs of victims should be facilitated by:

    (a)   Informing victims of their role and the scope, timing and progress of the proceedings and of the disposition of their cases, especially where serious crimes are involved and where they have requested such information;

    (b)   Allowing the views and concerns of victims to be presented and considered at appropriate stages of the proceedings where their personal interests are affected, without prejudice to the accused and consistent with the relevant national criminal justice system;

    (c)   Providing proper assistance to victims throughout the legal process;

    (d)   Taking measures to minimize inconvenience to victims, protect their privacy, when necessary, and ensure their safety, as well as that of their families and witnesses on their behalf, from intimidation and retaliation;

    (e)   Avoiding unnecessary delay in the disposition of cases and the execution of orders or decrees granting awards to victims.

7. Informal mechanisms for the resolution of disputes, including mediation, arbitration and customary justice or indigenous practices, should be utilized where appropriate to facilitate conciliation and redress for victims.

Restitution

8. Offenders or third parties responsible for their behaviour should, where appropriate, make fair restitution to victims, their families or dependents. Such restitution should include the return of property, or payment for the harm or loss suffered, reimbursement of expenses incurred as a result of the victimization, the provision of services and the restoration of rights.

9. Governments should review their practices, regulations and laws to consider restitution as an available sentencing option in criminal cases, in addition to other criminal sanctions.

10. In cases of substantial harm to the environment, restitution, if ordered, should include, as far as possible, restoration of the environment, reconstruction of the infrastructure, replacement of community facilities and reimbursement of the expenses of relocation, whenever such harm results in the dislocation of a community.

11. Where public officials or other agents acting in an official or quasi-official capacity have violated national criminal laws, the victims should receive restitution from the State whose officials or agents were responsible for the harm inflicted. *In cases where the Government under whose*

authority, the victimizing act or omission occurred is no longer in existence, the State or Government successor in title should provide restitution to the victims.[*]

Compensation

12. When compensation is not fully available from the offender or other sources, States should endeavour to provide financial compensation to:

(a) Victims who have sustained significant bodily injury or impairment of physical or mental health as a result of serious crimes;

(b) The family, in particular dependents of persons who have died or become physically or mentally incapacitated as a result of such victimization.

13. The establishment, strengthening and expansion of national funds for compensation to victims should be encouraged. Where appropriate, other funds may also be established for this purpose, including those cases where the State of which the victim is a national is not in a position to compensate the victim for the harm.

Assistance

14. Victims should receive the necessary material, medical, psychological and social assistance through governmental, voluntary, community-based and indigenous means.

15. Victims should be informed of the availability of health and social services and other relevant assistance and be readily afforded access to them.

16. Police, justice, health, social service and other personnel concerned should receive training to sensitize them to the needs of victims, and guidelines to ensure proper and prompt aid.

17. In providing services and assistance to victims, attention should be given to those who have special needs because of the nature of the harm inflicted or because of factors such as those mentioned in paragraph 3 above.

B. Victims of Abuse of Power

18. "Victims" means persons who, individually or collectively, have suffered harm, including physical or mental injury, emotional suffering, economic loss or substantial impairment of their fundamental rights, through acts or omissions that do not yet constitute violations of national criminal laws but of internationally recognized norms relating to human rights.

19. States should consider incorporating into the national law norms proscribing abuses of power and providing remedies to victims of such abuses. In particular, such remedies should include restitution and/or

---

[*] [Emphasis added by the editor.]

compensation, and necessary material, medical, psychological and social assistance and support.

20. States should consider negotiating multilateral international treaties relating to victims, as defined in paragraph 18.

21. States should periodically review existing legislation and practices to ensure their responsiveness to changing circumstances, should enact and enforce, if necessary, legislation proscribing acts that constitute serious abuses of political or economic power, as well as promoting policies and mechanisms for the prevention of such acts, and should develop and make readily available appropriate rights and remedies for victims of such acts.

COUNCIL OF EUROPE: RECOMMENDATION NO. R (84) 15 ON PUBLIC LIABILITY

Adopted by the Committee of Ministers on 18 September 1984 at the 375th Meeting of the Ministers' Deputies

The Committee of Ministers, under the terms of Article 15.*b* of the Statute of the Council of Europe,

Considering that the aim of the Council of Europe is to achieve a greater unity between its members;

Considering that public authorities intervene in an increasing number of fields, that their activities may affect the rights, liberties and interests of persons and may, sometimes, cause damage;

Considering that, since public authorities are serving the community, the latter should ensure reparation for such damage when it would be inappropriate for the persons concerned to bear it;

Recalling the general principles governing the protection of the individual in relation to the acts of administrative authorities as set out in Resolution (77) 31 and the principles concerning the exercise of discretionary powers by administrative authorities set out in Recommendation No. R(80)2;

Considering that it is desirable to protect persons in the field of public liability,

Recommends the governments of member states:

a.   to be guided in their law and practice by the principles annexed to this Recommendation;

b.   to examine the advisability of setting up in their internal order, where necessary, appropriate machinery for preventing obligations of public authorities in the field of public liability from being unsatisfied through lack of funds.

Appendix
Scope and definitions

1. This Recommendation applies to public liability, that is to say the obligation of public authorities to make good the damage caused by their acts, either by compensation or by any other appropriate means (hereinafter referred to as "reparation").

2. The term "public authority" means:

a.   any entity of public law of any kind or at any level (including state; region; province; municipality; independent public entity); and *b*. any private person, when exercising prerogatives of official authority.

3. The term "act" means any action or omission which is of such a nature as to affect directly the rights, liberties or interests of persons.

4. The acts covered by this Recommendation are the following:

a. normative acts in the exercise of regulatory authority;
b. administrative acts which are not regulatory;
c. physical acts.

5. Amongst the acts covered by paragraph 4 are included acts carried out in the administration of justice which are not performed in the exercise of a judicial function.

6. The term "victim" means the injured person or any other person entitled to claim reparation.

Principles

I

Reparation should be ensured for damage caused by an act due to a failure of a public authority to conduct itself in a way which can be expected from it in law in relation to the injured person. Such a failure is presumed in case of transgression of an established legal rule.

II

1. Even if the conditions stated in Principle I are not met, reparation should be ensured if it would be manifestly unjust to allow the injured person alone to bear the damage, having regard to the following circumstances: the act is in the general interest, only one person or a limited number of persons have suffered the damage and the act was exceptional or the damage was an exceptional result of the act.

2. The application of this principle may be limited to certain categories of acts only.

III

If the victim has, by his own fault or by his failure to use legal remedies, contributed to the damage, the reparation of the damage may be reduced accordingly or disallowed.

The same should apply if a person, for whom the victim is responsible under national law, has contributed to the damage.

IV

The right to bring an action against a public authority should not be subject to the obligation to act first against its agent.

If there is an administrative conciliation system prior to judicial proceedings, recourse to such system should not jeopardise access to judicial proceedings.

V

Reparation under Principle I should be made in full, it being understood that the determination of the heads of damage, of the nature and of the form of reparation falls within the competence of national law.

Reparation under Principle II may be made only in part, on the basis of equitable principles.

VI

Decisions granting reparation should be implemented as quickly as possible. This should be ensured by appropriate budgetary or other measures.

If, under domestic law, a system for a special implementation procedure is provided for, it should be easily accessible and expeditious.

VII

Rules concerning time limits relating to public liability actions and their starting points should not jeopardise the effective exercise of the right of action.

VIII

The nationality of the victim should not give rise to any discrimination in the field of public liability.

Final Provisions

This Recommendation should not be interpreted as:

a. limiting the possibility for a member state to apply the principles above to categories of acts other than those covered by the Recommendation or to adopt provisions granting a wider measure of protection to victims;
b. affecting any special system of liability laid down by international treaties;
c. affecting special national systems of liability in the fields of postal and telecommunications services and of transportation as well as special systems of liability which are internal to the armed forces,

provided that adequate reparation is granted to victims having regard to all the circumstances;

d. affecting special national systems of liability which apply equally to public authorities and private persons.

Explanatory Memorandum
Introduction

1. Recommendation No. R(84)15 relating to public liability is a logical sequel to the Council of Europe's work in the field of administrative law, aimed at protecting persons in their dealings with public authorities. Public authorities in all states are acting in an increasing number of fields; since their actions have a continuous and determining influence on the public's activities, rights and interests, many occasions of conflict and damage inevitably arise and the problem is to determine how far the injured persons can be required to bear the damage....

4. It was concluded that, besides the need of establishing a general rule according to which public authorities must be liable for their acts, specific principles are necessary in this field which would be appropriate to the particular nature of the activities of public authorities. Such principles are justified regardless of the question of whether public authorities are answerable before the same courts or whether, by statutory or case-law, they come under a separate system of liability.

5. Damage caused to persons may be the result either of "unlawful" or of "lawful" action by public servants or administrative bodies. The instrument accordingly contains principles providing for reparation in both cases. Nevertheless, since rules concerning reparation for damage caused by lawful acts may necessitate important changes in certain states' legislation and practice, the instrument provides for the possibility of limited application of Principle II in national systems with the possibility of a gradual extension.

6. The existence of a system of public liability constitutes an essential safeguard for persons, but it is equally important that the system should be so implemented as to allow those injured to obtain just and expeditious reparation. Thus the Recommendation, as well as laying down principles to govern the right to reparation, sets out ways of making such reparation effective and advocates that consideration be given to the desirability of setting up, where necessary, ways and means to prevent obligations in this field being unsatisfied through lack of funds.

Scope and Definitions

Paragraph 1

7. This paragraph states the scope of the Recommendation and, for this purpose, indicates that it applies to public liability; the latter is defined as the obligation of public authorities to make good the damage caused by their

acts. Such liability of public authorities is traditionally known in several legal systems as "State liability". However, this notion was rejected because the word "State" does not always denote the same political and institutional realities. In some systems, for instance, the notion of state applies to all institutions which govern or regulate the public life of the nation whereas in others it refers only to central government. The expression "public liability" is therefore preferable because it can apply in all legal systems to the type of liability covered by this instrument.

Paragraph 2

8. Public liability is characterised by the fact that its scope is limited to acts of public authorities.

The notion of "public authority" is defined by using a functional criterion, that is the exercise of powers or prerogatives exceeding the rights or powers of ordinary persons. The indication of the specific cases where this condition is met falls within the sphere of domestic law. In some legal systems, prerogatives of official authority are exercised in the performance both of activities traditionally viewed as falling within the sphere of public entities, such as the maintenance of public order, and of activities which can also be carried out by private persons, such as education or transport. Conversely, other systems consider that the prerogatives of official authority cannot be exercised in respect of the last-mentioned activities—which would consequently be subject to the liability system under ordinary law.

9. In some states, "public service" (*service public*) activities are also subject to a particular liability system.

The performance of tasks or activities which have special characteristics, or are of special interest to the community, is sometimes viewed as a public service. However, the notion of public service does not exist in all legal systems or does not always cover the same situations.

For this reason the Recommendation does not specifically provide for the system of public liability to be applied to such activities, but nothing should prevent its application to those states which recognize the notion of public service and consider that activities relating to it must be subject to a liability system different from that existing under ordinary law.

10. Public authorities within the meaning of this Recommendation may be both public law persons or entities and private law persons or entities, provided they come within the situation described above.... The public or private quality of an entity or person is therefore not decisive in giving rise to public liability. What matters is the nature of the powers it exercises....

Paragraph 4

12. This provision defines the scope of the instrument. It covers specifically some acts of public authorities but states may extend the application of the system of public liability to other categories of acts.

It follows from paragraph 4 that the legislative acts adopted by Parliament, and, in some states, by similar bodies of the entities forming the state which possess legislative power (regions, states in a federal state) are excluded from the scope of the Recommendation.

In many states, the executive authorities (Government, Ministers, other administrative authorities) can adopt normative acts of general application. Those acts are adopted either on the basis of a delegation of power by the body which possesses the legislative power or by virtue of a power which is derived from the Constitution.

According to paragraph 4, only acts of the executive bodies falling within "the regulatory authority" are covered by the Recommendation. The acts which fall within such a "regulatory authority" shall be determined in accordance with the law of each state.

Paragraph 5

13. Paragraph 5 draws a fundamental distinction between acts performed in the exercise of a judicial function and solely administrative acts carried out in the administration of justice. The former acts do not fall within the scope of this Recommendation. The latter acts, whether performed by the judge himself or by his ancillary staff, may be equated with one of the types of acts set out in paragraph 4. These acts are covered by the Recommendation.

Paragraph 6

14. The protection granted by the system of public liability can cover not only the injured person but also other persons, namely his or her heirs. For the purpose of this instrument all those who are entitled to claim reparation are called "victim".

Principles

Principle I

15. This provision defines the factors which must be present for public liability to arise. With regard to the basis of liability, the instrument follows is already established in the area of civil liability by the work of the Council of Europe's European Committee on Legal Co-operation (CDCJ), precedents which are in line with recent developments, especially recent court decisions, in a number of member states. This principle does not make use of the two criteria of unlawfulness and fault. Public liability should arise whenever damage is caused by a failure of public authorities to comply with the standards of conduct which can reasonably be expected from them in law in relation to the injured person. This makes it possible, *inter alia*, to protect victims having suffered damage caused by agents unknown or by a department acting collectively.

16. The standards of conduct which public authorities might reasonably be expected in law to observe depend on their tasks and the means at their disposal. The public administration in particular and public authorities in general are instruments to which the nation, through its representatives, entrusts functions for which they are assigned the means. Public authorities must consequently be in a position to perform a series of tasks and provide a number of services to the community, the definition, scope and nature of these activities being established by legal rules. When a public authority fails to comply with a duty required by the legal rules and damage to citizens ensues, it should be possible for the latter to obtain reparation from the public authority in question, regardless of any personal liability of the agents or officials who caused the damage.

17. The term "in law" means that the state's legal system must be considered as a whole. It refers to all applicable legal rules.... It is ... a matter for domestic systems to decide which rules may be considered as legal rules.

18. The definition of the term "act" in paragraph 3, considered in conjunction with the expression "reasonably in relation to the injured person" in Principle I, makes it clear that public liability does not arise in every instance of transgression of a legal principle or legal rule, since such principle or rule must be one that affects a right, freedom or interest of the injured person. Only such a transgression can give rise to reasonable expectation within the meaning of Principle I. Transgression of a rule which is concerned with an administration's internal organization and does not directly or indirectly create an individual right or interest does not give rise to liability under Principle I.

19. The presumption raised in this principle is confined, for reasons of legal certainty, to established legal rules. These are rules known at the time when the act was carried out. This excludes those rules defined by the courts by means of an overall interpretation of legal provisions after the carrying out of the act that caused the damage.

20. This presumption is rebuttable, and the public authority in question will not be liable if it can show that violation of the rule does not amount to noncompliance with the standard of conduct which it was bound to observe. This presumption helps to protect the victim, who is not obliged to investigate the conduct of the agent or administrative department responsible for the act causing the damage but has merely to prove that the public authority has failed to observe conduct prescribed by a legal rule....

22. It appears from the text of the provision that public liability arises only where damage is caused, which conversely means that the breach of a legal rule by itself is not sufficient to give rise to this category of liability. This should not prevent the possibility of liability of a different kind, for instance, criminal or disciplinary liability. The affirmation that the damage

must be "caused" by an act establishes the need for a causal relation between the act of the public authorities and the damage....

23. A special problem may arise where damage is caused by an official ostensibly acting in the public service, but in fact acting in his own interest; one must determine the criteria for defining what is referred to in some systems as separate personal fault (*faute personelle détachable*) and administrative error (*faute de service*). Where the appearance of normal activity of a public authority is sufficient to mislead reasonable and careful people, public liability must arise even if such an appearance subsequently proves to be untrue. This consequence is based on the fact that appearance is constituted by factors that are objectively linked to public administration or a public service. Thus, liability may arise if, in the particular case, the capacity of an administrative official and the circumstances of his action are of such a nature as to mislead the injured person.

Principle II

24. A person's rights and legitimate interests may be infringed and damage caused not only when a public authority fails to conduct itself in the way required of it but also, in certain instances, when it acts in a proper manner and cannot be accused of breach of duty. Such damage is the consequence of a risk inherent in all social activity, and criteria must be established for determining those instances in which the damage should be borne by the injured person and those in which, on the other hand, it should be the responsibility of the community.

25. A generally accepted principle of social solidarity requires persons to accept a whole range of inconveniences and damage as a normal consequence of life in society, when they are not excessively important or serious and they affect the population as a whole. Conversely, it seems unjust to require the injured person to bear damage to which the aforementioned qualifications do not apply and which constitutes an excessive burden for a specific person in relation to the principle of equality in sharing the consequences of public obligations....

Principle III

28. The provisions of Principle III are based upon those relating to the same subject in the European Convention on Products Liability in regard to Personal Injury and Death. The principle covers cases in which the injured person has himself contributed to the damage. The fault of the victim is the main cause that modified the liability. However, the case of the failure of the victim to use the legal remedies available to him, which might have prevented or reduced the damage, has been expressly mentioned. It will be for the court to determine in a specific case the contribution to the damage of the victim with a view to assessing the reparation or, if appropriate, disallow it.

29. The second paragraph states that reparation may also be reduced where the damage is the result of an act committed by a person for whom the victim is responsible under national law (for example, depending on the system: agent, minor).

30. Although the Recommendation does not expressly mention this matter, public authorities will, as a general rule, be exonerated from liability in the case of *force majeure*. *Force majeure*, an example of which arises out of atmospheric phenomena, is characterised by the fact that, since the cause of the damage cannot be attributed to the public authorities, the actual occurrence of the act causing damage is normally unpredictable and its consequences are unavoidable.... The causal link may, in certain cases, be broken by the intervention of a third person which would, for example, by preventing the action of an administrative body, consequently free the public authorities from liability.

Principle IV

31. This principle departs from the approach, now discarded by many states, whereby a person having suffered damage caused by a public activity or service had to bring a claim against the official or civil servant allegedly liable. This solution did not provide the victim with satisfactory protection because it was sometimes impossible to find the person who had actually caused the damage, or very often, that person was insolvent.

32. The liability of public authorities is at present the victim's basic guarantee that he will obtain proper compensation, but there are two different means whereby action can be taken. In cases where the official or person who has caused the injury can be identified, some legal systems allow the victim to claim either against the public authority for which the official was working at the time or against the official himself, or against both simultaneously. Under other systems, claims must always be brought against the public authority, which can then take action against the official or civil servant who has caused the damage. The instrument adopts a compromise solution, establishing that states could not hinder the victim in the exercise of his right to proceed directly against the public authority liable or bound to make good the damage, thus leaving it to the victim to choose in countries where direct action can be taken against the official in question. If the damage was the result of a lawful act, there would be no basis for recourse action of the public authority against the agent having caused the damage....

Principle V

34. This provision establishes the principle that reparation must be made in full, meaning that the victim must be compensated for all the damage resulting from the wrongful act which can be assessed in terms of

money, and be appropriately compensated for other damage. However, it leaves it to domestic law to determine the heads of damage, the nature and the form of the reparation. In most legal systems, however, reparation covers both immediate material damage (*damnum emergens*) and the loss incurred (*lucrum cessans*).

35. In the circumstances referred to in Principle II, in view of the characteristics of acts by public authorities which cause damage and having regard to the basis of the duty to make reparation, it may be appropriate for the injured person to bear a part of the damage. Indeed, since this provision specifically mentions cases in which it would be manifestly unjust for the injured person to bear the damage "alone", it follows that it may be just to make fair rather than full reparation. The amount of such reparation is to be fixed in the light of all the factors used in such cases to establish the degree of liability of public authorities and the consequent entitlement of the injured person.

Principle VI

36. The final decision recognizing the right of the victim to receive reparation does not always result in effective reparation being received without delay. Procedurally speaking, the enforcement of decisions in this field is made according to one of the following systems:

a. The decision can be immediately enforced and constitutes sufficient title to obtain reparation;
b. The decision cannot be immediately enforced and a special procedure is provided for in order to obtain effective reparation.

37. In principle, the first system permits fast reparation. Nevertheless, it was thought useful to lay down the general principle according to which enforcement of decisions in this field should be made as quickly as possible. If the second system is followed, the Recommendation emphasizes that the enforcement procedure should be easily accessible and fast. These two rules comply with the principles contained in Recommendation No. R(81)7 of the Committee of Ministers on measures facilitating access to justice.

38. However, practical or legal obstacles to obtaining an effective reparation may exist. One is represented by strict budgetary rules of the state or other public entities which might prevent the disposal of the funds necessary to comply with the decision. Another possible obstacle is the inertia or the officials of the administration. A third obstacle lies in the prohibition, in some states, of enforcement in respect of the public authorities.

39. The instrument does not describe specific measures to overcome such obstacles and recommends that states adopt budgetary or other appropriate measures. In some states, for example, budgetary rules provide

for orders to pay and, if necessary, the automatic entry in the following year's budget of the sums which are due to the victim. To remedy the inertia of malicious conduct of officials of the administration, some systems provide for the possibility of the personal liability of the agents concerned.

40. Procedural time-limits and rules relating to their calculation have the double aim of fixing the period within which a right of action must be exercised and of instituting a measure of legal certainty by reasonably limiting the possibility of affecting legal rights. In the sector of private law, the first factor prevails and, consequently, time-limits are usually long. Long periods may sometimes constitute an obstacle to the smooth operation and effectiveness of administration action and, at the same time, would not seem indispensable for the protection of individual rights. For this reason, states lay down shorter periods. The Recommendation recognises the need for this but it also underlines that such rules must not jeopardise the effective exercise of the right of action.

Principle VIII

41. The principles on public liability should be applied according to the same criteria and in a uniform way to all persons, regardless of their nationality, even if other states have a different legal provision. Progress in the protection of rights and legitimate interests of persons, in the spirit of the constant action of the Council of Europe, implies rejection of any discrimination in this field....

ALBANIA: LAW ON FORMER VICTIMS OF PERSECUTION

Law No. 7748 (July 29, 1993)

On the basis of Article 16 of Law No. 7491 of 29 April 1991 "On the Main Constitutional Provisions" and on the proposal of the Council of Ministers, the People's Assembly of the Republic of Albania decrees:

Definitions
Article 1

The status of formerly convicted and persecuted persons, hereinafter referred to as "status," is granted on the fundamental criteria and conditions of a person having been politically sentenced or persecuted, and involves rights and obligations in accordance with the degree of persecution.

Article 2

Political persecution, hereinafter referred to as "persecution," is considered to be any act or failure to act between 8 November 1941 and 22 March 1992 on the part of any armed formation or individual of the National Liberation Army, the State security service, the police, the Army, or a local government organ on the basis of an order or decree of the party, military, State, or judicial organs of the Albanian communists, when this act or failure to act led to loss of life, freedom, or civil rights or classification as kulak or declassed person, as well as any other debarment of the individual from political, economic, and social life because of his political or religious convictions or attitudes.

Classification of Those Formerly Convicted and Politically Persecuted
Article 3

On the basis of the Law "On the Innocence and Amnesty of Those Formerly Convicted and Politically Persecuted" No. 7516, amended by Laws 7660 on 14 January 1993 and No. 7719 of 8 June 1993, those with the status of victims of political persecution are divided into five categories:

(a) Persons who have lost their lives or are mentally ill because of persecution.
(b) Persons sentenced to imprisonment or who survived as outlaws within the country because of persecution.
(c) Persons sentenced to internment or deportation because of persecution; Albanians with foreign citizenship, now Albanian

citizens, who have lived in concentration camps especially built for them.

(d) Persons who have lost civil rights, village kulaks, declassed persons, and those who have suffered privations of various kinds because of persecution.

(e) Persons who, although fulfilling the conditions for inclusion in one of the above categories, do not gain the right to this status.

Article 4

Albanian citizens who lost their lives, freedom, or suffered other privations mentioned in Article 3, Paragraphs (a), (b), (c), and (d) outside the territory of Albania during the time they worked for the administration during the years of antifascist war, or later as a result of the impossibility of their remaining in Albania because of the persecution to which they were subjected, regardless of the fact that the final persecution was carried out by non-Albanian communist forces, gain the full rights guaranteed by this status.

Article 5

The persons categorized by Article 3 Paragraph (e) are:

(a) The high-level communist nomenclature under the criteria established by the Council of Ministers.

(b) State security service collaborators and witnesses at political trials whose activities led directly to such crimes as the murder, imprisonment, internment, deportation, etc. of citizens.

(c) Those convicted for political reasons whose sentences include a sentence for theft, plunder, murder, or serious assault equal to or greater than the political element of their sentence, and rapists.

(d) Those convicted or interned for political reasons whose political sentences include the common crimes mentioned under Paragraph (c) of this article and who, before this conviction, were sentenced twice for theft or plunder, regardless of the level of punishment.

(e) Person falling in the category of Article 3 Paragraph (d) who have lost the moral right to be so categorized because of public denial of their political convictions or renunciation of their ties with relatives falling under Article 3 Paragraphs (a), (b), (c), and (d), when this is testified in writing by the person himself defined as a victim of persecution under these paragraphs.

   If this person has died, the court decides this matter on the proposal of the presidiums of the Association of Former Political Prisoners and Victims of Persecution in the neighborhood or village where he lives or has lived.

(f) Those proved by the Appeal Court to have been officials of the authorities practicing violence, terror, or espionage and those who collaborated with the occupier.

Article 6

All family members or relatives of persons considered under Article 5 of this Law will be included under Paragraph (d) of Article 3 when they fulfill the relevant conditions, regardless of whether the person because of whom they were persecuted has acquired the right to this status or not.

Rights
Right to Material Compensation

Article 7

Material compensation for victims of political persecution will take the form of: immediate cash awards, life pensions, compensations for salary, land, business premises and other forms of material benefit that may be irrevocably given to the persecuted person or to his family, if he has died, in compensation for his loss of life and freedom and his unpaid labor and suffering, with the principal intention of creating conditions and possibilities of integrating him and his family into the normal economic and social life of our country. The form of material compensation will be decided by a special decree of the Council of Ministers.

Article 8

The material compensation defined in Article 7 covers the categories of people mentioned in Paragraphs (a), (b), and (c) of Article 3. Those victims of persecution included in Paragraph (c) who were paid for work performed during the time when their liberty was restricted do not gain this right.

Persons categorized under Paragraph (a), besides the right to a pension recognized by the above legal provision, are also given an immediate cash award. The amount to be granted will be determined by special provisions after the approval of this Law.

Article 9

The time for which compensation will be calculated will be the full length in days of the sentence according to Paragraphs (b) and (c) of Article 3.

Calculations of the amount of compensation for this period will be based on the highest basic pay rate in mines operative in the period between 1945 and 31 December 1990, corrected according to the average rate of price increases at the time when the compensation is calculated.

Article 10

The registration period for recognition of the right to this status will continue until 31 December 1993. Applications will not be considered after this deadline, except in cases of the total impossibility of applying, testified by a court decision.

Article 11

Material compensation will begin three months after this Law comes into effect. Compensation will be concluded by 31 December 1994.

Other Rights
Article 12

By special acts, the government will guarantee to all those persons included under Paragraphs (a), (b), and (c) of Article 3 concessions and priority consideration of their individual or collective demands in the following economic, financial, and social fields:

(a)   the privatization of State property.
(b)   grants of credit.
(c)   construction and housing.
(d)   tourism.
(e)   education and training.
(f)   employment within Albania and abroad.
(g)   the realization of various national and international economic and social programs.
(h)   the health service.

The date concluding the grant of these concessions will be decided by a special law.

Intermediate Provisions
Article 13

All persons categorized under Paragraphs (b), (c), and (d) of Article 5, although not recognized as having the right to this status, will be given material compensation in accordance with the provisions of this Law.

Article 14

The right to this status is personal. Property rights stemming from this status may be transferred to heirs according to the provisions of the Civil Code on inheritance, but only once and only to persons included under Paragraphs (a), (b), and (c) of Article 3.

The Organs and Procedure for Granting Status
Article 15

A trilateral commission will be created to grant the right to this status, consisting of:

(a) three representatives of the Justice Ministry.
(b) three representatives of the State Commission for Former Victims of Political Persecution.
(c) three representatives from the National Association of Victims of Political Persecution.

The level of representation and procedures for meetings will be decided by special provisions issued by the Council of Ministers.

Article 16

Documents recognized for the grant of the right of this status in the cases categorized under Paragraphs (a), (b), (c), and (d) of Article 3 are as follows:

For Paragraph (a):
—A certificate from the Commission of the Ministry of Public Order and the Justice Ministry in cases in which a person has been killed or has died as a result of persecution.
—A legal and medical report from the time when the persecuted person lost the power of judgement because of persecution and a current legal and medical report showing that this situation is still true today or continued until the date of death, if the persecuted person is no longer alive. The degree of incapacity at which a person acquires rights under Paragraph (a) will be determined by a commission specially created for this purpose by the Ministry of Health.

For Paragraph (b):
—A certificate of conviction from the Justice Ministry showing the length of time spent in prison.
—A decision from today's court testifying to the length of time spent as an outlaw, in the cases of persons living as outlaws within the country.

For Paragraph (c):
—A decision of the courts or the internment commissions of the Ministry of Public Order.

For Paragraph (d):
—Testimonies from the convicted or interned person who became the cause of the persecution of other persons. These other persons may not be more remote than nephews, nieces, grandsons, or granddaughters. Also valid are other forms of documentary evidence, not only court decisions, proving the persecution of anybody because of his blood or social ties with persecuted persons included under Paragraphs (a), (b), and (c) of Article 3 including cases covered by Article 6 of this Law.

In all cases where it is not possible to secure documented testimonies from the time the persecution task place, interested persons have the right to settle their cases in court.

Article 17

All documents described in Article 16 will be collected by the presidiums of the associations of former political prisoners and victims of persecution and the associations of former victims of political and economic persecution in neighborhoods, villages, and towns in cooperation with the State inspectors for victims of political persecution in the districts, who will send them to the Committee for Former Victims of Political Persecution. This committee will collate them and submit them for consideration at a meeting of the trilateral commission.

Article 18

On the basis of the proposals of the National Presidium of the Association of Former Political Prisoners and Victims of Persecution, the trilateral commission mentioned in Article 15 is given the right to consider special cases for the granting of this status to all persons excluded from this right under Article 5 of this Law. After the examination of these applications, the decision of this commission is final.

Article 19

Persons who unjustly acquire this status are obliged to return the sum of material compensation received according to the rights stemming from this status.

Persons acquiring this status with documents legally proved to have been falsified, besides returning the sum they have unjustly obtained, will also be subject to criminal prosecution according to the provision in force.

Final Provisions
Article 20

All legal provisions conflicting with this Law are annulled, except when considered otherwise by this Law.

Article 21

The State Commission for Former Victims of Political Persecution is the State authority responsible for the enforcement of the rights obtained under this status....

ARGENTINA: INDEMNIFICATION LAW

Law No. 24.043 (November 27, 1991)

Article 1

Those persons who during the period of the state of emergency were placed at the disposition of the National Executive Authority based on a decision of the latter, or in the case of civilians, who were incarcerated based on orders issued by military courts, whether or not they have filed claims for damages and loss, are eligible for the benefits prescribed by this Law, provided that they have not received indemnity of any sort based on a legal decision related to the events covered by the present Law.

Article 2

In order to have recourse to the benefits covered by the present Law, the persons mentioned in the preceding Article must comply with one of the following requisites:

(a) Having been placed at the disposition of the National Executive Authority prior to December 10, 1983.
(b) In the case of civilians, having been deprived of their freedom based on orders issued by a military court, whether or not a sentence of guilty was issued in the case.

Article 3

Applications for the benefits shall be submitted to the Ministry of the Interior, which will ensure in the customary way that all the requirements specified in the preceding Articles have been fulfilled, and will verify the period of time referred to in Article 2, paragraphs (a) and (b).

A decision to deny the benefit in total or in part shall be subject to appeal within ten (10) days after serving notice before the National Chamber of Appeals for Federal Administrative Litigation in the Federal Capital. The appeal must be submitted with supporting evidence, and the Ministry of the Interior shall forward it to the Chamber, along with its opinion, within a period of five days. The Chamber shall render its decision with no further procedures within a period of twenty (20) days after receiving the case.

Article 4

The benefit established by the present Law shall be equal to one-thirtieth (1/30th) of the monthly remuneration assigned to the higher category on the pay scale for civilian employees of the national public administration ... for every day included in the period during which the measure referred to in Article 2, paragraphs (a) and (b) took place, with respect to each beneficiary. For these purposes, the monthly remuneration shall be considered to include all the elements that constitute the monthly salary of the individual, such as retirement benefits, with the exception of particular additions (such as seniority increments, titles, etc.), calculated starting from the month in which the benefit was granted.

In order to calculate the period of time described in the preceding paragraph, it will be based on the Law of the Executive Authority that ordered the measure or the effective arrest of the individual without a directive from a competent judicial authority, and the Law that canceled the measure, whether it was a particular order or as a result of the lifting of the state of siege.

Cases of house arrest or liberty under surveillance are not considered as cancellations of the measure taken.

If a person described above died during the period in which he was subject to the measures referred to in Article 2, paragraphs (a) and (b), the benefit shall be established in the manner indicated above, with the period of time being calculated up to the moment of death. Without affecting the foregoing, in such a case the benefit shall be increased—simply because of the death—by an amount equivalent to that specified by this Law for being affected by the measures described in Article 2, paragraphs (a) and (b), for a period of five (5) years.

The benefit corresponding to persons who under similar circumstances suffered serious wounds, according to the classification indicated by the Penal Code, shall be increased to take this factor into consideration, by an amount equivalent to that specified in the preceding paragraph, less thirty percent (30%).

Article 5

The rights granted by this Law can be exercised by the persons mentioned in Article 1 or, in case of death, by their legal heirs.

Article 6

The application referred to in Article 3 of this Law must be submitted, in order to ensure its validity, within a period of one hundred and eighty (180) days from the date on which this Law goes into effect.

Article 7

In all cases, the payment shall be made in six (6) semi-annual installments, the first of which shall be due within sixty (60) days following the date on which the benefit was granted. The amount of the installments shall be indexed based on the increase in cost of living from the date of granting the benefit to the date of payment, based on the consumer price index published by INDEC, plus an annual interest rate of six percent (6%) on amounts due. For the purpose of calculations, the index used will be the one corresponding to the month previous to the granting of the benefit and the actual payment, respectively.

If the payment is not received within the specified period of time, the beneficiary shall have the right to file a legal claim, with no requirements for previous notification, mediation, or other actions, in application of the standards that regulate the implementation of a legal decision. The amount of the indemnities established by this Law shall be determined in accordance with the provisions of Law No. 23.982.

BRAZIL: 1988 CONSTITUTION— TRANSITIONAL PROVISIONS

(October 5, 1988)

The Transitory Constitutional Provisions Act
Article 8

Amnesty is granted to those who, during the period from September 18, 1946 to the date the Constitution is promulgated, have been affected, exclusively for political reasons, by institutional or supplementary acts of exception, to those encompassed in Legislative Decree No. 18 of December 15, 1961, and to those affected by Decree-Law No. 846 of September 12, 1969, ensuring the promotions, in their inactivity, to the office, position or rank to which they would be entitled if they were in active service, with due regard for the periods of continuous activity set forth in laws and regulations in force, respecting the characteristics and peculiarities of the careers of civil and military public servants and complying with the respective legal regimes.

Paragraph 1. The provisions of this article shall only generate financial effects as from the promulgation of the Constitution, any kind of retroactive compensation being forbidden.

Paragraph 2. The benefits established in this article are ensured to workers of the private sector, union officers and representatives who, for exclusively political reasons, have been punished, dismissed or compelled to leave the remunerated activities they had been performing, as well as to those who have been prevented from performing their professional activities by virtue of ostensive pressures or secret official procedures.

Paragraph 3. Reparation of economic nature shall be granted, as set forth by a law to be proposed by the National Congress and to become effective within twelve months counted from the promulgation of the Constitution, to citizens who were prevented from performing, as civilians, a specific professional activity by virtue of Reserved Ordinances of the Ministry of the Air Force No. S-50-GM5 of June 19, 1964, and No. S-285-GM5.

Paragraph 4. To those who, by virtue of institutional acts, have gratuitously exercised elective offices of city councilmen, the respective periods shall be computed for purposes of social security and retirement from civil service.

Paragraph 5. The amnesty granted under this article applies to civil servants and to employees at all levels of government or at its foundations, state-owned companies or mixed-capital companies under state control, except at the military Ministries, who have been punished or dismissed from professional activities interrupted by decision of their employees, as well as by virtue of Decree-Law No. 1632 of August 4, 1978, or for exclusively political reasons, the readmission of those affected as from 1979 being assured, with due regard for the provisions of paragraph 1.

Article 9

Those who, for exclusively political reasons, were disfranchised or had their political rights suspended during the period from July 15 to December 31, 1969, by an act of the then President of the Republic, may request the Supreme Federal Court to acknowledge the rights and advantages interrupted by the punitive acts, provided that they prove that such acts were marked by gross flaws.

Sole Paragraph. The Supreme Federal Court shall pronounce its decision within one hundred and twenty days as from the request of the interested party....

BULGARIA: LAW ON POLITICAL AND CIVIL REHABILITATION OF OPPRESSED PERSONS

(June 15, 1991)

Article 1

Political and civil rehabilitation is hereby declared for persons who have been unlawfully oppressed because of their national origin, or political and religious convictions during the period running from 12 September 1944 until 10 November 1989 to include the following:

1. persons sentenced for criminal acts with the exception of persons sentenced by the People's Court of 1944-1945;
2. persons who were unlawfully detained in subdivisions of the Ministry of Internal Affairs and other places;
3. persons interned in labor-education hostels, camps and other such places;
4. persons interned, deported or resettled under administrative rules;
5. persons sentenced under criminal proceedings for failure to meet State quotas;
6. students and pupils who were expelled;
7. persons oppressed in connection with forced change of name;
8. persons who disappeared without a trace.

Article 2

Persons in the categories listed above shall have the right to lump-sum compensation for the property and non-property damages they have endured as follows:

1. persons sentenced under the Law on Safeguarding National Power, chapters I and II of the Criminal Law in effect prior to 13 March 1951; chapter I—Crimes against the People's Republic of the Criminal Code in effect subsequent to 13 March 1951 and chapter I—Crimes against the People's Republic in effect after 1 May 1968 who have been granted amnesty for their actions;
2. persons sentenced for crimes and granted amnesty under Article 1 of the Law on Amnesty and Exemption from Serving Sentences Imposed (*State Gazette*, N° 6, 1990);
3. persons sentenced to imprisonment for failure to meet State quotas who have served prison terms;
4. persons interned in labor-education hostels, camps and other similar places;
5. persons who were interned, deported or resettled under administrative rules;

6. students and pupils who were expelled and who were not permitted to complete their educations.

Article 3

(1) If persons listed in Article 2, items 1-5 who have not received compensation for property damages have died, compensation shall be paid to their heirs to include children, spouse, parents.

(2) Heirs, to include children, spouse and parents of persons sentenced to death whose sentences were carried out, the heirs of persons who vanished after 12 September 1944 and those who died in connection with forced change of name shall receive lump-sum compensation for non-property damages.

Article 4

(1) The amount and procedures for payment of compensation shall be determined by the Council of Ministers.

(2) The right to restitution shall be established through appropriate written evidence.

(3) If said written evidence is missing as a result of circumstances under previous regulations, its establishment shall be carried out by central and regional commissions under procedures and in a composition determined by the Council of Ministers.

Article 5

(1) Requests for restitution shall be submitted to the Ministry of Finance within 3 years of the time when the Law takes effect.

(2) Restitution shall be paid out of the State budget.

Article 6

Restitution shall not be paid to persons who have received compensation under previous regulations.

Article 7

Length of labor service shall recognize the following:

1. the time during which persons under Article 1, items 1 and 2 were in prison, labor-education hostels, camps and detention sites;
2. the amount of time during which persons of legal majority did not hold employment while they were interned, deported or resettled.

Article 8

The heirs of persons who died, committed suicide or disappeared in connection with forced changes of name shall receive a survivor's pension until such time as there is lawful basis for its termination.

Additional and Final Regulations

§ 1. The following are rescinded:

1. Item 5 of the Decision on Political and Civil Rehabilitation for Persons Who Were Sentenced or Oppressed after 30 March 1990 (*State Gazette*, N° 30, 1990).
2. Item 5 of the Decision of the Parliamentary Commission on Review and Resolution of Certain Urgent Questions Associated with Allowed Infractions and Violations of the Law in State, Social and Economic Life (*State Gazette*, N° 44, 1990)....

§ 2. Actions under Article 4 shall be published by the Council of Ministers no later than 6 months after the Law goes into effect....

BULGARIA: LAW ON AMNESTY AND RESTORATION OF CONFISCATED PROPERTY AND IMPLEMENTING REGULATIONS

Law No. 167 (December 20, 1990)

Article 1

Amnesty is granted for the following crimes thereby eliminating their criminal nature:

1. Under the Law on Safeguarding National Power, Articles 2, 3 and Article 10, paragraph 1;
2. Under the Criminal Code which became the Criminal Code in effect after 13 March 1951: Article 71, items 1 and 2, Articles 73-80, 82, 83, 85, 87, 90, 92, 93, 95 and 96.

Article 2

Amnesty is granted which relieves persons convicted of the following actions of criminal responsibility and of the consequences of their sentence:

1. Under the Law on Safeguarding National Power: Article 9, paragraphs 1-3 and 5;
2. Under the Criminal Law in effect prior to 13 March 1951: Article 101, paragraphs 1-3 and 5;
3. Under the Criminal Law in effect after 1 May 1968: Articles 95, 98, 100, 101, 103, 104, 105, 107, 108, 109, 110, 269, 270, 272, 279, 320 and 386.

Article 3

Amnesty is granted for actions that were committed during the period from 17 March 1945 until 31 December 1989.

Article 4

Outstanding fines shall not be collected and court actions to collect fines shall cease.

Article 5

(1) Real property under Article 1 that has been confiscated shall be returned to the persons from whom it was confiscated or to their legal heirs if it is in the possession of the State or in the possession of a State or

municipal company in which the State owns at least a 51 percent share before this Law goes into effect.

(2) If the conditions of the preceding paragraph have ceased to exist or if the property has been destroyed, demolished or rebuilt, said convicted individuals shall be compensated with another piece of real property of equal value or with monetary compensation under rules and procedures determined by the Council of Ministers....

Article 7

Property seized prior to 22 May 1989 under the laws governing Bulgarian citizenship shall be returned to persons deprived of Bulgarian citizenship after its restoration under the conditions of Article 5.

Article 8

(1) Claims from convicted persons or their heirs for return of confiscated real property or for compensation shall be submitted within two years from the time this Law takes effect to the Municipal People's Council in the area where the confiscated property is situated.

(2) If a claim that has been submitted is not satisfied within a period of 6 months, interested parties may request a court judgment against the Municipal People's Council and the Ministry of Finance.

(3) In proceedings before a court, the circumstances of the verdict, the execution of the confiscation process, the type and cost of the confiscated property must be established from all types of proof allowable under the Code of Civil Procedure in situations where actions or the appropriate written documentation has been lost or destroyed.

(4) Proceeds under actions are exempt from State taxes.

Additional and Final Regulations

§ 1. Disputed issues that may arise from this Law shall be decided by the court issuing the judgment or in which proceedings on the respective crime are handled....

§ 3. The Council of Ministers shall issue regulations under Article 5, paragraph 2 within a period of 2 months.

§ 4. Implementation of this Law is entrusted to the Minister of Justice, the Minister of Finance and the Chief Prosecutor of the Republic.

This Law is hereby adopted by the Grand National Assembly on 20 December 1990 and is stamped with the State Seal.

Implementing Regulations

for application of Article 5, paragraph 2
of the Amnesty and Restoration of Confiscated Property Act

adopted by Resolution No. 139 of the Council of Ministers (July 18, 1991)

Article 1

The method and procedures for compensating persons granted amnesty under Articles 1, 6 and 7 of the Law on Amnesty and Restoration of Confiscated Property (*State Gazette*, No. 1, 1991) shall be determined by this Regulation....

Article 3

(1) Real property that has been confiscated or seized shall be returned to the persons from whom it was confiscated or seized or to their legal heirs if said property is in possession of the State before the Law on Amnesty and Restoration of Confiscated Property goes into effect.

(2) Real property that has been confiscated or seized which is being administered or managed by Municipal People's Councils, ministries, departments and other State institutions and organizations, by joint ventures with State or municipal shares of at least 51 percent and other State legal entities or which has been handed over by them under a loan, for lease or in which the right of use is vested before such time as the Law on Amnesty and Restoration of Confiscated Property takes effect is considered to be in the possession of the State.

(3) Agricultural property that has been confiscated or seized is considered to be in the possession of the State and subject to return under the procedures and in amounts not greater than the amount of land that can be owned under the Law on Ownership and Use of Agricultural Land, regardless of whether there has been a change in its character. If the rightful owners are foreign citizens or Bulgarian citizens permanently residing abroad, they must be compensated monetarily with such amounts to be determined in accord with the Bulgarian Law on Ownership and Use of Agricultural Land.

Article 4

(1) Ministries, departments and other State institutions, organizations and municipal companies, joint ventures with a State or municipal share of at least 51 percent and other State legal entities to which real properties have been conceded under Article 3, paragraph 2 must hand over these properties to the Municipal People's Council for return to their rightful owners within a period of 2 months after notification.

(2) If properties have been acquired as payment, the Municipal People's Council shall return amounts paid from transfer of the property reduced by

an appropriate amount for damages sustained and increased by the cost of any improvements made.

(3) If confiscated or seized real estate has been acquired without payment, the Municipal People's Council shall return only the amounts by which value has increased as a result of improvements made reduced by amounts for wear and tear and any damages incurred.

Article 5

When confiscated or seized real estate is not in possession of the State or in situations in which it has been destroyed, demolished or rebuilt, the rightful owner shall be compensated with other real property or with monetary payment.

Article 6

If real property has been granted to a joint venture with a State or municipal share of less than 51 percent, the rightful owner shall be compensated with some other piece of real property of their choice or with monetary payment.

Article 7

(1) Real property that has been confiscated or seized that has not been taken over by the State and is in possession of the rightful owner or possession of members of his family shall remain in possession of the rightful owner.

(2) When property under paragraph 1 is under the control of a third person without legal basis, said property is taken by the State under the procedures of Article 16 of the Law on Ownership and is transferred to the rightful owner.

Article 8

(1) Real properties that have been confiscated or seized are not subject to return and no compensation is owed for them if the State has paid the debts of a person who has been convicted or deprived of Bulgarian citizenship occurring prior to institution of criminal proceedings or before deprivation of Bulgarian citizenship.

(2) If the amount of payment for debt is less than the value of real estate that has been confiscated or seized, then any residue of the value of property prior to the date when the debt was paid shall be returned to the rightful owner.

Article 9

Confiscated or seized property is considered to have been destroyed if the following is true prior to the time of submission of the claim for their return:

1. said properties have been set aside for activities of the State, cooperatives or municipal organizations after construction and regulation plans have gone into effect and actions have been taken to realize such activities to include studies and design, yielding of right to construction or issue of permission for construction;
2. said properties are in areas consisting of beaches, reservoirs, ravines, rivers, lakes, preserves, parks, line facilities (roads, rail lines, electric power lines, etc.), type "A" sanitary protection zones of sources of for the public water supply, garbage dumps, other protected natural areas of national and international environmental protective significance to include lands under and on which archeological finds or cultural monuments are located.

Article 10

(1) Structures that have been eliminated are considered to have been destroyed and are not subject to compensation for confiscation or seizure as follows:

1. when they have become unfit for further use because of normal wear and tear or other circumstances, when they are threatened by collapse or have become dangerous in terms of health and hygiene and cannot be repaired, reinforced or made safe after the verdict of judgment took effect;
2. when frame structures ... have aged significantly and threaten the appearance of cities, industrial centers, health resorts and vacation areas, population centers of historic, ethnographic or architectural importance, streets and squares at the center of villages, republic roadways, railroads, stations, airfields, rest areas and tourist areas or when they hinder traffic safety;
3. illegal structures as well as those for which compensation is not due in cases of expropriation.

(2) In situations noted in paragraph 1, above, compensation is due only by right of ownership of the site or the right of construction.

Article 11

Confiscated or seized real estate is considered to have been rebuilt when the following is true at the time a claim for return is submitted:

1. the right to build on them has been conceded;

2. the overall structure, size, area or purpose of the property has been substantially changed as a result of reconstruction, addition or renovations or the value of the reconstruction, addition or renovations is greater than the value of the confiscated or seized property.

Article 12

(1) If confiscated or seized real estate is sold or building rights have been let after a verdict has gone into effect or after deprivation of Bulgarian citizenship, a monetary sum shall be returned to the persons from whom it was confiscated or seized or to their spouses.

(2) Rightful owners or their spouses who have acquired another residence or permission to construct a residence or country house from the State after the confiscation or seizure of real property shall owe the difference between the price for which it was sold or for which the right to build was purchased on property of the same type to the State if the seized property is returned or if compensation has been paid for a similar type of property at the time of return or payment of the price for acquisition of State property.

Article 13

Real property in the area where the confiscated or seized real property is located shall be offered as compensation to the rightful owner. With consent of the rightful owner, real property of another type in the same location may be granted to the rightful owner.

Article 14

If it is not possible to compensate the rightful owner with other real property, monetary compensation may be paid by decision of the executive committee of the Municipal People's Council where the confiscated or seized property is located.

Article 15

(1) Confiscated real property and real property given in compensation shall be appraised at the same rates at which the State sells or concedes the right to build on State properties of the same type to individuals at the time of return. Confiscated properties are also assessed at this rate in situations where monetary compensation is determined to be owing.

(2) The differences between the value of confiscated or seized real property and real property received as compensation is paid by the party receiving the more valuable property. In the case of property return, the rightful owner owes to the State the amount by which the value of the property has increased as a result of improvements made and reduced by

amounts for normal wear and tear and damages incurred. The conditions of paragraph 1 are used in determining the amount owing.

Article 16

Request from persons granted amnesty or their heirs for compensation shall be submitted to the Municipal People's Council. They shall prepare for a review by a committee consisting of the president who is the president of the Municipal People's Council or an individual appointed by him, and members to include the legal counsel of the Municipal People's Council and specialists from the "Architecture and Public Services", "State Property" and "Finance" departments. The regional prosecutor shall also be invited to take part.

Article 17

(1) The committee under Article 16, above, shall make an inventory of all confiscated and seized real estate within three months after this regulation goes into effect.

(2) Based on this inventory, the commission shall:

1. determine which of the confiscated or seized real properties is in possession of the State in the meaning of Article 3, paragraph 2 and which of them may have been destroyed, demolished or rebuilt;
2. calculate the value of existing real properties in the stock entitled "Real Property Reserves";
3. specify the ministries, departments, institutions, firms and other legal entities that are obligated to transfer confiscated or seized real estate entrusted to them for administration and management or assigned for rent or lease or for utilization;
4. review the claims of rightful owners for compensation by them with other real property of equal value or with cash.

Article 18

(1) Return of confiscated or seized real property is done on the basis of a written request from the rightful owner based on written proof in the hands of the council. If necessary, the committee may request that the person submit appropriate evidence to establish the claim.

(2) When it is not possible to establish or specify confiscated or seized property from the existing evidence, matters in dispute shall be established by court order.

Article 19

(1) A decision shall be made on a request submitted for compensation within a period of six months from the date of submission.

(2) Decisions from the Municipal People's Council are subject to appeal through court order under the Law on Administrative Procedure.

Article 20

(1) The return of properties in possession of the State is carried out by order of the Ministry of Finance on the basis of a proposal directed from the president of the Municipal People's Council in the area where the property is located....

(2) When a rightful owner is compensated with some other piece of real property of equal value, the transfer of ownership takes place on instruction from the president of the Municipal People's Council in the area where the property is situated on which basis a written contract is then concluded....

Article 21

(1) When a person who has been granted amnesty requests a review under the rules of oversight or reopening of a criminal proceeding and the verdict of not guilty is entered which means that no criminal act has been committed, he shall be compensated under the conditions and procedures of this regulation. This also applies to actions under Articles 1 and 6 of the Amnesty and Restoration of Confiscated Property Act.

(2) When persons who have been granted amnesty under Article 2 of the Law on Amnesty and Restoration of Confiscated Property request a review under the procedures of oversight or reopening of a criminal proceeding and a verdict of not guilty is granted, any confiscated real property shall be returned under the conditions of Article 151 of the Law on Imposition of Penalties.

Article 22

(1) When confiscated or seized properties taken in payment to ministries, people's councils, departments, other State institutions and organizations, State and municipal companies, joint ventures and other State legal entities are not subject to return and the rightful owners have been compensated with other property or monetary payment, the difference [in] value under which they were sold or the right to build on civil or State real property of similar type is released as well as any sums paid shall be restored to the State.

(2) If the properties under paragraph 1 are consigned without payment, their entire value shall be paid....

Article 23

An account marked "Return of Seized Property" shall be created for the Municipal People's Council. Assets in this account are collected from:

1. income under Article 12, paragraph 2, Article 15, paragraph 2 and Article 22;
2. income under account 1 in the "Residential Construction" fund in the case of the Municipal People's Council from the sale or release of building rights or building onto confiscated and seized real properties and from sales against payments for administration and management or from the right of use, for lease or rent of confiscated or seized real property;
3. assets transferred into the State budget from confiscated and seized personal property that has been liquidated in accordance with Article 71, paragraph 6 of the Regulations on State Property;
4. other sources as defined by the Council of Ministers based on the report of the minister of Finance.

Article 24

Assets in this fund shall be expended for:

1. the acquisition of real property from people's councils through purchases from individuals and legal entities needed to compensate rightful owners;
2. payment for the cost of residences taken out of the housing stock in circulation or left unsold under Article 117 of the Law on Regional and Urban Construction for the purpose of granting compensation to rightful owners;
3. financing and building new residences necessary for compensation of rightful owners;
4. payments of monies owing under Article 2, paragraphs 2 and 3, Article 8, paragraph 2, Article 12, paragraph 1, Article 14 and Article 15, paragraph 2....

Article 26

(1) An account entitled "Real Property Reserves" shall be created. This fund shall consist of:

1. confiscated real property that is in possession of the State at the time the Law on Amnesty and Restoration of Confiscated Property goes into effect;
2. real property acquired with assets of the account under Article 23;
3. newly constructed residential housing set aside by ministries, departments, municipal organizations, companies and other legal entities against the right to build on State land given up by them in return for construction of housing under Article 25, paragraph 1;
4. real property acquired from the State on the basis of Articles 6 and 100 of the Law on Ownership and Article 11 of the Law on Inheritance;

5. that portion of residential housing from the circulating stock given up by lease holders—owners are compensated as are other persons through acquisition of another residence;

6. residential buildings in good repair acquired from the State through expropriation which are used for non-residential needs;

7. that portion of State-owned building lots designated for single-family residences and construction of country [second or vacation] homes.

(2) Properties in the account entitled "Real Property Reserves" may not be sold and the rights to build on them may not be given up until two years have elapsed under Article 8 of the Amnesty and Restoration of Confiscated Property Act.

(3) After elapse of the period noted in paragraph 2, above, that portion of the properties which exceeds the claims submitted for property compensation may be excluded from the fund under Article 26 by decision of the executive committee of the Municipal People's Council....

Transition and Final Directives

§ 2. Actions having to do with transfer and other actions involving confiscated or seized real property in possession of the State or a State or municipal firm in which the State has at least a 51 percent share before the Law on Amnesty and Restoration of Confiscated Property are hereby stopped.

§ 3. Properties that have been sold or for which the right to build has been released to an individual after the Law on Amnesty and Restoration of Confiscated Property goes into effect but before this regulation takes effect are subject to return should the rightful owner request return of the same property within a period of two years. In this instance, individuals may be granted another piece of property from the State stock of housing to include properties from the fund marked "Real Property Reserves"....

CHILE: LAW CREATING THE NATIONAL CORPORATION FOR REPARATION AND RECONCILIATION*

Law No. 19,123 (January 31, 1992)

Title I
National Corporation for Reparation and Reconciliation
Paragraph I
Nature and Objectives
Article 1

It is hereby created the National Corporation for Reparation and Reconciliation, a decentralized public service subject to the supervision of the President of the Republic through the Ministry of the Interior. Its domicile will be in the city of Santiago.

The object thereof shall be the coordination, execution and promotion of the actions necessary for complying with the recommendations contained in the Report of the Truth and Reconciliation National Commission (*Comisión Nacional de Verdad y Reconciliación*), created by Supreme Decree Nr. 355, as of April 25, 1990, and the other duties set forth in the present Law.

Article 2

The specific duties of the Corporation shall be:

1. To promote the reparation of moral damages caused to the victims referred to in Article 18 and grant the social and legal assistance required by their families in order to have access to the benefits provided for in this Law.

2. To promote and cooperate in actions tending to determine the whereabouts and circumstances of the disappearance or death of the disappeared detainees and of those whose remains, although the legal recognition of their decease exists, have not been located. In the fulfillment of this objective, it shall gather, analyze and systematize any information useful for this purpose.

3. To keep under custody the background information gathered by both the Truth and Reconciliation National Commission and the National Corporation for Reparation and Reconciliation, as well as all such information that may be gathered in the future concerning cases and matters similar to those dealt with by the Corporation. Likewise, it may require, gather and process the overall information

---

* The English translation of Law No. 19,123 which follows was produced by the Ministry of Foreign Affairs of the Republic of Chile. Modifications to the translation are in brackets.

existing in the possession of public entities, and request it from private entities, in connection with the human rights violations or political violence referred to in the Report of the Truth and Reconciliation National Commission.

Access to the information shall ensure the absolute confidentiality thereof, without prejudice to the fact that the Courts of justice may have access to such information, in proceedings being heard by them.

4. To gather information and perform the inquiries necessary to render judgment in those cases investigated by the Truth and Reconciliation National Commission and in which it was not possible to attain certainty as regards the condition of victim of human rights violations or political violence of the concerned person, or with respect to cases of the same nature, of which it had no opportune knowledge or, having had it, the Commission did not issue an opinion due to lack of sufficient information. Concerning this matter, it shall proceed according to the same rules prescribed for said Commission in Supreme Decree Nr. 355 from the Ministry of the Interior, as of April 25, 1990, whereby it was created.

The cases referred to in the preceding paragraph of this number shall be communicated to the Corporation within 90 days following the publication of its internal Regulations in the Official Gazette, and they shall be settled within one year commencing from the same publication.

If the Corporation attains certainty of the condition of victim of a person, it shall communicate it immediately to the pertinent agencies of the State Administration, in order that they grant the rights and benefits provided for by the present Law to the beneficiaries.

5. To enter into agreements with non-profit Institutions or Corporations so that they may provide the professional assistance required to fulfill the objectives of the Corporation, including medical benefits.

6. To make proposals for the consolidation of a culture of respect for human rights in this country.

Article 3

In order to achieve its objectives, the Corporation may request the collaboration of the different agencies of the State, in [matters within their competence] and which are related to the duties pertaining to it.

Article 4

In no event shall the Corporation undertake jurisdictional functions corresponding to the Courts of Justice nor shall it interfere with proceedings pending before them. It shall not, therefore, decide on the responsibility that, according to the laws, lies on individuals.

If in the performance of its duties the Corporation should have knowledge of acts having the nature of a crime, it shall, without further steps, report them to the Courts of Justice.

Article 5

The acts of the Corporation shall be performed in a reserved manner, its advisors and officers being obliged to keep secrecy as regards the information and documents that may come to their notice in the fulfillment of their duties.

Article 6

It is declared that the location of the disappeared detainees, as well as that of the bodies of the executed persons and the circumstances of said disappearance or death, constitute an inalienable right of the victims' families and of the Chilean society.

Paragraph II
Organization of the Corporation

Article 7

The Management of the Corporation shall be the responsibility of a Higher Council, which shall be composed as follows:

- (a) a [Chairman], who shall preside over the Higher Council, appointed by the President of the Republic, and
- (b) six counselors, appointed by the President of the Republic, with the agreement of the Senate.

The Counselors, except for the Chairman, shall receive a salary amounting to one thirtieth of the remuneration corresponding to a Justice of the Supreme Court, 2nd degree of the Salary Scale established by Decree Law Nr. 3,058, as of 1979, for each meeting attended by them.

The Counselors shall be entitled to tickets and travel allowances. The amount of the travel allowances shall be assimilated to those corresponding to the second category of the judiciary.

The duties of Chairman of the Council and those of Counselors shall be compatible with any public office, excepting those established by the Constitution itself.

Nevertheless, incompatibility of remuneration shall apply to the Chairman of the Council in case he holds another employment or public office, and he will have to choose between the remuneration assigned to him in this Law and that of the other office or employment.

Article 8

The duties of the Higher Council are:

1. To exercise the [executive] management of the Corporation and approve the courses and programs of action of this entity for the fulfillment of its assignment.
2. To declare the condition of victim of human rights violations or of political violence.
3. To make the proposals referred to in Nr. 6 of Article 2.
4. To ensure compliance with the resolutions and directions to be adopted or issued by it.
5. To establish the internal Regulations of the Corporation, which shall state, *inter alia*, the procedure to which the requests for the investigation and decision of the cases referred to in Article 2 Nr. 4 will be submitted, the order of subrogation of the Chairman among the Council members, that the decisions thereof shall be adopted by a majority of the acting Counselors and that, in case of equality of votes, its Chairman shall have a casting vote.
6. To decide on the performance of such acts and contracts that, according to the laws, require that a special power of attorney be granted.

Article 9

The duties of the Chairman of the Council are:

1. To preside over the meetings of the Council.
2. To represent the Corporation judicially and extrajudicially.
3. To issue the [directions] necessary to comply with the resolutions and directions of the Council.
4. To administer the Corporation, with the agreement of the Council.
5. To periodically inform the President of the Republic of the work of the Corporation.
6. To appoint the Executive Secretary and the personnel, with the agreement of the Council.

Article 10

The Corporation shall have an Executive Secretary, whose duties shall be as follows:

1. To execute the resolutions of the Council and comply with the directions of the Chairman.
2. To act as Secretary of the Council and Commissioner for Oaths.

The Executive Secretary shall be entitled to speak at the meetings of the Council.

Paragraph III
Staff and Personnel
Article 11

The following staff for the National Corporation for Reparation and Reconciliation is hereby established:... [total number of staff: 15]

Article 12

The personnel of the Corporation shall be governed by the provisions of Law Nr. 18,834, Administrative Statute, and as regards remunerations, it shall be subject to the rules of Decree Law Nr. 249, as of 1974, and its supplementary legislation.

Article 13

The organs and services of the State Administration may assign officers of their respective agencies ... to the National Corporation for Reparation and Reconciliation....

The degrees of the salary scales ... of the aforementioned Corporation, may not exceed the maximum limit prescribed for the personnel of the several staffs referred to in Article 5 of Law Nr. 18,834.

Paragraph IV
[Assets] and Control
Article 14

The [assets] of the Corporation shall be composed of all kinds of real and personal property that it may acquire gratuitously or [by payment] and, in particular, by:

(1) The annual contributions allocated to it by the Budgetary Law;
(2) Other contributions, either national or international, and
(3) The proceeds of such property.

The gifts in favor of the Corporation shall not require ... judicial certification ... and shall be exempt from the payment of the gift tax....

Article 15

The Corporation shall be subject to supervision by the Office of the Comptroller General of the Republic as regards the examination and verification of its income and expenditures accounts and to control as to the legality of the actions relative to its personnel and the statutory regulations thereof.

Paragraph V
Extinguishment
Article 16

The National Corporation for Reparation and Reconciliation shall have legal existence for 24 months, commencing from the publication date of this Law. Once this period is elapsed, it shall extinguish by operation of law. Its property shall be taken over by the Fisco or one of its bodies, which shall be determined by Supreme Decree from the Department of the Interior. Without prejudice to the above, the President of the Republic may extend its effective period for a term not to exceed twelve months.

However, should the objectives of the Corporation be fulfilled before the term established in the foregoing paragraph, the President of the Republic shall, by decree signed by the Minister of the Interior, be empowered to terminate the Corporation as earlier as he may deem proper.

Title II
The Reparation Pension
Article 17

A monthly pension is hereby established for the benefit of relatives of the victims of human rights violations or political violence, who are named in the Second Volume of the Report from the National Commission for Truth and Reconciliation and those who are [declared] as such by the National Corporation for Reparation and Reconciliation, as provided by Articles 2, Nr. 4 and 8, Nr. 2.

Article 18

Eligible for the reparation pension will be those individuals declared victims of human rights violations or political violence, as provided for in the preceding paragraph.

Article 19

The monthly pension set forth in Article 17 shall amount to Ch. $140,000 plus the percentage equivalent to the health contributions; it shall be subject to no provisional contribution other than that, and shall be adjusted according to the provisions of Article 14 of Decree Law 2,448 as of 1979 or of the law rules in replacement of the said provision. Waiver may be made of this pension.

Article 20

Beneficiaries of the pension set forth in Article 17 shall be: the surviving spouse, the mother of the principal or his father if she has predeceased; the mother of the natural children of the principal or their father when the principal is their mother, and children under the age of 25, or disabled children regardless of age, whether legitimate, natural, adoptive or illegitimate who are included in the cases mentioned in Nr. 1, 2 and 3 of Article 280 of the Civil Code.

To the effects of this Law, disabled children will be those who suffer from a physical, intellectual or psychological damage or weakening of his physical or intellectual powers which bring about, on an assumably permanent basis, a reduction of at least fifty per cent of his capability to perform a normal job, according to his/her age, sex and current strength, capacity, training or level of instruction.

The declaration and [examination] of the disability shall be vested in the Preventive Medicine and Disability Committee of the respective Health Service as determined by the Regulations.

Supervening disability shall entitle [a beneficiary] to a pension regardless of the benefit having expired, as set forth in by Article 22, which shall, at any rate be consistent with any other social security benefit created by the law.

The said pension shall be allocated among the beneficiaries already mentioned as follows:

(a) 40% for the surviving spouse;
(b) 30% for the mother of the principal or for the father where she has predeceased;
(c) 15% for the mother, or the father, as the case may be of the natural children of the principal; if more than one, each of them shall be entitled to the percentage stated, even if in excess of the amount of the pension set forth in Article 19; and
(d) 15% for each child of the principal under the age of 25 and for disabled children of any age.

In case of more than one child, each and every one shall [receive] 15% of the pension, even if in excess of the amount set forth in Article 19.

In the event that upon the call being made there is only one beneficiary, he shall [receive] a total pension amounting to Ch. $100,000 plus the contribution and the adjustment set forth in Article 19.

If upon the call there is no one or more of the beneficiaries mentioned in letter (a), (b) or (c) of this Article and there is more than one child, the allocation that the missing beneficiary would have been entitled to shall be firstly allocated to the settlement of the whole or a part of the allocations corresponding to such children. If after following this procedure there shall be a remaining, it shall be preferentially allocated to the settlement of the whole or a part of the allocation corresponding to possible beneficiaries additional to that mentioned in letter (c) of this Article. If still a remaining exists, it shall increase the allocation of each existing beneficiary *pro rata* to his/her rights until completion of the total amount of the pension referred to in Article 19. Same increase shall apply in the event there are no children.

Should any of the beneficiaries decease or pursuant to this Law cease the enjoyment of, or waive the enjoyment of the benefit, the same increase shall operate so that the pension be allocated in its entirety, except where the remaining beneficiary is only one, in which event, the pension shall be reduced to the amount of Ch. $100,000 plus the contribution and the adjustment set forth in Article 19 of this Law.

Article 21

The enjoyment of the benefit shall be deferred at the time when the present Law comes into force, and beneficiaries shall be those individuals who, for the time being alive, have had at the time of decease or disappearance of the principal, any of the family links stated in the foregoing Articles....

Article 22

The victims' children shall enjoy the pension they are entitled to, with the proper increases until the last day of the year in which they turn 25 years of age.

As regards the other beneficiaries, including disabled children, the pension with its corresponding increases shall be for life.

The surviving spouse and the mother or father of the natural children of the principal, as the case may be, shall not lose title to this benefit by reason of marriage after the death or disappearance of the principal.

As regards the beneficiaries of principals declared as victims of human rights violations or of political violence in the report of the National Commission for Truth and Reconciliation the pension shall accrue from July 1, 1991, provided they request it within six months following the effective date of this Law; should the benefit not be claimed within this term, it shall accrue from the first business day following the date on which the right is exercised.

For the beneficiaries of the principals that the National Corporation for Reparation and Reconciliation declares as victims of human rights violations or of political violence, the pension shall accrue from the date of notice as referred to in the final paragraph of number 4 of Article 2, provided they request it within the six-month term counting from the said date.

Those who claim beyond that term shall begin to enjoy it, if there are already beneficiaries entitled to it, only from the first day of the month following the date on which such applications are filed.

Whenever new beneficiaries appear and are admitted to the benefit, the pension already determined shall be reallocated. Such reallocation shall only apply for future payments, without prejudice to the provisions of the fourth and fifth paragraphs of this Article.

Article 23

Notwithstanding the provisions of Article 17, a unique payment of compensation allowance is hereby awarded to the relatives of the victims as referred to in Article 18, equivalent to twelve monthly pensions, excluding the percentage for health contributions, which shall not constitute income for any legal purpose.

Said allowance shall not be subject to any contribution and shall be paid to the beneficiaries mentioned in Article 20, in the corresponding proportions and increases as set forth in the said Article.

This allowance shall be deferred to and its amount determined conclusively and irrevocably in favor of the beneficiaries who have filed the application prescribed for in the fourth and fifth paragraphs of the foregoing Article, within the terms established therein, and those beneficiaries who submit it beyond that time limit shall lose title to it.

Article 24

The reparation pension shall be consistent with any other, of any nature whatsoever that the respective beneficiary may be entitled to.

It shall also be consistent with any other social security benefit prescribed by the laws.

Article 25

To all legal effects, the Department of the Interior shall, at the request of the concerned persons or the Normalization Institute for Social Security, issue a certificate attesting that, the National Commission for Truth and Reconciliation or the Corporation established as per Title I in this Law has verily found that a certain person has been a victim of human rights violation or of political violence.

Article 26

The reparation monthly pensions set forth in Articles 17 and 19 and the compensation allowance prescribed by Article 23 shall be unseizable.

Article 27

For the purpose of this Law, it shall be understood that the date of death or disappearance of the principal is that determined by the National Commission for Truth and Reconciliation or that established by the National Corporation for Reparation and Reconciliation, if the former has failed to do it.

Title III
Medical Benefits
Article 28

Beneficiaries as referred to in Title II as well as the father and brothers and sisters of the principal where they are not beneficiaries, are hereby granted the right to receive free health care services set forth in Articles 8 and

9 of Law Nr. 18,469, which in the institutional assistance modality are provided in the institutions depending upon or adscribed [sic] to the National System of Health Services created by Decree-Law Nr. 2,763, as of 1979 and in the modality established by the Department of Health for a specialized assistance.

The Department of Health or the respective Regional Ministerial Secretary of Health, with the sole production of the documents accrediting the status as beneficiary, or of father or brother/sister of the principal, shall cause the issuance of a special credential or card containing the name, address and national identity card number of the beneficiary. Such individual card shall constitute an indispensable requirement for the health care institutions depending upon or adscribed to the National System of Health Services of any level to provide free health care to the beneficiary.

The provisions contained in the foregoing paragraphs are regardless of the benefits created in the contribution referred to in Article 19.

Title IV
Educational Benefits
Article 29

The children of a principal as referred to in Article 18 of this Law shall be entitled to educational benefits set forth in this Title.

The age limit to be admitted to these benefits shall be 35.

Article 30

The students of State-supported Universities and Colleges shall be entitled to the payment of enrollment and monthly fees. The cost of this benefit shall be defrayed by the Scholarship and Development Fund for Higher Education of the Department of Education.

The students of Universities, Colleges and Technical Training Centers without State support, and accredited by the Department of Education, shall be entitled to the payment of enrollment and monthly fees of each institution. The cost of this benefit shall be defrayed by the Scholarship Programme "President of the Republic", created by Supreme Decree Nr. 1,500 [of] the Department of the Interior, dated December 18, 1980.

Article 31

The students of secondary education as well as those mentioned in both paragraphs of the foregoing Article, shall be entitled to a monthly allowance equivalent to 1.24 monthly tax units. This allowance shall be payable while the student accredits his status as such and shall accrue during the school months of each year.

Title V
The Requirement of
Obligatory Military Service

Article 32

The legitimate, natural and adoptive children of the people referred to in Article 18 of this Law shall be classified in the category of available as referred to in Article 30 of the Decree Law Nr. 2,306 as of 1978, on Recruitment and Mobilization of the Armed Forces, when so requested directly by them or through the Corporation as set forth in Title I of this Law.

Title VI
Financing

Article 33

The Benefits set forth in Title II of this Law shall be administered by the Normalization Institute for Social Security and shall be financed out of the resources provided for in item 18-08-01-24-30.002 Concerning Retirements, Pensions and Widow's Pension of the Item of the Department of Labor and Social Security from the applicable Budget of the Nation.

Article 34

Without prejudice to the provision set forth in the preceding Article, the expenses incurred in the enforcement of this Law during 1992 shall be financed out of resources coming from item 50-01-03-2533-104 of the Complementary Operations Programme of the Public Treasury.

The President of the Republic shall, by a Supreme Decree issued through the Department of Finance, create the respective Chapter of income and expenditure of the budget of the National Corporation for Reparation and Reconciliation with the proper budgetary allocations....

CZECH AND SLOVAK FEDERAL REPUBLIC: LAW ON THE MITIGATION OF THE CONSEQUENCES OF CERTAIN PROPERTY LOSSES ("SMALL RESTITUTION LAW")

Act No. 403/1990 (October 2, 1990)

Part One:
Subject of the Adjustment
Article 1

The Act refers to the consequences of property losses caused to natural persons and private legal entities by the abrogation of ownership rights to real or movable property under Government Decree No. 15/1959 [Law Gazette] on measures relating to certain property used by organizations in the socialist sector, under Act No. 71/1959 on measures relating to certain private residential property, and through nationalization carried out on the basis of the decisions of certain ministries issued after 1955 and pertaining to the nationalization Acts of 1948.[1] Abrogation of ownership rights under this Act is also understood to mean the transfer of ownership rights on the basis of a purchase contract pursuant to paragraph 1 and 2 of Article 4 of Government Decree No. 15/1959.

Article 2

Mitigation of the consequences of property losses under this Act comprises restitution of property to the natural person or private legal entity from whom it was expropriated (hereinafter "the owner") on the basis of the regulations set forth in Article 1, the offer of financial compensation (Article

---

[1] Article 3 of Act No. 114/1948 Sb. on nationalization of certain additional industrial and other enterprises and facilities and on adjustment of certain conditions in nationalized and national enterprises.

Article 3 of Act No. 115/1948 Sb. on nationalization of certain additional industrial and other production enterprises and facilities in food industry and on adjustment of certain conditions in nationalized and national enterprises in this industry, in the formulation of Act No. 64/1951 Sb., which changed and appended regulations concerning nationalization of certain enterprises in food industry.

Article 6, paragraph 1 of Act No. 118/1948 Sb. on organization of wholesale activity and on nationalization of wholesale enterprises, in the formulation of Act No. 64/1951 Sb., which changed and appended regulations concerning nationalization of trade enterprises.

Article 3 of Act No. 120/1948 Sb. on nationalization of trade enterprises with 50 or more active employees.

Article 1, paragraph 2 of Act No. 121/1948 Sb. on nationalization in building trades in the formulation of Act No. 58/1951, which changed and appended regulations concerning nationalization of building trades.

Article 3 of Act No. 123/1948 Sb. on nationalization of printing enterprises.

Article 6 of Act No. 124/1948 Sb. on nationalization of certain restaurants, drinking establishments and lodging facilities.

14), or restitution of the purchase price (Article 15), or payment of the difference between the financial compensation and the purchase price (Article 16).

Article 3

Other Entitled Persons

(1) If the owner has died or has been declared to be dead, the expropriated property shall be restored to other entitled persons according to the following sequence:

    a)   the testamentary heir, if he is alive on the date of this Act's entry into force;

    b)   the owner's children and spouse who are alive on the date of this Act's entry into force; if none of the owner's children is alive on the date of its entry into force, their children (i.e. the children of the owner's children shall be the entitled persons in their place; if none of them are alive, their descendants [shall be the entitled persons]);

    c)   the owner's parents living at the time of the owner's death, if the persons mentioned under letter (b) are not alive;

    d)   siblings who are alive on the date of this Act's entry into force. In the event that none of the siblings is alive at the date of its entry into force, their living children shall be the entitled-persons in their place.

(2) If none of the persons mentioned in paragraph 1 is present, the expropriated property shall be restored to the owner's heir, or to the heir's living children if he is not alive.

(3) If the expropriated property belonged to the jointly owned property of several persons, the co-owners shall be the entitled persons according to the extent of their ownership share; if none of them is alive, the sequence of other persons entitled in their place shall be governed by paragraphs 1 and 2.

Part Two:
Restitution of Property

Article 4

Restitution under Articles 2 and 3 refers to property held prior to this Act's entry into force by legal entities (hereinafter "organizations"), with the exception of enterprises with foreign ownership participation[2] and commercial companies[3] whose partners are exclusively natural persons. This

---

[2] [omitted]
[3-5] [omitted]

exception shall not apply, however, in the case of property acquired by legal entities after 1 October 1990.

Article 5

(1) Organizations shall promptly restore property to an entitled person at his written request.

(2) Organizations and entitled persons shall draw up an agreement on restitution of property and on mutual settlement of claims under this Act.

(3) Agreements are subject to registration with a notary public; the notary public shall proceed here as with the registration of a contract on transfer of real property.[4]

(4) If an organization fails to meet its obligations, an entitled person may seek satisfaction of his claims in court.

Article 6

(1) The owner shall include with the written request for property restitution a document from the District National Committee within whose territory the real property is located (hereinafter "the District National Committee"), confirming expropriation of the item under Act No. 71/1959, or a document from a ministry confirming nationalization after 1955, or a decision from this ministry concerning nationalization and its extent and identifying the person from whom the property was expropriated. The place of these documents can be taken by an excerpt from a land register or by another credible document if it states the legal grounds for the expropriation and the name of the person(s) from whom the property was expropriated.

(2) In the case of transfer of real property pursuant to Government Decree No. 15/1959, the request must include a document from the District National Committee confirming expropriation of the property and identifying the person from whom it was expropriated. The place of these documents can be taken in the same manner as the documents in paragraph 1. The request must also include a document from the District National Committee confirming:

a) the amount of the sum paid (hereinafter "reimbursement") to the owner for the confiscated property,[5] together with the name of the organization that paid it;

b) whether the appropriate Ministry of Finance or competent Office for Property and Convertible Currency Affairs paid extraordinary compensation (hereinafter "compensation") out of the State budget for confiscated property, to whom it was paid, and in what amount.

(3) Other entitled persons shall also include with the request a document certifying their relationship to the owner (Article 3).[6]

---

[6] For instance, birth or marriage certificate, last will.

(4) If the entitled person is a permanent resident of another country (including both Czech and foreign nationals) he shall include with the request a document from the appropriate Office for Property and Convertible Currency Affairs confirming that the real property was not disposed of through interstate agreements.

Article 7

Within 60 days after conclusion of an agreement, the entitled person must return:

a) the reimbursement, either to the organization that paid it or to its legal successor;
b) the (provided) compensation to the appropriate ministry for the administration of national property and its privatization, to which he will return the reimbursement if the organization has ceased to exist and has no legal successor.

Article 8

The entitled person shall submit, together with the proposal for registration of the agreement, a document to the notary public certifying that the sums mentioned in Article 7 of this Act have been returned or that an agreement on payments has been reached.

Article 9

If there are more entitled persons, their share will be determined on the basis of Article 3 of this Act unless they have agreed otherwise in writing.

Article 10

(1) Property shall be restituted to the entitled person in the condition it was in on the date the agreement was reached. If the organization has signed before this date a contract involving construction work, reconstruction, or modernization of the real property to be restituted, or another agreement relating to this property, the contract must stipulate whether and to what extent the entitled person assumes the rights and obligations arising from this contract.

(2) If a building to be restituted has, in comparison with its condition at the time of expropriation, depreciated to such an extent as to be unfit for housing, production, business, or other services without immediate repairs, the entitled person shall also be entitled to financial compensation (Article 14).

(3) If the property in question is a building that has been appraised in such a way that its value, as determined by the date of the agreement and set in accordance with Announcement No. 73/1964 concerning the values of privately owned buildings and concerning compensation for expropriation

of real property, exceeds the compensation stipulated in Article 14(1), the entitled person shall have the option to accept this compensation or to request that the organization restitute the building while he shall pay back the difference between this set value and the compensation under Article 14(1) to the appropriate ministry for the administration of national property and its privatization.

(4) A plot of land containing a building that was not expropriated pursuant to the regulations in Article 1 shall not be restituted; the entitled person shall have the right to financial compensation (Article 14).

Article 11

Organizations may not pursue any financial or other claims connected with restituted properties against entitled persons. Likewise, an entitled person to whom a property has been restituted may not pursue claims against an organization in regard to this property, other than the claims mentioned in this Act. The surety rights and property liens placed against the property during its expropriation or its restitution shall not be considered.

Article 12

The Tenancy Act shall continue to apply to the current tenants of apartments or non-residential premises in restituted properties, and legal regulations governing the use of apartments and the renting and subletting of non-residential premises shall also remain in force.

Article 13

Restitution of Movable Property

(1) An entitled person may file a claim for restitution of movable property if he proves that it was expropriated on the basis of the regulations listed in Article 1 and documents its location by the date of this Act's entry into force.

(2) Movable property used in conducting activities inside restituted real property shall be offered for sale by the organization first to entitled persons at a depreciated price no later than the date stipulated in Article 19(2).

Part Three:
Financial Compensation
Article 14

(1) For a building that has been demolished, and for real property for which financial compensation is due under Article 10, the appropriate ministry for the administration of national property and its privatization shall offer the entitled person, at his request documented in accordance with

Article 6, financial compensation (hereinafter "compensation") in the amount determined according to its condition by the date of expropriation and on the basis of Ministry of Finance Announcement No. 73/1964 concerning the values of privately owned buildings and concerning compensation for expropriation of real property, with the addition of 3% of this sum for each year from the expropriation to the date of this Act's entry into force.

(2) This compensation shall be reduced by the reimbursed sum (Article 6(2a)) or by the extraordinary compensation (Article 6(2b)).

(3) Compensation offered under Article 10(2) shall be further reduced by the value of the restituted property as determined according to the Announcement mentioned in paragraph 1, and as calculated on the basis of the condition of the real property stipulated in Article 10(1).

Article 15

(1) If real property was transferred, in the period preceding this Act's entry into force, to the ownership of natural persons other than entitled persons, the right of those natural persons shall be preserved, and the entitled person may claim reimbursement of the purchase price from the organization that sold the property or from its legal successor. If the responsible organization no longer exists and has no legal successor, the entitled person may pursue this claim against the appropriate ministry for the administration of national property and its privatization. An entitled person who has bought real property prior to this Act's entry into force may also claim reimbursement of the purchase price.

(2) The ownership right of an enterprise with foreign ownership participation or of a commercial company whose partners are exclusively natural persons shall also be preserved, provided that this right was transferred to them before 1 October 1990. The entitled person may claim restitution from the appropriate ministry for the administration of national property and its privatization.

Article 16

If the purchase price to the payment of which the entitled persons have the right under Article 15 is lower than the compensation stipulated in Article 14, the appropriate ministry for the administration of national property and its privatization shall pay to these persons the difference between the compensation and the purchase price.

Article 17

If real property has been purchased by only one of the entitled persons, the rest of them may claim from the person who received the full purchase price a proportionate share of it or a proportionate share of the payment making up the difference between the compensation and the purchase price.

Article 18

Entitled persons shall not have the right to compensation for real property which they have failed to claim by the deadline set in Article 19(1).

Article 19

(1) The entitled person may request an organization to restitute property (Article 5) or reimburse a purchase price (Article 15) within 6 months after the date of this Act's entry into force, failing which his claim will be considered invalid.

(2) An organization shall conclude an agreement with the entitled person and restitute property or reimburse a purchase price to him no later than 30 days after expiration of the deadline given in paragraph 1.

(3) On or before the deadline given in paragraph 1, the entitled person may request the appropriate ministry for the administration of national property and its privatization to offer compensation under Article 14, to reimburse a purchase price under Article 15, or to pay the difference under Article 16.

(4) The appropriate ministry for the administration of national property and its privatization shall disburse sums pursuant to paragraph 3 no later than one year after receipt of a request.

Part Four

Article 20

This Act shall also apply to permanent residents of another country (including both Czech and foreign nationals) if property that was to be transferred to their ownership has not been disposed of through interstate property agreements.

Article 21

Necessary expenses connected with the provision of compensation to entitled persons shall be borne by the appropriate ministry for the administration of national property and its privatization.

Article 22

(1) An organization shall have an obligation to take proper care of the movable property stipulated in Article 13 (2) until its restitution to entitled persons; from the date of this Act's entry into force, it may not transfer these properties, parts of them, or rights over them to another person for ownership or use.

(2) The right to compensation for damages that an organization may cause through a breach of this obligation shall remain unaffected by the provision in Article 11.

(3) If an organization fails to satisfy the claims of an entitled person under this Act within the stipulated deadline (Article 19(2)), it shall reimburse the appropriate ministry for the administration of national property and its privatization the sum of 3,000 crowns for each day past the deadline. If the entitled person files a claim in court, the deadline shall expire 30 days after the court's decision has become effective.

Article 23

(1) Expenses connected with the signing of a Property Restitution Agreement shall be borne by the organization.

(2) Notary and administrative fees connected with property restitution under this Act shall not be assessed.

(3) Persons seeking redress against an organization under this Act shall be exempt from court costs....

Article 26

This Act enters into force as of 1 November 1990.

CZECH AND SLOVAK FEDERAL REPUBLIC: LAW ON EXTRAJUDICIAL REHABILITATION ("LARGE RESTITUTION LAW")

(February 21, 1991)

The Federal Assembly of the Czech and Slovak Federal Republic, in an attempt to redress the consequences of certain property and other injustices arising in the period from 1948 to 1989, aware that these injustices, even less the various injustices from previous periods, including injustices committed against citizens of German and Hungarian national origin, cannot ever be fully compensated for, and desiring nevertheless to confirm its desire that such injustices never happen again, has adopted the following Act.

Part 1
Object of the Reform
Article 1

(1) This Act concerns the redressing of the consequences of certain property and other injustices arising from legal actions and rulings in both the civil and labor legal spheres, and arising in the period between 25 February 1948 and 1 January 1990 (hereinafter the "period concerned") in conflict with the bases of a democratic society respecting the rights of citizens as expressed in the charter of the United Nations, the Universal Declaration of Human Rights, and applicable international agreements on civic, political, economic, social and cultural rights.[1]

(2) This Act regulates the conditions for the exercising of rights arising from the annulment of sentences confiscating real estate and items, or interdiction of items, as well as the means of compensation and the extent of the above rights.[2]

(3) This Act shall not be used for the redressing of injustices which are the subject of another Act.[3]

(4) This Act shall not be used for the redressing of injustices which arose in connection with agricultural land used for agricultural production, including buildings used for the same purpose, forest land, and areas of water.

(5) This Act shall not be applied in cases where property was acquired in the period of non-freedom by persons other than those representing the State, or acquired as the result of racist persecution.

[1-3] [omitted]

Part 2
Civil Law and Administrative Relations
Article 2

(1) The redressing of the results of property and other injustices caused by rulings in civil courts, by administrative decisions, or other illegal actions, occurring in the period concerned, shall be realized by the handing over of property, in the granting of financial compensation, or the revoking of certain directives, and possibly by adjustments in social security payments:

a) If such is explicitly stated in the law,
b) If the injustices arose as a result of legal regulations repealed by this Act,
c) If the injustices were the result of political persecution or of an action violating generally accepted human rights and liberties.

(2) Political persecution is, for the purposes of this Act, understood as the persecution of a person:

a) Directly connected to the person's democratically motivated political and social activities and civic positions or,
b) As a result of his or her membership in a specific social, religious, property owning or other group or social strata.

(3) For the purposes of this Act, violations of generally accepted human rights and liberties are understood to be actions which are in contradiction with the principles outlined in Article 1, paragraph 1 of this Act. If the property right has been withdrawn in accordance with the nationalization regulations dating from 1945-1948 during the period concerned, without adequate compensation, the afflicted persons shall assert their claims in accordance with the relevant law.

Section One: Relations in Civil Law
Article 3. The Entitled Person

(1) The "entitled person" is a natural person, whose possession became the property of the State under circumstances outlined in Article 6 of this Act, providing that such persons are citizens of the Czech and Slovak Federal Republic, and have their place of permanent residence in this country.

(2) In the case of the death of a person whose possession became the property of the State under circumstances outlined in Article 6 of this Act before the expiration of the period specified in Article 5, paragraph 2, or in the case of such a person being proclaimed as dead within the period specified in Article 5, paragraph 2, then the entitled persons, provided that they are citizens of the Czech and Slovak Federal Republic with their place of permanent residence in this country, shall be the natural persons in the following order:

a) The inheritor, according to a last will and testament, of the total worldly goods of the deceased, based on a will submitted to testamentary proceedings.

b) An inheritor who, according to a last will and testament, received a part of the deceased's worldly goods. In such a case the inheritor may claim only such a portion of restitution as corresponds to his or her share of the deceased's total legacy. The above does not apply where an inheritor is awarded only specific items or rights by the will. Where the inheritor is awarded by the will a certain portion of certain items, then he or she may receive restitution only concerning those items.

c) The children and spouse of the person whose property passed into the ownership of the State in the cases outlined in Article 6. All are entitled to the same share. Should a child have died within the period specified in Article 5, paragraph 2, then his or her right passes to his or her children. Should they also have died, their right passes in turn to their children.

d) The parents of the person whose property passes into the ownership of the State in the cases outlined in Article 6.

e) The siblings of the person whose property passed into the ownership of the State in the cases specified in Article 6. If any of them should have died, then their right passes to their children.

(3) In cases covered in Article 6, paragraph 1, letter (f), the entitled persons shall be persons specified therein. This definition also applies to paragraph 2, letters (c) through (e) as appropriate.

Article 4. The Obliged Person

(1) The "obliged person" is the State or a legal person/entity who, on the day this Act enters into effect, holds the property in question, with the following exceptions:

a) Enterprises with foreign capital participation and commercial organizations whose members or components are exclusively natural persons. This exception however, does not apply where the property in question was acquired from a legal person on or after 1 October 1990.

b) Foreign States.

(2) A natural person who acquired property or the right to use property from the State, within the definition of Article 6, is also an obliged person in cases where the person in question acquired the property either in contradiction with legal regulations valid at the time, or on the basis of an illegal bias towards the person in question, or of members of that person's household, should the property have been acquired with the aid of such persons.

Article 5. Surrender of Items

(1) The obliged person will surrender an item following the written request of the entitled person demonstrating his or her right to the transfer of the item and showing the way in which the item came into the property of the State. If the item is movable, then the written demonstration shall include the location of the item. If there is more than one entitled person, but only one or some of them claim their right during the period specified in paragraph 2 below, then these applicants are entitled to the whole item.

(2) The entitled person must call on the obliged person to surrender the item within six months of the date this Act enters into effect; otherwise the right to compensation expires.

(3) The obliged person shall enter into an agreement with the entitled person, and surrender the item to that person within thirty days after the expiration of the period specified in paragraph 2 above. In a case involving real estate, the agreement shall be registered by a notary public, who must proceed in the same manner as when registering an agreement on the transfer of property.

(4) If the obliged person does not act on the request within the period specified in paragraph 2 above, then the entitled person can pursue the claim in a court within a period of one year from the date this Act comes into effect.

(5) If an item was surrendered, then persons who made requests within the period specified in paragraph 2 above, but whose requests were not satisfied, can pursue their claims in court against the person or persons to whom the item was surrendered within a period of one year from the date this Act comes into effect.

(6) The fees normally charged by notaries public for their registration under paragraph 3 above, and administrative payments charged in connection with the surrender of real estate, are not levied.

Article 6

(1) The obligation to surrender an item arises in cases where, during the period concerned, an item came into the ownership of the State on the basis of:

    a)   Article 453A of the Civil Code, or Article 287A of Act No. 87/1950, in the version published as Act No. 67/1952,

    b)   A pronouncement and agreement to cede all claims in cases of emigration (the so-called declaration of renunciation),

    c)   Cases where a citizen remaining abroad abandoned an item on Czechoslovak territory,

    d)   Shortened-procedure auctions held to defray the claims of the State,

    e)   An agreement to donate real estate extracted under duress,

    f)   A court decision ruling that an agreement on the transfer of property was invalid in cases where a citizen before departure from the republic transferred ownership of the item to another person, should leaving the Republic have been the reason for the court so ruling. In such cases the entitled person is the receiver of the item under the original agreement, whether or not the agreement ever took effect,

g) A sale agreement closed under duress and with strikingly disadvantageous conditions,

h) A refusal to accept items, as a result of duress, left to the entitled person in a will,

i) Confiscation with compensation, in cases where the item still exists and never served the purpose of which it was confiscated,

j) Confiscation without compensation,

k) Nationalization carried out in contradiction with legal regulations in force at the time.

(2) The requirement to surrender an item also exists in cases not covered in paragraph 1 above, which fall under Article 2, paragraph 1, letter (c), and in cases where the State took ownership of an item without legal justification.

Article 7

(1) The item shall be surrendered to the entitled person on the day the written request for the surrender of the item is received by the obliged person.

(2) In cases where the obliged person has, before that day, negotiated an agreement for building, reconstruction or modernization work of real estate in question, or some other agreement related to this real estate, then an agreement specifying to what extent the entitled person takes over the rights and commitments arising from such agreements shall be concluded.

(3) Should surrendered real estate be, in comparison to its state at the time of transfer to ownership to the State, degraded to the point where it can no longer be used for accommodation, productions, trade, or other services without immediate construction work, then the entitled person may demand, instead of surrender of the real estate, financial compensation under Article 13.

(4) Should the real estate have increased in value to the point where, on the day the entitled person presents his or her written request, its value substantially exceeds its original value, then the entitled person may choose either to demand financial compensation under Article 13 or to demand the surrender of the real estate. Should the entitled person elect for the surrender of the real estate, then he or she must pay the obliged person the difference between the prices mentioned in the previous sentence. Both prices are to be calculated on the basis of legal regulations valid on the day this Act comes into effect.

(5) The same procedure as in paragraph 4 above will be followed in cases where the item in question has become an indivisible part of another item.

Article 8

(1) Structures which, as a result of fundamental reconstruction, have lost their original structural character shall not be surrendered.

(2) The obliged person shall surrender land on which a no-longer existing structure stood, unless the case falls under paragraph 3.

(3) Land on which there is now a building constructed since the land came into the ownership of the State shall not be surrendered.

(4) Land over which a right of personal use has been established shall not be returned to the entitled person.

(5) In cases covered by paragraphs 1 to 4 above, where the item is not surrendered, the entitled person receives financial compensation under Article 13.

(6) An item classified as a national cultural artifact shall not be surrendered until such time as the Czech National Council and Slovak National Council adopt a new law on the management and protection of cultural artifacts.

Article 9

(1) The obliged person shall treat items to be surrendered to an entitled person with the care of a normal owner. The obliged person may not, after the day this Act comes into force, transfer an item, its parts or fittings into the ownership of another person, or allow another person to make use of the item, with the exception of an agreement to give up and to take up an apartment, based on an agreement to exchange apartments. No such legal actions shall be considered valid.

(2) The right of the entitled person to compensations for damages which the obliged person owes because of the non-observance of his or her duties under paragraph 1 above are not affected by the provisions of Article 10.

Article 10

(1) An obliged person cannot exercise any financial or other claims connected to the surrender of an item against an entitled person. At the same time, an entitled person to whom an item is surrendered, cannot exercise against an obliged person any claims connected with the surrender of the item, other than those claims permitted under this Act.

(2) If, on the day of the property's take-over by the State, it was encumbered by any claims by financial institutions secured by the restriction or the right of transfer of the property and settled in accordance with specific regulations, the entitled person shall reimburse the amount settled by the State.

(3) If the item, at the time of its surrender, is encumbered by a lien, the obliged person shall settle the encumbrance or secure it in some other fashion.

(4) If the State paid a purchase price or compensation for the confiscated item, the person to whom the item is surrendered shall return that sum to

the relevant State administrative organ. Should such an entitled person demand financial compensation for a non-surrendered item, then the sum mentioned above should be deducted from any final compensation.

Article 11

If an item is surrendered by a person other than the State, that person has the right to the return of the purchase price. This right should be exercised against the relevant central State administrative organ of the Republic.

Article 12

(1) On the day of transfer of real estate, the entitled person takes on all the rights and duties of a lessor who has concluded an agreement on the giving up and taking up of an apartment or an agreement on the lease of non-residential premises after the transfer of property.

(2) The previous users of apartments and non-residential premises in surrendered real estate, where such apartments or premises serve for:

  a) The activity of diplomatic and consular missions,
  b) The carrying out of health and social services,
  c) The purposes of education,
  d) The carrying out of cultural activity,
  e) The rehabilitation and/or employment of physically disabled persons,

acquire the right, with regard to the entitled person, to the closing of an apartment, or on the lease of non-residential premises governed by the regulations of the Civic Code, Law on the Letting and Subletting of Non-Residential Premises, and related regulations. The entitled person may not withdraw from this agreement before ten years have elapsed from the day this Act enters into effect. This last obligation of the entitled person applies equally to any subsequent owners within the period concerned.

(3) Should the entitled person and the user of the apartment or non-residential premises as understood in paragraph 2 above be unable to agree on the amount of the rent and the conditions for its payment, then the relevant organ of the State administration will set the level of rent in accordance with the generally valid price regulations.

(4) A user of an apartment or non-residential premises whose right to use such premises ends, and who, in accordance with building regulations, has carried out at his or her own expense such works which have increased the value of the apartment or non-residential premises, has the right to compensations for that increase in value, to be estimated in accordance with valid price regulations.

Article 13

(1) Financial compensation will be awarded to the entitled person only for real estate which it is not possible to surrender, or if the entitled person requests financial compensation under Article 7, paragraphs 3, 4, 5 of this Act.

(2) In cases where the entire property of a citizen, which did not include real estate, was confiscated by the State on the basis of a legal decision which has been or will be overturned under Act No. 119/1990 on judicial rehabilitation, in the version published as Act No. 47/1991, or on the basis of a decision overturned under this Act, then the entitled person will receive compensation in the sum of 60,000 Crowns, to be paid in the form specified in paragraph 5.

(3) A written request for financial compensation must be submitted to the relevant central State administration organ of the Republic no later than one year from the date this Act enters into effect, or from the date when legal authority rules that an item may not be surrendered.

(4) The central organ of the State administration of the Republic will pay financial compensation to the entitled person within six months of the date of receiving a written request as specified in paragraph 3 above.

(5) Financial compensation may consist of a cash payment of up to 30,000 Crowns, and in the issuing of securities which are not State bonds. The amount of financial compensation to be paid in cash may be adjusted by the governments of the Czech and Slovak Federal Republics according to their own regulations. Financial compensation under paragraph 1 above shall be fixed according to the price regulations for the valuation of real estate in force on the day this Act comes into effect.

(6) If the entitled person is not an entitled person under Article 3, paragraph 1, but is under Article 3, paragraph 2, then financial compensation shall be made only in securities, but not in State bonds.

Section Two: Administrative Relations

Article 14

(1) Entitled persons are those persons defined in Article 3 of this Act, whose property came into the ownership of the State by means specified in Article 16 of this Act.

(2) Entitled persons shall also include natural persons who have suffered injustices committed by organs of the State administration whose decisions are repealed by Articles 16, 17, and 18 of this Act.

Article 15. Obliged Persons

Obliged persons are the State or legal persons according to Article 4, paragraph 1 and natural persons according to Article 4, paragraph 2 who received an item in question from the State, or acquired the rights to use the item in the manner set forth in Article 16, paragraph 1, and the relevant central organs of the State administration (Article 16 and 17, paragraph 2 of this Act).

Article 16

(1) Decisions based on Act No. 88/1950, concerning the punishment or forfeiture of assets are hereby repealed.

(2) Should a part of the assets mentioned above represent real estate, then the procedure set forth in the previous part of the Act applies. Should real estate not form part of these assets, the procedure specified in Article 13, paragraph 2 shall be applied.

(3) Compensation for imprisonment, both before and after sentencing and exceeding three months, is governed by Article 23 of Act No. 119/1990, in the version published as Act No. 47/1991. Such compensation is to paid by the relevant central State administration organ of the Republic.

Article 17

(1) Decisions to assign a person to a forced labor camp under Act No. 247/1948, except in cases where previous sentencing clearly shows that the individual concerned consistently committed property-related criminal activity, are also repealed.

(2) The relevant central State administration organ of the Republic is required to supply financial compensation for periods spent in forced labor camps or in labor formations in amounts such as those set forth in Act No. 119/1990, in the version published as 47/1991.

Article 18

(1) Military call-up orders under which soldiers were, for the period of their compulsory basic military service, assigned to auxiliary technical battalions between the years 1950 and 1954, and call-up orders to auxiliary technical battalions for exceptional military exercises under Article 39 of Act No. 92/1949, the armed services law, are hereby repealed.

(2) Decisions whereby pupils and students were expelled from secondary schools and universities, which were reached as a result of political persecution or by an approach violating generally recognized human rights and liberties, are hereby repealed. Educational rehabilitation shall be carried out according to the instructions of the relevant minister for that sphere.

Part Three
Relations Under Criminal Law
Article 19. Entitled Persons

(1) Persons rehabilitated under Act No. 119/1990, who fulfill the conditions set forth in Article 3, paragraph 1 of this Act, or should such persons be dead or be pronounced dead, then those persons who fullfill the

conditions set forth in Article 3, paragraph 2 of this Act, are considered to be entitled persons.

(2) The rights set forth in paragraph 1 above also accrue to persons for whom a right to compensation arises under Article 27, paragraph 1, letter (f) of Act No. 82/1968 on Legal Compensation, where such compensation concerns real estate which has not been returned to them.

Article 20. Obliged Persons

(1) Obliged persons are legal persons according to Article 4, paragraph 1 of this Act, natural persons according to Article 4, paragraph 2 of this Act who have acquired the rights to usage of an item from the State on the basis of a court ruling, and the relevant central State administrative organ.

(2) Obliged persons shall surrender items according to Article 5 and Articles 7-12 of this Act. Should this not be possible, the entitled person has the right to apply for compensation according to Article 13 of this Act.

(3) In cases of the exercising of rights to the surrender of property arising from the overturning of court rulings sentencing an individual to the forfeiture or confiscation of assets, where the decision to overturn becomes absolute when this Act comes into effect, then the period within which such rights must be exercised begins on the day that decision takes legal effect.

Part Four
Relations Under Labor Law and Social Security Relations
Article 21

(1) Legal acts during the period concerned which resulted in the termination of a person's employment or official responsibility, or membership in a cooperative (hereafter "Working Relationship") and which were the result of political persecution or of procedures violating generally recognized human rights and freedoms (Article 2, paragraphs 2 and 3), shall be deemed invalid, particularly:

a) Where the justification for such an Act is a conviction for a punishable offense (felony, misdemeanor, infraction) and where the court's sentence is overturned according to the second or third parts of Act No. 119/1990 on legal rehabilitation, in the version published as Act No. 47/1991, and where the legal sentence is lightened, or where the accused is cleared of all guilt,

b) If it was carried out according to the legal measure of the Presidium of the Federal Assembly No. 99/1969 on some transitional measures necessary for the strengthening and protection of public order,

c) If a person was dismissed according to Article 46, paragraph 1 of the Labor Code, No. 65/1965, in the version published as Act No. 153/1968, on the grounds that the employee, by his or her activities, disturbed the socialist social order and therefore could not command the trust necessary for the fulfilling of his or her position or job,

d) If a person was summarily dismissed according to Article 51, paragraph 1, letter (c) of the Labor Code, No. 65/1965, in the version published as Act No. 153/1968,

e) If a person signed an agreement to end a working relationship under the pressure of political persecution or under the pressure of a procedure violating generally accepted human rights and liberties.

(2) Judicial decisions rejecting propositions or accepting concessions in cases concerning the issue of the validity of the ending of a working relationship in the cases set forth in paragraph 1 above are hereby overturned.

Article 22

(1) At the request of the individual whose working relationship terminated for one of the reasons set forth in Article 21, the organization with which he or she had that working relationship or the legal representative of that organization, and should there be no legal representative then the central organ to which the organization is, or was at the time, dependent (hereinafter the "organization") will issue a statement to that effect. Should the individual mentioned above be no longer living, his or her spouse or child may make the request.

(2) The request mentioned in paragraph 1 above may be submitted up to six months after this Act comes into effect.

(3) Should the organization not issue the statement mentioned above within three months of the date it receives the request, then the person mentioned in paragraph 1 may, within two years of the day this Act enters into effect, ask a court to make a statement that the reason for the ending of the working relationship in question was one of those set forth in Article 21.

(4) A statement or any other document issued before the day on which this Act takes effect, including a judicial decision, shall also be deemed as a statement in the meaning of paragraph 2, if from that document it is clear that the working relationship in question terminated for one of the reasons set forth in Article 21....

(6) The annulment of a legal Act in accordance with Article 21 shall not restore the terminated labor relation and shall not result in any claim for compensation of lost income, damages, or any other performance connected with the duration of the labor relation.

(7) Should an individual whose working relationship was terminated for one of the reasons set forth in Article 21 request that the organization with which he or she had been in a working relationship take him or her back into employment, and makes such request within six months of the day this Act enters into effect, then that organization shall employ him or her in a position corresponding to the legal contract in force at the time when his or her working relationship was terminated, provided that he or she holds the

qualifications and requirements for the performance of such work and providing also that it is possible for the organization to employ him or her.

Article 23

(1) Decisions by which organs responsible for the provision of social security to artists resolved, for reasons outlined in Article 2, paragraphs 2 and 3 of this Act:

a) To terminate the participation of an individual in the artists' social security system, or that

b) An artist did not have the right to social security payments,

are hereby overturned.

(2) The decision as to whether a particular case is covered by paragraph 1 above shall be made, on request, by the relevant central State administrative organ of the Republic; the decision as to who in such cases should be considered to have been an artist is within the competence of the relevant central State administrative organ of the Republic.

Article 24

(1) Should the termination of a working relationship be considered invalid on the basis of Article 21, or a legal act leading to the termination of a working relationship be considered invalid under Article 22, then, for the purposes of calculating entitlement to a pension, the period from the termination of the working relationship to the date an individual becomes eligible for old age, partial or full disability pension, or to the date this Act enters into effect, whichever is the shorter, is counted in full.

(2) Should the decision of a relevant organ under Article 23 be considered invalid, then, for the purpose of pension insurance, the whole period from the date the decision acquired legal validity until the date when the individual in question became eligible for an old age, partial disability pension or disability pension, or until April 30, 1990 whichever is the shorter, is counted as the period of employment.

(3) Should employment classified as work Category I(II) for the purposes of pension insurance have been terminated for one of the reasons set forth in Article 21 of this Act, or terminated as the result of a legal act since declared invalid according to Article 22 of this Act, then the period of employment as defined in paragraph 1 is counted as employment in Category I(II), but this for a period no longer than that required to qualify as eligible for a pension in Category I(II). The categorization of particular employment shall be done according to paragraph 1.

(4) With the aim of redressing injustices committed against the persons specified in Article 18, paragraph 1, periods of time of military service, including military training in auxiliary technical battalions, shall be counted toward pension entitlement at double its length in the category in which the relevant work carried out was classified.

(5) With the aim of redressing injustices caused by the expulsion of university students from their studies, the number of years at that time considered necessary to graduate, but which were not completed or studied due to an individual's exclusion, count for the purpose of pension entitlement as a period of employment double their length.

(6) The average monthly earnings, for the purpose of calculating pension entitlements of persons for whom such calculation shall be made under paragraphs 1 or 2, shall be calculated on the basis of total real earnings during the year previous to the termination of employment, increased to take account of the wages growth in the general economy during the period before the individual achieved the right to a pension. The mechanism for the upward adjustment of real total earning shall be fixed by the government of the Czech and Slovak Federal Republic.

Article 25. Adjustment

The calculation of pension entitlement or adjustment of its amount shall be carried out only if it is more advantageous for the citizen concerned than treatment under the generally valid pension system, or under Article 25 of Act No. 119/1990, in the version published as Act No. 47/1991.

Article 26

Pensions already awarded before the day this Act comes into effect shall be adjusted, on request, in line with Article 24; in doing so, the pension shall be calculated according to the regulations under which it was granted.

Article 27

The amount of pension in accordance with the preceding provisions shall be modified at least as far back as the date of the pension installment payable after the day on which this Act takes effect.

Article 28

The procedures outlined in Articles 24 to 27 shall be applied in the calculation or adjustment of widow's and orphan's pensions.

Article 29

(1) Citizens who are rehabilitated according to Act No. 119/1990, in the version published as Act No. 47/1991, citizens for whom a legal conviction of the type outlined in Article 2 of Act 119/1990 was repealed before it came into effect, and citizens who were rehabilitated under Article 22 (C) of Act 82/1968 on legal rehabilitation receive, with the exception of rights to pensions, the same advantages as participants in the resistance.

(2) Citizens who were assigned to forced labor camps or work formations under decisions annulled by Article 17 of this Act are granted the

rights set forth in Article 25 of Act No. 119/1990. The measures outlined in the previous paragraph also apply.

(3) The measures outlined in paragraphs 1 and 2 above are to be applied only in the cases of citizens:

a) On whom a sentence of death was carried out, or

b) Who died in captivity, while serving a detention sentence, while suffering the illegal deprivation of civil rights under Article 33, paragraph 2 of Act No. 119/1990, or while serving in forced labor camp or a labor formation,

c) Who served at least 12 months in detention,

d) Who served at least 12 months in a forced labor camp or labor formation.

Article 30

In the case of an unlawful termination of an official post of a professional soldier or member of an armed corps, that person's social security rights arising from the law on official post conditions are calculated as if the person had been discharged for reasons of reorganization. The amount of such payments shall be calculated according to the period of service actually carried out, and the earnings achieved (the basic sum for the purpose of calculating social security payments). The exact details are to be set by the Federal Ministry of Defense, Federal Ministry of the Interior and the relevant central State administrative organs of the Republics.

Part 5
Common and Concluding Measures
Article 31

The Procurator General/Public Prosecutor may issue a protest against decisions, measures and other Acts which took place during the period concerned in contradiction with the law, and with other legal regulations and which led to political persecution or to preferential treatment for political reasons until December 31, 1992....

Article 34

If there is no entitled person, or if none of the entitled persons concerned exercises their rights to the surrender of an item within the period set forth in Article 5, paragraph 2, the State becomes the entitled person, and must exercise its rights within 18 months of the date this Act comes into effect. The procedure for the exercising of the State 's rights will be set forth in special regulations by the relevant organs of the Republics.

Article 35

This Act comes into effect April 1, 1991.

GERMANY: COMPENSATION ACTS

First Act for Rectification of SED Injustice
(October 29, 1992; as amended June 23, 1994)

Article 1
Act on the Rehabilitation and Compensation of Victims of Criminal Prosecution in Violation of the Rule of Law in the Territory of Accession (Criminal Rehabilitation Act)

Part One
Rehabilitation and Resulting Claims

§ 1. **Annulment of Rulings in Violation of the Rule of Law**

(1) A criminal ruling by a public German court in the territory defined by Article 3 of the Treaty of Unification (territory of accession) [the former German Democratic Republic] issued between May 8, 1945 and October 2, 1990 upon request shall be declared in violation of the rule of law and be annulled (rehabilitation) if it is incompatible with essential principles of a system characterized by freedom and the rule of law, in particular because

1. the ruling served the purpose of political persecution, usually applicable to convictions pursuant to the following provisions:

   a) Treasonous transmission of information (...*);
   b) Subversive man-trade[1] (...*);
   c) Subversive agitation (...*);
   d) Illegal establishment of contacts (...*);
   e) Illegal border crossing (...*);
   f) Agitation in order to promote boycotts (...*);
   g) Avoidance of military service and refusal of military service (...*);
   h) According to provisions that are equivalent in content to the aforementioned provisions; and
   i) High treason, espionage, allowing solicitation for purposes of espionage, treasonous activities as an agent, political crimes directed against an allied State, failure to report one of these

---

* [Editor's note: The Act here cites the pertinent provisions of the law of the former German Democratic Republic.]

[1] [Translator's note: This East German statutory language refers to persons who brought East Germans across the borders for compensation.]

crimes, betrayal of secrets (...*) or according to provisions equivalent in their content if the act was alleged to be committed for the Federal Republic of Germany, one of her allies or for an organization committed to the principles of a system characterized by freedom and the rule of law, or

2. the imposed legal sanctions are grossly disproportionate to the act for which they were imposed.

(2) The rulings of the Superior Court of Chemnitz, branch Waldheim, from the year 1950 ("Waldheim Trials") are incompatible with essential principles of a system characterized by freedom and the rule of law.

(3) If a ruling is based on the violation of several criminal provisions and if the conditions set by paragraph (1) apply only with respect to some of the criminal provisions, the ruling may be annulled in its entirety if the other violations of law were of subordinate relevance for the imposition of sanctions.

(4) If a complete annulment of the ruling is ruled out, the court annuls those parts of the ruling to which the conditions of paragraph (1) apply.

(5) The provisions of this Act apply *mutatis mutandis* to criminal measures other than rulings of courts....

§ 2. Rulings in Violation of the Rule of Law Concerning Imprisonment other than in a Criminal Proceeding

(1) The provisions of this Act apply *mutatis mutandis* to a judicial or administrative decision other than in a criminal proceeding ordering imprisonment. This applies in particular to the commitment to a psychiatric institution for the purpose of political persecution or for other extraneous reasons.

(2) Life under conditions similar to imprisonment and forced labor are considered equivalent to imprisonment.

§ 3. Resulting Claims

(1) The annulment of a ruling pursuant to § 1 serves as a basis for claims according to this Act.

(2) If the annulment concerns the seizure of objects or the impounding of assets, the return of the assets is governed by the Act on Assets and the Act on Investments.

§ 4. Termination of Enforcement

(1) If enforcement of a criminal ruling of a court of law has not yet been completed, it will terminate once the annulment ruling becomes final. The

---

* [Editor's note: The Act here cites the pertinent provisions of the law of the former German Democratic Republic.]

enforcement of a sanction that has not yet been carried out is not suspended by a request pursuant to § 1. The court may rule to suspend temporarily or interrupt the enforcement.

(2) Insofar as the ruling is not annulled, the court shall declare the enforcement as complete if the continuation of the enforcement would be disproportionate with respect to the amount of sanctions that have already been carried out....[2]

§ 6. Reimbursement of Fines, Costs of Proceedings and Necessary Expenditures of the Affected Person

(1) Insofar as a ruling is annulled, the reimbursement of fines paid, of the costs of the proceedings and of necessary expenditures of the affected person may be claimed at a ratio of two Marks of the German Democratic Republic to one German Mark. The claim is set off against reimbursements that have already been made.

(2) The sum of the reimbursement claim according to paragraph (1) may be estimated if a precise determination is impossible or would require disproportionate efforts....

Part Two
Judicial Proceedings
§ 7. Request

(1) The request pursuant to § 1 may be submitted until December 31, 1995

1. by a person whose rights are directly affected by the ruling in question and by the legal representative of such person,
2. after the death of the affected person by his/her spouse, his/her relative in straight ascending or descending order, his/her siblings or by persons with a justifiable interest in the rehabilitation of the person affected by the ruling, or
3. by the public prosecutor unless the person directly affected by the ruling has opposed such an application.

(2) The request may be submitted to any court of law either in writing or orally to be protocollized by the administrative office of the court. The request shall be substantiated.

(3) The request may be limited to specific objections.

(4) The parties to the proceedings listed in paragraph (1), numbers 1 and 2 may be represented by counsel. The attorneys admitted to the courts of law in the territory in which this Act has the force of law as well as

---

[2][Translator's note: § 5 provides for the entry of annulment decisions into the central crime register as well as the omission and deletion of East German entries that have subsequently been annulled.]

professors of law at German universities are eligible to be counsel. Other persons may be chosen as counsel with the consent of the court. With respect to legal aid, the same rules apply as in civil cases.

(5) If the affected person dies after the request has been submitted, the persons who hold the right to a request according to paragraph (1), numbers 2 or 3 may apply within six months for the continuation of the proceedings.

§ 8. Jurisdiction

(1) The jurisdiction for the decision according to § 1 lies with the District Court, or the Superior Court established in its location, in the district of which, according to the borders of October 3, 1990, the criminal trial of first resort or the investigative procedure had taken place. Insofar as the Highest Court of the German Democratic Republic had decided as a court of first resort, jurisdiction lies with the Berlin Superior Court....

§ 9. Composition of the Rehabilitation Panels or Rehabilitation Divisions

(1) The decisions of the District Court are made by panels of judges specifically assigned to rehabilitation cases; the decisions of the Superior Court are made by rehabilitation divisions, each of which consist of three judges.

(2) A person who had served as a professional judge or public prosecutor in the territory of accession is excluded by law from participation in decisions regarding rehabilitation matters, unless he has been appointed to the bench pursuant to the Act on Judges and the respective provisions of the Unification Treaty. No more than one judge who served as a professional judge or public prosecutor in the territory of accession may participate in any one rehabilitation decision.

§ 10. Investigation of Facts

(1) The court investigates the facts *ex officio*. Applying due discretion,[3] it determines the type and scope of investigations, in particular with respect to the introduction of evidence.

(2) The court may require the applicant to present or name documents and other types of evidence necessary for the determination and to present *prima facie* evidence for the facts alleged in the request....

(3) Upon request, the applicant will be provided with copies of the ruling under review and of the criminal indictment as far as those documents are available.

---

[3] [Translator's note: Discretion in German law does not have the same meaning as in common law systems. A discretionary decision under German law is structured and guided by a number of principles (such as adequacy and proportionality) limiting its free exercise, and the violation of these principles is subject to judicial review.]

(4) The court may transfer individual investigations to the public prosecutor.

§ 11. Court Proceedings

(1) A request shall be processed preferentially if this appears to be advisable considering the social urgency or the age of the applicant.

(2) Prior to handing down its decision, the court provides the public prosecutor with the opportunity to make a statement. If the request has been submitted by the public prosecutor, the applicant according to § 7, paragraph (1), number 1 must be heard.

(3) In general, the court decides without oral proceedings. The court may order oral proceedings if it considers them necessary for the determination of facts or for other reasons.

(4) The court may order the personal appearance of the applicant. If the applicant does not comply with such an order, the court may order the cessation of the proceedings. Within six months, the applicant may ask for the proceedings to be resumed.

(5) If it is to be expected that the decision regarding the request will directly impact the rights of a third person, this person must be included in the proceedings. Paragraphs (1) and (3) apply *mutatis mutandis*.

§ 12. Rehabilitation Decision

(1) The court decides by decree. The decision is issued in written proceedings unless the conditions of a proclamation pursuant to § 35, paragraph (1) of the Code of Criminal Procedure[4] apply.

(2) The decree shall include the names of the judges, the parties, and their representatives. Furthermore, the decree shall contain

1. the name of the ruling under review,
2. a statement as to which accusation and which sanction are grounds for annulment of the ruling under review,
3. the length of the unjust imprisonment suffered by the affected person,
4. the amount of the fine to be reimbursed pursuant to § 6 as well as a statement whether the conditions for a claim pursuant to § 6 have been met.

(3) The decree shall state the reasons for the decision insofar as the decree may be subject to appeal.[5]

---

[4] [Translator's note: § 35 mandates oral proclamation if the affected party is present at the moment the decision is issued.]

[5] [Translator's note: German law knows two different types of appeal: appeals with a complete review of factual evidence and law and appeals with review of law alone. The type of appeal referred to here and in the subsequent provisions is the former type.]

(4) The decree shall state the applicant's right to appeal and shall be served upon the participants in the proceedings.

§ 13. Appeal

(1) The decree may be appealed within one month after it has been served.

(2) The decree is not subject to appeal insofar as

1. a request for rehabilitation has been granted and none of the participants in the proceedings had objected to the request,
2. the court has unanimously and upon substantiated request of the public prosecutor ... determined that the sanctions of the ruling under review are not grossly disproportionate to the act for which they were imposed....

Sentence 1, number 2 [*sic*] does not apply if a successful appeal would lead to the reduction of the length of a sentence that remains to be served.

(3) The appeal is decided by the District Court or by the Court of Appeals of the district in which the state government has its seat; in Berlin this is the Berlin Court of Appeals *(Kammergericht)*. The decisions of the appeals court are made by special appeals panels for rehabilitation matters. § 9 applies *mutatis mutandis*.

(4) If the appeals panel intends to deviate in its decision on a question of law from the decision of another District Court or Court of Appeals or from the Federal Supreme Court, it shall submit the matter to the Federal Supreme Court....

§ 14. Costs of the Proceedings and Necessary Expenses

(1) No costs shall be imposed for the proceedings.

(2) If the request has been granted fully or partially, the necessary expenses of the applicant are covered by the Treasury. In all other cases the court holds the Treasury to be responsible for the necessary expenses of the applicant or a part thereof if it is considered unjust to burden the applicant.

(3) The decision pursuant to paragraph (2), sentence 2 is not subject to appeal....[6]

Part Three
Social Restitution

§ 16 . Social Restitution

(1) Based on his rehabilitation, the affected person obtains a claim to social restitution for hardship caused by imprisonment.

---

[6] [Editor's note: § 15 deals with applicability of the Act on the Administration of Justice and the Code of Criminal Procedure.]

(2) Social restitution pursuant to this act is not granted if the person entitled to it or the person from whom the entitlement derives has violated the principles of humanity and the rule of law or has abused his position for his own benefit or for the benefit of or to the detriment of others.

(3) Social restitution pursuant to paragraph (1) is granted upon request as capital restitution and support payments pursuant to §§ 17-19 and as pension payments pursuant to §§ 21-24.

(4) The benefits pursuant to §§ 17-19 are not considered income for the purpose of income-dependent social benefits.

§ 17. Capital Restitution

(1) Capital restitution amounts to 300 German Marks for each full or partial calendar month of imprisonment incompatible with essential principles of a system characterized by freedom and the rule of law. Beneficiaries whose domicile or place of permanent residence was in the territory of accession, shall receive an additional capital restitution of 250 German Marks for each full or partial calendar month.

(2) Restitutions made on the basis of other legal provisions, in particular those pursuant to the Prisoners Act, that have been made with respect to the same set of facts shall be set off against the capital restitution.

(3) From the moment of submission of the request, but not earlier than September 18, 1990, the capital restitution is transferable and subject to inheritance.

§ 18. Support Payments

(1) Persons entitled pursuant to § 17, paragraph (1) whose economic situation is particularly impaired shall receive support payments. The Foundation for Former Political Prisoners, founded pursuant to § 15 of the Prisoners Act, shall provide such payments.

(2) The Foundation Council of the Foundation for Former Political Prisoners shall draft guidelines for the distribution of funds determining under what circumstances and up to which amount support payments may be granted. The guidelines shall require ratification by the Federal Minister in charge of drafting this Act in conjunction with the Federal Minister of the Interior and the Federal Minister of Finances. §§ 22 and 23 of the Prisoners Act apply *mutatis mutandis*.

§ 19. Hardship Cases

If undue hardship results because no capital restitution or no additional capital restitution pursuant to § 17, paragraph (1), sentence 2 is paid, the agency in charge of such matters may grant such payments to the entitled persons.

§ 20. Costs

The Federal Treasury shall cover 65 percent of the expenditures accrued by the states [German Länder] through payments pursuant to this Act.

§ 21. Disability Pensions

(1) Upon request, an affected person whose health has been damaged as a result of imprisonment shall receive a pension for the health and economic consequences of the damage in *mutatis mutandis* application of the Federal Pensions Act. This does not apply if he already receives a pension based on the Federal Pensions Act or on the basis of statutes that apply the Federal Pensions Act *mutatis mutandis....*

(4) Damage to an aid worn on the body, such as glasses, contact lenses or dentures, is equivalent to health damaged pursuant to paragraphs (1)-(3).

(5) The probability of a causal connection is sufficient evidence for the recognition of a health impairment as a result of a damaging act. If this probability cannot be demonstrated solely due to the fact that medical science is uncertain about the causes of the ailment, the health impairment may be acknowledged as a consequence of a damaging act with the consent of the Federal Minister for Labor and Social Affairs; the consent may be given summarily for all similar cases. A recognition pursuant to sentences 1 and 2 and administrative acts based thereon may be revoked *ex post facto* if it is established beyond doubt that the health impairment is not a consequence of a damaging act. Payments received do not have to be reimbursed.

§ 22. Pensions for Surviving Family Members

(1) If the affected person has died from the consequences of the damaging act, the surviving family members shall upon request receive pensions in *mutatis mutandis* application of the Federal Pensions Act. This does not apply if the surviving family members already receive a pension based on the Federal Pensions Act or on the basis of statutes that apply the Federal Pensions Act *mutatis mutandis.* § 21, paragraph (3) of this Act and §§ 48 and 52 of the Federal Pensions Act are applied *mutatis mutandis.*

(2) If a death sentence has been executed as a consequence of a criminal ruling pursuant to § 1, paragraph (1) applies *mutatis mutandis....*[7]

---

[7] [Translator's note: §§ 23-27 deal with technical issues regarding a multiplicity of claims, jurisdictional details, transitional provisions, and abrogations and amendments to other statutes necessitated by this Act. Articles 2 through 7 contain minor technical amendments of the Federal Central Register Act, the Prisoners Act, the Income Tax Code, the Housing Subsidy Act, the Criminal Prosecution Restitution Act and the Federal Fee Schedule for Attorneys.]

Article 8
Effect

This Act shall come into effect on the day after its announcement.

⊷⊶ ⊨♦⊨ ⊶⊷

Second Act on the Rectification of SED Injustice
(June 23, 1994)

The *Bundestag* with the consent of the *Bundesrat* has passed the following Act:

Article 1
Act for the Annulment of Administrative Decisions in Violation of the Rule of Law in the Territory of Accession and the Claims Resulting Therefrom

§ 1. Annulment of Administrative Decisions in Violation of the Rule of Law

(1) Upon request, an official act with respect to an individual case ... in the territory defined by Article 3 of the Treaty of Unification (territory of accession) issued between May 8, 1945 and October 2, 1990 (administrative decision) that led to damaged health (§ 3), to an encroachment into assets (§ 7), or to an occupational disadvantage, shall be annulled if it is utterly incompatible with basic principles of a State based on the rule of law and if the consequences of the administrative decision continue to have an impact in a direct, severe, and overly burdening way. This Act does not apply to tax matters and to matters covered by the Act on Assets and the Act on Restitution Pensions....

(2) Acts that gravely violated the principles of justice, legal certainty, and proportionality and served the purpose of political persecution or were arbitrary in the individual case, are utterly incompatible with basic principles of a State based on the rule of law.

(3) Forced relocations from the border areas of the former German Democratic Republic based on the Ordinance concerning Measures near the Demarcation Line between the German Democratic Republic and the Western Zones of Occupation of May 26, 1952 (GBl. No. 65, p. 405) or the Ordinance concerning the Restriction of Residence of August 24, 1961 (GBl.II No. 55, p. 343) are utterly incompatible with basic principles of a State based

on the rule of law. The same applies to the encroachments upon assets in connection with forced relocations.

(4) If the act referred to in paragraph (1) consists of a rescission of an administrative decision, the act will only be annulled if an administrative decision with the same content could be reissued. Otherwise, a certification that the rule of law was violated shall be issued instead. Sentence 2 applies also to encroachments upon educational, vocational, and service relationships with the armed forces.

(5) The provisions of this Act apply *mutatis mutandis* to public acts other than those directed towards the creation of legal consequences. A certification that the rule of law was violated substitutes for the annulment of the act.

(6) The provisions of this Act apply *mutatis mutandis* to acts of the Socialist Unity Party of Germany and the parties and organizations dominated by it.

§ 2. Resulting Claims

(1) The annulment of an act pursuant to § 1 or the certification that it violated the rule of law serve as a basis for claims pursuant to this Act.

(2) Resulting claims pursuant to this act are excluded if the person entitled to it or the person from whom the entitlement derives has violated the principles of humanity and the rule of law or has greatly abused his position for his own benefit or for the benefit of or to the detriment of others....

(4) With respect to resulting claims, other restitution benefits awarded in connection with the same factual circumstances shall be taken into account insofar as they were actually received. In particular, this applies to restitution granted by the German Democratic Republic. Payments in Marks of the German Democratic Republic shall be converted to German Marks in the relation of 2 to 1. If substitute real property[8] has been transferred as restitution, the applicant must relinquish his property rights or pay its market value. If the applicant no longer holds title to the property, the relevant value is the value at the moment of the loss of title. Measures or legal acts concerning the substitute property done by the [subsequent] holder of the title are not considered in determining the market value. The Restitution Fund has the right to appropriate the substitute property or a claim to its market value as well as a claim to other restitution benefits that have to be relinquished.

§ 3. Disability Pensions

(1) Upon request, an affected person whose health has been damaged as a result of an act referred to in § 1 shall receive a pension for the health and economic consequences of the damage in *mutatis mutandis* application of

---

[8] [Translator's note: When German law talks about real property, the reference is to the land as well as the buildings attached to it.]

the Federal Pensions Act. This does not apply if he already receives a pension based on the Federal Pensions Act or on the basis of statutes that apply the Federal Pensions Act *mutatis mutandis*....

(4) Damage to an aid carried on the body, such as glasses, contact lenses or dentures, is equivalent to health damaged referred to in paragraphs (1)-(3).

(5) The probability of a causal connection is sufficient evidence for the recognition of a health impairment as a result of a damaging act. If this probability cannot be demonstrated solely due to the fact that medical science is uncertain about the causes of the ailment, the health impairment may be acknowledged as a consequence of a damaging act with the consent of the Federal Ministry for Labor and Social Affairs; the consent may be given summarily for all similar cases. A recognition pursuant to sentences 1 and 2 and administrative acts based thereon may be revoked *ex post facto* if it is established beyond doubt that the health impairment is not a consequence of a damaging act. Payments received do not have to be reimbursed.

§ 4. Pensions for Surviving Family Members

(1) If the affected person has died from the consequences of the damaging act, the surviving family members shall upon request receive pensions in *mutatis mutandis* application of the Federal Pensions Act. This does not apply if the surviving family members already receive a pension based on the Federal Pensions Act or on the basis of statutes that apply the Federal Pensions Act *mutatis mutandis*....[9]

§ 7. Encroachment upon Assets

(1) If the act referred to in § 1 resulted in the deprivation of an asset referred to in § 2, paragraph (2) of the Act on Assets, the retransfer or return of property or the restitution following the annulment or the certification of violation of the rule of law is governed by the Act on Assets, the Act on Investments, and the Act on Restitution....

(2) If, through a miscellaneous act referred to in § 1, an encroachment upon real property resulted in a reduction of its value, the owner may abandon the title to the property and choose restitution pursuant to the Act on Restitution instead. When the release of the title becomes effective, he is released from any obligations resulting from the condition of the property caused by the encroachment. The obligations are assumed by the state in which the property is located.

---

[9] [Translator's note: § 5 contains technical details about the computation of pensions and about multiplicity of claims; § 6 contains details about the *mutatis mutandis* application of the Federal Pensions Act.]

§ 8. Occupational Disadvantage

If an act referred to in § 1 had an impact on one's occupation or one's vocational training and caused harm as per § 1, paragraph (1) of the Occupational Rehabilitation Act or as per § 3, paragraph (1) of the Occupational Rehabilitation Act, the Occupational Rehabilitation Act is applicable after the annulment or the certification of violation of the rule of law has been issued. A severe and overly burdening consequence pursuant to § 1, paragraph (1) exists in particular when, as a consequence of an act, a compensation for disadvantages in the social security insurance pursuant to the Occupational Rehabilitation Act is possible.

§ 9. Request

(1) The request pursuant to § 1 may be made by a natural person whose rights have been directly impacted by the act and, after the person's death, by others who have a legal interest in the rehabilitation of the directly affected person.

(2) The request shall be made no later than December 31, 1995 and should be directed to the responsible rehabilitation authority. The deadline has been met if the request has been submitted within the period to another German authority within the country or to a German court.

§ 10. Contents of the Request

The request shall contain:

1. information about the surrounding personal and economic circumstances,
2. a description of the factual circumstances that justify the annulment of the decision,
3. a list of evidence,
4. statements about the type and extent of resulting claims, and
5. a statement indicating whether the applicant has already received other compensation payments and whether and where he previously submitted a request.

§ 11. Use of Personal Data

Personal data from a rehabilitation procedure ... may be processed and used insofar as necessary for other procedures with respect to rehabilitation, restitution, or benefits pursuant to the Act on Prisoners.

§ 12. Rehabilitation Authority

(1) The rehabilitation authority of the state in whose territory, defined by the borders of October 3, 1990, the act referred to in § 1 occurred issues the annulment of the act or the certification of the violation of the rule of law

as well as the decision concerning the exclusions pursuant to § 2, paragraph (2). If, according to this provision, the rehabilitation authorities of several states have jurisdiction, the first authority to have been approached shall decide. The conclusions of the rehabilitation authority are binding for those authorities that decide on resulting claims.

(2) Rehabilitation authorities shall be established in the States [German "*Länder*"] of Berlin, Brandenburg, Mecklenburg-West Pomerania, Saxonia, Saxonia-Anhalt, and Thuringia.

(3) For claims pursuant to §§ 3 and 4, the rehabilitation authority determines whether the act has violated the rule of law pursuant to § 1 and concerning the exclusions pursuant to § 2, paragraph (2). The authorities who enforce the Act on Pensions make the determinations required by the Act on Pensions. If jurisdiction lies with the administrative authorities in charge of pensions for victims of war, the procedure is governed by the provisions regarding pensions for victims of war.

§ 13. Administrative Procedure

(1) Witnesses are obligated to testify and expert witnesses are obligated to issue expert opinions in the proceeding before the rehabilitation authority. § 65 of the Act of Administrative Procedure applies *mutatis mutandis*.

(2) The decision may solely rely on statements of the applicant regarding the violation of the rule of law of the act referred to in § 1 if evidence does not exist, cannot be obtained or has been lost without fault of the applicant or the person from whom the applicant derives his rights, provided the statements of the applicant appear credible. [T]he rehabilitation authority may require an affirmation from the applicant in lieu of an oath pursuant to § 27 of the Act on Administrative Procedure.

(3) Unless otherwise stated in this Act, the provisions of the Act on Administrative Procedure, the Act on Administrative Service, and the Act on Administrative Enforcement apply until the respective state law has been issued.

§ 14. Costs

The administrative procedure before the rehabilitation authorities, including the appeal procedure, is free. If a request in the administrative procedure or an appeal is rejected as *prima facie* unfounded, the applicant may be burdened with the costs....[10]

§ 16. Course of Law

(1) The administrative courts decide on disputes pursuant to this Act....

---

[10] [Translator's note: § 15 contains a technical provision regarding the finality of administrative decisions.]

§ 17. Cost Distribution

The Federal Treasury covers 60 percent of the monetary payments of the states pursuant to this Act. Money dispersed in compensation for or in lieu of benefits in kind are not considered payments.

Article 2
Act on the Compensation of Professional Harm for Victims of Political Persecution in the Territory of Accession

Part One
General Provisions

§ 1. Concept of the Victim of Persecution

(1) Whoever could not at least temporarily practice his former profession, whether he had already begun or still intended to practice, demonstrated by the start of appropriate education or vocational training, and could not practice a socially equivalent profession between May 8, 1945 and October 2, 1990:

1. due to unjust imprisonment in the ... territory of accession ...,
2. due to deprivation of liberty pursuant to § 25, paragraph (2), sentence 1, numbers 1 and 2 of the Criminal Rehabilitation Act,
3. through an official act pursuant to [Article 1, § 1 of the present law], or
4. through another act in the territory of accession, if the act served the purpose of political persecution,

may claim benefits pursuant to this Act.

(2) In the cases referred to in paragraph (1), numbers 1-3, the period of an unjust imprisonment must have been certified in a rehabilitation of cassation procedure, or the period of deprivation of liberty must have been stated in a certification pursuant to § 10, paragraph (4) of the Act on Prisoners, or the annulment or certification of the violation of the rule of law of an act pursuant to the Administrative Law Rehabilitation Act must have been issued.

§ 2. Period of Persecution

(1) Periods of Persecution are:

1. the period of imprisonment or deprivation of liberty certified pursuant to § 1, paragraph (2), as well as

2. the period in which the persecuted person could not practice a former profession or fulfill intentions to practice or had received a reduced remuneration from his previous occupation due to an act referred to in § 1, paragraph (1), numbers 3 and 4 or as the consequence of an act referred to in § 1, paragraph (1), numbers 1 and 2.

The period of persecution referred to in sentence 1, number 2 is deemed terminated with departure from the territory of accession, at the latest at the end of October 2, 1990.

(2) Periods in which the victim of persecution was responsible for the continuation of his professional disadvantage are not considered periods of persecution.

§ 3. Persecuted Students

(1) Whoever, in the period referred to in § 1, paragraph (1) as a consequence of an act referred to in § 1, paragraph (1), numbers 1-3

1. was not admitted to an educational institution leading to qualification for university studies,
2. could not continue his education at an educational institution leading to qualification for university studies,
3. was not admitted to a final examination leading to qualification for university studies, or
4. was not admitted to a technical school or university,

may claim benefits pursuant to Part Two....

§ 4. Grounds for Exclusion

Benefits pursuant to this Act will not be awarded if the victim of persecution has violated the principles of humanity and the rule of law or has abused his position for his own benefit or for the benefit or to the detriment of others....

Part Two
Preferential Continuing
Vocational Training and Retraining

§ 6. Support Payments as Subsidies

(1) Victims of persecution who participate in continuing vocational training and retraining ... and do not receive support payments pursuant to § 44, paragraph (2) of the Labor Promotion Act, shall receive support payments in *mutatis mutandis* application of ... the Labor Promotion Act.

(2) If a victim of persecution received support payments pursuant to § 44, paragraph (2)(a) of the Labor Promotion Act for participation in continuing vocational training and retraining before this Act came into force, the loan will, upon request, be transformed into a subsidy insofar as the loan has not been repaid as of the day of the submission of the request. If a victim of persecution may continuously claim support payments pursuant to § 44, paragraph (2)(a) of the Labor Promotion Act, the loan shall be transformed upon request into a subsidy....

§ 7. Reimbursement of Costs

Recipients of support payments pursuant to § 6, paragraph (1) shall be reimbursed upon request for:

1. necessary tuition including costs for educational material not exceeding four German Marks for each hour of instruction,
2. child care expenses that have actually been incurred up to 60 German Marks monthly for each child.

Part Three
Restitution Benefits

§ 8. Conditions for Claims

(1) Victims of persecution pursuant to § 1, paragraph (1) who are domiciled or have their usual place of residency in [Germany] and who are particularly disadvantaged in their economic situation shall, upon request, receive restitution benefits in the amount of 150 German Marks monthly if, for the foreseeable future, they will not be able to earn more than marginal income through gainful employment due to the lack of possibilities to reenter the work force. Restitution benefits shall not be granted if the period of persecution established in the certificate pursuant to § 17 or § 18 ended before the end of October 2, 1990, unless the period of persecution lasted for more than three years.

(2) Victims of persecution who own assets that may be considered pursuant to § 88 of the Federal Welfare Act are not particularly disadvantaged in their economic situation. Income is considered marginal if it is not sufficient to cover the necessary living expenses pursuant to Part Two of the Federal Welfare Act.

(3) The restitution benefits shall be paid monthly in advance, beginning with the month following the request, but no longer than the onset of payment of pensions from [the victim of persecution's own] social insurance pursuant to the Sixth Book of the Social Code.

§ 9. Exemption from Set-Off and Attachment

(1) Restitution benefits pursuant to this Part shall not be considered as income with respect to income-dependent social benefits.

(2) The claim for restitution benefits is not subject to attachment.

Part Four
Restitution for Disadvantages in Social Insurance

Sub-Part One
General Provisions

§ 10. General Provisions

The provisions of this paragraph supplement the generally applicable provisions of the law of social insurance for the benefit of the victim of persecution. Benefits pursuant to this paragraph are granted upon request; in individual cases they may be granted *ex officio*.

Sub-Part Two
Pensions Pursuant to the Provisions
of the Sixth Book of the Social Code

§ 11. Periods of Persecution as Periods of Required Contributions

Required contributions for employment or self-employment in the territory of accession are assumed to have been paid for periods ... during which the victim of persecution, due to acts of persecution, did not hold employment or engage in self-employment activities that would have established an obligation to be insured and to make required contributions....

§ 12. Periods of Persecution as Credited Periods

(1) If the victim of persecution, due to an act of persecution, was unable to complete his technical school or university education, the education shall be assumed to be completed for the purpose of the recognition of this period as a credited period.

(2) If, due to an act of persecution, a grade school education, a technical school education or a university education was interrupted but taken up again at a later time and subsequently completed or a different education was taken up and completed, the periods of education shall be recognized as credited periods for up to twice the length of the usual maximum amount of time....[11]

---

[11] [Translator's note: §§13 to 16 contain technical details about the computation of social insurance claims with regard to periods of persecution.]

Part Five
Jurisdiction and Procedure

§ 17. Certificate of Rehabilitation and Jurisdiction of Administrative Authorities

(1) A certificate, to be issued upon request by the rehabilitation authority, shall serve as proof that the requirements of § 1, paragraph (1) or § 3, paragraph (1) have been met and that the grounds of exclusion pursuant to § 4 do not apply....

§ 18. Preliminary Certificate of Rehabilitation

(1) The rehabilitation authority may issue a preliminary certificate as a basis for benefits pursuant to Part Two or Three or as a basis for applying § 60, number 1 of the Federal Act for the Promotion of Education, if the issuance of a certificate pursuant to § 17, paragraph (1) will presumably require an extended period of time. This preliminary certificate must contain the information required by § 22, paragraph (1), numbers 1-3 or § 22, paragraph (2), numbers 1 and 2....

§ 19. Use of Personal Data

Personal data from an employment rehabilitation procedure may be processed and used insofar as necessary for other procedures with respect to rehabilitation, restitution, or benefits pursuant to the Act on Prisoners.

§ 20. Request

(1) The request for issuance of a certificate pursuant to § 17, paragraph (1) may be submitted by the victim of persecution and after his death by his surviving family members insofar as they have a legal interest in the request.

(2) The requests pursuant to § 17, paragraph (1) and § 18, paragraph (1) may be submitted through December 31, 1995. In the cases mentioned in § 1, paragraph (2) the request pursuant to § 17, paragraph (1) may also be submitted within six months after the decision required by § 1, paragraph (2) has become final.

(3) The request shall be submitted in writing to the rehabilitation authority. The deadline has been met if the request has been submitted within the period to another German authority within the country or to a German court.

§ 21. Contents of the Request

The request shall contain

1. information about the person [the applicant],

2. information about the applicant's education and vocational and employment history,
3. an account of the persecution,
4. statements about the extent to which harm in education and occupation was incurred,
5. a list of evidence, and
6. a statement as to whether and where the applicant had previously submitted an application.

§ 22. Contents of the Certificate

(1) In the cases of § 1, the certificate shall contain the following information:

1. the statements pursuant to § 1, paragraph (1),
2. a certification that grounds for exclusion pursuant to § 4 do not apply,
3. the onset and conclusion of the period of persecution (§ 2),
4. length of the interruption of technical school or university studies before October 3, 1990 due to persecution,
5. information about a technical school or university education or other vocationally oriented training that was not completed due to acts of persecution as well as the otherwise usual length of this education until graduation,
6. information about the employment or self-employment that would have existed without the persecution, including information about the:

   a) performance group pursuant to Appendix 1 through 16 of the Act on Pensions for Periods of Persecution prior to January 1, 1950,
   b) qualification group pursuant to Appendix 13 and the field pursuant to Appendix 14 to the Sixth Book of the Social Code for periods of persecution after December 31, 1949,
   c) actual or hypothetical (had it not been for the persecution) membership in a supplementary or special pension plan to be named in the certificate and the respective occupation or function.

7. information about employment or self-employment at the beginning of the persecution in a field mentioned in § 14....

(2) In the cases of § 3, the certificate shall contain the following information:

1. the statements pursuant to § 3, paragraph (1),
2. certification that grounds for exclusion pursuant to § 4 do not apply,

3. the period of unjust imprisonment (§ 1, paragraph (2)) and period of interruption of education due to persecution before October 3, 1990.

Insofar as the certificate is not required for presentation to the responsible authorities to enforce § 60 of the Federal Act for the Promotion of Education, statements with respect to numbers 1 and 2 are sufficient....

§ 23. Deadline for Benefits Pursuant to Parts Two and Three

A request for benefits pursuant to Part Two and Three may be submitted through December 31, 1998.

§ 24. Competence for Benefits Pursuant to Parts Two and Three

(1) Benefits pursuant to Part Two will be granted by the Federal Labor Office as an institution of the state in which the affected person resides....

(2) The local welfare authorities ... shall provide restitution benefits pursuant to Part Three....[12]

---

[12][Editor's note: Article 1, §§ 25-29 parallel §§ 14-17 of Article 1 of the present law. Articles 3-5 contain technical provisions amending the Social Code as well as of some specialized legislation dealing with pensions. Articles 6-10 contain amendments of various laws.]

HAITI: 1987 CONSTITUTION

Article 293-1

Any individual who was the victim of confiscation of property or arbitrary dispossession for political reasons during the period from October 22, 1957 to February 7, 1986, may recover his property before the court of competent jurisdiction.

In such cases, the procedure shall be expedited to for emergency matters, and the decision may be appealed only to the Supreme Court.

Article 294

Sentences to death, personal restraint or penal service of the loss of civil rights for political reasons from 1957 to 1986 shall constitute no impediment to the exercise of civil and political rights.

HONDURAS: ORGANIZATION OF AMERICAN STATES, INTER-AMERICAN COURT OF HUMAN RIGHTS: VELÁSQUEZ RODRÍGUEZ CASE— JUDGMENT ON COMPENSATORY DAMAGES

Judgment of July 21, 1989, Series C No. 7

[P]ursuant to Article 63(1) of the American Convention on Human Rights (hereinafter the "Convention" or "the American Convention"), Article 44(1) of the Court's Rules of Procedure, and in accord with the judgment on the merits of July 29, 1988, the Court enters the following judgment in the instant case brought by the Inter-American Commission on Human Rights against the State of Honduras.

1. The Inter-American Commission on Human Rights (hereinafter "the Commission") submitted this case to the Inter-American Court of Human Rights (hereinafter "the Court") on April 24, 1986. It originated in a complaint (No. 7920), against the State of Honduras (hereinafter "Honduras" or "the Government"), lodged with the Secretariat of the Commission on October 7, 1981.

2. In its judgment on the merits of July 29, 1988, the Court

> 5. Decides that Honduras is hereby required to pay fair compensation to the next of kin of the victim.
> 6. Decides that the form and amount of such compensation, failing agreement between Honduras and the commission within six months of the date of this judgment, shall be settled by the Court and, for that purpose, retains jurisdiction of the case.

(Velásquez Rodríguez Case, Judgment of July 29, 1988. Series C No. 4, para. 194).[*]

I

3. The Court has jurisdiction to order the payment of fair compensation to the injured party in the instant case. Honduras ratified the Convention on September 8, 1977, and recognized the contentious jurisdiction of the Court on September 9, 1981, by depositing the instrument referred to in Article 62 of the Convention. The Commission submitted the case to the Court pursuant to Articles 61 of the Convention and 50(1) and 50(2) of its Regulations, and the Court decided the case on July 29, 1988.

II

4. By Resolution of January 20, 1989, the Court decided:

---

[*] [Editor's note: Excerpts from the 1988 judgment appear earlier in the present volume.]

1. To authorize the President, should the State and the Commission fail to submit an agreement within the allotted time period, to consult with the Permanent Commission of the Court, to initiate whatever studies and name whatever experts might be convenient, so the Court will have the elements of judgment necessary to set the form and amount of compensation.

2. To authorize the President, should it be necessary, to obtain the opinion of the victim's family, the Inter-American Commission on Human Rights, and the Government of Honduras.

3. To authorize the President, should it be necessary, and following consultation with the Permanent Commission of the Court, to set a hearing in this matter....

6. The attorneys recognized as counselors or advisers to the Commission (hereinafter "the attorneys") asked the Court for a public hearing to receive a psychiatric report on the moral damages suffered by the victim's family and the testimony of one of the experts on the methods and conclusions of the report.

7. Citing paragraph 2 of the Resolution of January 20, 1989, Mrs. Emma Guzmán de Velásquez, the wife of Angel Manfredo Velásquez Rodríguez (also known as Manfredo Velásquez), submitted a pleading dated February 26, 1989, in which she asked the Court to order the Government to comply with the following points:

1) An end to forced disappearances in Honduras.
2) An investigation of each of the 150 cases.
3) A complete and truthful public report on what happened to the disappeared persons.
4) The trial and punishment of those responsible for this practice.
5) A public undertaking to respect human rights, especially the rights to life, liberty, and integrity of the person.
6) A public act to honor and dignify the memory of the disappeared. A street, park, elementary school, high school, or hospital could be named for the victims of disappearances.
7) The demobilization and disbanding of the repressive bodies especially created to kidnap, torture, make disappear and assassinate.
8) Guarantees to respect the work of humanitarian and family organizations and public recognition of their social function.
9) An end to all forms of overt or indirect aggression or pressure against the families of the disappeared and public recognition of their honor.
10) The establishment of a fund for the primary, secondary, and university education of the children of the disappeared.
11) Guaranteed employment for the children of the disappeared who are of working age.
12) The establishment of a retirement fund for the parents of the disappeared.

8. As required by the Resolution of January 20, 1989, the Commission submitted its opinion on March 1, 1989. It asserted that the just compensation to be paid by Honduras to the family of Manfredo Velásquez should include the following:

1. The adoption of measures by the State of Honduras which express its emphatic condemnation of the facts that gave rise to the Court's judgment. In particular, it should be established that the Government has an obligation to carry out an exhaustive

investigation of the circumstances of the disappearance of Manfredo Velásquez and bring charges against anyone responsible for the disappearance.

2. The granting to the wife and children of Manfredo Velásquez of the following benefits:

    a)   Payment to the wife of Manfredo Velásquez, Mrs. Emma Guzmán Urbina, of the highest pension recognized by Honduran law.

    b)   Payment to the children of Manfredo Velásquez, Héctor Ricardo, Nadia Waleska and Herling Lizzett Velásquez Guzmán, of a pension or subsidy until they complete their university education, and

    c)   Title to an adequate house, equivalent to the house of a middle class professional family.

3. Payment to the wife and children of Manfredo Velásquez of a cash amount corresponding to the resultant damages, loss of earnings, and emotional harm suffered by the family of Manfredo Velásquez, to be determined by the illustrious Court based upon the expert opinion offered by the victim's family.

9. On March 10, 1989, the attorneys submitted a pleading in which they assert that, in conformity with Article 63 of the Convention, reparation should be moral as well as monetary.

The measures they request as moral reparation are the following:

- A public condemnation of the practice of involuntary disappearances carried out between 1981 and 1984;
- An expression of solidarity with the victims of that practice, including Manfredo Velásquez. Public homage to those victims by naming a street, thoroughfare, school or other public place after them;
- An exhaustive investigation of the phenomenon of involuntary disappearances in Honduras, with special attention to the fate of each of the disappeared. The resulting information should be made known to the family and the public;
- Prosecution and appropriate punishment of those responsible for inciting, planning, implementing or covering up disappearances, in accord with the law and procedures of Honduras.

In their opinion, the cash indemnity paid to the family of Manfredo Velásquez should include the following: damages, two hundred thousand lempiras; loss of earnings, two million four hundred and twenty-two thousand four hundred and twenty lempiras, emotional damages, four million eight hundred and forty-five thousand lempiras; and punitive damages, two million four hundred and twenty-two thousand lempiras.

They especially request

> that Emma Guzmán de Velásquez and her minor children, Héctor Ricardo, Nadia and Herling Velásquez Guzmán, be recognized as the beneficiaries, and that the Government of Honduras be ordered to adopt special legislation making that determination, in order to facilitate the payment of indemnity without the need for judicial proceedings for a declaration of absence, presumed death or declaration of heirship. For that purpose, we formally state on behalf of those persons that there are no other persons with a superior claim to inherit from Manfredo Velásquez.

Moreover, they ask the Court to establish deadlines within which the Government should make moral reparation, and to reserve the right to see that they are met. Regarding the monetary reparation, they ask the Court to set "a deadline of 90 days for the execution of the judgment, and that a lump-sum payment be made prior to that date to Emma Guzmán de Velásquez."

10. On March 10, 1989, the Delegate of the Commission submitted a clinical report prepared by a team of psychiatrists on the state of health of the family of Manfredo Velásquez.

11. The Agent [representing the Honduran government] informed the Court on March 14, 1989 that, in payment of the indemnity, his Government was willing to apply the Honduran law of the National Social Security Institute for Teachers (*Instituto Nacional de Previsión del Magisterio*), which it considered the most favorable law in this case because it establishes the right to payment of thirty-seven thousand and eighty lempiras in life insurance, and four thousand one hundred and twenty lempiras as a severance benefit. In addition, the Government offered a voluntary contribution toward the indemnity to bring the total to one hundred and fifty thousand lempiras.

12. On March 15, 1989, the Court held a public audience to hear the parties regarding the indemnity to be awarded....

14. On April 26, 1989, the Government submitted its response to the Commission's submission of March 1, 1989.... The pleading also refers to matters that, in its opinion, should be taken into account in the indemnification of the family of Manfredo Velásquez. Regarding measures to express its condemnation of the facts that gave rise to the judgment and its obligation to investigate the disappearance of Manfredo Velásquez and prosecute those responsible, the Government believes the Court's judgment of July 29, 1988 "is very clear and precise regarding the obligation of Honduras to pay damages, which is to pay *just compensation to the family of the victim, and nothing more*" (underlined in the original). Insofar as the benefits the Commission believes should be paid to the wife of Manfredo Velásquez, the Government believes that such payment "is only admissible insofar as whatever may be provided for by the system to which Mr. VELÁSQUEZ RODRÍGUEZ may have been affiliated." It asserts that damages, loss of earnings, and emotional harm are inadmissible because their purpose "is not merely to compensate the VELÁSQUEZ RODRÍGUEZ family, but ... to pay the expenses of the intense media campaign waged against Honduras within and outside the country by national and foreign associations, and to pay the fees of lawyers and other professionals who cooperated with the Commission in this case."

III

20. The first question the Court must resolve is related to the implementation of resolutory point number 6 of the judgment on the merits, according to which it gave Honduras and the Commission six months from the date of the judgment of July 29, 1988, to reach an agreement on the form

and amount of just compensation to be paid to the family of Manfredo Velásquez....

21. In its pleading of March 1, 1989, the Commission reported on its attempts to reach an agreement with the Government. According to the Commission, only at the end of the six-month period was it possible to meet in the city of Tegucigalpa with a commission named by the President of the Republic of Honduras "to negotiate and determine the amount and form of payment of the compensation awarded in the Inter-American Court's judgment of July 29, 1988."

22. According to the record of that meeting..., the parties agreed only on the recognition of the beneficiaries of the compensation. The remaining points are simple declarations which establish no criteria for fixing the amount of the compensation and, even less, for payment. Therefore, resolutory point number 6 of the judgment on the merits of July 29, 1988, was not carried out.

IV

23. The written and oral arguments made to the Court show substantial differences of opinion insofar as the scope, bases and amount of the compensation. Some arguments refer to the need to rely upon the internal law of Honduras, or part of it, in determining or paying the indemnity.

24. Because of those disagreements and in order to implement the judgment on the merits of July 29, 1988, the Court must now define the scope and content of the just compensation to be paid by the Government to the family of Manfredo Velásquez.

25. It is a principle of international law, which jurisprudence has considered "even a general concept of law," that every violation of an international obligation which results in harm creates a duty to make adequate reparation. Compensation, on the other hand, is the most usual way of doing so (Factory at Chorzów, Jurisdiction, Judgment No. 8, 1927, P.C.I.J., Series A, No. 9, p. 21, and Factory at Chorzów, Merits, Judgment No. 13, 1928, P.C.I.J., Series A, No. 17, p. 29; Reparation for injuries Suffered in the Service of the United Nations, Advisory Opinion, I.C.J. Reports 1949, p. 184).

26. Reparation of harm brought about by the violation of an international obligation consists in full restitution (*restitutio in integrum*), which includes the restoration of the prior situation, the reparation of the consequences of the violation, and indemnification for patrimonial and non-patrimonial damages, including emotional harm.

27. As to emotional harm, the Court holds that indemnity may be awarded under international law and, in particular, in the case of human rights violations. Indemnification must be based upon the principles of equity.

28. Indemnification for human rights violations is supported by international instruments of a universal and regional character. The Human Rights Committee, created by the International Covenant of Civil and Political Rights of the United Nations, has repeatedly called for, based on the

Optional Protocol, indemnification for the violation of human rights recognized in the the Covenant (see, for example, communications 4/1977; 6/1977; 11/1977; 132/1982; 138/1983; 147/1983; 161/1983; 188/1984; 194/1985; etc., Reports of the Human Rights Committee, United Nations). The European Court of Human Rights has reached the same conclusion based on Article 50 of the Convention for the Protection of Human Rights and Fundamental Freedoms.

29. Article 63(1) of the American Convention provides as follows:

> 1. If the Court finds that there has been a violation of a right or freedom protected by this Convention, the Court shall rule that the injured party be ensured the enjoyment of his right or freedom that was violated. It shall also rule, if appropriate, that the consequences of the measure or situation that constituted the breach of such right or freedom be remedied and that fair compensation be paid to the injured party.

30. This article does not refer to or limit the ability to ensure the effectiveness of the means of reparation available under the internal law of the State Party responsible for the violation, so it is not limited by the defects, imperfections or deficiencies of national law, but functions independently of it.

31. This implies that, in order to fix the corresponding indemnity, the Court must rely upon the American Convention and the applicable principles of international law.

V

32. The Commission and the attorneys maintain that, in implementing the judgment, the Court should order the Government to take some measures, such as the investigation of the facts related to the involuntary disappearance of Manfredo Velásquez; the punishment of those responsible; a public statement condemning that practice; the revindication of the victim, and other similar measures.

33. Measures of this type would constitute a part of the reparation of the consequences of the violation of rights or freedoms and not a part of the indemnity, in accordance with Article 63(1) of the Convention.

34. However, in its judgment on the merits (Velásquez Rodríguez Case,... para. 181), the Court has already pointed out the Government's continuing duty to investigate so long as the fate of a disappeared person is unknown.... The duty to investigate is in addition to the duties to prevent involuntary disappearances and to punish those directly responsible (Velásquez Rodríguez Case,... para. 174).

35. Although these obligations were not expressly incorporated into the resolutory part of the judgment on the merits, it is a principle of procedural law that the bases of a judicial decision are a part of the same. Consequently, the Court declares that those obligations on the part of Honduras continue until they are fully carried out.

36. Otherwise, the Court understands that the judgment on the merits of July 29, 1988, is in itself a type of reparation and moral satisfaction of significance and importance for the families of the victims.

37. The attorneys also request the payment by the Government of punitive damages as part of the indemnity, because this case involved extremely serious violations of human rights.

38. The expression "fair compensation," used in Article 63(1) of the Convention to refer to a part of the reparation and to the "injured party," is compensatory and not punitive. Although some domestic courts, particularly the Anglo-American, award damages in amounts meant to deter or to serve as an example, this principle is not applicable in international law at this time.

39. Because of the foregoing, the Court believes, then, that the fair compensation, described as "compensatory" in the judgment on the merits of July 29, 1988, includes reparation to the family of the victim of the material and moral damages they suffered because of the involuntary disappearance of Manfredo Velásquez....

43. The Government argues that the compensation should be on the basis of the most favorable treatment possible for the family of Manfredo Velásquez under Honduran law, which is that provided by the Law of the National Institute of Social Security for Teachers in the case of accidental death. According to the Government, the family would be entitled to a total of forty-one thousand two hundred lempiras, to which it would contribute an additional amount to bring the compensation to one hundred and fifty thousand lempiras.

44. The Commission does not propose an amount, but rather asserts that the compensation should include two elements: a) the greatest benefits that Honduran legislation allows nationals in cases of this type and which, according to the Commission, are those granted by the Institute of Military Pensions, and b) a cash amount which should be set according to what is provided for by Honduran and international law.

45. The attorneys believe that the basis should be the loss of earnings, calculated according to the income that Manfredo Velásquez received at the time of his kidnapping, at the age of 35, his studies toward a degree as an economist, which would have allowed him to work as a professional, and the possible promotions, Christmas bonuses, allowances and other benefits he would have been entitled to at retirement. They calculate an amount which in thirty years would be one million six hundred and fifty-one thousand six hundred and fifty lempiras. They add to that the retirement benefits for ten years, according to life expectancy in Honduras for a person of that social class, calculated at seven hundred and seventy thousand seven hundred and sixty lempiras, which gives a total amount of two million four hundred and twenty-two thousand four hundred and twenty lempiras.

46. The Court notes that the disappearance of Manfredo Velásquez cannot be considered an accidental death for the purposes of compensation, given that it is the result of serious acts imputable to Honduras. The amount of compensation cannot, therefore, be based upon guidelines such as life insurance, but must be calculated as a loss of earnings based upon the

income the victim would have received up to the time of his possible natural death. In that sense, one can take as a point of departure the salary that, according to the certification of the Honduran Vice-Minister of Planning on October 19, 1988, Manfredo Velásquez was receiving at the time of his disappearance (1,030 lempiras per month) and calculate the amount he would have received at the time of his obligatory retirement at the age of sixty, as provided by Article 69 of the Law of the National Institute of Social Security for Teachers and which the Government itself considers the most favorable. At retirement, he would have been entitled to a pension until his death.

47. However, the calculation of the loss of earnings must consider two distinct situations. When the beneficiary of the indemnity is a victim who is totally and permanently disabled, the compensation should include all he failed to receive, together with appropriate adjustments based upon his probable life expectancy. In that circumstance, the only income for the victim is what he would have received, but will not receive, as earnings....

49. Based upon a prudent estimate of the possible income of the victim for the rest of his probable life and on the fact that, in this case, the compensation is for the exclusive benefit of the family of Manfredo Velásquez identified at trial, the Court sets the loss of earnings in the amount of five hundred thousand lempiras to be paid to the wife and to the children of Manfredo Velásquez as set out below.

50. The Court must now consider the question of the indemnification of the moral damages..., which is primarily the result of the psychological impact suffered by the family of Manfredo Velásquez because of the violation of the rights and freedoms guaranteed by the American Convention, especially by the dramatic characteristics of the involuntary disappearance of persons.

51. The moral damages are demonstrated by expert documentary evidence and the testimony of Dr. Federico Allodi..., psychiatrist and Professor of Psychology at the University of Toronto, Canada. According to his testimony, the above doctor examined the wife of Manfredo Velásquez, Mrs. Emma Guzmán Urbina de Velásquez and his children, Héctor Ricardo, Herring Lizzett and Nadia Waleska Velásquez. According to those examinations, they had symptoms of fright, anguish, depression and withdrawal, all because of the disappearance of the head of the family. The Government could not disprove the existence of psychological problems that affect the family of the victim. The Court finds that the disappearance of Manfredo Velásquez produced harmful psychological impacts among his immediate family which should be indemnified as moral damages.

52. The Court believes the Government should pay compensation for moral damages in the amount of two hundred and fifty thousand lempiras, to be paid to the wife and children of Manfredo Velásquez as specified below....

VII

54. As previously stated, the obligation to indemnify is not derived from internal law, but from violation of the American Convention. It is the result of an international obligation. To demand indemnification, the family members of Manfredo Velásquez need only show their family relationship. They are not required to follow the procedure of Honduran inheritance law....

VIII

56. The Court now determines how the Government is to pay compensation to the family of Manfredo Velásquez.

57. Payment of the seven hundred and fifty thousand lempiras awarded by the Court must be carried out within ninety days from the date of notification of the judgment, free from any tax that might eventually be considered applicable. Nevertheless, the Government may pay in six equal monthly installments, the first being payable within ninety days and the remainder in successive months. In this case, the balance shall be incremented by the appropriate interest, which shall be at the interest rates current at that moment in Honduras.

58. One-fourth of the indemnity is awarded to the wife who shall receive that sum directly. The remaining three-fourths shall be distributed among the children. With the funds from the award to the children, a trust fund shall be set up in the Central Bank of Honduras under the most favorable conditions permitted by Honduran banking practice. The children shall receive monthly payments from this trust fund, and at the age of twenty-five shall receive their proportionate part.

59. The Court shall supervise the implementation of the compensatory damages at all of its stages. The case shall be closed when the Government has fully complied with the instant judgment....

HUNGARY: LAW VOIDING
CERTAIN CONVICTIONS 1963-1989

Law No. 11 (February 19, 1992)

Provisions defining criminal acts against the State and public order remained in effect unchanged after 1963; based on these provisions an adjudicative practice in conflict with the basic principles contained in the then effective Constitution, and repugnant to generally recognized principles and rules of human rights and to society's system of moral values, has prevailed. The system violated all these tenets not only by using means available under criminal law, but also as a result of rules violation proceedings and other administrative processes.

The National Assembly condemns this legal practice and intends to provide moral satisfaction to all those who suffered as a result.

No opportunity exists to remedy all types of violations by law, but it is appropriate to provide political, moral, and legal satisfaction in a manner consistent with the principles of a constitutional State as provided for in the Constitution, to those who suffered as a result of criminal proceedings. Therefore, the National Assembly adopts the following Law:

Section 1

Convictions between 5 April 1963 and 15 October 1989 regarding the following criminal acts shall be declared null and void:

(a) Conspiracy (Sections 116-118 of Law No. 5 of 1961, the wording of Law No. 4 of 1978 until the wording of Law No. 25 of 1989 took effect—hereinafter in the context of this Law: Criminal Code of Laws—Section 139);

(b) Insurrection (Sections 120-122 of Law No. 5 of 1961, Criminal Code of Laws Section 140);

(c) Incitement (Section 127 of Law No. 5 of 1961, Criminal Code of Laws Section 148);

(d) Conspiracy, insurrection against another socialist State (Section 133 of Law No. 5 of 1961, Criminal Code of Laws Section 151);

(e) Offending an authority or an official person (Section 158 of Law No. 5 of 1961, Criminal Code of Laws Section 232);

(f) Offending the community (Section 217 of Law No. 5 of 1961, Criminal Code of Laws No. 269);

(g) Incitement against a law or action by the authorities (Section 216 of Law No. 5 of 1961, Criminal Code of Laws Section 268);

(h) Abuse of the right to associate with others (Section 207 of Law No. 5 of 1961, Criminal Code of Laws Section 212);

(i) Prohibited border crossing (Section 203 Paragraph (1), Paragraph (2) Subparagraph (b), Paragraphs (4) and (5), Criminal Code of Laws

Paragraph 217, Paragraphs (1) and (2), Paragraph (3) Subparagraph (b), and Paragraph (5));

(j) Refusal to return to Hungary (Section 205 of Law No. 5 of 1961);

(k) Crime against people's freedom (Section 136 of Law No. 5 of 1961, Criminal Code of Laws Section 154);

(l) Misdemeanors violating rules governing the press (Section 211 of Law No. 5 of 1961, Criminal Code of Laws Section 213);

(m) Scare-mongering (Section 218 of Law No. 5 of 1961, Criminal Code of Laws Section 270);

(n) Failure to report a crime or misdemeanor if the duty to report pertains to criminal acts under nullity provided for in Section 1 (a)-(m);

(o) Aiding and abetting [an offender] (Section 184 of Law No. 5 of 1961, Criminal Code of Laws Section 244) if the offense pertains to criminal acts under nullity provided for in Section 1 (a)-(n);

provided that the commission of the crime constituted an exercise of the basic rights enumerated in the International Covenant on Civil and Political Rights proclaimed by Decree With the Force of Law No. 8 of 1976, or the realization of the principles and goals contained therein.

Section 2

(1) Other convictions which took place within the time period defined in Section 1 and pronounced jointly with the convictions enumerated therein for crimes closely related to the above enumerated crimes, but not sanctioned by a more severe punishment, shall also be declared null and void.

(2) Convictions stemming from crimes not enumerated under Paragraph (1), but which were adjudicated jointly with and in relation to the crimes enumerated in Section 1, shall be declared null and void only insofar as they pertain to crimes enumerated in Section 1 (partial nullity). In case of partial nullity, the starting point for declaring convictions null and void shall primarily be the ratio between the upper limits of punishments which constitute the basis for the nonconcurrent sentences, and the nonconcurrent sentence shall be reduced with the content of the partially voided punishment, in due regard to this ratio.

(3) If, in the case described in Paragraph (2), a convict has not yet completed his sentence, the court shall resentence the convict in the course of a hearing, leaving intact the factual considerations and the guilty verdict relative to the crime not voided.

Section 3

(1) The provisions of Section 2 Paragraph (1) shall be observed even if the punishment based on crimes enumerated in Section 1 was included as part of nonconcurrent sentences for other crimes closely related to the crimes enumerated in Section 1, but not sanctioned by more severe punishment.

(2) The duration of nonconcurrent sentences specified under Paragraph (1) shall be reduced by the duration of sentences pronounced as a result of crimes enumerated under Section 1. The Provisions of Section 2 shall be observed if any judgment of a court pronounced a nonconcurrent sentence.

Section 4

(1) Except as provided for in Paragraph (2), the general rules for special proceedings, as contained in Section 356 of Law No. 1 of 1973 concerning criminal procedure shall be applied in the course of declaring convictions void.

(2) Paragraph (2) of Section 356 of the Law on Criminal Procedure shall be applied in the course of declaring convictions void, with the following changes:

(a) Proceedings shall be initiated on the basis of petitions filed by the convicts' relatives (Section 137 Subparagraph 5 of the Criminal Code of Laws);

(b) Court jurisdiction for conducting proceedings pursuant to Section 3 shall be established on the basis of jurisdiction of the court that pronounced a nonconcurrent sentence in the first instance, or, in case of multiple nonconcurrent sentences, the court that pronounced the last nonconcurrent sentence;

(c) Relatives may also appeal the judgment of the court;

(d) The cause for vacating specified in Section 356 Paragraph (2) Subparagraph (d) of the Law on Criminal Procedure shall not apply;

(e) The State shall pay court costs.

Section 5

Section 3 of Law No. 36 of 1989 shall be applied in the course of voiding convictions during the time period specified in Section 1 regarding political or other criminal acts subject to the authority of Law No. 36 of 1989.

Section 6

(1) This Law shall take effect on the day of its proclamation.

(2) A separate Law provides for the compensation of persons whose conviction has been voided based on this Law.

(3) The time allowed for submitting compensation claims shall begin on the day on which a final judgment of a court proclaims a conviction null and void.

HUNGARY: COMPENSATION LAWS

Law No. 25 (June 26, 1991)

*To settle ownership conditions, for the partial indemnification
of damages caused by the State to the property of citizens.*

Guided by the principle of constitutional statehood and in due regard to society's sense of justice and ability to accept burden, the National Assembly adopts the following Law to settle ownership conditions consistent with sales conditions, to establish entrepreneurial security under conditions of a market economy, and to mitigate unjust damages caused by the state to citizens to their property:

Scope of Law

§1(1) Natural persons whose private property has been violated as a result of enforcing legal provisions created by the State after 1 May 1939, as enumerated in Appendixes 1 and 2, shall be entitled to partial indemnification (hereinafter: indemnification).

§1(2) Based on this Law, natural persons, as defined in §2, whose private property has been violated as a result of enforcing legal provisions created after 8 June 1949, as enumerated in Appendix 2, shall be entitled to indemnification.

§1(3) Indemnification of damages caused by the enforcement of legal provisions created between 1 May 1939 and 8 June 1949, as enumerated in Appendix 1, shall take place pursuant to the provisions of a separate law to be enacted by 30 November 1991, in a manner consistent with the principles defined in this Law.

§2(1) The following persons shall be entitled to indemnification:

(a) Hungarian citizens,
(b) who were Hungarian citizens when they suffered damages, [or]
(c) who suffered damages in conjunction with the deprivation of their Hungarian citizenship, [and]
(d) non Hungarian citizens who in a manner akin to carrying on their lives resided in Hungary as of 31 December 1990.

§2(2) If the person entitled to indemnification [hereinafter: entitled person] defined in Paragraph (1) above (hereinafter [also]: former owner) has deceased, the former owner's descendant, or in the absence of a descendant, the former owner's spouse shall be entitled to indemnification.

§2(3) Descendants shall be entitled to indemnification exclusively after the deceased descendant and only to the extent of the descendant's entitlement, divided in equal portions among the descendants. No indemnification shall be made for a deceased descendant's share of property if such descendant has no descendant.

§2(4) The surviving spouse shall be entitled to indemnification if there is no descendant, provided that such spouse was married to and lived with the former owner when the former owner suffered the injuries and at the time of the former owner's death.

§2(5) A person whose claim has already been settled in the framework of an international agreement shall not be entitled to indemnification.

Determining the Extent of Damages

§3(1) The extent of damages shall be defined in the form of flat rates. Appendix 3 contains the flat rates applicable to certain types of property.

§3(2) The extent of damage involving arable land shall be determined pursuant to the provisions of §13.

§3(3) The flat rates mentioned in Paragraphs (1) and (2) shall include the value of movable property.

§3(4) Only one type of indemnification shall be due for each piece of property, but the owner shall have an opportunity to choose [between various types of indemnification].

Extent of Indemnification

§4(1) That part of the aggregate damages determined pursuant to the provisions of §3 shall be the subject of indemnification which is derived as a result of calculations based on the table provided in Paragraph (2) below, rounded to the nearest one thousand forints, and which does not exceed the amount specified in Paragraph (4) below.

§4(2) Extent of indemnification:

Extent of Damage	Extent of Indemnification
0-200,000 forints	100 percent;
200,001-300,000 forints	200,000 forints plus 50 percent of the amount over and above 200,000 forints;
300,001-500,000 forints	250,000 forints plus 30 percent of the amount over and above 300,000 forints;
500,001 forints and above	310,000 forints plus 10 percent of the amount over and above 500,000 forints.

§4(3) The amount of indemnification per piece of property and per former owner shall not exceed 5 million forints.

§4(4) In case of multiple owners, the extent of indemnification shall be determined based on the proportionate share of ownership held by the several owners.

Method of Indemnification

§5(1) An indemnification voucher shall be issued for the amount of indemnification. All indemnification vouchers issued to an entitled person shall bear the same serial designation. (§6(2)).

§5(2) The indemnification voucher shall be redeemable on sight, shall be transferable and shall constitute a security whose value corresponds with the amount of indemnification and whose face value shall constitute a demand against the State.

§5(3) An indemnification voucher shall earn interest for a period of three years beginning on the first day of the calendar year quarter in which it was issued. The rate of interest shall be 75 percent of the central bank's basic interest rate which prevails at any given point in time.

§5(4) Irrespective of the date of issue, interest shall accrue beginning on the effective date of this Law.

§5(5) The face value of an indemnification voucher shall be increased by adding the amount of interest [calculated on the basis of an interest rate] publicized monthly by the National Damage Claims Settlement Office, and shall be credited on the first days of subsequent months.

§6(1) An indemnification voucher shall contain the following:

(a) the designation "indemnification voucher";
(b) the face value of the voucher and a reference to crediting interest §5(5));
(c) a description of the method in which the indemnification voucher may be used (§7);
(d) the date and place of issue;
(e) designation of the serial issue (Paragraph (2)) and a serial number;
(f) the signature of the director of the National Damage Claims Settlement Office, [and]
(g) the denomination of the voucher (1,000 forints, 5,000 forints, 10,000 forints).

§6(2) Indemnification vouchers shall bear serial issue designations A through J. Individual series shall be issued in equal quantities and at an equal pace.

§6(3) The issuance and sale of indemnification vouchers shall be governed by the provisions of this Law.

§7(1) The State shall guarantee the ability of holders of indemnification vouchers to redeem such vouchers pursuant to conditions provided in this Law

(a) for the purchase of pieces of property, stock and business shares sold in the course of privatizing State property; and

(b) for the acquisition of arable land property.

§7(2) An entitled person may use indemnification vouchers to which he is entitled under this Law as method of payment whenever State-owned housing units, or, following promulgation of this Law, State-owned housing units transferred free of charge into the ownership of autonomous local governmental bodies, are sold. In such transactions, indemnification vouchers shall be exchanged at face value.

§7(3) The face value of indemnification vouchers shall be regarded as a person's own financial resource whenever a person borrows funds pursuant to the provisions of the Law concerning the small business ["Existence"] fund or when taking advantage of privatization loans.

§7(4) At the request of an entitled person, annuity payments may be provided during the entitled person's life in exchange for indemnification vouchers and in the framework of social security pursuant to a separate law.

§8(1) If so recommended by the State Property Agency [AVU], the government may suspend purchases in exchange for indemnification vouchers (§7(1)(a)) each year relative to a certain series of, or all, indemnification vouchers in circulation. The period of suspension shall not exceed six months per year, and suspensions may be made only until 31 December of the fifth full calendar year starting in the year when the indemnification vouchers are issued. Thereafter the use of indemnification vouchers for the purpose of making purchases shall not be restricted.

§8(2) A given series of indemnification vouchers may be suspended for identical periods of time as viewed in two-year averages, and the series of indemnification vouchers to be suspended shall be chosen in a public lottery drawing. The time period in which indemnification vouchers earn interest shall be extended by the time period during which a given series of indemnification vouchers was suspended.

§8(3) Indemnification vouchers shall be accepted as payment for a least 10 percent of the value of assets of a State enterprise in the process of transforming into a business organization—as the value of such assets is evidenced by the financial statement of such State enterprise, and of the value of State-owned assets sold directly. The AVU shall determine the extent to which indemnification vouchers may be accepted as payment for such property over and above the 10 percent minimum limit.

§8(4) Indemnification vouchers acquired by a cooperative pursuant to the provisions of §26 shall be accepted as payment to the extent of at least 20 percent of the assets of State food industry enterprises in the process of transforming into business organizations—as the value of such assets is evidenced by the financial statements of such enterprises.

§8(5) In the event that the AVU board of directors renders a decision concerning the direct sale to a single owner of a State enterprise in the process of transforming into a business organization or in regard to a piece of property owned by the State, the AVU may deviate from the minimum redemption levels specified in Paragraphs (3) and (4) above.

§9 A person entitled to indemnification shall enjoy pre-purchase rights whenever the AVU or a unit of local government sells that person's former property. Exceptions to this rule are as follows: Cases governed by Law No. 74 or 1990; instances when rental housing units owned by a local government or by the State are purchased by their present occupants; situations in which the property pertains to a right having pecuniary value (e.g. corporate, membership rights); or situations in which the AVU sells membership rights in a corporation which acquired such property or was established with the contribution of such property.

Procedural Rules

§10(1) With respect to cases arising under the authority of this Law, the county (Capital) damage claims settlement office shall act as the authority of the first instance, and the National Damage Claims Settlement Office (hereinafter jointly: Office) as the authority of the second instance.

§10(2) Authorities charged with the protection of the natural environment shall participate in the workings of the county (Capital) Office, and the Ministry of Environmental Protection and Regional Development in the workings of the national Office as the expert authorities of the first instance.

§10(3) Final determination rendered by the Office may be reviewed in court. Courts shall also be authorized to change the Office's determinations subject to challenge. Proceedings shall be governed by rules provided in Chapter 20 of the Code of Civil Procedure.

§11(1) Entitled persons may submit petitions for indemnification within 90 days from the effective date of this Law to the county (Capital) Office having jurisdiction.

§11(2) In the event that the property which serves as the basis for an indemnification claim includes real estate, the county (Capital) office having jurisdiction at the place where the real estate is located shall have jurisdiction.

§11(3) The Capital Office shall have jurisdiction to proceed if the entitled person permanently resides abroad.

§11(4) In case several county (Capital) offices have jurisdiction ... the county (Capital) office chosen by the entitled person shall proceed with respect to all of the claimant's property.

§12(1) Petitions for indemnification shall be submitted in writing. Failure to submit such petition within the deadline specified in §11(1) shall constitute the surrender of the right to file a claim.

§12(2) All documents or copies of documents which verify entitlement to property shall be attached to the petition. Lacking such documentation, reference shall be made to other evidence of ownership.

§12(3) In the event that a petition is filed in a manner inconsistent with the provisions of Paragraph (2) above, the Office shall return such petition to the entitled person by simultaneously granting an extension of time to file the petition together with the missing data. In the event that an entitled person returns the petition in response to the Office's request to provide additional data without such additional data, the Office shall judge the petition based on this available data.

§12(4) The county (Capital) Office shall provide a summary notice to the affected business organizations within two months from the deadline established in §11(1) concerning the Gold Crown value of claims filed against arable land owned or used by such business organizations and acquired in a manner subject to the authority of this Law.

§12(5) The Office shall proceed pursuant to the rules provided in Law No. 4 of 1957 concerning general rules of State administrative procedure, except for the following:

(a) the deadline for action shall be six months from the date of receipt of petition. This deadline may be extended by the head of the Office only once for a period no longer than three months;

(b) proceedings shall be suspended if, in his petition, or at the request of the Office, the claimant verifies that he has initiated necessary court or other official proceedings to establish ownership rights which serve as a foundation for his claim.

§12(6) Proceedings initiated before the Office on the basis of this Law shall be exempt from the payment of fees.

Special Rules Pertaining to Arable Land

§13(1) Whenever a claim involves arable land, the extent of damage shall be determined based on the cadastral net income of the arable land (hereinafter: Gold Crown value), so that the value of one Gold Crown equals 1,000 forints. Relative to forest land, the quadruple of this Gold Crown value shall be considered as the basis of calculations.

§13(2) If a former owner received land in exchange for his arable land, the extent of damage shall be established on the basis of the [applicable] Gold Crown value differential.

§13(3) In the event that Gold Crown data pertaining to part of the land cannot be found in earlier documents, the Gold Crown value shall be determined on the basis of the cadastral net income data of the town (city) which exercises authority over the area where the land is located. Calculations shall be made based on the average Gold Crown data determined at the close of the years 1982 through 1985.

§13(4) In the event that the whole or part of the original land was recorded as an area not under cultivation or as a fish pond, the extent of damage shall be determined on the basis of the Gold Crown value established for the lowest quality cultivated land ["plough cultivation branch"] in the [surroundings of the] town (city) which exercises authority over the area where the land is located.

§14 If the former owner received any kind of compensation (e.g. redemption price) for his arable land, the amount of such compensation shall be deducted from amount of damage to be indemnified calculated pursuant to the provisions of §4.

§15(1) In order to provide indemnification in the form of arable land, the cooperative or its legal successor (hereinafter: cooperative) shall designate the arable land area it owns or uses as of the day when this Law is promulgated, and which it acquired on the basis of legal provisions enumerated in Appendix 2. Such designation shall take place within 30 days from date of receipt of the notice described in §12(4) pursuant to the provisions of §§16-18 In the event that a cooperative fails to comply with the obligation to designate the arable land area referred to above, the entire arable land [acquired on the basis of the legal provisions enumerated in Appendix 2.7] and owned or used [by the cooperative] shall be regarded as designated arable land.

§15(2) Entitled persons shall have a right to purchase arable land designated pursuant to Paragraph (1) above....

§17(1) A land bank shall be established in the course of designating arable land for the purpose of transferring land to the ownership of members and employees of cooperatives, and of employees of State farms. The size of the land bank shall be determined by allocating land of an average value of 30 Gold Crowns to each member of a cooperative, and of 20 Gold Crowns to each employee of a cooperative or a State farm. The Gold Crown value of the land bank thus calculated shall not exceed 50 percent of the Gold Crown value of arable land owned by the cooperative or managed by the State farm.

§17(2) For purposes of calculating the [size of the] land bank mentioned in Paragraph (1) above, current members of cooperatives, or employees of cooperatives or State farms whose membership or employment relationship has already existed on 1 January 1991, and whose agricultural land property is smaller than the size of property defined in Paragraph (1) above shall be regarded as members of cooperatives or as employees of cooperatives or State farms.

§18(1) Arable land to be released shall be designated outside of protected natural reservations.

§18(2) In the event that the area available outside of protected natural reservations is not sufficient for purposes of designation, plough lands, gardens, orchards, vineyards or forests owned by the cooperative, and cultivated protected natural areas may also be designated. The exceptions in this regard are: national park areas and areas governed by international agreements or subject to intensive protection.

§18(3) The concurrence of the authority charged with the protection of the natural environment shall be obtained before designating protected natural areas.

§18(4) If in the course of indemnification a protected natural area is released or if some other restriction on land use already exists, the persons participating in the auction (§21) shall be so informed in writing.

§18(5) These provisions shall also apply with respect to areas that are planned to be classified as protected areas.

§18(6) Land areas protected as historical sites, originally not belonging, or not adjacent to agricultural buildings or structures, which were originally not regarded as arable land, shall not be designated.

§19 Simultaneously with, and after the auctioning of, cooperative lands the State shall also auction State-owned land. The Gold Crown value of land thus auctioned shall amount to at least 20 percent of the Gold Crown value of land auctioned by cooperatives.

§20(1) Arable land designated pursuant to the provisions of §§15-19 shall be sold at auction to entitled persons. If the land of the former owner is State-owned land and was transferred into the common use of a cooperative, the cooperative may also auction State-owned arable land under the common use of the cooperative.

§20(2) The initial and final dates for auctions shall be determined by the county (Capital) Office having jurisdiction in the area where the cooperative is headquartered, in due regard to the evaluation of petitions for indemnification.

§21(1) The following entitled persons may participate in the auction with indemnification vouchers to which they are entitled:

(a) persons whose expropriated arable land is presently owned or used by the cooperative;

(b) members of the cooperative as of 1 January 1991 who continue to hold such membership at the time of the auction;

(c) permanent residents as of 1 June 1991 of the municipality or city in which the auctioning cooperative's arable land is located.

§21(2) The official exercising State administrative authority in the county (Capital) Office having jurisdiction shall conduct the auction, and a notary public shall attest to the legality of the auctioning process.

§22(1) Participants at the auction shall bid by stating forint values corresponding to one Gold Crown value. The opening price shall be 3,000 forints per Gold Crown. If there are no bids at or above the opening price, the opening price may be lowered gradually, but to no less than 500 forints per Gold Crown value.

§22(2) The auctioning must be conducted pursuant to the provisions of the implementing decree.... Owners of detached farms entitled to indemnification shall enjoy a pre-purchase right regarding the arable land surrounding their detached farms.

§23(1) The right to purchase defined in §22(2) may be exercised by a person entitled to do so provided that such person commits himself to use the arable land for agricultural purposes and not to withdraw the land from agricultural production for a period of five years.

§23(2) Arable land acquired by exercising the right to purchase shall be taken away from the owner without indemnification and shall be sold at auction, in the event that such owner reneges on the commitment made pursuant to Paragraph (1) within five years from the date of acquiring the land.

§23(3) If arable land acquired by exercising the right to purchase is sold within three years from the date of acquisition, proceeds of the sale, offset by the amount of investment to increase the value of such arable land, shall be regarded as income from the standpoint of the owner's personal income taxes in the year when the arable land was sold. The sales value used for calculating [official] fees shall be regarded as the amount of proceeds.

§24(1) An entitled person as defined in §21 who agrees to register as an agricultural entrepreneur with the tax authority within 30 days from the date of the auction may file a claim for the difference between the extent of damage defined pursuant to §3 and the extent of indemnification defined pursuant to §4. This amount shall be paid as agricultural entrepreneurial support for the purpose of purchasing arable land at auction. The combined amount of indemnification and support shall not exceed 1 million forints.

§24(2) If a recipient of a support payment defined in Paragraph (1) above fails to register as an agricultural entrepreneur within the time limit specified, or if the tax authority determines within five years from the date when the arable land was purchased that the recipient does not conduct actual agricultural entrepreneurial activities, the support payment shall be reclassified into a loan and shall become due immediately.

§24(3) A five year lien in favor of the State and a prohibition to sell shall be recorded on land acquired by an indemnified person with the use of support [funds] mentioned in Paragraph (1) above. The lien in favor of the State and the prohibition to sell shall be cancelled if the indemnified person repays the amount of support within five years to the tax authority.

§24(4) At the request of an entitled person, the Office having jurisdiction shall issue a voucher for the amount of agricultural entrepreneurial support. Such vouchers may be used as payment at auctions in a manner similar to indemnification vouchers. A cooperative may request the county (Capital) Office having jurisdiction in the place where the cooperative is headquartered to issue indemnification vouchers [in exchange for agricultural entrepreneurial support] vouchers acquired by the cooperative from entitled persons in the course of auctioning land owned by the cooperative. Support vouchers may be exchanged only to the extent of the actual amount expended for the purchase of land....

§25(2) Expenses incurred in conjunction with the assignment of arable land, the development of the land as an independent piece of real property and the cost of recording such real property shall be paid by the buyer. The acquisition of property shall be exempt from the payment of official fees.

§26 Indemnification vouchers acquired by a cooperative in exchange for arable land designated pursuant to §§15-18 and sold at auction may be used by the cooperative in a manner consistent with the provisions of §7(1). This provision shall not apply to indemnification vouchers received by a cooperative for the sale of State-owned land used by the cooperative.

§27(1) State farms shall designate and auction arable land owned by the State and managed by the State farm pursuant to the provisions of §§15-26
§27(2) Any entitled person may use the indemnification vouchers to which he is entitled when State-owned arable land in addition to arable land designated by State farms pursuant to the provisions of §15(1) is auctioned....

§28 Indemnification vouchers obtained by cooperatives and State farms in the course of auctions in exchange for the sale of State-owned arable land shall be forwarded to the county (Capital) Office having jurisdiction within 30 days.

Closing Provisions

§29 The cabinet shall provide for the implementation of this Law, including the establishment of the Office and of rules for the functioning of the Office.
§30 This Law shall take effect 30 days after its promulgation, but the provisions of §§7(2) and §29 shall be applied beginning on the day of promulgation....

Appendix 3

...(b) Relative to firms, depending on the number of permanent employees

Number of employees	(Thousands of forints) value to serve as a basis for indemnification
0-2	150
3-5	500
6-10	700
11-20	1,000
21-50	1,700
51-100	2,500
100 and more	5,000

Official Explanatory Notes

On several occasions during the past five decades, in the course of changing periods of history, various State actions infringed upon the private property of citizens.

In conjunction with the system change, former owners expressed a strong need to remedy former injuries and private property damages they unfairly suffered. It is the moral duty of a State which recognizes and protects private property to take action and provide financial indemnification to those who suffered injuries in their property.

In the interest of developing appropriately settled ownership relations in a modern market economy, and to discontinue uncertainty relative to the ownership situation, the State intends to remedy the earlier private property injuries suffered not by returning (reprivatizing) the objects that constitute property, but by providing partial property indemnification to former owners.

This solution is justified by the nation's present ability to assume a burden, as well as by the circumstance that in the past not only property owners, but also individuals who did not own property suffered injuries. The financial implications of these injuries continue to affect their present living conditions. These cannot be remedied even on a partial basis. For this reason, indemnification is limited both in time and extent.

The Law declares a right to be indemnified for injuries suffered on the basis of legal provisions promulgated after 1 May 1939. Rules for indemnification for injuries suffered after 8 June 1949 are established in the framework of this Law, while injuries suffered prior to that date will be remedied on the basis of a law to be created by a certain date, using principles identical to those contained in this Law.

In order to facilitate calculations and to avoid disputes arising from such calculations, the Law defines the original (at the time of expropriation) amount of damages suffered in the form of flat rates. Only a small group of people can receive full indemnification. This is so in part because of the flat rate calculation of damages, but in addition to that, it was also appropriate to impose a limitation as a result of which the rate of indemnification declines as the value of expropriated property for which indemnification is claimed increases. Maximum limits for indemnification on a per person and per piece of property basis also had to be established.

Indemnification will be made in the form of interest-bearing negotiable securities and not in the form of cash because even the limited amount to be paid out is huge, and because the worth of indemnification must be protected against inflation.

Special rules for arable land were both justified and necessary. There is a limited supply of arable land, and arable land has an income potential that differs from average property and constitutes property of a peculiar legal character. The calculation of damages suffered in, and indemnification to be paid for, arable land property demanded a solution different from what could be applied to property in general. By establishing a requirement that arable land subject to indemnification be sold at auction to entitled persons, the Law provides a solution which permits the law of supply and demand to prevail when indemnification vouchers are exchanged. This solution also encourages the evolution of the market value of arable land.

Section by Section Analysis

§1

Section 1 of the Law declares that the State commits itself to indemnify natural persons who suffered injuries in their private property.

The Law intends to discharge obligations incurred as a result of injuries inflicted in different periods of history, based on various ideological and political principles and in various ways, in due regard to the situation that has evolved after the passage of a long period of time—including some irreversible changes, "renewed, by applying uniform principles under new legal authority, to a new extent and under new conditions (*novatio*)."

A rational limit had to be established regarding the retroactive effect of the obligation. Although injustices also occurred in prior history, the remedy of these today would be both impossible and unnecessary.

It is the intent of the Law to remedy injuries suffered as a result of legal provisions created after 1 May 1939.

A number of factors justify the establishment of that date as the threshold. On the one hand, this threshold ensures that persons who still live among us and who once suffered injuries, and who, together with their direct descendants, still suffer the consequences of those injuries receive indemnification to which they are entitled. At the same time, there is no realistic possibility to remedy possible injustices suffered by members of two prior generations. In contrast, it is still possible to review [and to formulate] retroactive [judgment] concerning the era that began on 1 May 1939. The so-called second Jewish Law promulgated on 5 May 1939 was the first legal provision to arbitrarily violate on an ideological basis the inviolability of private property and the principle of equality among citizens.

In addition to establishing a State obligation to indemnify [damages suffered] beginning on that day, the Law provides for the phased implementation of indemnification, in due regard to the country's economic situation and limited performance capacity. Consistent with this principle, injuries suffered on the basis of legal provisions created after 8 June 1949 will be remedied in the first phase. The National Assembly elected on the basis of antidemocratic processes in 1949 convened on that day. Legal provisions created in that period no longer contained the usual nationalization measures, but instead aimed for the systematic liquidation of private property and constituted politically motivated acquisitions of property with the character of reprisals on part of the State.

Injuries suffered on the basis of legal provisions created during the period prior to 8 June 1949 will be remedied by a law to be created by 30 November 1991, based on principles identical to those contained in this Law. Appendix 1 of the Law enumerates the legal provisions created in that era. These will serve as the basis for indemnification.

As its title indicates, the Law applies to the partial indemnification of damages caused to the property of natural persons and does not settle damages caused to the property of legal entities. This is so because on the one hand, a majority of these legal entities can no longer be found, while on the other hand separate laws settle property claims established by a certain group of legal entities, such as autonomous local governmental bodies, churches and social security.

§2

Only natural persons may establish claims for indemnification provided under the Law. When this Law takes force, an entitlement to receive indemnification vouchers may be established by Hungarian citizens, just as by persons who by now have become foreign citizens, but who were Hungarian citizens at the time the injuries were suffered, and further: by persons who prior to suffering of injuries were stripped of their citizenship, and by persons who do not hold Hungarian citizenship but who resided in Hungary as of 31 December 1990 in a manner akin to carrying on their livelihood. The latter provision recognizes Bulgarians, Poles, etc. who retained their foreign citizenship, but who have lived in Hungary for decades and suffered injuries identical to those suffered by Hungarians.

The Law provides for the enforcement of an indemnification claim not only by persons directly affected as a result of the application of the enumerated legal provisions, but also to the descendants of owners, or lacking descendants, to the former owners' surviving spouses. In regard to the indemnification of a former owner's descendant or surviving spouse, however, the inheritance rules of the Civil Code of Laws could not be applied for obvious reasons, because property taken away from a former owner prior to his death could not be made part of his bequest. Further, applying legal provisions pertaining to inheritance—rules pertaining to ancestral property, widows' rights, inheritance based on wills, etc. in particular—would expand the constituency entitled to indemnification—a matter voluntarily undertaken by the State—to an extent that it would exceed the present load bearing capacity of the country. This would also endanger the rapid achievement of the goal established as part of the Law; the settlement of ownership conditions.

Considering the above, the Law establishes *sui generis* rules, which extend to descendants based on considerations of fairness, but only in equal proportions among the descendants, to the extent to which their descendant would have been entitled, and provided that a descendant cannot claim the share of a deceased descendant of the same generation. Thus, for example, if one of the descendants of a former owner deceased without leaving further descendants, the still living descendant(s)' entitlement to indemnification does not extend to the share of the deceased descendant.

§3

In order to determine the amount of indemnification due on the basis of the Law, it is necessary to determine as a first step the extent of damage suffered.

The Law defines the extent of damage in flat rates with respect to the three types of property in which the application of the above mentioned legal provisions characteristically caused injury. Thus the Law provides flat rates for damages suffered in real property, enterprises and arable land. Practical considerations guided the establishment of flat rates for determining the extent of damage caused. It was apparent that by now the exact extent of damage incurred 30-40 years ago could not be determined, or if it could, such calculations would be highly debatable. The inclusion of the value of movable property related to a given real property, enterprise or arable land as part of the flat rate which expresses the extent of damage also reflects an endeavor to simplify matters, and to avoid unwarranted, time consuming law suits and disputes. This was also justified by the fact that even if the value of real property could be established with a certain degree of accuracy based on contemporary sales agreements and assessment records, providing the value of movable property found on real property would not be possible under any circumstance.

§4

The nation's capacity to carry a burden does not permit the full reimbursement of damages. Therefore the Law prescribes a fair method of regressively indexed tiers and defines the maximum amount of indemnification that may be paid per piece of property and per person entitled to indemnification.

§5

The Office having jurisdiction issues indemnification vouchers in the amount to be indemnified pursuant to §4 to the natural person who proves his entitlement....

The Law intends to preserve the value of indemnification vouchers by rendering these as interest bearing instruments. In a manner different from bonds and other securities, the interest—just as the indemnification voucher itself—does not increase the volume of money in circulation. For this reason interest accrued at a rate of 75 percent of the prevailing basic central bank interest rate is added to the face value of the indemnification voucher in the form of capital. A number of reasons justify the application of this interest rate. On the one hand, the relatively low interest rate stimulates the holders to quickly make use of indemnification vouchers, thus reducing possible threats presented by the presence of indemnification vouchers to the evolving securities market. On the other hand, it was appropriate to set the interest rate near the rate by which the value of productive capital goods which may be acquired with indemnification vouchers appreciates. The rate by which the value of capital goods increases falls well behind the inflationary price increases of consumer goods or the amount of interest that may be paid on deposits....

In order not to disadvantage persons entitled to indemnification as a result of possible delays in judging claims for indemnification vouchers, the Law determines the date when interest begins to accrue independent from the actual date of issue of indemnification vouchers.

Redemption of indemnification vouchers is stimulated by authorizing the payment of interest for a certain period of time only: for three years starting on the date when an indemnification voucher is issued....

§7

Not unlike a note, the indemnification voucher constitutes a demand. But the indemnification voucher authorizes its holder to purchase State property for the face value of the voucher plus accrued interest, and not for collecting cash. Purchase of State property may take place whenever a State enterprise is transformed into a business organization, or when pieces of State property are sold directly. Under the first alternative, an indemnification voucher may be exchanged for the stock (business share) of reappraised enterprise assets.... The second alternative permits the purchase of pieces of property (businesses) to be privatized and sold in public auctions....

The Law also enables the acquisition of ownership rights to arable land in exchange for indemnification vouchers....

Persons entitled to indemnification may use their indemnification vouchers primarily for the acquisition of [types of] property mentioned above. It was necessary however, to provide additional use opportunities for entitled persons.

Thus, indemnification vouchers may be used to pay for State-owned housing which is transferred free of charge to the ownership of autonomous local governmental bodies subsequent to the effective date of this provision of Law....

The possible use of indemnification vouchers is expanded by two additional considerations. In certain borrowing transactions indemnification vouchers must be considered as the borrower's own financial resource, and based on the provisions of separate law, indemnification vouchers may be exchanged for a sum annuitized for life.

By providing multipurpose use opportunities, the Law also serves the purpose of enabling certain larger organizations (local governments, financial institutions, social security, producer cooperatives) to utilize the accumulated indemnification vouchers in a more concentrated and more efficient way in the course of State property privatization. This intent is realized by the provisions of §8 of the Law.

§8

Ensuring that indemnification vouchers in circulation are exchanged at a pace consistent with the pace of State property privatization is of fundamental importance. This is so because property subject to privatization serves as collateral for indemnification vouchers....

§9

Reprivatization is not the purpose of this Law. Partial indemnification is. While maintaining and not exceeding this principle, the Law provides pre-purchase rights to a certain group of former owners. The grant of pre-purchase rights was regarded as appropriate because full indemnification could not be provided for reasons stated in the general intent, and because claims could be made for the reacquisition of property that may still be found in its original [condition]. This opportunity does not represent reprivatization either, it merely ensures a possibility for an entitled person appearing with his indemnification voucher to enjoy a civil law right vis-a-vis other entitled persons to pre-purchase his property....

§10

...Consistent with the Constitution, the Law provides for the judicial review of final decisions [rendered by the national office]. Courts are authorized to review and change such decisions in full.

§11

Indemnification claims must be filed within 90 days, according to the Law. This time period is needed to permit [entitled persons] to consider their claims.... It would be unnecessary to provide for a longer period of time for consideration, because that would unnecessarily prolong the assessment of actual damage claims, and as a result of that, the entire proceeding. This then would result in continued legal uncertainty....

The Law permits that all claims filed by any entitled person be dealt with in a single proceeding. Therefore, if more than one piece of real property is involved among the assets to be indemnified, and as a result of which more than one Office could have jurisdiction, the Law grants the jurisdictional choice to the entitled person....

§§20-22

It is the intent of the Law to resolve the sale of land by establishing equal conditions for all entitled persons to acquire land, while on the other hand, lacking an actual land market, it is the intent of the Law to create a situation which encourages the evolution of the market value of arable land.

This dual purpose is served by including auctioning in the framework of the indemnification process, prior to the exercise of the right to purchase.

The rule which requires that the sale of arable land designated for indemnification purposes takes place with the participation of entitled persons creates a competitive situation among participants. This serves the purposes of both indemnification and privatization....

§23

In creating special rules relative to arable land, an effort was made to find a solution which is acceptable to both the entitled person and to residents of villages, and which also serves the purpose of utilizing arable land, in addition to the goal of settling ownership conditions. For this reason, the Law grants the right to purchase only to those entitled persons who ensure the utilization of the acquired land in a manner consistent with the purpose of the such land.

The decision to be made by entitled persons regarding the exercise of the right to purchase is strongly influenced by strict rules provided as part of the Law which deal with the withdrawal of acquired land from agricultural production or the sale of acquired land....

§25

The nation's limited capacity to bear a burden warrants the requirement that entitled persons also accept a burden along and in conjunction with indemnification. For this reason, costs incurred in the course of assigning arable land, the development of the land as an independent place of real property and the recording of such real property are covered by the entitled person....

Law No. 24 (April 7, 1992)

To settle ownership conditions, to provide partial compensation for unjust damages inflicted by the State to the property of citizens as a result of enforcing legal provisions created between 1 May 1939 and 8 June 1949.

Guided by the principle of constitutional statehood, and in due regard to society's sense of justice and its ability to bear a burden, the National Assembly adopts the following Law pursuant to the provisions of Section 1 Paragraph (3) of Law No. 25 of 1991 in order to establish secure ownership conditions and to mitigate damages unjustly caused by the State to the property of citizens as a result of enforcing legal provisions created between 1 May 1939 and 8 June 1949:

Section 1

(1) Under this Law, natural persons whose private property had been violated by the State as a result of enforcing legal provisions created between 1 May 1939 and 8 June 1949 shall be entitled to partial compensation (hereinafter: compensation).

(2) The provisions of Law No. 25 of 1991 (hereinafter: Compensation Law) shall be applied in conjunction with compensating for damages referred to in Paragraph (1) above, together with the changes and supplemental provisions contained in this Law.

Section 2

(1) The force of this Law shall apply to damages suffered in ownership within the borders of Hungary, as those were established by the Paris Peace Treaty.

(2) No compensation shall be due to a person who was convicted on the basis of a final judgment [of a court] for war crimes or crimes against humanity, and whose property ownership was impaired in conjunction with such conviction.

(3) No compensation shall be due to a person whose impairment of property ownership has been remedied under legal provisions enumerated in Appendix 1 to this Law, or on any other ground....

Section 4

If a person entitled to compensation is eligible to apply for compensation on the basis of both the Compensation Law and this Law, the extent of compensation shall be determined as if all claims had been filed under the same Law.

Section 5

Irrespective of the date when compensation vouchers are issued, interest on compensation vouchers issued on the basis of this Law shall accrue beginning on the effective date of the Compensation Law.

Section 6

Persons entitled to compensation may file applications for compensation within 120 days from the effective date of this Law with the county (Budapest) damage claims settlement office.

Section 7

(1) This Law shall take effect 30 days after its date of proclamation....

ITALY: CONSTITUTION—
TRANSITORY AND FINAL PROVISIONS

(1947)

III

By a decree of the President of the Republic, for the first term the Senate will include among its members deputies of the Constituent Assembly who have the necessary qualifications by law for election to the Senate and who:

- have been President of the Council of Ministers, or Speaker or President of legislative bodies;
- have been members of the dissolved Senate;
- have been three times elected, including election to the Constituent Assembly;
- were dismissed during the session of the Chamber of Deputies of November 9, 1926;
- have suffered imprisonment for a period of not less than five years in consequence of sentences passed by the Special Fascist Court for State Defence.

Members of the dissolved Senate who were also members of the National Consultative Assembly are also nominated Senators, by decree of the President of the Republic.

The right to nomination as Senator may be renounced prior to signature of the decree of nomination. Acceptance of candidacy in political elections implies renunciation of the right to be nominated Senator.[2]...

---

[2] As a result of this Article, 107 Senators were nominated by right to the first Senate of the Republic.

LITHUANIA: LAW AND IMPLEMENTING RESOLUTION ON THE RESTORATION OF PROPERTY

Law on the Procedure and Conditions of the Restoration of the Right of Ownership of Existing Real Property

(June 18, 1991)

Chapter 1
General Procedures
Article 1. The Objective of this Law

This Law shall legislate the procedures and conditions of the restoration of the right of ownership to the citizens of the Republic of Lithuania to the property which was nationalized under the laws of the USSR (Lithuanian SSR), or which was otherwise unlawfully made public, and which, on the day of enactment of this Law, is considered the property of the State, of the public, of cooperative organizations (enterprises), or of collective farms.

The right of real property ownership shall be restored:

1) by giving over either the actual property or the equivalent of such property; or
2) in the event that it is impossible to grant the actual property or the equivalent of such property, or if the former owner does not desire the actual property, by financially compensating the persons specified in Article 2 of this Law, thereby enabling them to purchase an appropriate amount of State (public) property subject to privatization.

Article 2. Citizens Entitled to Restored Ownership Rights

The right of ownership to the existing real property shall be restored:

1) to the former owner of the property, provided that he is a certified citizen of the Republic of Lithuania and is a permanent resident of the Republic of Lithuania;
2) to the children (or adopted children), parents (or foster parents), or spouse of the former owner, in the event that he is no longer living. Upon the death of a child of a former owner, the right of ownership to his portion of existing real property shall be restored to his spouse and children, provided they are certified citizens of the Republic of Lithuania, and are permanent residents of the Republic of Lithuania (Amended 14 January, 1992).

Article 3. Property to which the Right of Ownership shall be Restored

Ownership rights to the following existing real property shall be restored to persons specified in Article 2 of this Law:

1) land;
2) forests;
3) structures used for economic and commercial purposes together with their equipment;
4) residential houses together with their equipment.

Chapter 2
Conditions and Procedures for the
Restoration of the Right of Ownership

Article 4. Conditions and Procedures for the Restoration of the Right of Ownership to Land Used for Agricultural Purposes

The right of ownership to land used for agricultural purposes shall be restored to persons specified in Article 2 of this Law, provided that they continue or resume farming on this land, according to the plans established for that territory.

Such persons must either: have been permanent workers of State or collective farms; work and permanently reside in a rural area; or demonstrate an intention to engage in farming (i.e. by settling in a rural area, by acquiring agricultural machinery or livestock).

In the event that such persons reside or work on an area of the farm other than that being restored, or if the plot of land cannot be given back for reasons specified in Article 12 of this Law, these persons shall be allotted, upon their request, a plot of land according to their place of residence, provided that there exists vacant State-owned land. All plots of land situated in that locality, which are not returned to persons specified in Article 2 of this Law, and which may be sold for private ownership under the Land Reform Law, shall be deemed a vacant lot of the State land fund. (Amended 14 January, 1992.)

Former owners shall be given plots of land equivalent in size to their previous property, either in the same or in different are in accordance with the procedure established by the Government. The restored plot of agricultural land must not exceed 50 hectares. The total area of the property restored to one owner (including forest and water bodies) cannot exceed 80 hectares. (Amended 14 January, 1992.)

The implementation of property ownership rights (the allotment of land) to persons entitled to this Right, may be postponed for a five year period. In such cases, the land shall be allotted from the State land fund without payment, and, if possible, the land shall be returned to the former owner.

The newly returned or allotted land must be used for agricultural production and cannot be sold or otherwise transferred, mortgaged, or leased within the period of five years from the day it was returned or allotted.

Land may be transferred to an agricultural company only in the event that the owner of the land is employed in this company or if he is a pensioner and falls under the category of persons specified in Article 2 of this Law.

If land is not used for agricultural production within one year (in spring or autumn) of its transferal, or if the conditions defined in Article 7 of this Law are violated, the land shall be relocated to the land reform fund. The former owner shall be financially compensated in accordance with the prices that were in effect at the time of the original restoration of ownership, as established by the Government of the Republic of Lithuania.

Article 5. Conditions and Procedures for the Restoration of the Ownership Rights to Land Situated Within the Limits of Towns and Urban Settlements

The ownership rights of land within the boundaries of towns or urban settlements shall be restored to persons specified in Article 2 of this Law as follows:

1) in cases where the property was within the boundaries of a town or urban settlement, a plot of land shall be allotted in the same vicinity for the construction of a private house. The property shall be free of charge, and shall be assigned in the size and manner established by the Government of the Republic of Lithuania;

2) in cases where the former plot of land was ascribed to the territory of a town or urban settlement, a plot of land shall be allotted in the town or urban settlement of the territory to which the land was ascribed, for the construction of a private house. The property shall be free of charge, and shall be assigned in the size and manner established by the Government of the Republic of Lithuania.

In cases as defined in paragraphs 1 and 2 of this Article, if persons specified in Article 2 of this Law possess private houses by the right of ownership, they may be given ownership rights to the land surrounding their present residence rather than being given their previous property, if they so desire:

3) in the case that persons specified in Article 2 of this Law own a house situated on land which they formally had rights to, and if they actually utilize this land (according to the data of inventory cases), the property right to that plot shall be restored, but not exceeding 0.2 hectares in Vilnius, Kaunas Klaipéda, Siauliai, Panevézys, Alytus, Marijampolé, Druskininkai, Palanga, and

Birstonas and not exceeding 0.3 hectares in other towns and urban settlements, not including the land occupied by buildings.

Article 6. The Conditions and Procedures for the Restoration of Ownership Rights to Forest Areas

Property rights of forest areas not exceeding 10 hectares shall be restored to persons specified in Article 2 of this Law according to land-planning projects devised in the established manner to carry out land reform.

The forest area which is returned to the former owner must be cared for, utilized, and reforested according to the forest planning project. Within five years from the day it was returned or allotted as a compensation, the area cannot be sold, mortgaged, or otherwise transferred without the approval of the body authorized by the Government of the Republic of Lithuania.

Violators of the conditions defined in paragraph 2 of this Article shall be held responsible in accordance with the laws of the Republic of Lithuania.

Article 7. Procedure for the Restoration of Ownership Rights to Structures Used for Economic and Commercial Purposes

The ownership rights to structures used for economic and commercial purposes together with their equipment shall be restored to persons specified in Article 2 of this Law by returning the aforesaid buildings as well as the plots of land, provided that it was private property, or by allotting securities (shares), in accordance with the procedure established by the Government of the Republic of Lithuania.

Article 8. Conditions and Procedures for the Restoration of Ownership Rights to Residential Houses

The ownership rights to residential houses (or a portion thereof) shall be restored to persons specified in Article 2 of this Law by returning the actual houses (or a portion thereof), or by compensating their value.

The procedure and time limits for the restoration of residential houses (or portions thereof) which do not fall under the category of houses defined in Article 14 of this Law shall be established by the Government of the Republic of Lithuania, pursuant to the provision that the residential houses shall be returned in case that:

1) they are reconstructed into premises unfit for human occupancy of if they are vacant;
2) tenants, occupying houses subject to being returned, and which are occupied by more than one family, are familiar with all of the laws guaranteeing their rights, and with their option to move under conditions proposed by the local government and set forth in

Article 21 of this Law, or under the conditions guaranteed by the former owner of the house;

3) the residential house consists of a single dwelling unit;
4) the former owners reside in the house which is subject to being returned.

Persons specified in Article 2 of this Law may, rather than reclaiming their former property, acquire ownership rights of their present dwelling (i.e. if they are currently renting from the State or public housing fund), if they so desire.

If a person so requests, their property right to a residential house may be substituted with the transferal of a dwelling unit other than their current residence to their ownership in the manner prescribed by the Government of the Republic of Lithuania if:

1) the floor area of the current State or public housing unit does not exceed 15 square metres per occupant;
2) they reside as subtenants in houses belonging to State or public housing funds or as tenants in houses belonging to house building cooperatives or to private housing funds, and if they possess no other place of residence;
3) they live in hostels or other office premises fit for residential use;
4) they live in houses which do not comply with sanitary and technical requirements;
5) they do not possess any place of residence in the Republic of Lithuania because of previous deportation or imprisonment as the result of resistance to occupational regimes.

Persons defined in Article 2 of this Law, along with their family members, must vacate dwelling units rented by them from the State or public housing funds upon the return of their former residential houses or upon the allotment of an equivalent dwelling.

In the event that a person, as defined in Article 2 of this Law, is given only a portion of the formerly owned residential house, or if the dwelling unit transferred to their ownership in another house does not equal the value of the formerly owned residential house, their right of ownership shall be supplanted by an allocation from the State, if the person so desires and consents. The amount of State allocation shall be determined by the commissions of initial privatization in accordance with the procedure established by the Government of the Republic of Lithuania.

In such cases, the property right to the formerly owned plot of land shall be restored in the manner provided for in Article 5 of this Law.

The provisions of this Article shall not apply to persons who, at their own will moved from residential houses formerly owned by them to dwelling units owned by State or public housing fund.

Article 9. Documents Confirming the Right of Ownership

Excerpts from mortgage books, conveyance deeds, court decisions, deeds of property nationalization, as well as certificates issued by State archives and other documents established by the Government of the Republic of Lithuania (Amended 14 January, 1992) may serve as documents confirming the right of ownership.

Article 10. Procedure for Filing Petitions to Reclaim Property

Persons defined in Article 2 of this Law may file petitions to reclaim the real existing property, or for the compensation thereof, with the boards of the town or district in which the existing real property is located, prior to March 31, 1992. (Amended 11 February 1992). Citizens who fail to file a petition within this period shall lose their right to reclaim the property under this Law, with the exception of persons having no place of residence because of deportation or imprisonment as a result of resistance to occupying regimes.

The statute of limitation—three years from the enforcement of this Law—shall apply to claims for compensation for unreclaimed property.

Citizenship documents, as well as documents confirming the ownership of property, must be presented together with the petition. The Government of the Republic of Lithuania may extend the period for filing documents confirming the ownership of property.

Article 11. Contents of Petitions

Petitions to reclaim existing property, or for the compensation thereof, shall contain the following information: the citizen's full name and place of residence, the type of the existing real property, its size, its location, the grounds for the entitlement to the ownership rights of the property, the present owner of the property, as well as the date and the way that the ownership right was lost.

The petitioner shall state in his petition other persons known to him who are entitled to reclaim this property under this Law, and whether the petitioner wishes to recover the actual property or to be compensated therefor.

Chapter 3
Conditions by which the Existing Real Property shall be Bought out by the State
Article 12. The Buying out of Land

Land required for State needs as well as other land shall be bought out from persons defined in Article 2 of this Law in the manner specified in Article 16 of this Law if:

1) it is occupied by roads, airports, military units, or is required for the protection of State borders.

    The land occupied by underground line communications or pipelines may be given over for limited use, if persons specified in Article 2 of this Law give their consent;

2) it is occupied by bodies of water which were made and financed by the State budget, by gardens of gardeners' associations, or by industrial gardens of State enterprises that are being established;

3) it is in a rural area, has been allotted to a farmer under the enforced laws, and is occupied by a personal plot, house or other structures to which the farmer has the right of ownership;

4) on the day of enforcement of this Law, it was within the limits of a town, urban settlement, or township which, according to development projects, is planned to be expanded, or if it is determined by the government that this land is essential to the recreational needs of the people residing in the given area;

5) it is allotted in the established manner to scientific or educational institutions for carrying out experiments or for other scientific purposes;

6) it is in the territory of investigated mineral deposits, confirmed in the established manner.

    Such Plots may be given back for limited use, provided the persons specified in Article 2 of this Law give their consent thereto;

7) it is located in a nature reserve.

    The territory of existing nature reserves and national parks as well as the territory which is being considered as such according to the all-around nature protection scheme, and the preserved land of natural, cultural and historical monuments may be given back for limited use, provided that the persons specified in Article 2 of this Law, the Inspectorate of Cultural Heritage of the Republic of Lithuania, and the Department of the Environmental Protection of the Republic of Lithuania give their consent thereto;

8) State-owned facilities that are built or are planned to be built thereon, as well as sites corresponding to the norms and standards of environmental quality wherein waste is planned to be stored;

9) the plot contains structures of agricultural enterprises and optimum land area necessary for their operation.

In the case that only a portion of the land subject to restoration is occupied by buildings or other structures, this portion of land maybe given back as well, provided that the persons specified in Article 2 of this Law and the users of this land agree on the transference of the right of ownership of buildings and other structures.

Article 13. The Buying out of Forests

Forests required by the State shall be bought out (or compensated for) from persons specified in Article 2 of this Law in the manner established in Article 16 of this Law, provided that these forests are assigned to Group 1 forests under the laws of the Republic of Lithuania.

Article 14. The Buying out of Residential Houses

Residential houses shall be bought out (or compensated for) by the State from persons specified in Article 2 of this Law in the procedure established in Article 16 of this Law, provided they are required by the State or if:

1) they have been expanded, rebuilt, or reconstructed into uninhabitable premises and have thereby been given to scientific, medical cultural, educational institutions or communications companies;
2) it is a wooden residential house which has been substantially improved or if the house has been augmented, rebuilt, or reconstructed, thereby increasing the gross floor area by more than 1/3, in a manner which makes it impossible to separate the additional gross floor area from the original one.

Article 15. The Buying out of Economic and Commercial Structures

Structures of economic and commercial purposes which have been substantially reconstructed shall be bought out by the State from persons specified in Article 2 of this Law in the manner established in Article 16 of this Law.

Chapter 4
The Buying out of Existing Real Property
Article 16. The Methods of Buying out Existing Real Property

The State shall buy out the existing real property by:

1) giving the owner, free of charge, rights to different property of the same type or value;
2) reimbursing the owner or by allotting shares;
3) making void financial liabilities of a citizen to the State which were incurred after the appropriation of real property.

The method of buying out shall be chosen by the owner with the exception of cases specified in Articles 7, 8, 14 and 15 of this Law.

Article 17. The Amount of Financial Reimbursement

In buying out existing real property, the amount of financial reimbursement shall be based on the actual value of the property at the time of purchase, less the amount needed for improvement. The procedure for the calculation of payments, as well as for their allocation, shall be established by the Government of the Republic of Lithuania.

Chapter 5
Consideration of Petitions for the Restoration of Ownership Rights

Article 18. Institutions which Consider Petitions for Citizens for the Restorations of Ownership Rights

Petitions to reclaim land used for agricultural purposes or to reclaim forest area shall be considered by the ministry authorized by the Government of the Republic of Lithuania, taking into consideration the recommendations of the town (district) board of the territory in question.

Petitions to reclaim residential houses, economic and commercial structures, as well as equipment therein, shall be reviewed by the town (district) board which has control over the structure in question, in accordance with the procedure established by the Government of the Republic of Lithuania.

Petitions to reclaim economic structure, commercial structures, or houses occupied by scientific, medical, cultural, or educational institutions, or by communication companies, shall be considered by the ministry or agency which has jurisdiction over the area in which the object in question is located.

Institutions considering petitions for the restoration of ownership rights, in the cases provided for in this Law, shall determine the amount of compensation on the basis of rates established by the Government of the Republic of Lithuania.

Article 19. Adoption Of Decisions on the Restoration of Ownership Rights

Institutions specified in Article 18 of this Law must consider petitions of citizens, and adopt decisions concerning the restoration of ownership rights, within three months of the day that the documents confirming the right of ownership are submitted.

In the event of a dispute between citizens regarding the method of restoration of ownership rights, the decision shall not be adopted. Upon the receipt of citizen applications, such disputes shall be considered in court.

Article 20. The Procedure to Appeal Decisions

Decisions adopted by the institutions set forth in Article 18 of this Law concerning the restoration of ownership rights, or compensation for these rights, may be appealed in court within 20 days.

In such cases the parties shall be exempt from State duties.

Article 21. Guaranties for Tenants who Reside in Houses Subject to Restoration

Tenants residing in houses which were returned to the former owner shall pay rent according to an agreement between the parties but which does not exceed the maximum amount established by the Government of the Republic of Lithuania.

In addition to rent, tenants shall pay for public utilities according to rates approved in the established manner.

Deadlines for the payment of rent and utilities shall be determined by an agreement between the parties in question.

In the cases provided for in subparagraph 3 of paragraph 2 of Article 8 of this Law, the owner shall be prohibited from evicting the tenants of the house for ten years from the day of restoration of ownership.

Persons who reside in a residential house which has been returned to the owner shall be provided with a place of residence by the local government of the respective town or district, pursuant to the programme prepared and carried out by the Government of the Republic of Lithuania.

Tenants residing in houses which have been returned to their former owners shall be entitled to obtain, free of charge, a plot of land for the construction of a house, to join a housing construction cooperative, and to get credit on easy terms for these purposes.

In the event that a house is being sold by the original owner, the tenants of this house shall have priority in the purchase of it. The restrictions prescribed by paragraph 4 of this Article shall apply to the purchaser of the house.

Any actions intended to compel tenants to move from a newly returned house, without safeguarding guarantees defined in this Article, shall be prohibited, and the violator(s) shall be held responsible by laws.

Chapter 6
Final Provisions

Article 22. Guarantees to Persons whose Property is Bought Out by the State

Payments of allocations or of securities for the property bought out by the State must be made no later than 3 months after the decision to buy out the property has been adopted.

On the decision of the Government of the Republic of Lithuania this time limit may be extended.

Article 23. The Prohibition on Use of Budgetary Resources

It shall be prohibited to use budgetary resources for payments of property bought out by the State.

⇥✦⇤

Implementing Resolution

(July 16, 1991)

The Supreme Council of the Republic of Lithuania resolves:

1. To put this Law into effect on August 1, 1991.

2. That the requisite of permanent residence in the Republic of Lithuania, as set forth in Article 2 of this Law, shall not apply to deportees (and their children), or to persons who were deported or imprisoned as the result of resistance to occupational regimes.

3. That tenants occupying houses subject to restitution, as defined in subparagraph 2 of paragraph 2 of Article 8, shall be informed of their option to move, at their own will, by settling on a dwelling unit allotted to them which complies with the requirements set forth in Article 94 of the Housing Code of the Republic of Lithuania.

4. That tenants who, at their own will have moved to dwelling units proposed to them by their local government because their previous place of residence was restored to the original owner, shall have the right to buy this new unit within six months, on the basis of the house building prices of 1989, by applying the indexation coefficient....

Residential houses which are not returned to their former owners under the Law of the Republic of Lithuania on the Procedure and Conditions of the Restoration of the Right of Ownership of Existing Real Property, shall be privatized in accordance with the procedures of the Republic of Lithuania.

5. That in the event that persons specified in Article 2 of this Law are proving their ownership rights in court, the period for filing the property ownership documents shall be one month from the day of the court decision.

6. That the provisions defined in Article 8 of this Law shall apply to persons specified in Article 2 of this Law if they were compensated according to the laws which have hitherto been valid, in the absence of another option. In such cases the amount of compensation must be returned.

7. That land occupied by personal plots which were allotted pursuant to the July 26th, 1990 Resolution of the Supreme Council of the Republic of Lithuania "On the Expansion of Personal Plots of Farmers" shall be also designated as land occupied by personal plots, as specified in paragraph 3 of Article 12 of this Law.

8. That a person shall own any lake (of the size determined by the Government of the Republic of Lithuania), water reservoir, canal, pond, and other surface water body, if it is surrounded on all sides by his property.

In such cases, the area of the body of water shall be included in the total area of the reclaimed land or of the newly allotted land.

The regulations concerning the recreational use of such bodies of water shall be established by the Government of the Republic of Lithuania.

Land owners must utilize their land, as well as the bodies of water situated therein, in compliance with the requirements of nature protection.

9. That territorial land-planning projects shall be developed in compliance with land reform requirements.

10. That in the event that persons specified in Article 2 of this Law do not satisfy the conditions set forth in Article 4 of this Law, they must be compensated for their portion of the land by the person (or persons) to whom this land was allotted.

11. That property, with the exception of land and residential houses, which was not returned (either because it was not claimed, or because the claims were inadequate), shall be privatized in accordance with the procedure established in the Law of the Republic of Lithuania on the Initial Privatization of Property.

12. To commission the Government of the Republic of Lithuania:

1) by 1 August, 1991 to establish the procedure and time limits for the payment of State allocations for the real property subject to be bought out;

2) by 1 August, 1991 to establish the procedure and stages of the giving over of residential houses (or portions thereof), as well as the procedure for the allotment of plots of land surrounding these houses if previously they were not the property of the house owner;

3) by 1 August, 1991 to establish the procedure for the allotment of plots of land in towns (townships) for the construction of a private house;

4) by 1 August, 1991 to allocate credits on easy terms for tenants, occupying houses which have been returned to former owners, if they desire to build a private house;

5) by 1 August, 1991 to establish the procedure for the giving over structures used for economic and commercial purposes together with their equipment or for the allotment of securities (shares) for said property;

6) to establish the procedure in accordance with which the provision of paragraph 3 of part 1 of Article 16, pursuant to which the existing real property, if a person gives his consent thereto, may be bought out by the State by making void financial liabilities of a person to the State, which were incurred after the appropriation of real property, shall be implemented.

13. To obligate the Government of the Republic of Lithuania to submit proposals to the Supreme Council of the Republic of Lithuania concerning the compensation of persons whose real property was nationalized and which does not exist any longer.

14. To commission the Government of the Republic of Lithuania to establish the procedure in accordance with which documents certifying the right of ownership, upon the request of a citizen and after he has paid a duty in the established manner, shall be ordered by the board of a local government.

In such cases the archives which are under the jurisdiction of the Board of Directors of the Archives of the Republic of Lithuania shall furnish the documents in due time.

15. To establish that the guarantees provided for in parts 5 and 6 of Article 21 of this Law shall also apply to cases where former owners shall be restored their ownership right of residential houses by court's decision.

16. To commission the Ministry of Justice of the Republic of Lithuania to supervise the implementation of this Law.

ROMANIA: INTERNATIONAL LABOUR ORGANISATION REPORT ON COMPENSATION*

(March 28, 1991)

Chapter 1
Filing of the Complaint and Establishment of the Commission

Filing of the Complaint

1. On 27 June the Director-General of the ILO received communication dated 26 June 1989 in which ... delegates respectively of Côte d'Ivoire, United States, Spain, Italy, Zambia, Venezuela, Switzerland, Japan, Canada, United Kingdom, France, Federal Republic of Germany and Denmark, to the 76th Session of the International Labour Conference, stated that they were filing a complaint against the Government of Romania under article 26 of the Constitution of the International Labour Organisation [for non-observence of Convention No. 111].

The complaint is based upon the following facts:

1. A significant minority of Romanian citizens of Hungarian origin (more than 2 million persons, or 9.5 per cent of the population) are subjected to particular discrimination in the political, cultural, social and employment spheres.

2. Members of ethnic minorities, in particular the Hungarian minority, are currently being forcibly dispersed from their places of birth and assigned by the authorities to employment not of their own choosing. Population transfers are carried out as a rule without previous notice and without informing those concerned where they are being sent. Persons of Hungarian origin are barred from a number of cities.

3. The programme of rural systematization gives rise to considerable damage in cultural as well as social terms; villages are destroyed only to be replaced by agro-industrial centres; Transylvania has been particularly affected by this process. Citizens are forced to destroy their own houses and are resettled elsewhere with their families in crowded, low-quality buildings.

4. Restrictions are deliberately imposed in the field of Hungarian language education; access to higher education and training is restricted. The prohibition of the Hungarian language in public life goes hand in hand with the gradual elimination of Hungarian cultural institutions.

---

* Excerpted from International Labour Office, "Report of the Commission of Inquiry Appointed under Article 26 of the Constitution of the International Labour Organisation to Examine the Observance by Romania of the Discrimination (Employment and Occupation) Convention, 1958 (No. 111)," *Official Bulliten*, Vol. LXXIV, 1991, Series B, Suppl. 3. Copyright © 1991, International Labour Organisation, Geneva.

5. Youth of the Hungarian ethnic minority as well as those of other minorities (Germans, South Slavs, Slovaks, Ukrainians, Jews and Gypsies) are discriminated against in education, training and employment. Young people who request to leave the country are conscripted into the army and sent to unhealthy forced labour camps.

6. The Hungarian minority, among which there are more than 300,000 unemployed, is affected by suppressions of jobs or whole enterprises, and restrictions on employment through the use of a *numerus clausus*. Moreover, and as a result of economic difficulties, wages are paid only in part, and Hungarian nationals do not benefit from special premiums paid by way of compensation in enterprises.

In view of the foregoing, the ... Workers' delegates ... request the appointment of a Commission of Inquiry in order to ensure the effective observance by the Government of Romania of Convention No. 111, which it has ratified, They reserve the right to supply at a later stage further elements in support of this request....

Measures Taken by the Governing Body
Following the Filing of the Complaint

...6. The observations of the Government of Romania were transmitted in a letter from the Chargé d'affaires *ad interim* of the Permanent Mission of the Socialist Republic of Romania in Geneva dated 7 October 1989 and received on 9 October 1989. The text of these observations is contained in Annex I of this report.

7. At its 244th Session (November 1989), the Governing Body ... decided that the question should be referred back without any further discussion to a Commission of Inquiry appointed in accordance with article 26 of the Constitution. The Governing Body ratified the following recommendations made by its Officers:

(a) the members of the Commission should be nominated in accordance with the same criteria, and would serve in the same conditions, as the members of commissions previously appointed under article 26 of the Constitution. They would serve as individuals in their personal capacity, would be chosen for their impartiality, integrity and standing, and would undertake by solemn declaration to carry out their tasks and exercise their powers as members of the Commission honourably, faithfully, impartially and conscientiously.

A solemn declaration in these terms would correspond to that made by judges of the International Court of Justice;

(b) the Commission should establish its own procedure in accordance with the provisions of the Constitution.

Composition of the Commission

8. At its 244th Session (November 1989) the Governing Body adopted the proposals made by the Director-General[3] concerning the composition of the Commission:

> Chairman: Mr. Jules Deachênes (Canada), Chief Justice, Superior Court of Quebec. Lecturer in private international law, University of Montreal. Former expert of the Sub-Commission on Prevention of Discrimination and Protection of Minorities of the United Nations Commission on Human Rights.

> Members: Mr. Francesco Capotorti (Italy), professor of international law at the Law Faculty of the University of Rome (La Sapienza). Former expert on the Sub-Commission on Prevention of Discrimination and Protection of Minorities of the United Nations Commission on Human Rights, and former judge and advocate general at the Court of Justice of the European Communities (CJEC).

> Mr. Budislav Vukas (Yugoslavia), professor of public international law and Director of the Institute of Comparative Law at the Law Faculty of the University of Zagreb. Member of the Permanent Court of Arbitration. Member of the ILO Committee of Experts on the Application of Conventions and Recommendations.

[Editor's Note: The report points out that subsequent to the appointment of the ILO Commission of Inquiry, the December 1989 Romanian revolution brought an end to the Ceausescu government against which the charges had been brought.]

Chapter 15
Reparations

471. In view of its undertaking to respect human rights, the new Government has been seeking means of remedying the consequences of human rights violations committed by the previous regime and of redressing the wrongs suffered. Equality of opportunity in employment and occupation had, in a number of cases, been nullified or impaired. The reparation measures are a manifestation of the Government's will to restore this nullified or threatened equality. Not all the measures adopted to repair human rights violations concern the application of the Convention. However, some of them are designed to remedy the consequences of discriminatory practices in areas covered by the Convention.

472. Reparation measures relating to the application of the Convention have taken various forms: amnesties, establishment of ad hoc committees to settle cases of persons claiming to have been wronged, adoption of regulations designed to remove discriminatory measures, re-examination of certain verdicts, compensation granted by the tribunals. Numerous other measures to redress wrongs suffered as a result of the application of

---

[3] GB.244/4/26.

discriminatory measures have been enacted in specific instruments. Thus, section 2 of Legislative Decree No. 35 of 19 January 1990, concerning the modification of certain regulations on wages, provides for a full reimbursement of wage deductions made during 1989, to paid-in installments spaced out over 1990 and 1991. This partial reparation, however, applies only to wage deductions effected in 1989.

Amnesty Measures

473. An amnesty covering political offences committed between 30 December 1947 and 22 December 1989 inclusively was granted by Legislative Decree No. 3 of 4 January 1990, respecting amnesty for certain offences and remission of certain penalties. Under the terms of section 1, political offences, as defined in the Penal Code and special laws, committed since 30 December 1947 are amnestied. Included under the definition of political offences subject to amnesty within the meaning of the Legislative Decree are: actions in connection with the expression of opposition to the dictatorship and the personality cult, the terrorism and abuse of power committed by those who held political power. The definition also covers actions committed in connection with respect for human rights and fundamental freedoms, with the demand for civil and political, economic, social and cultural rights, and the abolition of discriminatory practices.

Activities of the Provisional Council of National Unity Committee

474. In accordance with section 3(p) of Legislative Decree No. 82 of 13 February 1990 respecting the composition of the Provisional Council of National Unity (PCNU) and its Executive Board, and of the Council's specialized committees, a specialized committee was formed "to inquire into abuses and violations of human rights and to rehabilitate the victims of the dictatorship". This Committee elected Mr. Nicu Stancescu as its chairman and worked from March to May 1990.

475. During the three months of its proceedings, the Stancescu Committee received over 18,000 claims for reparation of human rights violations committed by the previous government. It examined and settled between 4,000 and 5,000 cases.[4] The Commission of Inquiry was unable to meet or speak to Mr. Stancescu during its visit to Romania as he was out of the country on a mission.

476. One witness, a member of the Stancescu Committee, said that several hundred files concerned cases of abuse at the workplace. He also stated that it had been impossible for the Committee to conduct its proceedings efficiently, largely owing to lack of personnel and the inordinate number of cases. He also referred to a certain lack of co-operation on the part of those whose duty it was to help solve the cases.[5] In reply to a question by the government representatives, the witness stated that relations between the

---

[4] Interview with the Secretary of State for Justice, L. Stingu, Bucharest, 9 October 1990.

[5] Andreescu, VII/8-9.

Stansecsu Committee and the various ministries concerned, notably the Ministry of Labour, had been satisfactory. Relations with the Public Prosecutor's Office[6] had been more difficult. When the Committee discontinued its proceedings shortly before the elections of 20 May 1990, there were some 14,000 claims for reparation still outstanding. The witness spoke of Mr. Stancescu's complaint that, since that date, the files had been left in such a state that it would be difficult to resume them for examination by the competent departments in each ministry.[7]

477. The PCNU Committee has not published a general report on its proceedings, but it reported periodically to the Provisional Council of National Unity on its activities and on the difficulties encountered. The Government has not communicated more detailed information on the results achieved by the PCNU, under the chairmanship of Mr. Stancescu, as requested in a letter from the Chairman of the Commission of Inquiry dated 16 October 1990.

Legislative Decree No. 118 of March 1990

478. The Provisional Council of National Unity adopted, on 30 March 1990, a Legislative Decree to grant rights to persons persecuted for political reasons by the dictatorship established on 6 March 1945. In accordance with this Decree, time spent in detention or in work not corresponding to the training received is taken into account for the calculation of seniority or years of service or employment. The provisions of this Decree are analysed in paragraphs 478 to 495.

Scope

479. Employed or retired persons charged with political offences who have found themselves in one of the following six situations may apply to the departmental committees for recognition of their rights to benefit from the provisions of the Decree:

- deprivation of liberty, pronounced on the basis of a final decision of the court or on the basis of a detention order for offences of a political nature;
- deprivation of liberty as a result of administrative measures or to serve the needs of an inquiry by the forces of repression;
- psychiatric internment;
- house arrest;
- forcible transfer from one place to another;
- first or second-degree disability arising during or following any of the above five situations, and preventing the person from finding work.

---

[6] ibid., VII/16.
[7] ibid., VII/17.

480. By virtue of section 8 of the Legislative Decree, persons who were not able to engage in their occupation or employment during the period leading up to their political arrest, or during the investigation of their case by the forces of repression, may also claim their rights under this Decree (section 8).

481. Under the terms of section 9, the provisions of this Decree also apply to repatriated persons and Romanian citizens in other countries, on condition that they take up permanent residence in Romania.

482. In accordance with the single section of Act No. 38 of 13 December 1990, the provisions of Legislative Decree No. 118 are extended to persons deported after 23 August 1944. This category includes persons considered as prisoners by the Soviet side from that date.

Exclusions

483. Excluded from the scope of the Legislative Decree, in accordance with section 11, are persons convicted of crimes against humanity, though the article in question does not specify by what tribunals and under the provisions of what laws these persons may have been convicted. Section 11 also excludes persons who have conducted "proven fascist activities" as members of an organisation or movement of that type. This provision refers to persons who were involved in such activities in the past and not persons currently involved in these activities. The concept of "proven fascist activity" is sufficiently vague to cover the manifestation of opinions or beliefs, or even membership of any kind of opposition organisation or movement, without any criminal or illegal act having been committed. Finally, the wording of section 11 of the Decree, "in the framework of [a fascist] organisation or movement", leaves the door open to the establishment of distinctions on the basis of membership or support of an organisation or movement described as being fascist.

484. The epithets "fascist" or "legionary"[8] were frequently used in the past by the authorities of the Socialist Republic of Romania to describe the activities of all the former political parties subscribing to the liberal, Christian democratic or social democratic ideology or nationalist. More recently, these terms were widely used by the mass media during the events of June 1990 in Bucharest, though the "fascist" or "legionary" nature of the persons or parties thus referred to was by no means established.

Nature of the Situation and Means of Proof

485. It must be established that the persecution was conducted on political grounds, but the Legislative Decree fails to define what is meant by political grounds.

486. Under the terms of section 6, proof of the situations referred to in section 1, paragraph 1, must be supplied by the party concerned, on the basis

---

[8] This term refers to the iron guard movement which was an ultranationalist movement between the two World Wars.

of official documents issued by competent authorities or, where this is not possible, by any legal means. The formulation of this section makes it difficult to produce proof in the case of an unexplained refusal on the part of the competent authority to issue an "official document", especially in cases where no conviction had been pronounced by any court. The wording of section 8 raises a similar question: the proof that a person was unable to engage in his occupation during the period leading up to his arrest, when he was being prosecuted for political reasons by the forces of repression, must also be substantiated by a judicial decision.

Nature and Scope of Reparations

487. The reparations provided for under the Legislative Decree are of three kinds: the taking into account of the duration of the persecution or its consequences in the calculation of seniority in employment; financial indemnities proportionate to the duration of the persecution; and entitlements in respect of medical care and housing accommodation.

488. Section 1, subsection 2, of the Legislative Decree stipulates that each year of detention or internment under the circumstances listed in paragraph 1 shall be considered as one year and six months of service or employment. In order to claim this right, persons who were under house arrest or forcibly transferred from one area to another must supply proof that they are unable to engage in employment "in posts for which they had received vocational training". Seniority thus calculated is considered as continuous employment (uninterrupted seniority) in the same "work unit" (subsection 5). This seniority is taken into account in the calculation of the retirement pension[9] and other entitlements accruing with seniority: remuneration level (Labour Code, section 82.2), bonuses, paid leave (Labour Code, section 125), severance pay, for example. Seniority is also a factor in the allocation of certain goods or services (housing, vacations in works holiday centres, purchase of certain consumer goods, etc.).

489. Employed or retired persons, covered by the definitions contained in section 1, are entitled to a monthly allowance of 200 lei for each year of detention, internment, house arrest or forcible transfer. The amount of 200 lei per year of detention was considered very low by the Association of Former Political Detainees.

490. Persons receiving the financial indemnities provided for under section 3 are also entitled to free medical care and medicaments from the state health services. Moreover, persons who have been in situations referred to in section 1 are given priority in the allocation of housing "from the state housing property, subject to the legal provisions in force". The original part of this state property consists of buildings confiscated from their former owners, frequently for political reasons.

---

[9] Act No. 3/1977 respecting state social insurance pensions and social assistance; Act No. 4/1977 respecting pensions and other social insurance entitlements for members of agricultural production co-operatives; Act No. 5/1977 respecting pensions and other social insurance entitlements for individual farmers not belonging to cooperatives.

491. Furthermore, according to section 36 of Act No. 18 of 19 February 1990 concerning landownership, persons whose lands were confiscated and given over to the State following a criminal conviction under the terms of Legislative Decree No. 118, or the heirs of such persons, may receive shares in companies established under Act No. 15/1990 of 7 August 1990 on the reorganisation of state economic undertakings, up to an amount equivalent to the value of ten hectares of land per family.

Committee Composition and Procedure

492. The machinery set up for the implementation of the Legislative Decree comprises committees established at county level and composed of government officials and representatives of the parties concerned (the Association of Former Political Detainees and Victims of the Dictatorship), assisted by a secretariat provided by the decentralised departments of the Ministry of Labour and Social Security. A national committee is responsible for the coherence of the entire procedure, but has no function whatsoever in respect of appeals against decisions taken by the county committees.

County Committees

493. County committees have been formed in each county and in Bucharest. They are composed of six members (two government officials from the Directorate of Labour and Social Security and four representatives of the Association of Former Political Detainees and Victims of the Dictatorship) and one chairman, who must be a lawyer. The method of designating the chairman is not explained…. The committee must pronounce a well-founded verdict within 30 days on the claims referred to it (section 5, subsection 6). Two-thirds of the members form a quorum, and the decision is taken on the majority vote of those present. Both the claimant and the Directorate of Labour and Social Security may appeal against the decision before the county tribunal or the Bucharest Tribunal, within 15 days from the day on which the decision is published. The decision of the tribunal is final.

National Committee

494. The National Committee is composed of seven members (one representative of the Ministry of Justice, one representative of the Ministry of Labour and five representatives of the Association of Former Political Detainees and Victims of the Dictatorship) and elects its chairman from among these members (section 5, subsection 3). The role of the National Committee is to co-ordinate the activities of the local committees (subsection 4): to this effect, it supervises the composition of the local committees and gives them the assistance necessary for the solution of the cases referred to it (subsection 5). The nature of this assistance is not specified, any more than are the hearing procedures of the National Committee. The National Committee organised a seminar in mid-June 1990 for the benefit of members

of the local committees, to co-ordinate the decision-making criteria decided upon.

Implementation of Decisions

495. According to section 7, the enterprises that employ the persons concerned, the departments of Ministry of Labour and the municipal councils shall carry out the final decisions adopted by the committees or the tribunals....

496. The Government has provided the Commission with information concerning the implementation of Legislative Decree No. 118. On 25 August 1990, 9,312 reparations claims were registered throughout the country, 5,430 of which have been settled; 3,882 cases are still pending.

Measures Enacted in Higher Education

497. In a document communicated to the Commission,[10] the Government stated that certain injustices in higher education, inherited from the period of dictatorship, had been eliminated. Students who had previously been excluded from higher education for political or religious reasons, or who had not passed examinations on ideological questions, were reintegrated in their universities. The Commission requested the Government to provide further details on these cases at its second session. In its reply,[11] the Ministry of Labour indicated that all students who had been expelled for political or religious reasons had, without any discrimination, been re-enrolled in the academic course and level of the year in which they had been expelled. The Government added that teachers who had been persecuted for political or religious reasons now enjoyed their full rights.

498. The Commission has not been able to gather any more detailed information concerning, in particular, the number of students and teachers reinstated in their right to pursue an education, without discrimination on the basis of political opinion or of religion. During the talks it was able to conduct, both with government officials and private individuals, the Commission detected a certain reticence on the subject of re-enrollment measures. A number of persons, including one of the witnesses, continued to assert that, under the former regime, the only criteria for access to higher education had been competence and merit.

Action Taken in Favor of Members of National Minorities

499. In accordance with section 16 of Act No. 18 of 19 February 1991 concerning land ownership, "Romanian citizens belonging to the German minority, who were either deported or transferred and dispossessed of their

---

[10] Delegation of Romania, CSCE Copenhagen: *White Paper concerning the actions taken for promoting fundamental human rights in Romania*, p. 11; document attached to the communication of 29 June 1990.

[11] Letter of the Minister of Labour and Social Security, dated 17 September 1990.

lands by a prescription enacted after 1944", if they so request, shall be awarded priority in the allocation of an area of land not exceeding ten hectares per family from the land reserves placed at the disposal of commissions in the localities from which they originated. Should the lands of which they were dispossessed have become state property, they may, on request, receive a number of shares proportionate to the value of ten hectares of land per family.

Special Cases Brought to the Notice of the Commission

500. Detailed information was referred to the Commission concerning the situation of the workers in Brasov, who, in November 1987, had demonstrated against the government in power. On 3 December 1987, the Brasov District Tribunal convicted 61 workers of outrage to public decency and disturbance of the peace ("*hooliganism*"), under section 321, subsection 2 of the Penal Code. In addition, the majority of these 61 workers were forcibly transferred to other areas, to more arduous and lower-paid jobs. Furthermore, these workers declared that they were ill-treated during their arrest and detention. They fear that they were irradiated during their detention after being exposed to radioactive substances. They stated that one of them died after showing symptoms of having been irradiated: loss of hair, diarrhea, skin problems; two others show similar symptoms. They requested a medical examination to be carried out by an international organisation in order to analyse the symptoms and to determine if others in the group had been irradiated.

501. These 61 persons were able to return to Brasov in the final days of December 1989. At this time they formed an "Association of 15th November 1987" and lodged an extraordinary appeal with the Public Prosecutor, for the reversal of the decision of the Brasov District Tribunal. The Public Prosecutor considered that the appeal could be brought before the court. The Supreme Court of Justice pronounced its ruling on 23 February 1990, quashing the penal sentence of the Brasov District Tribunal. The persons convicted in December 1987 were consequently acquitted of the charge of outrage to public decency and disturbance of the peace. However, the 61 persons concerned felt that this decision did not do justice to their case, in that it did not recognize the political nature of the actions for which they had been condemned.

502. The Commission heard the testimony of one of the members of the "Association of 15th November 1987" of Brasov, Mr. Miroea Sevaciuc, who explained the reasons for the appeal lodged with the Public Prosecutor for the redefinition of the charges brought against them in December 1987.[12] The Commission is gratified to note that the Supreme Court, in a ruling of 5 March 1990, redefined the charges and recognized the political nature of the demonstration of 15 November 1987 in Barsov and the actions carried out on that occasion.

---

[12] Sevaciuc, IX/14-16.

503. Following the first decision of the Supreme Court on 23 February 1990, the members of the association requested the authorities to make good the financial losses they had suffered as a result of their conviction and transfer.

504. After their request had been examined by the enterprises and the ministries responsible for the latter, the Ministry of Labour, on behalf of the Government of Romania, gave a definitive reply on 13 September 1990. This decision recalled the provisions of section 13 of Legislative Decree No. 35/1990 concerning the modification of certain regulations on wages. The remuneration of persons excluded from employment for political reasons is calculated in conformity with the provisions of section 200, subsection 2, of Act No. 57/1974 respecting remuneration based on the quality and quantity of work in state units, handicraft and consumer co-operatives, at the level of the fixed wage on the day on which the labour contract was terminated, and taking into account length of continued employment (uninterrupted seniority) in the same enterprise on that same date, with a view to awarding the corresponding seniority bonus. The decision also recalls that under the terms of section 136 of the Labour Code, the unit is bound to reinstate the person whose contract was wrongfully terminated and pay him compensation calculated on the basis of his average wage during the last three months preceding the termination of his contract and to grant him all individual rights of which he was deprived. These rights are as follows:

- payment of the difference between the wages paid before the termination of the labour contract and those paid since termination of contract or transfer;
- payment for days not worked during custody and police investigation and until reinstatement in employment;
- payment of premium for uninterrupted seniority in the same unit;
- restitution of wage deductions in the case of persons condemned to serve their sentence at their place of work;
- paid leave calculated on the basis of the conditions applicable before termination of the contract;
- payment of children's allowances for the periods during which these allowances were not paid in full or in part;
- allowances for transfer in the interest of the service; transport costs incurred by visits to their families, in the case of persons transferred to localities other than the locality in which their family is domiciled;
- restitution of monies representing rents paid to workers' hostels in the enterprises in which the persons in question were accommodated.

505. On the other hand, claims concerning the recovery of wives' wages, compensation for moral wrongs, supplementary payments for work with toxic substances, and legal costs cannot be covered. All the monies mentioned above are to be paid by the undertakings in which the persons concerned were employed on 15 November 1987.

506. The decisions of the Brasov District Tribunal, to which the members of the Association had applied, with a view to obtaining compensation for the wrongs suffered as a result of the decisions taken in December 1987 and reversed by the Supreme Court, were pronounced on 10 September 1990. According to these decisions, the monies due should not be payable by the undertakings in which the workers were employed, but by the Romanian State. The Tribunal bases its decision on the "fact that the decision (to dismiss the workers) was not signed by the manager of the undertaking, which proves that the undertaking was not responsible for terminating the labour contract, the operation having been carried out, in defiance of the law, by the personnel department at the command of the state authorities and the Securitate". The State retains the right to recover the sums paid to those who took the decisions at that time. The Tribunal recognizes the claims of the complainants and awards them a sum in respect of the difference in wages, for allowances, for seniority bonuses retroactive over three years, for legal costs and for compensation for moral wrong, taking into consideration the complainant's distance from his family, home, friends, etc....

Chapter 18
Recommendations

616. Having carefully examined the facts stated by the complainants in the light of the provisions of the Discrimination (Employment and Occupation) Convention, 1958 (No. 111), of the International Labour Organisation, and having regard to the general conclusions of the inquiry as set forth in Chapter 17 of this report, the Commission deems it appropriate to recommend that the Government of Romania adopt a number of measures which could help it to conform fully to the Convention. In the opinion of the Commission, the essential premises for the attainment of this aim are as follows:

- that the concept of the rule of law be gradually strengthened in Romanian society;
- that the principle of separation of the legislative, executive, and judiciary powers be laid down in the Constitution;
- that the legal and material conditions be created to ensure an independent judiciary and bar;
- that there be absolute equality between litigants, even if one of them is the Romanian State or a public institution linked to that State;
- that the enforcement of judicial decisions be secured in law and in practice;
- that the Constitution guarantees the rights recognised for all persons by the Universal Declaration of Human Rights and by the International Covenants on economic, social and cultural rights and on civil and political rights;

- that freedom of association and the freedom to bargain collectively be observed in public, private and mixed enterprises in the application of Acts Nos. 11/1991 on collective contracts and 15/1991 on collective labour disputes;
- that a permanent structure for dialogue between management and trade unions be established by law in such enterprises;
- that the assets previously belonging to the General Federation of Trade Unions of Romania be distributed fairly among the new trade union organisations to enable them to establish themselves and to draw up the programs called for by the current situation;
- that Decree No. 153/1970 which provides for penalties in the case of certain offences against the laws of communal social life and public law and order be repealed;
- that a competent body be entrusted with the task of receiving and settling some 14,000 complaints which remained pending after the dissolution of the Commission of the Provisional Council of National Unity "to investigate abuses and infringements of fundamental human rights and to rehabilitate the victims of the dictatorship".

617. The Commission hopes that all of these premises will be achieved and maintained within the framework of the democratic rule which the Romanian people has expressed the will to establish in its country. On the basis of these premises, the Government of Romania should adopt as soon as possible, in accordance with Convention No. 111, measures aimed at:

1. Ending all discrimination in employment and occupation based on any of the criteria set out in Article l(a) of the Convention, and in particular on political opinion.
2. Dismantling all instruments of the policy of assimilation and discrimination against members of minority groups pursued in the past by the Government of the Socialist Republic of Romania.
3. Putting an end to all use of the personal records which workers had to fill out under the former regime and to publicise widely information on the present and future status of such records.
4. Putting an end to the effect of discriminatory measures in employment and restoring equal opportunity and treatment which was suspended or altered to the persons concerned....
6. Guaranteeing an efficient and impartial follow-up to the requests for medical examinations made by the persons who went on strike on 15 November 1987 in Brasov, who have been rehabilitated by the courts.
7. Reinstating the workers who, under the Labour Code provisions on imprisonment for over two months, lost their jobs as a result of being arrested following the June 1990 demonstrations and of not being released until after more than two months, despite the absence of evidence.

8. Adopting all the necessary measures to promote dialogue and an attitude of conciliation between the Romanian majority and minorities....

10. [I]mplementing in practice the right of minorities to their cultural identity, traditions and the use of their respective languages....

18. Assisting citizens wishing to rebuild their houses destroyed as a result of the systematisation policy declared by the previous regime.

19. With regard to the January 1992 census, ensuring that representatives of minorities are involved in choices of methodologies, census-taking operations, processing of results and decisions concerning their publication.

20. Informing the supervisory bodies of the International Labour Organisation of the results achieved as regards reparations for the discrimination suffered by members of national minorities (in particular, under section 16 of Act No. 18/1991 respecting landownership) or by persons persecuted for political reasons (in particular, Legislative Decree No. 118/1990, as amended by Act No. 38/1990; section 36 of Act No. 18/1991).

21. Taking the measures recommended by the Commission and supplying detailed information as soon as possible on all developments in the annual reports on the application of Convention No. 111 submitted under article 22 of the Constitution of the International Labour Organisation.

Geneva, 28 March 1991.

RUSSIA: LAW ON REHABILITATION OF VICTIMS OF POLITICAL REPRESSION

(October 18, 1991, as amended December 17, 1992)

During the years of Soviet power millions of people became victims of the arbitrary actions of the totalitarian State and were subjected to repressive measures because of their political and religious convictions and according to social, national, and other indicators.

Condemning the many years of terror and mass persecution of our people as incompatible with the ideas of law and justice, the RSFSR Supreme Soviet expresses its deep sympathy to the victims of unjustified repressions and their friends and relatives, and it declares its unwavering desire to achieve real guarantees of legality and human rights.

The purpose of the present Law is to rehabilitate all victims of political repressions on the territory of the RSFSR since 25 October (7 November) 1917, to restore their civil rights, to eliminate other consequences of arbitrary rule, and to provide compensation for material and moral harm to the best of our ability at the present time.

I. General Provisions

Article 1

Political repressions are considered to be various measures of coercion taken by the State out of political motives in the form of deprivation of life or freedom, forced treatment in psychiatric institutions, expulsion from the country and deprivation of citizenship, resettlement of groups of population from their customary place of residence, exile, banishment, and deportation, compulsory labor with restrictions of freedom, and also any other deprivation or restriction of the rights and freedoms of individuals who have been declared to be socially dangerous to the State or political system because of class, social, national, religious, or other factors, which have been imposed by decisions of the court of other organs performing judicial functions or administratively by organs of executive power and officials.

Article 2

As it pertains to rehabilitation procedure, this Law applies to citizens of the Russian Federation, citizens of States which are former USSR Union republics, and foreign citizens and persons without citizenship, who were subject to political repression in the territory of the Russian Federation since 25 October (7 November) 1917; persons permanently residing in the territory of the Russian Federation who were repressed by Soviet judicial and administrative organs functioning beyond the borders of the USSR, or by military tribunals or central courts of the USSR and extrajudicial organs

(USSR Supreme Court and its collegiums, OGPU [Unified State Political Directorate of the Soviet of People's Commissars of the USSR to Combat Political and Economic Counterrevolution, Espionage, and Banditry], Special Conference of the NKVD [People's Commissariat of Internal Affairs]—MGB [Ministry of State Security]—MVD [Ministry of Internal Affairs] of the USSR, Commission of the USSR NKVD and USSR Procuracy on Investigations); foreign citizens who were repressed by decision of the USSR courts or extrajudical organs outside USSR borders, having been accused of acts against USSR citizens and USSR interests. Matters of the rehabilitation of foreign citizens who were repressed by decision of USSR courts or extrajudicial organs outside USSR borders on the basis of international laws, for acting against the interests of the United Nations during the Second World War, are resolved in accordance with international agreements between the Russian Federation and the States involved.

Article 3

Those subject to rehabilitation include individuals who, because of political reasons, were:

a) convicted of a State or other crime;
b) subjected to criminal repressions by decisions of organs of the VChK [All-Russian Extraordinary Commission for Combating Counterrevolution and Sabotage], the GPU-OGPU [State Political Administration-Consolidated State Political Administration], KGB [Ministry of State Security], Ministry of Internal Affairs, the procuracy and their colleagues, commissions, "special conferences," *dvoykas* [special commission of two], *troykas* [special commission of three], and other organs performing judicial functions;
c) administratively subjected to exile, banishment, deportation, and forced labor under conditions of restriction of freedom, including in "labor colonies of the NKVD [People's Commissariat of Internal Affairs]," and also other restrictions of rights and freedoms;
d) by decisions of courts and nonjudicial organs, committed to psychiatric institutions for compulsory treatment.

Article 4

Individuals listed in Article 3 of the present Law who have been justly convicted by the courts and also those subjected to punishment by decisions of nonjudicial organs in cases where there is adequate proof to convict them of the following crimes are not subject to rehabilitation:

a) betraying the homeland in the form of espionage, divulging military or State secrets and deserting by military servicemen; committing espionage, terrorist acts, sabotage;
b) committing violent acts against the civilian population and prisoners of war and also aiding and abetting traitors to the homeland and

fascist occupation troops in committing these acts during the Great Patriotic War;

c) organizing gangs and participating in their commission of murder, theft, and other violent crimes;

d) committing war crimes and crimes against law and order.

Article 5

The acts listed below are regarded as not containing social danger, and individuals convicted of them are rehabilitated regardless of whether or not there was actual justification for the conviction:

a) anti-Soviet agitation and propaganda;

b) dissemination of false rumors maligning the Soviet State or social system;

c) violation of laws on separation of the church from the State and the schools from the church;

d) encroaching on the persons or rights of the citizens in the guise of performing religious rites,

that is, under Articles 70 (in the edition in effect before the decree of the Presidium of the RSFSR Supreme Soviet of 11 September 1990), 190-1, 142, and 227 of the RSFSR Criminal Code and analogous norms of legislation previously in force.

II. Procedure for Rehabilitation

Article 6

Applications for rehabilitation may be submitted by repression victims themselves and also by any other individuals or public organizations. The applications are submitted at the location of the organ or official who adopted the decision to apply the repressions; with respect to individuals indicated in point (c) of Article 3 of the present Law—to internal affairs organs; and [with respect to] other victims of repression—to procuracy organs.

The time period for consideration of the applications for rehabilitation must not exceed three months.

Article 7

Internal affairs organs, on application from interested individuals or social organizations, establish the facts, the exile, banishment, or deportation or forced labor under conditions of restriction of freedom or other restrictions or rights and freedoms established administratively, and issue a certificate of rehabilitation.

In the absence of documentary evidence of the fact of the application of repressive measures can be established judicially on the basis of testimony.

A decision of internal affairs organs to refuse to issue a certificate of rehabilitation may be appealed in court according to the procedure envisioned for appealing illegal actions of State administrative organs and officials who encroach on the rights of citizens.

Article 8

Procuracy organs, and State security and internal affairs organs enlisted on their instructions, establish and verify all cases involving decisions of courts and nonjudicial organs that have not been revoked before the introduction of the present Law against individuals subject to rehabilitation in keeping with points a), b), and d) of Article 3 and Article 5 of the present Law. The procedure for the indicated work and the distribution of the responsibilities are determined by the RSFSR procurator general.

From the materials of the inspection, the procuracy organs draw up conclusions and issue certificates of rehabilitation to applicants, and if there are none of these, they submit information on rehabilitated individuals for publication in the local press.

In the absence of justification for rehabilitation, when there are applications from interested individuals or social organizations, the procuracy organs send the case with a conclusion to the court in keeping with Article 9 of the present Law.

Article 9

Decisions on cases envisioned by Paragraph 3 of Article 8 of the present Law are applied:

a) to convicts—by the courts which made the last judicial decisions. Cases for which the sentences, determinations, and decrees were made by courts that have been abolished or reformed and also military tribunals with respect to civilians are turned over for the consideration of those courts that had jurisdiction over these according to legislation in effect. The territorial jurisdiction of the case is determined in the place where the last judicial decision was made.

b) individuals subjected to nonjudicial repressive measures; with respect to civilians—by the supreme courts of the autonomous republics, the oblast and kray courts, the courts of the autonomous okrugs; and with respect to military service personnel—military tribunals of the districts or fleets on whose territory the corresponding nonjudicial organs functioned.

In the event of a dispute concerning jurisdiction, cases may be transferred from one court to another on instructions from the chairman of the RSFSR Supreme Court.

Cases envisaged in Part 3 of Article 8 of the present Law which were resolved by the former USSR Supreme Court are reviewed by the Russian

Federation Supreme Court; those resolved by judicial collegiums of the USSR Supreme Court are reviewed by judicial collegiums of the Russian Federation Supreme Court; those resolved by the Plenum of the USSR Supreme Court—by the Presidium of the Russian Federation Supreme Court. The Presidium of the Russian Federation Supreme Court may also review cases in this category for which they themselves rendered and earlier decision.

Article 10

Cases coming to the court with a negative conclusion of the procuracy are considered at judicial meetings according to the rules for revising judicial decisions under the policy of oversight established by existing criminal procedural legislation of the RSFSR with the exceptions envisioned by the present Law.

As a result of the consideration of the case, the court declares that the individual is not subject to rehabilitation or confirms that the individual was unjustifiably subjected to repressive measures and overrides the decision that was made, and the case is closed. The court may also make changes in previous decisions.

With respect to individuals declared by the court not to be eligible for rehabilitation, the applicants are given a copy of the determination (decree) of the court, and in the event that the individual is declared to have been unjustifiably subjected to repressive measures—a certificate of rehabilitation. The determination (decree) of the court may be protested by the procurator and appealed by the interested parties and social organizations to the higher court.

Article 11

Rehabilitated individuals and, with their consent or in the event of their death, their parents, have the right to look over the materials from the closed criminal and administrative cases and to obtain copies of the documents of a nonprocedural nature. Other individuals are allowed to see the materials according to the policy established for familiarization with materials from State archives. The use of the information to the detriment of the rights and legal interests of the individuals involved in the case or their relatives is not allowed and is prosecuted according to the procedure established by Law.

Rehabilitated individuals and their heirs have the right to obtain manuscripts, photographs, and other personal documents kept in the files.

Upon receipt of a petition from the applicants, the organs providing for archive storage of the files related to the repressive measures must report to them the time and cause of death and the place where the rehabilitated individual is buried.

III. Consequences of Rehabilitation
Article 12

Persons who are rehabilitated are granted restoration of the sociopolitical and civil rights they lost in connection with repression, as well as military ranks and special titles. State awards are returned to them. They are afforded benefits and compensation is paid them in accordance with procedure as established by this Law and other normative acts of the Russian Federation.

Restoration of the rights of persons who were repressed outside the borders of the Russian Federation but who permanently reside in its territory, the affording to them of benefits and payment to them of compensation—are effected, unless decisions on rehabilitation taken in their regard by organs of States/former USSR Union republics empowered to do so are contrary to Russian Federation legislation.

When a person is deemed to have been unjustifiably subjected to repressive measures for only part of the accusation made against him, the rights violated in connection with the unjustified political accusations are restored.

Article 13

The right is recognized for rehabilitated individuals to reside in the areas and population points where they lived before the repressive measures were taken against them. This right extends also to members of their families and other relatives who lived with the victims of repressive measures. In the absence of documentary data, the fact of the forced resettlement of relatives in connection with repressive measures may be established by the court.

Article 14

Citizenship in the RSFSR is restored to all residents of the RSFSR who were deprived of their citizenship against their will. Their citizenship is restored according to the procedure envisioned by legislation of the USSR and RSFSR.

Article 15

Individuals subjected to repressive measures in the form of deprivation of freedom, and rehabilitated in keeping with the present Law by social security organs in the place of their residence, are paid, on the basis of a certificate of rehabilitation a monetary compensation of 180 rubles [R] for each month of their incarceration, but no more than R25,0000, out of funds from the republic budget.

Compensation is made both as a one-time payment and according to other procedures established by the RSFSR Council of Ministers under the condition that no less than one-third of the overall sum is paid within the first three months after the appeal of the rehabilitated individual to the social security organs and the rest is paid within three years.

No compensation is paid to heirs except in cases when the compensation was assigned but the rehabilitated individual did not receive it.

For individuals to whom the decree of the Presidium of the USSR Supreme Soviet of 18 May 1981, "On Reimbursement for Damages Caused to a Citizen by Illegal Actions of State and Social Organizations and also Officials When Performing Their Official Duties," applies, compensation is paid minus the sums paid on the basis of this decree.

Procedure for the payment of compensation as envisaged by this Article applies to persons who were repressed outside the borders of the Russian Federation but who permanently reside in its territory. Payment of compensation to these persons is effected on the basis of documentation concerning rehabilitation and time spent in prison which was issued in States/former USSR Union republics or by State organs of the former USSR. Payment or recomputation of compensation amounts is not effected for persons who received such in States/former USSR Union republics.

Article 16

Rehabilitated persons and members of their families have the right to first-priority obtainment of housing in instances where they lost the right to residential premises they occupied in connection with repression and are presently in need of improved housing, as well as in instances where they lost the right to residential premises they occupied in connection with repression and are presently in need of improved housing, as well as in instances indicated in Article 13 of this Law. Rehabilitated persons residing in rural localities are afforded the right to obtain interest-free loans and first-priority receipt of construction materials for housing construction.

Persons subject to political repression in the form of imprisonment, exile, deportation, directive to a special settlement, order to undergo forced labor under conditions of restricted freedom, including "labor colonies of the NKVD," and other restrictions of their rights and freedoms, as well as persons placed without justification in institutions of psychiatric treatment and later rehabilitation, who are invalids or pensioners—have the right to:

- priority in obtaining passes for sanitarium-health resort treatment and recreation;
- extra medical treatment and a 50-percent reduction in the cost of prescription medicine;
- free provision of a motor vehicle of the class ZAZ-968M when medically indicated;
- free travel on all kinds of urban passenger transportation (except taxis) and in rural areas within the administrative region in which they reside;
- a free trip (back and forth) once a year on rail transportation, and in regions that do not have rail transportation—by water, air, or

> interurban automotive transportation with a 50-percent discount from the cost of the trip;
> - a 50-percent reduction of payments for housing and municipal services within the norms envisioned by existing legislation;
> - priority in installation of a telephone;
> - priority membership in gardening societies and housing-construction cooperatives;
> - priority admission to boarding houses for the elderly and disabled and habitation in them with full State support while retaining no less than 25 percent of their assigned pension;
> - free manufacture and repair of dental prostheses (with the exception of prostheses made of precious metals), and preferential provision of other prosthetic-orthopedic devices;
> - preferential provision of food and industrial goods.

Individuals rehabilitated in keeping with the present Law have the right to free legal consultation on questions related to rehabilitation.

Rehabilitated individuals who have the right to the privileges envisioned by the present Law are issued a standard certificate which is approved by the RSFSR Council of Ministers.

Article 17

Articles 12-16 of the present Law extend to victims of political repressions who were rehabilitated before the adoption of the present Law.

Article 18

Lists of individuals rehabilitated on the basis of the present Law with an indication of their basic biographical information and the charges from which they are deemed to be rehabilitated are [to be] published regularly by press organs of the local soviets of people's deputies, the supreme soviets of the republics included in the RSFSR, and the RSFSR Supreme Soviet.

Workers of the organs of the VChK, GPU-OGPU, UNKVD-NKVD, MGB, procuracies, and courts and members of commissions, "special conferences," "dyokas," "troykas," workers of other organs exercising judicial authority and judges participating in the investigation and examination of cases concerning political repressions bear criminal liability on the basis of existing criminal legislation. Information on individuals who, according to the established procedures, have been deemed to have falsified cases, applied illegal methods of investigation, and committed crimes against justice is published periodically by press organs.

IV. Final Provisions
Article 19

The Commission of the RSFSR Supreme Soviet on Rehabilitation is created to monitor the execution of the present Law. It will be given complete access to the archives of the courts, military tribunals, procuracies, State security and internal affairs organs, and other archives located on the territory of the RSFSR.

The Commission on Rehabilitation has been granted the right to extend the application of Articles 12-16 of the present Law to individuals rehabilitated through the general procedure when there is cause to regard their court appearance and conviction as political repression.

[signed] President of the RSFSR B. Yeltsin

RUSSIA: STATUTE OF THE COMMISSION ON REHABILITATION OF VICTIMS OF POLITICAL REPRESSION

1) The Commission under the Russian Federation President for Rehabilitating Victims of Political Repression (hereinafter "the Commission") is a consultative body that coordinates, in the name of the Russian Federation President, the activity of federal bodies of the executive branch in implementation of the RSFSR law of 18 October, 1991, "The Rehabilitation of Victims of Political Repression," and also prepares and presents to the Russian Federation President appropriate papers and recommendations.

2) The Commission's basic tasks are:

- Analysis and coordination of the activity of federal bodies of the executive branch for implementing the RSFSR Law of 18 October, 1991, "The Rehabilitation of Victims of Political Repression";
- Full and comprehensive study, analysis and assessment of political repression that is aimed against all social groups and representatives of political parties and public movements;
- The preparation of reports to the Russian Federation President on the execution of the RSFSR Law of 18 October, 1991, "The Rehabilitation of Victims of Political Repression," by federal bodies of the executive branch;
- The preparation of papers and recommendations on improving the work of federal bodies of the executive branch on the rehabilitation of victims of political repression; and
- Informing the public about the scale and nature of political repression.

3) For purposes of executing the tasks that face it, the Commission has the right:

- To require State bodies to furnish any documents and papers that relate to the problem of political repression;
- To enlist scientific collectives, as well as various specialists and consultants, including foreign, for the work, on a contractual basis;
- To adopt, in coordination with interested ministries and agencies, decisions on the declassification of documents and papers that related to the problem of political repression; and
- To turn over for publication documents and materials that relate to the problem of political repression.

4) The Commission consists of the Chairman of the Commission, the Secretary of the Commission, and members of the Commission.

The Chairman of the Commission is named by an edict of the Russian Federation President.

The Secretary of the Commission is named by a directive of the Russian Federation President.

Ex officio members of the Commission are the Russian Federation Ministry of Security, the Russian Federation Ministry of Internal Affairs, the Russian Federation Ministry of Foreign Affairs, the Russian Federation Ministry of Defense, and the Chairman of the Russian State Archival Service. The Russian Federation President, at the recommendation of the Commission Chairman, can include supervisory State bodies, scientific institutions, as well as public figures and specialists in the Commission.

5) The Commission Chairman:

- Directs the Commission's work;
- Has the right to report directly to the Russian Federation President on the progress and results of the Commission's work;
- Concludes, in the name of the Commission, contracts with scientific-research collectives and individual specialists for execution of work necessary for realizing the tasks set for the Commission; and
- Approves the structure and staff schedule of the Section on Problems of the Rehabilitation of Victims of Political Repression.

6) The Administration of the Russian Federation President provides organizational and equipment support for the Commission's work.

URUGUAY: AMNESTY LAW AND IMPLEMENTING DECREE

Law 15.737 (March 8, 1985)

Chapter I

Article 1

Amnesty is decreed for all political, common and related military crimes committed after January 1, 1962. Concerning the perpetrators and coperpetrators of intentional homicides committed, the amnesty will function only with the objective of enabling the revision of sentences on the terms envisioned in Article 9 of this Law.

Article 2

For the purposes of this Law, crimes considered political will be those committed with motives directly or indirectly political, and common and military crimes related to political crimes will be those that share the same objectives or have been committed in order to facilitate, prepare, consummate, augment the effects of, or impede the punishment of these crimes. Also considered related crimes are those that coincide in any manner (real or formal recidivism or concurrence without recidivism) with political crimes.

Article 3

This amnesty expressly includes:

a) The crimes of Article 60, paragraphs I, II, III, IV, V, VI, VII and XII, of Chapter 6 of the Military Penal Code, incorporated in this by Article 1 of Law 14.068, of July 10, 1972.

b) The crimes specified in Titles I and II of Volume II of the Ordinary Penal Code; and organizations for the purpose of committing crimes (Articles 150 and 152 of the Penal Code and Article 5 of Law 9.936, of June 18, 1940) if they had been created for political purposes.

c) Those [crimes] classified in the Military Penal Code when they have been committed with motives directly or indirectly political, or when as a result of these crimes civilians have been investigated, prosecuted or sentenced.

d) Crimes occurring within military units during a state of declared war.

e) In general, without prejudice to the crimes described heretofore, all crimes, whatever the legal tenet violated, that have been committed with direct or indirect political motives.

Article 4

All persons to whom the commission of these crimes has been attributed, whether as perpetrators, co-perpetrators or accomplices, and accessories to these, whether or not they have been convicted or processed, and even though they be recidivists or habituals, are included in the effects of this amnesty.

Article 5

Excluded from the amnesty are those comparable or similar crimes committed by police or military officials who may have been perpetrators, co-perpetrators or accomplices in inhuman, cruel or degrading treatment, or in the detention of persons who subsequently disappeared, and about whom they may have concealed any of this behavior.

This exclusion extends in the same manner to all crimes committed with political motives by persons acting with the backing of the power of the State in any form, or under orders of the government.

Article 6

All principal and cumulative penalties, all penal actions, administrative and retirement sanctions, debts attributable to expenses of imprisonment and any other sanction imposed by an authority of the State by virtue of the forgiven crimes are hereby declared null and void.

Article 7

Starting with the proclamation of this Law, the following will be terminated immediately and definitively:

a) All systems of surveillance of persons included in the amnesty, whatever the nature of the surveillance and the authority by which it was imposed. Said persons will be automatically exempted from any obligation directly or indirectly related to the type of surveillance to which they were subjected.

b) All pending orders for capture and summons, whatever their nature or the imposing authority, issued against persons benefited by this amnesty.

c) All restrictions in force regarding the entry to or exit from the country which affect said persons.

d) All investigations of acts that may characterize any of the crimes included in the amnesty.

Article 8

The Supreme Military Tribunal, within 48 hours of the proclamation of this Law, will send to the Supreme Court of Justice the listing of the detainees held, indicating the crimes of which they have been accused or convicted and the place of their confinement.

The Supreme Court of Justice will implement the immediate release of these prisoners with the exception of perpetrators or co-perpetrators of completed intentional homicide, who will remain in its custody until the Supreme Military Tribunal remits their respective cases, which must be done within five working days of the proclamation of this Law.

Having received the cases, the Supreme Court of Justice will set these persons free and distribute the cases equitably among the three Penal Courts of Appeal.

Article 9

The Penal Courts of Appeal will have a period of one hundred and twenty days to decide whether or not the conviction has merit, being able to pass sentences of either absolution or conviction. In the latter case the new sentence will be liquidated at the rate of three days of the term for each day of deprivation of freedom actually suffered.

The Courts of Appeal can evaluate freely the proofs resulting from the summary instruction and will pass sentence based on the merits of their free convictions, the previous citation of the accused serving as a measure to assist the decision.

In any case the debts incurred for expenses of incarceration will be nullified.

An appeal for dismissal may be filed against the sentence.

Article 10

The order to release will be implemented also in regard to persons detained due to the implementation of illegitimate emergency security measures that were adopted by a *de facto* authority and not communicated to the General Assembly or to the Permanent Commission, or by virtue of another administrative decision, whatever the agency or authority from which it emanated or the place of detainment.

Article 11

The military or police official who fails to comply with or delays the execution of, the order to release referred to in Articles 8 and 10 will be guilty of the crime specified in Article 286 of the Penal Code (violation of personal freedom by a public official in charge of a prison).

Article 12

The seizures, injunctions, abductions and precautionary measures of any nature that affect persons covered by this amnesty or their property, that have been ordered as a direct or indirect result of accusations of any of the crimes referred to in Article 3, will be cancelled or dismissed as of the date of proclamation of this Law. In the same manner, the personal bonds that may have been exacted and levied in relation to these persons will expire.

Within one hundred and twenty days of the proclamation of this Law, all property of pardoned persons that has been seized, attached or confiscated, with the exception of the proceeds of the crime or the instruments of its execution, will be restored.... In cases where restitution is rendered impossible because the attached or confiscated property has been destroyed, made useless, sold or deeded to the State in accordance with the Decree-Law 14.373 of May 13, 1975, the responsibility of the State and of the acting functionaries will be governed by Articles 24 and 25 of the Constitution, and this will include the case in which the property has deteriorated or been rendered useless through bad administration or continued use.

Article 13

In the same period of one hundred and twenty days, the Executive Power will arrange for the return of money deposited as bonds and that collected for expenses of imprisonment, duly accounted by the regulations described in Decree-Law 14.500, of March 8, 1976 and charged to General Revenues. The return of these funds must be completed within a maximum period of one year from the proclamation of this Law.

Article 14

The Executive Power will control the procedural measures that result from this Law of amnesty, determining which judicial authority must issue the stay of proceedings necessary for the closure of the cases of pardoned persons.

Chapter II
Article 15

The American Convention on Human Rights, called the Pact of San Jose of Costa Rica, signed in the city of San Jose, Costa Rica, on November 22, 1969, whose text forms a part of the present Law, is approved.

Article 16

The legal authority of the Inter-American Commission for Human Rights is recognized for an indefinite period of time, as is that of the Inter-

American Court of Human Rights, over all cases relating to the interpretation or application of this Convention, under the condition of reciprocity.

Chapter III

Article 17

Articles 1, 2, 3, 4, 5, 6, 11, 12, 13, 14, 15, 37, 40, 41, 42, 43, 45 and 46 of the Law of State Security, 14.068, of July 12, 1972; Decree-Law 14.493, of December 28, 1975, and Decree-Law 14.734, of November 28, 1977, are revoked....

Chapter V

Article 20

The pardon that nullifies the crime and brings about the dismissal of the case will be granted by the Supreme Court of Justice while visiting the prisons and cases, which they will do at least once a year.

On these occasions it will also be able to release on bail those being prosecuted, whatever the nature of the accusations.

Both powers will be exercised officially or by request of one of the parties.

Article 21

Article 328 of the Code of Criminal Procedures will be modified and will read as follows:

> The Supreme Court of Justice may grant early freedom to those convicts who have been deprived of their freedom in the following cases:
>
> 1) If the sentence is imprisonment and the subject has completed half of the term imposed.
> 2) If the relapsed penalty is imprisonment or fine, whatever the period of confinement endured.
> 3) If the prisoner has completed two thirds of the term imposed the Supreme Court of Justice will grant early release. It can only deny this through an admissible decision in cases where there are no evident signs of rehabilitation of the condemned.
>
> The petition should be presented to the directors of the prison facility where the condemned is confined.
> The petition will be submitted to the executing judge within five days, with a report from the management of the facility concerning the evaluation of the petitioner as an inmate.
> Once the petition is received, the judge will request the report from the Institute of Criminology, which will be delivered within thirty days.
> When the records of the case have been returned, the judge will issue a well founded opinion and the processing will continue

in accordance with that which is established in the fourth paragraph of the preceding Article.

If the Supreme Court of Justice grants early release, the judgment will be carried out immediately and it will be recorded that the person freed has been advised of the obligations imposed by Article 102 of the Penal Code, and the case will be returned to the judge of execution.

Article 22

Once the Supreme Court of Justice is constituted in accordance with Article 236 of the Constitution, it will proceed immediately with a visit to the prisons and cases in order to exercise the right of pardon accorded by Article 20 of this Law....

Chapter VI

Article 24

There will be created a National Commission for Repatriation, on an honorary basis and with the commitment to facilitate and support the return to the country of all those Uruguayans who so desire.

This Commisson will function within the Ministry of Education and Culture, which will provide it with the material means and the human resources necessary for its operation.

The Commission will be composed of one delegate from the Ministry of Education and Culture, one delegate from the Ministry of Foreign Affairs, one delegate from the Ministry of the Interior, one delegate from the Ministry of Labor and Social Security, one delegate from the Mortgage Bank of Uruguay, one delegate from the Commission of Reconciliation and a person who will be designated by the President of the Republic and who will assume the chairmanship.

The Executive Power will specify, through regulation, the duties and faculties of the Committee.

Chapter VII

Article 25

The right of all public officials deposed under the application of the so-called institutional Law No. 7 to be restored to their respective positions is declared.

Chapter VIII

Article 26

The present Law takes effect with the official confirmation by the Executive Power....

—•—⚔—•—

Decree Implementing Amnesty Law
Decree 256/985 (June 27, 1985)

Considering: the proclamation of the Law 15.737 of March 8, 1985....

Article 1

Within a period of seventy days starting with the publication of this Decree, the agencies of Military Justice that have knowledge of the cases and the crimes specified in Article 3 of Law 15.737 of March 8, 1985 will proceed with the official cancellation of the means of seizure, interdiction or prevention used, releasing the corresponding documents.

Within the same period, the acting body will provide for the return of the seized properties that are at the disposal of the court.

Within the same period they must submit proof of the payments made for bail and confinement expenses with specific indication of the amount and date of the payment.

In the documents submitted in accordance with the provisions of Articles 8 and 9 of Law 15.737, the measures established earlier, as well as those described in the third and ninth Articles of the present Decree, will be specified by the acting body to the extent they are pertinent.

Article 2

The pardoned persons who have made payments for confinement expenses should appear before the Ministry of National Defense with a certificate made out according to the specifications in the first Article to the effect that the Executive Power, in accordance with the Ministry of Economy and Finance, may issue a resolution determining the date of the payment and the amount of the restitution adjusted in conformity with Article 2 of Decree-Law 14.500 of March 8, 1976. The same procedure will be followed for the return of funds paid in the form of bail.

In both cases, the ministry that makes the payment will communicate this circumstance within a period of thirty days counting from the occurrence of same, to the Supreme Court of Justice, with an indication of the date, the amount, and the person to whom the payment was made.

Article 3

Once the provisions of the first Article are complied with, the records pertaining to the political, common and military crimes related to those that come under the jurisdiction of Military Justice organizations will be remitted to the Supreme Court of Justice, which will distribute them among the penal trial courts of first instance, which will be competent to understand the effects of Article 14 of Law 15.737 and other provisions of this Decree, as well as those related to the return of the properties that were seized, attached or confiscated in the respective cases.

Article 4

Within the period referred to in the first Article, all the State Institutions, Autonomous Entities, Decentralized Services and Departmental Governments will remit to the Interior Ministry a listing of the personal property or real estate under their control that have been seized, attached or confiscated from the persons pardoned by the law being implemented.

The personal property as well as the documents that establish the ownership of rights to the real estate will remain at the disposal of the Ministry of the Interior for their return.

Article 5

The real estate will be restored, after a detailed inventory describing its current state, to the person who can prove ownership of the property.

In any case, the delivery will be verified under bond in which the state of the properties will be confirmed and which will be signed by the recipient and the intervener.

Article 6

The personal property that has been seized, attached, or confiscated from persons pardoned by Law 15.737 of March 8, 1985 by any administrative or judicial authority taking part in the proceedings shall be restored to those who owned it at the moment of seizure or to those who have inherited their rights.

The items involved in the crime and the documents of its execution are to be excluded from these provisions unless one or the other belongs to a third party, dissociated from the act (Article 105, letter (a) of the Penal Code). In case of controversy about the nature of the property or the document of the crime, the Provincial Penal Court will have jurisdiction in the case.

Article 7

In those cases in which the seizure, attachment or confiscation of the properties has been effected outside of all jurisdictional procedure, the restoration will be resolved by the Executive Power in accordance with the Ministry of the Interior.

Article 8

Aside from the case described in paragraph 2 of Article 6 and when the restoration is not possible for any of the reasons enumerated in Article 12 of the Law being implemented, as in the case of deterioration or uselessness, the person interested may present himself before the Ministry of the Interior in order to apply for the appropriate indemnification (Article 24 of the Constitution of the Republic), without prejudice to his right to claim the indemnity directly before the Judicial Power.

Article 9

In the case where the pardoned persons may not yet have withdrawn the evidence referred to in the first Article, the acting Provincial Penal Court will order, within a period of thirty days, starting from the date on which it assumed jurisdiction, the deposit of the sums received in the way of expenses of confinement and bail demanded by the Military Justice institutions in a special assets account in the Mortgage Bank of Uruguay to the order of the court. The owners of the deposits, without prejudice to the provisions of the second Article, can file the respective documents and the acting agency will issue the corresponding payment order.

The Provincial Penal Court will communicate both measures to the Ministries of National Defense and Economy and Finance....

URUGUAY: DECREE ESTABLISHING THE NATIONAL COMMISSION FOR REPATRIATION

Decree 135/985 (April 11, 1985)

Considering: the provisions of Article 24 of Law 15.737 of March 8, 1985.

Whereas: the standard referred to establishes that the Executive Power will specify through regulations the duties of the National Commission for Repatriation and its authority.

The President of the Republic, acting in the Council of Ministers, decrees:

Article 1

The National Commission for Repatriation will have as its duties:

a) to produce a Registry of Uruguayan citizens living abroad who express an interest in being repatriated.
b) to produce programs that tend to facilitate and support the return to this country of all citizens who wish it.
c) to submit to the Government agencies, Central, Departmental and Decentralized Administration, the recommendations it deems pertinent to the accomplishment of its objectives.
d) to propose the allocation of available resources for the repatriation of Uruguayan citizens abroad.
e) to provide the information required by interested parties concerning the possibilities of resettlement in the national territory.
f) to coordinate the activities of the various organizations the operations of which are similar to those of the Commission.
g) so study and recommend official support, when it is deemed appropriate, for the projects and programs developed by organizations with ties to the Commission.
h) to carry out the projects and programs with which it is entrusted and administer the funds that are intended for these purposes. To this end, it is authorized to maintain accounts in national or foreign currency in the Bank of the Eastern Republic of Uruguay.

It may also include in its programs representatives of public, international or private organizations that it deems appropriate.

Article 2

The decisions of the National Commission for Repatriation will be adopted by a majority of the members. In case of a tie, it will be decided by the Chairman of the Commission.

Article 3

The delegate from the Ministry of Education and Culture will serve as Vice-Chairman of the Commission and will substitute for the Chairman in case of leave, temporary absence, or excuse.

Article 4

The Commission is empowered to communicate directly with all the State, para-State and international agencies, diplomatic representatives and private entities, obtaining the information required for the fulfillment of its duties.

Article 5

The Chairman of the National Commission for Repatriation, or the Vice-Chairman, in case of substitution, will represent it for the purposes expressed in Article 5 [*sic*]....

COUNTRY INDEX

Volume I: General Considerations

Contents

Volume II: Country Studies

Contents